D0204224

Environment & Behavior

To my three Ladies,
Beverly, Amanda, and *Carrah.*

They endured much.
They forgave much.
And they still loved me.
I feel very blessed.

Environment & Behavior
An Introduction

Robert B. Bechtel

SAGE Publications
International Educational and Professional Publisher
Thousand Oaks   London   New Delhi

For information address:

SAGE Publications, Inc.
2455 Teller Road
Thousand Oaks, California 90321
E-mail: order@sagepub.com

Sage Publications Ltd.
6 Bonhill Street
London EC2A 4PU
United Kingdom

Sage Publications India Pvt. Ltd.
M-32 Market
Greater Kailash I
New Delhi 110 048 India

Printed in the United States of America

Library of Congress Cataloging-in-Publication Data

Bechtel, Robert B.
    Environment and behavior: An introduction / Robert B. Bechtel.
      p. cm.
    Includes bibliographical references (p.) and index.
    ISBN 0-8039-5795-5 (cloth: acid-free paper)
    1. Environmental psychology. 2. Man—Influence of environment.
    3. Human ecology. I. Title.
  BF353.B42 1997
  155.9—dc20   96-25246

97 98 99 00 01 02 03 10 9 8 7 6 5 4 3 2 1

Acquiring Editor:	Alex Schwartz
Editorial Assistant:	Jessica Crawford
Production Editor:	Astrid Virding
Production Assistant:	Karen Wiley
Copy Editor:	Janet Brown
Typesetter / Designer:	Janelle LeMaster
Indexer:	Jean Casalegno
Cover Designer:	Ravi Balasuriya

Contents

Part I: Beginnings

Part II: Conceptual Areas of Study

Part III: The Study of Environments

Part IV: Conclusions

List of Figures

List of Tables

Preface

In 1962, my first internship as a graduate student in psychology at the University of Kansas in Lawrence was at the Midwest Psychological Field Station at Oskaloosa under Roger Barker. So imbued was I with ordinary psychology that it took me another three years to understand I was in the midst of the most radical departure from psychology since it was founded.

Meantime, about my third year of graduate school, Larry Good, an architect practicing in Lawrence and redesigning a mental hospital ward in Topeka, asked me to join him in what later became the Environmental Research and Development Foundation. My professors warned me that this could only be a sideline at best but it was already too late for me.

When I received my Ph.D. in 1967, the field of environmental psychology was yet to be born but already several of us were working in it. Those were heady days. The excitement of discovery was everywhere and it took me beyond my wildest expectations, to remote corners of the Earth like Nanisivik, Northwest Territories of Canada; Shay Gap, Australia; Eastern Saudi Arabia; Iran; Alaska; and many others. I was in full-time research for 10 years until 1976 when I moved to the University of Arizona.

I first taught Introduction to Environmental Psychology in 1980 and this book is a direct result of 15 years of interacting with students over this stimulating subject. It will be immediately apparent that this book is not like other textbooks. Some will say it goes beyond the topic as conventionally taught. I certainly tried to go beyond the narrow scope the field is being given in other texts. Others will say it has too many references. More will be shocked by the first chapter. And, horror of horrors, I placed the chapter on theory at the end. I am happily guilty of all these transgressions of the accepted way.

It became very apparent to me early in the course that students were not aware of the nature and magnitude of the threats to life on Earth. Despite all the publicity, despite many books and television programs, students did not have a comprehensive picture of how dangerous our environment had become. It was as though the constant barrage had created a kind of immunity. The first chapter attempts to deal with this lack of perspective. It is by no means complete, but judging from student response, it seems to do the job. Only after this sober appraisal were students ready to take up the topic of environment and behavior. My approach was that environmental psychology is not a simple branch of psychology but a plan for survival.

It also became evident that most texts "talk down" to the students, presenting too simplified a view of complex problems and definitions that papered over the authors' own difficulties. I make no apologies for revealing the ambiguities and contradictions that exist with even the most popular topics, and the references are readily there for any student to look up the facts and discussions. Science should be supported by evidence that can be verified. Students appreciate being able to do so.

Finally, after trying it both ways, I put theories at the end. Every professor will say theories should go at the beginning. That is how the professors were taught. That is how they teach. But students do not begin with the knowledge range of a professor. When I put theories at the beginning, there was nothing to "hang them on." They just floated in space with no connections to facts. When placed at the end, however, there were many "aha" experiences and the building of networks to each theory.

There are probably 10 more chapters in this book than in the comparable texts. This is so the teachers can pick and choose rather than have to resort to additional readings.

Goals are listed at the end of each chapter to point out the most important concepts and studies. Questions appear at the end of each chapter and could be used for essay questions.

Acknowledgments

———◁▷———

Foremost, I want to recognize the thousands of students who helped shape this text with their many questions and comments as well as their helpful written evaluations. Many colleagues influenced my writing further with their own comments. Bill Ittelson was first because he was the earliest to encourage me to write. Paul Gump provided comments, pictures, and data. Gary Evans sorted out the mediator-moderator tangle. Amos Rapoport and Setha Low relentlessly pressed the anthropological view. Riley Dunlap filled out the sociological perspectives, especially the HEP-NEP. Burgess Ledbetter was my guardian angel of the Arctic and Australia. Mark Flamm was the untiring programmer for Nofim. David Hattis invited me to Iran, and Harry Broley got me into the inner sanctums of Saudi Arabia. Dan Levi offered his expertise on energy. My friend Alvaro Gonzalez introduced me to the *barriadas* and Altiplano of Peru. Sheila Ornstein piloted me through her many POEs in Brazil.

Ultimately, it was Larry Good who invited me into the field, and it was Roger and Louise Barker who taught me the meaning of human behavior.

All these people showed me that environmental psychology was not just psychology but environmental anthropology, architecture, archaeology, geography, and sociology. The title is an attempt to include all of these.

Alex Schwartz and Jessica Crawford shepherded the text through Sage. Janet Brown did the capable copyediting. Sara Miller McCune asked me to "write a textbook."

Part I

Beginnings

1

The Environment Will Get You
If You Don't Watch Out!

Introductory Note

Environmental psychology, with its counterparts, environmental sociology, environmental anthropology, and the larger field of environmental studies as a whole, had their beginnings in the 1960s in the United States. The field was one of the results of a combination of social and political forces that made not only psychologists but the population as a whole more aware of the environment. In addition to the antiwar movement and the civil rights movement, there was an environmental movement, and what this movement uncovered was nothing less than a threat to human existence as real and even more serious than the (then) current threat of atomic war. Yet, despite continuing publicity, few people are aware of the total sum of threats to our existence that continue to grow, or of the progress that has been made in alleviating some of these threats. This chapter will lightly survey the threats to human life that human behavior has introduced into the environment. These may not seem light to the reader, but keep in mind that this is only a cursory survey, not anywhere near a complete list.

This chapter is necessary so that the reader will become aware of the breadth and diversity of the dangers that humans have introduced into the environment before going on to the main topics of environmental psychology. To skip over or not connect these threats would be to miss the main impetus and urgency of all environmental studies: survival. It answers the question: What is behind the need to study the environment in relation to human behavior? The answer is not just another academic topic for college credits but to understand the fundamental human influences on the environment and their interactions with behavior ultimately to save human life and make that human life more amenable to existence on this planet.

What Is Out There to Get You?

Environment means all that surrounds us. Not all that surrounds us is good. Finding and avoiding that which is harmful is a matter of survival. Aside from the more obvious hazards such as tornadoes, floods, and earthquakes, all of us who live on this planet are confronted with an invisible array of dangers to our lives. It seems almost daily that new dangers are discovered. Some food or food additive is found to be cancer producing. Waste products dumped into the soil or rivers seep into and pollute the water supply. It seems there is a never-ending stream of these threats. Yet seldom does anyone stop to add up the total sum of these threats. Even though some of these environmental threats are a fairly recent phenomenon, they already add up to a confused and complex picture of global danger. How did it happen so quickly?

What follows is a convenient catalogue of these dangers as they exist in the four familiar elements of the environment most commonly known: air, water, food, and land. These are artificial divisions because they all overlap. Acid rain comes from the air and pollutes the waters of lakes; gases come from waste dumps on land and pollute the air; and both may contaminate food. Keep in mind that what Train (1978) said is still true: "What we do not know, still far exceeds what we do know" (p. 320).

Air Quality: Outdoor Environments

The Greenhouse Effect

For the urban dweller, the most easily recognized threat to air quality is the brown haze that seems to settle over many cities. This danger seems

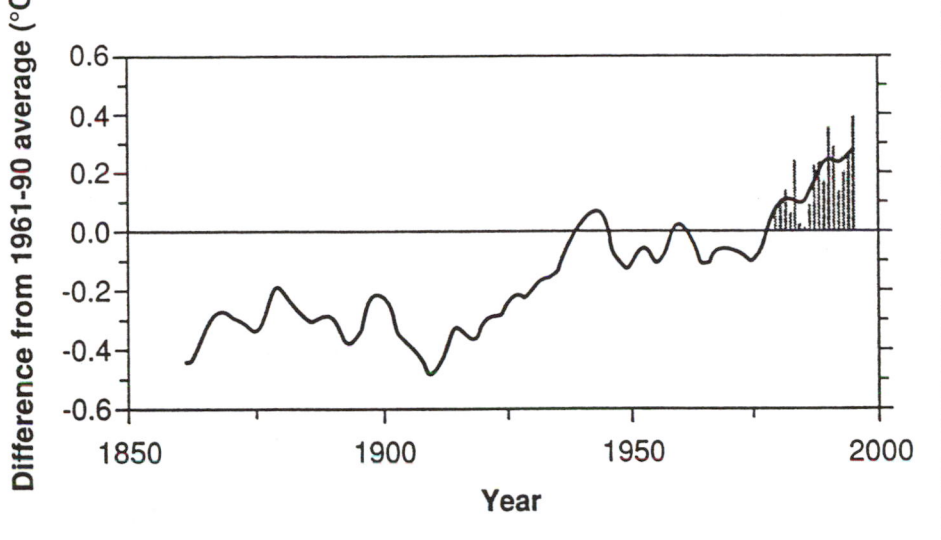
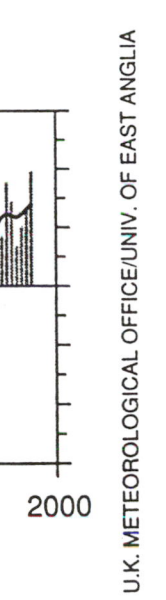

Figure 1.1. Global Temperature Trend
SOURCE: Kerr (1996).

immediately recognizable and urgent; however, invisible pollutants are even more dangerous.

Carbon dioxide (CO_2) buildup in the atmosphere is considered by many scientists to be the most serious environmental threat to our existence on this planet (Hansen et al., 1981; Jones & Wigley, 1990; Trefil, 1990). The effect of carbon dioxide buildup is called the "greenhouse" effect because, just like the glass in a greenhouse, the carbon dioxide lets the sun's rays into the atmosphere but blocks their reflection back out into space, thus keeping the heat on the Earth's surface. Figure 1.1 shows the rise in temperature 1850 to 1995, with 1995 as the warmest year.

Hansen et al. (1981) claim the global temperature rose by .2 degrees Celsius from the middle 1960s to 1980. It is easy to conclude that this increase is due to carbon dioxide pollution but Hansen et al. maintain it is actually due to a combination of volcanic emissions and changes in the sun's radiation. Only at the end of the century will human contributions catch up with nature. Without our help, nature is already warming the planet and this effect will produce more dry deserts in North America and Central Asia as well as a melting of the ice caps and a rise in ocean levels that will flood many coastal cities (Revelle, 1982). The magnitude of this threat is no less great because its main effect is in the future and it is happening so gradually.

Ramanathan (1988) has pointed out that trace gases (gases produced in small quantities) such as chlorofluorocarbons (CFCs) are more effective at absorbing infrared rays than CO_2 and therefore contribute more to the greenhouse effect than previously realized. If the increase in these gases continues at the current rate, global warming could increase by 5 degrees Kelvin by the next century.

A threshold of public awareness was crossed by NASA's James Hansen during a congressional hearing when he announced in June 1988 that the greenhouse effect was already evident in our climate. He pointed out that the five warmest years in the past century have occurred within the last decade. Although scientists are still divided over whether the greenhouse effect is measurable, the coincidence of droughts and high temperatures since 1988 made the statement credible to the public. Hansen predicted a record high temperature for the first three years of 1990-1992 and won his bet in 1990 (Kerr, 1991).

We are contributing to the buildup of carbon dioxide not only by burning fossil fuels but also by the destruction of forests and ocean flora that use CO_2 and convert it to oxygen. Revelle (1982) claims that human activities have increased the amount of CO_2 by 15% in the last century. There is some evidence, however, that aerosols and particles produced from industry may have a cooling effect (Kerr, 1995).

Ozone

Oxygen occurs naturally as O_2 but is often found as the more reactive O_3 (ozone). At 35,000 to 150,000 feet above the Earth's surface is an ozone layer that shields us from ultraviolet rays, especially the UV-B rays, which take apart organic molecules. These rays cause cancer and harm the immune system. Were the ozone shield removed, most plants exposed to the sun would literally burn up in a few moments and humans would require constant shielding from the sun while outdoors. Estimates by the National Academy of Sciences in 1979 (NAS, 1983b) were that if the release of chlorofluorocarbons (CFCs, the chemicals used in aerosol cans as propellants) continues at the rate of 1977 levels, the reduction of the ozone shield would be about 8% by 2030.

The role of CFCs in the reduction of the ozone layer is now clear (Anderson, Tooney, & Brune, 1991). If the use of these compounds is increased only by 7%, the reduction of the ozone would be as much as 30%. The possible result would be to cause several more thousand cases of melanoma, a particularly fatal type of skin cancer. But the effects on animal life would be more devastating. Certain seafood species and microorganisms at the base of the food chain would be harmed. Furthermore, the depletion of ozone would also heat up the Earth.

One chlorine molecule can destroy 100,000 ozone molecules before it falls back to the Earth as HCL (hydrochloric acid). It can take 15 years for a CFC molecule to work its way into the ozone.

With the report of the Ozone Trends Panel (NASA, 1988), it became evident that the depletion rate was greater than predicted. Ozone depletion for 1969-1986 was 1.7% to 3% over most of Europe and the United States but it was more severe in winter (2.3% to 6.2%).

The discovery of an "Ozone Hole" over Antarctica created a sensation when it was realized that 50% to 95% of the ozone was missing inside the hole. A smaller hole was discovered over the Arctic (Weisburd, 1986), and there is every reason to believe both these holes will increase if current conditions are not altered (Brune et al., 1991). The depletion of ozone is further aided by gases from the burning of the Brazilian jungles. An area the size of Austria was burned in Brazil in 1987 alone.

Ozone in the lower atmosphere is itself a pollutant and it is one of the pollutants most often in the unhealthful range. Between 1973 and 1978, it was the only pollutant to remain constant while the other main pollutants decreased. In the 1990s, ozone pollution had spread even to rural areas such as the Maine countryside (Kerr, 1994). The ambient air quality standard for ozone is .12 parts per million. Most cities have not yet met that standard (Russell et al., 1995).

A new twist was added to the age of jet travel when passengers and crew came up with symptoms of ozone poisoning. Broad (1979) described how ozone can affect humans who fly into the ozone layer. Coughing, chest pains, headaches, dizziness, eye irritation, and burning of the nose and throat were experienced when airliners flew above 35,000 feet. Ironically, airliners were tending to fly at these altitudes because the lack of air resistance saved fuel. Ozone in the passengers' cabin may go up to four times the level considered safe, yet no standard has been set for this kind of exposure. Instead, charcoal filters and catalytic converters were installed in the jet liners to handle the problem.

The United Nations Environment Program sponsored an effort that resulted in the Montreal Protocol on Substances That Deplete the Ozone

Layer, signed by 24 countries in September 1986. Unfortunately, the protocol had so underestimated the amount of depletion that dangerous amounts of ozone loss would occur even if the agreement were fully implemented by all nations (Benedick, 1991). As a result, new negotiations were opened and a new treaty signed by 93 nations in June 1990. The chief aim of the new treaty was to end all production of CFCs by 2000. A special fund was created to help developing countries buy CFC substitutes. This provision was the key to getting cooperation from Third World countries.

The sobering thought that may nullify this success at international cooperation is that if even one country continues to manufacture CFCs, the rest of the world will still be subject to the effects of ozone depletion. Further, even if all manufacture is stopped, there are enough CFCs already in the atmosphere to continue to affect the ozone layer well into the next century.

Fortunately, there is evidence that the chlorine level is "topping out" as a result of these efforts and this becomes another bit of evidence that the environmental effects of dangerous chemicals *can* be turned around (Kerr, 1996).

Automobile Pollutants

Automobile exhaust is a major contributor of certain air pollutants such as carbon monoxide (CO), various hydrocarbons (HC), and nitrogen oxides (NOX). Carbon monoxide is one of the most insidious pollutants because it combines with red blood cells to form carboxyhemoglobin and, in sufficient quantities, will suffocate a human being. In lesser quantities, such as those often found in heavy traffic, it puts a strain on the heart by causing it to pump faster. In heavier quantities, it affects coordination, slows reaction time, and affects mental abilities.

Hydrocarbons and nitrogen oxides in sunlight combine to form photochemical oxidants (Grad et al., 1975). It is thought these chemicals have much the same effect as carbon monoxide but it is not known exactly how they operate. It is these photochemical oxidants that are largely responsible for the brown haze over most cities of the world. There is some early evidence that these pollutants are already declining because of the introduction of catalytic converters in automobiles (Speth, Yarn, & Harris, 1980). Once more, we have an example of how a concerted effort can reduce pollution.

Lead is one of the chief pollutants from gasoline consumption, yet the story of how it has been reduced is one of the great successes in restoring the environment. When human blood is measured for amounts of lead, automobile exhaust is responsible for 20% of the amount. Although there are other sources of lead such as paint or solder in food cans, the prevalence of lead from auto exhaust is such that it reduces the tolerance level for doses from such other sources.

Currently, lead content in gasoline has been reduced to the point where only 1% or less of gasoline on the market contains any lead. A study by Houk (reported in Marshall, 1982) at the Center for Environmental Health linked lead levels in children to lead levels in gasoline. Children from 60 cities showed a mean lead level decrease in blood of 25.6% from 1977 to 1980. The only exposure factor that changed in that time was a 30% reduction in the amount of leaded gasoline used in the United States. Research shows a relationship between amount of lead ingested and problems of thinking and learning. This effect occurs under what is considered "safe" levels of exposure.

Needleman et al. (1979), in a classic study, asked teachers in Boston schools to play tooth fairy and collect a baby tooth from each pupil. When these teeth were analyzed for lead content, the mean IQ of the high lead group was four points lower than in the low lead group. In addition, teachers rated high-lead children as worse on 11 behavioral qualities. These results were duplicated in West Germany and England.

The effects of lead poisoning are particularly devastating because they seem to cause permanent intellectual deficits. Needleman, Bellinger, Schnell, Leviton, and Allred (1990) tested 132 of the subjects 11 years later and still found the same deficits. These same subjects were also more likely to have dropped out of school. Houk claims no childhood disease even approaches lead poisoning in breadth and impact. Needleman's work was attacked but upheld (Lewis, 1995).

The reduction of lead in the atmosphere and its removal from paint by the Lead-Paint Poisoning Prevention Act is one of the great success stories in the battle against pollutants. Eventually all lead will be removed from gasoline in the United States.

Diesel exhaust looms as a critical pollution source because a number of automobiles in the United States were built with diesel engines in the belief that diesel exhaust was less polluting. Although much lower on emission of CO, diesels emit 20 to 100 times more particles than gasoline engines and these particles remain in the lungs for some time. Some

ETTA HULME

ETTA ©1992 FORT WORTH STAR-TELEGRAM
HULME
NEA.

YOU ARE HERE ⇒ X

ENVIRONMENT

SOURCE: Reprinted by permission of Etta Hulme/*Fort Worth Star Telegram.*

research shows these particles to be carcinogenic (Nesnow & Huisingh, 1974). The move to diesels has slowed in the United States but picked up in Europe so that about 18% of engines burn diesel fuel there.

Even if you avoid the daily pollutants, if you manage to have an accident, the ambulance that comes to pick you up can provide more than your share of carbon monoxide. In the May 1984 issue of the *American Journal of Public Health,* unacceptable levels of CO were reported at the head of the stretcher in 22.6% of the ambulances tested. The gas gets into the vehicle when the exhaust pipe is mounted close to the rear doors. In no case should rear windows ever be opened. The researchers call for redesign of ambulances.

Industrial Pollutants

By March 1980, there were 27,000 major stationary sources of air pollution. A major source is one that releases more than 100 tons per year

Table 1.1 Air Pollutants From Energy Sources in Generation of Electricity

Technology[a]	Conversion Efficiency (percentage)	Emissions (grams per kilowatt hour)		
		NO_2	SO_2	CO_2
High-sulfur, coal-fired steam plant (without scrubbers)[b]	36	4.3	21.1	889
High-sulfur, coal-fired steam plant (with scrubbers)[c]	36	4.3	2.1	889
Low-sulfur, coal-fired fluidized bed plant	32	0.3	1.2	975
Oil-fired steam plant (uncontrolled)	33	1.4	1.6	794
Integrated gasification combined cycle plant (coal gasification)	38	0.2	0.3	747
Gas turbine combined cycle plant (current)[c]	43	0.3	0	416
Gas turbine combined cycle plant (advanced)[d]	55	0.03	0	331

SOURCE: Worldwatch Institute, "Air Pollution From Various Electricity Generating Technologies," *State of the World*, 1992, p. 36. Reprinted by permission.
a. The figures in this table are for particular plants that are representative of ones in operation or under development.
b. Burning coal with 2.5% sulfur content.
c. Using steam-injected gas turbines.
d. Using intercooled chemically recuperated gas turbine with reheat to improve the efficiency of converting exhaust steam into fuel energy.

of any pollutant. Pollutants from electricity-generating plants alone account for a major and growing source of pollution.

Table 1.1 shows energy source and air pollutants from the various kinds of energy used to generate electric power. It is obvious from this chart that natural gas is the preferred energy source in terms of saving the atmosphere. Coal is by far the most serious pollution source. Table 1.2 shows the levels of the principal pollutants in the atmosphere as established by the Pollution Standards Index (PSI). Seven additional substances emitted into the atmosphere have been listed as hazardous by section 112 of the Clean Air Act: asbestos, mercury, beryllium, vinyl chloride, benzene, radionuclides, and arsenic.

Toxic metals are a major part of the hazards from industrial emissions. Ore smelting produces arsenic. Coal ash yields zinc, copper, and mercury. Many power plants drop selenium, cadmium, and nickel from their stacks. These metals do not degrade; they remain wherever they are deposited. Nriagu and Pacyna (1988) claim the amounts already deposited constitute a "silent epidemic of environmental metal poisoning." Fortunately, levels of lead, zinc, cadmium, and copper dropped in the middle 1970s but the problems from these metals are increasing in underdeveloped countries.

Table 1.2 Comparison of PSI Values, Pollutant Levels, and General Health Effects

PSI value	Pollutant level TSP (24-hr) μg/m	SO (24-hr) μg/m	CO (8-hr) mg/m	O (1-hr) μg/m	NO (1-hr) μg/m	Descriptor	Health Effects	Warning
400 and above	875 and above	2,000 and above	46.0 and above	1,000 and above	3,000 and above	Hazardous	Premature death of ill and elderly. Healthy people will experience adverse symptoms that affect their normal activity.	All persons should remain indoors, keeping windows and doors closed. All persons should minimize physical exertion and avoid traffic.
300-399	625-874	1,600-2,099	34.0-45.9	900-1,099	2,260-2,999	Hazardous	Premature onset of certain diseases in addition to significant aggravation of symptoms and decreased exercise tolerance in healthy persons.	Elderly and persons with existing diseases should stay indoors and avoid physical exertion. General population should avoid outdoor activity.
200-299	375-624	800-1,599	17.0-33.9	480-899	1,130-2,259	Very unhealthful	Significant aggravation of symptoms and decreased exercise tolerance in persons with heart or lung disease, with widespread symptoms in the healthy population.	Elderly and persons with existing heart or lung disease should stay indoors and reduce physical activity.
100-199	260-374	365-799	10.0-16.9	240-479	NR	Unhealthful	Mild aggravation of symptoms in susceptible persons, with irritation symptoms in the healthy population.	Persons with existing heart or respiratory ailments should reduce physical exertion and outdoor activity.
50-99	75[a]-259	80[a]-364	5.0-9.9	120-239	NR	Moderate		
0-49	0-74	0-79	0-4.9	0-119	NR	Good		

SOURCE: U.S. Environmental Protection Agency, "Guideline for Public Reporting of Daily Air Quality—Pollutant Standards Index," 450/2-76-013 (Washington, DC, 1976).

NOTE: NR = No Index values reported at concentration levels below those specified by "alert level" criteria.

a. Annual primary NAAQS.

Air Quality: Indoor Environments

Nero (1988) lists the most common indoor pollutants as cigarette smoke, asbestos fibers, radon, formaldehyde, and other organic chemicals. Also there are indoor live inhabitants such as dust mites, fungus, and bacteria that contribute to allergy symptoms. At least 27 kinds of fungi in ventilation systems are known to cause illness. The EPA designates buildings with such pollutants as "sick buildings" (Hutchison, 1990).

On July 31, 1995, the Registry and Motor Vehicles building in the Roxbury district of Boston was closed permanently because a number of pollutants had made employees sick. Starch in the ceiling tiles had fermented from the moisture and produce butyric acid, which made the building smell like vomit. In addition, there were latex particles in the air to which some were allergic.

Latex allergy was a factor in sending 47 nurses on disability leave from the Brigham and Women's hospital in the same city. Fifty employees filed lawsuits partly because of the kind of antibiotics used and the latex contamination from the more frequent use of rubber gloves. (See the video *Can Buildings Make You Sick?* 1996.)

Smoking

The fact that smoking is hazardous to health has now been established beyond any doubt (U.S. Department of Health, Education and Welfare, 1979). Smoking is now considered the greatest single factor in causing cancer and is a prime contributor to heart disease (Kannel & Thomas, 1982).

Between 1950 and 1963, there was a tenfold increase of deaths among men due to chronic obstructive pulmonary disease (emphysema and bronchitis) and the number of deaths from these two diseases plus asthma continued to increase until they passed that of lung cancer in 1977 (Berkow et al., 1977). All these diseases have smoking as the primary cause, with environmental pollution as the second ranked cause (Enstrom, 1979). Even though the total number of smokers is decreasing, the ratio of female smokers is increasing.

There is conclusive evidence that mere exposure to cigarette smoke, even though one does not smoke, produces measurable effects on the body (Wald et al., 1984). Children of smokers have a 20% to 80% greater risk

Box 1.1

The Medical Effects of Tobacco Consumption

Discovered in the early 1800s and named nicotianine, the only essence now called nicotine is the main active ingredient of tobacco. Indeed, researchers recognized in 1942 that smoking dried tobacco leaves was basically a means of administering nicotine, just as smoking opium was a means of obtaining morphine. Nicotine, however, is but a small component of cigarette smoke, which contains more than 4,700 chemical compounds, including 43 cancer-causing substances. Condensates of tobacco smoke suspended in acetone and applied to the skin of mice for long periods cause papillomas or carcinomas at the site. Toxins in cigarette smoke cause breaks in the DNA of cultured human lung cells. In some cases, these carcinogens greatly accelerate the mutation rate in dividing cells, which in turn can lead to tumor formation.

Unfortunately for the smoker, no threshold level of exposure to the toxins has been found. What is clear is that years of cigarette smoking vastly increase the risk of developing several fatal conditions. In addition to being responsible for more than 85 percent of lung cancers, smoking is associated with cancers of the mouth, pharynx, larynx, esophagus, stomach, pancreas, uterine cervix, kidney, ureter, bladder and colon. Cigarette smoking is thought to cause about 14 percent of all leukemias and 30 percent of new cases of cervical cancer in women. All told, cigarette smoking is responsible for 30 percent of all deaths from cancer and clearly represents the most important preventable cause of cancer in the U.S. today.

Smoking also increases the risk of cardiovascular disease, including stroke, sudden death, heart attack, peripheral vascular disease and aortic aneurysm. Cigarettes caused almost 180,000 deaths from cardiovascular disease in the U.S. in 1990. Components of cigarette smoke damage the inner lining of blood vessels, which can lead to the development of atherosclerosis. The toxins can also stimulate occlusive elements in coronary arteries, thus promoting clots to form and triggering spasms that close off the vessels. In this regard, the smoking of a single cigarette can profoundly disturb blood flow to the heart in patients with existing coronary artery disease.

Furthermore, cigarette smoking is the leading cause of pulmonary illness and death in the U.S. In 1990 smoking caused more than 84,000 deaths from pulmonary disease, mainly resulting from such problems as pneumonia, emphysema, bronchitis and influenza.

Passive smoking—the breathing of sidestream smoke (emitted from the burning tobacco between puffs) or of smoke exhaled by the smoker—poses a similar health risk. A 1992 Environmental Protection Agency report emphasized the dangers, especially of sidestream smoke. This type of smoke contains more particles of smaller diameter and is therefore more likely to be deposited deep in the lungs. On the basis of this report, the EPA has classified environmental tobacco smoke as a "group A" carcinogen, to which radon, asbestos, arsenic and benzene belong.

of respiratory problems than children of nonsmokers. People married to smokers run a 30% greater chance of getting lung cancer than those married to nonsmokers.

Of the 12,000 deaths due to lung cancer in 1985, 2,400 were caused by environmental smoke (National Research Council, 1986). Some researchers feel there is conclusive evidence that smoking is the reason males don't live as long as females.

Box 1.1 Continued

Of the estimated 53,000 annual deaths in the U.S. caused by passive smoking, 37,000 come from associated heart disease. A nonsmoker living with a smoker has a 30 percent higher risk of death from ischemic heart disease or myocardial infarction. Lung cancer risk also skyrockets. Any exposure from a spouse who smokes is associated with at least a 30 percent excess risk of lung cancer. Increasing daily amounts and the number of years of smoking significantly heighten the risk. The figure jumps to 80 percent if the spouse has been smoking four packs a day for 20 years. Another recent study points out that 17 percent of the cases of lung cancer among nonsmokers can be attributed to exposure to high levels of tobacco smoke during childhood and adolescence.

The health consequences of smoking among women are of special concern because of the deleterious effect on reproduction. Unfortunately, the fastest-growing segment of smokers in the U.S. is women younger than 23 years. Smoking reduces fertility, spurs the rate of spontaneous abortions and stillbirths, can cause excessive bleeding during pregnancy and results in lower birth weights in infants. Moreover, children of smokers do not grow as large or attain the same level of educational achievement as unexposed children.

Smoking is a significant cause of cardiovascular diseases and strokes in women, especially if they also use oral contraceptives. Lung cancer has now surpassed breast cancer as the primary cause of death from cancer among women. In 1993 lung cancer claimed an estimated 56,000 deaths, whereas breast cancer took 46,000 lives.

The elderly also faced special harm from smoking. Among those older than 65, the rates of total mortality among current smokers are twice those among people who have never smoked. A 1992 *Time* magazine article noted that three life insurers owned by tobacco companies charge smokers nearly double for term insurance.

Smoking is associated with a variety of other ailments: cataracts, delayed healing of broken bones, periodontal maladies, predisposition to ulcer disease, hypertension, brain hemorrhages and skin wrinkles, to name just a few.

Recently some studies have suggested that cigarette smoking ameliorates symptoms of Alzheimer's disease. It is not surprising that with its powerful effect on the central nervous system, nicotine may influence the condition. Yet methodological flaws plague many of these studies. Moreover, other researchers suggest that smoking may increase the risk of Alzheimer's, in that it accelerates the natural consequences of aging. With its many and potent toxins, cigarettes would in any case be an inappropriate vehicle for delivering nicotine should the compound ever prove valuable in treating Alzheimer's.

There is much to be gained by those who kick the habit. After a year, mortality from heart disease drops halfway back to that of a nonsmoker; by five years, it drops to the rate of nonsmokers. A person's risk of lung cancer is cut in half in five years; by 10 years, it drops almost to the rate of nonsmokers. Such gains make sense, however, only if smokers quit in time, before they show any signs of tobacco's lethal effects.

The Working Place Atmosphere

Where you work has a critical effect on the air you breathe. Industrial environments are notorious for containing workplace pollutants. Several million workers are exposed to silica dust, a comparable number are exposed to asbestos, and hundreds of thousands to cotton dust in textile mills; 12½% of miners suffer from pneumonoconiosis (black lung) (National Institute for Occupational Safety & Health [NIOSH], 1975). Not only do these various dusts contribute to lung disease but toxic gases such as oxides of nitrogen, sulfur, ammonia, chlorine, and ozone contribute to lung irritation and disease.

Noise in the Workplace

The modern world is increasingly noisy. Jet planes (Cohen, Krantz, Evans, Stokols, & Kelly, 1981) and rock concerts (Lipscomb, 1982, as quoted in Raloff, 1982) are only two of the more dramatic examples of industrial technology that have harmful effects on hearing. On the more moderate level, EPA standards state that any interference with normal activities constitutes a noise level that should be avoided. Sound levels are measured in decibels. Table 1.3 shows the decibel (dB) levels of common noise sources.

Sound is carried by the atmosphere so that without the presence of atmospheric gases, there can be no noise. Noise is now considered the most widespread occupational hazard facing American workers. Hearing can be permanently damaged by exposure to noise levels above 75 dB during an 8-hour workday.

About 53% of U.S. workers are exposed to dB levels of 80 or more and 5.1 million work in environments at the 90-dB level. The insidious fact about loss of hearing is that it doesn't hurt while the hearing capacity is being damaged, and the loss is permanent. The sensitive hair cells of the inner ear do not regenerate. The person who suffers hearing loss is seldom aware it is taking place until the damage is noticeable and at an advanced stage. Furthermore, the more hearing is damaged, the easier it is to damage it more. This is why continuous exposure to high sound levels like those found in many workplaces is particularly harmful: The damage is progressive in nature. Also, intermittent loud noises seem to be just as harmful as the steady noise.

Noise is also a factor in raising blood pressure and causes ulcers and neurological disorders. Coupled with this, it is known that certain drugs, among them aspirin and antibiotics, will interact with noise to impair hearing further.

The capstone for all this injury caused by noise is that it increasingly intrudes into daily life. The President's Council on Environmental Quality estimates that at least 13.5 million people are exposed to vehicular noise of 75 dB or more—a level sufficient to cause permanent damage. And it

Table 1.3 Sources of Noise

Sound Levels (decibels)		
Harmful to hearing	140	Jet Engine (25m distance)
	130	Jet takeoff (100m away) Threshold of pain
	120	Propeller aircraft
Risk hearing loss	110	Live rock band
	100	Jackhammer/Pneumatic chipper
	90	Heavy-duty truck Los Angeles, 3rd floor apartment next to freeway Average street traffic
Very noisy	80	Harlem, 2nd floor apartment
Urban	70	Private car Boston row house on major avenue Business office Watts—8 mi. from touch down at major airport
	60	Conversational speech or old residential area in LA
Suburban & small town	50	San Diego—wooded residential area
		California tomato field
	40	Soft music from radio
	30	Quiet whisper
	20	Quiet urban dwelling
	10	Rustle of leaf
	0	Threshold of hearing

SOURCE: U.S. Environmental Protection Agency (1974).
NOTE: Because the decibel scale is a logarithmic measure of sound intensity, values don't add in the usual way: a 60 dB sound played atop another 60 dB sound corresponds to 63 dB noise. And a 10 dB difference means one sound is 10 times louder than the other, so that the ratio between 140 dB and 0 dB is roughly 100 trillion to 1. Readings for cities (above) represent levels actually measured by EPA and expressed as a day-night average.

seems these levels will only increase in the future, for example, from aircraft noise (see Figure 1.2).

Indoor Atmosphere of Homes and Public Places

Research on the indoor atmosphere of homes is relatively recent. Americans spend about 80% of their time indoors, including work, shop-

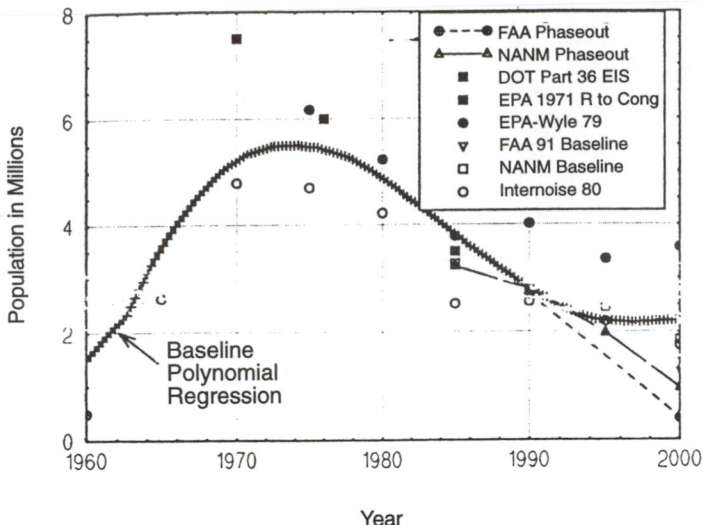

Figure 1.2. Population Estimated to Reside in Areas Where the Day-Night Sound Level Exceeds 65 dB
SOURCE: Council on Environmental Quality (1980).

ping, and recreation. This makes the potential for exposure to pollution greater for the indoor environment than out-of-doors. The evidence for exposure to tobacco smoke has been so convincing (Repace & Lowrey, 1980) that smoking in many public places has been prohibited or limited.

For indoor home environments, radon has been shown to be the most prominent pollutant. Radium 226 decays to produce radon gas. Even though radium is only a trace element, it is widely found in rocks and soil. Thus any house contains a significant amount in its building materials and the soil beneath the foundation. Tests indicate that indoor concentrations of radon are significantly higher than outdoors. The EPA estimates that as many as 10% of all deaths from lung cancer could be caused by radon exposure.

As a result of a nationwide survey in 1987, the EPA found 21% of 11,600 homes had radon levels above the point at which some action should be taken. This amounts to one in five houses, making radon clearly the number one danger on the indoor home pollution list (Kerr, 1988b).

Formaldehyde is best known as an embalming fluid. It is also a common ingredient in foam insulation, furniture, carpets, drapes, and other common household items. It is widely used as a bonding agent in plywood and particle board. When natural gas is used, it is a byproduct of combustion.

Formaldehyde can produce nausea, eye irritation, and respiratory impairment in the short term, or cancer in the long term. Indoor levels of formaldehyde in the United States exceed .12 ppm, in some cases going beyond 3 ppm. The Netherlands set a standard for indoor air at .1 ppm. In an energy-efficient house, when the house was empty, formaldehyde levels were below 120 mg/m3, but when furniture was added, the level tripled. The Consumer Product Safety Commission has received over 500 complaints about health-related problems connected with foam insulation and formaldehyde.

Asbestos tile floors and ceilings sprayed with crocidolite materials release asbestos particles into the indoor air. In a sample of 122 buildings, concentrations of asbestos fibers in the air were found to be significantly higher than outdoors (Sebastian, Bignon, & Martin, 1982). Most of the particles come from the normal wearing of asbestos tile flooring as people walk on it.

Recently, Mossman, Bignon, Corn, Seaton, and Gee (1990) asserted that only one form of asbestos, amphibole, is responsible for its pathological effects while chrysotile, a more prevalent form, has little or no danger. This has been called the *Amphibole Hypothesis*. The hypothesis was immediately challenged (Brody, 1990; Crump, 1990; Nicholson, Johnson, Harington, Melius, & Landrigan, 1990). The National Academy of Sciences lists chrysotile as cancer causing, and the above cited researchers claim Mossman et al. ignored records that showed chrysotile workers to be susceptible to cancer. An apparent problem with chrysotile is that it does not remain in the lungs as long as amphibole and hence is not given credit for the damage it does.

Modern construction methods have unwittingly increased the problems of indoor pollution by the new efficiency in creating airtight windows, walls, and doors. An example of how these methods cause problems is provided by the ancient custom of the *coursi* in Iran. In a classical Iranian house, a room was built just for the practice. In fact, some wealthy homes still have such rooms. The coursi is practiced by gathering around a small table that contains a bed of charcoal underneath. The members of the family and/or friends sit with their feet toward the table and cover themselves with heavy blankets. It was a cozy way to warm up. Unfortunately, with modern construction seals on the doors and windows, not enough air gets into the room so that practitioners of this custom began dying of carbon dioxide asphyxiation. So many people were dying from this custom that it had to be outlawed. It did not occur to anyone to return to the old, inefficient, and draftier methods of construction.

Sometimes efforts to remedy environmental problems themselves result in increased risks. For example, to counteract the cost of fuel oil and exhaustion of the wood supply, the kerosene heater was reintroduced into the American home. Unfortunately, testing of these heaters (Leaderer, 1982) showed they "can result in exposures to air pollutants in excess of ambient air quality standards and in some cases in excess of occupational health standards" (p. 1113).

OSHA, the Occupational Safety and Health Administration, estimates there are 16,000 to 18,000 indoor firing ranges. The lead from bullets pollutes the air of these ranges to a significant extent by about 40 times the acceptable level of 50 micrograms per cubic meter (Valway, Martyny, & Miller, 1989).

Space: The Final Frontier (Escape?)

The ultimate escape from all this atmospheric pollution and dust, noise, and danger is to flee to outer space! Wrong!

The shuttle astronauts missed being blitzed by dangerous radiation from sun spots (Rust, 1982). In fact, the atmosphere and the Earth's magnetic field combine to protect us from frequent showers of deadly particles. Cosmic rays, whose origins are still unknown, frequently bombard us and leave a tiny track of dead tissue to mark their passage through our bodies. The atmosphere absorbs these rays to some extent but astronauts aboard the shuttle experience them more frequently and more strongly as flashes of light when they pass through the retina.

Sunspots release such a deadly shower of particles that if an astronaut had gone outside the shuttle on the third test flight during a sunspot storm, he would have been overcome with nausea and vomiting, the symptoms of radiation sickness.

Added to this is the greatest problem of space travel to date: the dissolving of calcium from the bones into the blood and the accompanying atrophy of muscles. Because U.S. astronauts have had relatively short flights, this phenomenon has been hard to observe. But when the Russian astronauts land from their long space flights, they must be carried to the waiting vehicles because they can no longer walk on their own power.

Without gravity, the muscles shrink and the bones lose their strength. Muscles and bone must be constantly used under the force of gravity to keep them at their normal strength. Some of the same experience comes from staying in bed for a long period but this is not nearly as profound as that experienced by the Russian astronauts. Although these effects may be somewhat alleviated by exercise, the problem is to get exercise equal to the gravity level of Earth.

So, dear readers, there is no escape in outer space.

Water Quality

Acid Rain

Next to the CO_2 buildup in the atmosphere, the second largest threat to the environment (even larger than the loss of ozone) comes from the recently discovered phenomenon known as acid rain. It is hard to exaggerate the potential damage that acid rain can do. The principal causes of acid rain are the expulsion of sulfur dioxide (SO_2) and nitrous oxide (NO_2) into the atmosphere from tall smokestacks. These gases combine with water in the air to form sulfuric and nitric acid. The acid falls to the Earth as dry particles, combines with water to fall as acid rain, dew, or even snow, or combs through trees on mountaintops as acid clouds. Acidic clouds can be 10 times more acidic than rain. Tall stacks transport these particles for long distances with the result that Canada has charged the United States with destroying its lakes. The concentration of these tall stacks in the eastern, North Central, and South Atlantic regions of the United States makes New England and Eastern Canada prime targets of acid rain.

Measurement of acidity is calibrated on a pH scale, 7 being neutral. Distilled water measures exactly 7. Vinegar measures 3 and lemon juice 2.2, but each unit on the pH scale represents an increase of 10, making vinegar, at 3, 100 times more acidic than a substance with a pH of 5. Lakes in the Adirondacks measured 5.6. Acid rain kills fish, the organisms they feed on, and, eventually, the plants of the entire ecosystem. With increasing pressure to use coal in the building of new generators of electricity (look at Table 1.1 again), these emissions have increased even though controls have decreased their volume from existing plants. Thus, even though controls have been put in place, there is a net gain in pollution because of the number of new plants (*State of the World,* Flavin & Lenssen, 1994). Currently, rains are falling on the northeast two thirds of the North American continent with 10 times the acidity of normal rain.

Current attempts to control SO_2 and NO_2 do not affect the level of sulphate particles (SO_4), which may turn out to be a significant contributor to acid rain. Sulphate particles are especially important, not only because they have not decreased with the decrease of SO_2 but because they can only increase with the use of high-sulfur coal. Thus the use of coal as a solution to the energy problem may produce even more acid rain (Amdur, 1976).

In Canada, 140 lakes have had fish killed due to acid rain. In Nova Scotia, nine rivers are barren. It is estimated that thousands of lakes could become devoid of fish by the end of the decade (Conservation Foundation, 1982). The identification of tall smokestacks as the primary source of acid rain was made over 10 years ago (National Academy of Sciences [NAS], 1983a).

Schindler (1988) points out the interaction of acid rain with toxic metals. The higher acidic level helps dissolve them where they can concentrate in still bodies of water such as lakes. Recent studies (Likens, Driscoll, & Buso, 1996) indicate that the effects of acid rain are more long-lasting and costly than anticipated. Long-term data show that calcium and magnesium were leached from the soils of forests, and this means the 1990 amendments to the Clean Air Act of 1970 may not be sufficient to stop the effects of acidic leaching.

Polychlorinated Biphenyls (PCBs)

PCBs are oily or waxy substances manufactured in the United States from 1929 until 1977 when they were banned because of their cancer-causing properties. These substances continue to be used as cooling liquids in electrical transformers and capacitors. Supposedly, because the systems are closed, they will no longer be released, but the problem of their eventual disposal remains. At one time, PCBs were also used as heat transfer and hydraulic fluids, dye carriers in carbonless copy paper, additives in paints, adhesives and caulking compounds, sealant and dust control road coverings, and as pesticide extenders. In short, they were nearly everywhere and—they linger on.

PCBs are among the most chemically stable substances known, which means they won't decay or lose their cancer-causing capacity. The EPA estimates there are 150 million pounds of PCBs dispersed throughout the United States gradually working their way into water tables and water systems. An additional 290 million pounds are in landfills and an additional 750 million pounds in various pieces of equipment from voltage regulators to electromagnets. These latter represent the closed systems that must one day be reckoned with.

As these chemicals work their way into the food chain, they contaminate various animals. For example, fish from the area that drains the Redstone Arsenal in Alabama show a concentration of from .36 to 3.32 ppm of PCBs per liter of blood serum. Although no data are yet available, EPA officials estimate that every person in industrialized countries has accumulated some level of PCBs in the blood.

More serious is the appearance of PCBs in the breast milk of Inuit women in the Arctic and the resulting lowered immunity of children (DeWailly et al., 1989).

A dramatic incident of PCB contamination occurred in 1965 when about 1,000 Japanese developed skin lesions, dark splotches on their skin, eye discharge, and peripheral nervous disorders after eating rice oil contaminated with a mixture of PCBs. Since they were first used in 1929, 1.25 billion pounds of PCBs have been produced. In May 1983, the EPA announced that the fraction of Americans with "high" levels of PCBs declined from 9.7% to 1% in 1981.

PBBs

Polybrominated biphenyls (PBBs) are another source of contamination. Their potency became evident recently when 35,000 cattle and other livestock had to be slaughtered in Michigan because of the accidental mixing of PBBs into cattle feed. The cattle developed bizarre symptoms of hoof lesions, loss of milk, and staggering behavior. Shortly after, humans who had eaten the meat became affected with loss of concentration and memory. The result was the largest case of contamination in history, with virtually every resident in the state of Michigan (9,000,000) contaminated in some way (Eggington, 1982).

EDB

Ethylene dibromide (EDB) is a pesticide that had been under investigation for 7 years when it was finally banned in the state of Florida in 1984. The EPA tried to control its use as far back as 1977 but protests from manufacturers and lack of response from federal officials in the Reagan administration resulted in no federal action. Aunt Jemima and

Chemicals: How Many Are There?

Like it or not, the world around us is filled with chemicals. The clothes we wear, the foods we eat, the magazines we read, and virtually all of the other things that nurture our civilization are made possible by the use of chemicals. Recognition of these facts, and of some of the potential dangers of chemicals, often prompts the question How many chemicals are there? A definitive answer to that question has proved elusive, but one measure of the answer is provided by the American Chemical Society's Chemical Abstracts Service (CAS). As of November 1977, CAS's unique computer registry of chemicals contained 4,039,907 distinct entities. The number of chemicals in the register, moreover, has been growing at an average rate of about 6000 per week.

CAS began the computer registry in 1965 to assist in the indexing of chemical substances reported in the scientific literature. The system identifies chemicals on the basis of an unambiguous computer-language description of their composition and molecular structure and automatically assigns a permanent identifying number to each unique substance. The registry contains all compounds that have been mentioned in the literature since 1965.

The system is not set up to provide a detailed breakdown of different classes of chemicals. Some broad generalizations can be made, though. About 96 percent of the chemicals, for example, contain carbon. The average compound in the registry, if it is possible to define such a thing as an average compound, contains 43 atoms, 22 of which are hydrogen. The fictitious average compound also contains one and a half ring systems with eight atoms per ring.

About 3.4 million of the chemicals are organic or inorganic chemicals whose structures are fully defined. Some 3 million of these contain at least one ring system. Another 258,000 entities are coordination compounds, which require a somewhat different registration procedure. About 59,000 are organic compounds whose structures are not completely defined; these generally are compounds in which the exact location of a substituent or a double bond or the site of an esterification is uncertain. About 120,000 entries are listed only by name or molecular formula; these are specifically identified substances for which not enough is known or has been disclosed about structure to permit machine structure registration. The registry also lists 72,000 alloys, 120,000 polymers, and 10,000 mixtures with specific names.

The list contains some apparent duplication in that stereoisomers are listed individually. There are, for example, four listings for aspartic acid: D-aspartic acid, L-aspartic acid, DL-aspartic acid, and aspartic acid of unspecified stereochemistry. Since each of these has its own biological characteristics, however, they can justifiably be considered distinct entities.

The vast majority of chemicals in the registry are esoteric materials that have been isolated from natural products or synthesized for research purposes. A more interesting problem, then, might be to define the number of chemicals that are in everyday use. That problem is much more difficult, but at least a partial answer may soon be available. As part of the Toxic Substances Control Act, the Environmental Protection Agency (EPA) has been charged with maintaining an inventory of chemical substances manufactured, imported, or processed in the United States for commercial purposes. Because there are so many different names for many of the chemicals used in industry, EPA has contracted with CAS to process reports submitted by manufacturers, determine the precise identity of the reported chemicals, and create and maintain a computer file on the chemicals and their manufacturers.

To initiate the project, CAS has submitted to EPA a preliminary list of some 33,000 chemicals that are thought to be in common use. The complexity of the registration problem is illustrated by the fact that CAS has already found in its files more than 183,000 different names for those chemicals. Current estimates from EPA, moreover, indicate that there may be as many as 50,000 chemicals in everyday use, not including pesticides, pharmaceuticals, and food additives. EPA estimates that there may be as many as 1500 different active ingredients in pesticides. The Food and Drug Administration estimates that there are about 4000 active ingredients in drugs and about 2000 other compounds used as excipients to promote stability, cut down on growth of bacteria, and so forth. FDA also estimates that there are about 2500 additives used for nutritional value and flavoring and 3000 chemicals used to promote product life. The best estimate thus is that there are about 63,000 chemicals in common use. Small wonder then that determination of the safety of all commonly used chemicals is a massive project that may never be completely finished.

—THOMAS H. MAUGH II

SOURCE: Reprinted with permission from *Science*, Vol. 199, January 13, 1978. Copyright © 1978 American Association for the Advancement of Science.

Pillsbury products were pulled off the shelves of Florida groceries because of contamination with EDB.

The use of EDB has stretched over 40 years for such purposes as fumigating milling machinery, killing nematodes (worms) in soil, and an

Table 1.4 Observed Latency Period in 78 Workers Exposed to Aromatic Amines

Length of latent period in years	Percentage of workers with tumors, by length of exposure in years					
	Up to 1	1	2	3	4	5 and over
Up to 5	0	0	0	0	0	0
10	0	0	0	0	0	11
15	0	17	22	0	10	45
20	4	17	22	40	30	69
25	9	17	22	70	70	88
30	9	17	48	70	80	94

SOURCE: Wilhelm Hueper, *Medicolegal Considerations of Occupational and Nonoccupational Environmental Cancers,* chapter 7 in Charles Frankel and James G. Zimmerly, *Lawyers' Medical Cyclopedia* (1992). Charlottesville, VA: Michie Butterworth.
NOTE: For example, of those workers who were exposed for two years 30 years ago, 48% had tumors.

insecticide against the medfly. California fumigated all its exported citrus with EDB. The EPA estimated 30% of all packaged grain products showed contamination.

The EPA studies in the 1970s showed EDP was highly toxic and carcinogenic to a number of animals. Because it had been used so long, it never received the scrutiny of new chemicals.

Other Industrial Wastes

Every year, new chemicals are invented for industrial and domestic use. Currently there are over 63,000 chemical substances throughout the world used as drugs, insecticides, industrial solvents, paints, hair conditioners, and in many other functions. As many as 1,000 of these substances are known carcinogens with new ones being discovered annually (see the box on chemicals). For example, a few years ago, a flame retardant known as triphosphate was used on children's pajamas to make them flameproof. Then it was found to cause cancer in laboratory animals. Saccharin is another example of a substance once commonly used (as a substitute for sugar) that was found to be cancer causing.

The most serious problem with many chemicals is their latency effect. It often takes a long time before the harmful effect is noticed. Table 1.4 shows the long-term effects of aromatic amines, 0 to 30 years. Clearly, by the end of 30 years, the greatest amount of tumors were generated. With only short-term studies, it would have been impossible to observe these effects. An example of how long-term effects complicate the elimination of cancer-causing substances was the government case against Reserve Mining Company for dumping asbestos wastes into Lake Superior. The town and most of the workers opposed the EPA because it meant the loss of jobs in the area. Most simply did not believe there were long-term effects of exposure to asbestos. None of them had yet experienced it.

More recently, a trailer park in Globe, Arizona, had to be evacuated because it was built on an asbestos waste dump. The EPA paid to evacuate the residents. The developer testified that he did not believe asbestos caused cancer. Asbestos is known to be the sole cause of mesothelioma, a lung cancer. This is one of the few cases where a specific disease can be linked to a specific chemical. Most environmentally caused diseases are much more ambiguous.

Antibiotics

At first, it may seem unbelievable that antibiotics could be an environmental pollutant. After all, antibiotics are the reason most of us no longer die of communicable disease. The problem occurs when they were used as a regular supplement to animal feed. Research showed that cows, chickens, pigs, and other animals grew to a larger size and developed faster when antibiotics were used with their food. But with prolonged use of antibiotics, bacteria can grow resistant strains in just a few generations. Evidence was forthcoming in 1983 when salmonella-resistant bacteria infected people in a Minnesota town who ate meat from a particular farmer's cows. The farmer had been using antibiotics in his feed (Sun, 1987).

Lead Again

Recently, standards have been developed for lead in drinking water that lower the acceptable level from 50 ppb to 15. Beginning in 1992, municipal water suppliers had to monitor lead levels at the faucet. This came about from the discovery that lead in the solder used on the pipes dissolves into drinking water. Lead was banned from all new plumbing in 1987 but the majority of all plumbing up to that point remains with its old solder. Water suppliers have up to 15 years to replace the old plumbing.

More recently, the use of electric cars has been questioned on the premise that more lead would be introduced into the atmosphere than would have occurred with the continued use of leaded gasoline. The source is the lead plates used in batteries (Lave, Hendrickson, & McMichael, 1995).

And Radon Again

EPA experts estimate that 40% of public drinking water is contaminated by radon that seeps out of rocks. Radon in water is estimated to cause 30 to 600 excess deaths from lung cancer annually, making radon the number one polluter of water supplies (Cothern & Ohanian, 1987; Cothern & Smith, 1987).

Rivers Run Through It

Measuring water quality from over 300 locations, Smith, Alexander, and Wolman (1987) observed changes from 1974 to 1981 that showed decreases in fecal bacteria and lead but increases in nitrate, chloride, arsenic, and cadmium. Nitrates originate largely from agricultural chemicals and increases in air pollution. Highway salt has influenced sodium and chloride increases, but the Colorado River declined in salinity. Arsenic and cadmium come largely from midwestern locations as combustion products. If anything, this lesson shows that as we improve one area, vigilance cannot be relaxed on others.

The Ocean

The nations of the world have long considered the oceans a limitless source of food and a limitless waste disposal facility. It was inevitable that a harvest of waste be the outcome. For centuries, the various oceans have been the recipients of raw sewage, garbage, and industrial effluents. Even to this moment, the raw sewage and sludge that remain after treatment are dumped into the oceans. Added to this are the residues from rivers and harbors, the radioactive wastes from certain countries such as Britain, Belgium, Netherlands, and Switzerland, and the washings from oil and chemical tankers as well as occasional oil spills.

The dumping of ocean wastes, when regulated by the EPA, decreased from 10.8 million tons in 1973 to 8.7 million tons in 1974. But dumping of municipal sludge has increased largely because more cities are now treating their sewage.

One seldom thinks of harbor and river dredging as a significant pollutant, but in 1979, 72.8 million cubic yards of waste materials were dumped into the ocean from U.S. harbors and rivers. A significant portion of these wastes are contaminated with toxic chemicals.

Radioactive waste disposal has been controlled by international agreement since 1967. A minimum depth for disposal of 4,000 meters has been recommended (but not enforced). Also, only low-level wastes are disposed at sea. Nations disposing of radioactive wastes must notify an international agency (OECD) and give access to all disposal sites.

Unfortunately, not enough is known about what happens at all these disposal sites. Do modern containers decay and allow these wastes into the food chain? To date, few investigations have been made. More than 600,000 curies of mixed wastes have been dumped with annual totals ranging around 85,000 curies.

Oil spilled from tankers reached a peak of 724,000 metric tons in 65 incidents in 1979. The Campeche well blowout in the Gulf of Mexico was the largest oil spill in history (about 425,000 metric tons) until the Exxon tanker spill in 1989. The Exxon accident is a good illustration of how ill prepared industry and government are to deal with these episodes even after a long history that predicts a continuing series of spills (Weber, 1993).

Coupled with the losses due to pollution is the disastrous loss due to overfishing. The situation became so desperate that the Canadian government began seizing vessels at gunpoint in April 1994 to save what once was the largest fishing resource in the world, the Grand Banks of Newfoundland.

In the last few years, more than 100,000 fishermen have lost their way of earning a living and the remaining 20 million are feeling threatened (Weber, 1994). Some fisheries have dropped by as much as 30% while all but two areas in the world have experienced an annual loss that is increasing. Fourteen major fish species are so seriously depleted it would take 5 to 20 years to recover if all were fishing stopped. Unfortunately, most governments still support expansion of their fishing industries, and the overcapacity of those industries continues.

The Land

Chemical Dumps

Disposal of hazardous wastes has been a long-term problem since the industrial revolution, but only fairly recently, through such dramatic incidents as Love Canal (A. Levine, 1982), has the threat they are to human life been recognized. It is estimated that there are now 75,700 active industrial landfills in the United States. An estimated 50,644 active and inactive sites may have potentially hazardous wastes (Hart & Associates, 1979). An assessment of 25,749 sites was made in 1979 (Silka & Brasier, 1980) and it was found that for 95% there was no groundwater monitoring system to detect contamination. By 1989, action had begun only on 250 sites identified as having national priority (Department of Energy, 1989).

The problems from chemical dumps illustrate the artificiality of separating water quality from land quality because it is this contamination from the land that contributes so dramatically to the pollution of groundwater and streams and rivers. Figure 1.3 shows the various processes whereby groundwater is contaminated.

In 1980, an estimated 56 million metric tons of hazardous waste was generated nationwide. Over half of this amount (60%) came from 10 states: New Jersey, Illinois, Ohio, California, Pennsylvania, Texas, New York, Michigan, Tennessee, and Indiana.

Of all these wastes, 90% are being disposed of in an "environmentally unsound" manner (Subcommittee on Oversights and Investigations, 1979). This includes unsecured landfills, improper incineration, and illegal dumping. Illegal dumping involves a company contracting with an individual or organization to dispose of its hazardous wastes. This professional disposer then dumps the waste at an illegal place such as federal land, the ocean, or any vacant lot, and then, conveniently, goes out of business. The hazardous wastes are then on some public land to be moved at taxpayer expense while no one can be found who is legally responsible. A new business is then formed and the practice continues. Municipal waste reached 302 million tons in 1970 and grew to 420 million tons by 1990 (Meadows, Meadows, & Randers, 1992). Most is still dealt with in an "environmentally unsound manner."

In a sample of 39 cities in the United States, the most common pollutant in groundwater supplies was found to be trichloroethylene

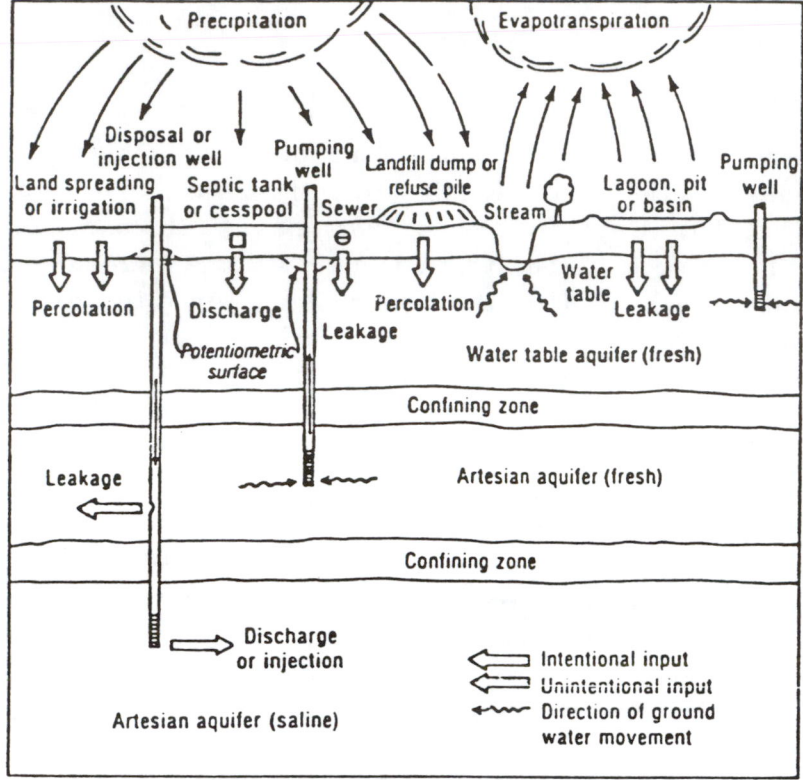

Figure 1.3. Sources of Groundwater Contamination
SOURCE: Council on Environmental Quality (1980).

(TCE). By March 1980, state agencies throughout the United States had tested hundreds of wells and found TCE to be the most prevalent contaminating substance. Private wells are being closed throughout the United States because of TCE contamination (EPA, 1979).

The cost of removing the wastes from the ground is staggering. A $45 million lawsuit was used just to clean up Love Canal. Yet many thousands of these sites exist. The EPA estimates the total cost of removing waste ranges from $20 to $1,000 per metric ton depending on the method. With estimates of from 27 to 54 million metric tons per year of such wastes, this averages to over 550 pounds per person in the United States, or a cost of $10,000 per person per year at the higher cost method. But it is difficult to arrive at verifiable figures (Conservation Foundation, 1982). These estimates do not deal with the considerable social and psychological problems of people in communities exposed to chemical dangers (Edelstein, 1988).

Table 1.5 Total U.S. Industrial Hazardous Wastes

Source	Percentage of total
Chemical and allied products	60
Machinery (except electrical)	10
Primary metals	8
Paper and allied products	6
Fabricated metal products	4
Stone, clay, and glass products	3
All others	9

SOURCE: U.S. Environmental Protection Agency, Office of Water and Waste Management, *Everybody's Problem: Hazardous Waste* (Washington, DC: Government Printing Office, 1980), p. 14.

Table 1.6 Common Hazardous Wastes

Chemical	Use	Manufacturing hazard
C-56	Bug and Insect killer	Acutely toxic, suspected carcinogen
Trichloroethylene (TCE)	Degreaser	Suspected carcinogen
Benzidene	Dye industry	Known human carcinogen
Curene 442	Plastics industry	Suspected carcinogen
Polychlorinated biphenyls (PCBs)	Insulators, paints, and electrical circuitry	Acutely toxic, suspected carcinogen
Benzene	Solvent	Suspected carcinogen
Tris	Fire retardant	Suspected carcinogen
DDT	Bug and Insect killer	Acutely toxic
Vinyl chloride	Plastics industry	Known human carcinogen
Mercury	Multiple Uses	Acutely toxic, suspected carcinogen
Carbon tetrachloride	Solvent	Acutely toxic, suspected carcinogen
Polybrominated biphenyls (PBBs)	Fire retardant	Effects unknown

SOURCE: Sharp and Hall (1979, p. 19A); reprinted by permission of *Detroit Free Press.*

The EPA has 7,200 waste disposal sites under investigation. The nature of these wastes is detailed in Tables 1.5 and 1.6.

Landfills

In 1978, 14,000 active municipal landfills were identified in a national survey (Eldridge, 1978) and only 35% of these were found to be in compliance with their state's laws. These data do not include landfills already covered and abandoned. In addition, there are 19½ million home units in the United States still using on-site disposal systems such as septic tanks. These release an estimated 1 trillion gallons of waste a year. Septic tanks and cesspools are the largest polluters of the land and are the most frequent source of fecal, toxic, and other kinds of contamination. They frequently contaminate nearby wells—often the well owned by the same person who uses the septic tank or cesspool (Council on Environmental Quality [CEQ], 1980).

Because sludge buildup in septic tanks can cause the growth of harmful bacteria, homeowners often buy septic tank cleaning fluids that dissolve the sludge. Unfortunately, the solvent contains trichloroethylene (TCE), benzene, or methyl chloride, which dissolves the sludge and then contaminates the groundwater. An estimated 400,000 gallons of these cleaners were used by home owners on Long Island in 1979 (CEQ, 1980, pp. 90-91).

Insecticides and Herbicides

Since Rachel Carson's *Silent Spring* (1962), the public has been made aware of the increasing hazards of insecticide use, particularly DDT. As a result of public outcry, DDT was banned in 1977, but not before it had covered the globe. Traces of DDT were found in Antarctic penguins. It seemed to bring about the near extinction of the peregrine falcon on the eastern seaboard of the United States and has had detrimental effects on the brown pelican and many species of fish. Since its ban, concentrations of DDT have decreased in the United States, but it is still exported to countries that have not outlawed it and sometimes comes back to the United States on imported foodstuffs! Furthermore, the waning influence of DDT has more than been made up for by the increasing use of other insecticides and the exponentially increasing use of herbicides.

The legal case against the herbicide Agent Orange provides an example of the destructiveness of herbicides. In Vietnam between 1962 and 1970, a mere 368 pounds of dioxin was accidentally included in an herbicide used to defoliate certain areas of the country. By 1972, complaints about harmful effects from exposure to Agent Orange began to be received by the Veteran's Administration from soldiers who had been exposed in Vietnam. Sampling 22 persons who claimed exposure, it was found that 10 had traces from 3 to 57 ppm. By September 1979, there were 4,800 complaints and 750 had filed for compensation. Claims were not paid because the causal role of dioxin in human cancer had not been proven.

Nevertheless, the VA set aside a fund to eventually pay all claimants without admitting a causal link.

By 1994, dioxin was linked to the following diseases: soft tissue sarcoma, non-Hodgkin's lymphoma, and the already known chloracne. The VA has added Hodgkin's disease and porphyria cutana tardia (a liver disease) as linked to exposure to dioxin. These conclusions were the result of a National Academy of Sciences study of 6,000 abstracts on dioxin and 230 epidemiological studies. By July 1993, 40,097 claims had been filed with the VA related to Agent Orange.

A dramatic contamination from dioxin was discovered at Times Beach, Missouri, in 1983 when someone tried to dampen the dust of the town with a dioxin-laced liquid. The town was ordered evacuated by the EPA and 2,200 people were moved to new homes. Times Beach was only 1 of 15 known dioxin-contaminated sites in Missouri, with 80 more suspected.

Food

"You are what you eat" is a common saying. But what if the food you eat is poisoned? Lead is one of the chief environmental poisons. Symptoms of severe lead poisoning include convulsions, coma, and death. Chronic exposure to low levels produces fatigue, headache, poor appetite, clumsiness, and diminished mental capacity. A high source of exposure to lead is food, chiefly through the lead solder used on cans that hold the food. This source has greatly decreased since 1970.

Caffeine recently has been considered a hazard in food. It is primarily found in coffee, tea, chocolate, and cola drinks. Although caffeine has been adjudged safe by many experts, the caffeine in three cups of coffee consumed in succession may impair verbal performance, and higher levels of consumption may produce symptoms of anxiety and neurosis (Grden, 1974). Currently, the question of whether caffeine causes birth defects is unsettled. The *Diagnostic and Statistical Manual* (*DSM-IV,* 1994) of the American Psychiatric Association lists caffeine as an intoxicant.

The National Research Council (1982) points to several components of the U.S. diet that are potentially harmful. Fats as a whole, not just cholesterol, seem to point to increased risk of cancer.[1] Consumption of salt-cured, salt-pickled, and smoked foods should be reduced because of the linkage with cancers of the stomach and esophagus. Excessive consumption of alcohol has been linked with cigarette smoking as cause of cancers of the upper respiratory and gastrointestinal tracts and other health problems. Especially avoid drinking any alcohol during pregnancy as this has been definitely linked to fetal alcohol syndrome.

Among other problems of diet are the more than 3,000 food additives used with the 12,000 that are by-products of processing and packaging. Weiss (Moses, 1989) exposed children to food coloring considered acceptable by FDA standards and observed significant behavioral responses including crying, shortened attention span, and hyperactivity.

An unintentional additive is dioxin. FDA research (Raloff, 1989) shows most people get their daily dioxin dose from such commonplace objects as milk cartons and coffee filters. The chief source of the dioxin is the bleaching that is part of any paper-making operation.

Despite the many news reports of famines, there is actually a world surplus of food (Abelson, 1987) that is expected to last up to the year 2,000, but at great cost (see below).

Pollution by Foreign Species

Many times in the history of most countries, exotic plants and animals have been introduced from other ecosystems. Often these introduced species multiply out of control because they do not have natural predators or conditions to keep them in check. All species in any ecosystem have had a long history of balancing with other species until each surviving species establishes itself in an ecological niche where it lives in harmony with the rest of the system.

A good example of an introduced species out of control is the so-called western U.S. tumbleweed plant. This seems so much a part of the western United States that there are even cowboy songs about it ("Tumbling Tumbleweed").[2]

Other examples include the European sparrow, the starling (Page, 1990), the black rat, and the Norway rat. The Hawaiian Islands have probably suffered the most of any U.S. territory because of their fragile ecosystem derived from eons of isolation. The Asian mongoose was introduced to control rats and instead ate up exotic local lizards and eliminated two rare species of ground-dwelling birds. Other examples include the walking catfish of Florida, tropical snails, fire ants (Conniff, 1990), and, of course, the relentless movement north of the "killer" bees.

Plants in addition to the Russian thistle have proliferated in other parts of the United States. The Japanese kudzu vine, introduced to stop erosion, has long irritated southerners while crabgrass and dandelion have long bothered lawn growers.

Invaders are a constant threat to agriculture and the evidence from the medfly invasion, the white fly, and others mean there can be no relaxing the constant vigil at the borders of every country.

Depletion of Resources

Not only are we threatened by a surplus of harmful chemicals and invasions by foreign species, the erosion of topsoil and the depletion of fossil fuels and necessary minerals are also a significant part of the environmental crisis. The Club of Rome report served to focus attention on these losses with a projected crisis of depletions coming together sometime in the next century (Meadows, Meadows, Randers, & Behrens, 1972). Twenty years later, Meadows et al. did a recalculation of their original research on depletions and concluded that the losses have progressed even faster than predicted. We are now beyond the limits of sustainability (Meadows et al., 1992)!

Currently, most arable land is already under cultivation and at best an increase of only 4% may be possible (CEQ, 1980; Ruttan, 1992). In fact, Ruttan and his associates claim that although all previous increases in agriculture in the past were due to the use of new land, *all* increases in the future will have to come solely from higher yields on land already in use. The truth is that the actual amount of land cultivated has dropped slightly in the last 20 years.

A false picture of the world food supply, reinforced by the current surplus, has occurred because of a tendency to deal only with crises such as Somalia and a misconception that problems of supply can be handled by technological innovation such as the genetically superior grains produced by the "green" revolution. Unless greater world cooperation can be worked out quickly, the 75% of the world's population living in developing countries will be subjected to increasing restraints on their food supply. So far, any gains in food supply in these countries has been more than offset by increases in population (Meadows et al., 1992).

1. Desertification, worldwide, is turning productive grassland and croplands into deserts at the rate equivalent to the size of Belgium each year.

2. Deforestation is occurring at the rate of 17.1 hectares per year, resulting in a estimate that 40% of forests in developing countries will be gone by 2000.

3. Per capita water supplies will decrease one third by 2000.

4. The need for wood as a fuel in developing countries will exceed available supplies by 35% in 2000.

5. As many as 20% of the remaining species on Earth may be extinct by 2000.[3]

6. One third of U.S. cropland is eroding at rates that threaten productivity. The impact of this loss is hidden by intensive use of fertilizers and insecticides. In 1977, erosion averaged 4.8 tons of topsoil per acre of cropland (U.S. Department of Agriculture: Soil and Water Resources Conservation Act, 1980).

7. Salinization, the accumulation of salts through irrigation, is rapidly poisoning valuable cropland. In 1973, it was estimated every arid land country was in some stage of salinization (Raloff, 1984). Salinization of the Caspian Sea is Russia's second highest ecological disaster.

Following a worldwide conference on desertification held at Nairobi in 1977, a conference on arid lands was held at the Office of Arid Lands Studies in Tucson, Arizona, in 1985. Gilbert White, renowned conservation expert, noted that little progress had been made since the earlier conference or, in fact, since 1969 (White, 1988). Unfortunately, because of extensive irrigation, it appears salinization is increasing.

Overpopulation

Central to all problems is the increasing population of the world. Population increases nullify reductions in pollution and increases in food supply. From 1971 to 1991, the population increase in the world was reduced only from 2.1% to 1.7%. In the 1980s, 75 million people were added to the Earth each year, but by 2000 there will be 100 million added per year. The poorer countries of the world will have 79% of this increase.

Population is a compounded problem because neither resources nor services can keep pace with population growth. As population increases, the percentage in poverty rises. By 2000, the poorer countries of the world are expected to average only $600 per capita. The gulf between rich and poor will be wider than ever. The United States averaged $22,560 in 1991 and was only the tenth richest nation per capita behind the first, Switzerland.

Over 30 years ago, von Foerster, Mora, and Amiot (1960) predicted that the Earth's population would reach infinity. The article was titled "Doomsday: Friday 13, 2026." The article received wide publicity and was scoffed at as impossible. Later, Umpleby (1987) used the same formula to calculate whether von Foerster's formula was able to predict accurately the populations for 1975 and 1980. He found the actual population figures for 1980 exceeded von Foerster's formula by 445 million, more than the population of the United States. Of course, von Foerster doesn't believe the Earth's population will reach infinity. Economic and social catastrophes will prevent this, but the point was to show how population increase defeats any attempt to remedy Earth's problems.

The Built Environment

Increasingly, the lives of humans have been forced indoors since the world became largely urban in the latter half of the twentieth century. The result is that most of our lives are lived in an artificially created environment to which our adaptation is an open question. Urban life has become increasingly threatening. The most obvious threats are crime, gangs, an increase in communicable diseases, traffic accidents, pollution, and the other benefits of modern civilization. Added to these are the consequences of poor planning and design. In a strict sense, all of the above problems can be attributed to poor planning and design.

No one foresaw the consequences of waste disposal, industrial effluents, crowding, urban poverty. There is resistance to planning for them even now.

Such was the case in the summer of 1981 when 113 persons died and 186 were injured in the collapse of two suspended walkways at the Kansas City Hyatt Regency Hotel. Another dramatic case was the "popping windows" from the Hancock Insurance building in Boston that shed its $500 windows into the streets below (Fitch quoted in Merzbach, 1975). These examples were technical violations of building practice in which people died or were injured, and, as such, they are relatively rare.

Table 1.7 Impacts of Modern Buildings on People and the Environment

Problem	Buildings' Share of Problem	Effects
Use of Virgin Minerals	40 percent of raw stone, gravel, and sand; comparable share of other processed materials such as steel	Landscape destruction, toxic runoff from mines and tailings, deforestation, air and water pollution from processing
Use of Virgin Wood	25 percent for construction	Deforestation, flooding, siltation, biological and cultural diversity losses
Use of Energy Resources	40 percent of total energy use	Local air pollution, acid rain, damming of rivers, nuclear waste, risk of global warming
Use of water	16 percent of total water withdrawals	Water pollution; competes with agriculture and ecosystems for water
Production of Waste	Comparable in industrial countries to municipal solid waste generation	Landfill problems, such as leaching of heavy metals and water pollution
Unhealthy Indoor Air	Poor air quality in 30 percent of new and renovated buildings	Higher incidence of sickness—lost productivity in tens of billions annually

SOURCE: Roodman and Lenssen (1995); reprinted by permission of Worldwatch Institute.

Much more common is the simple neglect of everyday needs, which, although less dramatic, accumulates daily and reduces the quality of human life for untold numbers. An example of this kind of environmental harm to human life was the Pruitt Igoe public housing complex in St. Louis. It had to be demolished in 1973 because it was unlivable. Other examples abound yet are less known because they do not make the headlines but instead create daily hardships for those who live in them.

Roodman and Lenssen (1995) point out that the environmental costs of the building industry have largely been ignored. But the increases in building activity are accelerating. Turkey increased its construction 13-fold between 1963 and 1993. Construction in South Korea increased by 50% in the same period. Even in the United States, the floor space available per person doubled from 1949 to 1993.

Disasters are revealing building code violations that show housing was sloppily built even in the United States. Hurricane Andrew did $30 billion in damage but much of it was due to contractors who did not follow building codes. The recent earthquake in Kobe, Japan, showed a similar pattern. Roodman and Lenssen detail the impacts of modern buildings on people in Table 1.7.

Conclusions

It should be obvious that there are only two possible conclusions to this chapter: Either humanity will recognize its peril and take steps to survive or we shall perish from one form of poisoning or another.

But for every person who reads this chapter, there is the illusion of a third choice: avoidance. Many still see threats to their lives from the environment as actually coming from "environmentalists," people who have some special cause and are seen as just another interest group. Many feel constrained to say, "It can't be that bad." Indeed, it is possible to find public officials and some writers and radio talk show hosts who say just that. One former interior secretary felt that alarm over the ozone layer was exaggerated. "Just wear a broad brimmed hat and sunglasses," was his comment. Fortunately, the public ridicule that arose in response to that remark did much to publicize the danger.

Nevertheless, it must be noted that this chapter is only a brief list[4] of environmental threats, and any doubting person is urged to pursue the topic further with the list of references at the end of the book. Sooner or later, any individual must come to grips with the following personal responses:

(1) Shock and dismay. For those who have never read a report on environmental problems, a common response is to be shocked at the variety and magnitude of the threats to their lives. Air, water, land, food—all seem to be polluted. Is there no end? Danger threatens from every conceivable place. There is literally no place to escape to. This is shocking, frightening, and disheartening. And such a response is a true response to a true condition.

(2) Anger and outrage. Shock, fear, and dismay do not last long. Sooner or later, they give way to anger at how this could happen. How did it happen? Who let it happen? How was it allowed to happen?

(3) Feeling trapped. Beneath whatever emotional response there may be is the realization that we are all trapped. We are all stuck on this planet and cannot escape the poisons placed there. Behind this is the more paranoid fear of some sinister force—politicians, conspiracies, foreign governments, *someone*—that has done this to us. Yet, whatever or whomever is responsible, there is no escape.

(4) Feeling stupid. Somewhere among all these feelings is the eventual realization that all of us are actually stupid to have let this happen. How could we (anyone) be so stupid as to let us drown in our own filth? How could we be so shortsighted? Can't we see the simple effects of smoke, sewage, and trash? Yet, has anyone thought about where the shampoo goes when it is rinsed down the drain?

(5) Disbelief and denial. Whether it happens at first or later, the temptation to disbelieve or deny the magnitude of the threat is persistent. Sometimes we grab any straw to make us feel more comfortable. A scientist admits a certain poison is not as powerful as he first thought. A politician tries to get our vote by asking us to choose between owls and people (as if that were *ever* the choice). Sooner or later, all of us will flirt with denial.

(6) Hopelessness is another response. The weight of all the evidence and the avoidance of public officials both work toward making us feel helpless against an overwhelming tide. It is easy to find refuge behind the question, "What can one person do?"

(7) Resolution to act in some fashion is actually the only mature way to respond to a threat to your life. All other responses require a forfeiting of current life and life in the future. In addition, there is a psychological price of denial that is added to giving up on life. Denial of the magnitude required can become much more stressful than the most vigorous action to save life.

What action and what behavior are appropriate?

1. In 1989, the Earth Works Group published a book titled *50 Simple Things You Can Do to Save the Earth*. It contains simple suggestions about everyday things such as saving water while brushing teeth, getting a more fuel-saving car and energy-saving appliances. Of course, these are not enough, but think of the enormous effect if every human did these small things every day.

2. Vote for candidates who promise to save the environment. This works perhaps better than any other action. Remember that laws passed in the 1970s were responsible for the reduction of lead in children's blood (Marshall, 1982), the 39% reduction in pollution in 23 cities (CEQ, 1982), the decline of persons with high levels of PCBs in the blood from

9.7% in 1977 to 1% in 1981. The environment *can* be cleaned up by legislative action.

3. Join an environmental action group. The Sierra Club, the Audubon Society, the National Wildlife Federation, and many other groups have agendas that suit any person who wants to take part in the struggle to save life on our planet. And one doesn't necessarily have to join all of these groups to benefit from their work. The Worldwatch Institute publishes an annual book-length review of environmental conditions called *State of the World*. A subscription costs $30.00 payable to Worldwatch Institute, 1776 Massachusetts Ave., Washington, DC 20036-1904. The National Wildlife Federation publishes a state of the environment every February in its journal *National Wildlife*.

Finally, consider what must take place on Earth for each of us to survive. Herman Daly (1991) states there must be three conditions for survival:

1. The use of renewable natural resources cannot exceed the rate at which renewable resources are developed.
2. The use of *non*renewable resources also cannot exceed the rate at which they are developed.
3. Rates of pollution cannot exceed the assimilative capacity of the environment.

These are three simple rules by which any human enterprise can be judged, but what must be changed is *human behavior*. Consider that all of the pollutants, all of the chemical environmental disasters, were caused by some human being or group of humans doing something to the environment—whether it was intended or not. Stopping pollution will not save the environment unless the human motivation for causing the pollution is changed. The target must be human behavior if we are to survive. The descriptions of threats in this chapter did not include the initial human behavior, only its consequences. This is, perhaps, the most frequently misunderstood of all aspects of the environment. There was nothing wrong with the environment as it existed before a large human population. What is wrong with the environment is what we have done to it. What we must do is understand how human behavior could have brought us to the point of our own destruction.

NOTE: Research has shown that it is more beneficial for students to look up definitions in the text or library than to have them conveniently arrayed at the end of a chapter. Hence, at the end of each chapter under the chapter's goals are listed the important concepts and definitions and the critical studies. These should be looked up in the text.

Notes

1. To calculate the actual percentage of fat in any food, first look at the number of calories per serving. Next, look at the number of grams of fat per serving. Multiply the number of grams times 9 (the number of calories per gram of fat). Take this product, the number of calories of fat, and divide it by the total number of calories per serving to get the percentage of fat in each serving. Do not calculate fat as a percentage of weight in grams because fat is very high in calories and it is the percentage of calories that is the true measure of the amount of fat.

2. The tumbleweed of the U.S. West is actually the Russian thistle introduced in the 1870s. It has become so successful and such a nuisance most people think of it as a native plant and even sing songs about it.

3. Since the 1992 modeling of the depletion of Earth's resources by Meadows et al. (also known as the Club of Rome), it has been discovered that many frog species (Blaustein & Wake, 1995) and songbirds (Askins, 1995) have been steadily declining in many parts of the world. Although all the causes of this decline are not known, loss of habitat is emerging as a prime suspect.

4. The list has not included such things as tampons (Sun, 1982), salt in the diet (Kolata, 1982), heptachlor contamination (Smith, 1982), temik (Marshall, 1985), pollution from ranching and mines (Gold, 1985), more carbon monoxide (Newell, Reichle, & Seiler, 1989), and the destructive effects of off-road vehicles (Iverson et al., 1981), just to mention a few.

GOALS

Definitions and Concepts

Greenhouse effect

Chlorofluorocarbons

Ozone layer

Ozone hole

Pollution Standards Index

Heavy metals

Radon (creating two sources of pollution)

Passive smoking

Pneumonoconiosis

Formaldehyde

Agent Orange

Noise

pH scale

Acid rain

Latency period

Immunity to antibiotics

Groundwater cycle

Hazardous waste disposal schemes

Fat in diet calculation

Behavior-environment interaction

Diesel exhaust particles

Salinization

Asbestos (two kinds)

Dioxin

OSHA

PCB

EDB

Landfill

Love Canal

Times Beach

DDT

Important Studies

Hansen (1988)

Hansen et al. (1981)

Ramanathan (1988)

Anderson et al. (1991)

NASA (1988)

Needleman et al. (1979)

Needleman et al. (1990)

National Research Council (1986)

Mossman et al. (1990)

Silent Spring (Carson, 1962)

Roberts (1991)

Meadows et al. (1972)

Meadows et al. (1992)

von Foerster et al. (1960)

QUESTIONS

1. What are considered to be the most serious environmental threats to life on Earth?

2. What is the primary cause of most danger from the environment?

3. Why don't people wear seat belts in automobiles?

4. Does this attitude have anything to do with why we are in such a dilemma today?

5. Is there a world food shortage?

6. What is the price being paid for current food production?

7. What is happening to the oceans?

8. What are the possible new sources of lead pollution?

9. What has been the most successful area in environmental improvement?

10. What are you doing to help the situation?

2

Evolution: The Product of an Environmental Exchange

Definition

Evolutionary psychology is a new topic (Caporael & Brewer, 1991). The purpose of this branch of psychology is to better understand human behavior through evolutionary theory. In the past, much of the impetus for such a branch in psychology came from assertions that the physical traits of various races placed members of these races at various advantages to each other; that is, one race has a larger brain, therefore it is superior (Rushton, 1991). The evolutionary psychologists feel this view as well as sociobiology (Wilson, 1975) are without sufficient evidence.

But what evidence is there for human behavior that was inherited and can be seen as a product of the evolutionary process? Kaplan (1972) proposed that preference for natural versus human-made environments was a product of evolution. Kaplan (1987) has consistently found humans usually choose a natural environment in preference to one that was modified by humans. Appleton (1975) suggests that the evolutionary drama has been played out in the savannah-type landscape such that humanity prefers savannahs over any other kind of landscape. Balling and Falk (1982) submit evidence that children prefer savannahs and assert that this is more important than evidence from adults because children are less influenced by learning and more influenced by their inheritance. They found a preference for savannahs among their two youngest age groups, the 8- and 11-year-olds.

Balling and Falk argue that preference for a savannah is inherited because of our long experience in evolving in such an environment. This preference is strongest in childhood and then is modified by the kind of environment one is most in contact with. They also hypothesize that with increasing age, the preference for savannahs takes over again. They state that at no time does the preference for familiar environments exceed that for savannahs.

Bouchard (1994) tries to summarize the consensus about human behavior as contained in the "Big Five" human traits, extroversion, neuroticism, conscientiousness, agreeableness, and openness. But Cloninger proposes a big four—novelty seeking, harm avoidance, reward dependence, and persistence—and, so far, he seems to have most of the evidence (Cloninger, Svaric, & Prysbeck, 1993). Ebstein et al. (1996) report linking novelty seeking with a gene, D4DL, and replicating the finding. An argument will be presented toward the end of this chapter concerning the second trait, harm avoidance.

Historical Perspective

There are two basic problems that have to be overcome before human behavior can be linked to an evolutionary process. When Charles Darwin published *Origin of Species* in 1859 and its subsequent five editions, evolution was accepted as a fact. The first of the problems was to find a way to link evolution with some mechanism that would explain how it happened. Mendel published his paper on genetics in 1865 but it was not until 35 years later that it was accepted. In the 1930s, genetics came to be seen as the mechanism by which evolution worked.

This still left the second problem: how to link behavior with genetics. Up to the present time, the problem is seen as having been solved only for animals. Other than inherited deficiencies, there was no human behavior identified with any known genetic source such as a gene until Cloninger's studies.

On the other hand, human behavior is thought to be the result of a long process of evolution. Put another way, it is inconceivable that the long process of evolution could have occurred without coding some genes on human behavior.

The most extreme view of genetic influence on behavior is proposed by the *sociobiologists,* and is expounded by Wilson's *Sociobiology* (1975). Others such as Dobzhansky (1964) claimed there was no evidence for gene control of any human behavior. This is known as the *nature versus nurture* controversy, which continues to be argued for both sides up to the present time.

One does not need to take either side to consider persistent forms of behavior that seem to be characteristic of all humans across all cultures (Brown, 1991). What form might such behavior take?

Brown argues that in the past there has been the assumption that culture was a distinct phenomenon that could not be reduced to explanation by psychology or biology. Further, it was assumed that culture was the sole determinant of human behavior. Also, culture was thought to be arbitrarily evolved for each cultural entity. Brown tears down these assumptions by examining evidence that was built up in the past and shows it to be false. Color classifications are not arbitrary; female adolescents are not stress-free in Samoa; and there are not true reversals of male-female roles among the Tchambuli. Also, the time concepts of the Hopi are not radically different than that of the dominant U.S. culture. To anyone educated in the anthropological literature, these uncoverings are a spectacular revelation. Apparently, much of the foundation on which modern anthropology rests was the result of personal errors of anthropologists in the field. Brown embraces evolutionary psychology as the new pathway to understanding human behavior. Brown has a long list of behaviors that need investigation. Barkow, Cosmides, and Tooby (1992) take a similar view.

One does not have to look far to observe candidates for evolutionary behavior, for example, my own back yard.

The Rich Response Repertoire

My house is located in the foothills of the Catalina Mountains in southern Arizona. Temperatures here range from a low of below freezing in winter to highs over 110 degrees Fahrenheit (43°C) in the shade during summer. In summer, the normal period of temperatures over 100°F every day may go unbroken for as long as 10 weeks. From the windows of my house, it is possible to watch a drama that is as old as evolution itself—the attempt of animals to cope with this harsh environment.

In my front yard, the western cottontails and jackrabbits begin their day before dawn by eating grapefruit leaves that I have unintentionally provided them. They also feed on Palo Verde tree shoots, which is an accomplishment considering the piercing odor these shoots give off when I break them. Eating at dawn is wise, not only because it is the coolest time of day but also because it is the only time when there is a chance of any moisture being on the leaves except, of course, when it rains. The rabbits stand on their hind legs and eat away a space up to a foot above the ground under each tree. This also provides a shady spot where they can lie during the hot part of the day.

As the day grows warmer, the rabbits seek out the coolest spots to be idle in until evening. They increase their comfort by scratching off the top layer of soil and planting their bellies in it. They prefer places under the plants I have just watered. As the day gets hotter, they dig deeper and stretch out their legs to increase heat loss. The western cottontails have longer ears than their eastern cousins and this aids in cooling blood through a greater exposure of skin and blood vessels.

Once the sun goes down, the temperature decreases and the rabbits become active again. When a dog or coyote gives chase, the rabbits run at right angles and makes sudden stops to confuse the pursuer, who is focused on movement. Their small size and fur permit them to slip under cactus stalks, where larger predators cannot follow. And, of course, rabbits are noted for their burrows in the earth, which are also cooler. Rabbits are known for their breeding habits. These particular ones have their young near the house, where coyotes are more reluctant to probe.

Even from observing these few facts about cottontail behavior, it is easy to be impressed by the variety of responses a small mammal is capable of to the many challenges a harsh environment can offer. No single response or pattern of responses can account for the rabbits' success. It is the ability to respond in several ways to many challenges that enables the rabbit to prosper in this demanding locality. The cottontail has learned to eat new kinds of food since humans came, to find cool spots that did not exist over its period of evolution, and to take advantage of many things offered by humans that were never part of its evolutionary environment. How can such a small creature do this? Doesn't this prove the behavior could not be part of the rabbit's evolutionary heritage? Humans have only lived in this part of the Catalinas less than 100 years.

Louw (1971; Louw & Seely, 1982) observed the same kind of variety of responses in desert animals in one of the most extreme deserts on Earth, the Namib in Africa. "Moreover, their survival in the desert is often due to several favorable adaptations acting in concert rather than a single adaptation" (Louw & Seely, 1982, p. 84).

It is also quite likely that Louw's desert lizards and mammals could adapt to the foothills just as easily as the rabbits did because their responses are not too environmentally specific. It is the ability to create many responses to new situations that is the best candidate for an evolutionary behavior pattern.

This concept of developing many responses to a situation needs a label that will do it justice. *The Rich Response Repertoire* (RRR) is ripe with meaning and easy to remember. The concept of repertoire comes from acting and opera. The *repertoire* of an actor or singer is the number of roles or songs that can be performed from memory. The richness of the responses is the key to evolutionary success, and collecting them into a repertoire provides the kit for survival.

There is another aspect to the RRR. Each animal is *motivated* to develop and collect a large number of responses. Skinner's belief (1984) is apropos here: He sees the collection of responses, their organization, change and adaptation to new circumstances as self-rewarding in its own right. Skinner was talking about children and the learning process. His research points to *self-reward* as the most effective way of learning. He could have been talking about the RRR, a motive to acquire, organize, and adapt a repertoire of responses because it is self-rewarding to do so.

The RRR is the key to survival in any changing environment, and all environments change. It is the only way behavior could be inherited given the background of a changing environment. The behavior had to be adaptable to change and could not be too environmentally specific. The more choices among responses, the greater the chances of survival.

But the rabbit's method of survival seems too simple and direct. How has our own civilization gotten so far removed from this simplicity such that any one of us who was placed in the same environment with the same limited resources could not survive? Does this mean we should return to such a simple, direct relationship? Some believe this to be the case. But the question remains: Why couldn't humans survive as well as a rabbit in a harsh environment?

The Survival Package

Every human body and brain form a survival kit that is the product of more than 20 to 40 million years of traceable testing of the environment (Lovejoy, 1981) (see Figures 2.1-2.3). The human anatomy is the result of selection and accidents through many different models that could not adapt.

At various times, certain physical characteristics have been proposed as the single most important response to account for success in evolution. These include (a) the highly developed brain, (b) the opposable thumb, (c) bipedal locomotion, (d) molar dentition, (e) technology, and (f) sexual and reproductive behavior. Without going into a detailed explanation of why each of these aspects of human adaptation is the single reason humans have successfully evolved, let us agree it is already obvious that all of them in concert have contributed to human survival. In short, the reason humans evolved is that all of these contribute to the richness and variety of the Rich Response Repertoire.

In more psychological terms, the RRR is seen as intrinsic (inside the person) motivation similar to Skinner's (1984) self-rewarding mechanism, White's (1959) and Harter's (1978) innate need for competence, or de Charms's (1968) view that intrinsically motivated behaviors are the result of a desire for personal causation. Put another way, the human brain evolved a wide variety of behaviors, was predisposed toward none in particular but motivated to solve as many problems as possible, to respond to situations of challenge, and to overcome obstacles rather than avoid them. Very important is the large brain that provides for a huge capacity of responses compared with the rabbit.

At this point, it is necessary to examine more closely the concept of "success" in evolution. Success in our culture is too closely linked with the imperatives for competition and "winning." Success in the evolutionary sense can also come about by pure accident (Gould, 1989). In other words, not every trait of the human being is necessarily in place because it is part of a "winning team" of traits. Some traits survive merely by accident and have no discernable value. It is easy to reason backward from every aspect of human behavior and say it has evolved because it served an evolutionary purpose. This is called the logical fallacy of *affirming the consequent* (Handwerker, 1986).

To look at "success" in evolution another way, consider that there are about 30 million species known to have lived on this Earth to date. Of all

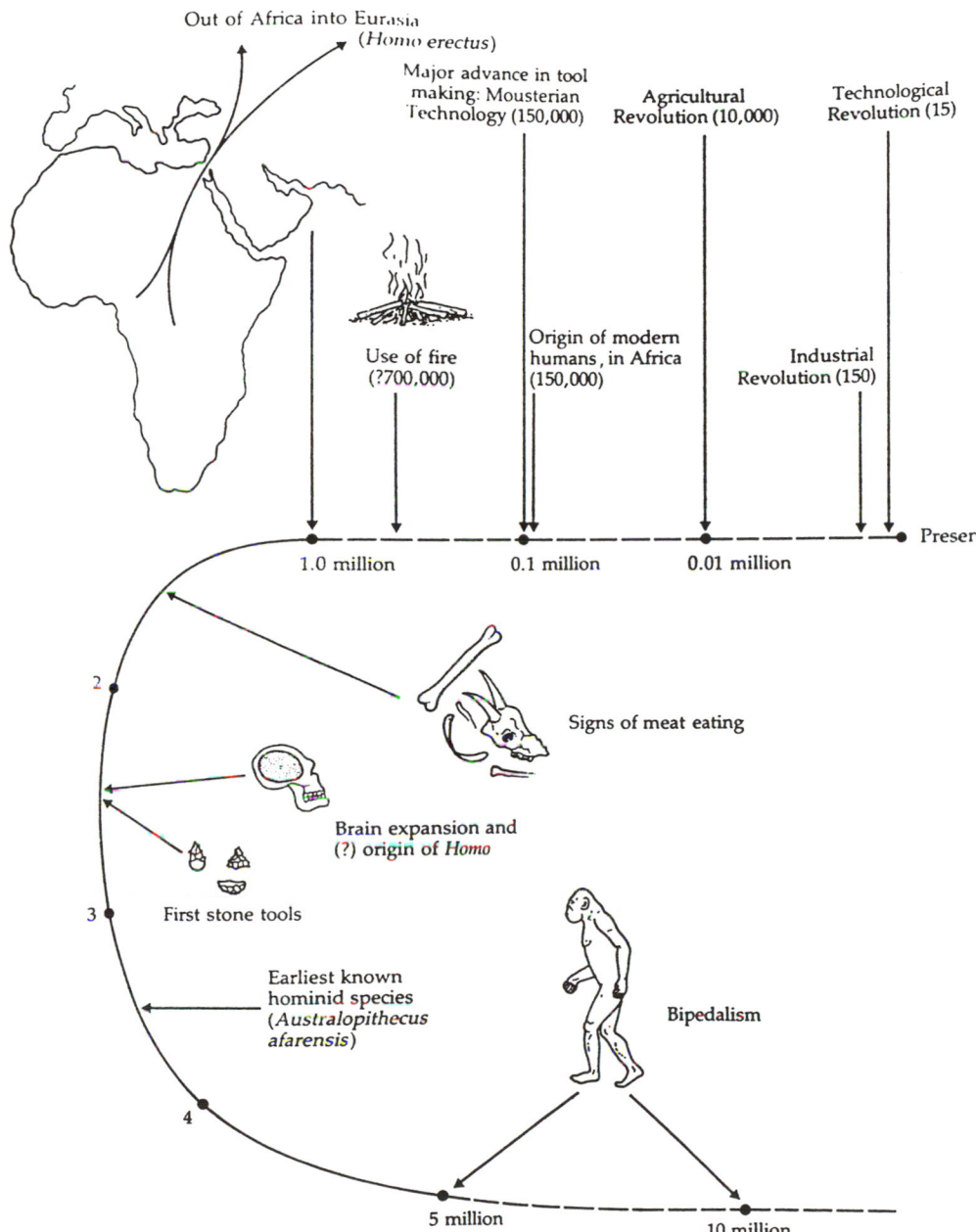

Figure 2.1. Milestones in Prehistory
SOURCE: R. Lewin (1989), *Human Evolution: An Illustrated Introduction* (2nd ed.), inside front cover; reprinted by permission of Blackwell Science, Inc.

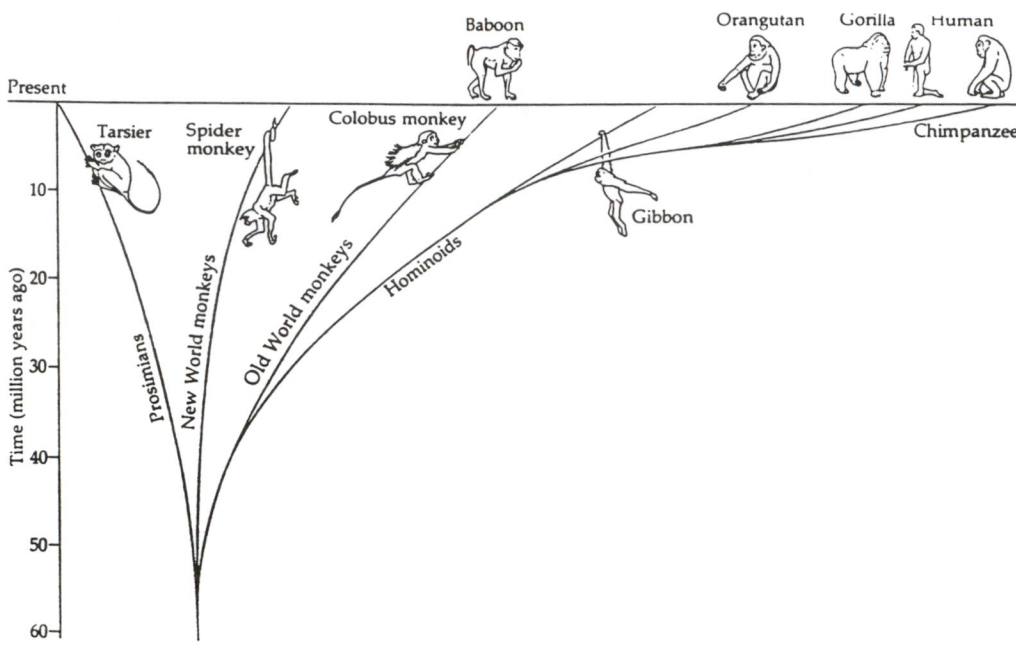

Primate family tree.

Figure 2.2. Human Ancestry Model
SOURCE: R. Lewin (1989), *Human Evolution: An Illustrated Introduction* (2nd ed.), p. 32; reprinted by permission of Blackwell Science, Inc.

these 30 million, only 1% are alive today—actually less than 1% (Lewin, 1989). That means evolution as a success story is a 99% failure! Lewin portrays the popular view of evolution as a "hero myth" epic where the one-celled animal evolved in the sea, became a multicelled animal, became a fish, then crawled unto the land to become an amphibian, then a mammal, and then, finally, human. The scientific evidence for this myth is decidedly lacking.

The reason no simple line of evolution like the "hero myth" can be followed is the evidence for widespread catastrophic losses of many species at several times in evolutionary history (Gould, 1989). Thus it is not possible to trace any line of descent for any long period of time. The interruptions are too many. It is not clear when many kinds of species actually began.

Specialization often occurs when two extremities of environment exist: great abundance and great scarcity. With great abundance of a certain

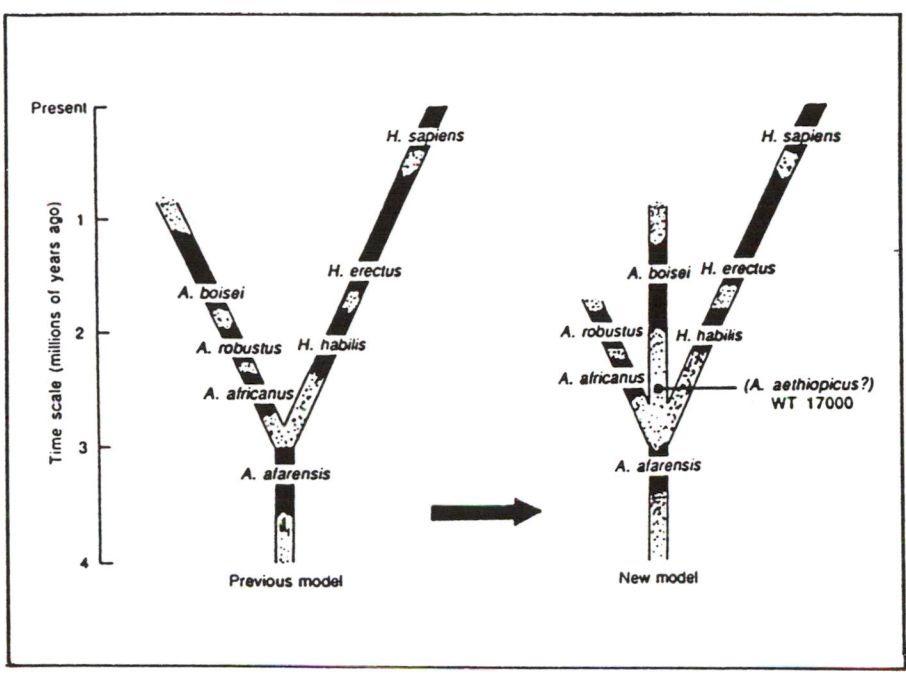

Figure 2.3. Evolutionary Paths

food, a species can adapt by losing its ability to forage for other kinds of food. The many flightless birds of New Zealand are an example.

With scarcity, a species can take advantage of a particular niche by "downsizing." The deer is an example of an animal that has grown larger or smaller to meet the circumstances of scarcity or abundance (Weintraub, 1991). It is tempting to see the same analogy in human pygmies, but it must be remembered the pygmies may have evolved just by accident.

Specialization, although temporarily successful in certain conditions, can ultimately trap a species when the conditions that fostered it change too quickly. Thus the RRR is the most successful pattern in the long term because it is the most quickly adaptable to the largest number of changes.

But to return to the original question of why a human could not last as long as a rabbit in the desert, we are even more compounded in dilemma now because the larger RRR of a human should make survival much easier for a human. Why doesn't it?

"May I remind you that ninety-nine percent of all species that ever existed are today extinct."

SOURCE: Reprinted by permission of N. Downes. © 1992 by Nick Downes.

Something is lacking when we try to account for evolutionary success in humans solely through the RRR kit. This is because we have accepted the traditional Western view of the human as a single, solitary individual confronting a hostile environment. This view is too simple to fit the evidence. It also leads to the absurdity that a single human could not outperform a rabbit.

The "new" archaeology recognizes that humans were never solitary in their evolutionary development. Leakey and Lewin (1977) note that even fossil traces of humans occurred in groups and the insight to be gained from them is important, but achieving this insight also requires the views of social psychology and other disciplines, and more than just the simple vision of how people might have made a living in a world without machines.

All that is encompassed by the term *social psychology* includes language, technology, attitudes, beliefs. These are even better included under the term *culture*. Struever and Holton (1979) define culture from the perspective of the new archeology:

> The new archaeologists define culture as a nonbiological system which human beings develop to cope with their environment. Culture is seen as a series of interlinked behavior patterns and material items. All parts of the cultural system—economic, social, political, religious—are interdependent. The total system serves the people who develop it as a buffer between them and their environment. It permits them to shape the environment to meet their ends, to protect themselves against danger, and to exploit potentially valuable aspects of the environment effectively, including not only animals and plants but other cultures as well. (p. 107)

Handwerker (1989) sees culture more simply as ideational thinking that maximizes resources. So it seems that every aspect of our culture is derived from an attempt to deal with the physical environment: the economic to wrest a living from it, the social to organize the activities, the political to organize the power relationships of those who control the means of getting a living, and the religious to ascribe values to the environment and environment-derived behavior. Despite the large capacity of the human brain, the largest part of the RRR is not contained within an individual human being but in the culture itself. No single human being could begin to duplicate all the responses a culture is capable of. This provides an even more severe contrast to the rabbit. The cottontail carries within its brain and genes nearly all the responses the species is capable of. The average human, although capable of many more responses than the rabbit, could not survive out of context in a harsh environment alone. The bulk of the RRR is contained in the culture, and most of it is neither in the brain of any one individual nor in the genes.

Each rabbit carries within itself all the genetic inheritance and nearly all the behavior it is capable of, and nearly all examples of the same species have virtually identical behavioral performance coded into the genes.

Humans, by contrast, have developed faster than lessons could be coded into the genes. The bulk of human learning is coded into books, papers, stories, and computers, and it is far more than any one person is capable of learning. Humans are locked into a complete dependency on one another to survive. Very few individuals from an industrialized society could survive if plucked out of their everyday environment and

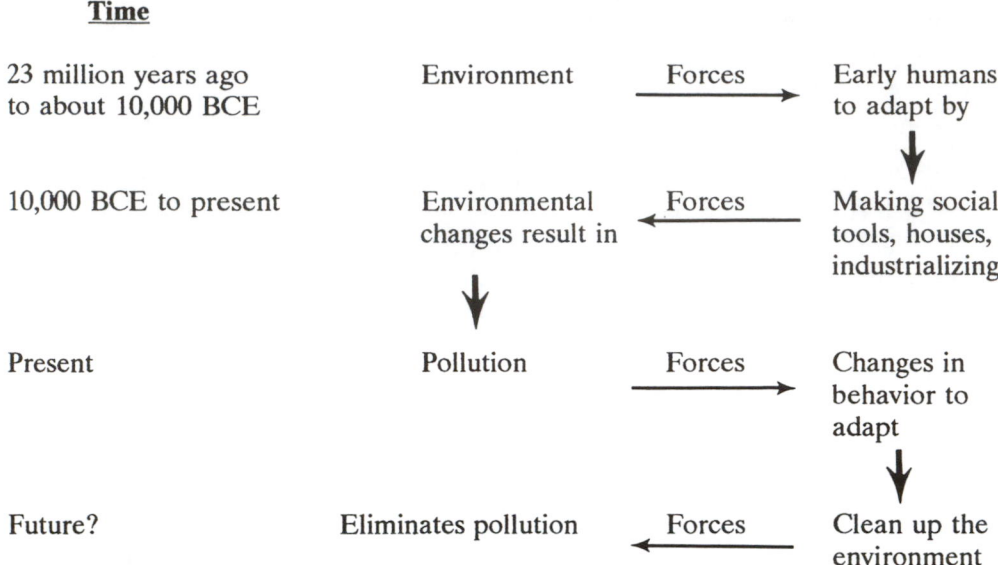

Figure 2.4. The Evolutionary Exchange Between Humans, Culture, and Environment

placed in a desert because they have not learned the simple facts of how to survive alone.

The picture is still not complete. The acts of technology—creating new tools and using them—change the environment itself. Forests are felled; rivers are polluted; the air is filled with noxious gases. These effects on the environment, as a result of a culture derived from the environment, change it in such a way that its effect on the culture also changes. In other words, a feedback system develops.

The picture that emerges is one of complex interaction between the physical environment and culture. Figure 2.4 illustrates that interchange in the evolutionary time sequence. What is important to remember is that the pace of this interchange is accelerating. Changes are occurring at a faster rate, and the number of changes increases over time as well.

Although these changes are often characterized as technological (Toffler, 1980), they also include social, political, and economic cultural changes. Huxley (1974) felt that changes have become so rapid that there is no time for ordinary evolution, and social evolution is now what takes place in human society. That view is not held by all scholars. Lumsden and Wilson (1981) feel 50 generations, or 1,000 years, is sufficient to produce genetic change. In any case, the survival kit depends on culture and its interchange with the environment.

Until recently, this view of evolution as taking a long time was accepted universally. More recently, however, as Weiner (1994) reveals, there has been considerable evidence that evolution can take place much more quickly, even within a year. Weiner describes the work of Peter and Rosemary Grant, who have worked for more than 20 years in the Galapagos measuring the beaks of finches. What they discovered was that in a year of severe drought, the lack of food can quickly eliminate all the birds on one island except those that can eat the very toughest seeds. Thus, in one year, the size of the beaks jumped three quarters of a millimeter and only those birds with the large beaks would survive to propagate.

By contrast, in a later year with excess rain, it seemed the hybrid finches had an advantage. The Grants' conclusion was that environmental conditions can produce a significant change in species within one year!

The reader may feel that these results are far removed from daily life and human survival. On the contrary, this same principle of rapid change is what accounts for the response of insects to insecticides and bacteria to penicillin. As soon as these killing agents are introduced, they set in motion the evolutionary process toward a superspecies, one that cannot be killed by these very agents. The result is drug-resistant bacteria and insects that have immunity to insecticides.

One of the ironies of our time is that the very states who are trying to outlaw the teaching of evolution are the ones whose cotton crops are being threatened by the insects immune to the sprays used to control them, a practical consequence of an evolutionary process.

The Social Cushion

Culture (which includes such things as outlawing the teaching of evolution) becomes a *social cushion* against the physical environment. It prevents each individual from having to be naked against the wilderness. It clothes, educates, biases, and values each person by consensual criteria and demands everything in payment for this protection. So immersed in the social cushion does each person become that the physical environment is lost as a separate reality. The social cushion becomes the only eyes through which to see the world.

Evidence exists (Reiss, 1961) that as industrialization takes place, the individual becomes more affiliated with organizations related to the work setting, while in agricultural societies, the farmer is closer to being an independent person dealing with nature. Industrial society becomes increasingly immersed in the social cushion.

Two different points of view can emerge at this point. One sees the physical environment as never having been experienced directly in the first place. This lack of direct experience with *anything* is seen as an essential fact of perception. The other view is that the physical reality of the world can be experienced as it exists and as a separate entity. The social cushioning effect would seem to be such that, regardless of which view is correct, the results are the same. Because no individual exists outside of a social context, no individual is free of the social distortion, and therefore an individual cannot view the physical environment without the lens of culture. The problem is that the social situation in any industrial culture has gotten out of touch with the physical state of its environment.

Whatever intrusions the physical environment may make into the cushion become meaningful only by their social definition. For example, floods, earthquakes, and crop failures become defined within the particular social context where they occur. For one person, a flood is a consequence of poor farming practices along a drainage system. For another, it is a punishment for past sins. The environment means what people agree it should mean. Such definitions are arrived at for most people by social consensus, not by testing whether the definition fits the environment itself.

The social cushion is a kind of protective cocoon, directing attention away from the physical environment to the realities created within the culture. Within each culture, there are additional forces inside the cushion that restrict outside information even further. These are the myopic cultural view (ethnocentrism) and the role myopia had in the inversion of social status.

Ethnocentrism

Every culture sees itself as the center of the universe and this restricts its ability to see other cultures as being of equal value but, more important, even of equal reality (Campbell, 1965; Murdock, 1931). It is a universal characteristic of each culture to think of itself as "the" people or the "real" people and to characterize foreigners as of lesser value, or not of the same reality. For example, the word *sioux* among the plains Indians of that tribe means simply "the people." Others are nonpeople. The Yanomamo Indians believe only their world is real and all other worlds are not of the same reality. The !Kung call themselves the "real" people and others not real. Similar definitions can be seen throughout hundreds of cultures and examples within national groups inside many cultures. It is too painfully apparent how whites in the United States view blacks, how Arabs and Jews view one another, and how Bosnians and Serbs view one another. The fractionation of ethnic groups seems almost limitless, and therefore the ability to consider ideas and values outside one's own culture becomes problematic.

Inversion of Social Status

The picture of the social cushion is one of cocoons within cocoons, each layer preventing or filtering information from the outside until finally the amount and kind of information reaching the individual is a travesty of reality. Only within such an overcushioned context is it possible to bring about that inversion in modern society that values least those on whom it depends most—those who work directly with the natural environment. Valued most are those who are at the top of the social pyramid—those who are furthest removed from any natural contact and who are innermost within the social cushion. Farmers and miners are valued least in all societies because they are in closest contact with the natural environment. Laborers and factory workers are next in line because they get their hands "dirty." Hence the concerns of those most in contact with the dirtiest parts of the environment, and their firsthand knowledge of the environment, are not only furthest from the center of power but also stigmatized by several layers of the social cushion so their needs are seen filtered through several layers.

The irony of this inversion of status is that no society has ever been free of a total dependence on the natural environment. Every society must still depend on the land, and therefore farmers to grow its food, and only modern industrial societies have managed to remove a majority of its citizens from having to work as farmers. Yet, even though every human in the world depends on the farmworker for existence, those who depend most, in industrial society, place farmers at the bottom of the status hierarchy. Reiss (1961) shows that in using two schemes for weighting prestige scores for major occupation groups, the group that includes farm laborers and foremen comes out on the bottom in both schemes. Census categories also place farm and nonskilled farmworkers on the bottom.

Kornhauser (1965) shows that the lower the occupational level of the worker, the lower his or her mental health regardless of education, prejob background, or personality.

Thus things of the soil are seen as farmerish and uncouth. We block out a whole series of environmental messages by making them socially beneath us. We literally won't dirty our hands for dirty hands are the mark of dirty labor in the soil.

The box shows how information coming from the environment is distorted in passing through the various layers of the social cushion, or does not get through at all. In addition, information from surrounding cultures, institutions, and organizations is distorted by the particular group context of the individual.

It is also possible to argue that ethnocentrism and inversion of status have had their positive benefits in social evolution. The inversion of status lets those at the top of the status hierarchy feel they are very special. The question is whether this series of comfortable horse blinders is still functional in a world where hunting-gathering bands have long vanished and large-scale international cooperation is necessary for survival. It seems as though our cherished social comforts must give way.

The competitive responses considered so healthy in our society help us to see our group, our nation, our culture as superior and not in need of any adjustment to accommodate others.

It is these perceptions in particular that must give way if cooperative efforts in dealing with limited resources are to succeed. Sociologists have a term, *pluralistic ignorance,* to describe the many kinds of ignorance that abound concerning other peoples, cultures, and so on. The social cushioning is more dynamic, actually screening out and selecting information about which we will remain ignorant. Many individuals feel they know the correct path for a reconciliation between society and the environment, but how to traverse that path is the dilemma.

In any case, humanity stands at a threshold in evolution. The survival kit that carried it through 20-40 million years of testing was compromised when the social cushion took over. We are citizens of two worlds, the world we know through the social cushion and the physical environment that

Box 2.1

Distortion of Information From the Environment or, YOU WON'T GET THE MESSAGE

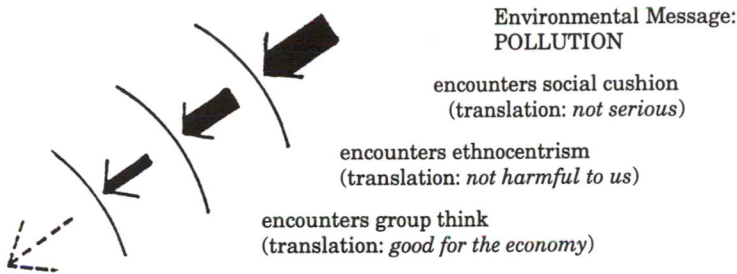

Environmental Message: POLLUTION

encounters social cushion
(translation: *not serious*)

encounters ethnocentrism
(translation: *not harmful to us*)

encounters group think
(translation: *good for the economy*)

Result: does not teach the individual as an intelligible message from the environment

Explanation

First Level: Since the message originates in the environment, it is not recognized as having a constituency inside the social cushion. Therefore, it need not be considered seriously.

Second Level: Since every culture considers itself supreme, the message may be a threat to less supreme beings but not to us. A second level might be that we supreme beings would not be capable of such errors.

Third Level: We must think positive. It means someone is doing something industrious, therefore, it must be good for the economy.

Finally: The message is so weakened by the time it reaches the individual, it can easily be avoided.

Of course, in contrast to this chart, the individual can receive a message directly from the environment. For example, pollution could be discovered in anyone's backyard. This, however, would require communicating with the various agencies of local, state, and federal goverments where the responses and distortions of the message would be the same. It doesn't matter at which point in the system the message enters, the distortion is consistent because there are no norms for dealing with the environment outside of the needs of the various layers of the social cushion.

Many writers, reporters, and researchers see these kinds of responses as a conspiracy (e.g., Frank Kaler's film, *In Our Water*, or the Michigan PBB incident (J. Eggington, *The Poisoning of Michigan*). The reason they seem so consistent and deliberate is that the principals involved are responding to the norms of the social cushion. The norms for responding to the environmental messages don't exist yet.

vaguely seems to surround us somehow but of which we have little real personal knowledge.

Each person must be in harmony with both these worlds, yet this can only come about through major change in the social cushion, change in the structure of society that Meadows et al. (1992) talk about. Thus the main focus is not the environment but the society that ruined the environment. Unless that society is changed, the damage cannot be reversed.

Human Motivation

Our study of human evolution is not yet finished. Before we can focus on the societal changes, we must examine more closely the process whereby each individual is reinforced by and in turn reinforces those elements of society that bring about the damage. This involves studying human motivation in more detail.

Motivation is sometimes thought of as purely physiological, even gene dominated as with the sociobiologists (Wilson, 1975). But it is more accepted to see human motivation arising from forces both within the individual and within the environment. Human motivation can be seen as a synthesis of these two forces in a transaction. The *transactional view* as expounded by Altman (1992; Altman & Rogoff, 1987) sees any psychological process as embedded and inseparable from its physical and social context. There is also a temporal context to every event but there are no actors or linear causes; continuity and change are constant elements. These elements are not separable into variables as is the common custom in experimental psychology; they belong together so intrinsically that to separate them destroys their meaning. Meaning is only found in context, and context is constantly changing.

If we follow human development from infancy, we can see that motives develop around eating, the parent-child relationship, and child-child relationships. As Kelly (1955) points out, the human is constantly testing the environment and trying to organize it into a coherent pattern. If one were to ask the child what it wants most, and the child were able to respond coherently, as many are, it would say a "home" with everybody it knows in it, love, and everything needed. The reference is to a *place* with an attached social context, and both are related and inseparable from need satisfaction.

A middle-aged person might reply in a similar fashion to this question. If he or she were asked what was wanted most, the answer would no doubt involve some aspect of "home" but it would also include some parameter of a job or work that is useful and satisfying. Both these concepts still involve places and social contexts. The satisfaction of needs is still embedded in the social context.

Finally, if someone were to ask an elderly retired person what he or she wanted most, it would most likely still involve some kind of "home" but because of the possibility of approaching disability of some sort, which is more feared than death, he or she would want a place with some assurance of being cared for.

These places where needs are best taken care of become idealized and often reified (made more meaningful than reality justifies) in the metaphor *refuge*. Humans at any age idealize a place of refuge. For children, it is a secure home; for adults, home and work; for the elderly, a place secure from health concerns. The motive is continuous throughout life; it is to find a *place* in the environment that is not only secure from adverse forces but that provides maximum satisfaction of needs. For many, this is an idealized home, but eventually this becomes more social as in the metaphor for utopia.

Mannheim (1956) feels that humans cannot lead a meaningful life without a utopia, and without a vision of the future, the present is meaningless. Notice that this ideal as a motivating force is contrary to most of the current psychological theories: One is reminded of the Freudian motivation to return to the womb. Although this is an inadequate metaphor in many ways, it fails most in limiting human vision to the past. Normal individuals are motivated more by the future and present than the past. Even in the poorest cultures, children want to grow up and elders want a place of respect in the eyes of others. In literature, the utopian ideal is constantly re-created for each generation as the City of God, Shangri La, Walden II, or even Arcosanti. Many people also have tried to create perfect societies in the present, for example, the communistic societies (Nordhoff, 1960) or more recent religious communes.

The primary impetus for the motive to gain refuge is the perception of the unrelenting demands of the social cushion. A person must work to earn a living. No human can escape the existential perception that the need to do work will at some time exceed the ability to perform it. Sickness and old age are doubly feared, not only because of inconvenience and pain but primarily because they deprive one of the work that must be done to remain a valued member of society. It is only natural to fantasize a place where the demands of work cease, where one has finally paid up the dues, and where reward finally exceeds effort.

When the human is young, dependence on others is accepted as necessary for survival. But this is an inferior state that the child becomes conscious of and wishes to get over, to become independent (Erikson, 1963). By the time the child is able to take his or her place as an adult, however, it is already clear that this productive period will last only a specified time until old age will have its crippling effects and he or she will become dependent again. In Western societies, the common goal is to amass enough wealth (retirement funds) during the productive period so that the dependent period is provided for in some comfort. In Eastern societies, the goal is to have enough children to be one's caretakers in old age.

The ideal is to attain some place of refuge at all stages in life, otherwise life is an overwhelming struggle against the demands of society—a constant planting and harvesting, or daily attendance at a job, in constant fear of losing security. Refuge from this fear is achieved at least in fantasy by holding out one's own carrot as a vision.

The most important aspect of the refuge concept is its institutionalization within the social cushion. Houses become a symbol of security and so do places of work. Successful designs of the refuge must communicate strength, success, invulnerability, and some sense of permanence. Public places like restaurants, hotels, and resorts advertise themsevles as attractive places of temporary refuge.

As the individual is motivated, so does the social cushion mirror a transactional reflection. Organizations and governments are motivated to provide refuge to gain popular support. The more affluent the society, the greater is this demand. Japanese society is conscious of refuge needs (Cole, 1971) and Japanese workers in the most successful companies are guaranteed a job for as long as they live once they are employed. What is often not mentioned, however, is that this security only exists for the top companies. Smaller, dependent companies provide virtually no job security. Yet the ideal is the goal for all workers, even though most do not actually enjoy it.

Similarly, the modern history of governments shows a tendency to provide more security for its citizens. Social security and medical insurance are just two examples of benefits that modern governments are wrestling with in the attempt to provide more security. The question is whether there are enough resources to provide even these forms of security.

Religions provide further evidence of the universal motive for refuge. Christianity, Judaism, and Mohammedism establish heaven as the ultimate refuge and reward for faithful followers. Many religions also see a refuge on Earth provided by divine intervention in the form of a messiah or some form of millennium.

Yet we are still not finished with the inventory of human motivation related to evolution. One large aspect of behavior needs to be accounted for, the ability to escape danger, which Cloninger calls harm avoidance (Cloninger et al., 1993).

Throughout the course of human and animal evolution, the avoidance of harmful stimuli is the most critical of all responses. If the organism is killed, it cannot breed and evolve. Avoiding stimuli that can harm is the primary survival response.

Avoidance Learning

Consider the importance of learning to avoid an extremely harmful stimulus. This kind of experiment cannot be done with humans, and today's animal rights groups have made us conscious of how unacceptable such experiments would be with animals. Yet some early studies can be instructive. Solomon and Wynne (1953) administered subtetanic shock to dogs. *Subtetanic* means it nearly kills. Dogs were placed in a box and shocked. After only one of these extreme shocks, the dogs learned to avoid the box. No matter how many times the dogs are placed in the box after that one experience, they immediately jump out. The dogs never wait to see if they will be shocked a second time; hence there is no chance to learn whether the box has ceased to be a threat. It is always regarded as a threat after one contact.

Avoidance Motivation

Another dimension of avoiding a negative stimulus is provided by the work of Neal Miller (1944). After a series of experiments matching

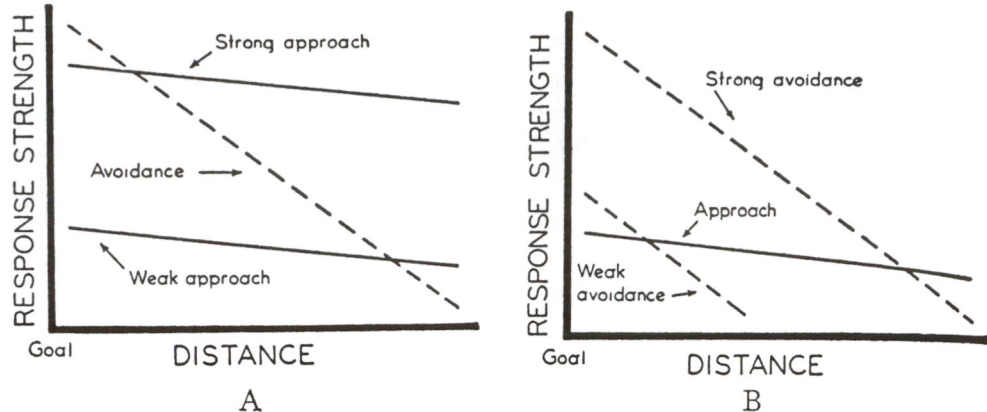

Figure 2.5. Dominance of Avoidance Motive Near a Goal

SOURCE: J. M. Hunt (1944), *Personality and Behavior Disorders.* New York: John Wiley. Copyright © 1944 John Wiley. Reprinted by permission of John Wiley & Sons, Inc.

NOTE: Diagram A demonstrates that with an increase in the strength of approach tendencies the intersection is not only moved nearer to the goal but also occurs at a higher point on the avoidance gradient. Diagram B demonstrates that within the limits in which the two gradients cross, decreasing the strength of avoidance increases the height of the point of intersection. Thus in both cases the amount of avoidance actually aroused will be increased.

positive and negative stimuli, Miller showed that as the animal gets closer to the goal, if there are negative stimuli associated with the goal, the negative elements will rise in strength faster than the positive and overwhelm the positive motivations, which causes a sudden reversal of motives. Figure 2.5 illustrates the nature of this imbalance. Try to imagine the classically reluctant bride or groom on the wedding day. As he or she first thinks of marriage, it looks rosy and glorious. As the date of the marriage gets closer, however, the avoidance (negative) aspects climb faster in strength and on the day of the event he or she has very strong avoidance behavior and leaves the partner at the church.

Are humans actually like this? Do they practice one-trial learning for traumatic stimuli and do they become overwhelmed with avoidance toward what seemed to be a positive goal?

There is clinical evidence for one-trial learning for many traumatic experiences. To answer whether people experience a negative reversal, it is better to ask whether people change their minds toward what was once a positive goal. The answer is obvious.

One form of avoidance is studied under the term *negativity bias*. Negative adjectives have greater importance than positive ones (Anderson, 1965; Feldman, 1966; Hodges, 1974; Kanouse & Hanson, 1971; Rokeach, 1968). Not only is negative information weighed more heavily in impressions we form of others, but it seems negative impressions are more resistant to change (Richey, McClelland, & Shimkanas, 1967). It also seems that psychological subjects (at least) concentrate more on not losing than they do on winning (Katz, 1964; Rettig & Pasamanick, 1964; Slovic & Lichtenstein, 1968). Thus winning isn't everything, *not losing* is! This research points out that there is a general tendency to respond more strongly to negative stimuli than to positive ones.

Taylor (1991) confirmed these findings and rounded out the dimensions of the picture of responses to negative stimuli by formulating the *mobilization-minimization* hypothesis. This hypothesis means that when we meet something negative, we are highly mobilized to act, and then after the stimulus passes, we minimize the strength of the stimulus.

Taylor summarizes research showing we have more emotions connected with negative stimuli than positive ones; we narrow and focus our attention more on negative stimuli and we count the impact of negative stimuli more strongly than positive ones. The human response mechanism is asymmetrically tuned more toward negative than positive things. What is just as intriguing is the tendency to deny this is the case, to deny that one was afraid after the event. These tendencies hinder our ability to remember and evaluate the true value of negative events after the fact.

Taylor's findings are summarized in Figure 2.6. Note that this figure is a complement to Miller's (1944) study, and they could be placed back-to-back to create a symmetrical image for modeling approach and egress from negative events. The point at which the negative responses overcome the positive in Miller's curve is the equivalent of Taylor's maximizing of negative events. Her own curve shows how we minimize negative events afterward. In other words, preceding or following negative events, we don't see them as they are.

Matlin and Strang (1978) found people recall positive events more than negative ones, in agreement with Taylor's minimization half of her hypothesis, and they call this the *Pollyanna Principle*. They found positive material is recalled faster than negative.

Taylor (1991) calls this tendency the "undoing" of negative events. Taylor reviews evidence that people resist negative moods and negative information about self.

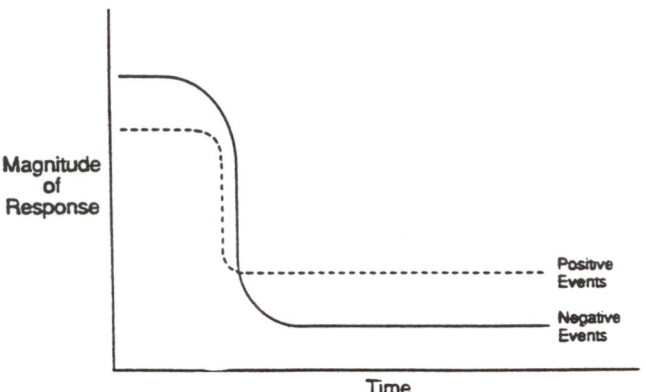

Figure 2.6. Taylor's Mobilization-Minimization Hypothesis
SOURCE: S. Taylor (1991, p. 76). Reprinted by permission.

How is this general tendency explained? Kanouse and Hanson (1971) cite evidence that negative stimuli stand out in a figure-ground relationship. In other words, any negative stimuli within a field of other stimuli are more easily noticed. Is this because noticing negative stimuli has had survival value? It is tempting to say so. But Kanouse and Hanson claim it is because the usual expectation is that all stimuli are positive, hence negative stimuli are noticed because they are such a contrast to most stimuli and the expectation about most stimuli. Evidence for a positive expectation is convincing (Boucher & Osgood, 1969; Bradburn, 1969); therefore, negative stimuli could be a contrast to positive prevalence.

Unfortunately, the research done on positive expectations has a social rather than environmental context. Generalizing the positive expectancy to the environment must await more research.

Klein (1991) showed that negative information on political candidates has more power in getting people to vote against the opponent than positive information in getting votes for the candidate. A negative trait was more predictive of evaluations of candidates than strengths. A trait was more predictive when it fell below the mean of other traits rather than above. In short, negative campaigning works because we respond more to negative information about a candidate than to positive information. Klein (1991) concludes: "Thus, character weaknesses were more important than strengths in determining the public's evaluations of the candidate and the ultimate vote" (p. 412).

Although candidates may not be environments, they can be people who vote for environmental solutions and the information about them can be tailored by an opposing party to reflect on them negatively.

In a more mundane area, fear of crime, there is evidence that one-trial learning in the form of news of a rape or mugging can influence attendance at a park or recreational area (Malt, 1972). Once a park has gained a reputation for crime, residents will avoid it for years, never learning whether crime has actually decreased.

Another example is a study done of a high-rise public housing project (Roth & Bechtel, 1972). At the beginning of the study, residents would avoid hallways and outside areas as much as possible; laundry trucks would not deliver on site; and taxis would not pick up at the front door to the building, all because of a stated fear of crime. After a period of "vertical policing" in which guards were introduced and seen to patrol the areas most feared, resident behavior changed. Laundry trucks began delivering and taxis would pick up at the door. Yet the actual crime rate had not significantly altered. The only variable that changed was the *belief* that crime had decreased. Ironically, once people repopulated the area, crime did diminish.

Thus there is some evidence that people may have a negativity bias about environments, avoiding them when there is a harmful aspect perceived and doing so disproportionately to the actual threat.

There is also evidence of how sensitive humans are to negative stimuli, even to the point of avoiding them without knowing it! McGinnies (1949) exposed subjects to a series of words at speeds so fast they could not be recognized. When negatively valent words like *bitch* or *penis* were shown, however, the subjects' palms sweated as though they had actually seen the words. It must be remembered that the subjects had been carefully measured as to exposure thresholds so they were not physically able to recognize words at the speeds they were shown.

Psychologists call this discrimination without awareness. So sensitive is the avoidance mechanism that it can respond to a negative stimulus even though the person cannot recognize the stimulus. Sullivan (1945) independently recognized this phenomenon in his patients and called it a "radar mechanism" that is used to avoid a negative stimulus without our being fully aware it is present. With such an apparatus, we negotiate our daily lives, not knowing the many unpleasant stimuli we have avoided. Thus the world seems more pleasant by such avoidance.

What is the conclusion from research on negativity? Consistent with both Miller (1944) and Taylor (1991), human beings seem to be creatures that *have a difficult time giving up positive present benefits to avoid future negative events*. This picture of motivation will have consistent consequences throughout the remainder of the book.

Increasing Differentiation

Another principle of evolution that seems to be pervasive is the principle of *increasing differentiation*. This is evident in the increasing differentiation of species, the increasing differentiation of nervous tissue as it develops, and the increasing differentiation of behavior at many levels. The latter is at least partly due to the RRR. Gould (1989) points out that the proliferation of species is cut off by the mass eliminations caused by such things as asteroids or volcanoes. Otherwise we would have considerably more evidence of species diversity than we do now.

In human behavior, increasing differentiation occurs at many levels such as art, science, and language. Each makes increasingly finer distinctions: Art moves simplistic to Baroque, science moves from Rutherford to Einstein, and language follows with increasing numbers of words.

Conclusion

Finally we are prepared for a comprehensive view of the range of possible behaviors that may be candidates for evolutionary derivation. First is the only demonstrated link established by Ebstein et al. (1996) as related to Cloninger's theory, novelty seeking. The second trait of Cloninger's theory is harm avoidance, and Miller's and Taylor's research may provide the behavioral evidence but so far there is no genetic link.

The RRR system motivates learning and adaptation; the avoidance system operates to keep us away from harmful stimuli but it is the social cushion that buoys us up from the environment and provides a minienvironment for everyone. Enough reality permeates the cushion so that each person must work, but the individual and society become motivated by metaphors of refuge, and the unreality of the cushion inverts the social order.

Langer (1983) terms the complex motives of the RRR the *psychology of control*. She finds that people are motivated to control each situation they encounter. Inability to control leads to problems of identity. When people cannot control events, they often resort to the illusion of control provided in such terms as *luck* and *fate*. This leads her to use the term *perceived* control to encompass all those situations in which there is true control and the illusion of control as well. Implied in this term is the notion that we may not always know when we actually are in control. Langer also feels that the true aim is actually mastery rather than simply control. Mastery provides a true understanding of any situation and allows recognition that there may be no controlling certain situations. Mastery is understanding relationships rather than just having power over them. All humans and their institutions are motivated to create a refuge within the social cushion. The particular metaphorical term this refuge takes depends on the culture. But no culture completely takes into account all the empirical environmental messages because of the layers of ethnocentrism and social inversion. The social cushion that has been so successful in past evolution has become maladaptive in the accelerating changes of industrial society. It is clear that survival depends on changing the very institutions within societies that have produced the environmental crisis. But very few people have thought out what those changes will involve (Meadows et al., 1992). It sounds simple to say we must change the way we derive and use materials and energy from the Earth. Involved in this kind of change is not only the technology invented to exploit the Earth but the fundamental belief systems that support each culture. Think of what it means to give up ethnocentrism, to admit that your enemy, a stranger, an unknown person has the same value as a person within your own group. It is one of the most difficult things to do. It goes against what most people believe is the source of survival, their own identity. Finally, it becomes even more difficult to give up present rewards to avoid future calamities. As Taylor (1991) demonstrates, negative events are glossed over and minimized.

Environment and behavior research is part of the Rich Response Repertoire response to the environment. It arises within the social cushion but also begins to push against it. How this kind of research evolved is the subject of the next chapter.

GOALS

Definitions and Concepts

- Culture
- Ethnocentrism
- Intrinsic motivation
- Negativity bias
- Mastery
- Negative avoidance mechanism
- Pollyanna Principle
- Differentiation
- RRR
- Affirming the consequent
- Social cushion
- Inversion of social status
- Refuge
- Mobilization-minimization hypothesis
- Psychology of control
- Transactional viewpoint
- Novelty seeking
- Harm avoidance

Important Studies

- Darwin (1859)
- Huxley (1974)
- Solomon and Wynne (1953)
- Neal Miller (1944)
- McGinnies (1949)
- Langer (1983)
- Taylor (1991)
- Wilson (1975)
- Mendel (1865)

QUESTIONS

1. What would your own ideal refuge look like? If you were to imagine the best possible environment for yourself, would it be a true refuge?

2. What things do you think you avoid via the avoidance mechanism?

3. What are successful ways to use to change the social cushion?

4. Which are the most important problems of the social cushion?

5. Which ideologies promise the most compatibility between the limitations of the physical environment and the demands of the social cushion?

6. How are positive and negative responses different?

7. What peculiar limitation in human motivation is there in regard to future disasters?

8. Why do people find it difficult to give up smoking?

9. What is the relationship between RRR and mastery?

10. What is the best environmental message, given what you know about human motivation?

3

The History and Promise of Environment and Behavior Research

If you were given the task of changing your society to make it more aware of and responsive to the environment, how would you go about it? Sit down and give it some thought. Perhaps your conclusions would agree with the course of history of environment and behavior research.

Essentially, to change our society, the leaders in the field chose the following five methods:

1. Create a body of new and useful research findings.
2. Create new organizations to conduct and apply the research.
3. Promote the research through new journals, magazines, and newsletters.
4. Organize the practitioners of the new knowledge.
5. Set up educational programs.

The following chapter describes how the people who founded environment behavior research set about to change their world. The five pioneers began by creating a new and useful body of research; new organizations sprung up to enlarge the research; journals and newsletters began publishing the new findings. The practitioners organized themselves, and, finally, educational programs began in several universities. Although this was not a deliberately planned sequence of events, its spontaneity more than made up for its original lack of direction.

The history of environment and behavior research is presented as an interdisciplinary movement that grew from the work of five pioneers, Barker, Hall, Lynch, Sommer, and Alexander; picked up impetus from the environmental concerns of the 1960s; and flowered into five original centers for education and research. A "convergence of disciplines" period followed in which researchers from various academic pursuits contributed to a core of studies that reached a high level of practical knowledge. Then the field began spawning its own specialties with environmental perception, postoccupancy evaluation (POE), and environments for the elderly as specialties, and nascent specialties began to emerge. The primary goal, to put environment into the person-behavior equation (environment-person-behavior), seems to be nearer realization.

Environment behavior (EB) research has been called many names from the point of view of its many constituents: Architectural psychology, psychological architecture, socioarchitecture, environmental psychology, ecological psychology, environmental sociology, environmental anthropology, sociophysical technology, design research, environment behavior design research, environmental design, and man-environment relations are just a few. In addition, each discipline debates whether the entity is part of a larger field or only a specialty of its own discipline.

The environmental psychologists, for example, debate whether environmental psychology is actually interdisciplinary. Some, like Russell and Ward (1982), see environmental psychology as a specialty of psychology and want to exclude other disciplines while others (Bell, Fisher, Baum, & Greene, 1996; Bell, Fisher, & Loomis, 1978; Proshansky, 1973) see environmental psychology as interdisciplinary by nature. Barker at one time proposed it should be a separate field by itself, "eco-science."

This kind of debate goes on in many academic departments throughout the world as some, professors and students alike, struggle to determine where their work truly belongs while others are no longer concerned. Practitioners worry less about such distinctions but even they have some identity problems.

Thus we have a field of research and practice that borrows ideas, methods, and personnel from many diverse areas. But make no mistake about the true nature of the cloth, environment and behavior research is interdisciplinary in its daily operations, whatever attempts there may be to unravel threads for academic examination.

Despite the eclectic nature of environment and behavior research, it has many blind spots. Human factors (Sanders & McCormick, 1993) has been clearly an environmental discipline for longer than EB research, yet except for luminaries such as Walt Kleeman (1981), it is largely ignored by the field as a whole. Despite the admonitions of Amos Rapoport (1974), environmental anthropology remained outside of most EB research until recently.[1] And most central of all, despite the constant efforts of EB researchers and practitioners, very few design firms in the United States use social science as a part of their everyday practice.[2]

Environmental sociology, on the other hand, has had a healthy evolution on its own. Dunlap and Catton (1994) describe the history of environmental sociology since the 1970s and its "revitalization" in the 1980s. Environmental sociology has made many conceptual contributions to E&B research, not the least of which is the Human Exceptionist Paradigm (HEP; see Chapter 4), a view held by many that humans are outside the forces of nature.

It is also fair to say that most EB researchers are aware of these blind spots and feel free to borrow from many fields. It is this diverse weaving together, widely borrowing, and the deep sense of mission that still characterize the field and makes it exciting for its participants. Environment and behavior research still has the flavor of a frontier to be explored.

The Five Pioneers

Although there are many antecedents, and these have been amply described by Stokols (1977a), environment behavior research had its beginnings with five pioneers[3]: Barker, Hall, Sommer, Lynch, and Alexander. The analogy of threads-without-awareness is applicable here for none of these pioneers was aware he was relating to environment behavior research, and, of course, such a field did not exist when they began. These five, however, set the field in motion with new and unusual research findings that did not fit into the ordinary molds.

The earliest pioneer was Roger G. Barker (Figure 3.1). He was a student of the great social psychologist Kurt Lewin (see Lewin, 1951). Barker, as well as a number of colleagues, came to the University of Kansas in 1947 when he was offered the job of chairman. Herbert Wright

Figure 3.1. Roger G. Barker

and Roger Barker teamed up to found the Midwest Psychological Field Station, a study center established in a small town for the purpose of discovering all the influences of society on child development. Wright went on to live in the town while Barker stayed in Lawrence to shepherd the department for the first few years. Then he moved there also and the two began a long series of studies of the town.

The first technique, largely developed by Wright, was called *behavior specimen recording* and was used to record the behavior of a child during an entire day. *One Boy's Day* (Barker & Wright, 1951) was the first record of a child's behavior during a complete day. Eventually, 17 such daily records were collected for study. By 1955, however, *Midwest and Its Children* was published by Barker and Wright, and this text marked a radical departure from anything that psychology, sociology, or anthropology had seen before. Behavior specimen records were mentioned but the text described new units for studying behavior called *behavior settings*. By the time the second text *Ecological Psychology* was published (Barker,

1968), the field of ecological psychology had fully developed. To this day, some still confuse environmental psychology with ecological psychology. Holahan (1982) even credits Barker with founding environmental psychology. Nevertheless, the methods of ecological psychology remain a separate system, while environmental psychology has become a new branch of psychology (within E&B research) that uses many methods including Barker's.

The influence of Barker is hard to overestimate.[4] His colleagues Paul Gump and Phil Schoggen coauthored books of studies (*Big School, Small School* by Barker & Gump, 1964; *Qualities of Community Life* by Barker & Schoggen, 1973; *Habitats, Environments and Human Behavior*, 1978, by Barker et al.). His pupils Wicker, Bechtel, and Willems have continued and expanded the methods (Bechtel, 1977; Wicker, 1979; Willems & Raush, 1969). Although ecological psychology has had a large influence, it is fair to say that the influence has been more by citation than through actual application of the methods (see Kaminski, 1983). The latest text is Schoggen's revision of the 1968 book (Schoggen, 1989).

Hall's influence (Figure 3.2) stems from his two books, *The Silent Language* (1959) and *The Hidden Dimension* (1966), particularly the former, which is the "best-seller" in the entire field.[5] Hall's work is given the name *proxemics*, and it introduces the concept of *personal distance* and the various social distances people adopt while conversing, greeting, caressing, and the various other forms of human discourse. As an anthropologist, Hall observed that different cultures make different uses of the sensory zones that surround the body. One has to be at a certain distance before one can smell another (olfactory space) or touch another (tactile space) or feel another's body heat (thermal space) or recognize a face (visual space). Distances between bodies were divided into intimate (touching to 18 inches), personal ($1\frac{1}{2}$ to 4 feet), and social (4 to 12 feet) with each distance divided into close and far phases. The research was formalized in a handbook (Hall, 1974).

Sommer (1969a) picked up on Hall's more general notion of personal distance and began a series of experiments on the behavioral response when *personal space* was invaded. He found people attempted to preserve a certain amount of space in their placement of books in libraries or would move away when strangers sat too close. Sommer's book *Personal Space* (1969a) is also one of the best-sellers in the field. Osmond (1957), Sommer's mentor, coined the terms *sociofugal space* to label large, open indoor areas such as train stations that did not foster intimate or social distance

Figure 3.2. Edward T. Hall

encounters, and *sociopetal space* for environments like restaurants and living rooms, which did. Izumi (1957) translated these principles into a new mental hospital design.

Rapoport's *House Form and Culture* (1969), although not directly influenced by Hall, is a further example of the anthropological tradition in E&B research but, in retrospect, was a rather lonely voice until the 1980s.

Lynch's *Image of the City* (1960) had a profound influence on the architectural and planning professions. Lynch used the simple method of *cognitive maps* to determine how people "held" an image of the city. When people drew these maps, they tended to use common elements that were *paths, edges, districts, nodes*, and landmarks to orient themselves.

Cognitive mapping became a research area of its own, and even though the original concept began with Tolman (1938), its use by Lynch gave birth to a widespread practical and research application (Downs & Stea, 1973, 1977). Lynch's book remains another best-seller in EB research.[6]

Of the five pioneers, Christopher Alexander is probably the least well known outside of architectural circles. His influence began when he collected a remarkable group of students at Berkeley in 1963, and from this class two of the most influential organizations were born (DMG and EDRA; see the section on organizations below). Alexander published later than the other three pioneers; *Notes on the Synthesis of Form* (1964) and *A Pattern Language: Towns, Buildings, Construction* (with Silverstein, Angel, Ishikawa, & Abrams, 1977) were highly influential. Gary Moore[7] and Charles Rusch were two of his pupils who later made contributions. Pattern language was the first attempt of an architect to systematically link units of behavior to architectural elements, and it is still used by some architects today, especially on the West Coast.

Institutional Beginnings

While the five pioneers were doing their work independently, the American Institute of Architects (AIA) was beginning to feel the need for social science in the practice of architecture. On December 3, 1956, the research committee of the American Institute of Architects submitted a proposal to the National Science Foundation to have a conference "to analyze the relationships of the physical, biological and social sciences in the problems of optimum created environment for human activities" (Magenau, 1959, p. 5).

That conference was held at Ann Arbor, Michigan, March 10-12, 1959. (Prior to this, the AIA convention in Cleveland for 1958 had a seminar in research that foreshadowed the Ann Arbor conference.) Attendees were from architecture, psychology, sociology, structures engineering, planning, and environmental health. The conference outcome was to propose an agenda for basic research in architecture whose purpose was to include the findings of the social and biological sciences in the designed outcome of buildings. This was the first of many conferences in the years that followed. It is significant that it originated within the architectural profession to fulfill a need for help from the social sciences. That theme has been a strong central focus within environment behavior research. In 1958, Ewing Miller, an architect, and Lawrence Wheeler (1985), a psychologist, began the first collaboration of an architect with a social scientist. Their product was a truck depot, and their collaboration was so successful they went on to design dormitories for the University of Indiana.

The Five Early Centers

By 1965, three centers had been funded by the National Institute of Mental Health (NIMH) to do research and educate people in the discipline of EB research, and two universities developed centers on their own. The National Institute of Mental Health fully realized that to promote this new knowledge, new organizations must be supported.

The first of the three funded centers was begun at Brooklyn College in 1958 (later moved to City University of New York in 1967) to do research on the environment of the mental hospital and its effect on patient behavior. The first grant was awarded for the 1958-1959 academic year and was renewed in 1960. The report of this project was titled *Some Factors Influencing the Design and Function of Psychiatric Facilities* (Ittelson, 1961). A program was begun by Ittelson and Proshansky and it remains the only one of the original five still functioning. This program produced the first text in the field, *Environmental Psychology* (1970) by Proshansky, Ittelson, and Rivlin, and the first journal, *Environment and Behavior*, edited by Gary Winkel, in 1969. This center of study emphasized *behavioral mapping* as a method and specialized in urban and institutionalized environments. Its early influence was pervasive (Figure 3.3).

Figure 3.3. CUNY Environmental Psychology Program, 1975

The second of these centers, in Salt Lake City, began primarily as an educational program for dual degrees in architecture and psychology and was founded by Roger Bailey, an architect, and Calvin Taylor, a psychologist, with early assistance from Hardin Branch, a psychiatrist. The Utah group convened the first conference in environmental psychology. It was called *Architectural Psychology and Psychiatry, a National Exploratory Research Conference* and was held February 24 and 25 at Salt Lake City (Bailey, Branch, & Taylor, 1961).

It is worth taking note of this conference as the first gathering of research scholars in the field.[8] It brought together William Ittelson, Humphrey Osmond, Kyo Izumi, Lawrence Good, and several others who later figured prominently in environmental research. Following the conference, Bailey and Taylor applied to the National Institute of Mental Health for a training grant. The grant was awarded for six trainees per year from 1962 through 1967 and received a 2-year extension. It did not turn out to be a dual degree, as originally planned, but granted a Ph.D. in psychology with a large minor in architecture or an allied field. The first graduate was Robert Wehrli in 1967. John Archea and John Collins were also students in the program. In that year, the newsletter *Architectural Psychology* was first published under the editorship of John Archea. This newsletter later merged with another publication (see MES).

The third center began when architect Lawrence Good received a grant from the Topeka State Hospital Research Fund to construct a model for an experimentally flexible mental hospital ward renovation. This was called the Kirkbride Day Hall Project, from Thomas Kirkbride, who designed the mental hospital ward in most prevalent use at that time. An interested interdisciplinary group collected at Topeka State Hospital, hosted by superintendent Alfred Paul Bay. Among these were anthropologists Robert Squier and Edith Zeller, psychologists Saul Siegal, Robert Bechtel, and Rajendra Srivastava, and sociologists Charles Warriner and David Boyd. Some of this group formed the Environmental Research Foundation (ERF) on July 21, 1965, with Lawrence Good as president. ERF was the first organization brought into existence solely to research the behavior-environment link. It was supported at first by a 5-year grant from NIMH. Unlike the Utah group, this grant was not for training but to establish a center for research. ERF's work was influential in changing the design of nursing stations on mental hospital wards (Bechtel, 1977) and in developing a different concept for mental hospital wards as a whole (Figure 3.4).

ERF moved from Topeka, Kansas, to Kansas City, Missouri, in 1970, changed its name to Environmental Research and Development Foundation (ERDF), and expanded its research scope into urban problems (Dumouchel, 1971).[9] It began publishing a quarterly magazine, *Milieu*, in October 1965. Closely following the establishment of ERF, several practitioners began doing business using social sciences in the design process. These include Deasy and Bolling in 1966 and Brolin and Zeisel in 1967. George Agron, of Stone, Marraccini, and Patterson, began his studies of hospital designs in 1966, and Lou Gelwicks left the University of Southern California and set up Gerontological Planning Associates in Santa Monica in 1972.

Although separated geographically in the West, Midwest, and East, the three earliest organizations cooperated by exchanging students, research papers, and ideas and by holding conferences at which principals from all three organizations attended. At Topeka, Kansas, on March 11, 12, and

Figure 3.4. ERF in 1965

13, 1963, ten researchers gathered from all three organizations. These included William Ittelson from New York, Calvin Taylor of Utah, Roger Barker, and Lawrence Good. The results were published in a book, *Therapy by Design* (Good, Seigel, & Bay, 1965).

Utah held its second conference at Park City in 1966 and over 200 attended with the above three organizations well represented, including dozens of other universities and organizations (Taylor, Bailey, & Branch, 1967) (Figure 3.5).

The fourth group gathered around Jack Wohlwill in psychology and Robert Kates in geography at Clark University in 1965 and lasted into the mid-1970s. Actually, it was not an organization at all but can be thought of as a "critical mass" in the departments of geography, sociology, and psychology at Clark. Robert Beck in sociology, Seymour Wapner and Jack Wohlwill in psychology, and Robert Kates and James Blaut in geography cooperated in a series of studies partly culminating in the special issue on the physical environment of the *Journal of Social Issues* in June 1966 (Kates & Wohlwill, 1966).

Figure 3.5. Second Utah Conference

Ken Craik was also a visiting fellow at Clark (1970-1971). As a climax to the Clark research, a conference called "Experiencing the Environment" was held on January 7-8, 1975. These papers were later collected and published as *Experiencing the Environment*, edited by Wapner, Cohen, and Kaplan (1976).[10]

The fifth organization was both an independent firm established to do research and practice in the field (the Research Design Institute) and a teaching program with the principals holding teaching positions at the Rhode Island School of Design. Ray Studer was instrumental in this organization and he and David Stea (at Brown University at this time) collaborated until Stea moved to Clark. The Rhode Island school published the first directory of EB researchers in 1965.

It is ironic that, although only one of the five original groups has survived (CUNY), there are again five groups dominating the field 30 years later: the CUNY Graduate School Program in Environmental Psychology, the School of Social Ecology at the University of California,

Irvine, Environmental Cognition at the University of Arizona, the Environment-Behavior Studies Program at the University of Wisconsin, Milwaukee, and the Architectural Design Program at the Georgia Institute of Technology.

Further Attempts to Organize

The Environment and Behavior Task Force

When a new discipline does not have a home, it suffers personal identity crises and many problems of organizing research and literature. To address these difficulties and to try to bring a better sense of unity to the field, an ad hoc committee of the American Psychological Association called the committee of Newly Emerging Areas of Research (NEAR) created the Task Force on Environment and Behavior. Members were Irwin Altman (chair), Robert Helmreich, Edwin Willems, and Joachim Wohlwill. The *Environmental Task Force Committee* was created by the American Psychological Association (APA). The task force was only one of several task forces that APA was creating for newly emerging areas in the mid-1970s. Another was the task force on population, which eventually led to Division 34 (Population Psychology), and a third group was on health (Medical Psychology).

Willo White, longtime Executive Director of EDRA, was then an employee of the APA working on the board of scientific affairs. Irwin Altman was also on this board as a social psychologist. White suggested that a task force be formed, and a group met at the 1974 APA convention. The task force was set up to last for 3 years with Altman as chairman. It got a 1-year extension, and its work was extended again for another year. Willo White's book *Resources in Environment and Behavior* (1979) was a product of the task force and marks its end point. Altman feels the real success of the task force was in bringing together new researchers and giving them a national forum.[11]

White and Altman disagreed on the proper place for E&B research; Altman felt a separate division of APA was proper, while White did not feel a division of APA would be capable of enfolding the various disciplines. Altman then negotiated with Division 34 (Population Psychology) to merge with environmental psychologists. Division 34 changed its name to Population and Environmental Psychology and began publishing the

Population and Environmental Psychology newsletter in 1974. See Altman's comments on complacency 8 years after the merger with the Task Force and Division 34 (*Population and Environment Newsletter*, Fall-Winter, 1982).

Meanwhile, there were other efforts at organizing the field. Organizations sprang up in an attempt to provide professional contacts, identity, and an outlet for literature. Three of these were most prominent: the Design Methods Group, the Environmental Research Design Association, and the Association for Man-Environment Relations.

Organizations

DMG. The Design Methods Group (DMG) had its first informal meeting on June 7, 1966, at the University of Waterloo in Canada. Founding members were Marvin Manheim, Martin Krampen, Charles Owen, Allen Bernholtz, Serge Bouterline, Robert Gay, and Gary Moore. Gary Moore and Marvin Manheim were elected cochairs. They began publishing the DMG newsletter in December 1966. That first issue contained a list of over 150 people interested in the field. This newsletter later (1968) became the journal *Design Theories and Methods*, which is still being published. In September of that year, 30 to 40 of the DMG group met informally at MIT to discuss computer-aided building design. DMG was concerned with the design process and has fairly consistently tried to refine it and look for ways to include new methods.

EDRA. DMG had its first annual conference at MIT on June, 2, 3, 4, 1968. About 250 attended. From these, about 30 individuals met together on June 4 to discuss broadening the content of the DMG newsletter and to integrate with the newly forming ASMER (the Association for the Study of Man-Environment Relations) and new journals such as *Environment and Behavior*. They decided to hold a conference and form an organization called the Environmental Design Research Association (EDRA). Henry Sanoff, an architect from North Carolina State University at Raleigh, and Sidney Cohen were elected cochairmen of the conference committee. Sanoff and Gary Moore were to be cochairs of the organization. Others in the core group included Marvin Manheim, Gerald Nadler, and Stuart Silverstone. Daniel Carson and Gary Winkel were not present but were elected, along with the others, to a nine-person steering committee. Their first annual meeting was held at Chapel Hill, North Carolina, on June 8, 9, 10, 1969 (Sanoff & Cohen,

1969). An invitation was broadcast on November 12, 1968. EDRA incorporated as a nonprofit corporation on January 19, 1972. It was first intended that the DMG group be a part of the EDRA conference but DMG attendance dropped off after the first annual meeting.

EDRA is the largest and most successful of all the organizations spawned during the convergence period. It has held annual meetings continuously since 1969, has accumulated thousands of pages of annual conference proceedings, and remains the principal annual gathering of environmental researchers and practitioners. Its list of boards of directors (new ones elected every 3 years on a staggered basis) contains virtually all the famous names in the field[12] and its practice of locating its conferences in universities with relevant programs ensures maximum exposure for environmental design research throughout the country. From the very beginning, it has attracted international researchers, and it is common to have attendance from a dozen foreign countries.

EDRA has attempted to bring direction to the field, most recently with Moore and Howell's *A Research Agenda for the Eighties* (1982). A series of annual summaries was planned to begin in 1986 (see Zube & Moore, 1989).

ASMER. The Association for the Study of Man-Environment Relations sprang from the 1967 meeting of the American Association for the Advancement of Science. Aristide (Hans) Esser, a psychiatrist, was the stimulating force. At that time, he was employed at the Rockland State Hospital in Orangeburg, New York. Irwin Altman chaired the meeting at the headquarters of the American Geographical Society. A second meeting was held the next day at the Americana Hotel. The group requested affiliation with the AAAS, but for some reason it was never granted. Their first newsletter went out in January 1965. Eventually this newsletter became *Man-Environment Systems*, a review of literature in the field. MES, as an organization, devoted itself largely to publication of *MES*, the review. In 1981, it completed a comprehensive review of the literature in a special project (Murtha, 1988).

Directories

In a further effort to help unify the field and increase communications, various groups issued directories. The research Design Institute of Providence, Rhode Island, issued the first directory in 1965. The directory was revised in 1967 and again in 1969. Subsequently EDRA produced several lists of its members and continues to do so. MIT compiled a directory of all persons interested in the field in 1971. ASMER compiled an international directory of EB researchers in 1974. Willo White's (1979) resource volume was the last comprehensive directory until the first *EDRA Membership Handbook* was published (White, 1984). Although EDRA continues to publish annual lists, Saarinen and Sell (1987) produced the most comprehensive list of all, attempting to gather all researchers worldwide.

The Diplomats

No field of endeavor can grow without a group of diplomats who not only contribute research and train students but also found organizations, promote growth by bringing interested persons together, and serve as continual salesmen for the field among various professions. William Ittelson stands out as the first diplomat by helping to found the first environmental psychology field at (what is now) CUNY and assembling the first textbook (Proshansky, Ittelson, & Rivlin, 1970) with an introductory text (Ittelson, Proshansky, Rivlin, & Winkel, 1974) and also a revision of the original text (Proshanky, Ittelson, & Rivlin, 1976). Ittelson also began the first research project to receive government funding (Ittelson, 1961). Ittelson's contributions as a diplomat span from the early 1960s through the 1980s (Hagino & Ittelson, 1980). The contributions also cover a countless number of conferences and influence through many graduates of the environmental program at CUNY. Harold Proshansky certainly shares this spotlight as cofounder and senior author. Proshansky became director of the program at CUNY and has produced summaries of the field (1987).

Irwin Altman is an outstanding diplomat whose record as the chairman of the Environmental Task Force helped to shape the field in a critical period. Altman's research began in the 1960s, and his work as editor of two series published by Brooks/Cole and Plenum (Altman & Wohlwill, 1976) has helped to present environment and behavior research as a coherent field of work. Altman also had a principal role in the founding of ASMER and served as head of Division 34 (APA) as well as in numerous other roles and as a chief supporter of EDRA.

Dan Stokols carved a role as diplomat by founding the social ecology program at Irvine and writing a book that defined the state of the art (Stokols, 1977a) as well as numerous research reports on stress and crowding (Stokols, 1976, 1978b). Stokols and Altman collaborated on the

---

Box 3.1

Some Firsts in Environmental Psychology

First Text:	*Introduction to Environmental Psychology* by Proshansky, Ittelson, & Rivlin, 1970
First Conference:	AIA Research Conference, Ann Arbor, March 10-12, 1959
First Journal:	*Environment and Behavior,* 1969
First Newsletter:	Design Methods Group newsletter
First Organization:	Design Methods Group, 1966
First Collaboration:	Miller and Wheeler, 1959
First Directory:	Rhode Island School of Design, 1965
First Attempt at Legislation:	Senate Bill 2080, 1979
First International Conference:	Dalandai Conference, Great Britain, 1969

Handbook of Environmental Psychology published by John Wiley (Stokols & Altman, 1987). The Irvine program has turned into the School of Social Ecology.

At this point, it must be recognized that the *environment* in EB research did not then (in the late 1950s and early 1960s) have the meaning that it has today. The five pioneers and the five organizations concerned themselves largely with the human response to the built environment. Indeed, *environment* had not yet become the worldwide concern that it became in the late 1960s and 1970s. Although the geographers always had a larger definition when they studied floodplains and disasters, even they did not include energy, nuclear accidents, and the broad range of topics considered in current EB research. This larger view of the environment as a whole was a product of the converging disciplines, a period of EB research that stretched from the late 1960s through the 1970s and into the 1980s.

The Convergence of Disciplines Period

The explosion of growth that occurred in the late 1960s through the 1970s is best characterized as a convergence of disciplines. Social psychologists, geographers, sociologists, anthropologists, architects, interior designers, planners, ethnologists, psychiatrists, and even a few engineers converged on the field and overwhelmed the three original institutions. This period is seen as a convergence rather than an expansion because, although the researchers and practitioners worked "in" the field, most did not leave their home disciplines. Important papers were not primarily addressed to the new audience but were published within the old disciplinary journals, with consciousness of addressing and keeping the respect of peers. Publication in EDRA proceedings, for example, was seen as a secondary source, less prestigious, and not worthy of a major effort. The result of this curious convergence of bodies at conventions was a dispersion of papers throughout various journals and a failure to centralize the field. Few saw themselves as full-time researchers in EB. I can remember the advice given by my social psychology professor during this period: "It's OK to do that as a hobby, but not for your career." That advice was already too late in the mid-1960s, but the "real" careers were still within the disciplines. Unfortunately, some of this remains true today. Many of the researchers in environment behavior still see themselves as primarily affiliated with their home disciplines.

The Period of Retrenchment

One of the first acts of the Reagan administration upon possession in 1980 was to remove the solar panels placed on the White House roof by Jimmy Carter. This was followed by an announcement from Budget Director David Stockman that funding would be cut for all social sciences.

With the funding cuts of the Reagan administration and the subsequent pruning of new programs in many universities, it might at first seem as though the loss of programs and personnel in EB research was merely a reflection of this national trend. Departments of psychology were withdrawing into the traditional professions and making it more difficult to gain tenure for the more interdisciplinary environmental psychologists. Some schools of architecture were letting go of the EB researchers they had hired in the more ebullient 1960s, and Fred Krimgold of the National Science Foundation announced at the EDRA 13 meeting in Ames, Iowa, that "interdisciplinary projects" were no longer favored. Most of the personnel at the design research branch of the National Bureau of Standards were dismissed or transferred. The Man-Environment Systems Program (MER) at the Pennsylvania State University was eliminated.

Yet, with a little historical perspective, it can be seen that at least some retrenchment in the field had begun in the mid-1970s. In their study of housing postoccupancy evaluations (POEs), Bechtel and Srivastava (1978) showed a decline in housing POEs since 1974 when 23% of all published POEs on housing were done (up to 1978). Also by the 1973 EDRA (EDRA IV at Blacksburg, Virginia), the maximum attendance at EDRAs was reached with 480 registered conference members and about 700 in total attendance. EDRA attendance has leveled off since that time to just under 300.

In 1979 and 1980, Senate Bill 2080 was introduced into and passed the U.S. Senate with a wide majority, but both times was never voted out of committee by the House. This bill attempted to require POEs of all federally funded buildings. It represented a high-water mark in EDRA's effort to influence national policy.

Were these signs actually a period of retrenchment or merely the shifting of forces? In the midst of the drastic cuts, two new programs sprang up, one at the University of Wisconsin in Milwaukee and the other at the Georgia Institute of Technology. At the same time, another new journal, the *Journal of Environmental Psychology*, came into being (March 1981) with joint editorship in Great Britain and the United States, and new organizations were springing up in many foreign countries.

International Research

As David Canter is fond of reminding Americans, Europe and the rest of the world are not a homogeneous region. Each country has its own history of EB research. Nonetheless, Europe as a whole appears more outgoing in its research endeavors than the United States, holding many international conferences and incorporating the use of social sciences within governmental structures at a faster pace than in the United States.

Kruse reports environmental psychology in Germany as dating back to the 1920s (Kruse & Arlt, 1984; Kruse, Grauman, & Lantermann, 1990). Curiously enough, it is still called ecological psychology (Ökologische psychologie), a point of confusion between Germany and the United States.

When Saarinen and Sell (1987) did their review of environmental perception research, they found no less than 66 countries had reported

Table 3.1 Growth in E&B Researchers Worldwide

World Region	1967		1974		1985	
	N	%	N	%	N	%
Africa	0	0	2	.2	66	2.2
Anglo-America	216	88.5	801	84.4	1432	48.5
Asia	0	0	0	0	281	9.5
Australasia	0	0	13	1.4	137	4.6
Eastern Europe	0	0	1	1	74	2.5
Latin America	0	0	12	1.3	65	2.2
Western Europe	28	11.5	114	12.2	896	30.4
Totals	224	100	949	100.2	2951	99.9

SOURCE: Saarinen and Sell (1987, p. xiv, Table 1); reprinted by permission.

research efforts. This is a fair estimate of the extension of the field to other countries. (See Table 3.1, from Saarinen and Sell, for a listing of increased numbers of researchers since 1967.)

In 1983, Australasia formed an association called People and the Physical Environment Association (PAPER). It has been meeting annually since. Ross Thorne of Australia was the first chair. John Daish and Duncan Joiner were on the board from New Zealand.

The European countries got together and formed the First International Conference on Architectural Psychology held at Kingston, Great Britain, in 1970; the second was held at Lund, Sweden, in 1973; and the third at Strasbourg, France, in 1976. This group was headed by Gilles Barbey of Lausanne, Carl Graumann, head of Heidelberg's Psychology Institute, Lenelis Kruse of Heidelberg, and Perla Korosec-Serfaty of Strasbourg.

In 1969, a European group held the Dalandai Conference in Great Britain. These conferences continued every 2 years until they became officially organized in 1981 as IAPS, the International Association for the Study of People and Their Physical Surroundings. There was considerable overlap of membership among the European organizations. Only IAPS survived and continues to hold conferences.

At a meeting funded by the U.S. National Science Foundation in Tokyo in 1980, a gathering of Japanese psychologists and architects announced the formation of the Man Environment Research Association (MERA). MERA has continued to do local and international research and is always represented at EDRA, IAPS, and PAPER. The Japanese have a keen interest in traffic safety and publish annual summaries of their work through the International Association of Traffic and Safety Sciences (IATSS), with its journal *IATSS Research*.

The collection of Japanese and U.S. psychologists that first met in Tokyo in 1980 continued to have meetings every five years: 1985 in Tucson, Arizona; 1990 in Kyoto, Japan; and in 1995 at Clark University in Worcester, Massachusetts. The 2000 meeting will be in Japan.

Japan has a history of environmental concern that goes back at least to 1212 when Kamo-no-Chomei published a book titled *Hojoki*. Yoshitake (1990) describes how the priest continued reducing the size of his dwelling to conform more closely to his needs and at the same time making fewer demands on nature. He finally arrived at a small 100-square foot dwelling called a *hojo*, which was a dwelling completely in harmony with nature.

In the 1960s, Ualfrido del Carlo, former dean of the School of Architecture at São Paulo University in Brazil, attended the Sorbonne in France and learned to do POEs. Immediately upon returning to Brazil, he set about doing POEs, marshalling government support, and enrolling colleagues. He began his first POE in 1972 and produced what may be the most voluminous one to date, over 400 pages. By 1990, Sheila Ornstein, one of del Carlo's pupils and a professor at the School of Architecture, was involved in no less than 11 POEs at various stages. Most of these were supported by either university or government funds, including the work of undergraduates. São Paulo had become the POE capital of the world.

Although much has been written about the fall of the Soviet Union, work in E&B research began there long before the period of *glasnost* and *perestroika*. Toomas Niit was one of the academics centered at Tallinn in Estonia. Much of this work was concerned with housing (Liimets, Niit, & Heidmets, 1983; Mikkin, 1988).

Conclusions

In the more than 30 years since its birth in the early to mid-1960s, EB research has flourished and produced an imposing array of literature. It has now become staple fare in many universities in one form or another, whether taught as environmental psychology, social ecology, or social science in architecture. Environmental psychology is a section of or chapter in most introductory texts and is usually a chapter in social psychology texts.[13] It is reviewed about every 4 or 5 years in the annual review of psychology and is standard fare at APA and applied psychology conventions. Even the learning psychologists have begun to recognize the importance of the environment (Balsam & Tomie, 1985). During the course of these more than 30 years, four trends have developed, some of which show the maturity of the field while others show its continuing youth.

Trend 1: Diversification of Subjects and Convergence of Methods

Ross and Campbell (1978) surveyed 8 years of EDRA proceedings from 1969 to 1978 and discovered the trend of diversification. It seems that E&B research has moved from a concentration on housing and buildings to a smorgasbord of topics including the recent proliferation of computers in offices (Kleeman, 1983, 1991) and environmental problems of workplaces (Becker, 1982), nursing homes (Koncelik, 1976), high-rise buildings (Conway, 1977), hospitals (Trites, Galbraith, Sturdavant, & Leckwert, 1970), bathrooms (Kira, 1976), offices (Wineman, 1982), and streets (Appleyard, 1981) in the daily world. Altman's Plenum series has produced 10 volumes in such areas as children, transportation, the elderly, home environments, and public spaces. But the journey has not been solely one of specialized applied topics. Defensible space (Newman, 1972) has been combined with environmental overload in cities (Milgram, 1970), and territorial behavior, crowding, and privacy were borrowed from social psychology and put together in various ways in Stokol's (1983) special issue of *Environment and Behavior*, a collection of new theoretical concerns. Finally, the *Handbook of Environmental Psychology* (Stokols & Altman, 1987) attempts to summarize the field in the United States and abroad.

There has been an evolution of methods as well. The research in the early EDRA volumes had very few empirical studies and seldom made use of statistics other than chi-square. Almost no control groups grace the early literature. By contrast, the more recent literature boasts sophisticated multivariate techniques. This is only the natural course of maturation that one would expect. The outstanding feature of the methodological development has been the rise of the postoccupancy evaluation (POE).

As was typical of the field as a whole, no one knew what to call POEs at first. England coined the term *desk appraisal*, architecture professors called them *design evaluations*, psychologists used *needs assessments* for a while, and a brave attempt was made to take the sting out of evaluations by calling them postoccupancy *assessments*. By the late 1970s, however, the term solidified to indicate that a *postoccupancy evaluation* was an attempt to measure whether a building's design suited the occupants' needs. Zimring and Reizenstein's (1980) definition is "the examination of the effectiveness of occupied designed environments for human users." For a while there was a brief debate over whether one needed to know the designer's intentions before a "true" evaluation could be made, and some still question whether POEs can be used in basic research.

The problem with viewing the POE as a method is that it is actually several methods combined, but seemingly often not the same methods in each use. Bechtel and Srivastava (1978) found the majority of POEs used an average of three different methods to collect data. Thus there is potential to draw conclusions from a *converging* model (á la Campbell & Fiske, 1959), but as Starr and Danford (1979) point out, instruments must be able to *discriminate* between environments. Discriminant validity was equally important with convergent validity in the Campbell and Fiske model. Daniel and Ittelson (1981) note that many self-report measures do not discriminate between a verbal concept and an actual environment. Starr (1979) brought this to a reductio ad absurdum by having subjects report on *anything* in one condition, and did not get significant differences from the anything condition and certain other more specific environments.

Trend 2: The Development of Independent Areas

A measure of a field's maturity is its development of subject topics that become areas of investigation on their own and independent of the field itself. The prime candidate for independence is environmental perception (EP). Saarinen and Sell's (1981) review makes clear that this topic has some followers and practitioners who have never even heard of EB research and feel no need to ally with it. There may even be some question as to whether EP was ever a part of the main body of EB research. The geographers (Burton, 1962) who began hazard perception studies were actually a part of the field of geography and to a large extent still are. Whichever view one might take, it is clear that the EP topic has a following of its own, had its own newsletter, and is growing in its own directions. Saarinen and Sell finished an international directory of 2,951 names from 66 countries (Saarinen & Sell, 1987).

A second candidate for independent offspring is the POE area. There have been separate POE conferences (Zimring & Reizenstein, 1980), and practitioners of the POE operate on a contractual basis, independent of any organization. There is a handbook on POE use (Bechtel, 1978a) and another published by Preiser, Rabinowitz, and White (1988). See also Bechtel's (in press) defense of the POE as a paradigm.

Implementations of the POE system have proceeded in countries such as Sweden and New Zealand. Although New Zealand's was influenced by U.S. participation, Sweden's was entirely independent, and Sweden issues regular reports on new findings that are systematically made part of the government housing system (Bechtel & Srivastava, 1978).

And it can be said without equivocation that the POE is very much a product of EB research. There still may be a question as to how independent it is, because although there is a POE network within EDRA, there are no POE newsletters or regular POE conventions. Nevertheless, it has become a clear topic of its own and is presented at nearly every EB meeting in some form.

One can see other topic areas growing. The environment of the elderly has become a specialized field. But this is not entirely an offspring candidate because it has always had the Gerontological Society behind its development. It is more nearly characterized as a semiadopted offspring. Practitioners make the gerontology meetings a higher priority than they do EDRA meetings.

Other candidates for future independent offspring would be the childhood city movement, wayfinding, energy conservation, museums and zoos, and housing. These topics are at various stages of taking off on their flights to independence.

Trend 3: The Continuing Struggle to Bridge the Social Science Gap

A consistent theme of EB research from its earliest beginnings has been the motive to use the tools of social science in the design process. The very first AIA research conference in 1959 was a plea for social scientists to apply their skills to design practice. And from its first meeting in 1969, every EDRA convention since has had several symposia, workshops, and/or papers concerned with that issue in some way. Foremost among the champions of this cause have always been the architects themselves. Lynch, Alexander, Agron, Deasy, Conway, Gelwicks, Pena, Sauer, and many others have consistently pleaded the case while the vast majority of the design professions (with the exception of landscape architecture) have remained largely indifferent up to the present time.

The struggle continues unabated, however, and is still clearly seen as a large motive in EB research. The recent surge in the practical applications of social science to energy issues (Baum & Singer, 1981; Geller, Winett, & Everett, 1982) is a manifestation of the same motive. Even though the Department of Energy has severely cut back support for research in this area, it continues to be done through other sources. Of interest, even though the energy research had success in modifying human behavior, it has not been accepted by policymakers just as (and perhaps for some of the same reasons) architects have not accepted social science.

It is a particular irony that, although architects are not seen as accepting social science, government agencies (Eichinger, 1985; Reinsel, 1985; Vischer, 1985) and industry (Picasso, 1985) seem to be making POEs part of their operating procedures.

Trend 4: The Disciplinary Conflict

The final and fourth trend is potentially destructive but it too has been a recurring one. It is a problem that goes back to the very beginnings of EB research. In July 1965, the very year and month that ERDF was founded, a new researcher visited Topeka who was traveling the entire United States from Maine to Florida, California to Oregon, and stops between. When asked why he was making such an exhausting trip, he said, with a touch of desperation, "to find some colleagues."

That same drama is being enacted on a much smaller scale in various departments of architecture and psychology, various design firms, and governmental agencies. The EB researchers still have trouble finding colleagues because the power of the traditional disciplines and the forces against interdisciplinary projects are very strong. Many compromise by remaining allied with a parent discipline and treating EB as an avocation. The drama is compounded when some EB practitioners fail to get tenure or lose their jobs because they are not seen as firmly established in the traditional disciplines.

So the conflict with the disciplines continues. David Canter claims, however, that it is not the case in Britain, where E&B research is accepted. Germany, Sweden, Australia, and New Zealand have developed successful programs of their own. EB research may soon face the same situation as American car dealers—the crush of foreign imports.

Some of the conflict with the disciplines is due to the applied nature of much EB research. Within many of the traditional academic disciplines, applied research is still frowned on as being a form of prostitution. Therefore, some EB research is seen as not quite respectable. This bias will tend to disappear as more theory is built, but it is true that a great deal of EB work is applied and will continue to be so because a great deal of the success in the field is that it now can offer concrete advice in specialized areas.

Perhaps this dilemma will never be solved. It may be that EB research will become an area of its own that will never "marry" with the other disciplines despite its avowed intentions to do so. After all, this has been the course that all of the so-called disciplines have traditionally taken. But if this becomes the case, it will mean that a good part of the original impetus of EB research will not be consummated, for it was the original vision that the problems of the environment-behavior interface could only be understood and solved by an interdisciplinary effort, and the belief in the reality of that vision seems as strong as ever 20 or more years later.

Yet there is a larger goal that grew within the movement, and although it has never been as clearly articulated, its aim was to redress the balance in psychological studies as a whole. This has not been as pressing a need in sociology, with its ecological concerns (Hawley, 1950), or with anthropology (see Hieb, 1977), but in the field of psychology it has been much as Little (1972) observed: "Were an alien being to attempt to draw a picture of man's environment from the information contained in personality journals it would appear as a set of disembodied significant others floating in a sea of abstractions" (p. 95).

Some success has been achieved in redressing that balance and placing people in an environment. Most introductory psychology texts list environmental psychology as a section of a chapter, and most social psychology texts now devote a significant part of a whole chapter to the topic. Evans (1979b) listed 20 formal graduate programs and 43 less-than-formal programs. White (1984) listed 36 formal programs in the United States and 8 in foreign countries. In a very substantial way, the proponents of the field have had an impact in the literature, in academia, and in the professions.

Notes

1. Hieb (1977) has made a bibliography on anthropological research in EB research.

2. Possible exceptions to this statement are Farbstein and Associates of San Luis Obispo and Min Kantrowitz and Associates of Albuquerque. Yet these firms would not be classified as purely design firms because they do EB research as well. Another exception might be BOSTI, the Buffalo Organization for Social and Technological Innovation. This organization, founded in 1972, does both design work and social science research separately and in combination. It is connected with SUNY at Buffalo and is headed by Mike Brill.

3. Canter and Stringer take the view that the famous Hawthorne studies (Roethlisberger & Dickson, 1939) were the first work in EB research. Industrial psychology also claims this as their first work.

4. In a count of citations in 14 EB texts in 1978 excluding all of Barker's texts, Barker was the researcher most cited ($N = 601$).

5. Hall's *Silent Language* sold over 1 million copies in paperback alone by 1987. *Hidden Dimension* sold over 400,000 paperback and hard cover through 1987.

6. Lynch remains the best-selling author for the MIT Press years after his death. *Image of the City* sold over 143,000 copies in eight editions through 1992.

7. Moore feels his 1968 book *Emerging Methods in Environmental Planning* was directly inspired by Alexander (letter to author not dated but in 1983).

8. But, of course, second to the previously mentioned AIA conference at Ann Arbor in 1959. This conference, however, was research oriented and reported on research projects while the Ann Arbor conference was essentially for planning.

9. ERDF, which was the only one of the original five organizations to win the AIA research medal in 1975, went out of existence by 1990. Its archives are stored in the Spencer Library at the University of Kansas, Lawrence.

10. Other outstanding students at the Clark enclave were Ann Buttimer, Saul Cohen, David Lowenthal, and Jeremy Anderson in geography and David Stea in psychology. Also present were Ervin Zube, Roger Hart, David Seamon, Art Patterson, Albert Mehrabian, and Gary Moore. See the special issue on Clark University in *Journal of Environmental Psychology* (Vol. 7, No. 4, 1987).

11. The task force began as the Task Force on Man-Environment Relations but changed its name in December of 1973 to Task Force on Environment and Behavior. "We feel that this name more accurately reflects our mission and removes any hint of chauvinism which was not intended in the original name" (memo from Willo White dated December 17, 1973).

12. A roster of board members and publication list is available by writing EDRA, P.O. Box 7146, Edmond, OK 73083-7146, phone: (405) 330 4863; FAX: (405) 330 4150; e-mail: amsedra@aol.com

13. In 1987, of 35 texts in introductory psychology, 23 had sections on EB, 3 with full chapters. Although 12 did not list EB separately, the subject matter was spread throughout.

GOALS

Definitions and Concepts

Ecological psychology

Proxemics

Personal space

Sociofugal space

Sociopetal space

Pattern language

EDRA

CUNY

Division 34

POE

Convergence of disciplines

Sensory zones

Cognitive maps

Social science in architecture

Retrenchment period

Environmental perception

Important Studies

Barker (1968)

Hall (1954)

Sommer (1969a)

Lynch (1960)

Proshansky et al. (1970)

White (1979)

Saarinen and Sell (1987)

Stokols and Altman (1987)

QUESTIONS

1. What was the origin of environment behavior research?

2. What was the significance of the contributions of the five pioneers?

3. Why was the convergence period more of an implosion than an explosion?

4. What is the significance of the year 1973?

5. What problems does any interdisciplinary movement face?

6. Why was an original goal of EDRA never met?

7. What was the all-time best-seller in the E&B field?

8. What educational program had the longest life?

9. What future directions is E&B research likely to take?

10. What has remained a steady but frustrating purpose?

Part II

Conceptual Areas of Study

4

Values, Beliefs, and Attitudes About the Environment

And God blessed them and God said unto them, Be fruitful and multiply, and replenish the earth and subdue it: and have dominion over the fish of the sea and over the fowl of the air and over every living thing that moveth upon the earth.

(Genesis I, 18)

Iitoi known as Elder Brother, came down from Baboquivari and took the red clay from his mother, the Earth, and formed man. He made the head first so that man might be wise. When he finished, he put the forms in the hot sun to bake. Then Iitoi went back up to Baboquivari to unleash the wind that lived in the cave on the sacred mountain.

Above Baboquivari a large dark cloud formed, and moved down the mountain. A wind blew over the man and lifted the mold up. It looked as if it might blow away, but the wind stopped. The man sat up and looked around. Iitoi greeted him and told the man that he was the child of earth, sun and wind. He cautioned the man not to harm the earth or she would cease to give him all the things he needed.

(Tohono O'odham myth from Fisk, 1983, p. 5)

Contrast these two stories of creation. One treats the Earth as an inanimate object, the other as a living entity with power to withhold the necessities of life. Which view is most likely to result in pollution and which is most likely to result in preservation? It is tempting to say that the Tohono O'odham myth, like so many Native American beliefs, results in less harm to the environment. However, the evidence is not persuasive. The evidence seems to support the proposition that *no matter what* your religious belief, you will harm the environment. Martin and Klein (1989) take the view that the gentle hunters of prehistoric America were responsible for the extinction of the large fauna on the North American continent. Evidence is accumulating that the Maya Indians exhausted their environment with wars and overpopulation (Schele & Friedel, 1990). All this points to an underlying set of values that undergird treatment of the environment across all religions and cultures based on the hunting-gathering tradition.

Some would say that the human, patriarchal-centered view given in Genesis is primarily responsible for the state of the environment today (White, 1967). What is the evidence?

Coward (1995) reviews Judaism, Christianity, Islam, Hinduism, Buddhism, and Chinese religions and concludes that although all religions except Buddhism and Chinese religions have urges to irresponsible population increases, all have, nevertheless, tended to "temper our aggressiveness toward nature" (p. 297). Thus the blaming of religions for environmental depredation is a false trail. There are, however, beliefs and values that cut across many religions and cultures, and bear examination.

Kluckhohn and Strodtbeck (1961) administered the Variations in Value Orientations (VVO) scale to several cultures and showed that Eastern cultures valued harmony with nature more than Western cultures but this generalization must be tempered with the fact that many persons within Western culture also value harmony with nature. In a more recent survey of world values, Schwartz found a more universal pattern of benevolence conflicting with power in all cultures (Schwartz, 1994; Schwartz & Bilsky, 1990; Schwartz & Sagiv, 1995). Western cultures tend more toward the power end of the matrix and are thus less benevolent.

But what are values, and how do they influence our treatment of the Earth? Schwartz and Sagiv (1990) define *values* as "transsituational goals (terminal or instrumental) that express interests (individual, collective, or both) concerned with a motivational type and that are evaluated according to their importance as guiding principles in a person's life" (pp. 93-94). Note several important distinctions. Values go across situations; they are not "stuck" in any one circumstance. Values express an interest that can be at an individual or a collective level, or at both at the same time. Values are concerned with a motivational type. Motivational types were found by factor-analyzing Schwartz's questions into 10 elements: hedonism, achievement, power, self-direction, stimulation, universalism, benevolence, security, conformity, and tradition. Spirituality was at first thought to be an eleventh type but eventually was shown to be diffused throughout the other types. *Hedonism* is, of course, concerned with pleasure or sensuous gratification in a healthy way. *Achievement* relates to personal success through competence within social standards. *Power* refers to social status and prestige, control or dominance over people and resources. This is a type expected to be highly rated in Western culture. *Self-direction* refers to being independent in thought and action and not being constrained by external limits. *Stimulation* refers to novelty, excitement, and challenge. *Universalism* refers to understanding, appreciation, tolerance, and protection for the welfare of all people and nature. *Benevolence* refers to the preservation and welfare of all those one comes in immediate contact with. *Security* is concern with safety, harmony, and stability of society, relationships, and self. *Conformity* is restraint of actions, inclinations, and impulses that are likely to harm or upset others or violate social expectations. *Tradition* is respect for the customs and norms of one's own culture. Schwartz sees these types in a dynamic relationship (Figure 4.1). Thus, among the evidence collected so far, Western industrial civilization seems to have values that are less likely to conserve Earth's resources.

Also, Eastern cultures see conformity and tradition as being related to maturity while Western cultures do not. This raises the interesting question of whether Western cultures would be less likely to conform to environmental regulations.

A further distinction must be made when considering values. Schwartz's schema owes a great debt to Rokeach's (1973) distinction between terminal and instrumental values. A *terminal value* is one that expresses an end-point goal in life such as salvation or success. An *instrumental value* is one that is lived daily in the process of reaching the terminal value, such as honesty. Rokeach's system has shown that a change in terminal values is more important and difficult than one in instrumental values and that there is a hierarchy of terminal over instrumental.

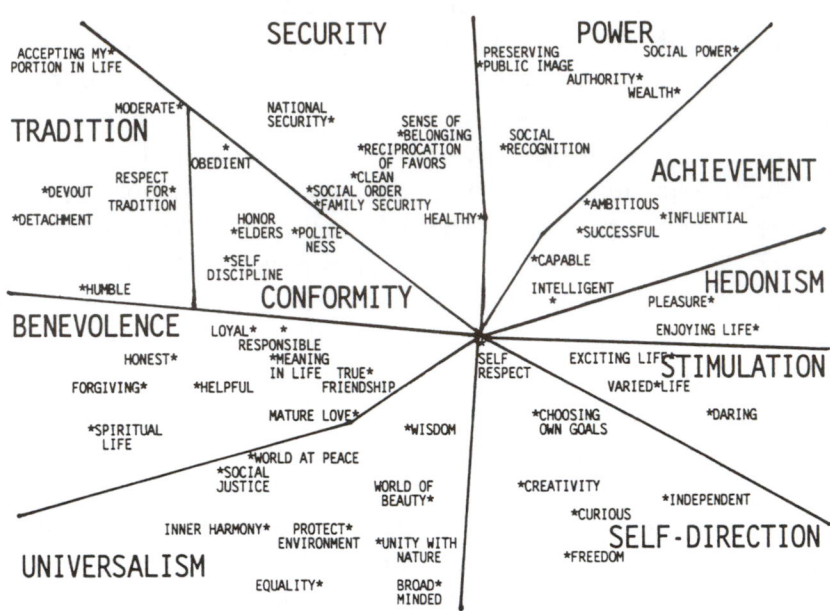

Figure 4.1. Schwartz's Value Relationships
SOURCE: Schwartz and Sagiv (1995).

Beliefs

One of the most persuasively argued beliefs discovered in recent years is described in Melvin Lerner's *The Belief in a Just World: A Fundamental Delusion* (1980). Because belief is more a matter of fact than values, a belief is more subject to question and challenge. People believe in the existence of God or they do not. Lerner claims the belief in a just world is the chief method by which the world of experience is ordered and has meaning. All things that happen are arranged according to what is believed to be just. People get what they deserve. Lerner's research deals with how people reconcile this belief with an unjust world. This is often done by extending the time frame to an ultimate justice.

Belief in science is assumed to be a cornerstone of our society (Whitehead, 1961). Yet it was Korzybski (1958) who pointed out that our industrialized society does not believe in scientific data as a way of determining truth. He claims that science is only used when the culture benefits from it. Otherwise, science is a captive of the culture and is, in fact, often seen as antithetical to cultural values.

Numerous types of evidence would seem to support Korzybski's thesis that science is not believed when it goes contrary to cultural beliefs. Faust and Ziskin (1988), and Dawes, Faust, and Meehl (1989), for example, point out that expert testimony from psychologists and psychiatrists is accepted in courts of law even though there is compelling evidence their testimony is no better than that of laypersons with no training. Actually, this information has been known for some time. Gough (1962) reviews a number of studies that show actuarial (scientific) methods to be superior to expert judgments. There are several reasons these experts do not believe or follow scientific data and one of them is the belief of their own superiority over the data in making judgments. Thus, even among the scientifically trained, there is sometimes a distrust of scientific data and this comes out in testimony.

Vonnegut (1981), in an essay, described the fate of Ignaz Semmelweiss, who tried to make physicians wash their hands because of germs on them. Semmelweiss was ignored even when he killed himself as a demonstration of contamination.

Shadish (1984) points out how the recent social problem of emptying out the mental hospitals ignored several scientifically demonstrated solutions because these went contrary to the prevailing wisdom in the professions. Burnham (1987) documents how the public information on health has been taken over by nonscientific reporting given to "unreasoned" assertions rather than supportive data.

The evidence from these many areas seems to indicate that the beliefs in our society are such that Korzybski's assertion is true: Science is a captive of the culture (social cushion) and is only attended to when it supports the prevailing wisdom.

Toffler (1980) describes a more complex set of beliefs that he refers to as preindustrial, industrial, and postindustrial. Citizens in our world are caught in these forms of thinking that are not adequate to deal with modern technology. What is important about Toffler's observation is that various segments of any society are caught in preindustrial kinds of thinking; others are barely into the industrial age itself before having to face a postindustrial way of thinking. For many, as Toffler observed, the changes are too many to endure (future shock).

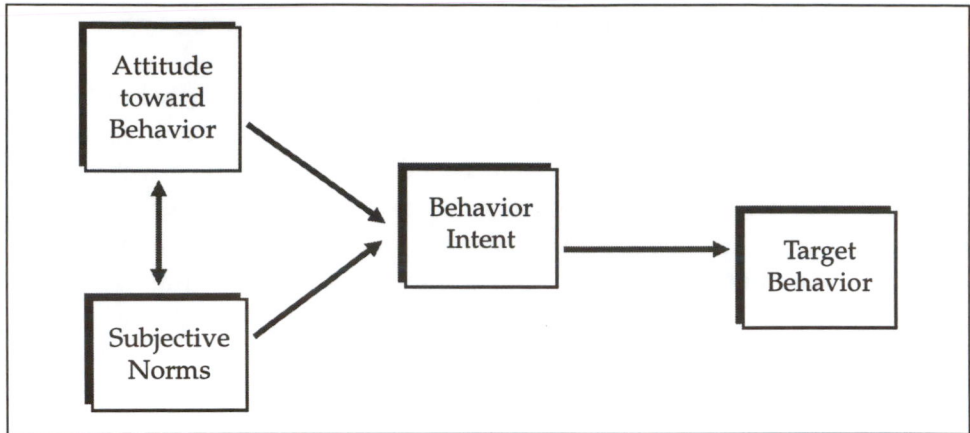

Figure 4.2. Fishbein-Ajzen Model

Attitudes

Social psychology has a long history of research on attitudes. Unfortunately, until relatively recently, the connection between attitudes and behavior has been questionable (Wicker, 1969a) despite the amount of research. Perhaps the evidence that behavior was not related to attitudes went too much against prevailing wisdom. In any case, a model was finally developed (Fishbein & Ajzen, 1975) that not only explained why previous research had been so bad but actually led to studies in which high predictability was demonstrated. The main principle that led to this discovery was called "levels of correspondence." Figure 4.2 shows the elements of the Fishbein-Ajzen model.

The model shows a direct interaction between the attitude toward a specific (target) behavior and subjective norms. If the behavior is against these norms, it will likely not take place. This interaction feeds into behavioral intentions in which one decides whether the target behavior will take place. Put more simply, previous research did not take into account some factors (norms, intentions) that contributed to whether the behavior would happen. More important, the levels of generality or specificity at which both attitudes and behaviors were held were not matched. Often, voting would be predicted by the global attitude inferred from what party a person belonged to rather than the attitude toward the particular candidate. When the attitude toward a specific candidate was matched with the behavior of voting for that candidate, predictions improved. In other words, once the levels of attitudes and behaviors corresponded, the relationship between attitudes and behavior was much more clear. For example, Bowman and Fishbein (1978) were able to account for 85% of the variance on a nuclear safeguards bill in Oregon. The correlation between the attitude measure and voting was .91.

The levels of correspondence is only one feature of the attitude-behavior relationship, however. Weigel and Newman (1976) demonstrated that if several behaviors are used as a criterion, the predictability can increase from .29 to .62. In other words, once the attitude is known, a person's behavior as a pattern is more predictable than for any single behavior.

Recent research (Madden, Ellen, & Ajzen, 1992) indicates that the amount of control a person feels in a situation *(perceived control)* also has an influence on predicting behavior. Langer (1983) reports a series of experiments that demonstrated that increasing control has beneficial psychological and health effects.

Attitudes Toward the Environment

Gray (1985) proposed a model for attitudes toward the environment. This is currently the most comprehensive model in the literature (Figure 4.3).

The elements of Gray's model include the following:

General environmental concern. The pressing need for humanity to act in concert is the unifying theme.

Primitive beliefs. These include the belief that humanity is above and apart from nature, and the interdependency of all life is rejected. Another is the belief in progress and growth. Bigger is always better. Whatever happens, science will create a technology to solve any problem (the technological fix). Actually, these beliefs may be separate or together in the same person. This is the kind of belief that would underlie religious belief.

Costs/benefits. This includes both long-term and short-term aspects of the magnitude of any personal or societal threat.

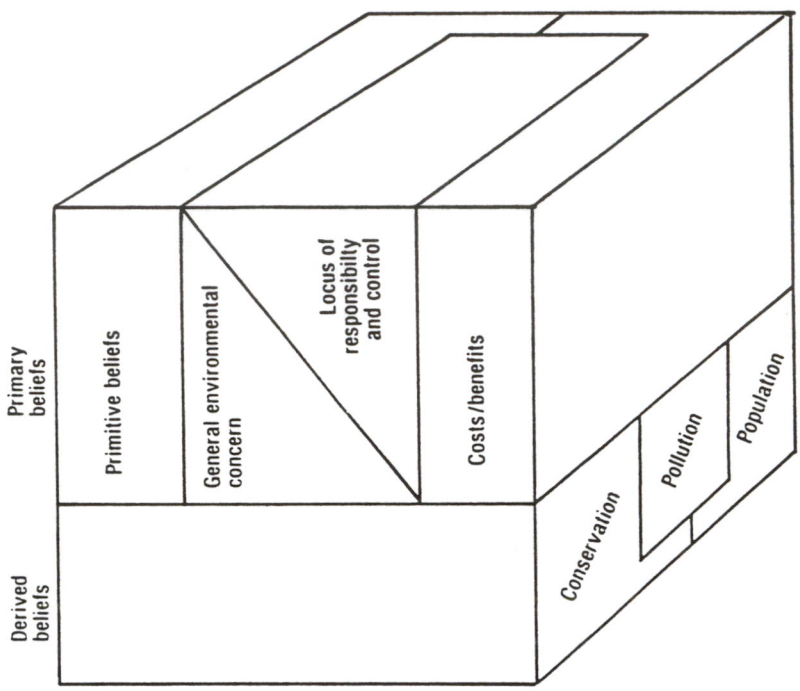

Figure 4.3. Gray's Environmental Attitudes Model
SOURCE: David B. Gray, *Ecological Beliefs and Behaviors,* reprinted with permission of Greenwood Publishing Group, Inc., Westport, CT. Copyright © 1985 by David B. Gray, Richard J. Borden, and Russell H. Weigel.

Locus of responsibility and control. What difference can one individual make, and are there areas where a person can have an influence as opposed to others?

Conservation, pollution, and population are seen as derived beliefs. Thus *conservation* refers to all attempts at reaching harmony with nature; *pollution*, the intrusion of synthetic substances into nature; and *population* refers to the finite capacity of the Earth. Two tests of the model are reported (Gray, Eckles, & Fuehrer, 1982).

The Environmental Response Inventory

McKechnie's Environmental Response Inventory (ERI) is a different approach in that it attempts to classify personal dispositions toward the environment (McKechnie, 1974, 1978). The dispositions are as follows:

Pastoralism is opposition to development, concern about population growth, preservation of natural resources.

Urbanism prizes high-density living, the variety of cultural and interpersonal experiences in the city.

Environmental adaptation sees the environment to be modified to suit one's own needs, with opposition to government control, and use of technology to solve environmental problems.

Environmental trust denotes being responsive and open to the environment, feeling competent in it, as opposed to seeing the environment as fearful and unsafe.

Antiquarian denotes enjoyment of old things, history, a tendency to collect historical artifacts.

Need for privacy is the need for physical isolation, enjoyment of solitude.

Mechanical orientation is enjoyment of working with hands, liking mechanical things, an interest in technology.

Communality actually is only a validity scale recording attention to test taking and responding in a modal fashion.

NIMBY

A discussion of attitudes about the environment would not be complete without reference to a growing attitude that seems to be present in every culture. The attitude is best expressed by the thought that, yes, these things (whatever they may be) are necessary and I support them but *not in my back yard* (NIMBY).

This attitude is encountered when an environmental project such as a landfill, a hazardous waste disposal site, or a nuclear plant is proposed for the immediate neighborhood. Then, it is often found that although the local populace support the project in principle, they strongly object to it being in their immediate neighborhood.

An example of this occurred when the State of Arizona agreed to build a hazardous waste disposal plant in a fairly remote section of the state. Once citizens became aware of the plant, protest gained momentum until the state government bought out the entire facility at great expense rather than allow it to begin operation.

SOURCE: Reprinted by permission of the *Cincinnati Post* and Jeff Stahler.

Environmental Ethics

In an influential paper, Hardin (1968) set forth a concept that defined, more or less, an environmental ethical dilemma for the world. He termed this the "tragedy of the commons." The commons was the green area of the New England village (many still have a commons area) where members of the village could graze their livestock. The commons was owned by everyone in the village so everyone had a right to use it. Yet, when one person would begin grazing more than the normative share of livestock, it would be to the detriment of others because, if they did the same, the green quickly would be used up and all would starve. What is so compelling about this example is that it is perfectly logical for the individual to increase the number of livestock to gain the immediate advantage at the expense of others. The initiator assumes the others will not follow by increasing their herds. Therein lies the dilemma. The others, stimulated by the example, increase their herd and the commons is depleted. Hardin sees this dilemma as a metaphor for the Earth with each nation competing for the commons (Earth's resources) until it is exhausted and we all perish.

Astute readers will see a similarity to this dilemma and the results of Miller's (1944) and Taylor's (1991) combined work on the relative force of positive and negative motives in Chapter 2. The conclusion was that humans have a particular difficulty giving up present rewards so as to prevent future negative consequences. The reason for this dilemma is that the negative consequences are undervalued both prior to and after the event so that it is difficult to weigh the actual effects of negative events. There is a tendency to devalue the negative strength of any event. This is very much the same dilemma that Hardin portrays. The user of the commons is unable to give up raising more sheep because the future negative consequence is less potent than the present reward.

Platt (1973) sees the tragedy of the commons as only one of several *social traps*. According to Platt (1973), a social trap arises in situations of opposition between highly motivating reward or punishment in the short term, and consequences postponed to the long term. Types of traps are as follows:

One person traps.   This is the simplest trap because it involves only one person and a significant time delay in reversing reinforcers. Cigarette smoking is the best example of the one person trap. It involves reversing reinforcers because the chemical pleasure and perhaps social reinforcement are replaced by the negative result of cancer. Overeating is another example.

Another subtype of the one person trap involves ignorance of the long-term results. Certainly, no one can say smokers are ignorant of the eventual results of smoking, but the worker handling an insecticide may not know of its long-term effects on health.

Sliding reinforcers are yet another subtype. This occurs when the reinforcement becomes less and less pleasurable the longer it is used. Drugs are a good example as the body adapts to their effects.

The missing hero.   When group benefit is blocked by a negative reinforcer for anyone who takes action, the result is a dilemma calling for a missing hero. Platt's example (borrowed from Schelling, 1971) is a mattress falling off a truck in the middle of rush hour. Most people are unaware of the problem but those who see the cause are reluctant to get out in the danger of traffic and remove the mattress.

Collective traps. These, of course, are exemplified by the tragedy of the commons situation where everyone acts in immediate self-interest to the long-term detriment of all. Other examples are the prisoner's dilemma, where each of two prisoners is separated and each offered a plea bargain to testify against the other. Each one usually does testify even though it results in both being convicted. Brechner (1977) has devised a commons-type situation as an experiment where a tube of quarters is placed in front of subjects and they are told that a percentage of the quarters in the tube will be added to at a specified time interval. Hence the greatest amount of money can be earned by leaving the quarters in the tube. But there is the rub. The subjects are also told that to win the game, one person must acquire the most quarters and each person is free to take as many quarters out of the tube as they like whenever they like. The "game" is never finished because once a subject reaches into the tube, others follow and the quarters are quickly gone. This is an experimental analogue to the commons dilemma and pretty convincing evidence that, at least in this situation, humans would not give up immediate rewards.

Nested traps. Finally, a special kind of trap occurs in social situations when the behavior is rapidly accelerated because the rewards come from going faster. Examples of this are gang violence, violence on TV programs, and extremes of advertising. In these cases, a feedback mechanism operates to accelerate the behavior. The gang members begin with a casual or accidental episode of violence but this quickly accelerates in response to others' responses. The bombing in World War II is another example.

What are the resolutions to all these dilemmas, traps, values, attitudes, and beliefs that lead to exploitation of the environment? Ehrlich and Ehrlich (1970) and Odum (1971) propose deriving an environmental ethic from three basic "laws" of ecological sciences. These are simple observational aspects of the environment as a whole.

Laws of Ecological Science

The Law of Interdependence

It is clear from all scientific evidence presented that the entire biosphere is interrelated perhaps in ways that we don't yet know about (Lovelock, 1978). Hardin (1968) claims that we can't ever do only one thing. Any action has unforeseeable consequences in many places and sets in motion forces over which we have no control. Lovelock (1978) proposes that the entire Earth acts like an organism to regulate the atmosphere. This includes the amount of oxygen, which, he claims, has been relatively constant since Precambrian times. This constancy of atmosphere maintained largely by bacteria is termed the "GAIA hypothesis." Although not many scientists subscribe to it (Mann, 1991), the hypothesis represents a literal form of the interdependence rule.

Diversity

If everything is interdependent, then everything that exists has a place in the scheme of things. One principle apparent from evolution (Lewin, 1989) is that diversity seems to be a prominent way of nature.[1] The law of diversity seems to be widely applicable to things as far apart as agricultural crops and investment portfolios.

The Law of Limitation and Irreversibility

When all the oil is gone, there will be no new discoveries. When a species dies out, there is no recovery. When the environment is damaged, it may not always be true that it can't be repaired, but it must be clear that some things cannot be replaced and in our ignorance we must act as if all things are irreplaceable.

HEP-NEP

Dunlap and Van Liere (1978b) describe basic attitudes toward the environment in the *Human Exceptionist Paradigm* (HEP) and a *New Environmental Paradigm* (NEP), which differentiate those who are willing to help save the environment from those who are unwilling to take part in conservation because they still see humans as outside nature's influence.

Their short, 12-item questionnaire (see Table 4.1) has received considerable currency since its first publication and has become an unofficial standard for basic human attitudes toward environmental problems. A total score of 12 indicates a complete rejection of the New Environmental

Table 4.1 HEP-NEP

1. We are approaching the limit of the number of people the earth can support	SA	MA	MD	SD
2. The balance of nature is very delicate and easily upset.	SA	MA	MD	SD
3. Humans have the right to modify the natural environment to suit their needs.	SA	MA	MD	SD
4. Mankind was created to rule over the rest of nature.	SA	MA	MD	SD
5. When humans interfere with nature it often produces disastrous consequences.	SA	MA	MD	SD
6. Plants and animals exist primarily to be used by humans.	SA	MA	MD	SD
7. To maintain a healthy economy, we will have to develop a "steady state" economy where industrial growth is controlled.	SA	MA	MD	SD
8. Humans must live in harmony with nature in order to survive.	SA	MA	MD	SD
9. The earth is like a spaceship with only limited room and resources.	SA	MA	MD	SD
10. Humans need not adapt to the natural environment because they can remake it to suit their own needs.	SA	MA	MD	SD
11. There are limits to growth beyond which our industrialized society cannot expand.	SA	MA	MD	SD
12. Mankind is severely abusing the environment.	SA	MA	MD	SD

SOURCE: Dunlap and Van Liere (1978b).
NOTE: SA = strongly agree; MA = mildly agree; MD = mildly disagree; SD = strongly disagree. Circle the one you agree with best. Count SA = 4; MA = 3; MD = 2; SD = 1. Reverse items 3, 4, 6, and 10.

Paradigm while a score of 48 indicates complete acceptance of it. Take the test and find out where your belief in NEP resides.

Voluntary Simplicity

Has anyone tried to put environmental ethics into effect in a practical way? Elgin (1981) promotes the way of life characterized as *voluntary simplicity*. Although this concept had its origins as far back as Thoreau and Gandhi, it received impetus from the social changes and environmental consciousness of the 1960s and 1970s. Elgin lists 18 ways in which a person simplifies life such as by (a) lowering the overall level of consumption, (b) buying products that are less polluting and needing less repair, (c) eating foods that require less processing, (d) getting rid of material possessions not used, (e) boycotting firms that are not ethical,

(f) recycling all objects possible, (g) favoring worker-operated stores and cooperatives, (h) doing work that contributes to the well-being of the world, (i) developing self-reliance skills, (j) trying to choose smaller scale places to live and work in, (k) striving for equality of sexes, (l) trying to promote extended families, (m) trying to develop the full spectrum of one's potential, (n) participating in holistic health care practices, (o) getting involved in compassionate causes like world hunger, (p) using public transportation, (q) employing appropriate technologies, and (r) questioning the traditional teachings in public schools. Although one does not hear as much about voluntary simplicity since the 1980s, it is still very much alive in many communities and many of these principles are becoming part of our lives such as recycling, appropriate technology, holistic health care, and many others. It is important to note that Elgin emphasizes voluntary simplicity is not self-imposed poverty but a realistic appraisal of what is one's fair share of the Earth's resources, regardless of cultural imperatives.

Belief Systems

Belief systems arise as a response to environmental and social conditions. People do not hold attitudes, values, and beliefs as separate items, they are organized into *belief systems* that can be as large as a whole culture or as small as a cluster of attitudes. There are also different kinds of belief systems. Spicer (1971) points out the *identity systems* held by a group of humans who want to be seen as a "people." Others constitute a system of beliefs about things such as a proper scientific way of doing things (Kuhn, 1970). Stern, Dietz, and Guagnano (1995) found that the NEP constitutes a belief system that correlates with Schwartz's values as well as awareness of environmental consequences. This makes the NEP a primitive belief in Gray's scheme. Stern et al.'s proposed model ties together things such as position in the social structure, values, general beliefs (like NEP), specific beliefs and attitudes, behavioral commitments, and behavior. Generally the causal relationship is top to bottom but they allow for influence the other way. What this means is that the general beliefs may influence the specific but the specific may also influence the general. Contrast this with the Fishbein-Ajzen model (Figure 4.2), which emphasizes levels of correspondence. Thus we have

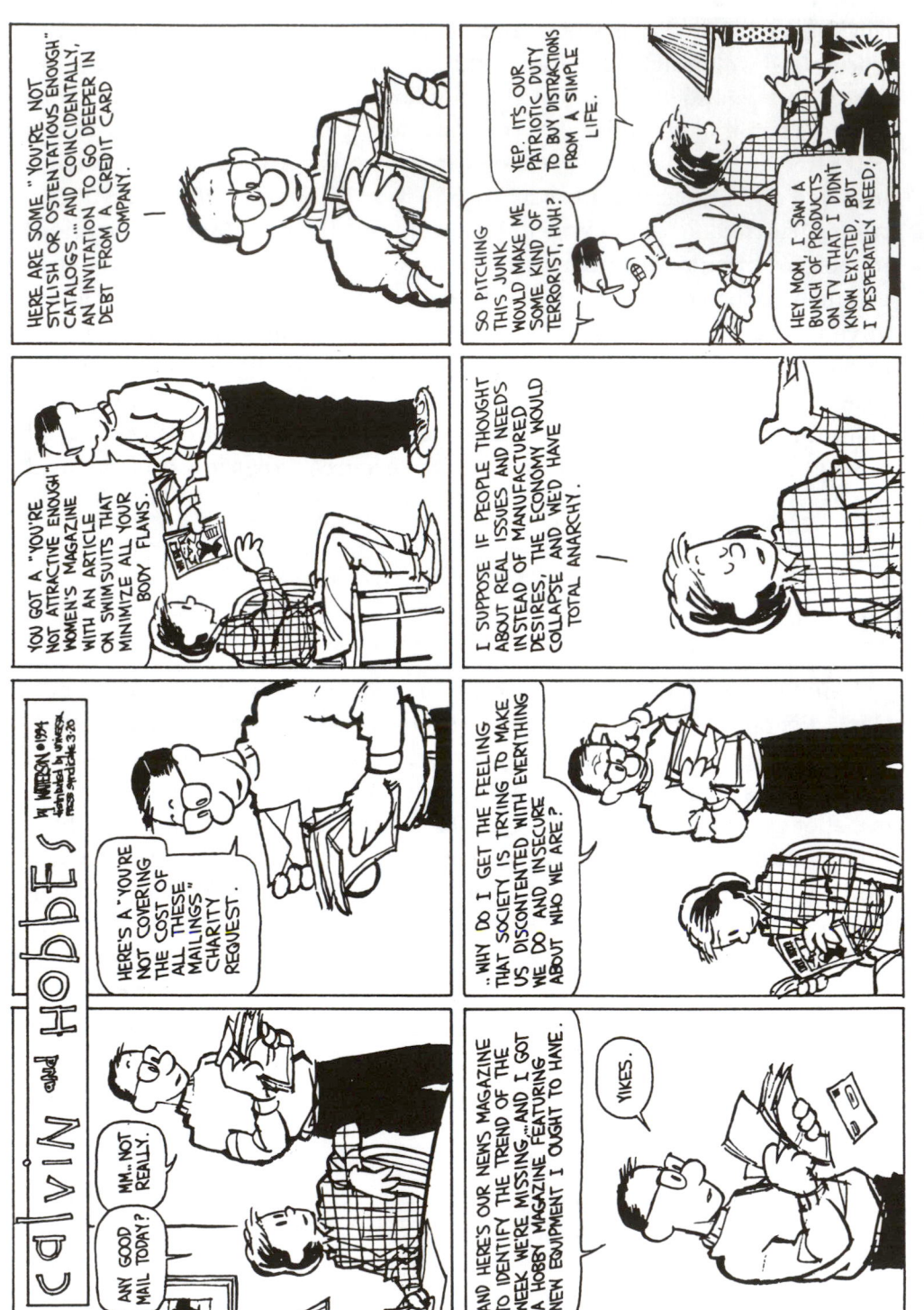

SOURCE: *Calvin and Hobbes* © 1994 Watterson. Distributed by *Universal Press Syndicate*. Reprinted with permission. All rights reserved.

SOURCE: © 1989 Willis—San Jose Mercury News. Used by permission.

two views of belief-value-attitude causality—the more specific levels of correspondence versus the more global belief systems that allow influence from general to specific and specific to general. It must be emphasized that the more specific models have more evidence while the larger models are still in the formation stage.

It is hard to overestimate the importance of belief systems. One does not have to look far to see their compelling nature. A good example is the Jonesville tragedy in which hundreds of ordinary people committed suicide at the command of their leader. It is one of the qualities of many belief systems that they are considered more important to uphold than human life. In older cultures, belief systems were preserved as "tradition," a concept still held by many societies today.

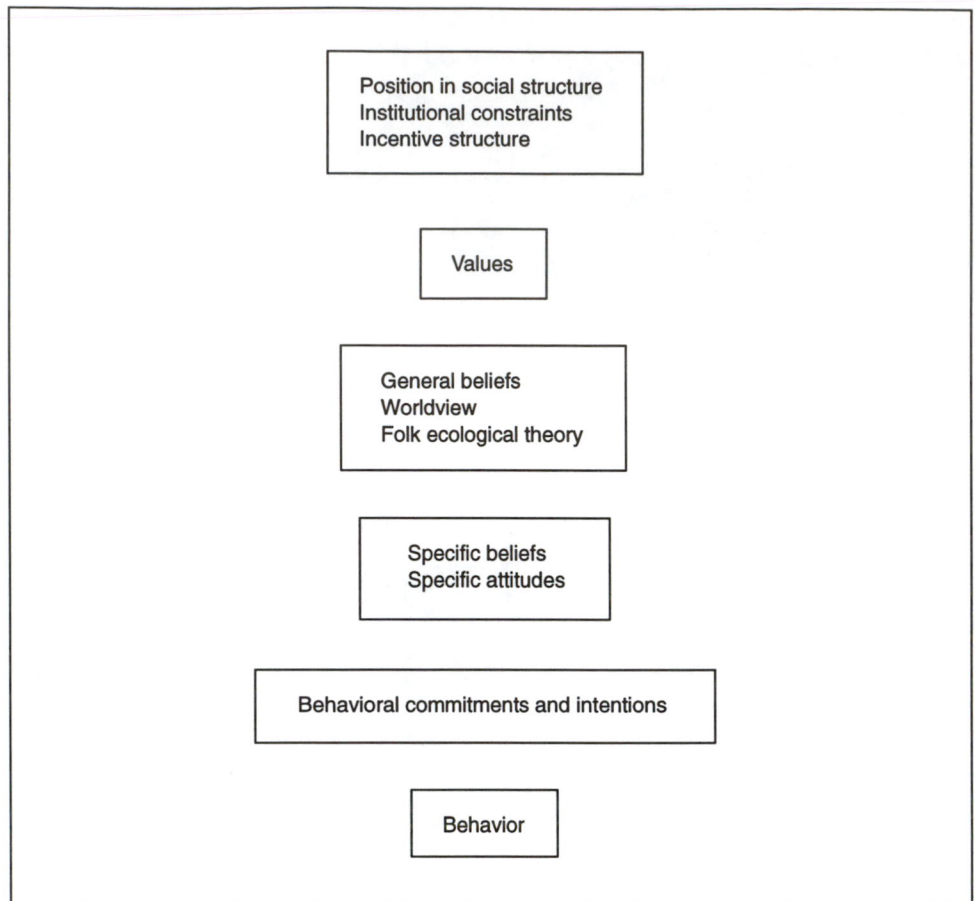

Figure 4.4. Stern et al.'s Causal Model of Environmental Concern
SOURCE: Stern et al. (1995).

Conclusions

Values, attitudes, beliefs, and belief systems are ways we have of organizing our knowledge of and responses to the environment around us. It appears that regardless of values, religious beliefs, or cultures, human abuse of the environment has been universal. Much of this is attributable to the view that humans are above or outside nature (HEP). Unless this view is replaced by the new environmental paradigm (NEP), it does not seem likely that the environment can be saved because human behavior seems to follow these current belief systems. Although the understanding of the attitude-behavior link is better because more research has been done on it, the wider belief system concept would seem to be more useful in understanding the larger causes of human behavior as they are anchored in social systems.

Note

1. See Gould (1989, pp. 39-42) for an explanation of how diversity is often misused in describing evolutionary matters.

GOALS

Definitions and Concepts

Values
Terminal values
Instrumental values
Primitive beliefs
ERI
NIMBY
Environmental ethics
Social traps
Three laws of ecological science
Diversity
HEP-NEP
Belief systems
VVO
Fishbein-Ajzen model
Gray's model
Nested trap
GAIA
Just world
Tragedy of the commons
Rule of interdependence
Spirituality

Important Studies

Korzybski (1958)
Schwartz and Bilsky (1990)
Kluckhohn and Strodtbeck (1961)
Rokeach (1973)
Kuhn (1971)
Lovelock (1978)
Brechner (1977)
Hardin (1968)
Platt (1973)
Dunlap and Van Liere (1978b)

1. Is there a relationship between religious belief and attitudes toward the environment?

2. What was the central problem in predicting behavior from attitudes?

3. Is there any research support for the tragedy of the commons metaphor?

4. What are the most central values in Western civilization?

5. What is the evidence that scientific information will change attitudes and beliefs?

6. What is the central concept of the NEP?

7. How are Gray's primitive beliefs related to HEP-NEP?

8. Explain voluntary simplicity.

9. What does the rule of interdependence mean in your life?

10. Are there any universal human values?

5

Environmental Perception
and Aesthetics

In their recent review of modern research on perception, Banks and Krajicek (1991) describe three areas of important influence: artificial intelligence, neuroscience, and the Gestalt tradition. Environmental perception work has drawn heavily from the last of these three, the Gestalt tradition, and especially from J. J. Gibson.

But who was Gibson, and why has his work been so influential in the environmental aspects of perception? Gibson's life and work are somewhat idealistically portrayed in Reed (1988), perhaps less idealistically represented by Lombardo (1987), and his collected works are presented by Reed and Jones (1982). His work that bears most directly on environmental perception is the 1979 book *The Ecological Approach to Visual Perception*. But, in actuality, all of Gibson's post-1960 work was ecological and he was the first truly environmental perception theorist.

Neisser (1990) pointed out that Gibson was the first researcher in perception who introduced something actually *new* to modern psychology. A little background is necessary to understand why Gibson's work was so different. Much of perceptual research involved (and still involves) defining and studying perception as a response to a specific stimulus. A visual

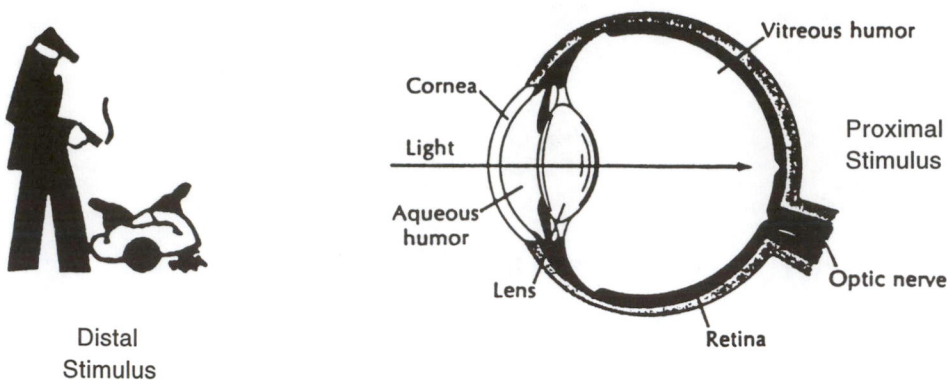

Figure 5.1. Distal and Proximal Stimuli

model was used to help conceptualize the stimulus-response links as in Figure 5.1.

In the model in Figure 5.1, however, it will be quickly noted that there is a *distal* stimulus in the environment and a *proximal* stimulus at the receptor, in this case, the retina. The same idea would hold for hearing, touch, smell, and so on. The principal idea is that most of theory construction and research involved understanding the proximal stimulus. Not only did Gibson depart from the distal stimulus, he expanded the concept to the entire visual array and made it *move*! This was what he tried to convey in his concept of the *ambient optical array*. Gibson, who worked at understanding how pilots could take off and land airplanes, wanted to start with an accurate portrayal of the ecology. What was then so radical was that if we could understand more accurately what was in the ecology, we would clearly see that it directly caused perception. This was too much for the perceptual psychologists and many still do not accept this approach.

Neisser (1990) explains that the optic array is not a (proximal or distal) stimulus, a retinal image, or an intervening variable, not a cognitive structure or a stage of processing, not a neural network or a projected meaning. But it is, essentially, the environment through a lens, and although it may not be a completely precise reconstruction of the environment, it (Gibson believed) explains perception directly. We perceive an indescribable variety in the optic array and it is always moving.

But do we perceive the optic array in its entirety always or do we focus on parts of it? Gibson claims we first perceive parts that move and separate these from parts that don't move. This distinction provides depth perception. Then, there are qualities in the optic array called *affordances*. These are very simply places where we can sit because they have sit-onable qualities, places where we can run because they have run-onable qualities, and so on. Thus the optical array is further divided by these affordances. Gibson was reminding psychologists of something that in truth they had never realized: Perception takes place in an ever-changing environmental context.

It is important to understand further the reductionist thinking psychologists had immersed themselves in so as to understand the uncomprehending response they had to Gibson's ideas. Much of perception research had been done by *reductionistic methods*. For example, if one wanted to study how people perceived the distance of an object, one first took the subject to the laboratory and began by reducing the number of cues available to judge depth perception (reducing to the basic elements). Then the sum of these elements became the solution to the problem of depth perception.

The first cue to be removed might be to cover one eye. Then, the accuracy of depth perception with one eye subtracted from the accuracy with both eyes constituted the contribution of *binocular disparity* to depth perception (Wheatstone, 1828, 1852). The next cue to be removed would be to restrict head motion by strapping the head into a vise. This would produce the contribution to depth perception from *head motion parallax* (Redding, Mefford, & Wieland, 1967). Certainly, Gibson would have no trouble saying all of these things contribute, but he would emphasize that the main cues come from movement in the optical array, and depth of an object would most likely be judged by its position in the *textural gradient*. The optical array has a feature of texture. Everything closer (grass, buildings, dirt) has a coarser and more detailed quality. Everything farther away has a finer and less detailed quality so that it is clear how far away an object is by how it is placed in the textural gradient. And, because the optical array is always moving, motion parallax will also play a role. This is very different, however, than a reductionist analysis. In effect, the binocular disparity would probably not enter into the equation unless the person was in a fixed or a standing position.

Gibson was influenced by Egon Brunswik, especially by Brunswik's concept of *ecological validity* (Brunswik, 1956), the idea that an experi-

Figure 5.2. The Gestalt Principle of Closure

ment in perception must be grounded in the environment to be valid. Brunswik was better known for his concept of *probabalistic functionalism*, the idea that we learn depth perception and other functions by learning probabilities that are constantly being revised. Gibson rejected Brunswik's probability notions because he felt the environment was more directly perceived.

The Gestalt View

The gestaltists also reacted to the reductionist methods by insisting that perception was more holistic. They amply convinced the world by a series of demonstrations. For example, in Figure 5.2, what is it that you see? Most people will answer, "rectangles." The gestaltists claim this is because of a principle called *closure*. One does not just see two three-sided figures arranged at right angles, one "sees" a rectangle. Other principles are similarity, proximity, common fate, objective set, inclusiveness, and good continuation (Metzger, 1966). It is worth noting that the gestaltists did very little research as such but conducted many "demonstrations."

The Transactional View

Adelbert Ames (1951) invented a series of demonstrations not unlike the gestaltists' but aimed to uncover some very basic assumptions about perception that can deceive the eye. These include the Ames window (Figure 5.3) and the Ames room (Figure 5.4).

In a typical demonstration, the window appears to revolve up to a point and then reverse itself, but, in fact, it moves continuously. Ames says this exposes the assumptions involved in observing what appears to be a

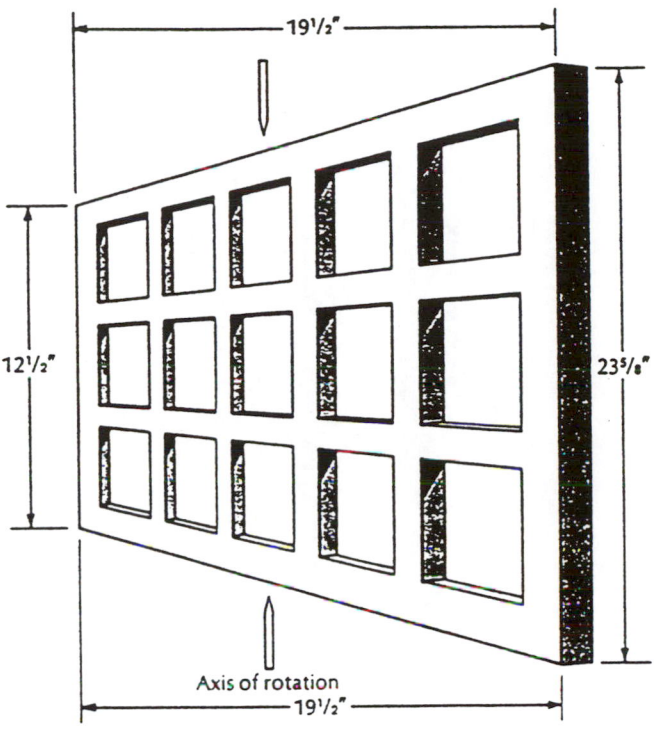

Figure 5.3. The Ames Window
NOTE: One side of the Ames trapezoidal window shown perpendicular (frontoparallel) to the line of sight. (After Ames, 1951.)

normal window. When the subject is informed of the abnormal shape, he or she can then actually see the continuous movement, and experiences a sensation of discovery. The Ames room is much more startling. The subject is put in place and then looks through what appears to be a window into what appears to be a normal room. Two people are inside the room. Suddenly, one begins to walk toward the back wall and seems to grow to gigantic proportions with each step. The subject is startled and often gasps. He or she literally cannot believe what is happening. Once again, the assumptions of normality are violated. The room is constructed so as to look normal to someone peering through the window but in actuality is a trapezoid along converging visual lines to fool the eye into thinking it is rectangular.

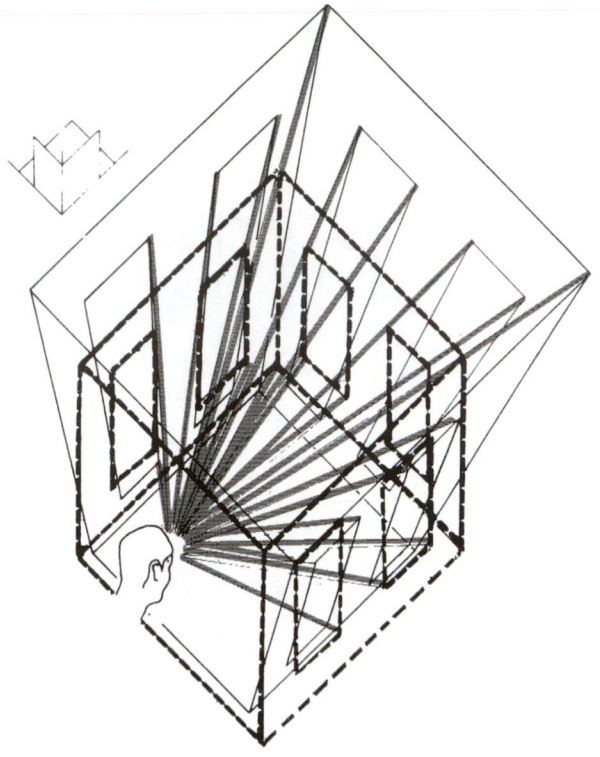

Figure 5.4. The Ames Room

SOURCE: Figure from *An Introduction to Environmental Psychology* by William H. Ittelson and Harold M. Proshansky, copyright © 1974 by Holt, Rinehart and Winston, Inc., reproduced by permission of the publisher.

NOTE: [Drawing:] The Ames distorted room has been widely used as an artificial environment that produces varied and unusual experiences. [Photograph:] One of the visual effects found in the Ames distorted room.

Ames founded what is called the *transactional school* of perception. Essentially, this school views perception as a transaction between organism and environment. It is not just a simple stimulus-response mechanism but a true transaction between assumptions, perceptions, and environment.

In some ways, Ames seems to have anticipated Gibson's affordances with his concept of the perception of *choices*. Ames felt that what we actually perceive in the environment are a series of choices as we negotiate our way.

Applications

Appleyard and Craik (1978) created the Environmental Simulation Laboratory at Berkeley to simulate environments based on perceptual cues learned from research. The attempt was to simulate environments realistically enough that the reaction could be measured without having to build the environment itself, thus saving the cost. The laboratory would not have been possible without the "fisheye" camera lens, which permits filming a scene the size of a model and creating a plausible reproduction because the view is not too distorted. Figure 5.5 shows the simulator above a model of a section of West Way, New York. The environment can be simulated by moving the lens through the model's streets.

Other problems of perception may not be so easily simulated. King, Marans, and Solomon (1982), for example, simulated an operating room with a full scale mock-up because the bodily motions of the doctors and patients needed to be measured at true scale. De Long (1981) claims that a half-scale model can reproduce meaningful movements but these studies have not been replicated.

Adaptation Level

Why can't you smell your breath? Why do colors seem to lose their brilliance after a few seconds? Harry Helson (1964) discovered this was because our senses quickly adapt to many stimuli. A good demonstration is to take a piece of colored paper and cover half of it with a neutral paper or cardboard. Stare at the place between the colored and covered side for over 20 seconds and then remove the neutral paper. The colored paper

Figure 5.5. The Berkeley Simulator Above a Model
SOURCE: © Berkeley Environmental Simulation Laboratory, Bosselman.

will now appear to have two colors, the one you were staring at and a new color at the place that was covered.

This demonstrates why we see true colors after a few seconds of wearing colored glasses. Strangely, adaptation level is left out of most descriptions of environmental perceptions even though Wohlwill (1974) argued for its importance.

In a rare example of use of the adaptation principle, Russell and Lanius (1984) combined the affective appraisal of Russell and Pratt (1980) with the contextual dimension of Helson's theory. They demonstrate how the pleasantness or unpleasantness of a stimulus can be influenced by introducing pleasant or unpleasant stimuli prior to a target. For example, a neutral scene can be made slightly unpleasant by introduction of a pleasant scene prior to exposure. The formerly neutral scene then shifts in evaluation to a slightly unpleasant one because of adaptation to a new context. The importance of using Helson's adaptation level is to demonstrate that the same stimulus can have several different affective appraisals depending on the context in which it is found, a fact that seems to be ignored by most researchers.

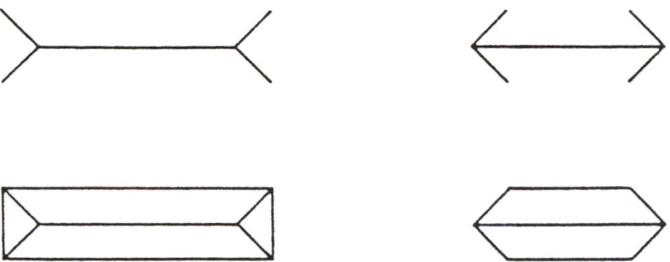

Figure 5.6. The Muller-Lyer Illusion

Perception and Language

Only recently have psychologists rediscovered the fact that human learning has an environmental context (Balsam & Tomie, 1985). Some time ago, Benjamin Whorf put forth the hypothesis that as we learned a language, we learned to shape our perceptions by that language (Carroll, 1956). This hypothesis, which became known as the Whorfian hypothesis, had much to support it from common sense. Eskimos (now called Inuit) had 20 or more words for snow, so they could "see" snow, presumably, in ways the ordinary person could not. The hypothesis did not prove out, however. When cross-cultural studies were done, it was shown that several cultures with differing vocabularies for various objects and colors could equally distinguish among these same objects and colors even though they may not have had the "proper" words.

This is not so for certain illusions, however. When a group of anthropologists and psychologists took part in the first interdisciplinary expedition to the Torres Straits in 1899 (Haddon, 1901), they came across the Trobriand Islanders, who were spear fishermen. When these people were tested with a number of psychological instruments, it was discovered they were not susceptible to the Muller-Lyer illusion (Figure 5.6).

In this illusion, the subject is shown two lines; the one on the left has lines extending outward at angles, the one on the right has lines extending at angles inward. It was always assumed that the average person would see the right line as shorter. In fact, both lines are equal. That the Trobrianders were not fooled was attributed to their experience as spear fishermen where they supposedly felt the converging lines looked like their spear points. This fact establishes the influence of learning on perception, or perhaps it is just the perceptual assumptions Ames speaks of. Would a Dogon of Africa who has lived in round houses all his life be fooled by the Ames window or room?

Perception of Hazards

For some time, geographers have studied people who live in flood plains, earthquake zones, tornado "alleys," and other hazardous areas of the Earth (Burton, 1962; Burton, Kates, & White, 1978; Turner, Nigg, Paz, & Young, 1980). As technological problems increased, the hazard studies extended to human-made hazards (Harris, Hohenemser, & Kates, 1978; Orr, 1979). From the beginning, a major concern of these studies was to discern why people would continually expose themselves to the same dangers. One unexpected discovery was the false belief that after a particularly devastating flood (hurricane, earthquake), the chances of having another soon were very remote. Hence the risk in moving back to the dangerous area was perceived to be low.

In a landmark study, Sims and Baumann (1972) discovered that people in the South were especially prone to injury from tornados because of their somewhat fatalistic beliefs. They tended to take less precautions than people living in the Midwest, who had more of a belief in their own ability to influence events.

Generally, the findings remain consistent that people tend to live in hazardous areas and do not take proper precautions despite educational efforts (Burton et al., 1978; Mangelsdorf, 1985). Rubonis and Bickman (1991) reviewed 52 studies of disaster effects on psychopathology and estimate a rate of 17% psychopathology in the wake of disasters. Curiously, they find the harmful effects greater if the disaster is natural as opposed to human caused.

Perceived Environmental Quality

Russell and Pratt (1980) distinguish the perceptual-cognitive meaning versus the affective meaning of environments. Affective meaning is usually measured by having subjects rate affective words in relation to a particular environment. Russell and Ward derive a two-dimensional bipolar space with eight affective variables named by the words: *pleasant, exciting, arousing, distressing, unpleasant, gloomy, sleeping*, and *relaxing*. Russell, Ward, and Pratt (1981) attempt to classify the affective quality attributed to environments into two bipolar factors of affective quality, *pleasing* and *arousing*. Russell and Pratt (1980) found these two factors to have a split-half reliability of .97 for pleasantness and .97 for arousingness for 20 environments. These factors are seen as not necessarily stable over every situation but are considered similar to the *evaluation and activity* factors of the semantic differential (Heise, 1969).

This contrasts to the more specific attempt by Canter and Tagg (1980) to classify building attributes. Canter and Tagg go beyond adjectives and use activities and physical aspects (furniture, heating, lighting) as part of the classification. In their study, 31 bipolar adjectives, with 6 aspects of function × 5 evaluations of each function, were combined with activities as self-reported by users of the spaces. Finally, subjects were asked to furnish 16 rooms with a selection of furniture. The conclusion is a surprisingly limited range of activities, evaluations, and furniture for each room. The physical environment puts more constraints on what we can do and even where we place our furniture than we might at first think.

These two approaches show a contrast in how environmental quality is evaluated in studies. Actually, the Russell and Ward approach is the most common with adjective lists predominating.

The PEQI

Craik and Zube (1976) and Zube (1980) created an adjective list to evaluate the quality of environments. The attempt was to develop a universal list that could be applied to any environment. This was called the Perceived Environmental Quality Index (PEQI). Sometimes the list would be combined with more objective measures of air or water quality. Eventually it became apparent that no single list could be applied to all environments.

Aesthetics

Michelson (1968) discovered that the average person tended not to like modern architecture for the very reason architects praised it: its simplicity. Instead, when given the choice between a decorated house or building and a simple one, most people chose the "fancier" one. Actually, it was not the "fancy" aspect that was chosen. Michelson noticed people seem to prefer "cluttered" over unadorned environments. Berlyne (1963) seemed to explain this in a series of comparisons of choice by demonstrating that most people would choose complexity over simplicity. Going even further, Information Theory proponents explained the preference for complexity and clutter as due to the fact that such environments contain more information.

Results in environmental aesthetics seem curiously opposed to object aesthetics. Sears (1983) demonstrates a *person positivity bias* in the evaluation of objects. That is, as objects tend to resemble or remind one of persons or have personal characteristics, they are favored more over those objects that are not so endowed. By contrast, Clamp (1976) and Brush and Palmer (1979) find that human influence tends to decrease liking for natural environments. Anderson (1981) and Hodgson and Thayer (1980) found that natural landscape photos were rated lower when they were accompanied by labels indicating human influence such as "tree farm" as opposed to "forest growth." This trend is somewhat mitigated by the fact that human influences that tend to belong in the environment can sometimes even increase its rating (Wohlwill, 1979; Wohlwill & Harris, 1980; Zube, Pitt, & Anderson, 1974). The increase in value due to human intervention seems to occur when the intervention is deemed "appropriate."

Herzog (1989) studied preferences for urban areas. He exposed 354 subjects to 70 color slides of urban environments and factor-analyzed the results into factors called older buildings, concealed foreground, tended nature, and contemporary buildings. Tended nature was by far the most preferred. Using a regression analysis, Herzog found three variables to be predictors of his results: coherence, mystery, and nature. He interpreted his findings as supporting the Kaplans' (1982) informational model.

Appleton (1975) proposed that humans prefer a savannahlike environment because this is the environment we evolved in. Similar support for such a theory is provided by Orians (1980, 1986), Kaplan (1987), and Ulrich (1983).

The SBE

Daniel (1976) and his associates (Brown & Daniel, 1984; Daniel & Boster, 1976) developed a different approach to measurement of scenic quality by using the psychophysical model. This means, instead of word lists with a bipolar scale, a numerical scale of 1-10 was used with the prescribed task of rating the environment by assigning a number (1 or 10 being the most beautiful possible). Daniel painstakingly validated his methods by comparing slides with reality and calibrating his scale by paired comparisons. This method avoids some of the ambiguities and un-reliabilities of the word lists (Daniel & Ittelson, 1981; Starr & Danford, 1979). It is called the *scenic beauty estimate* (SBE).

Perhaps the most significant trend in the aesthetics of environment literature is the finding that natural environments not only reduce stress but actually foster better health. Ulrich's (1984) landmark study showed that patients exposed to a view of trees recovered from surgery faster than patients with the same ailment, in the same hospital, who were exposed to a view of a brick wall. Moore (1982) compared inmates in a prison who had a view of farmland from their cells versus those who looked on the prison yard, and found those who viewed farmland to have fewer sick calls.

Ulrich and Simons (1986) and Ulrich (1979) exposed stressed individuals to either natural or urban environments during recovery that was monitored by physiological measurements. Recovery was quicker and more complete among those exposed to the natural environments.

Parsons (1991) reviews the literature on the healthful influences of exposure to natural environments and concludes: "Exposure to natural environments can be stress reducing" (p. 1).

Application

The scenic beauty estimate (SBE) of Daniel and his colleagues is an instrument of practical value that is used in the management of forests and national parks. Using a random method for selection of points within a given park or forest, the scenic beauty profile can be constructed as a three-dimensional graph that can direct the cutting of timber, the placement of roads, the placement of scenic viewpoints, and the location of visitor centers. Figure 5.7 shows such a three-dimensional graph.

Attribution Theory

Attribution theory has been referred to as the theory about how people make sense out of their environment. The influential work that began attribution studies was Fritz Heider's (1958) book, *The Psychology of*

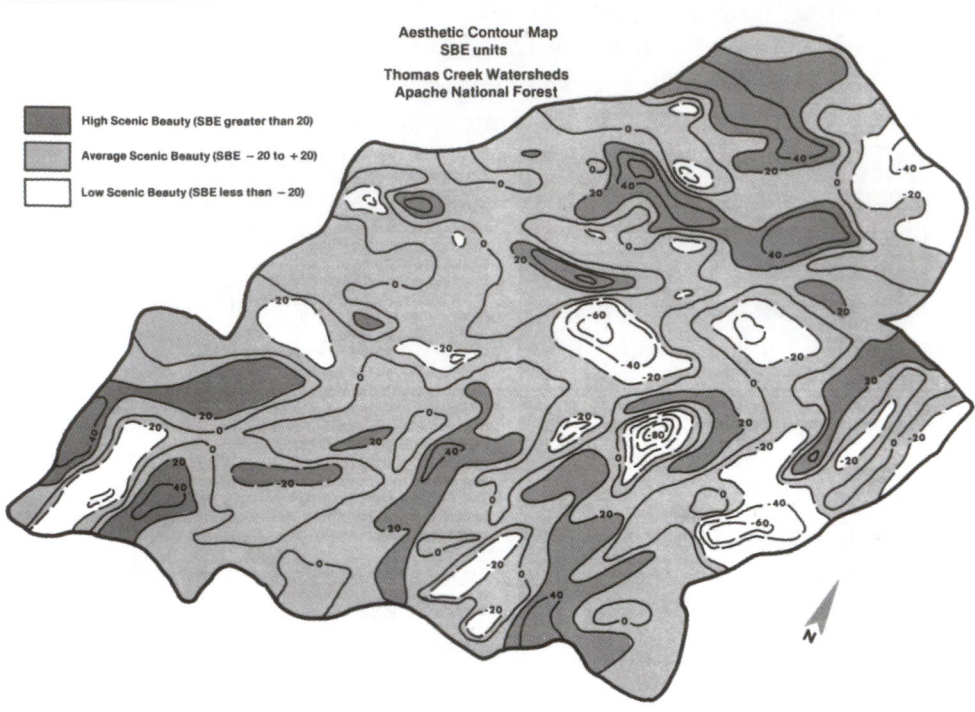

Figure 5.7. Three-Dimensional Scenic Beauty Graph
SOURCE: Daniel and Boster (1976); reprinted by permission.

Interpersonal Relations. Heider proposed a "naive" analysis of the way people made sense out of what went on around them. As such, some might think attribution theory belongs in the next chapter on environmental cognition, but many researchers feel attribution is so closely tied with perception as to be very much like the closure, goodness of fit, and other principles of the gestaltists.

Heider developed a film showing triangles, squares, and circles moving about in random fashion (Heider, 1944). When subjects were asked to describe what they saw, they would say things like, "The square chased the circle," or "The triangle hit the square." In other words, the subjects attributed motives to describe the random motion. No one described the events by saying they saw objects moving randomly. This illustrates the main principle of attribution theory, that people *attribute* qualities to stimuli to make sense out of what happens. Although most of the research done on attribution focuses on person and self-perception, enough

Box 5.1

Aesthetic Mapping

[Figure 5.8] is what might be called an aesthetic or scenic beauty map. The area is the Thomas Creek Experimental Watersheds, which cover 1,073 acres on the Apache-Sitgreaves National Forest in Arizona. The contours represent lines of equal scenic quality; the zero (darker) contour represents the average scenic quality for these watersheds. The higher the number of a contour (darker areas), the more aesthetically pleasing is the view from that line relative to the average; the lower the value (lighter areas) the less pleasing. Note that a contour on a topographic map represents the elevation *at* each point along that contour. In contrast, a contour on the scenic beauty map represents the scenic qualities of the view *from* each point on that contour.

This map was prepared in much the same way as a topographical map: SBEs were determined at specific ground points, and transferred to a map of the area. Contours were then drawn connecting points of equal value. To obtain the SBEs, randomly directed photos were taken at each of the 250 equally-spaced stakes. The resulting slides wre randomized and shown to groups of observers who rated them on scenic beauty. The SBE mathematical methodology had to be modified somewhat to permit this application; SBEs were computed for each stake based on the four slides.

We believe the concept of an aesthetic contour map is valid, but we are concerned with and presently working on several important questions. For example, how close to one another do the sampling ground points need to be, and how many photos are necessary to adequately represent the scenic quality from a point? Answers to these questions for Thomas Creek will not necessarily hold for other areas. We are also uncertain of the obvious influences of dramatic changes in viewing depth across an area. None of these problems, however, seem insurmountable.

The design of scenic road and trail systems is but one application of such a map; the location of scenic vistas is another. The feasibility of overlaying a scenic beauty map with other resource maps offers the possibility of a direct interface with other resources and products. The effects of seasonal changes on aesthetics could also be readily determined.

SOURCE: Daniel and Boster (1976); reprinted by permission.

is involved with situational or environmental aspects to see emerging relationships.

Heider, and others that followed, said people made *dispositional* attributions to infer what a person was like. *Situational* attributions were made about the surrounding environment. Heider described environmental forces and personal forces. These often took the form of words such as *can* and *trying* to describe what people are doing. Observing that a person was trying hard usually meant the person *wanted* to. These were commonsense interpretations that people could describe in ordinary language.

Kelley (1967) became more formal with these commonsense rules by saying people were like scientists in that they tested hypotheses and made comparisons over time. They paid attention to consistencies over time, took into account a consensus of opinion, and would *discount* hypotheses if there were alternative explanations.

Bem (1972) made an important contribution by showing that his subjects tended to infer their own attitudes by observing themselves (If I'm eating pizza, I must like it!). Furthermore, there is a tendency to forget information that is contrary to these self-observed conclusions.

Ross (1977) describes the *fundamental attribution error*, which is "the tendency for attributors to underestimate the impact of situational factors and to overestimate the role of dispositional factors in controlling behavior" (p. 183). In other words, people tend to overestimate their own influence and to underestimate the environmental influence over them. In fact, Seligman and Miller (1979) say people opt for high perceived choice and control situations so as to enable them to match their own internal states with external events. This is called the "comforting illusion." This illusion becomes less comforting the more that is learned about it. For example, depressed and neurotic people are more realistic about their chances of controlling events than "normal" people. However, the fundamental attributional error is thought to be culturally specific because when Cha and Nam (1985) tested Koreans, they found a reverse tendency because Koreans placed much more emphasis on situational factors and less on their own personal control. Hamilton et al. (1983) found the same results with the Japanese, and Miller (1984) found the same with Hindus, who place much greater emphasis on role obligations.

Fiske and Taylor (1991) point out that not only is there a fundamental attribution error in our culture, it has an egotistical twist in that people's explanations for others' behavior tends to be dispositional but for themselves is more situational. In other words, when *you* do things, it is because of something in you, but if *I* do things, it is usually because something beyond my control made me do it.

Conclusions

Environmental perception emphasizes the ecological aspects of perception first brought out by J. J. Gibson. This model is far different than the reductionism formerly practiced in psychology. Gibson's view of perception was much more dynamic, emphasizing the constantly moving nature of the ambient optical array, the textural gradient by which depth was perceived, and the affordances that were opportunities for behavior in the environment. The gestaltists and Ames provided demonstrations showing there was no one-to-one relationship between the distal and proximal stimuli. The simulation lab and recent computer developments are producing virtual environments of extraordinary quality based on these principles.

Environmental aesthetics has developed into practical tools for management of forests and parks via the scenic beauty estimate (SBE). Environmental aesthetics, however, has gone beyond measuring perceptual responses and is now concerned with the healing and stress-reducing qualities of being in contact with natural environments. Theories behind this range from Appleton's prospect and refuge to the biophilia hypothesis.

Attribution theory goes beyond Gibson's affordances and claims that we see motives in the environment and conceive these to be causal in nature. Chief of these is the fundamental attribution error, which ascribes more power and importance to human actions than to situational forces. This is a view consistent with the HEP of the previous chapter. The fundamental error seems to be a product of our own culture because it is not reported in others.

The perception of the environment has at once a healing and soothing quality while at the same time its importance is diminished in preference to human powers by our own belief systems.

GOALS

Definitions and Concepts

Distal stimulus

Proximal stimulus

Ambient optical array

Affordances

Gradient

Binocular disparity

Probabalistic functionalism

Ecological validity

Closure

PEQI

Attribution

SBE

Transactional school

Reductionism

Adaptation level

Whorfian hypothesis

Person positivity bias

Psychophysical model

Savannahlike environments

Fundamental attribution error

Important Studies

Gibson (1979)

Brunswik (1956)

Ames (1951)

Appleyard and Craik (1978)

Helson (1964)

Burton et al. (1978)

Sims and Baumann (1972)

Rubonis and Bickman (1991)

Ulrich (1984)

Daniel and Boster (1976)

Heider (1958)

1. Does laboratory research on perception create a view of the world that will not accept Gibson's theories?

2. Does the Gestalt view of perception only demonstrate the effects of learning?

3. A man who wears colored glasses claims he can see true colors. Why?

4. A researcher claims he has developed a universal scale to rate outdoor environments. What do you say to him?

5. The financier of a hospital says you have to cut the funds for the trees surrounding the hospital because there isn't enough money for the building. What do you say?

6. A forest ranger claims it doesn't matter where a new scenic road goes in his forest. It's all beautiful, he says. Response?

7. Why were the Trobriand Islanders immune to Muller-Lyer?

8. What features of his work made Gibson the first environmental perception researcher?

9. What is the relationship between cognition, perception, and the proximal and distal stimuli?

10. What are the limitations of environmental simulation?

6

Environmental Cognition

If perception is apprehension of the immediate environment through sensory input, then cognition is apprehending without the necessity of an external stimulus. Imagining, creating, remembering, thinking, learning are all the province of cognition. E&B research, however, has not cast such a wide net but has focused on the cognitive tools people use to move about on the Earth.

In the history of psychology, Ulrich Neisser's (1967) book *Cognitive Psychology* is seen as the beginning of the cognitive revolution. But what was it a revolution against? Largely it rebelled against the behavioristic notion that what went on in the head was irrelevant. The behaviorist view was caricatured as seeing the head as a "black box" with no discernable processes taking place within. Against this, Neisser and others insisted human beings had a "mind" and could think and behave cognitively.

But this was during the same time environment and behavior research was evolving so the cognitive revolution in psychology and environment-behavior research merged at several points.

Prior to Neisser's book, Kevin Lynch (1960) published his influential *Image of the City*. The main thesis of Lynch's book was that a city had to be legible for a person to grasp a *cognitive map* of the place and find his or her way around in it. There were certain elements in a city that were used by people to find their way. These were *landmarks, paths, nodes, edges*, and *districts*. Landmarks are the easily recognized features of an environment that stand out and have an identity of their own. The Empire State Building in New York has been replaced by the Trade Center Towers as the most popular landmark but both remain recognizable landmarks of that city. Paths are the routes people take to get places. Freeways through town are often paths, but any street, subway route, or waterway can be a path. Nodes are places where paths come together. Times Square in New York is probably the most famous node, but any intersection can be a node. Edges are any definable physical thing that serves to separate. Streets often serve as edges as well as paths. Physical barriers such as railroad tracks are also often seen as edges, and so are freeways. Finally, districts are any recognizable places in the city or region. Chinatown is often a recognizable district. But there are also tenderloins, the Bowery, historical districts, and many others. Furthermore, people organize these elements to form an image of the city that is used like an internal map.

Tolman (1948) coined the phrase *cognitive maps* and did research on rats to demonstrate that even these diminutive animals had such capabilities. What Tolman discovered was that rats were smarter than psychologists gave them credit for. Instead of just learning the stilted series of left and right turns psychologists built into the maze, the rat raised his head above this and saw the relationship of the food reward to the placement of the ceiling light in the experimental room. In short, as Tolman discovered, the rat had learned relationships. This was the stuff of cognitive psychology. A cognitive map was stored somewhere in the brain. There is no evidence, however, that Tolman influenced Lynch. There was no reference to Tolman in Lynch's book. It was later workers such as Downs and Stea (1973) who recognized both Tolman and Lynch.

The bulk of cognitive research in the environmental area has consisted largely of some aspect or other of Lynch's original thesis of the use of cognitive maps and the five elements or *cues* found in the urban environment. Lynch continued with the theme of the legible city (1981) and proposed it as an ideal form for all cities. You might say that Lynch proposed cities become user friendly.

Meanwhile, O'Keefe and Nadel (1978) discovered evidence that cognitive maps were located in the hippocampus of the brain. Persons with a damaged hippocampus could not use cognitive maps. But more general in importance was the rediscovery that *all learning* was environment specific. Animals and people perform better in the place they receive training than in any other place. This is why it is better to take an exam in the place where you learned the material. Nadel et al. theorize that this occurs because the environment provides many more associations for learning that were part of the original learning stimulus. In other words, when we learn, we involuntarily incorporate stimuli from the environment along with the things we focus on learning. Then, when it is time to remember, the peripheral cues in the environment help the memory.

The Five Cues

Research on the five cues described by Lynch has largely focused on how the cues are organized in a cognitive map. Usually this involves exposing subjects to an environment and then asking them to draw a map. The analysis of the maps provides the data.

Golledge (1978) and Spector (1978) proposed the *anchor point hypothesis*. This means that the person picks one of the cues, usually a landmark, and organizes the other cues around it such as the paths, nodes, districts, and edges. Essentially this finding was confirmed by Coucelis, Golledge, Gale, and Tobler (1987). Wilton (1979) and Maki (1981) found similar results but called it *clustering*.

Hart and Moore (1973) and Siegel and White (1975) found that children develop primary, secondary, and tertiary nodes with paths. These are also similar to anchor points. The home, work, shopping node is primary and the rest develop from the primary node, connected by paths.

Aragones and Arredondo (1985), in Spain, tested the five cues and essentially confirmed them, but other studies have not demonstrated the importance of all five cues. Norberg-Schulz (1971), for example, found two clusters: a structured center to the city consisting of paths, landmarks, and nodes, and a periphery composed of districts and edges. They felt that the edge as a cue was the most difficult and only seemed to operate at the edges of the city, not inside it. Siegel and White (1975) found their cues fell into three categories: routes, nodes, and configurations.

Rovine and Weisman (1989) concluded that, regardless of clustering or anchoring, each unit of information has in its center a landmark. Figure 6.1 shows the types of maps their subjects drew.

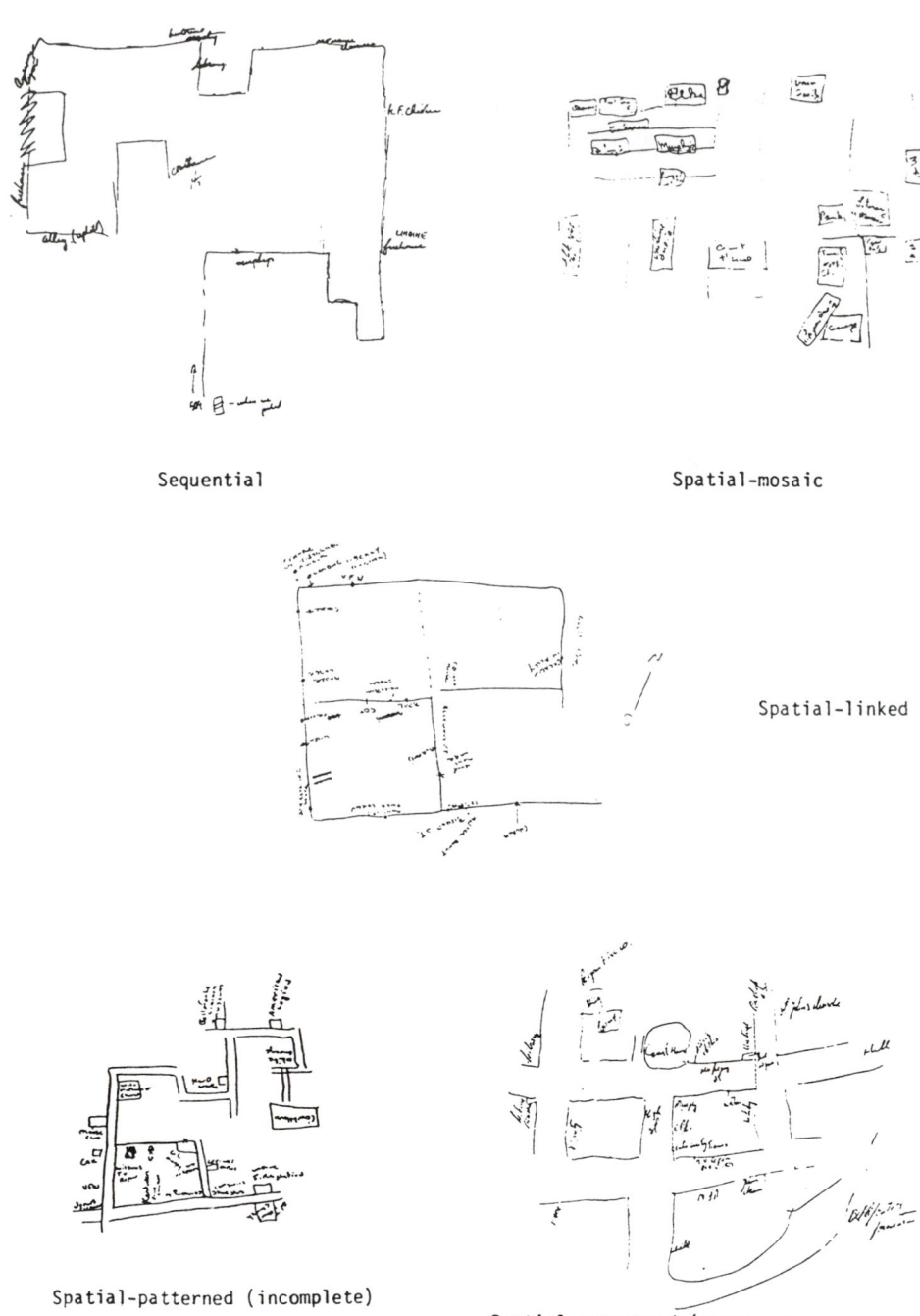

Sequential

Spatial-mosaic

Spatial-linked

Spatial-patterned (incomplete)

Spatial-patterned (complete)

Figure 6.1. Cognitive Maps
SOURCE: M. Rovine and G. Weisman (1989). Used by permission.

Errors

All cognitive maps contain errors simply because most people are not expert mapmakers. It became evident fairly quickly that certain kinds of errors seemed to predominate. Downs and Stea (1973) described the errors that continue to occur.

Incompleteness, or leaving something out, is the most common error. When people draw cognitive maps, they will always include those things that are known and familiar to them and leave out those things they never noticed or learned.

Distortion is also very common. Very seldom can anyone draw a map without some form of distortion. Size will be exaggerated or diminished. Usually those things best known will appear bigger and, of course, in more detail.

Augmentation is the least common and most puzzling of the errors. Augmentation occurs when something is added that doesn't belong there. This often happens when a person confuses one place with another and includes items from both.

Distance Judgment

Anooshian and Siegel (1985) tested whether judging distance was related to how well people liked a place. What seemed to happen was that this effect was lost after a time because of familiarity with the route. Thus, when freshmen were asked to judge the distances to places on campus, they overestimated distances to places they liked, but this did not occur for upperclassmen. These results were confirmed by Herman, Miller, and Shiraki (1987).

Distance judgment seems related to the anchor points, or clusters, of the cues. Wilton (1979) and Maki (1981) found response times in making distance judgments was greater across clusters than within. Hirtle and Jonides (1985) found distances that are equal are judged to be shorter within regions defined by clusters of landmarks. Allen (1981) had the same finding.

Route Angularity Effect

A peculiarity of distance judgment is what is called the route angularity effect (Sadalla & Magel, 1980). It was discovered that when subjects were asked to judge distances of routes of equal length, they would judge the route with more angles in it as longer than the straight one.

Downs and Stea (1973) called this phenomenon *route segmentation*. They theorized that subjects tended to cognitively segment the routes they traversed and thus remembered routes with the most segments as longer. Milgram (1973) explained this by an *information storage model*. Routes that had more bits of information (people, signs, whatever) tended to be remembered as longer than those with fewer bits. Sadalla and Staplin (1980) supported the information model by having subjects traverse two identical routes with 15 intersections. The only difference was that one route had easy-to-learn names for the streets while the other had very uncommon names. If it was information that was influencing the distance estimation, then the easy-to-learn route should be remembered as longer. This is exactly what happened. Subjects could not remember the hard names and therefore had less information stored for that route.

Herman, Norton, and Klein (1986) were unable to replicate the route angularity effect with children. Heft (1988) felt it was because their route only had direction changes and not the usual amount of possible decisions that go with "real" wayfinding. Heft also feels the angularity aspect is misleading because there actually is a lot of information at turns. Herman (1988), however, felt he *was* testing angularity because all his turns only contained direction changes.

Heft's criticism is similar to Cadwallader's (1979) earlier demonstration that all distance estimates are questionable because of their dependency on the method used and that this is true even at the ordinal level of measurement. Cadwallader goes on to question whether human beings perceive the world in such a way as to be able to "possess cognitive representations of the physical world that have the mathematical properties of metric space" (p. 560). In other words, humans just don't think in terms of miles, feet, and meters when it comes to perceiving the world.

Montello (1991) took a different interpretation of route angularity and concentrated on the confusing aspects of oblique angles in route changes. Montello noticed that in past research, subjects tended to remember turns as right angles even when they weren't. He hypothesized that oblique angles would be confusing and set up a field experiment where he stopped subjects at oblique and right-angle intersections and asked them for directions to landmarks that were not visible. Subjects at the oblique-angled intersections made more errors in pointing out the direction than did those asked the same questions at right-angled intersections. None of the landmarks was visible so all pointing was done from memory.

Slope

Okabe, Aoki, and Hamamoto (1986) demonstrated, at least for Japan, that all subjects, both adult and children, overestimate traversed distances, whether walking downhill or uphill, relative to walking on a flat plane. This might be called the "slope effect."

Wayfinding

According to Passini (1984), wayfinding involves three distinct abilities:

1. A cognitive mapping ability
2. A decision-making ability
3. A decision execution that results in behavior

All three of these abilities have been studied in some form or other in wayfinding studies.

Rovine and Weisman (1989), however, point out that the majority of cognitive map studies treat the maps (Passini's number one ability) as a dependent variable, that is, as the data that the environment influenced. They proposed using the cognitive map as an independent variable to see how the map influenced *wayfinding* behavior (Passini's number three).

When Rovine and Weisman used behavior of the subjects as their data, they found that the ability to accurately portray the relationships of buildings to one another accounted for 59% to 62% of the variance in wayfinding, a strong association for these kinds of studies.

A problem with studying children (Waller, 1986) is that children (like the rats before them) often have been underestimated in the skills they can bring to bear on wayfinding. Typically, the children could find their way around better than the maps they could draw. Waller points out this is because children learn and develop along several dimensions and the typical measure was too narrow to pick up the multidimensionality of the learning.

Several models of wayfinding have been proposed. Gärling (1989) describes the *traveling salesman's problem* in which subjects must plan a trip to several locations and attempt to minimize the overall distance traveled.

Hayes-Roth and Hayes-Roth (1979) proposed the local minimizing of distance model *(LMD)* in which the person simply tries to minimize distance between each point without regard to the total distance. Presumably, the traveling salesman pays more attention to his total mileage than the person in the LMD. Thus the traveling salesman model is more a planning strategy while the LMD is a series of independent decisions. Both models have some success in predicting how subjects plan and carry out trips.

Passini (1984) also distinguishes between recreational, resolute, and emergency wayfinding. Sime (1980) points out the constrained nature of emergency wayfinding from his discovery that emergency routes should always be the same as familiar entry routes because in panic conditions people always choose the familiar route to escape.

Wayfinding Indoors

Finding one's way around public buildings is an interesting problem for designers to see from the point of view of the first visitor. Distress and confusion are sometimes alleviated by posting signs. But how many signs? Carpman, Grant, and Simmons (1984) experimented with the comfort and endurance of hospital visitors. They set up a situation that tested how long people can go before feeling uncomfortable without a sign. The problem for subjects was to find the cyclotron in a complex hospital building. Presumably, here, none of the subjects had enough knowledge of physics to know that a cyclotron was totally inappropriate for a hospital. In any case, by watching subjects carefully, she discovered that about 50 feet was the distance down a corridor where people began to feel uncomfortable and looked for another sign.

ONeill (1991) looked at complexity of floor plans to see if this alone would predict difficulty in wayfinding. He developed an objective method for measuring complexity of a floor plan by counting the number of interconnections at every choice point in the plan. These were then averaged for an *interconnection density* (ICD) measure and this directly related to map accuracy and wayfinding performance. Weisman (1981) found simplicity of a floor plan was a strong predictor of reported way-

finding behavior. Weisman also concluded that legibility was the most important ingredient of wayfinding, and whether this is defined as simplicity or density of decisions, there is a clear relationship to difficulty in finding one's way.

Wayfinding for the Blind

Passini and Proulx (1988) compared congenitally blind subjects with sighted ones and found that the blind subjects were not too different than the sighted in being able to find their way around, given the same instructions. The blind differed mostly in paying more attention to environmental cues and planning their routes more thoroughly.

Previous research with the blind used tactile maps (Herman, Norton, & Roth, 1983; Leonard & Newman, 1970). Preiser (1985) experimented with a radio-guided cane that followed an activated strip and had recorded messages at checkpoints.

You-Are-Here Maps

Levine (1982; Levine, Marchon, & Hanley, 1984) is the originator of you-are-here map studies. His research looked at the placement of these maps in relation to the environment. He found that placing a you-are-here map out of alignment with the building was worse than having no map at all. In other words, these maps must be perfectly aligned with the environment, north pointing to true north and so on, or they will have a disorienting effect. Further, most people assume that all YAH maps *are* oriented correctly so they never check to tell whether the maps are out of alignment.

Conclusions

Environmental cognition has concerned itself largely with wayfinding and the problems associated with wayfinding such as using cues, estimating distances, and developing strategies. Although the original five cues of Lynch's work did not hold up over time, the strategy of clustering around landmarks seems to have currency. Many practical aspects of distance judgment have been discovered such as the effects of oblique-angled streets, slopes, and information collected along the way. Milgram collected these findings under the information storage model, which seems to have held up over time.

Wayfinding indoors is a special problem. People need signs every 50 feet to reassure them they are going in the right direction, and density of information at intersections is directly related to wayfinding indoors. Blind people use many of the same cues as sighted people except they are more attentive to environmental cues and plan their journeys more carefully.

Examples of Perceptions or Cognitions

"I saw it on TV once, but it looked littler."

SOURCE: Reprinted with special permission of King Features Syndicate.

"This is like a church, Mommy. Everyone's whispering."

SOURCE: Reprinted with special permission of King Features Syndicate.

GOALS

Definitions and Concepts

Landmarks

Paths

Nodes

Districts

Edges

Anchor points

Sketch map errors

Information storage model

Oblique angle confusion

Cognitive map

LMD

Traveling salesman's problem

ICD

Edge problem

Context of learning

Wayfinding

Important Studies

Neisser (1967)

Lynch (1960)

Tolman (1948)

Golledge (1978)

Okabe et al. (1986)

Montello (1991)

Levine (1982)

QUESTIONS

1. What fact tied the cognitive map to the hippocampus?

2. What is the common thread in the work of Lynch, ONeill, and Weisman?

3. How does Montello differ from Sadalla in his interpretation of angles?

4. What did Rovine and Weisman find predicted wayfinding behavior?

5. What did Carpman et al. find was the optimum distance for signs in corridors?

6. What is worse than having no YAH map?

7. How do blind people differ from the sighted in wayfinding?

8. What theory seems best to explain the angularity effect?

9. What is the most unexpected error in cognitive maps?

10. Explain the "failure" of the Whorfian hypothesis.

7

Personal Space

Historical Background

The term *fight or flight distance* was first coined by Cannon (1932). This term was given greater elaboration by Hediger (1950, 1955), who described the behavior of wild animals he hunted and those he observed in captivity. Hediger noticed that he could approach birds and animals fairly closely before shooting at them, but after once firing his gun, the birds and animals gave him a much wider berth. This is an insight lost on much of the work that became later known as *personal space*.

Hediger watched the behavior of animals in zoos. He noticed that as a keeper approached an animal, the keeper would reach a certain point at which the animal gave full attention to the approaching figure. Then, at another point, the animal would either flee or charge the keeper. Animals in zoos almost never charged a keeper. This was more appropriate for wild animals.

Notice that there are two important observations from Hediger's notes: The flight distance increased dramatically when the animals were shot at, and there were actually two zones an approaching figure crossed. One was the zone where the animal became fully alert to the approaching figure. The other was the zone where the animal chose either to flee or to charge. These two lessons were not very well accommodated in later research. Almost always, the research that followed conceptualized only a single line or "bubble" around the organism and paid no attention to the "alert zone."

Edward T. Hall (1959, 1966) was an anthropologist hired by the U.S. State Department at the end of World War II to help bring together the disparate cultures of the "enemy" nations, Germany and Japan, with the United States so that the occupation and further cooperative ventures could move more smoothly. It was thought an anthropologist could explain differences in culture that could easily lead to misunderstandings. Hall discovered that one of the prime sources of misunderstanding that occurred when Germans and Japanese tried to talk with Americans was the distance at which conversation took place.

Hall elaborated the concept of distance between humans into what he called *proxemics:* "the study of how people unconsciously structure microspace." Hall elaborated the distance between people into sensory zones according to what they could see, hear, smell, and touch. A chart of these zones appears in Figure 7.1.

The zones permitted four basic kinds of human interaction: intimate, which occurred at 0 to 18 inches; personal, which occurred at 18 inches to 4 feet; social, which was 4 feet to 12 feet; and public, which was 12 to 25 feet. Only at personal and intimate distances could one use olfactory and temperature cues (and temperature only at intimate distance). The remaining zones used diminishing oral and visual cues with distance.

Hall had convincing pictures of how Arabs preferred to "smell each other's breath" while talking and of how a marriage broker for an Arab male would smell the skin of a prospective bride and find the best compliment to be that it smelled like fresh bread.

These were cited as evidence the Arab cultures preferred a more intimate space for interaction than North Americans.

Sommer (1969a) took up the personal space distance and refined it to "the emotionally charged bubble of space which surrounds each individual" (p. viii). Sommer's research began with observations in public places followed by experiments in seating arrangements. In 1963, he began invading personal space to see at what point the person would flee an intruder. A bench would be marked so distances could be seen at a glance and Sommer or some other researcher would approach the person sitting on the bench, sit down, and move closer until the target person fled.

Another aspect of personal space research was the seating arrangements at a table. Sommer would show subjects a drawing of a table and ask them where they would sit to prevent anyone else from sitting at the

CHART SHOWING INTERPLAY OF THE DISTANT AND IMMEDIATE RECEPTORS
IN PROXEMIC PERCEPTION

FEET	0	1	2	3	4	5	6	7	8	10	12	14	16	18	20	22	30

INFORMAL DISTANCE CLASSIFICATION: INTIMATE (CLOSE / NOT CLOSE) — PERSONAL (NOT CLOSE / CLOSE) — SOCIAL – CONSULTIVE (CLOSE / NOT CLOSE) — PUBLIC. MANDATORY RECOGNITION DISTANCE BEGINS HERE. NOT CLOSE BEGINS AT 30' – 40'.

KINESTHESIA:
- HEAD, PELVIS, THIGHS, TRUNK CAN BE BROUGHT INTO CONTACT OR MEMBERS CAN ACCIDENTALLY TOUCH. HANDS CAN REACH & MANIPULATE ANY PART OF TRUNK EASILY.
- HANDS CAN REACH AND HOLD EXTREMITIES EASILY BUT WITH MUCH LESS FACILITY THAN ABOVE. SEATED CAN REACH AROUND & TOUCH OTHER SIDE OF TRUNK. NOT SO CLOSE AS TO RESULT IN ACCIDENTAL TOUCHING.
- ONE PERSON HAS ELBOW ROOM.
- 2 PEOPLE BARELY HAVE ELBOW ROOM. ONE CAN REACH OUT AND GRASP AN EXTREMITY.
- JUST OUTSIDE TOUCHING DISTANCE.
- OUT OF INTERFERENCE DISTANCE. BY REACHING ONE CAN JUST TOUCH THE OTHER.
- 2 PEOPLE WHOSE HEADS ARE 8' – 9' APART CAN PASS AN OBJECT BACK & FORTH BY BOTH STRETCHING.

THERMAL RECEPTORS: CONDUCTION (CONTACT). RADIATION — NORMALLY OUT OF AWARENESS. ANIMAL HEAT AND MOISTURE DISSIPATE (THOREAU).

OLFACTION: CULTURAL ATTITUDE
- WASHED SKIN & HAIR — OK
- SHAVING LOTION–PERFUME — OK — TABOO —
- SEXUAL ODORS — VARIABLE — TABOO
- BREATH — ANTISEPTIC OK, OTHERWISE TABOO
- BODY ODOR — TABOO
- FOOT ODOR — TABOO

FEET	0	1	2	3	4	5	6	7	8	10	12	14	16	18	20	22	30

VISION

DETAIL VISION (VIS ∠ OF FOVEA 1°): VISION BLURRED DISTORTED. ENLARGED DETAILS OF IRIS, EYEBALL, PORES OF FACE, FINEST HAIRS. DETAIL OF FACE SEEN AT NORMAL SIZE, EYES, NOSE, SKIN, TEETH CONDITION, EYELASHES, HAIR ON BACK OF NECK. SMALLEST BLOOD VESSELS IN EYE LOST. SEE WEAR ON CLOTHING. HEAD HAIR SEEN CLEARLY. FINE LINES OF FACE FADE. DEEP LINES STAND OUT. SLIGHT EYE WINK. LIP MOVEMENT SEEN CLEARLY. ENTIRE CENTRAL FACE INCLUDED. SHARP FEATURES DISSOLVE, EYE COLOR NOT DISCERNIBLE, SMILE–SCOWL, VISIBLE, HEAD BOBBING MORE PRONOUNCED. SNELLEN'S STANDARD FOR DISTANT VISION - EMPLOYING ANGLE OF 1 MIN. GUILD OPTICIANS OF AMERICA EYE CHART. A PERSON WITH 20/40 VISION HAS TROUBLE SEEING EYES & EXPRESSION AROUND EYES THOUGH EYE BLINK IS VISIBLE.

CLEAR VISION (VIS ∠ AT MACULA 12° HOR, 3° VERT): 25" × 3" ON EYE, NOSTRILS OR MOUTH. 3.75" × .94" UPPER OR LOWER FACE. 6.25" × 1.60" UPPER OR LOWER FACE. 10" × 2.5" UPPER OR LOWER FACE OR SHOULDERS. 20" × 5" 1 OR 2 FACES. 31" × 7.5 FACES OF TWO PEOPLE. 4'2" × 1'6" TORSOS OF TWO PEOPLE. 6' 3" × 1' 7" TORSOS OF 4 OR 5 PEOPLE.

60° SCANNING: 1/3 OF FACE, EYE, EAR OR MOUTH AREA SEEN DISTORTED. NOSE PROJECTS, WHOLE FACE SEEN FACE-DISTORTED–DISTORTED. UPPER BODY CAN'T COUNT FINGERS. UPPER BODY & GESTURES. WHOLE SEATED BODY VISIBLE. PEOPLE OFTEN KEEP FEET WITHIN OTHER PERSON'S 60° ANGLE OF VIEW. WHOLE BODY HAS SPACE AROUND IT, POSTURAL COMMUNICATION BEGINS TO ASSUME IMPORTANCE.

PERIPHERAL VISION: HEAD AGAINST BACKGROUND. HEAD & SHOULDERS. WHOLE BODY MOVEMENT IN HANDS–FINGERS VISIBLE. WHOLE BODY. OTHER PEOPLE SEEN IF PRESENT. OTHER PEOPLE BECOME IMPORTANT IN PERIPHERAL VISION.

HEAD SIZE: FILLS VISUAL FIELD FAR OVER LIFE SIZE. OVER NORMAL. NORMAL SIZE. NORMAL TO BEGINNING TO SHRINK. VERY SMALL. NOTE: PERCEIVED HEAD SIZE VARIES EVEN WITH SAME SUBJECTS AND DISTANCE.

ADDITIONAL NOTES: SENSATION OF BEING CROSS-EYED. PEOPLE & OBJECTS SEEN AS ROUND UP TO 12' – 15'. ACCOMMODATIVE CONVERGENCE ENDS AFTER 15' PEOPLE & OBJECTS BEGIN TO FLATTEN OUT.

TASKS IN SUBMARINES: 67% OF TASKS IN THIS RANGE. 23% FALL IN THIS RANGE. DIMMICH, F.L. & FARNSWORTH, D. VISUAL ACUITY TASKS IN A SUBMARINE, NEW LONDON, 1951.

ARTISTS' OBSERVATIONS CF GROSSER: VERY PERSONAL DISTANCE. ARTIST OR MODEL HAS TO DOMINATE. A PORTRAIT. A PICTURE PAINTED AT 4 – 8' OF A PERSON WHO IS NOT PAID TO "SIT". TOO FAR FOR A CONVERSATION. BODY IS 1/3 SIZE. FULL LENGTH STATE PORTRAITS. HUMAN BODY SEEN AS A WHOLE, COMPREHENDED AT A GLANCE, WARMTH AND IDENTIFICATION CEASE.

ORAL AURAL: GRUNTS GROANS. WHISPER. SOFT VOICE INTIMATE STYLE. CONVENTIONAL MODIFIED VOICE CASUAL OR CONSULTIVE STYLE. LOUD VOICE WHEN TALKING TO A GROUP, MUST RAISE VOICE TO GET ATTENTION FORMAL STYLE. FULL PUBLIC SPEAKING VOICE FROZEN STYLE.

NOTE: THE BOUNDARIES ASSOCIATED WITH THE TRANSITION FROM ONE VOICE LEVEL TO THE NEXT HAVE NOT BEEN PRECISELY DETERMINED.

Figure 7.1. Chart of Proxemic Locations
SOURCE: From Hall (1969, pp. 126-127); reprinted by permission.

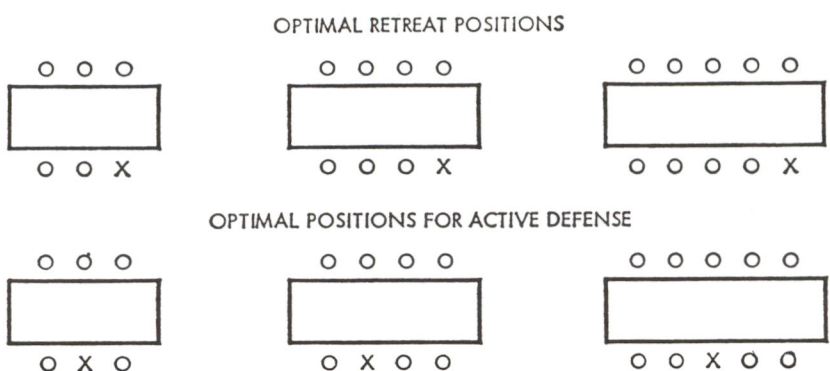

Figure 7.2. Optimal Offensive and Defensive Positions
SOURCE: From Sommer (1969, p. 49); reprinted by permission.

table or where they would sit to be alone. He found that people chose the middle chair to prevent others from sitting at the table and an end chair to signal being alone. See Figure 7.2.

Seating arrangements were a way to achieve dominance over space and people. It was found that the person who sat at the head of a table tended to be chosen foreman of a jury (Strodtbeck & Hook, 1961). This research combined with social psychological findings has developed into a new field of jury selection. Some see this as adding adversity to the justice system by having each side battle over selection of jurors favorable to their side.

Definition

Nearly every reviewer of personal space research has problems with definition. Hall (1966) did not emphasize the distance per se but instead the use of visual, olfactory, and oral cues in communication. In other words, it was the cultural imperative of which cues to use that determined the distance. North Americans tend to be offended by odor and try to stay outside the olfactory zone. "Contact" cultures like those in South America try to stay within touching distance, which is also closer than their *Norte Americano* cousins.

Patterson (1975) first suggested that the term *personal space* is misleading. The use of the space is actually more *interpersonal*. Aiello (1987) suggests the use of *interaction distance* because the space between two or more persons is involved and it is the interaction that defines the space.

Recent reviewers (Aiello, 1987; Hayduk, 1983) agree that the bubble concept is misleading and unsupported by research. The interactive space is flexible, mutually adjustable, and situationally influenced. Further, there are language aspects not sufficiently explored by research. Sussman and Rosenfeld (1982) measured the distance between bilingual subjects and found they sprang apart going from Spanish to English but moved closer together when switching from English to Spanish. This suggests a choreography that is learned with the language. Such a concept was promoted by Birdwhistell (1970) and the *kinesics* research but the interpersonal aspect was not followed and it concentrated (just like the personal space research) on observing and measuring the target individual rather than pairs or aggregates. Kinesics is the study of body language.

It seems then that a more appropriate definition of personal space is actually *interaction distance* with all the dynamic and multivariate aspects that an interaction implies. Aiello (1987) is reluctant to give up the personal space label because of its long-term use, but the facts of research should speak for themselves.

Because researchers often are not clear about differentiating *interaction distance* from *social distance, territory, privacy*, and *crowding*, the reader must be cautioned to be alert to the lack of clarity in many studies. Ciolek (1983) points out that there are 140 terms used in the area of personal space and proxemics, and all of these are in need of greater consistency and refinement.

The point to keep in mind is that Sommer visualizes personal space as an "invisible bubble" that accompanies the person everywhere.

Problems of Methods

Sommer's invasive technique remains in use up to this time, but more often it has been replaced by the *stop-distance method*. In the stop-distance method, a subject approaches a target person until the target person reg- isters discomfort. Aiello (1987) questions the validity of this method when compared with naturally observed interaction distances but Hayduk (1985) finds it to be stable.

Many studies have used projective techniques. Kuethe (1962) developed the flannel figures schema as a projective test of interaction distance. Subjects placed cutout flannel figures on a flannel background in imitation of real-life settings. Other techniques such as placement of dolls in models (De Long, 1981) or on a stage or platform (Sinha & Mukerjee, 1990) use the same principles but use three-dimensional objects. Holz, Brannigan, and Schofield (1980) used the kinetic family drawing technique; Edwards (1980) had subjects place figures in a room diagram; Sanders, Thomas, Suydam, and Petri (1980) had subjects listen to approaching footsteps; Scott (1984) used photographs of rooms and asked people to point out where they would sit; and Codol, Jarymowicz, Kaminska-Feldman, and Szuster-Zbrojewicz (1989) used interpersonal distances drawn by subjects on maps.

Hayduk (1983) summarizes research that shows the projective techniques have questionable validity. Love and Aiello (1980), Slane, Petruska, and Cheyfitz (1981), and Peterson, Roscoe, and Draper (1982) came to the same conclusion. Aiello (1987) asserts that "more than half" of the findings in all of personal space research are questionable because of the use of projective techniques. Therefore, it would seem prudent to reach conclusions based only on research that involves direct observation or controlled laboratory studies. The projective techniques are not trustworthy.

Special Populations

Many studies observe the interactive distances of children and conclude that interaction distance increases with age. Sommer (1969a) wants to avoid an inference that interaction space is inherited behavior. Instead, most researchers assume it is learned as the child grows older.

Children

Smetena, Bridgeman, and Bridgeman (1978), using 113 children aged 2 to 5½ years, found consistent spacing with a small increase in age. Speelman and Hoffman (1980) found an increase of interpersonal space with age. Willis, Carlson, and Reeves (1979) also found an increase of space with age. Many studies found a difference with sex of children, with male children having larger personal space (Folarin, 1983, 1989; Severy,

Forsyth, & Wagner, 1979), but Pegan and Aiello (1982) found no consistent sex differences. Also, researchers report that distances between children are influenced by a number of factors such as dominance (Eisenberg-Berg, Hand, & Haake, 1981), reduced space and resources (Sanchez-Bedolla, 1981), standard versus colloquial speech (Waller, 1984), and even the health of the child (Ludlow & Levy, 1984). Nevertheless, the evidence points to personal distance increasing with age in children.

The Mentally Ill

In a study of suicides, Niemi (1975) suggested the observation of communication distance would be useful. Generally, researchers find people with various mental illnesses keep larger personal distances than normal controls. Adler and Granbert (1976) found this to be true for Australian patients in a mental hospital. Fukui (1983) found that different kinds of mental illnesses were related to different personal space distances. For example, he found 66.6% of the depressives followed a voluntary bedridden style while 83% of the neurotics were freely communicative, and the schizophrenics tended to follow many different styles.

Noshpitz (1984) found narcissistic patients have greater reactivity to invasion of personal space. Cooper (1984) found chronically institutionalized nonverbal clients are also more reactive to invasions. Therefore, they should have more provision for living space and use of their own clothes.

Both Melges and Swartz (1989) and Akhtar (1990) found borderline personality disordered clients have a central problem with maintaining optimal personal distance.

Srivastava and Mandal (1990) reported schizophrenics have larger personal distance and take comfort from the greater space. This agrees with earlier studies by Grant (1965).

Mentally retarded people also maintain personal spaces (Burgess, 1981; Edmonson & Han, 1983; Iwai, 1986) and this seems to be true of even the profoundly retarded with IQs of less than 36 (Paslawskyj & Ivinskis, 1980).

The evidence on personal space distance among the mentally ill seems to vary with the kind of illness. Most important is the evidence that the mentally ill keep distances that seem inappropriate to the situation, producing discomfort in others.

The Elderly and Handicapped

Burgess (1983a), in an observation of 2,008 persons in eight malls and two downtown sidewalks, found senior adults had the closest interpersonal spaces. Phillips (1979) observed that elderly males had larger personal spaces than females.

Handicapped persons seem to get a wide berth when it comes to personal space. Most people tend to keep a larger distance from a handicapped person than from a person with no visible handicaps although Perkins and Marsha (1978) found sixth-grade children narrowed the gap as they increased their knowledge of the handicapped.

Hayduk and Mainprize (1980) observed that blind people keep the same interpersonal distances as sighted persons and that sex, age, and income do not influence the distance. Sanders et al. (1980) observed that both blind and sighted persons kept strangers farther away when approached from the front.

Jones (1985) observed that hearing-impaired children maintained greater distances than similarly aged children with no hearing problems.

Albrecht, Walker, and Levy (1982) found 150 professional managers expressed greater social distance from deviants such as alcoholics and drug addicts than from disabled people such as paraplegics and the blind. Stephens and Clark (1987) found that students in a classroom show significant movement away from a person with a physical disability. Conigliaro, Cullerton, Flynn, and Roeder (1989) show personal space increased in the presence of a stigmatizing artifact such as a white cane. Holmes, Karst, and Erhart (1990) maintain these social barriers hurt the rehabilitation of handicapped people.

Even pregnancy seems to be a handicap in terms of personal space. Davis and Lennon (1983) observed that pregnancy "functions similarly to a physical stigma" when it comes to personal space; that is, people maintain a greater distance from pregnant women.

In summary, while elderly reduce personal distance, elderly males still seem to have larger distances than females. The handicapped in general seem to be given a wider berth than the nonhandicapped.

Cross-Cultural Differences

Iwata (1978) found females in Japan have shorter interpersonal distances than males. Fukuhara (1977) found eye contact increased with interaction distance and that females show more eye contact. Iwata (1980) also showed that Japanese who exhibited "strong" territorial behavior are more prone to experience crowding. Higashiyama and Ono (1988) propose that Japanese interpersonal distances are determined by the Japanese words *koko, soko*, and *asoko*, which designate spaces between speakers.

Maykovich (1980) shows evidence that social distance is influenced by news of international events. For example, the recognition of communist China influenced people of Taiwan to increase personal distances from U.S. personnel. Cline and Puhl (1984) observed that Chinese on Taiwan prefer side seating as contrasted to U.S. people. Taiwanese see the corner seating preferred by U.S. people as aggressive.

Balogun (1991) shows Muslims require less space than Christians. Noejirwan (1978) observed smaller personal space use by Indonesians, with more touching, more smiling than in those from the United States.

Comparing Hellenics with Hebrews, Markus-Kaplan and Kaplan (1979) found the avoidance gradient steeper than the approach gradient for Hellenics while it was the opposite for Hebrews. *Hebrew* and *Hellenic* refers more to a personality style than to persons living in Israel or Greece. Thus Hebrews seemed to approach people using less distance.

Ogunlade (1980) found the Yoruba of Nigeria had closer social proximity to their own group than strangers.

Smith (1981), however, found the cross-national commonalities in territorial patterns of France and West Germany to be more important than any within-culture variations.

Kinloch (1986) looked at social distance in Hawaii, an island with many mixtures of cultures, and found social distance among smaller and less established groups was determined by the length of residence rather than social origin. For larger, more established groups, the reverse was true.

Rustemli (1986) studied Turkish library users and found males placed greater distances between themselves and intruders of both sexes but that females distanced themselves further and escaped faster from opposite sex intruders, thus exhibiting the "traditional female modesty" of the culture.

In another study, Rustemli (1988) found neither the impressions nor decisions of interviewees were influenced by the distance of the interviewer but feelings were influenced and interacted with the sex of the interviewer, the closer male being seen as most negative. Similar to Rustemli, Sanders, Hakky, and Brizzolara (1985) found few differences between U.S. and Egyptian males but found Egyptian females highly reactive to male invasions.

Keating and Keating (1980) watched spaces between persons seated on benches in San Francisco, Tangier, Seville, and Nairobi and found no significant differences in spaces between persons on benches across these countries.

Although there are many variations across cultures, the "touch" cultures keep shorter distances in interactions while the "no-touch," such as ours, keep larger distances, consistent with Hall's observations. Many cultures emphasize sex separation such that the distances males keep from females are greater than in same-sex interactions.

Family Personal Spaces

Finighan (1980) studied 225 householders and found values of privacy to be similar regardless of family stage or income. Hill, Blackman, and Crane (1982) observed 37 couples and found the husband-wife combination requires significantly less space than any other combination. Crane, Russell, and Griffin (1983) found chair placement among 24 married couples was associated with marital adjustment. In fact, chair placement was associated with divorce potential, that is, the further away, the more likely a divorce. Frew (1983) had similar findings and found that "clear boundaries" were related to greater levels of intimate contact and marital adjustment. Morris and Smith (1980) found affection produces closer proximity.

DeCarlo, Sandler, and Tittler (1981) indicated that therapy could result in increased distance between pairs. Wood and Talmon (1983) had findings that agreed with this and talked about a reorganization of proximity and hierarchy that takes place during therapy. Apparently the changes that take place in a relationship during therapy seem to be reflected in changing interaction distances and seating arrangements.

Distance between children and parents is another aspect of family social interactions. Sigelman and Adams (1990) found that the presence of other children in the family reduces the closeness between parent and child. Larson and Lowe (1990) found the spatial distance between parents and older adolescents was greater than with younger adolescents. Spigelman and Spigelman (1991) found that the "vulnerability of body boundaries" appears to persist even years after a marital breakup, meaning that there is a long-term effect for children of either sex.

Goldsmith and Hill (1986) found that a family's home space affects their behavior according to a framework of access to dimensions of space in the home. In other words, who has access to what spaces has a large influence on family behavior.

Family personal spaces relate to space in the home, number and age of children, and history of traumatic events such as divorce. Couples who keep the greatest distance from each other seem to have the greatest likelihood of divorce. But distance of separation cannot always bode ill because therapy also increases the distance couples keep from each other.

Prisoners and Violence

O'Neal, Brunault, Marquis, and Carifio (1979) found that angered persons prefer more distance, especially in front. Gilmour and Walkey (1981) report that interpersonal distance is the next best discriminator between violent and nonviolent offenders. He also finds no difference in this respect between Polynesians and European whites. Wormith (1984) studied 49 incarcerated males over 3 years and found no changes in his personal space distance measures. He found the *behind* distance the largest, however (in contrast with O'Neal), and that age was inversely related to personal space area. Large personal spaces were found to correlate with recidivism. McGurk, Davis, and Grehan (1981) also found personal space distance largest in the rear.

Eastwood (1985) found no significant difference between violent and nonviolent persons in personal space size but did find an interaction with intelligence. Low intelligence went with higher personal space area. Cavallin and Houston (1980), consistent with other researchers, did find maladjusted and aggressive males preferred more personal space with a stranger.

Most research associates violence and anger with larger personal spaces, especially with strangers.

Sex and Personal Space

Fairly consistently researchers find a difference between males and females such that the males have larger personal spaces than females.

Although there are some exceptions, this finding seems to hold across many cultures as well.

Barnard and Bell (1982) showed female dyads are closer than males; Wittig and Solnick (1978) found women have less personal space than males; Lombardo (1986) observed males were more affected by face-to-face invasion by other males than by females; Bell, Kline, and Barnard (1988) found male-male dyads had greater distances than female-female or female-male; Balogun (1991) found different-sex dyads require greater distances even with familiarity.

But it is not always simple. Murphy-Berman and Berman (1978) found more "intentional" males (males who seemed to have some purpose in mind) were seen as more negative than nonintentional ones. Females displayed larger social spacing than males toward groups of three, according to Pederson (1978). Eliot and Cohen (1981) revealed a sex-by-distance interaction with invasion such that males are seen more positive under moderate distances, and females at close and far distances. Mandal and Maitra (1985) observed that facial expressions of happiness, sadness, and fear separate sexual responses such that men prefer to be closer to happiness, women approach both happiness and sadness, and both sexes avoid fear. Young and Guile (1987) reported women had shorter latencies of departure when their space was invaded by low-status intruders regardless of sex.

Everything changes for short people! Caplan and Goldman (1981) found that females invade the personal space of short people more than males.

Touch is another separator of the sexes. Apparently women feel more comfortable with touch than men. Sussman and Rosenfeld (1978) had confederates touch subjects under what appeared to be justified versus unjustified conditions and the unjustified touch lowered the performance of males on an experimental task regardless of the sex of the intruder. Fromme, Jaynes, Taylor, and Hanold (1989) also found females more comfortable with touch and found that active interpersonal style and more satisfactory social relationships were also related to comfort with touch.

It is generally found across most cultures that men have larger personal spaces than women and that women are more comfortable with closeness than men.

Psychological Factors

Eye Contact

In a church setting, Campbell and Lancioni (1979) had stooges attempt to get pew seats by staring. After 98 such invasions, it was concluded that staring increases the likelihood of people moving away in the pew or returning the gaze. Ahmed (1979) observed that people retreat faster from male than from female starers although females retreat from all starers sooner than males.

Kaplan, Firestone, Klein, and Sodikoff (1983) observed that women tolerate male invasions assisted by staring (from the males). Tobiasen and Allen (1983) found a continuous gaze made people sit farther away. Rosenfeld, Breck, and Smith (1984) see the relationship of gaze and close proximity to be regulated by the amount of movement, the role of the conversation, acquaintanceship, and gender. Rivano-Fischer (1988) watched the watching of people in buses and concluded that there is a lot of avoidance of eye contact.

Kleinke (1980) tried to use eye contact as a method to get greater compliance when asking for money for a phone call versus money for a candy bar. It worked for the phone call but not for the candy bar. Going on to ask for gum, it was found people gave more gum when not gazed at or touched.

Fukuhara (1977) observed that eye contact in a dyad is affected by interaction distance and the need for affiliation (n aff). Eye contact was increased with interaction distance in both high and low n aff females, but females generally use more eye contact than males and use more eye contact than males when listening.

Avoiding eye contact is a way to maintain personal space. People who stare tend to intimidate others, especially when a male stares at a female.

Personality

Cavallin and Houston (1980) found maladjusted and aggressive subjects preferred more personal space with a stranger than less maladjusted and aggressive subjects. Underestimation of body size was related to size of personal space.

Wellens (1979) correlated interpersonal liking with measures of distancing from others. Snyder and Endelman (1979) proposed a curvilinear relationship between similarity and interpersonal distance. Being very similar is as bad as being very different. Positive attraction lies between these two extremes; hence, so does personal distance.

Bharucha-Reid and Kiyak (1979) administered Rotter's IE scale (Rotter, 1966) to subjects and found externals more comfortable with invasions because they were used to being controlled more.

In a later study, Bharucha-Reid and Kiyak (1981) applied Brehm and Brehm's (1981) reactance theory to explain why internals move more. The externals are more aware of and react to a loss of freedom.

Roger (1982) managed an experimentally induced, enhanced self-esteem situation, which resulted in lower penetration and social distance scores than those with reduced self-esteem. Clarke (1986) found an inverse correlation between self-actualization and conversational distance.

In a deindividuation (loss of identity) condition, Kaminska-Feldman (1988) measured the physical distance as larger between self and others. Carducci and Webber (1979) claim the very shy maintained greater personal distance, particularly with the opposite sex.

Strube and Werner (1983) say the distance is greater from others when one wishes to avoid control by others. They go further and assert that *there is no relationship between interpersonal distance and size of personal space*. The reader will note that most researchers have been treating interpersonal distance and personal space as almost synonymous. In a later study, Strube and Werner (1984) describe how people expand personal space in the direction from which a threat comes. This seems to be even more consistent for Type A personalities (see Chapter 11).

Kline, Bell, and Babcock (1984) find that field-dependent personality types (those who relate to a perceptual frame) stand further away than those who are field independent. Finally, Ray (1984) measures conservatives as standing farther away than liberals.

Most important is the Strube and Werner admonition that personal space is *not* interaction distance even though many researchers treat the two as one. People whose personality type is easily threatened, such as with shyness, are more likely to keep larger personal spaces.

Helping

Latane and Nida (1981) review 10 years of studies of helping behavior and conclude one's best chance of being helped is when there is only one other person present. Adding just one more person begins the dilution of responsibility. To this literature the studies of personal space add a small amount. DeBeer-Kelston, Mellon, and Solomon (1986) find when subjects' personal space was invaded, they were less likely to help anyone. Harada and Araragi (1981) arranged a clever ruse at bus stops by dropping a pen either nearer to or further from a target person and watching for a helping response. Increased distance decreased the likelihood of helping. By contrast, Jackson and Latane (1981) found distance had no effect on the success of door-to-door solicitors.

Willis and Hamm (1980) used touch as an aid to a request for compliance and discovered it was useful when the request was difficult and the person being asked was of the same gender. Anderson and Sull (1985) claim attitudes toward communication, particularly touch, determine spatial intimacy. Greenbaum and Rosenfeld (1980) observed 152 greeting dyads and found that female-female contacts last longer and involve more touching of lips and faces, have more embraces, and hand-to-upper-body touches.

Getting help is more directly related to numbers of people available than personal space. Distance research in helping yields contradictory results. It does seem clear that touching solicits help best among females.

Density and Crowding

Studies of personal space often have used the intrusion of personal space as the definition of crowding. Sometimes the definition includes a measure of social or physical density. The important concept seems to be incursion into personal space. For example, Levitt and Leventhal (1978) describe density and the intrusion upon personal space as it affects the perception of crowding. Thalhoffer (1980) merely describes how the spacing norm is violated in high social density and that this results in honoring fewer social expectations, not dissimilar from Milgram (1970).

Lange, Mueller, and Donnerstein (1979) describe interference density as affecting both performance and mood. Ciolek and Furnham (1980) observed that the seating in churches, lectures, and cinema is arranged in order of decreasing proximity. Lange et al. conclude that setting density is situationally defined. Burgess (1983b) observed distances between walking companions was inversely correlated to density. In other words, when the mall is crowded, people walk closer together. This is not surprising!

Jain (1987) feels that when spatial density is greater, it leads to a feeling of encroachment of personal space. Much as in the more general crowding studies described in Chapter 9, the experience of encroachment on personal space is directly related to the kind of situation. The same situation can seem crowded to one person and not crowded to another, much like a football game.

Seating

Kline and Bell (1983) feel that relationships are more evident face-to-face than side-by-side.Gifford and O'Connor (1986) repeated Sommer's earlier studies and found judgment of seating arrangements strongly related to distance but not orientation. By contrast, Patterson, Roth, and Schenk (1979) observed that L-shaped tables create more nervousness in the form of self-manipulation, postural shifts, and pauses in communication.

In classroom seating, Byrd and Guyot (1979) discovered that students maintain the serial order of their seats but not the adjacency. Haber (1980) claimed central seats were more defended than peripheral seats.

Glaser (1985) wrote that regulars in a tavern demonstrated a greater need for social distance and avoidance of social intimacy. Collet and Marsh (1980) observed that seat choice is affected by group size. Larger groups are less likely to find seats of their choice. Singles tend to choose peripheral seats while pairs seem to have no preference.

The clarity of Sommer's earlier studies on seating seems to have slipped with time but at least the distance factor has held up even though the corner seating relationship has produced contradictory findings.

Stress

There seems to be a general finding that invasion of personal space causes stressful responses in a variety of ways. Kanaga and Flynn (1981) conclude that spatial invasions are stress producing. Thompson, Aiello, and Epstein (1979) observe that it is the intermediate distances that seem more comfortable while the nearest and farthest produce most of the discomfort. Observing 264 undergraduates under conditions of stress, Slane, Dragen, Crandall, and Payne (1980) observed differences in eye contact as a response to stress. Yaezawa and Yoshida (1981) observed changes in heart rate, eye blinks, subjective feelings, anxiety, and tension at the approach of another person. In this case, the other person was simulated by a model.

Ugwuegbu and Anusiem (1982) describe how stress affected their subjects' tendency to approach in a simulated interview situation. Mildly stressed subjects seemed to distance more than those with no stress. Long (1984) observed personal space in eight natural settings rated on degrees of psychological tension and concluded that persons in four of the high-tension waiting places had a preference for significantly more distance. In fact, self-reported tension correlated significantly with distances preferred across all eight situations.

Ajdukovic (1988) concludes that people use compensatory responses (eye contact, shifts in position, and so on) to reduce the stress of personal space invasion. Vargas (1984) concludes there is an interaction between environmental factors, stress, and personal space.

The studies of stress and personal space seem more directly related to the original concept rather than to interaction distance. Clearly, invasion of personal space produces some measurable amount of stress.

Distance Estimation

How do people estimate these distances of interpersonal space? Ford and Hoebeke (1980) reported their subjects overestimated the actual distances between themselves and others when distances moved beyond the preferred level. Gifford (1983) reported the perceived interaction distance to be larger than the distance as objectively measured. Subjects believed they were further apart than they actually were.

Codol (1985) claims that distance judgment actually depends upon the reference point. His subjects tended to perceive persons as closer to themselves but perceived themselves as further from others. This tendency becomes greater when there is a large number of people in a room. So it seems generally true that people overestimate the distances between themselves and others compared with an objective measure.

Miscellaneous

Does being outdoors influence personal space? Apparently so because Cochran and Hale (1984) found the stop-distance technique produced less discomfort out of doors than in more vertically restricted areas, that is, places with ceilings. Rivano-Fischer (1984) wrote that the invasion of personal space occurs less in outdoor settings.

Smokers get their due in personal space. Kunzendorff and Denney (1982) measured intruders as stopping farther away from smokers than nonsmokers. They found the number of packs smoked per day correlated with a desire for more personal space.

Rachlinski, Foltin, and Fischman (1989) investigated marijuana smoking's decreasing effect on verbal behavior, which also causes increased personal space.

Is there nothing that hasn't been studied? Apparently not.

Sanders (1978) describes personal space as larger during menstrual flow. O'Neal, Schultz, and Christenson (1987) were more precise and find this greater distance only in midcycle.

Theories

Three theories have been proposed to explain personal space distance. Argyle and Dean (1965) were the first to propose a dynamic theory of *equilibrium*. Personal space is maintained by a series of methods such as eye contact, facial expression, distance itself, and verbal behavior. As can be seen from the previous list of studies, many of these behaviors are clearly related to maintaining and changing personal space or interaction distance. There are both interpersonal and intrapersonal qualities to this dynamic. Either person in the transaction can exhibit equilibrium behaviors or both can interact in their behaviors. This theory attempts to deal with the original limitations of the bubble concept and helps account for the many fluctuations of personal space that occur under many circumstances.

Attribution theory comes from social psychology and attempts to deal with an important aspect of interaction space that is not too often taken into account, namely, what one person thinks the other person's motive is. The reader must have puzzled many times about what the hapless persons thought about all these invaders and intruders of either sex. Is this guy going to hit me? Is she trying to seduce me? Almost as an afterthought, the social psychologists began to ask this question in personal space invasion studies.

Smith and Knowles (1978) describe how an invader is rated negatively and then specific intentions are attributed to him or her. Manaster,

Cleland, and Brooks (1978) claim that the emotions that move people away or toward each other are self-attributed and interactive. Webb, Worchel, and Brown (1986) conclude that people use attributions to enhance perceptions of control over the environment.

Expectancy theory also comes via social psychology and encompasses the concept of norms and violations. Aiello (1987) has already said that the protective function of personal space has been overemphasized and perhaps the expectancy theory of Burgoon and Jones (1976) that deals with violations would be better balanced by Gouldner's (1960) reciprocity norm. Kaplan et al. (1983) list four rules of dyadic exchange of intimacy and the first of these is reciprocity. Reciprocity seems to be used with likable interviewers or invaders, and compensation with those not liked. In any case, expectancy has to deal with the unexpected and it does not do so very well. For example, Ruback (1987) had subjects remain longer in a library aisle when they were invaded than the uninvaded control. Personal space invasion does not always lead to retreat.

There is yet another possible theory and this too comes from social psychology. It is Brown's (1967) concept that distancing in social relationships is founded in *language* and forms of address. There is actually a fair amount of evidence accumulated to demonstrate this. Reid (1980) found that distances in a classroom were related to the verbal interaction, that it was the verbal interaction itself that determined these distances. Meltzer (1983) concluded that the social distances he measured were controlled by use of vocabulary, refinement, and images.

Smith and Cantrell (1988) found that physical distance was only anxiety arousing if combined with verbal intrusion. In fact, verbal intrusion evoked anxiety regardless of distance. Higashiyama and Ono (1988) describe how the Japanese demonstratives *koko* (near the speaker) and *soko* (which includes both the place near the listener and the outer boundary of koko) control the distance between speaker and listener. The koko area (closest to the concept of personal space) did not increase with increasing distance. Waller (1984) describes how the perceived distance between speaker and listener was determined by the use of standard versus colloquial language. There is some evidence then that distance between speakers and listeners is at least partially controlled by *language*. This is a situation not only envisaged by Brown but also the research of Birdwhistell (1970).

It must be said, as it can be said about many psychological theories, that they are all true at least in some sense. Personal space or, more accurately, interaction distance, as it has been studied by many researchers, is affected by forces for equilibrium, attribution, expectancy, and the use of language. What is needed is a theory to bring all of these together.

Meanwhile, a knowledge of personal space can have very practical results. Hern (1991) reports how the court, in deciding to station demonstrators outside an abortion clinic, listened to the advice of no less a person than Edward T. Hall himself before deciding to keep the demonstrators far enough away so they would not interfere with the social distance of persons going to the clinic.

And a further footnote: If you are arrested for being in such a demonstration, or for any other reason, please be careful when the policeman invades your interaction distance. Winkel, Koppelaar, and Vrij (1988) documented that police interpret defensive behavior that occurs when such space is invaded as expression of being a true suspect of whatever crime is the subject of the interrogation.

Conclusions

There remains confusion between *personal space* and its bubble concept and the *interaction distance* proposed as a better term. The interaction distance is more related to Hall's proxemics and thus subject to the many influences of culture and language. It is not clear whether the bubble invasions are nothing more than defensiveness against bodily threats or truly a part of interaction phenomena. It is important to keep in mind that many of the invasive studies are subject to the attribution theory interpretation. It may be that people assume there is a potential threat until the so-called invader begins to speak and redefines the situation.

In any case, these studies have generated a large body of literature that at the very least demonstrates the importance of the distance between people, whether interacting or not, and how this distance is influenced by the particular way the situation is defined by culture, assumed motive of the invader, and presence or absence of other persons.

GOALS

Definitions and Concepts

Personal space (Sommer, 1969a)

Proxemics (Hall, 1966)

Personal distance (Hall, 1966)

Intimate distance (Hall, 1966)

Interaction distance

Kinesics (Birdwhistell, 1970)

Fight or flight distance

Alert zone

Invasion of personal space

Stop distance

Flannel figures

Important Studies

Hall (1966)

Sommer (1969a)

Birdwhistell (1970)

Hayduk (1983)

Higashiyama and Ono (1988)

Finighan (1980)

Goldsmith and Hill (1986)

Caplan and Goldman (1981)

Sussman and Rosenfeld (1982)

Strube and Werner (1983)

Latane and Nida (1981)

Hern (1991)

Thompson et al. (1979)

Argyle and Dean (1965)

Smith and Knowles (1978)

Hediger (1955)

Kunzendorff and Denney (1982)

Winkel et al. (1988)

QUESTIONS

1. Do sex differences in interaction distance reflect sex roles?

2. Of what importance is the motive of the invader in personal space research?

3. Is *social distance* different than *personal space* as Sommer defines it?

4. What is the evidence that invasion of personal space is stressful?

5. How is interaction space influenced by density?

6. What is the relationship between interaction distance and good mental and emotional adjustment?

7. What is the relationship between interaction distance and mental illness?

8. What is the relationship between interaction distance and age?

9. What are the differences between Hediger's early observation of fight or flight distance and later research on personal space?

10. What uses could be made of personal space in the design of environments?

8

Territorial Behavior

Definition

The word *territory* has many meanings. It is any tract of land. It can be land or waters belonging to a state. In the United States, it is the name for an area not yet a state. It can be a thought, a sales district, and, finally, an area that an animal defends. It is this last meaning that has been the basis of much research and speculation in environment and behavior research. U.S. citizens in particular resonate to ideas of territoriality because of our cultural emphasis on private property.

Territory must be distinguished from personal space, privacy, and crowding. In the last chapter, we read that Sommer (1969a) defines *personal space* as an invisible bubble people carry around with them. Territory is a fixed, geographic space and therefore is separate from personal space although both may be defended when invaded. Territory is often, if not always, marked by boundaries that are discernable.

Privacy is defined by Altman (1975) as access to self. This can be visual, auditory, or even informational. Yet, privacy is essentially boundary-free. Yes, a person can feel a loss of privacy when territory is invaded, and in that sense the concepts overlap, but privacy is control over access that goes far beyond geographic boundaries to photographs, rumors, past events, even future events, and many other dimensions not contained in the concept of territory.

Crowding is, or can be, experienced if a person feels personal space has been invaded. Thus crowding is a special kind of invasion that relates to density as defined by cultures. And, of course, crowding can result in a loss of privacy. See the next chapter for a more full explication of crowding.

But definitions of territory and territorial behavior are not so easy to delineate. An understanding of animal territories will illustrate these difficulties.

Animal Studies

Ardrey (1966), a journalist, popularized territoriality through his best-seller *The Territorial Imperative*. Ardrey pointed out that many ideas about territory were stereotypes derived from observing just a few species. For example, most people writing about territorial behavior used examples of lonely males defending a piece of earth against mating rivals. In actuality, many species do not resemble this stereotype. Moor hens defend their territory as a pair. So do some gulls. And kob antelopes, after fighting each other, occupy a tuft of grass as an *arena* that is a territory for attracting females but that is not further defended. The kob simply ignores the other males when the female leaves to choose another. Bower birds in New Guinea build elaborate nests to attract females. The concept of an *arena* is to build or occupy some area and/or display to attract mates. This does not fit the stereotype of defense.

There are many other examples that also help to confuse the definition of territory. *Home range* is the area an animal may occupy in a year or a lifetime (Jewell, 1966). But the home range is related to density of animals and may or may not be defended. *Home range* can be the same as the hunting or grazing territory, which usually will be defended. Furthermore, the hunting or grazing territory changes with seasons. Many animals migrate to follow food growth from winter to summer or in rainy and dry seasons.

Nice (1941) describes seven types of territories just for birds:

Mating and nesting with feeding ground for young

Mating and nesting *without* feeding ground for young

Mating station only

Restricted only to the area surrounding the nest

Winter territories

Roosting territories

Collective command territories (added later by Carrick, 1963)

Ardrey points out that roe deer pair up *after* mating, which negates the concept of territory as exclusively for sex possession of females by the male. The grebe continues its defensive display long after nesting has taken place, which is another example of display not linked exclusively to mating.

Ardrey (1966) goes on to claim that one of the important functions of territory is to provide a *periphery*, a boundary, at which animals can congregate to vilify neighbors. Carpenter's (1934) study of howler monkeys "rendered obsolete the assumption that sex was the preoccupation of primates" (Ardrey, 1966, p. 213). Howlers love to congregate at borders with cacophonous results. Presumably, the integrating factor of primate life is defense of territory. This congregating at the periphery Ardrey calls a *noyau*. Then he goes on to describe Italy as a noyau, which makes one wonder if he was entirely serious.

Ardrey's conclusion is that human morality is so closely tied to territoriality that it is questionable whether morality is possible without territory. This follows the assumption that human behavior has an element of inherited territorial behavior. This assumption is far from accepted.

Another aspect of territorial behavior is *marking*. Most animals have some way of marking the boundaries of their territory so that other animals can detect the boundary. And, because most animals do not carry paint cans and brushes to put up signs, they mark with the only natural materials they possess: urine and feces or glandular secretions. Farley Mowat (1963), in his best-seller *Never Cry Wolf*, describes a charming scene where he unknowingly set up his tent in the territory of a wolf. The result of this intrusion was that the wolf constantly invaded the tent, sniffing out its contents and lavishly splashing it with urine. Mowat, no stranger to the ways of wolves, understood that the only way to stop these intrusions short of killing the wolf was to mark his own territory. This meant reinforcing himself with an unbelievable supply of tea to produce enough urine to mark the boundaries of his tent. Sure enough, once the wolf detected the human urine boundary, the intrusions stopped. Mowat had communicated to the wolf in a language the wolf could understand. Think about it campers, the next time you want to avoid animal intrusions.

Figure 8.1. Making the Best of It When the Bull Has You Down
I am indebted to Ayhan LeCompte for telling me about *La Querencia*. This phrase refers to the first place where the bull will go after he enters the ring. The bull will go to a spot and turn around or even sit down. Once the spot is selected, the bull fighter knows to get the bull *outside* the Querencia because inside he will fight much more intensely. Hence one of the secrets of fighting bulls is to closely watch for the selection of the Querencia and then instruct the *picadors* to force him outside. Of course, as the photo shows, it doesn't always work.

Human Homologues

The word *homologue* is used to describe human territorial behavior in recognition that there is no evidence that any of the human behavior described is inherited. A *homologue* is a near or partial similarity with no causal connection implied.

Home Range

Home range is not taken up by many researchers in relation to human behavior. Birdsell (1953) describes how the hunting-gathering territories of Australian Aboriginals were determined by the carrying capacity of the land. Dewar (1984) expands this carrying capacity of the land to mean that the energy available per unit of land space is the relative determiner of population density complicated by demographic and cultural factors. Thus home range is always closely connected with the amount of food available over a given territory but this is always complicated by human behavior. Barker (1968) describes the *behavioral range* of individuals in a community (see Chapter 10). The behavioral range is simply the number of behavior settings a person enters in a year. This is very similar to a home range except it includes entire behavior settings, not just the geographic space the individual occupies. Because behavior settings are standing patterns of behavior tied to specific places and times, these are literally all the behaviors a person engages in over a year, hence behavioral range. Behavioral range has usefulness (Bechtel, 1989) in describing a person's lifestyle and in making an individual aware of the amount of activity (or lack of it) in a given time frame.

Altman's Three Types

Altman (1975) is often quoted for his distinction of three types of human territories: *primary, secondary*, and *public*. Primary territories are those over which one has most control, such as one's own house. Primary territories are usually owned or, at least, the person feels a sense of ownership. Secondary territories are those that are more public but occupied exclusively for a time such as a favorite table at a tavern or a park bench one habitually occupies. Public territories are those one temporarily occupies such as a park or a table in a restaurant. If these are favorite or frequented with regularity, they become secondary territories.

Lee's Neighborhoods

Lee (1968, 1978) describes *neighborhoods* as the preferred territories of humans. Taylor (1988) sees the street block as the largest reference for human territoriality. The urban bias of these last two researchers is evident from the territorial problems ranchers have with the Bureau of Land Management, with the reactance of western states to the federal government in the "Sagebrush Rebellion" (White, 1991), or with the nationhood emphasis so often seen as a cause of war.[1]

Defensible Space

The term *defensible space* was first coined by Newman (1972). Essentially, this is a minitheory, which relies heavily on how a potential robber perceives a neighborhood, building, or any part of these. If the robber sees a place that has lots of *informal surveillance* and that has clear territorial markers, he will be deterred from going further in his intentions.

Newman describes four characteristics of defensible space: *territoriality*, as manifested by architectural barriers and markers; *surveillance*, as defined by what people can see from windows, or lines of sight; *image*, which is conveyed by architectural design, presence or absence of trash and vandalism, and evidence of maintenance; and *milieu*, which is the numbers and kinds of people and the frequency of their habitancy. This theory is not without its critics (Taylor, 1988) but continues to be applied (Cisneros, 1995; Moran & Dolphin, 1986) and seems to hang on (see Figure 8.2).

Newman's principles were applied to urban neighborhoods in St. Louis and Dayton, Ohio, and have been shown to successfully lower crime rates. The "claim" to the territories (streets) is operationalized by erecting iron gates across streets so that access is only through one gate and the visitor must completely retrace the route to leave. Presumably, the extra exposure discourages drug dealers and other criminals.

Brown and Altman (1983) found that houses robbed had less territorial displays than those not robbed. MacDonald and Gifford (1989) had convicted robbers assess photographs of houses as likely targets and found that surveillance was a reported deterrent but that highly marked territory was also an indication the owner had something worth stealing.

Perkins, Meeks, and Taylor (1992) tested the "disorder" thesis of Skogan (1990) and found that neighborhoods that were experiencing incivilities felt less capable of defending their territory, and this led to attracting more criminals. This thesis was upheld as a perceptual reality by their data.

Home Territories

Sebba and Churchman (1983) describe territories in the home. For children and teenagers, the bedroom is the *primary* territory (to borrow Altman's term). The authors define four areas:

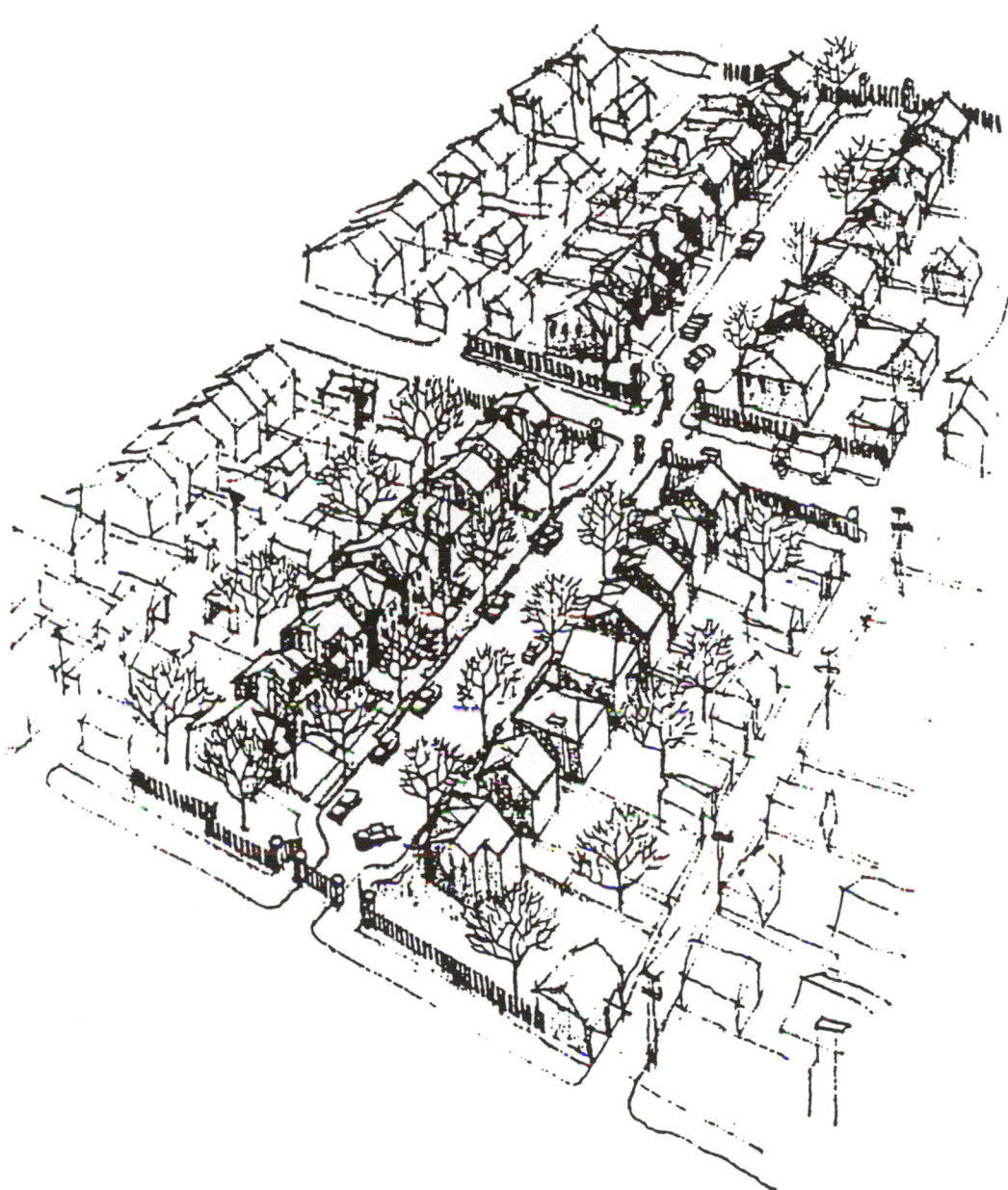

Figure 8.2. Aerial View of a Typical Set of Private Closed Streets in St. Louis, Missouri
SOURCE: Oscar Newman (1980) in Cisneros (1995).
NOTE: Street closures by residents have reduced crime and stabilized communities.

Figure 8.3. To Whom Does the House Belong?
SOURCE: Copyright © 1943 James Thurber. Copyright © 1971 Rosemary Thurber. From *Men, Women, and Dogs*, published by Harcourt Brace.

Individual: This type of area consists of bedrooms of a single child, the father's study.

Shared: This one consists of the parents' bedroom and all shared bedrooms.

Public: The living room was named by 96% of people interviewed, and this type also includes hallways, bathrooms.

Jurisdiction: The kitchen was named by 56% as primarily the mother's responsibility even though the whole family uses it.

Curiously, the one most left out of these territories is the father; 40% of the fathers felt nothing in the dwelling represented them (see Figure 8.3) while only 18% of the mothers felt that way. Sebba and Churchman point out that caring and being responsible for a particular area of the house is an important aspect of whether one feels control over it.

Personalization

Personalization is another human behavioral homologue often compared with marking a territory. All markings, however, are not personalization. Sommer (1969a) describes how library users mark their spaces in the library with books, jackets, sweaters, and other personal possessions. Strangely, however, these marked territories are almost never defended if someone (usually the psychologist's graduate student) takes them. Outside of psychology experiments, most people respect these markings.

Personalization usually refers to more than just marking. When a person moves into an office, the desk is immediately decorated with pictures, a name plate, or some other object that conveys personal possession of the occupant. Pictures are hung on the wall; books placed on the shelves (with art objects often among the bookshelves). Conversely, when a person leaves an office, these items are his or her responsibility to remove to make room for the next tenant, who will establish his or her possession with similar markings.

In every sense, these items of personalization are also a *display*. Although Ardrey (1966) and others may assert that humans are not *arena* animals, there is certainly no doubt that humans are indeed display oriented. As Joan Kron (1983) points out, U.S. culture is ashamed of admitting to material display, but, nevertheless, display is one of the hard facts of life. Ever since Thorstein Veblen's (1899) phrase *conspicuous consumption* characterized the material display of the upper classes, display of wealth has been an official part of our culture. Anthropologists (Rathje & Murphy, 1992) recognize that material goods are often the defining qualities of life, and have recently begun studying garbage to assess the castoffs of our affluent society.

But our society is not alone in material display. I remember well the hundred thousand dollar rugs and gold plates of my Iranian hosts (pre-Khomeini), and even the highly personalized doors of the lower classes (see Figure 8.4); the fine homes in India and Egypt amidst incredible poverty; and the chains of gold coins on women displaying family wealth in rural Turkey. It seems that most if not all cultures have display traditions.

I also recall the dismay of one of my Australian guests at my home on seeing I had Aboriginal artifacts on my coffee table. He acknowledged that he also had similar objects, but added with some feeling, "But we don't *display* them!" Australians are much closer to the taboo customs of the Aboriginals.

Display raises the important issue of purpose. Why do people display? Veblen (1899) had no problem with this, seeing it clearly as *dominance*.

Many animals have dominance displays. Sometimes these displays are physical threats as in the baboons' baring of teeth (Washburn & Devore, 1961), and wolves do much the same (Mowat, 1963). And it must be remembered that in most of the animal territories, it is the dominant

Figure 8.4. Personalized Doors in Iran

animal that gets to occupy the best territory, gets to mate, gets the best food. Territory and animal dominance are closely linked. Although in humans the analogue is much less physically threatening, it nevertheless can be intimidating. How do you feel when you see a Rolls Royce or a Bentley? No doubt it depends on your family income and perhaps even ethnic background. Few middle-class whites can understand the intimidation an urban black man might feel at the sight of such an automobile.

Strangely, as Sommer (1969a) noted, most humans do not defend their public territories. Ruback, Pape, and Doriot (1989) suggest the reason for this is that most field experiments are done with persons who are idle and not involved with some task. Ruback et al. did five experiments with callers at public telephone booths. Under these circumstances, subjects vigorously defended their public territories, and Ruback et al. conclude that people will defend "specific public territories and will continue to do what they have been doing before they are threatened by an intruder" (p. 232).

Box 8.1

When a rich corporation, which will remain unnamed, decided to build its corporate quarters in a large city, it hired a world-renowned architect, also unnamed, who agreed with the president and the board of directors that the design of the new building would be "pure," that is, no pictures or personal items on display.

Once the building was complete, the employees noted that although they could not decorate, the office of the president had cabinets to display his antique clock collection.

A campaign of vandalism began that did not end until the management had to relent and allow personalization. The question remains: Had it not been for the president's lapse, would the attempt to have a "pure" design without personalization have succeeded?

One of the most vivid displays of wealth was not in Beverly Hills or Buckingham Palace but at one time was in the homes of the Kwakiutl Indians of the Northwest Coast of North America. Their culture developed a ceremony known as the potlatch (Benedict, 1959) at which the invited guest would be seated and the host would proceed to destroy by fire as great a number as possible of blankets, coppers, and other items of wealth. The guest would sit in agony knowing that it would next be his turn to play host and that to save face he would have to burn up an even greater number of valuable items. Here is a display that would put even the wealthiest U.S. citizen to shame.

Possessions

The relationship of possessions, that is, physical objects, to territoriality in humans has been considered at some depth by Csikszentmihalyi and Rochberg-Halton (1981) and Rochberg-Halton (1984).[2] Rochberg-Halton surveyed 82 three-generational families comprising 315 individuals and catalogued the significant material objects in their lives (see Table 8.1). What was surprising was the few differences between social classes and the regularity of change of objects over the life span. Children

Table 8.1 Special Objects Mentioned at Least Once by Respondents of Three Generations

Children (N = 79)	Percent Mentioned	Parents (N = 150)	Percent Mentioned	Grandparents (N = 86)	Percent Mentioned
1. Stereos	45.6	1. Furniture	38.1	1. Photos	37.2
2. TV	36.7	2. Visual Art	36.7	2. Furniture	33.7
3. Furniture	32.9	3. Sculpture	26.7	3. Books	25.6
4. Musical Instruments	31.6	4. Books	24.0	4. TV	23.3
5. Beds	29.1	5. Musical Instruments	22.7	5. Visual Art	22.1
6. Pets	24.1	6. Photos	22.1	6. Plates	22.1
7. Miscellaneous	20.3	7. Plants	19.3	7. Sculpture	17.4
8. Sports Equipment	17.7	8. Stereos	18.0	8. Appliances	15.1
9. Collectibles	17.7	9. Appliances	17.3	9. Miscellaneous	15.1
10. Books	15.2	10. Miscellaneous	16.7	10. Plants	12.8
11. Vehicles	12.7	11. Plates	14.7	11. Collectibles	11.6
12. Radios	11.4	12. Collectibles	12.0	12. Silverware	10.5
13. Refrigerators	11.4	13. TV	11.3	13. Musical Instruments	10.5
14. Stuffed Animals	11.4	14. Glass	11.4	14. Weavings	10.5
15. Clothes	10.1	15. Jewelry	11.3	15. Whole Room	10.5
16. Photos	10.1				

SOURCE: Rochberg-Halton (1984).

would pick "ego-centric" objects that were action oriented such as stereos (46% actually chose stereo sets), while as one goes up the age scale objects become more contemplative until at old age the objects were photographs and other memorabilia (37% of grandparents chose photographs). Almost half of these objects are in the bedroom for children (aged 8-14), then they migrate outside the bedroom in adulthood (only 11%), and then come back into the bedroom in old age (24%).

Winnicott (1958) introduced the concept of the transitional object, which Rochberg-Halton amplified. A *transitional object* is one a person takes from one environment to another. One of the most famous transitional objects was Dorothy's dog "Toto" from the *Wizard of Oz*. Many college students will take some transitional object from home to college and place it in the college dorm room. This object is not necessarily displayed because it represents home to the individual and helps soften the contrast between one place and another. Rochberg-Halton's theory of the use of objects concerns how they help define identity. His theory takes off from the more Freudian interpretations of symbols such as "breast substitute" for transitional objects to considering the object as very similar to what serves as a *role model*.

Rochberg-Halton claims a person has conscious or unconscious dialogues with these special objects and that they serve to help define the self. It is much like the American Indian customs of having a vision and choosing a name from that vision.

Kron (1983) emphasizes that these transactions between self and object always involve at least a third party who must affirm what the person intends the object(s) to mean. Often these third parties are parents and friends. A great day in the life of a young person is when the parents first come to visit the new home. Even elder people invite friends to a housewarming party to celebrate new decorations. A part of every social visit is the toting out (if they are not already on display) of the sacred objects of identity. This ceremony may not come until the visitor is trusted not to ridicule or disapprove the intended meaning of the objects.

Conclusions

The studies of human homologues to territorial behavior are rich and various. So far there is no evidence that any of this behavior is inherited. Yet, as many researchers point out, the use of spaces organizes human behavior and allows a multitude of tasks to be performed without inter-ference. Furthermore, the richness of human spaces and possessions seems to be closely tied to the process of developing identity. Having one's own space is as important to children growing up as it is to the elderly and the parents of children. Perhaps territoriality can be seen as part of a privacy management mechanism via Altman's (1975) model. Or it may be merely a culturally defined way of distancing via Hall's proxemics, which is extended to geography in addition to spaces between people. Whichever view one takes, it would seem premature to fix on any one explanation at this time.

Notes

1. "Is it a false sense of human history which teaches us that nationalism is still the strongest force in the world, stronger than the hydrogen bomb and stronger than humanity?" (quoted from Dyson, 1984, p. 19, referring to Oppenheimer's questions about the atom bomb and its possible dangers).

2. Lee (1968) defines *neighborhood* as a synthesis of *physical objects*, social relation-ships, and space, so it must be remembered that objects and space definitions are not exclusive of each other.

GOALS

Definitions and Concepts

Privacy

Territory

Home range

Marking

Behavioral range

Primary, secondary, public
  territories

Home territories

Arena

Transitional object

Defensible space

Informal surveillance, disorder
  thesis

Personalization

Carrying capacity

Display

Noyau

Objects as role models

Important Studies

Altman (1975)

Veblen (1899)

Sommer (1969a)

Taylor (1988)

Brown (1987)

QUESTIONS

1. What is the evidence that humans defend territory?

2. How do the concepts of territory, privacy, and personal space differ?

3. How does display differ from territorial marking?

4. What is a home range?

5. How does home range differ from hunting territory?

6. What is a behavioral range?

7. How do possessions of older persons differ from those of younger persons?

8. What is the connection between territory and identity?

9. What is the connection between territory and environmental pollution or destruction?

10. Are wars caused by defense of territories?

9

Crowding

Figure 9.1 is a picture of participants in the civil rights demonstration called the March on Washington in April 1963. Are these people experiencing crowding?

Definition

Yakov Epstein (1981) claims there were over 200 studies of crowding in the 1970s. What became evident from these studies was the conflicting definitions used. The most obvious definition of crowding was number of persons per square unit of space. This was called *density*. The difficulty with such a simple definition is that it runs up against the *Hong Kong* problem.

Hong Kong is a British Crown colony leased from China and about to revert to China when the lease runs out in 1997. It occupies only 398 square miles on the southeast coast of China and has become legendary for its high density. In 1960, only one Standard Metropolitan Statistical Area (SMSA) in the United States had a higher density than Hong Kong (Jersey City). Today this is no longer true; U.S. SMSAs have lost population to the suburbs while Hong Kong continued to grow in population.

Figure 9.1. Crowd at the Base of the Washington Monument During the March on Washington, April 1963

However, the density of housing in Hong Kong is concentrated in a small space with most of the land unused (see Figure 9.2).

The housing consists of high-rise buildings (Figure 9.3). These buildings have 10 persons in 400 square feet of space compared with the American Public Health Association recommendation of 85 square feet per person (Mitchell, 1971). Mitchell found no evidence of deficits in emotional health related to such density. For persons who lived above the sixth floor, in households that contained two or more unrelated families, however, there was evidence of emotional illness and hostility.

Because it is the custom among the poor to share apartments with one or more families to be able to afford the rent, it is the norm for these apartments to hold two, sometimes three families. What Mitchell found was an interaction between height and presence of unrelated families. Thus it is incorrect to say that Chinese living in Hong Kong can all tolerate conditions that would be intolerable to Westerners.

But it is nevertheless true that, for some reason, Chinese living below the sixth floor with strangers, and even above the sixth floor with

Figure 9.2. Hong Kong Island Showing Open Land

Figure 9.3. High-Rise Housing in Hong Kong

relatives, *can* tolerate conditions that would be unacceptable for people in the United States, Europe, and many other countries. If density is to be a viable definition of crowding, it must be a constant and unvarying cause of crowding and not be unpredictably variable from place to place.

Many authors distinguish *social density* from *spatial density* (Baum & Paulus, 1987; Bell et al., 1990). Social density is critical to understand because it refers to number of persons in a confined space and usually results in unwanted interactions with persons. It is this concept of large numbers of uncontrollable interactions that forms the basis for many theories of crowding.

Spatial density refers to the way the physical space itself can feel crowded because it is too small to accommodate even a small number of people. Chalsa Loo (1992) noted that a number of her Chinatown informants reported feeling crowded even though they lived alone. This is an excellent example of spatial density.

Crowding is also defined as the *experience* (Stokols, 1976) of too many people present, meaning that the same situation may be experienced as not crowded.

A third form of crowding is often not dealt with in either field or environmental studies. This is physical constraints. For example, many people report not using seat belts in automobiles because they feel "crowded" by them. In this form of crowding perception, the individual may actually have enough space and not be pressed by unwanted social interactions but nevertheless feel crowded because of physical restraints in the environment.

To consider these three physical conditions with the proposition that each situation can have one to all three interacting and be experienced as either crowded or not, the logical possibilities are pictured in Figure 9.4.

But these three variables refer only to physical properties of the setting. The individual who moves into the setting carries a set of *predisposing attributes* as well.

Predisposing Attributes

Culture

The Hong Kong problem makes definition from density alone very difficult. The way most authors get around this problem is to say that density is defined by culture, that Hong Kong tolerates a higher density

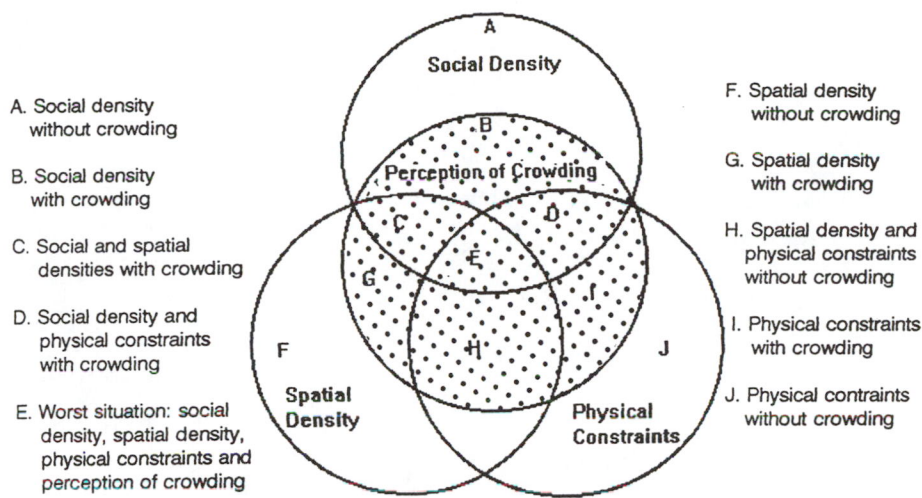

A. Social density
   without crowding

B. Social density
   with crowding

C. Social and spatial
   densities with crowding

D. Social density and
   physical constraints
   with crowding

E. Worst situation: social
   density, spatial density,
   physical constraints and
   perception of crowding

F. Spatial density
   without crowding

G. Spatial density
   with crowding

H. Spatial density and
   physical constraints
   without crowding

I. Physical constraints
   with crowding

J. Physical contraints
   without crowding

Figure 9.4. The Ten Situations of Crowding From Three Variables

than the United States, but that both places suffer stress from crowding in the context of their own culture. Thus culture is a predisposing attribute to crowding that each person within a culture carries as part of that culture. All this does not mean that the people in Hong Kong did not *feel* crowded. Indications are they did, but it did not produce the same severity of outcome that would occur in a Western culture.

Prior Experience

Booth (1976) found that men who grew up in Toronto in crowded households were less likely to experience stress-related diseases under conditions of high social density than those raised in less dense households. Similar results were found by Sundstrom (1978) and Nagar, Pandey, and Paulus (1988). This means that even within the culture, the tolerance for crowding varies according to early exposure. It becomes even more difficult to define crowding if the people within a culture are going to vary in their reactions to crowding.

Motivation

Helmreich (1974) studied aquanauts under extremely cramped and obtrusive conditions. The aquanauts had to live in a frustrating, noisy,

Figure 9.5. The Tektite Lab

humid environment with unusual conditions such as everyone sounding like Donald Duck because of the helium atmosphere. Nevertheless, under these seemingly intolerable conditions, the aquanauts performed work at a level higher than their normal workload. The reason was that these career-oriented professionals were highly motivated. The experience was seen as an important step in career advancement and as a justification for their special status as aquanauts.

The predisposing attributes of crowding are culture, prior experience, and motive. The setting conditions are discussed in the next section.

Box 9.1

**Why Motivation Is Such an
Important Variable in Crowding:
The Peace Corps Study**

MacDonald and Oden (1973) divided two groups of Peace Corps volunteers (five married couples each) into a hotel residence group and another group who lived in a 30′ × 30′ room. The "crowded" group had barely enough room to pitch tents and sleep separately. These were all young couples with normal desires. The frustration level was high.

When the 12-week training period was over, the hotel group rated themselves significantly below the crowded group in enhanced marital relations and tended to pick members of the crowded group as socioemotional leaders.

Contrary to expectations, the crowded group did not show any decrement in academic or language-learning settings.

The crowded group also expressed more regret at having to leave their quarters.

These results are exactly opposite of what anyone would have predicted. But, similar to the aquanauts, Peace Corps people are highly motivated and will tolerate extreme conditions.

MacDonald and Oden attributed these results to a theory of adaptive cognition.

Setting Conditions

Behavior

Fleming, Baum, and Weiss (1987) found density to be even more complicated when they compared two areas of equal residential density and found a difference in crowding perception due to differences produced from the presence of stores. The area where there were more stores reported more perceptions of crowding and less ability to regulate social interactions. What is important to realize here is that both areas compared were of equal density by the usual methods of measurement. Yet the presence of stores produced a greater perception of crowding because of the greater flow of people. Hence the behavior of the people also influences perceived density. People moving around makes the setting seem more crowded than people standing.

Social Density

Although relative to cultural definitions, high density is an assumed feature of crowded settings. Some studies involve the social density of residential settings (Wilner, Walkley, Pinkerton, & Tayback, 1962) while others artificially manipulate social density in laboratory settings (Baldassare & Fisher, 1976).

Physical Constraints

Physical constraints interfere with the ability to perform tasks. Seat belts are a good example. Some people feel that seat belts interfere with the task of driving by impeding their movements. Another example is being unable to use the telephone because there are too many coins in the slot.

Physical constraints on persons in a setting are the second physical feature that can produce the perception of crowding.

Organization

Wener and Kaminoff (1983) demonstrated that the perceived crowding in a setting is highly influenced by the way the setting is organized. They took a visiting room at a prison and decreased the perceived crowding by putting up signs that gave participants a better sense of order.

Thus the setting aspects that contribute to crowding are behavior, density, physical and spatial constraints, and organization. When the predisposing attributes that a person brings to the setting interact with the setting conditions, a complex situation arises in which all factors can interact to alleviate or exacerbate the perception of crowding.

Many theoretical approaches (Stokols, 1976) see crowding as that which is experienced under several of the above circumstances. Others feel these elements interact to produce stress, loss of control, or stimulus overload as intermediary variables to pathology. For example, a person entering a high social density situation with certain predisposing attributes might experience stress due to perceived crowding while another person with different attributes and/or different setting variables might not experience crowding.

Box 9.2

Freedman's Bombshell

Jonathan Freedman did a series of studies on crowding and wrote a book titled *Crowding and Behavior* (1975). The research world of crowding was shocked when Freedman suggested that crowding was not the villain portrayed in current research. He cited a series of studies in which he placed subjects in crowded conditions to determine whether the crowding would have an effect on the performance of various tasks. The results showed no effect of crowding.

Freedman claimed researchers were exaggerating the effects of the animal studies (Calhoun, 1962) and making extrapolations to human behavior that were not justified.

Were Freedman's results obtained because of motivation? Had he uncovered the artificial conditions described by Baldassare and Fisher (1976)? Or were the results of other studies in error?

The effect of the bombshell on crowding research was not detectable despite the credibility of Freedman's data.

Freedman attributed the effects of crowding to the *intensification hypothesis*. Whatever the prevailing mood or circumstance, crowding would intensify it. If people were having a good time, crowding would make them have a better time. If they were bored, crowding would make it more so.

It should be clear by now that measures of density alone cannot always produce the experience of crowding. The reader should now have some feeling for the complications involved in trying to come to a conclusion about whether crowding causes pathology. Perception of crowding can depend on the complex interaction of what the person brings to the situation and the physical and behavioral aspects of the situation over time.

There are many views of the way to study crowding (Evans & Lepore, 1992). Some emphasize the larger populations of an ecosystem or species or human populations in cities or nations (Faris & Dunham, 1939). Others focus on smaller segments of human or animal situations and either observe behavior in the field or create laboratory circumstances (Calhoun, 1962).

There are two traditions of research that cut across all these: animal studies and correlational studies.

Animal Studies

Just as in territorial studies in the previous chapter, crowding studies have a tradition of animal subjects. The most influential in recent times was by John Calhoun (1962). Through a series of studies, Calhoun tried to unravel the changes in behavior that overpopulation causes. First, he placed a colony of wild Norway rats in a quarter-acre enclosure with an abundance of food and lots of places to live and observed that they stabilized at a population of 150 rather than the 5,000 that would seem "normal." The reason was clear: The young rats died in great numbers. Calhoun tried to find out why.

In another series of six studies with an albino strain of Norway rats, he attempted the same experiment under more controlled conditions. This time it became apparent why the young rats were dying. As the population increased, the numbers of animals were such that they interfered with the female rats as they tried to reproduce and raise young. The females stopped building adequate nests and neglected the young, not feeding them properly so they died of starvation.

These and other changes in behavior Calhoun called the *behavioral sink*, which he defined as the outcome of any behavioral process that collects animals together in unusually great numbers. The central concept of the behavioral sink is the purposeful collecting together of animals for its own sake, to be "sociable." In other words, by actual social density count, the conditions *are not* crowded. There is ample room for the animals to feed, drink, mate, and so on. But they congregate together in a central space because they have learned this behavior from a proximity that does not normally exist in nature.

The elements of a behavioral sink all derive from the greater numbers of animals in an abnormal social situation. The daily behaviors of eating, drinking, and sleeping become socially oriented so that the animals tend to congregate together, abandoning other elements of the environment, and making the congestion even worse.

In Calhoun's study, the rats would gather to eat at one pen even although others were available and unused. This made it impossible for all to be present at once. The dominant animals would attack the less dominant and drive them off. These attacks produced a group who would stop trying, the "withdrawns." The withdrawns tended to become either passive or hyperactive probers. The passives would tend to eat or drink only when others were not around. The probers became pansexual and cannibalistic, trying to mate with anything and eating the abandoned pups.

The bulk of the population tried to eat in a single pen while the passives (males and females) avoided them and the probers circled and intruded from adjacent pens. Dominant males tended to collect a harem of females and sit at the passageway leading to the section of the pen they occupied. These "sultan" rats tolerated some of the hyperactives because they did not challenge their dominance. The passives ended up as the "beautiful people" because they did not get in fights and had the best coats of hair.

The temptation to anthropomorphize and attribute these activities to human behavior is just as strong in the crowding studies as it was in the territorial studies. We see humans who seem all too readily to fit into stereotypes of "sultans," "beautiful people," "hyperactives," and "passives." But on closer examination, the etiology seems different. When we think of beautiful people, they are usually more active and outgoing, and passives seem anything but beautiful.

But it is well to consider the ultimate behavior that Calhoun's studies produced. Many reviewers and compilers of crowding studies ignore the later studies that Calhoun felt were the most important.

In a study called "Death Squared," Calhoun (1973) repeated some of his conditions but used mice instead of rats. By 700 days, the colony had stopped breeding and was essentially dead.

This process occurs when the behavioral sink interferes with behavior: All young are prematurely rejected by their mothers and never develop adequate affection bonds. Reproduction slows and then stops, and the remaining mice die of old age. In short, the behavioral sink has interfered with the passing on of proper birthing and raising of young from one generation to the next. When this occurs, even though mice are placed in new, "normal" environments, they fail to reproduce.

Whether the rats learned their maternal behavior from others and the behavioral sink interfered with it, or the instinctive maternal behavior was unlearned or replaced by new "social" learning, the results are the same: There is a failure to transmit the behavior necessary to reproduce the species.

These results seem devastating if literally translated to larger animals like humans. They predict the death of any species if subjected to similar conditions. Calhoun (1976) warns that "if at any time you know how many years it has taken for the world to double its size—it will take only that number of years more before the world population may be subject to an ultimate pathology like that experienced by our mice" (p. 4).

What is the evidence for this? When Christian, Flyger, and Davis (1960) did the Sika deer study, the deer were isolated on an island and the experiment did not continue long enough to determine whether population death would occur. The human population has actually doubled since Calhoun's experiments, and some might say that urban migration is a sign of the behavioral sink, and urban gangs, the behavioral pathology. Yet, since 1980, urban areas in the United States, and since 1990, urban areas in other countries, are actually losing population.

For human conditions to approximate those of Calhoun's experiments, the physical limits of Earth would have to be reached so that all humans would be forced into a behavioral sink. We add 92 million per year. It is possible.

Correlational Studies

In their classic report, Park and Burgess (1925) saw urban life as "subversive and disorganizing" to our traditional culture. This theme has been picked up by the correlational studies. Faris and Dunham (1939), for example, found a "definite linking" of specific mental disorders to specific physical environments in the city. For example, paranoid schizophrenia was linked to rooming house districts, manic-depression to higher rent districts, and so on.

Studies like these were found to suffer from a series of problems of interpretation called *ecological fallacies* (Dogan & Rokkan, 1969). The study assumed that because the crowding and pathological condition existed in the same place (ecology), they were linked causally when some other factor such as poor economic conditions could explain the cause.

Wilner et al. (1962) reviewed 40 selected studies and came to much the same conclusion: Social economic conditions could explain the linkage of crowding with pathology. They proceeded to select two large urban poverty samples, matched them for socioeconomic conditions, and moved the test group into improved (public) housing from a slum. They then followed the two samples for 10 years. Their results were not simple correlations between poor health and the slum or between better housing and better health, but were a mix between age and sex groups.

For example, schoolchildren seemed to benefit from moving to better housing because they had fewer problems that kept them from school. Hence, because they attended school more, they did better in school than those who stayed behind in the slum. Similarly, males under 20 showed better health records in the test group than those left in the slums, but communicative diseases in both sexes at the 20-34 age group were no different than in the test group or the slum. There were fewer accidents in the newer housing.

A problem with the Wilner study is that public housing ages quickly and the "new" housing of the test group soon became the ghetto of public housing known today. Furthermore, the Wilner study actually was a housing study that did not control for social or spatial density.

Other, and more recent, studies have failed to find effects of good or poor housing as opposed to other variables. For example, Ruback and Pandey (1991) found that household density had few effects on health in a study done in India. Yeung (1977) found no relationships between crowding, high-rise housing, and pathology. Kirmeyer (1978) agrees with this and so does Choldin (1978). But still other studies—Giel and Ormel (1977), McCarthy and Saegert (1978), Gove, Hughes, and Galle (1979) —do find some relationships between residential crowding and social pathology.

The Midtown Manhattan study (Srole et al., 1975) reported a high level of mental impairment for a high-density urban area, but Leighton (1959) established the fact that mental impairment was not exclusively an urban phenomenon. His study of rural Nova Scotia showed a similarly high incidence of mental illness.

More recent studies of the effects of housing such as Evans, Palsane, Lepore, and Martin (1989) stress the social support system as a mediator of the isolating effects of crowding. The urban areas may be crowded, but if the social support system is available, it helps ameliorate the effects of crowding. This agrees with Robins's (1966) earlier finding that the friend-family system helps alleviate juvenile delinquency. In a similar fashion, Homma (1990) sees these same social density forces as diminishing the traditional coping strategies of the Japanese.

Notice that the correlational studies focus more on immediate relationships between physical conditions and poor health while Calhoun emphasized more the long-term effects of failure to transmit behavior essential to the survival of the species. Even though there is plenty of seeming social pathology in the rats and mice, the end result of species death is the most important finding. The main body of rats and mice were not actually so pathological in their behavior. The pathological behavior was more in the withdrawn and reactive animals. It was the social gathering together of the main body of animals that taught them to be together and that therefore interfered with the essential birthing and rearing tasks. This does not imply the animals had to be sick for the species to die. The failure to attend to birthing and rearing killed the mouse colony.

By contrast, the correlational studies assume it is the social pathology that is the direct and most important result of crowding. In all fairness, however, it should be pointed out that the earlier studies such as Park and Burgess (1925) did emphasize the loss of traditions. They did not have the insight from the later animal studies that loss of certain behaviors (traditions?) could lead to species death.

Theories of Crowding

Stokols (1976) first posited the concept that crowding had to be *experienced* before the harmful effects could result. Models since that time have emphasized both the conditions of crowding in the setting and the variables that could modify or increase the experience of crowding. Evans and Lepore (1992) in their review of crowding research point out that many studies have failed to distinguish between those variables such as personal control that acted as a *moderator* of crowding as compared with those studies that emphasized *mediators* of crowding such as behavioral constraints. Moderators tend to influence the perception of crowding or lessen its effects. They don't explain the effects of crowding. Mediators such as behavioral constraints, however, tend to try to explain *how* crowding works its negative effect by interfering with behavior.

Thus Evans and Lepore would posit a model like the one in Figure 9.6. Such a model helps to clarify that some variables should be understood as moderating crowding while others help to explain its cause, but the evidence is more complicated. For example, the tendency to see the world as controllable or uncontrollable, as measured by Rotter's (1966) I-E scale, can be seen as a predisposing variable, and hence as a moderator of crowding conditions. On the other hand, a setting can be objectively confusing and uncontrollable, which produces loss of control in most

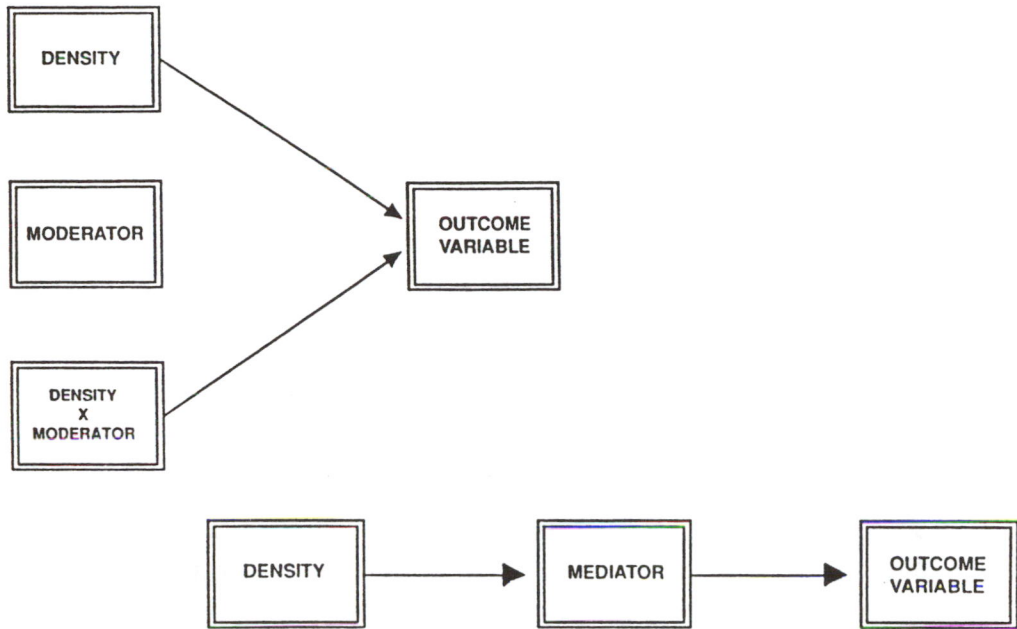

Figure 9.6. Moderator and Mediator Variables and Crowding
SOURCE: Reprinted by permission of Academic Press.

people, which acts as a mediator to stress. Thus control can be both moderator and mediator depending on whether it is predisposing or a quality of the setting. Furthermore, the outcome variables in most of the human laboratory and correlational studies have been short term (less than one generation), aimed at measuring more immediate negative results such as mental or physical illness. Very few have considered the long-term (multigenerational) outcomes emphasized by Calhoun. Therefore, a more inclusive model would take all these elements into account (see Figure 9.7).

It is important to understand from this model how short-term outcomes may or may not be related to long-term outcomes, which include traditional culture and species death. These may or may not be related to the pathologies measured as short-term outcomes. Although short-term outcomes such as communicable disease and mental illness may sound devastating in their own right, they are not necessary for long-term outcomes to occur. In other words, the human race could go, if not happily, at least somewhat placidly toward species and/or cultural death.

On the other hand, the short-term outcomes could easily be the cause or mediators of the long-term outcomes. The mental illness, stress, and

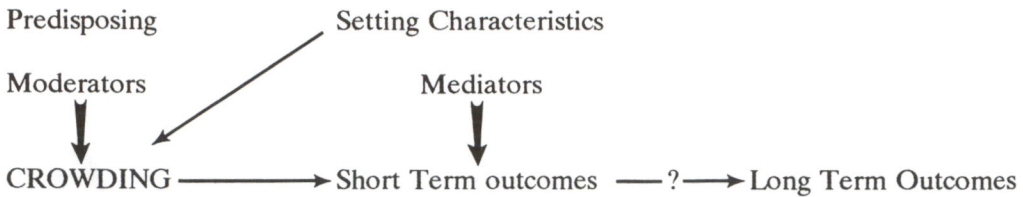

Figure 9.7. Crowding Model

malaise of the times could directly bring about the loss of culture (Lerner, 1958).

What are some of these mediators that tend to explain the effects of crowding? Evans and Lepore (1992) name *behavioral constraints, control,* and *overload/arousal* as the three most commonly used in crowding studies.

Behavioral constraints occur when experienced crowding interferes with any task a person or group may be doing. The negative outcome comes from being blocked from accomplishing that task. Presumably, being interfered with on one task at one time is not going to produce lasting negative effects, but being interfered with over time will produce frustration, depression, or anger, which eventually can lead to mental or physical illness or both. It is important to realize that no studies have followed this process to a long-term outcome.

Control, as has been pointed out, can be either a predisposing variable in the person or a condition of the setting.

Overload/arousal models see crowding as overwhelming the sensory or adaptive capacity, or being aroused so strongly that it causes undue stress. Either is essentially a stress model.

All three of these models fit under either the moderator or the mediator designation. Control is the only model seen as both moderator and mediator. Both behavioral constraint and overload/arousal are explanations of why crowding results in a negative outcome.

Practical Effects of Crowding

Socially dense, short-term situations can produce a variety of responses in people. Increased heart rate and blood pressure were found by Evans (1979a), D'Atri (1981), and Fleming et al. (1987). Sweating was found by Aiello, Epstein, and Karlin (1975) and Cox, Paulus, McCain, and Karlovac

(1982). Sickness of various kinds was found to be associated with socially dense situations by Stokols, Ohlig, and Resnick (1975), Baron, Mandel, Adams, and Griffen (1976), and Dean, Pugh, and Gunderson (1975, 1978). Freedman and Perlick (1979), in support of his intensification hypothesis, found that laughter was more contagious under crowded conditions.

But the most significant effects of crowding were found to be with children. Rodin (1976) found that crowded, lower-class children showed higher levels of learned helplessness and were competitive even when this meant they would lose rewards. It was found earlier that scarcity of resources as exists among poor children increases the likelihood of competitive behavior and that lower class children are therefore at greater risk. This is supported by Jouriles, Bourg, and Farris (1991) and Stone, Fitzgerald, and Kinsella (1990). Liddell and Kruger (1989) find that children from crowded homes are most susceptible, and Zuravin (1986) uncovers evidence that child neglect and abuse is related to crowded homes.

Thus, although crowding is a complex issue with many ramifications in theory and method, the "bottom line" seems to be that children and especially lower-class children are the ones most affected.

Next most affected by crowding are those in prison. A whole host of studies find a relationship between crowding and various pathologies in prison: Ganjavi, Schell, Cachon, and Poporino (1985), Paulus (1991), Wener and Keys (1988), Supancic (1988), Schaeffer, Baum, Paulus, and Gaes (1988), Poporino (1986), Ekland-Olson (1986), Ruback, Carr, and Hopper (1986), Cox, Paulus, and McCain (1984), Ruback and Carr (1984), Paulus and McCain (1983), Gibbs (1983), Paulus, McCain, and Cox (1978), and Megargee (1977). Much of this comes from placing three persons in cells intended for two or one and the various other strategies used to accommodate the high numbers of people the United States puts in prisons (see Chapter 16).

Finally, males seem to be more sensitive to overcrowding than females. Wachs (1979) claims proper male development from childhood is dependent on noncrowded situations. Males seem especially bothered in situations such as lines (Insel & Lindgren, 1978).

But Burch et al. (1978) found females are more anxious in crowded conditions than males. Patterson et al. (1979) claim this is because females react more to mixed-sex situations. Aiello et al. (1981) found that females seem to be affected more than males in crowded dormitories because they spend much more time there than the males. These contradictory findings indicate that much of the confusion results from failure to specify the situations and compare them across studies. At this time, we will have to be satisfied with the conclusion that some situations of crowding seem to affect men more than women while others affect women more than men.

There are some practical findings on crowding, at least from dormitory studies. Valins and Baum (1973) and Baum and Koman (1976) found that students who lived in suites rather than in rooms off long corridors had fewer perceptions of crowding, seemingly because there were fewer unwanted interactions. They also found that cooperative atmospheres produced less crowded perceptions while competition exacerbated the perception of crowding.

Conclusions

Despite much confusion over definitions of crowding, most studies use a social density concept of too many persons per unit of space even though this may be defined differently in different cultures and situations and even though the perception of crowding may differ among individuals.

The animal studies of Calhoun emphasized the harmful nature of long-term multigenerational effects of high social density while nearly all other studies, even when called "long term," looked at effects well within a single generation. The housing studies came up with questionable results due to the ecological fallacy. Laboratory studies emphasized short-term variables that seemed to have most measurable effects with children.

Theories of crowding have emphasized mediator effects, which modify the situation or conditions, and moderators, which change the perception. The finding, across dormitories and children, that competitiveness exacerbates perceived crowding and its effects is significant because it underlines the earlier criticism of the tragedy of the commons, that is, if our society were more cooperative, there would be less of a problem in the way we treat the environment. Put another way, competition makes us less tolerant of one another and less considerate of the environment.

SOURCE: *Ziggy* © 1995 *Ziggy and Friends, Inc.* Distributed by *Universal Press Syndicate*. Reprinted with permission. All rights reserved.

GOALS

Definitions and Concepts

Density

Social density

Spatial density

Physical constraints

Behavioral sink

Intensification hypothesis

Ecological fallacy

The Hong Kong problem

Moderators

Mediators

Predisposing conditions

Setting conditions

Order (Wener & Kaminoff, 1983)

Important Studies

Mitchell (1971)

Freedman (1975)

MacDonald and Oden (1973)

Helmreich (1974)

Rodin (1976)

Faris and Dunham (1939)

Wilner et al. (1962)

QUESTIONS

1. Are there signs of a behavioral sink in some human populations?

2. What are the most crowded conditions you have experienced?

3. How would you react in the conditions of the Peace Corps study?

4. What accounts for the recent population loss in the cities?

5. Where do you stand on the issue of population control?

6. Why are there so many high-rise buildings if people don't want to live in them?

7. Are there more than 10 situations of crowding from the three most prominent variables?

8. What is the connection between urban crowding and pathology?

9. Who are the people most affected by crowding?

10. What is the relationship between culture, crowding, and upbringing?

10

Ecological Psychology

In July 1947, Roger Barker and Herbert Wright of the University of Kansas at Lawrence founded the Midwest Psychological Field Station at the town of Oskaloosa about 25 miles northwest of Lawrence. Both men were child psychologists and their purpose was to find a town small enough that they could observe all the influences on children as they grew up.

Their first research involved learning to observe children with as little contaminating influence on their behavior as possible. They followed the children from their homes into the community and school and observed and recorded whatever happened.

This might sound rather obtrusive. What child is not going to be influenced by an adult standing around with a clipboard, attentive to every move? Yet, it was found that after a period of adjustment, the children learned to ignore the observer just as they would a piece of furniture. Such adjustment did not take place without parental cooperation and preparation. The parents explained to the child what was going to happen and told them to ignore the observer. Of course, as everyone knew, the children did not. But, after the observer would refuse to interact or answer the child's questions, the child eventually gave up and started on his or her round of activities, observer trailing behind.

Figure 10.1. Observing and Recording Child Behavior
SOURCE: Photograph by Paul Gump (which previously appeared in *Environment and Behavior,* Vol. 22, page 447); reprinted by permission.

Observation was exhausting. After about 20 minutes, the writing would get blurred and the activities would start to scramble. Two or more observers would act as a team and spell each other (Figure 10.1)

This technique of recording children's behavior was called collecting *specimen records* (Figure 10.2). These were specimens of behavior taken from the natural environment just as a physician takes a specimen from

8. Making own bed	7:03. Mary came back to her room.
	She seemed more purposeful.
	She took the two pillows off her double bed.
	Then she smoothed out the sheet and pulled up the covers on that side.
	She walked around to the other side and smoothed out the sheet and pulled up the covers on that side.
	She put the pillows on and pulled the spread over the pillows.
	7:04. After Mary got it fixed, she stood back and looked at her bed critically. It didn't suit her.
	She went back and pulled the spread over farther and smoothed it.
	She then went around again to the other side and straightened the spread over the pillows.
	The end result, from an adult point of view, was just fair. There were some wrinkles in the spread, particularly over the pillows.
	Mary stopped, looked at it again critically, and was apparently satisfied.
	7:05 She went into the kitchen.
9. Remarking about mother's apron	Noticing her mother wearing her apron, she chuckled and said, "Oh, Mommie, a big person like you in my tiny apron."
	Her mother said, "Yes, I know, but that is all I could find."

Figure 10.2. Specimen Record
SOURCE: Barker et al. (1978).

a living creature. Barker's philosophy of science was to collect data without interfering with it and without a preconceived notion of how the data should fit into a theory. This was a radical approach. Most psychologists collect data to confirm a theory. Barker calls this being an *operator*. When an operator has a theory, only those facts that relate to the theory are collected. This excludes information that may be more important than the theory itself. Barker's view of the way to collect data was to be a *transducer*, that is, to let the data flow through the recorder without imposing any form on them. Presumably, you can discover the natural form the data take without imposing your ideas.

Barker and Wright collected specimen records of children in their midwestern town and published the first record of a child's day. It was called *One Boy's Day* and was published in 1951. They went on to collect about 20 such records and stored them in a safe in the old bank building that

Figure 10.3. Old Bank Building Housing the Field Station

was the field station headquarters (Figure 10.3). Graduate students from the University of Kansas visited the field station to learn the techniques of observation. A number of these reflected on the experience at the fortieth anniversary of the founding of the field station (Bechtel, 1989). Phil Schoggen and his wife Dikkie were the first students at the field station (Schoggen, 1989).

Barker and Wright abandoned the observation of individual children, however, because they discovered a better unit for observation, the *behavior setting*. The transducer method led them to this "natural" unit of human behavior. Behavior settings were units of behavior that seemed to determine the observable behavior of individual children. Individuals were not the primary units of behavior because whenever they behaved, whenever they did *anything*, it was as part of a behavior setting. Barker and Wright found themselves drawn to these supraindividual units because they discovered that behavior was tied to places. Behavior always occurred at a specific place and at given times. You could always go to the place and see the behavior. The people who were in the place could change but the behavior would stay relatively the same. The units had a life of their own. They were parts of the community that people would go to to accomplish the daily business of life.

Behavior settings were natural because the people who lived in them could recognize them and call them by name. Behavior settings were the Boy Scout meeting, the lawyer's office, the grocery store, the Green's house, the streets and sidewalks. Each of these behavior patterns happened at a specific time and place, and if one counted all of the behavior settings in a town, it was possible to describe *everything* that happened in the town in the course of a year.

A year was chosen as the proper time period in which to count behavior settings because after a year they began repeating themselves. If one observed for less than a year, important behavior settings would be lost such as the Christmas Eve church service or New Year's office party.

It is easy to miss the significance of behavior settings because they have not been incorporated into psychology as yet and they contain a basic challenge to experimental methods. Experimental psychologists assume that human behavior is like a seamless web that can be pinched off or cut out and examined in an experiment. The discovery of behavior settings contradicts that basic assumption.

If all behavior occurs in behavior settings, then what behavior setting is a psychological experiment? The answer is that an experiment creates its own new behavior setting. The major question then becomes how the experiment relates to the rest of human behavior. Under the old assumption, an experiment can examine only a part of behavior, because it will relate to the whole. Under Barker's new reality of behavior settings as the basic unit of human behavior, the experiment, the new behavior setting, must somehow be connected to other behavior settings. The danger is that the experiment has created a new behavior setting that in no way connects with any other behavior settings. Once the assumption of human behavior as a seamless web is dropped, the experimental method encounters extreme difficulty.

An example of this difficulty was provided by Barker's own student, Clifford Fawl (Fawl, 1978), when he reexamined an earlier experiment (Barker, Dembo, & Lewin, 1941) that had become the standard reference to demonstrate childhood regression. In the experiment, children played with toys for a time and then an experimenter would pull down a screen and observe the children's behavior when frustrated by removal of the toys. According to observations, the children appeared to "regress" in their behavior. This experiment became a classic and was quoted in many textbooks.

When Clifford Fawl became Roger Barker's graduate student, he examined the behavior specimen records of the children of Oskaloosa to search for examples of frustration and regression. But there were no situations comparable to the experiment. Children would suffer frustrations but never the kind depicted in the experiment. Furthermore, the children never reacted to frustrations in any way that could be interpreted as regression. In other words, the experiment had created a behavior setting with conditions that did not exist in any other behavior settings known at that time.

This does not mean that experiments can't be done on human behavior but that the experimenter must take caution not to create a behavior setting that is not related to other behavior settings. That is a completely new way to look at the study of human behavior.

By the mid-1950s, Barker and Wright had abandoned mainstream psychology and taken up behavior settings as the base for all human behavior. Their *Midwest and Its Children* (Barker & Wright, 1955) was the first textbook in ecological psychology. Actually, the name *ecological psychology* was not coined until Barker's second text by that name published in 1968. A more up-to-date text is Phil Schoggen's *Behavior Settings* published in 1989.

Behavior settings were studied through a behavior setting survey. This is not a survey as we ordinarily think of them, but a true count of behavior settings in a community during the period of a year. It is actually a census of behavior. This method employs participant observation by going to the behavior settings and taking part in them while counting hours and people; by using informants, that is, people who attend the behavior settings and can describe them; and by using public documents such as newspapers, church bulletins, school yearbooks, and government records as sources of behavior settings. By having so many sources of data, the behavior setting survey uses most of the methods for establishing psychological validity. *Validity* is determined through independent confirmation of a behavioral phenomenon. The behavior setting survey uses virtually all of the independent sources of data, and thus is one of the most valid methods in psychology.

Underpopulation Theory

All this is fine, but of what practical use are behavior settings? They may be fundamental units of human behavior, but what does this tell us that is new? For one thing, once the behavior in behavior settings is learned, it is possible to predict well over 90% of the behavior of any one person! No other psychological approach can claim such predictive utility.

But think about what that predictability means. The behavior in behavior settings depicts the daily behavior of human beings. Daily behavior is not something psychology has been concerned with. From the earliest times, psychologists have attempted to fathom the workings of the innermost thoughts and feelings of individuals. It was assumed these led to and would explain all of human behavior. The problem was that measures of these innermost elements seldom produced predictable behavior. But as Shadish (1984) points out, psychology only accepts what fits with the prevailing wisdom of the day.

Nevertheless, Barker's research led to discoveries that have had wide theoretical and practical importance. Chief among these was the discovery of *underpopulation theory*.[1] The discovery of underpopulation was first reported in Barker's chapter in the Nebraska Symposium for Motivation in 1960. The principal data that led to this discovery resulted from comparing the behavior settings and occupants of the midwestern town with a town in England. Barker went there in 1963 to make a comparative study and discovered some peculiar differences. The residents of Oskaloosa, his midwestern town, had a smaller population (830) than Leyburn, the British town (1,310), but there were 1.4 as many behavior settings available to the residents in the Midwest. Barker looks at behavior settings as "resources," which meant there were 40% more behavioral resources available to the residents of Oskaloosa compared with the British town. But what does this mean in terms of daily life? It means there were more things to do, more places to go to do things one wants to do, and a greater variety in the lives in the midwestern compared with the British town.

But the term *variety* can be confusing. On the surface, the British town seemed to have more variety. It certainly had more behavior settings operating on any given day than did the midwestern town. Yet, because the British town had more people, there was less access to settings per person. This is an important distinction to make because it creates a "size illusion" that makes bigger entities appear to have more variety (and they do) but the fact is that the variety is less accessible than in a smaller entity like a town.

Another important difference is discovered when one examines the roles played by the residents of each town. Every behavior setting has leaders and followers. When one compares the leader roles in the midwestern town as compared with the British town, the midwestern town has *twice* as many leader roles per person as the British town.

Further investigation revealed differences in segments of the population in terms of what was available. Children took part in more settings in the midwestern town, but, it seemed, were excluded from more settings in the British town. A similar pattern existed for the elderly. Not only was this true in terms of numbers of settings available, it was also true of the kinds of behavior. More specifically, leadership roles were more available to children and the elderly, and to the population as a whole, in the smaller midwestern town. The net result of these differences was that the residents of the midwest town had a higher participation level than the people in the British town.

Barker reasoned the principle behind these differences was that the smaller community made people work harder at their lives than the larger community. Put another way, it seemed as though the larger community had a surplus of labor and seemed to exclude people from participating.

In a later study, Wright (1971) reported differences between children who lived in small towns with fewer than 1,000 persons versus a larger town of 33,000. Wright had the children come into a large empty room and "build" their communities with toy blocks; then he walked with the children in the community surrounding their homes and questioned them about the people who lived there. Small-town children were considerably more knowledgeable about their communities than the children of the larger town (Figure 10.4). They knew more behavior settings, more details about settings, more persons, and more details about persons than their large-town counterparts. The reason for these differences seemed to be that, although the large-town children entered more and more

Box 10.1

Why Small-Town Boys Make Good

What do Dixon, Boise, Saint Johns, Mission, Westminster, Shirkieville, Floresville and Clio have in common? If, understandably, the light does not dawn, try this: Laurinburg, Walters, Rumford, Mitchell, Everett, Doland and Pocantico Hills. In case the riddle is still not solved, two more names should give it away: Plains and Grand Rapids.

The list, of course, includes the birthplaces and/or home towns of current and former Presidential Hopefuls (in order) Reagan, Church, Udall, Bensten, Shriver, Bayh, Connally, Wallace, Sanford, Harris, Muskie, McGovern, Jackson, Humphrey, Rockefeller, Carter and Ford.

All qualify, with only a little imagination here (Rockefeller) and there (Ford), as small-town boys. They ran off to Washington or their state capitals, which must tell us something about small towns as well as the men. But it is a fact that with the exception of John Kennedy, every President of this century since Taft was born or reared in a small community. Which leads one to wonder why, in our age of ultimate urbanization, we end up with men who never had firsthand experience living right down in the crowded center of Megalopolis.

True, a couple of people's places were omitted—Cleveland and San Francisco. But Milton Shapp did not go far; Jerry Brown remains an oddity in the down-home parade of 1976.

"We exaggerate the citification of this country," says Irving Kristol, the New York University urban expert. "We do have an urbanized culture, but we are not a city people." Those fellows running for the White House are more a profile of America than we commonly recognize. The Census Bureau says that 80% of our population live in communities of less than 500,000 people, a city size not all that big.

In the suburbs and in many smaller cities, the folks still think a lot in small-town terms, insists Kristol, even while indulging in the urban world to work and go to concerts. The professor adds that this vast majority of people are not beset with the metropolitan problems that have dominated our public dialogue for years. More moderate sized cities, like Minneapolis, can actually solve their garbage, traffic and downtown commercial problems. This leads people like former Mayor Hubert Humphrey to believe that they can work wonders from the White House.

Daniel Boorstin, Librarian of Congress and a Pulitzer prizewinner for his book *The Americans: The Democratic Experience*, says that life is "more graspable" in smaller places. He believes that the immense cities often overwhelm the people who grew up there, discouraging them before they reach the age of leadership. In smaller places, he reckons, hope, a certain confidence and an ability to cope are nurtured. Boorstin is intrigued at how some of the open-air, back-fence values of Editor William Allen White, the Emporia sage of the 1920s, have re-entered the national discussion and how the small-town wisdom and wit of Will Rogers have been rekindled on the stage with amazing success by James Whitmore (who also does a nice impression of the man from Independence, Harry Truman).

(continued)

Box 10.1 Continued

"I think a person gets a better grip on himself and on the world when he spends those early years in a smaller place," muses Bill Moyers, public television's impresario, who was raised in Marshall, Texas. He says that solitude, knowing friends and enemies intimately, having a more hospitable environment—all provide a gentle entry into the harsh world. "People in towns get a better sense of themselves, their places. The families stay closer, the landmarks last longer."

In small places most people survive easily, and many who live so close to church, flag and mother leave home charged with what Moyers describes as a strain of Calvinism. It is composed of equal parts of missionary zeal to help others and fierce self-interest. It was best described, he says, in the admonition that Rebekah Baines Johnson, formidable matron of Johnson City, delivered frequently to her son Lyndon. "Do good," she said, "and you will do well." Onward Calvinist soldiers from Plains and Dixon and Grand Rapids and . . .

SOURCE: *Time* (May 24, 1976). © Time Inc. Reprinted by permission.

different behavior settings, the small town children encountered the same behavior settings and people more often and learned more about them. Therefore, mere repetition of exposure is enough to explain why the small town children learned more about their communities.

School Studies

To test whether this principle of size-determining participation worked in organizations below the community level, Barker and his colleagues and students (Barker & Gump, 1964) studied students at the junior year in several high schools in Kansas. The high schools were chosen because of their contrast in size. High schools like those in Valley Falls and McClouth had a student population of a few hundred while high schools in Topeka had over 1,000.

The theory was supported by the data collected on extracurricular activities. Juniors in the small schools reported having twice as much "pressure" to take part in these activities and reported 2.5 times as many positions of responsibility than those of the larger schools.

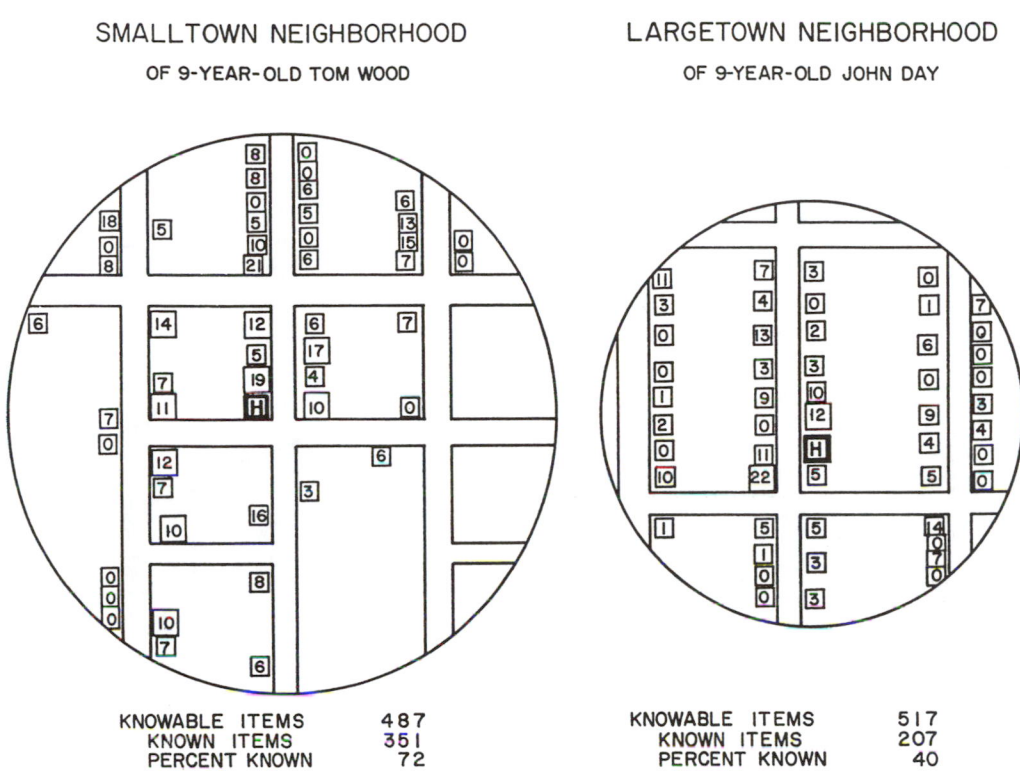

Figure 10.4. Comparison of Knowledge About Environments Between Small Town and Large Town Boys
SOURCE: Wright (1969).

A good example of the quality of this pressure is provided by the marching band in one of the small high schools. As was the custom (and still is), the band practiced at 7 a.m. in the morning before school started. It was observed that a number of the clarinet players did not touch the instruments to their lips. When asked why they didn't play their clarinets, the students replied, "Oh, we can't play the clarinet." In other words, the demand for bodies in the marching band was so great that they had to take people who couldn't play the instruments. Contrast this to the larger school where many good clarinet players can't get into the band because there isn't room.

Consider the other extracurricular activities: The small school students have more than one chance to get into the senior class play because

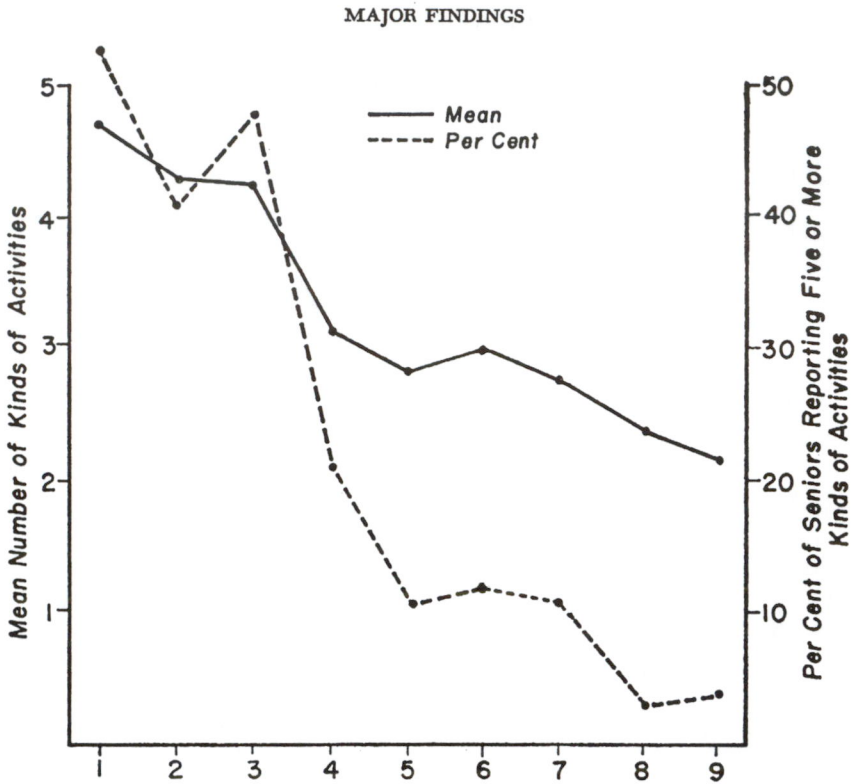

Figure 10.5. Extracurricular Versatility of Graduating Seniors in Schools of Different Sizes
SOURCE: Reprinted from *Big School, Small School: High School Size and Student Behavior* by Roger G. Barker and Paul V. Gump with the permission of the publishers, Stanford University Press. © 1964 by the Board of Trustees of Leland Stanford Junior University.

there aren't enough seniors to fill all the roles and they have to recruit juniors. Once again, by comparison, in the larger schools most of the seniors can't take part in the senior class play because there are too many of them. This produces a senior class with richer experiences in the smaller school (Figure 10.5).

Thus the net result is that students in the small schools have many more experiences and a greater variety of experiences than students in the larger schools. The small school student has a longer list of activities and a greater leadership role in those activities than his or her large school counterpart. There just aren't as many opportunities per person in the large school.

But the illusion of more activity in the larger school persists. Looking at any high school yearbook, one can easily see that the list of activities for the large school is longer. The small school can't afford to hire as many language teachers or as many multitalented teachers to head these activities. It appears that the small school is actually deprived because of its lack of such variety. Yet, the figures are inexorable. There are simply not enough activities available in the large school to include the student population at the same level of involvement as in the small school. Furthermore, the numbers of dropouts and absences are higher in the large school, and grades are lower.

Satisfaction with school events did not differ between the large and small schools, but the kind of satisfaction did. Small school students reported more satisfaction with being competent, challenged, and doing "important" things. Nevertheless, despite this evidence, the popular notion that "bigger is better" continues to influence school decisions.

To test these findings on a nationwide scale, Baird (1969) obtained data from a sample of 21,371 students who took the American College Test (ACT). Students in small high schools had significantly higher levels in four of six areas: drama and speech, leadership, writing, and music. There was no difference in science and art. Downey (1978) had similar findings with freshmen entering college.

Wicker (1979) reports similar data from 320 churches. Members of smaller churches attend more regularly, have more positions of responsibility, and report more satisfaction with their church than members of larger churches. However, the church studies showed that in some instances the expected differences between large and small churches did not occur. This was because in some behavior settings, such as the main church service and Sunday school, where the leaders are few and the audience many by comparison, the pressures to attend are not as great because the forces operate mostly on the few leaders.

Industry and Other Organizations

Wicker (1974), Oxley and Barrera (1984), and Bechtel (1977) generally find that the same conditions exist in the work settings in regard to underpopulation theory. Job enrichment has a wide literature that also provides many examples of underpopulating. Davis and Cherns (1975) describe the essence of job enrichment: "The central idea of job enrichment applied at the plant was to give employees as much responsibility and opportunity to make decisions as their competence and talents enabled them to use" (p. 270).

When the Volvo plant in Sweden tried job enrichment, the assembly line workers were told they would have to clean up their own spaces and repair their own machines as well as hire their own employees. The former positions in personnel and maintenance were eliminated and these tasks were assumed by the assembly line workers. In other words, job enrichment was behavior setting enrichment, creating more forces to participate in the behavior settings and placing the workers in greater positions of responsibility.

But the investigations of Curran and Stanworth (1978) provided a contradiction to the usual results of underpopulating studies. They studied 145 respondents from small businesses in England with populations under 200. One would expect these employees to show the benefits derived from being in an underpopulated situation based on size of organizations alone. However, the average employee complained of lack of important work and poor self-identity. They were not overworked so it could not be from extreme underpopulation. Upon further investigation, Curran and Stanworth found the owners of these small businesses were marginal people who were unable or unwilling to share responsibility with their workers and often the workers were not willing to take on any further responsibility.

The findings of Curran and Stanworth are critical. They show that there is nothing magic about having a small organization. The persons in power must be willing to *share* responsibility or the benefits of underpopulating cannot take place. Conditions of smallness only set up the situation where the benefits of the theory *can* take place, but it is dependent upon the willingness of the setting leaders to share their power.

A summary of underpopulation findings is presented in Figure 10.6. Positive benefits (feelings of responsibility, self-worth, and so on) are on the vertical axis while size of group is on the horizontal and is expressed in number of persons per setting. Benefits start low, with extreme underpopulation, increase to maximum benefit, and then decrease with overpopulating.

Note that the overall effect of underpopulation is an inverted "U-shaped" curve, a favorite way for psychologists to depict psychological effects. This means that on the left side of the curve, where there are too few persons,

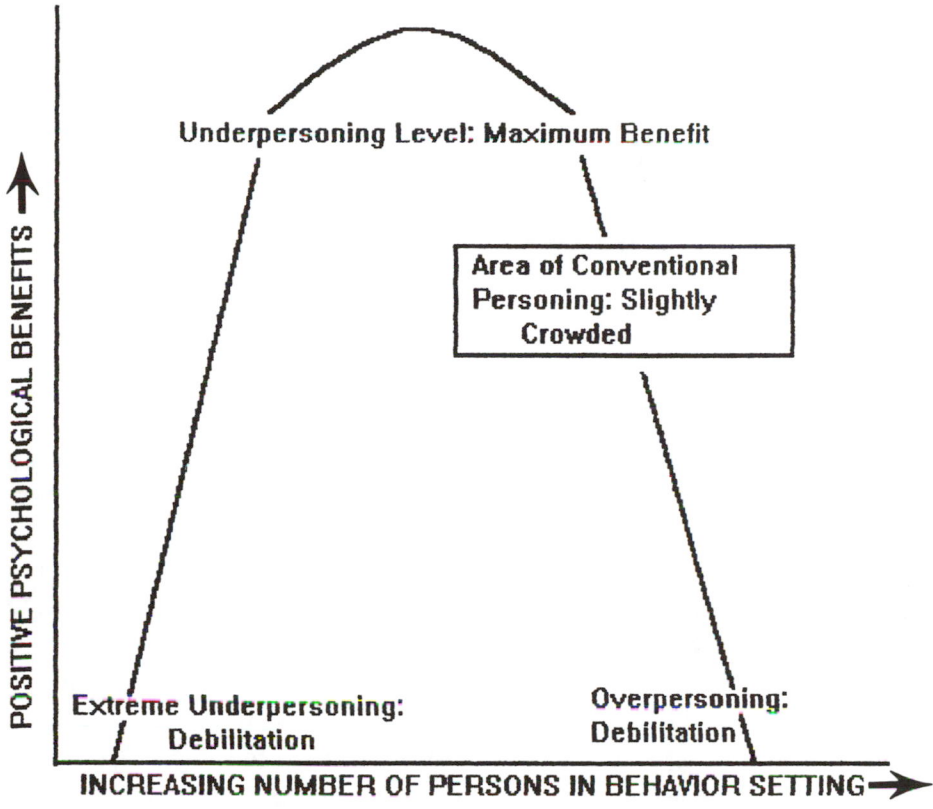

Figure 10.6. Undermanning Effects and Size of Settings in Organization

the effects of extreme underpopulating are felt and people are too heavily pressed to perform. This is a debilitating circumstance. Situations cannot be severely underpopulated without negative consequences. However, as the number of persons increases to a point where there are enough to do the job but not, perhaps, as many as people would like, the benefits of underpopulating reach maximum. It is important to realize that people in these circumstances are not necessarily *happy* with the situation. They may complain they need help or that there should be more people to do the job better. Yet, because of these pressures, they feel needed, that they are doing important work, and that they *must* be present so as not to let down their fellow employees.

Note also that as the curve moves to what we would ordinarily consider to be a proper number of people for any given setting, the benefits of underpopulating begin to decrease and we quickly move to the overpopulated situations where pressures to drop out and not perform are being felt.

We must also realize that, as Curran and Stanworth (1978) have shown, there is no guarantee that underpopulating effects will be felt when size of unit is small; the size condition merely sets up the circumstances under which it *can* occur. The key is whether persons in power are willing to share responsibility.

Behavioral Focal Points

Early in their studies of the town in the Midwest, Barker and Wright discovered that the drugstore served as the most central behavior setting of the town. It became a favorite spot for field station employees to take their breaks. The most central behavior setting became a way to "anchor" other behavior settings in the town in terms of how they related to it. One issue that had to be dealt with was the relationship of behavior settings to each other. A fundamental problem was determining if one behavior entity (called a *synomorph* to indicate a behavior-environment link) was actually a separate behavior setting or whether it merged with another

It was easily observed that behavior settings had a collection of prop-erties. They had a population, leaders, objects that people used, a time schedule, and other properties that could be observed and quantified. These properties were formalized into seven dimensions called the K-21 scale (Figure 10.7).

The properties of the K-21 scale are such that if the seven dimensions overlap more than 50%, the two synomorphs tend to be one behavior setting. That is, they get a score of less than 21. If the dimensions do not overlap, the score is 21 or over and the two synomorphs are actually two different behavior settings. Bechtel (1977) found that two adjacent syno-morphs with K-21 scores between 18 to 25 tend to have boundary prob-lems and ought to have a physical barrier between them.

By using the K-21 scores of all behavior settings against the most central behavior setting, it was possible to arrange the entire town's behavior settings in a polar coordinate map (see Figure 10.8)

The size of the circles on the map is determined by another concept: *environmental richness*. Think of richness as kinds of people plus kinds of behavior multiplied by person hours and divided by 100. The size of

THE INTERDEPENDENCE SCALE FOR
JUDGING VALUE OF K

Scale for judging the degree of interdependence of any pair of behavior settings A and B. On all criteria, a low rating indicates interdependence, and a high rating indicates independence of setting A and setting B.

1. Rating of population interdependence, i.e., of the degree to which the people who enter setting $A(P_B)$ are the same as those who enter setting $B(P_B)$. The percent overlap is judged by the following formula:

$$\frac{\text{Percent}}{\text{Overlap}} = \frac{2 P_{AB}}{P_A + P_B}$$

Where P_A = Number of people who enter setting A,
P_B = Number of people who enter setting B,
P_{AB} = Number of people who enter both setting A and setting B.

This percent overlap is converted to an interdependency rating by the following scale:

Rating	Per Cent Overlap
1	95–100
2	67–94
3	33–66
4	6–32
5	2–5
6	trace–1
7	none

2. Rating of leadership interdependence, i.e., of the degree to which the leaders of setting A are also the leaders of setting B.

This is judged in the same way as population interdependence for persons who penetrate to Zones 4, 5, or 6 settings A and B.

3. Rating of spatial interdependence, i.e., the degree to which settings A and B use the same or proximate spatial areas.

Rate on the following scale. In the case of scale points with two definitions, the most appropriate one applies; if more than one applies, give the lowest scale rating.

Rating	Per Cent of Space Common to A and B	
1	95 to 100	
2	50 to 94	
3	10 to 49	or A and B use different parts of same room or small area.
4	5 to 9	or A and B use different parts of same building or lot.

Figure 10.7. K-21 Scale
SOURCE: From Barker and Wright (1955).

the circle gets bigger as the numbers of people and behaviors gets larger (see Barker, 1968, p. 70, for a more precise definition).

This map shows the behavior of the entire town in relation to this most central setting. It shows how people organize their behavior by the frequency of contacts with each other. The most central behavior setting

Rating	Per Cent of Space Common to A and B	
5	2 to 4	or A and B use areas in same part of town.*
6	trace to 1	or A and B use areas in same town but different parts of the town.*
7	none	or A in town, B out of town.

4. Rating of interdependence based on behavior objects, i.e., the extent to which behavior setting A and behavior setting B use identical or similar behavior objects.

Rate on the following scale. In the case of scale points with two definitions, the most appropriate one applies; if more than one applies, give the lowest rating.

Rating		
1	Identical objects used in setting A and setting B; i.e., all behavior objects shared.	
2	More than half of the objects shared by A and B	or Virtually all objects in A and B of same kind.**
3	Half of the objects shared by A and B	or More than half of the objects in A and B of same kind.**
4	Less than half the objects shared by A and B	or Half the objects in A and B of same kind.**
5	Few behavior objects in A and B identical	or Less than half the objects of A and B of same kind.**
6	Almost no objects shared by A and B	or Few behavior objects of same kind** in A and B.
7	No objects shared	or Almost no similarity between objects in A and B.

5. Rating of interdependence based on molar action units, i.e., degree to which molar behavior units are continuous between setting A and setting B.

The molar behavior in behavior settings A and B may be integrated in two ways. The inhabitants of setting A may interact across the boundary with the inhabitants of B, e.g., the person

*Three parts of Midwest were identified: (a) south of the square (approximately 15 square blocks); (b) area of town square (approximately 5 blocks); (c) north of the square (approximately 15 blocks).
**Objects of the same kind are different instances of objects that have the same dictionary definition; e.g., spoons are used in the behavior setting School Lunch Room and the setting Clifford's Drug Store Fountain, but they are different spoons.

Figure 10.7 (Continued). K-21 Scale

is the one where all the people of the town have the most contact with each other. Ranged next to this behavior setting are the behavior settings close to it, and at each successive outer level the behavior settings become less related and tend to form separate clusters on their own.

in the cytosetting Preacher interacts directly with the members of the cytosetting Congregation in the Church Service. On the other hand, behavior begun in one behavior setting may be completed in the other, e.g., delivering lumber for a construction project starts at the setting Lumber Yard and is completed at the setting House Construction. Scales are provided for both kinds of behavior integration. For each kind of behavior integration, use the highest per cent which applies. The average of the two ratings is the final rating.

Rating	Per Cent of Behavior in A Having Direct Effects in B, or Vice Versa. (Highest Per Cent Counts)	Per Cent of Behavior Actions Beginning in A Which are Completed in B, or Vice Versa. (Highest Per Cent Counts)
1	95–100	95–100
2	67–94	67–94
3	34–66	34–66
4	5–33	5–33
5	2–4	2–4
6	trace–1	trace–1
7	none	none

6. Rating of interdependence based on temporal contiguity, i.e., the degree to which settings A and B occur at the same time, or at proximate times.

Most behavior settings recur at intervals. Any pair of settings, therefore, may occur close together on some occasions and be temporally separated at other times. For example, the American Legion meets monthly, while the Boy Scout Troop meets weekly; once a month their meetings occur during the same week. The closest temporal proximity of setting A and setting B determine the column to enter in the table below. The per cent of contact at the point of closest proximity determines the interdependence rating in the column at the right. The per cent of contact is computed as the ratio between the number of occurrences of both settings at this closest point of contact divided by the total number of occurrences of both behavior settings.

Scales for Rating Temporal Interdependence

Interdependence Rating	(Closest Temporal Proximity Per Cent of Contact)					
	Simultaneous	Same Part of Day	Same Day	Same Week	Same Month	Same Year
1	0.75–1.00					
2	0.50–0.74	0.75–1.00				
3	0.25–0.49	0.50–0.74	0.75–1.00			
4	0.05–0.24	0.25–0.49	0.50–0.74	0.75–1.00		
5	0–0.04	0.05–0.24	0.25–0.49	0.50–0.74	0.75–1.00	
6		0–0.04	0.05–0.24	0.25–0.49	0.50–0.74	0.50–1.00
7			0–0.04	0.05–0.24	0.25–0.49	0–0.49

Figure 10.7 (Continued). K-21 Scale

Bechtel (1977) observed that a community can be mapped by this technique to show how internally integrated the residents are with each other. A community that is not well integrated will have a most central behavior setting low in richness, without other behavior settings around it, and with many richer settings in the outer layers of the diagram. By

Example: The Boy Scout Troop met every Monday night during the survey year. The American Legion met the first Wednesday of every month. The closest temporal proximity of these settings was "Same Week." Enter column headed "Same Week." The 12 Scout and the 12 Legion meetings which occurred in this close contact were added and the sum divided by the sum of the 12 Legion meetings and the 52 Scout meetings, as follows:

$$\frac{\text{12 Scout Meetings} \quad \text{12 Legion Meetings} \quad 24}{\text{52 Scout Meetings} \quad \text{12 Legion Meetings} \quad 64} = .37$$

In column "Same Week," .37 falls at scale point 6. The temporal interdependence score, then, is 6.

7. Interdependence based on similarity of behavior mechanisms, i.e., the degree to which behavior mechanisms are similar in setting A and setting B.

Ratings are based on the following 12 behavior mechanisms:

Gross Motor	Writing	Eating
Manipulation	Observing	Reading
Verbalization	Listening	Emoting
Singing	Thinking	Tactual Feeling

The interdependence score is determined by the number of behavior mechanisms present in one setting and absent in the other as indicated in the following table;

Interdependence Rating	Number of Mechanisms Present in One Setting and Absent in the Other
1	0–1
2	2–3
3	4–5–6
4	7–8
5	9–10
6	11
7	12

The total interdependence score K is the sum of the separate interdependency ratings; the value of K can vary between 7 and 49.

Source: From R. Barker and H. Wright, Midwest and Its Children (Row, Peterson, 1955). Reprinted by permission of R. Barker and H. Wright.

Figure 10.7 (Continued). K-21 Scale

contrast, a well-integrated community will have a very rich most central behavior setting with many behavior settings near it and with few clusters of isolated behavior settings (see Figure 10.8).

Bechtel (1977) calls the most central behavior setting a *behavioral focal point* because it is literally the focal point of behavior for the community. A "good" behavioral focal point has the following qualities:

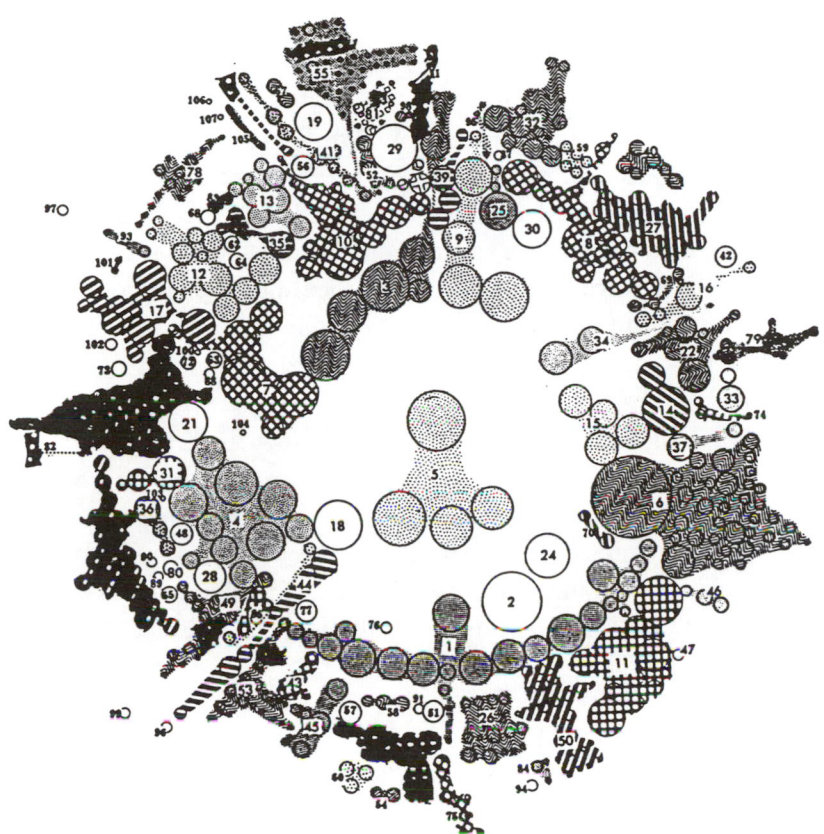

Figure 10.8. Polar Coordinate Map of Midwest Behavior Settings
SOURCE: From Barker and Wright (1955).

1. It is centrally located with easy access for everyone.

2. It is at a crossroads of traffic, specifically pedestrian traffic.

3. It is behaviorally rich, with a mix of many different kinds of behaviors and people.

4. It has maximum visual access so people can see and be seen.

5. It has provision for lots of seating. Very often this means some kind of food and drink is served.

Put all these qualities together and one has the primary framework on which to design a community. But this raises some interesting theoretical questions. The first question is how big a behavioral focal point can be before it is no longer integrating. This question also has overtones of underpopulation theory. It is important to remember that the essence of the behavioral focal point is that *it provides a place where the members of a community meet face-to-face.*

This principle echoes findings from Wright's (1971) studies in which it was discovered that small town children knew more about their communities than large town children because the children in small towns had more opportunities to meet the same people and see the same places more frequently. In other words, the behavioral focal point provides the chance for everyone to get to know and recognize each other as belonging to the same community.

But the question remains: At what point does it become too difficult for people to recognize each other? It is easy to show that, by these criteria, cities and large towns are not integrated, but where is the critical population point? At the present time, just as the specifics of underpopulation are vague, it is not possible to specify at what size population people can no longer retain memories of who belongs. It is also critical to consider how often people can come in contact and over what period of time.

Conclusions

Ecological psychology has opened a new dimension in human behavior, establishing the parameters of behavior from a community rather than from individual points of reference. Following the kinds of data that can be collected from this viewpoint, it was discovered that size of the social unit (town, school, church) has a direct influence on the behavior of individuals, not just on the way they perform their tasks but also on the way they think about themselves and each other.

Ecological psychology finds that the places where people go to behave are the determinants of behavior and that these place-time-behavior units (behavior settings) are the best predictors of human behavior and also make up the fabric of daily life.

Note

1. The original term was *undermanning* but this has become a sexist term because *underwomaning* is just as applicable. Following Schoggen's (1989) suggestion, I term it *underpopulation* or *underpopulating theory.*

GOALS

Definitions and Concepts

    Behavior settings

    Transducers

    Operators

    Synomorphs

    Underpopulation

    K-21 Scale

    Richness

    Behavioral focal points

    Giving up responsibility

Important Studies

    Barker and Wright (1951)

    Barker and Gump (1964)

    Barker (1968)

    Baird (1969)

    Wright (1969)

    Schoggen (1989)

QUESTIONS

1. What is the difference between a transducer and an operator?

2. Is the behavior setting a theory, a fact, or a scale?

3. Why does a behavior setting survey take so long?

4. What is the relationship between organizational size and setting size?

5. What are the so-called benefits of underpopulating?

6. What are the negative aspects of underpopulating?

7. Can people ever be outside of behavior settings?

8. What is the importance of richness?

9. Why should a community have a behavioral focal point?

10. What was the most influential behavior setting in your life?

11

The Stress of
Living in an Environment

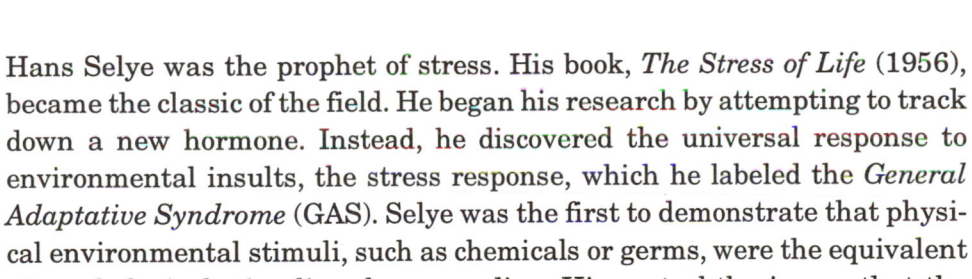

Hans Selye was the prophet of stress. His book, *The Stress of Life* (1956), became the classic of the field. He began his research by attempting to track down a new hormone. Instead, he discovered the universal response to environmental insults, the stress response, which he labeled the *General Adaptative Syndrome* (GAS). Selye was the first to demonstrate that physical environmental stimuli, such as chemicals or germs, were the equivalent of psychological stimuli such as crowding. His central thesis was that the body responded to these many different insults by a single set of responses (the GAS), a *nonspecific response*.

Selye began his experiments by injecting rats with an irritating chemical called crotonic acid. He observed the rats had a lowered immune defense, developed ulcers, and had enlarged adrenal glands. Being a good scientist, he had a rat control group that was being injected with a salt solution. Salt solutions do not produce a body defense the way crotonic acid does. Yet his control group was showing many of the same signs as his experimental rats. Any ordinary scientist would have scrapped the experiment and started over.

But Selye was convinced nothing had gone wrong. Instead, his rats were acting as though they had been injected with the same irritating substance. But he knew they had not. What was the common denominator? It was the huge experimenters pulling the rats out of the cage and injecting them daily. This was traumatic enough to produce injured-type responses across all animals.

What should Selye call this phenomenon? He looked to engineering and borrowed the term for forces placed upon metals: *stress*.

The Physiological Model

In response to some environmental stimulus, the pituitary gland produces a hormone called adrenocorticotropic hormone (ACTH). This causes the adrenal gland to produce two hormones, epinephrine, which is called adrenaline, and norepinephrine, which is called noradrenaline. Adrenaline causes the heart to beat faster and blood pressure to rise. It relaxes the smooth muscles of the digestive system but contracts others. Noradrenaline contracts the small arteries. Both hormones release fatty acids into the blood. Adrenaline also increases the metabolism of sugars in the muscles and liver. These effects increase oxygen utilization as well as production of carbon dioxide and raise the body temperature. There are consequences directly related to coronary heart disease (CHD). It is thought that constant stress is directly related to processes that cause arterial clogging.

The physiological model has a mechanical quality to it (see Figure 11.1). The organism is exposed to a stimulus that elicits the stress response, then goes through a period of adaptation and the stress is reduced, or, if it cannot adapt, becomes exhausted and after repeated exposure and exhaustion, may die. Selye (1976) sees this sequence as the main elements of his GAS. But this led to defining stress as "the nonspecific response of the body to any demand" (p. 55).

There are three bodily secretions that have become the hallmark of stress and these are typically measured in the urine: adrenaline, noradrenaline, and cortisol. When these are detected, they are considered a valid measure of stress, and are considered to be a more accurate measure than the subjective measures. Frankenhaeuser, Lundberg, and Mardberg (1986) consider cortisol to be a measure of *distress* while adrenaline and

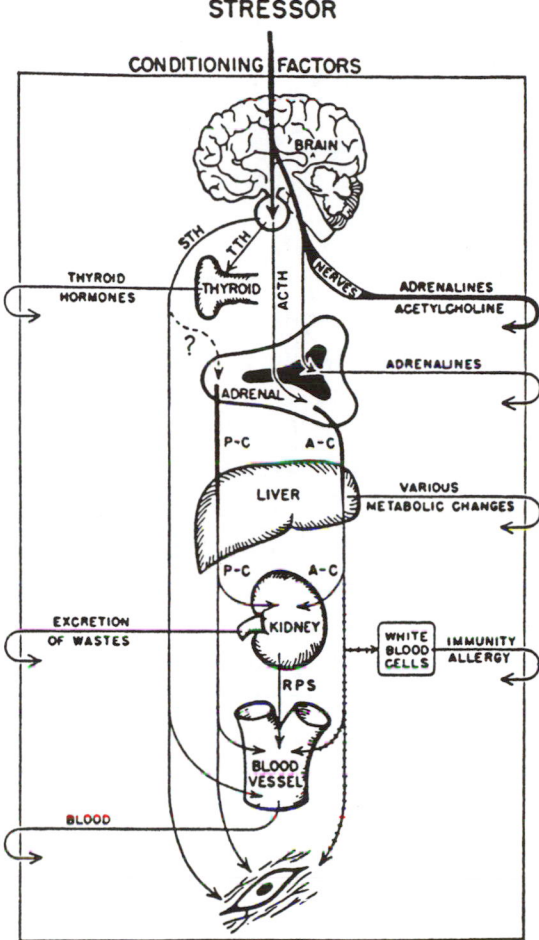

Figure 11.1. The Physiological Model of Stress
SOURCE: H. Selye (1956). *The Stress of Life*. Copyright © The McGraw-Hill Companies. Used by permission.

noradrenaline seem to be more a measure of *effort*. Cortisol is often measured by collecting saliva, a less obtrusive method than urinalysis.

The Psychological Model

Several researchers have pointed out that humans have the ability to evaluate many stressful stimuli, a process called *cognitive appraisal*. Humans can appraise the threat from any stimulus and decide whether

Figure 11.2. The Psychological Model of Stress

it is serious or not. This is only one of several ways in which humans have to *cope* with a stressor. After appraising the stimulus, the person can flee or overcome it by direct action, and this is called *instrumental coping*. Another way is to decide that the stimulus is not so harmful under closer examination, and this is called *palliative coping*. If one hears a loud noise outside, closing the window is an example of instrumental coping while appraising it as a passing parade that can be ignored is palliative coping. The psychological model is shown in Figure 11.2.

The psychological model does not displace the physiological one, it includes it as part of the process. It places emphasis on the more varied choices of behavior that humans enjoy over animals. The problem with the psychological model is that, although it more clearly defines the larger response repertoire of human behavior in stressful situations, it complicates the definition of the harmful stimulus that will produce stress. For one person, jumping out of an airplane is an extremely stressful event to be avoided except in dire emergency. For another, it is weekend recreation and sought and paid for. Thus the psychological model increases the sophistication of the process at the expense of increasing the confusion over what initiates the process.

Selye's insistence that the GAS is nonspecific is challenged by Mason et al. (1976) and Lacey (1967). They try to show that certain stimuli evoke more specific responses as a function of how the stimuli are appraised and/or coped with.

The Moderator-Mediator Issue

Just as with crowding (Chapter 9), there are moderators and mediators of stress. These follow naturally from the psychological model because humans can respond to a great variety of variables that can have an influence on how stressful an event can be. Evans and Cohen (1987) see all cognitive aspects as mediators of stress. Most of these are aspects of the appraisal process.

The most investigated mediator of stress is perceived control (Glass & Singer, 1972; Langer, 1983). When humans feel they can control events, even if they actually cannot, stress is measurably reduced. Many mediators have this cognitive quality; they tend to explain or reinterpret the physical stimuli.

Moderators, by contrast, are variables that exist outside the cognitive realm. One of the most interesting of these was discovered accidentally by Broadbent (1971) when he was testing for the effects of noise on performance. He discovered that students who came to the experiment with a lack of sleep were less bothered by the noise during their performance. Thus lack of sleep is a moderator of certain kinds of stress. Most moderators are either environmental variables or physiological ones but they can also be psychological, such as previous exposure to some stress.

The Measurement of Stress

Although there are many subjective measurements of stress (Dohrenwend, Dohrenwend, Dodson, & Shrout, 1984), their use as self-report measures and their potential confounding with other variables force researchers to rely more heavily on physiological procedures such as the measurement of catecholamines and cortisol in urine. *Catecholamines* are the collective term for adrenaline and noradrenaline. This is important to consider because it makes research in stress difficult, expensive, and obtrusive by having to collect urine before and after stressful events. Thus urinalysis becomes the baseline for measuring stress if one wishes to have a valid measure of chronic stress.

Evans and Cohen (1987) point out, however, that subjective measures may be better predictors in some circumstances, such as testing the effects of noise under low or moderate conditions of stress.

In addition to self-report and physiological measures, a few researchers have investigated indices of task performance and, less commonly, nonverbal observations such as facial expressions, repetition of movements, fidgeting, and scratching.

Life Events, Daily Hassles, and Ambient Stressors

Joan Campbell (1983) was the first to point out the taxing effect of background stressors that are just barely noticeable but that sap our ability to respond to more stressful events. She called these background stimuli *ambient stressors*, which can include pollution in the air or background noise. It is important to realize that they can be noticed if one makes a special effort, but usually they are not attended to and are accepted as part of the environmental ambience.

Daily hassles are behavioral episodes consisting of events such as commuting to work, dealing with the boss, marital arguments, and minor irritating events. These also take their toll in stress but are stronger stimuli and more attended to than the ambient stressors.

Life events claim the highest price in the stress market. These are the rare but life-wrenching events such as losing a job, getting divorced, a death in the family. Holmes and Rahe (1967) (see the box) were the pioneers in the development of the stressful life events concept. They developed a Social Readjustment Rating Scale. Each "life event" was given a scaled score (divorce = 73, getting fired = 47). When a person reached 300 points, he or she was considered to be in danger of physical or mental illness. Yet many people scored this high without becoming ill or needing to see a psychiatrist. Life events would seem to be the most clearly defined stimulus to provoke a stress response, yet even here there are complications because of individual differences in appraisal.

Brown and Harris (1989) developed a new scale for measuring life events called the Life Events and Difficulties Scale (LEDS). This scale tried to take differences in appraisal into account, yet it is difficult to score (Hansell, 1991) and the link between life events and illness remains not entirely clear. Although stressful life events have been linked to a variety of health problems (Dohrenwend & Dohrenwend, 1974; Rabkin & Streuning, 1976), it is also clear that many people who undergo stressful life events do not become ill. In fact, Aldwin and Stokols (1988) point out that many negative events can have positive outcomes for the people experiencing them. Helmreich (1992) compared the life adjustments of 140,000 survivors of the Holocaust now in the United States and found they fared better than a matched native Jewish group. They had more stable marriages and only 18% had seen a therapist versus 31% for comparable U.S. Jews. Why is it that many people can respond positively to stressful events?

Box 11.1
How's Your Stress Score?

Some stress is necessary for life, but too much stress is harmful. Drs. Thomas M. Holmes and Richard H. Rahe at the University of Washington Medical School developed a scale for measuring stress in terms of 43 "life events." They say a person scoring less than 150 on their scale has only a 37% chance of becoming ill during the next ten years. A score of 150 to 300 raises the odds of illness to 51%, and a 300+ score means you have an 80% chance of becoming seriously ill.

To find your score, check the events that have applied to you during the past 12 months. Then add up the total values.

Rank	Event	Value	Your Score
1	Death of a spouse	100	_____
2	Divorce	73	_____
3	Marital separation	65	_____
4	Jail term	63	_____
5	Death of close family member	63	_____
6	Personal injury or illness	63	_____
7	Marriage	50	_____
8	Fired from work	47	_____
9	Marital reconciliation	45	_____
10	Retirement	45	_____
11	Change in family member's health	44	_____
12	Pregnancy	40	_____
13	Sex difficulties	39	_____
14	Addition to family	39	_____
15	Business readjustment	38	_____
16	Change in financial status	38	_____
17	Death of close friend	37	_____
18	Change to different line of work	36	_____
29	Change in number of marital arguments	35	_____
20	Mortgage or loan over $10,000	31	_____
21	Foreclosure of mortgage or loan	30	_____
22	Change in work responsibilities	29	_____
23	Son or daughter leaving home	29	_____
24	Trouble with in-laws	29	_____
25	Outstanding personal achievement	28	_____
26	Spouse begins or stops work	26	_____
27	Starting or finishing school	26	_____
28	Change in living conditions	25	_____
29	Revision of personal habits	24	_____
30	Trouble with boss	23	_____
31	Change in work hours, conditions	20	_____
32	Change in residence	20	_____
33	Change in schools	20	_____
34	Change in recreational habits	19	_____
35	Change in church activities	19	_____
36	Change in social activities	18	_____
37	Mortgage or loan under $10,000	17	_____
38	Change in sleeping habits	16	_____
39	Change in number of family gatherings	15	_____
40	Change in eating habits	15	_____
41	Vacation	13	_____
42	Christmas season	12	_____
43	Minor violations of the law	11	_____
	Total		_____

SOURCE: Reprinted with permission from *Journal of Psychosomatic Research*, Vol. 11, T. Holmes and R. Rahe, "The Social Adjustment Rating Scale," 1967, Elsevier Science Ltd., Pergamon Imprint, Oxford, England.

Hardiness

Kobasa (1979) first suggested that the reason many people who are stressed do not fall ill is a trait called *hardiness*. People who have this trait are said to possess a sense of commitment, a feeling of control in their lives, and accept stressful events as challenges. Roth, Wiebe, Fillingham, and Shay (1989) found an association between both hardiness (negative) and stress (positive) and poor health. They suggest hardiness may influence health indirectly by influencing the interpretation of stressful events, such as by acceptance of them as a challenge.

Funk and Houston (1987) criticize the hardiness scale because it uses negative scores—that is, a low score on alienation to measure commitment—and claim hardiness is not well operationalized by the use of such scales.

Wiebe (1991) found a sex difference in hardiness. In an evaluative threat test, she discovered males who scored high in hardiness had less elevated heart beats than those who scored low in the scale. No such difference was observed among women.

The "Fatal" Type A

In large studies linking causal factors to heart disease, it was discovered that a personality type called "A" had a consistent relationship to coronary heart disease (CHD) (Friedman & Rosenman, 1959; Rosenman et al., 1975). Type A was a continuously self-stressed person whom Matthews (1988) defined as showing a sense of time urgency evidenced in strong voice and physical mannerisms, as being extremely competitive, hostile, and aggressive, and striving for achievement. If you find yourself cursing drivers who cut in front of you in traffic, if you have to take something to read with you every time you go to the bathroom to save time (not for pleasure), and if you find you are constantly pressed to get things done and just as constantly held up by people who get in your way, and who make you furious, you are probably a full-blown Type A.

Once this relationship was found between the time compression lifestyle and heart disease, a small industry arose to teach people to be more like Type B. Type B is simply a person who does not feel the time urgency of the Type A, which is the constant source of frustration to the Type A person. Friedman et al. (1986) report success in the effort to reduce Type A behavior and the subsequent incidence of coronary heart disease.

But all was not well with the Type A definition or its supposed links to CHD. Studies done after 1978 tended to find no link between Type A and CHD, and Ragland and Brand (1988) did a 22-year follow-up study of CHD patients and found the link with Type A seemed to vanish over time. More recently, however, Miller, Turner, Tindale, Posavac, and Dugoni (1991) did a review and meta-analysis of 61 studies and found there were several complex reasons for these null findings. Among them were tendencies to use what they called a disease-based spectrum, self-report measures, and the use of myocardial infarction (MI) as a criterion for prediction. In sum, Miller et al. found that 46% of middle-aged males (+ or − 2%) in healthy populations could be classified as Type A while 70% (+ or − 2%) among those with CHD were type A.

Two central concepts emerge from the Type A studies: One is an unrealistic need for control over the environment to achieve in the quickest time possible. The other is the anger that occurs when these attempts at success or control fail. Research indicates that anger is probably the most important factor.

Apparently Type A, although seemingly universal in its relationship with CHD, is a personality type especially prevalent in the United States (Rosenman, 1986). Furthermore, Eaker and Castelli (1988) found that Type As in the United States also had fatal heart attacks at a younger age than Type Bs. Therefore, they conclude, culture influences the rate of Type A but not its connection to heart disease.

What then are the methods to reduce Type A behavior among the U.S. citizens who are rushing toward their first heart attack? Ornish (1990) claims heart disease can be reversed by a low-fat diet to take care of the cholesterol as well as exercise and meditation to reduce stress levels. His arguments cite many independent studies. The solution seems to be to become free of time compression pressures and to learn to enjoy life more, not a small effort in a competitive, achievement-oriented society.

The Thrill Seeking Type T

T stands for *thrills*. The Type T personality is the one that enjoys jumping out of planes on a Sunday afternoon (with parachute, preferably). Farley (1990) studied this type of personality and sees it as a continuum on which all of us fit at some place. At one end of the continuum is the "Big" T, who goes out for major thrills, high risks, and constant stimulation. At the other end is the "small" t, who at most takes small risks and avoids thrills and high stimulation. The other dimension is a negative, or self-destructive risk-taking type, versus a positive, healthy, and constructive risk taker. Farley (1990) believes "Type T is at the basis of both the most positive and constructive forces in our nation and the most negative and destructive forces, vandalism, crime drug and alcohol abuse, drinking and driving, etc." (p. 29).

Type Ts are measured by a variety of instruments. In a maze test, the Type Ts constantly vary their routes even though they may have found an exit. Type Ts tend to make complex patterns or prefer complex patterns in figure tests. If you like to ski on increasingly dangerous slopes, climb increasingly difficult rock cliffs just for fun, and, yes, if you belong to a sky diving club, you are likely to be a Type T. On the other hand, if you are a citizen of the United States, you are also likely to be a Type T because Farley believes the United States is a Type T nation.

Critics maintain the construct validity of the Type T is weak and its relationship to stress not demonstrated.

Stress at Work

What is the most stressful situation people find at work? Evans and Carrere (1991) studied bus driving as one of the highest stress occupations. They report that nearly one fourth of the cost of public transportation is related to the absenteeism of bus drivers. But what is it that is so stressful? Evans and Carrere observed the driver's stress was highest at peak traffic conditions exactly when he had greatest pressure to make a great many decisions with little choice. The interpretation was that this was the point at which he had least perceived control of his situation. Karasek and Theorell (1990) did a study of Swedish workers and found the jobs most associated with illness were those with high demand but little control such as being a nurse. The researchers also repeated this study with U.S. workers and found a correlation between low-status jobs and heart attacks among 4,800 workers.

Thus the myth that the executive has the highest-stress job is exactly the opposite of reality. Executives have high workload demands but this is moderated by control of their situations. Karasek and Theorell (1990) claim lawyers and doctors have control over almost anything they do.

More relevant to a total stress concept was the attempt to measure *total workload* by Mardberg, Lundberg, and Frankenhaeuser (1990) and Frankenhaeuser et al. (1990). They looked at the demands on the job plus the other demands of unpaid duties such as commuting, raising children, doing laundry, cleaning house. The results clearly show the greater chronic stress load of women, especially with children living at home. Further, the stress load will be evident at work but will be due to the greater load from unpaid work.

Stress of the Designed Environment

We are so accustomed to the designed environment of buildings and public spaces that we don't notice the stress they place upon us except at critical moments when we are in an emergency or lost. Zimring (1981) points out how the design of buildings can be a contributor to or a moderator of stress. Actually, findings on stress from building designs is one of the oldest results of environmental psychology research. Osmond (1957) proposed a radial design for mental hospitals to give mental patients a choice between more public (sociofugal) and more private (sociopetal) spaces. This set the tone for many research studies to follow, and *choice* became a key word in designing environments that alleviated stress. Sommer (1969b), for example, found that people waiting in airports wanted space both for intimate conversation and, essentially, for being alone.

Lack of physical boundaries is another common problem in built environments. Bechtel (1977) illustrates an example from an office where a sergeant had to take men out of the room to counsel them because of a lack of privacy. Lecompte and Willems (1970) describe a rehabilitation hospital where staff erected physical barriers around their operations to create privacy. Open offices (Brookes & Kaplan, 1972) and open schools (Gump, 1974) are notorious for not having barriers to create privacy. Many of these offices now have been "landscaped" by office furniture that provides shoulder-high barriers.

Wayfinding is a great source of stress in the environment when people get lost in cities and buildings. Added to this stress is the cross-sex battle between males who hate to ask for directions and females who insist on it. Carpman et al. (1984) found that people become uncomfortable in

---

Box 11.2

Advice for Coping With Jet Lag

- Be well rested prior to flights
- Change your wrist watch on boarding the plane
- Avoid caffeine, alcohol and smoking
- Drink plenty of fluids
- Get out and about in daylight
- Stay up until normal destination bedtime
- Keep a midnight snack and earplugs handy
- Allow jet lag adjustment time on your return
- Consider staying on home time

SOURCE: Monk (1987); reprinted by permission.

hospitals if they go 50 feet without seeing a sign. Thus signs should be placed at least every 50 feet to reassure visitors.

Levine et al. (1984), who did research on you-are-here signs, discovered that if the signs are not matched exactly with the environment (i.e., unless north in the map points to north in the environment), the YAH map can cause more distress than if there were no sign at all. Getting lost can be a frightening experience in cities and especially in foreign countries where one does not know the language.

Another stress introduced in a technological society is the phenomenon of jet lag. Travelers skipping from one time zone to another four or five time zones away find themselves becoming disoriented, sometimes having stomach upset, and possessed by an overwhelming desire to sleep at the times to perform while an inability to sleep hits at the times when sleep is expected in the new time zone. These effects may last over a week for some. See Box 11.2 for some advice from Monk (1987).

A serious problem with environmental design studies is that no one has considered how these various problems—ambient stressors, daily hassles, life events, wayfinding, and other sources—add together. What is the total impact of all this stress? Milgram (1970) postulated his overload hypothesis to explain how people deal with stimulus overload in the city, but this did not deal with the measurement of how stressful all these impacts were. It only dealt with how people managed the load by trying to control the inputs from the environment.

Indirectly, both Chapin (1974) and Michelson (1985) conducted studies that dealt with stress in a total environment. The approach used random samples to find out who had the most free time. One result of both studies was the discovery that the people who had the least free time were working women with children. They were the most stressed in the samples from Washington, D.C., and Toronto, Canada. And they got little help from men, who had the most free time. In many ways, the environment also worked against them because they had to get children to school yet get to work on time, fetch children from school, and then come home to prepare meals. They also had to perform chores such as getting to bank when the hours were not convenient. Some of this has been alleviated by more recent changes in banking hours and the advent of 24-hour stores and gas stations but the working mother, single or married, remains the most stressed category in our society. These findings parallel findings from the Swedish studies on total workload, cited above.

Agarwal (1988) cites surveys from India that show the dismal plight of women in Third World countries. In these countries, the role of collecting fodder, fuel, and water is left to women, and as the environment erodes, these tasks become increasingly difficult and take more and more time. In many parts of India, all women have to work 11-16 hours every day of the week. Most do not have time to go to a clinic for illness. Agarwal points out that the invasion of a cash economy forces men into the city. The women left behind often have to fend for the children alone, and in certain areas such as Ranchi, they may be able to eat only every other day. Similar conditions exist in East and West Africa. Agarwal (1988) describes the plight of such woman:

> The women wake up early in the morning about 4 a.m. and soon after they begin their trek to the forest. On reaching the forest, some 8-10 km away, they begin collecting firewood. By the afternoon, having collected the firewood, they do not return home but go off to Ranchi in a train. They spend the night at the Ranchi railway station, which these days is an extraordinary sight. Then early next morning they sell the wood, a load of some 20-25 kg. For this entire load they get Rs. 5-6, a third of which they lose in bribing the forest guard on a fixed weekly rate and the train conductors who allow them a free ride. With the remaining money, the women buy some salt, kerosene for lighting and other vital household

necessities and return home. That evening they cook food and eat the first freshly cooked meal in two days. Next morning the two day cycle begins afresh. (pp. 115-116)

Kaplan (1994) predicts this combination of increasing population and erosion of resources will force many countries into the kind of anarchy already existing in Rwanda. Not many studies of stress measure the constant strain experienced by people in these countries.

Predictability

Weiss (1970) was one of the first to demonstrate that the predictability of an aversive stimulus like electric shock reduced the amount of stress. An animal could accommodate to shocks that came at predictable times. The critical variable seemed to be knowing when to relax. Abbott, Schoen, and Badia (1984) pointed out, however, that this situation was not similar for humans. In fact, often, when humans had to undergo predictable shocks for a long period of time, the expected shocks became just as stressful as the unpredictable ones. Abbott et al. criticized previous studies because they were relatively short and did not allow the long-term effects of predictable shock to occur. Arthur (1986) claims that *all* predictable shock is stressful whether long or short term, but Abbott and Badia (1986) disagree, saying that many studies show predictability can act as a safety signal.

Salutogenesis

Antonovsky (1979) proposed the term *salutogenesis* to mean the genesis of health. He criticized studies of stress and health for ignoring the obvious fact that most people do not get sick from stressful events. What must be studied is why people don't get sick from these events. There is more to be learned from healthy response than from studying pathology. Only then can pathology be truly understood in its larger context of health. Health and sickness are at the ends of a continuum. What pushes people toward one end of the continuum as opposed to the other?

Antonovsky claims that stress is a normal part of daily life, but that this normal aspect is actually only *tension* while stress, per se, enters the picture when tension is not managed. But how is tension managed?

Antonovsky proposes it is managed by acquiring a *coherent* view of the universe and one's place in it. This is the chief way by which a person gains the perspective of gaining control of his or her own life. Once again, we meet the perspective of control.

Conclusions

In summary, stress is caused when we lose control of a situation because the environment presents more demands than we can meet at the moment. This can occur through getting lost, losing a loved one, fighting through traffic, or many of the crises encountered in modern life. Stress can also occur from background circumstances such as poisoned environments. Humans, unlike animals, have many resources through which they can escape stress or overcome it. Cognitive ability to discern real danger from imagined is just one of many. The most important of these is the feeling of having control of one's life, whether it is gained through direct coping, palliative manipulation, or having a coherent view of the universe.

Different personality styles complicate responses or make it easier to cope with stress. Type As bring more stress onto themselves than is necessary. Type Bs are better copers with stress. Type Ts think stress is fun. Nevertheless, there is no denying the link between stress and ill health and the changes in lifestyle that may be needed for many in our society to provide themselves a healthier existence.

GOALS

Definitions and Concepts

Stress

Physiological model

Psychological model

Catecholamines

Type A

Type T

Salutogenesis

Moderators

Mediators

How to measure stress

Life events

Ambient stressors

Daily hassles

Hardiness

Important Studies

Abbott et al. (1984)

Aldwin and Stokols (1988)

Karasek and Theorell (1990)

Friedman et al. (1986)

Selye (1956)

Zimring (1981)

QUESTIONS

1. What was the most stressful experience in your life?
2. What is the main difficulty in defining stress?
3. How do moderators and mediators of stress differ?
4. What is the chief feature of the psychological model of stress?
5. What are good strategies to reduce stress?
6. How many stress points do you earn for being fired?
7. What are the problems in measuring hardiness?
8. What is a Type A person? Type B?
9. Does laughing and having a good time cause stress?
10. What is the relationship between psychological control and stress?

12

Energy: A Missed Opportunity

———— ⚜ ————

Historical Perspective

The Energy Crisis (That Caught Us Napping)

As is always the case when a major crisis occurs, experts come forward to sing a chorus of "I told you so." Many experts had been predicting an energy crisis for years. Conservation critics had forecast energy shortages since the 1940s (Vogt, 1948). The Club of Rome (Meadows et al., 1972) collected data to show a crisis of crises beyond the turn of the century. The energy crisis never became real to the United States, however, until the Arab Oil Embargo of 1973 when oil shortages forced millions to wait in gas lines and the subsequent price rise made scarcity evident. It is significant that the evidence for shortages was always there but virtually ignored even after the embargo.

Halberstam (1986) describes how Charley Maxwell, an oil industry expert advising the firm of Cyrus Lawrence on Wall Street, traveled to Detroit in June 1973 to warn the three automobile manufacturers about the coming shortage of oil. He claimed that the kind of car in the future would not be the large type being manufactured by Detroit but small, more gas-efficient cars. He was virtually ignored. Then, on October 6, 1973, the crisis began.

This theme of attending primarily to present successes and being unable to plan for the prevention of future negative events is by now a familiar one. It continues to be the main theme in energy as an environmental topic.

The Lessons of the 1970s
(When We Learned a Lot)

Looking back at the 1970s, Baum and Singer (1981) proposed three categories for energy studies: social trap analyses, conservation strategies, and the energy system as a hazard. The tragedy of the commons (see Chapter 4, "Environmental Ethics" section) was studied experimentally by Brechner and Linder (1981) and Stern and Kirkpatrick (1977). Platt (1973) proposed expanding the concept to include more varieties of social traps. Wilson's (1977) solution for the Maine lobster fisheries was to turn the commons area into private property for which owners were responsible. This produced a solution in that the fishermen no longer overfished the areas over which they had domain.

Yet there remain many examples of the commons dilemma still operating. The oceans of the world are the best example, followed by the burning of the rain forests, the killing of elephants, and the disappearance of many species.

Communication of information is one way out of the dilemma. When subjects received information about the depletion of the resources and could communicate with one another about this in the Brechner experiments, they acted more responsibly to prevent further loss of resources (Brechner & Linder, 1981).

Dividing the resource into territories as Wilson (1977) did seems a viable solution. Monbiot (1994) points out that the commons dilemma is not necessarily inevitable behavior. A cooperative society would not tolerate such selfish, individual pursuit of gain. However, this seems belied by cooperative societies' overfishing of the oceans. Apparently there is a difference when the resource is seen as limitless.

The Lesson of the 1980s
(When We Lost It)

One of the first acts of the Reagan administration in 1980 was to take down the solar collectors on the roof of the White House. This was symbolic of things to come. David Stockman, head of the Bureau of the Budget, announced that the social sciences would no longer be funded by the federal government. The 1983 budget cut alternative energy programs by 97% (see more consequences in the section on retrenchment in Chapter 2).

The Lesson of the 1990s (When We Hope We Don't Have to Learn It Over Again)

Stern (1992) summarizes energy research in the 1970s and 1980s as being more focused on energy use in households when actually much bigger savings could be made by targeting industry. Households account for only one third of U.S. energy consumption while industry accounts for the remaining two thirds. He claims looking for behaviors outside households will have a bigger payoff for the future.

Stern lists three categories of behavior to target:

1. Direct energy use actions such as driving a car or turning on lights are small for each person, but multiplied by the millions who perform these actions, there is a potential for great savings.

2. Technology choices such as more energy-efficient homes, cars, and appliances have a large potential impact on energy use.

3. Policy choices such as legislating lower auto emissions, taxing energy use to promote conservation, and regulating air pollution from manufacturers have the greatest potential impact of all. Unfortunately, this is the area where social scientists have had the least influence.

Kempton, Darley, and Stern (1992) point out that low gasoline prices in the United States have weakened motives to conserve energy. But Kempton et al. paint a new picture of the energy crisis from the 1970s and 1980s. It was then a crisis of economics while now it is a crisis of environmental degradation. This is illustrated by the way coal was perceived as a solution to the earlier crisis but a cause of much of the current crisis because of its polluting properties.

Stern and Oskamp (1987) proposed a psychological model of energy use (see Figure 12.1). The principle we can gain from this model is that the important behaviors to target for change must be determined first.

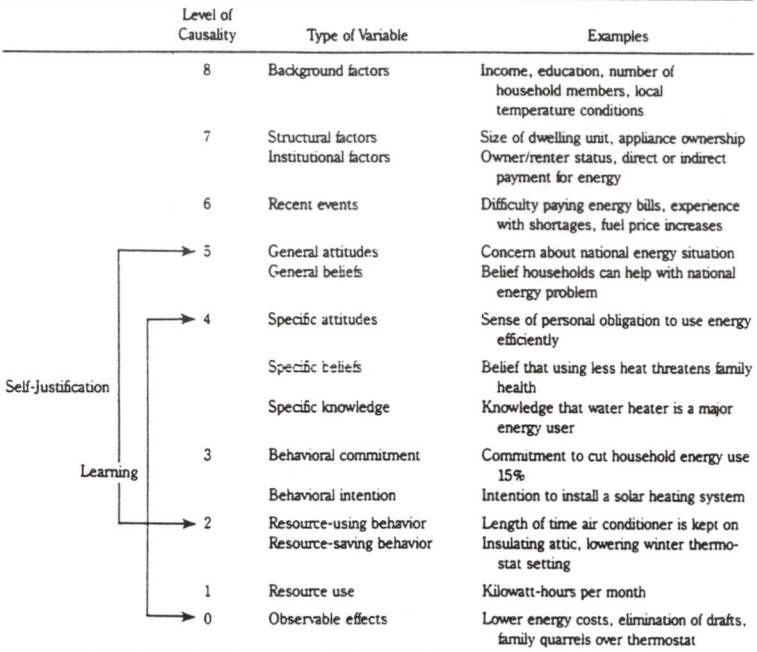

Level of Causality	Type of Variable	Examples
8	Background factors	Income, education, number of household members, local temperature conditions
7	Structural factors / Institutional factors	Size of dwelling unit, appliance ownership / Owner/renter status, direct or indirect payment for energy
6	Recent events	Difficulty paying energy bills, experience with shortages, fuel price increases
5	General attitudes / General beliefs	Concern about national energy situation / Belief households can help with national energy problem
4	Specific attitudes	Sense of personal obligation to use energy efficiently
	Specific beliefs	Belief that using less heat threatens family health
	Specific knowledge	Knowledge that water heater is a major energy user
3	Behavioral commitment	Commitment to cut household energy use 15%
	Behavioral intention	Intention to install a solar heating system
2	Resource-using behavior / Resource-saving behavior	Length of time air conditioner is kept on / Insulating attic, lowering winter thermostat setting
1	Resource use	Kilowatt-hours per month
0	Observable effects	Lower energy costs, elimination of drafts, family quarrels over thermostat

Self-Justification · Learning

Figure 12.1. Psychological Model of Energy Use
SOURCE: Stern and Oskamp (1987, 1991 reprint, p. 1063); reprinted by permission.

Previous studies have produced a number of methods of energy conservation. Geller et al. (1982) presented a series of over 150 studies that were a tour de force for conservation. For example, people can be taught not to litter (Dodge, 1972; Heberlein, 1974) but it is not easy to get them to pick up litter (Finnie, 1973; Geller, Witmer, & Orebaugh, 1976; Geller, Witmer, & Tuso, 1977).

Geller and his associates found that Keep America Beautiful (KAB) was the most successful litter control agency in the world. It operated through a plan called the Clean Community System (CCS) in 207 U.S. communities and six other countries. The KAB was supported by over 100 companies, labor unions, and other organizations. Each community paid $125 for a training workshop, various manuals, and bulletins. An analysis was then made of the community's existing practices and rules, which were changed if necessary to produce more conservation, and the results were evaluated. These steps involve a complex and sometimes costly procedure for communities to follow. One criticism of the KAB has been its failure to support bottle bills, which would also help reduce litter.

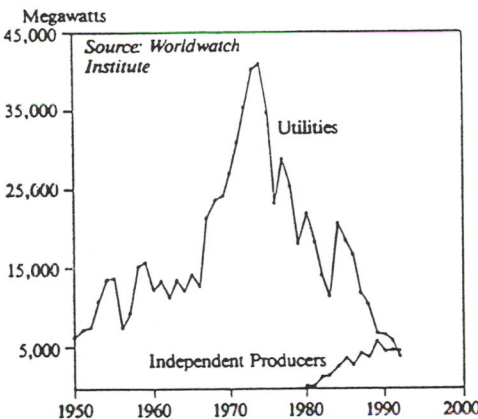

Figure 12.2. Additions to U.S. Installed Generating Capacity by Utilities and Independent Power Producers 1950-1992
SOURCE: Flavin and Lenssen (1994, p. 18, Figure 2); reprinted by permission.

Geller et al. (1982) also describe studies of recycling waste oil from automobiles, the use of a worm bin to recycle household garbage, and the recycling of other wastes such as glass, paper, and metals. However, they lamented the lack of awareness of how behavioral methods can be applied to these methods of conservation. Since the time of these studies, much progress has been made in recycling.

Electric Power

On September 6, 1882, Thomas A. Edison threw a switch in a converted warehouse in New York and lit up 156 lightbulbs in nearby office buildings. Thus began the electric power industry, which has grown to encompass the world. Today's electric power industry's value is estimated at $800 billion (Flavin & Lenssen, 1994; Figure 12.2).

The history of this industry follows the pattern of most industries: the pursuit of exponential growth. This actually seemed to occur until high fuel prices, overproduction of appliances, and public disfavor of nuclear energy resulted in a "bust" by the early 1980s.

Flavin and Lenssen (1994) describe changes in the power industry that have come about due to the passage of the Public Utility Regulatory Policies Act of 1978 (PURPA). This act allows companies other than the

Figure 12.3. "Windmill Valley" in California

utilities to construct their own power plants and sell the electricity to the utilities. Many companies took advantage of this act to the extent that demand for electricity fell off, and by the 1990s these independent companies had equaled the amount of electricity produced by the utilities (see Figure 12.2). This has resulted in the use of smaller generating plants and alternatives such as wind power (see Figure 12.3).

Another result of PURPA has been technological innovation in electric power generation. New "combined cycle" plants are being built that have energy efficiencies of 53% as opposed to the conventional coal-fired plant's 40%. These plants have a gas turbine that uses the excess heat of operation to run a steam turbine, thus the combined cycle.

To counter the constant push for expansion, a demand side management strategy (DSM) has been developed to demonstrate that in many cases it is economically more profitable to decrease demand for electricity than to build new plants. State governments are allowing utilities to make profits from the "saved" electricity. Although this may sometimes mean higher rates, the consumer benefits through having to buy less electricity.

Stern and Gardner (1981) list the behaviors that the average householder can use to reduce energy consumption (see Table 12.1). Geller et al. (1982) also described a number of behaviors. Socolow (1978) claims that following these procedures can reduce energy consumption by 50% in the average household. These procedures involve essentially two strategies: antecedents and consequents.

Antecedent procedures refer to something done *before* the expected behavior. Antecedents include *information* in the form of such materials as pamphlets, brochures, and ads. *Modeling* uses role performances as examples to follow. *Expectancies* as a strategy involve changing the way people view a situation to get them to conserve.

The general conclusion is that information by itself is not sufficient to cause much change in conservation behavior (Stern & Gardner, 1981). Modeling, via the Bandura (1979) concept, has not had much testing, but Winett et al. (1981) report success in getting subjects to save 26% in electricity use.

The expectancy strategy involves disabusing people of a false belief and then substituting correct information. A major false belief, for example, is that certain temperatures are necessary to maintain good health. Even though the evidence against this belief is substantial (Bell et al., 1978), there does not seem to be any evidence that correcting false impressions like this one has any effect on conservation.

Prompts involve things such as slogans and promotions to conserve. These can be such short aphorisms as "Save Energy" to a small label above a light switch that reads, "Turn Out Lights." Prompts are more effective if they are specific (Winett, 1978) about what to do and who should do it. The most important lesson to learn is that all these strategies are most effective as part of a larger program that has prompts coordinated with information and modeling.

Consequence procedures are rewards that follow a behavior and tend to reinforce it. These include rebates, recognition for achievement, and other forms that reward the behavior. Consequences have some degree of success (McClelland & Belsten, 1979; Winett, Neale, & Grier, 1979; Winett, Neale, Williams, et al., 1979).

Feedback, a form of consequence, seems to be the most successful energy-conservation instruction method. Cherulnik (1993) cites this method as an example of success with psychological techniques. The consumer merely receives information quickly about how successful the efforts have been to save energy. This can be in the form of a daily postcard

Table 12.1 Estimated Percentage of Current Household Energy Consumption That Can Be Saved by 30 Different Conservation Behaviors

End use	Curtailment	%	Increased efficiency	%
Household transportation				
Automobile	Carpool to work with one or two others	4-6	Buy more efficient auto (27.5 vs. 14 mpg)	20
	Cut shopping trips to one-half current mileage	2	Get frequent tune-ups	2
	Alter driving habits with mpg or vacuum feedback	2 (or more)	Maintain tire inflation pressures at correct level	1
Inside the home				
Space heat	Set back thermostat from 72° to 68°F. days and to 65° nights	4	Insulate and weatherize house	10
Water heat	Set back thermostat by 20°F.	1	Install more efficient heating equipment	8
Refrigeration/freezing	Decide on items you want in advance and open/close doors quickly	.5	Clean refrigerator coils frequently.	1
	Thaw frozen foods in refrigerator before cooking	.1		
Lighting	Do not leave porch light on all night	.3	Change one half of all incandescent bulbs to fluorescent	1.0
	Replace all hall and ceiling lights with 40-watt bulbs	.1	Clean bulbs and fixtures regularly	.3
Cooking	Do not use self-cleaning feature of oven	.2	Buy more efficient unit	.9
	Use right-size pots and do not open oven door to check food	.2		
Air conditioning	Set back (up) thermostat from 73° to 78°F.	.6	Buy more efficient unit	.7
			Insulate and weatherize home (see above under "Space heat")	
Drying	Do not use dryer 6 months of the year	.5	Buy more efficient unit	.2
Miscellaneous	Do not use garbage disposal unit	less than .1	Fix all dripping hot water faucets	.1
			Replace leaking refrigerator door seal	.1

SOURCE: Stern and Gardner (1981). Used by permission.

a. Figures in the right-hand column that refer to more efficient autos, appliances, and other equipment indicate energy savings that would result if all consumers purchased equipment that was among the most energy efficient currently on the market or likely to be on the market in the next year so two. The table assumes that more efficient appliances, autos, and other equipment are purchased when old equipment wears out and would normally be replaced. Hence, uniform, nationwide adoption of new equipment would require approximately 10 years to complete. The same time span is assumed as a minimum for dwelling insulation and weatherization. "Most energy efficient" is defined according to the following guidelines: (a) automobiles—the 27.5 miles-per-gallon (mpg) average new-car fuel economy federally mandated for 1985, a level of efficiency achieved by many of the most efficient autos now on the market; (b) appliances—the 1976 Federal Energy Administration (now part of the Department of Energy) projected efficiency averages for 1990 . . ., figures that were chosen on the basis of information from DOE's Office of Conservation and Solar Applications . . . concerning likely mandatory appliance minimum efficiency levels that will be in effect by 1981; and (c) insulation and weatherization—an estimated 35% decrease in energy consumption from current levels resulting from the installation of attic and wall insulation, storm windows, and weather stripping, a figure that assumes a mixture of dwelling types and levels of insulation in existing housing stock as of the early 1970s (does not include greater efficiency increases possible in new-home construction) . . .

b. Data were compiled or estimated [from various sources including the Office of Energy Preparedness and Office of Technology Assessment].

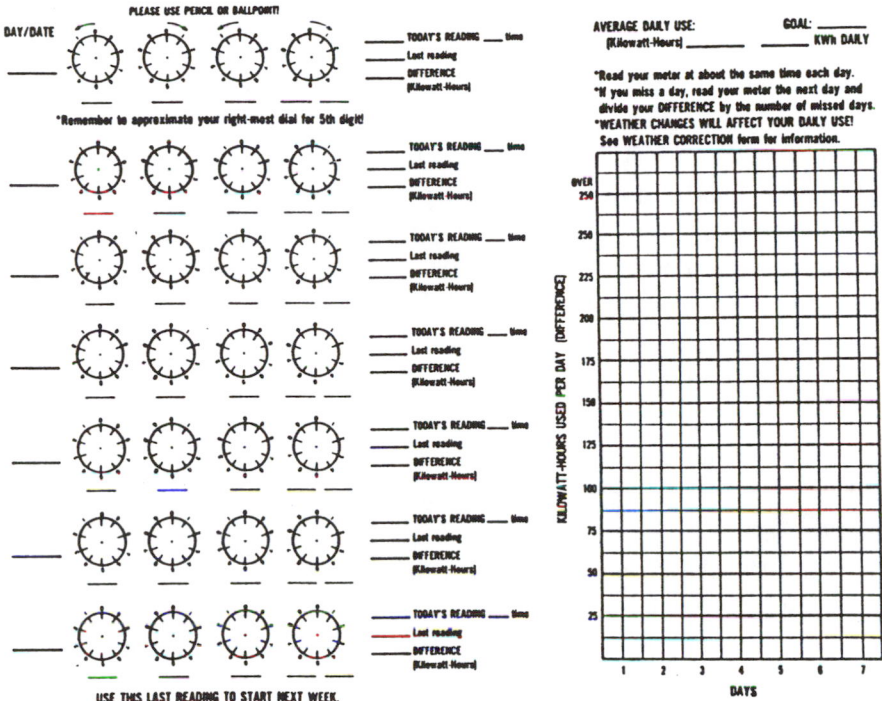

Figure 12.4. A Self-Monitoring Form for Consumers to Record Daily Readings on Their Electricity Meter Dials
SOURCE: Stern and Gardner (1981). Used by permission.

with electric or gas usage data compared with the previous year, week, or month, or a chart or some other easily comprehended way of measuring achievement. In fact, so successful has this method been that most utilities in the United States now include such charts in their monthly bills, comparing this month with last month and the year before (Figure 12.4).

Devices such as alarms for overload can be used as well as special digital meters. Self-monitoring is the most economical form of feedback and an example used for electrical monitoring is shown in Figure 12.4.

Nuclear Power

On September 16, 1954, while addressing the National Association of Science Writers in New York, Lewis Strauss of the U.S. Atomic Energy Commission declared that atomic energy would make electricity so available it would be "too cheap to meter." This expression, erroneous as it proved to be, was an example of the early enthusiasm over atomic energy. It would be more accurate to cite the atomic energy effort as the best example of an energy system that proved to be a hazard.

The most significant turning point for atomic energy came in March 1979 when radioactivity was released by accident into the atmosphere by the Three Mile Island nuclear power plant in Pennsylvania. Prior to this episode, surveys showed the public generally in favor of nuclear energy, but from this point on, support for nuclear energy declined (Mitchell, 1980).

In 1978, two new nuclear plants were ordered but twelve existing orders were canceled. In 1979, no new plants were ordered and an additional three units were canceled. In the first 3 months of 1980, three more units were canceled. It is estimated that out of the original 192 nuclear power plants built or planned in the United States, only 166, or possibly as few as 136, will ever operate (Council on Environmental Quality, 1980).

Webber (1982) did an analysis of California voters and found that their attitudes toward nuclear power seemed to be separate from attitudes toward the environment in general and that there was a larger potential for nuclear power opposition than for environmental concerns. By contrast, Goldhaber, Houts, and Disabella (1982) did not find a mass exodus of residents from the Three Mile Island area but did find an influx of residents who were more favorable toward nuclear power.

Much is made of the supposed fact that residents in general do not "logically" respond to the actual risks of nuclear power (see box). Slovic, Fischoff, and Lichtenstein (1981) point out that public reactions to nuclear risks are quite logical given the information available. The experts who estimate the risks are often proven wrong (see the section on the risks of nuclear waste, below) and the president's commission investigating TMI criticized the Nuclear Regulatory Commission for its lack of attention to safety issues.

The quotation from Weinberg (1976) seems even more true today:

> As I compare the issues we perceived during the infancy of nuclear energy with those that emerged during its maturity, the public perception and acceptance of nuclear energy appears to be the question we missed rather badly. . . . This issue has emerged as the most critical question concerning the future of nuclear energy. (p. 19)

And then came Chernobyl. In 1986, the nuclear plant at that location in what was then the Soviet Union went critical and sent 50 million curies

---

Box 12.1

Fear and Loathing of Nuclear Power

Advocates of civilian nuclear energy have long maintained that the public doesn't accept such plants mainly because it is fundamentally ignorant of the way risks are assessed. If people understand the facts, they say, opposition to nuclear power will dissipate in the clear light of reason. But a recent study shows that educating the public about these risks can have just the opposite effect.

In 1989, Taiwan's state-operated power corporation, Taipower, undertook a 4-month "risk communication program" to convince the public of the need for a new nuclear power plant. Taipower spent over $460,000 to produce 150 lectures, debates, and discussion groups at schools and cultural centers, as well as a series of public television programs emphasizing the merits of the new plant. In addition, the corporation offered to compensate residents living near the plant by over $6 million a year during the 10-year construction period and $4.6 million a year thereafter.

Researchers Jin Tan Liu of the Academia Sinica in Taiwan and V. Kerry Smith of North Carolina State University found, however, that instead of leaving the public more receptive to the idea of nuclear power, Taipower's campaign only "increased respondents' perceptions of the seriousness of risks posed by nuclear plants." Their survey of 404 households interviewed before and after the Taipower campaign revealed that "increased risk perceptions after the debate made respondents less likely to favor the plant."

These conclusions hold clear implications for the U.S. nuclear industry, Smith says. "You have to do more than just provide people with facts." Smith adds that his research into the related problems posed by nuclear waste disposal suggest another way of swaying the public. "There are clear indicators that when local authorities have the power to oversee and to shut things down, the more acceptable the whole notion becomes."

---

of radiation into the atmosphere. By 1992, 200,000 people had to be evacuated and the estimates of death due to cancer from irradiation range from 14,000 to half a million. Attitude surveys after Chernobyl showed the lowest support for nuclear energy ever recorded (Eiser, 1990; Peters, 1990; Verplanken, 1989).

Nuclear Waste

Despite the fact that the "atomic age" began in 1942 when the first chain reaction took place in a football stadium in Chicago, the governments of the world still have not worked out a way to dispose of nuclear waste. Even the waste from that first chain reaction has yet to find a safe disposal site. Meantime, literally hundreds of thousands of tons of nuclear waste have accumulated and been temporarily stored on the site of each nuclear facility. Some of these storage containers are inadequate and some have even exploded and caused disasters on their own. In September 1957, one of the steel tanks holding nuclear waste from atomic weapons manufacture in the Soviet Union exploded and caused the evacuation of 11,000 people. Governments continue to search for a solution but as yet none is apparent in the foreseeable future.

The most extensive research on the effects of radiation on humans is the long-term study of the victims of Hiroshima and Nagasaki. As a result of these studies and others that have come to light, the estimates of allowable exposure to radiation have been drastically revised downward. In 1934, the allowable radiation exposure for a worker was 30 centisieverts per year over the whole body. By 1990, this was revised to only 2 centisieverts, a multiple reduction of 15 times.[1]

The earliest scheduled year for a country to have a disposal plan for nuclear wastes is 2010 for France, India, and the United States. The latest is 2040 for Argentina, Italy, and the Netherlands. Other countries set their dates in between.

Plant Disposal

Perhaps even more controversial than nuclear waste is the problem of how to dispose of a nuclear power plant after it has outlived its usefulness. The more polite term used is *decommissioning*.

The process of decommissioning is itself laborious and not entirely satisfactory. For example, the expected life of a nuclear plant is 40 years, yet some have had to close after only 16 years. The average plant takes up about 40 acres of land and the structure is either dismantled and removed from the site or dismantled and "entombed" on the site by being sealed in a monolithic concrete structure. The latter solution means that the site must be guarded for 33 years, in one estimate, to 10,000 years in another.

Although it may seem that complete dismantling and removal is preferred, this method has some problems with exposure of the workers and the issue of removing and storing the contaminated waste. On the other hand, entombment has the perpetual cost of guarding the site.

A third solution is merely to close the doors and guard the plant in perpetuity. Obviously, this problem, just like the one of nuclear waste, has yet to be worked out.

The Sun Also Rises

Solar energy is another example of the technological fix solution. The American Solar Energy Society, based in Boulder, Colorado, publishes an annual review called *Advances in Solar Energy* (see Prince, 1993). The International Solar Energy Society is devoted to the advancement of solar energy and boasts membership in 90 countries (see Goetzberger, 1993). Optimistic as it may be about replacing all the world's electric plants with solar cells, it also seems clear that the solar cell cannot yet compete economically with current methods for generating electricity when it comes to more global usage such as air-conditioning and general household electric use. However, solar hot water heaters are another matter. Many countries use solar hot water heaters as a common method, and although the U.S. advertises more costly commercial models, a simple one can be built for under $100.

At one time, the National Energy Act allowed household owners to deduct the cost of solar installations from their income tax but this was just one of the many energy-saving consequence methods that vanished in the 1980s. Hoagland (1995) found that, because the public tended to view energy as less of a crisis in the 1980s, the motive to use solar technology declined.

Energy and Lifestyles

Lifestyles have a direct bearing on energy use. The U.S. lifestyle, which emphasizes ever-increasing consumption, takes a disproportionate share of energy. Mazur and Rosa (1974) compared lifestyle indicators with energy consumption in 55 countries and found the indicators highly associated with energy consumption among the 19 developed countries but not among the remaining undeveloped countries. Their conclusion was that it is likely energy can be conserved without markedly reducing lifestyles, but there will be some economic dislocation. Kruskal (1975) criticized this study but there was no disagreement that industrialization and energy consumption are closely related. Johnson, Stolzfus, and Craumer (1977) describe the Amish agricultural practices in their communities in the United States.

Their religious beliefs dictate energy use. They most often have horses instead of tractors with an average of eight horses or mules per farm; they don't use automobiles, and they maximize human labor. In short, they are a good group to study if one wants to compare the effects of an austere lifestyle on energy use and agricultural productivity. Although the study was not able to measure many of the side products of Amish life such as vegetables, shoofly pie, and so on, the chief advantage the Amish had over a comparison with British farmers was their low consumption of energy. The conclusion was that the Amish could survive easily without the support of the industrial society around them. Further, the Amish are prospering at a time when many small farmers, some even in the same locale, are going bankrupt. This labor-intensive, energy-conserving lifestyle is highly efficient. For example, the English farmers used 83% more energy to produce a unit of milk than the Amish. On the farms, the yield of the Amish in Pennsylvania was 4% greater than that of the English. It was interesting to compare the "new" order Amish with the old order. The Nebraska Amish (new) were 49% higher in energy use than the old order but their yields were 47% lower. Thus, even among the Amish, the older ways are more efficient. Johnson et al. conclude that the Amish would be the best able of any group in U.S. society to survive in agriculture if energy were to become scarce or more costly.

Revelle (1976) reported on energy use in India, an area that would seem obviously less energy consuming. The United States consumes 11.15 tons of U.N. coal equivalents per person compared with only .346 tons of the same units in India. Also, the villagers of India supply 89% of their own energy while virtually 100% of the energy use in the United States is from burning fossil fuels or hydroelectric power. But Revelle's conclusion is that this low-energy lifestyle virtually enslaves the Indians so that they cannot be free from the burdens of human labor required simply to be alive. Thus this study suggests that too much investment in human labor in agriculture does not allow for the amenities that most of us feel are necessary for civilization. The principal question this raises is how to strike a balance between the slavery to food production found in India versus the overconsumption found in the United States?

Gladhart, Zuiches, and Morrison (1978) found that family income was the best single predictor of energy consumption but concludes that *"those with the greatest economic incentive to save (the poor) . . . are the least able . . . and the upper income . . . have less incentive."* This principle is as true now as ever (Stern, 1992). Morell (1981) found that the middle income are those most likely to believe in conservation of energy. Morell's conclusion is that, based on the evidence available, economic incentives alone are not adequate to get people to save energy in the face of current institutional and political barriers to conservation. Changing lifestyles would likely not be supported by the existing infrastructure of the culture.

The Center for Science in the Public Interest published a lifestyle index (Fritsch & Castleman, 1974) that enables any individual to calculate his or her energy output. Part I, the Personal Inventory, is shown in the box.

Energy and Buildings

One significant area remains in which E&B research can contribute to energy conservation: designing buildings to conserve energy. The National Bureau of Standards (1973) maintained that the energy use of any building can be reduced by 20% merely by more careful operational practices and maintaining conservation procedures. Hirst and Hannon (1979) agreed with this figure. But much more can be accomplished by designing new buildings with energy conservation in mind. Further, if improved design is included with new energy-saving appliances, this savings in new buildings can be increased to a conservative 30% or even to 50% or more.

Rosenfeld and Hafemeister (1988) estimate that energy savings of $50 billion per year can be sustained by building energy-efficient buildings and that, most important, *this does not have to be at either a lowering of the standard of living or a sacrifice in comfort*. Snell, Achenback, and Peterson (1976) list four areas of design that help increase energy efficiency: (a) using insulation; (b) decreasing air flow through the building by caulking and sealing joints to increase the efficiency of insulation; (c) reducing the window area and using thermal panes (in severe climates, triple panes are cost effective); (d) landscaping to provide balanced shade and wind protection.

Box 12.3

PART I

a. Precise Household energy Expenditures

The most precise method of calculating energy expenditures is to take your fuel bills and convert to Energy Units (E.U. values) for comparison. Energy conversion factors are applied in this and many of the following sections. These are applied in order to account for energy lost in mining, refining, processing and conversion to electricity.

1. Take electric bills from last 12 months: Sum numbers of kilowatt hours of electricity; Multiply by 0.368 (conversion factor);
Your household's precise electric use in E.U.'s is _____ E.U.

2. Take your natural gas bills; Total the cubic feet used; Multiply by 0.038 (conversion factor);
Your household's precise gas use is _____ E.U.

3. Take your annual fuel oil bill; Total the number of gallons used; Multiply by 4.5 (conversion factor);
Your household's precise fuel oil bill is _____ E.U.

        Subtotal   _____ E.U.

If you have done (a) you may omit the rest of this section except for the last part, b-5 (Residential Building Material(s). Also you may omit PART 2, e (Preparing and Preserving Food) and PART 3, c (Electronic Appliances).

b. Approximate Household Energy Expenditure

1. Home Appliances (Refs. 1, 2)

The values listed are average annual use per item. Multiply by the number of items in the home. Food preparation items will be figures in PART 2, c-5.

Electric Appliances:

clock	(6)	_____
floor polisher	(6)	_____
sewing machine	(4)	_____
vacuum cleaner	(17)	_____
air cleaner	(80)	_____
bed covering	(54)	_____
dehumidifier	(128)	_____
heating pad	(4)	_____
humidifier	(60)	_____
germicidal lamp	(52)	_____
hair dryer	(5)	_____
heat lamp (infrared)	(5)	_____
shaver	(0.7)	_____
toothbrush	(0.2)	_____
vibrator	(0.7)	_____
clothes dryer	(365)	_____
iron (hand)	(53)	_____
washing machine (automatic)	(38)	_____
washing machine (non-automatic)	(28)	_____
water heater (standard)	(1555)	_____
water heater (quick recovery)	(1770)	_____

Gas Appliances:

gas clothes dryer	(277)	_____
gas water heater	(1170)	_____
Subtotal		_____ E.U.

2. Home Lighting (Refs. 3, 4)

Average electric use for lighting in the home is (268 E.U.).
This is equivalent to burning (54) 100 watt bulbs for four hours per day.

Ornamental lights (average annual	(668)	_____
(average annual use)		_____
Subtotal		_____ E. U.

3. Cooling and Ventilation (Refs. 1, 2, 3)

Fan (attic)	(107)	_____
Fan (circulating)	(16)	_____
Fan (rollaway)	(51)	_____
Fan (window)	(58)	_____
Electric air conditioner (room)	(510)	_____
Gas air conditioner	(1046)	_____

Central Air Conditioning:

New England	(755)	_____
Mid Atlantic	(957)	_____
East North Central	(905)	_____
West North Central	(905)	_____
South Atlantic	(1510)	_____
East South Central	(1560)	_____
West South Central	(1710)	_____
Mountain	(1058)	_____
Pacific	(1210)	_____
Subtotal		_____ E.U.

4. Space Heating (Refs. 2, 5, 6-8)

If you have not used the precise method (a) then use the following chart for approximate estimate of space heating energy expenditrure:

	Electric	Nat. Gas	Oil	Oil / Solar
Northeast	6480	5360	6380	
Middle Atlantic	5800	4800	5720	2210
East North Central	6030	4900	5940	2290
West North Central	5350	4440	5280	2040
South Atlantic	4460	3700	4400	1700
East South Central	4040	3330	3660	790
West South Central	2900	2400	2660	570
Mountain	4910	4060	4840	1870
Pacific	3800	3140	3740	1440

5. Residential Building Materials (Refs. 2, 8-14)

If your residence has been built in the last 25 years, add the following for building materials.

single dwelling	(844)
two- to four-unit apartment	(842)
five-plus unit apartment	(668)
public housing	(700)

Home additions and alterations also take energy. Multiply the dollar expenditure you incurred this past year by 1.1 E.U. per dollar spent.

Lawn and garden gasoline engines	(50)	_____
Subtotal		_____ E.U.

SOURCE: Fritsch and Castleman (1974, pp. 10-14); reprinted by permission.

Added to these four should be proper site orientation and building configuration to take advantage of the angles of the sun. In cold climates, the building should face the sun for maximum advantage, but in warm climates, the sun exposure should be minimized. Ralph Knowles (1981) analyzes sites by latitude and longitude to take best advantage of sun angles.

Snell et al. (1976) also recommend use of the heat pump because it saves one third to one half the costs of a total electric system. Heat pumps are best used in intermediate climates but are not very efficient in cold climates.

Finally, the use of underground buildings takes advantage of the more stable temperature of earth. Wells (1977) recommends underground houses and offices for energy savings. There exists more than a little prejudice against underground housing and it does cost more for construction. But the savings in energy more than compensate for the initial higher cost.

Conclusions

It seems that physical and social science technology are at a point where it would be relatively easy to implement many innovations in energy savings. Why doesn't this happen on a broader scale? There is a puzzling lack of support for a national energy program. Perhaps we need the motivation of a new energy crisis; yet, twice since 1973—in 1979 when there was another oil crisis and in 1990 when Desert Shield created an oil shortage—there was opportunity to declare a need for energy savings. Why didn't it happen? The governmental agencies continue to be consumer and economic growth oriented. This sets the tone for the rest of the society.

There are other reasons in addition to governmental will. Becker, Seligman, Fazio, and Darley (1981) noted the "comfort barrier," a belief that conservation requires a sacrifice of comfort. Add to it the unwillingness of those who can save energy to do so because of a lack of incentive (Gladhart's axiom). The sum is two powerful forces against conservation. Yet behind these remains the lack of government action.

Note

1. One centisievert is the equivalent of 1 rem, another unit to measure biological effects on the body. This is also equal to 1 roentgen, an equivalent in X rays. The different units are used to designate whether the radiation is from ionization or some other form. A centisievert measures the effects on the body of different types of radiation so it means the effects from several sources.

DOONESBURY

by Garry Trudeau

GOALS

Definitions and Concepts

Social trap

Conservation

Antecedent

Consequent

PURPA

Comfort barrier

Tragedy of the commons

Information program success

Prompts

TMI

Chernobyl

Decommissioning a nuclear plant

Lifestyles and energy

Gladhart et al.'s (1978) axiom

Important Studies

Geller et al. (1982)

Brechner (1974)

Wilson (1977)

Stern (1992)

Mazur and Rosa (1974)

Revelle (1976)

Knowles (1981)

QUESTIONS

1. What behavior in your own lifestyle uses the maximum amount of energy? (See the lifestyle analysis in the third box.)

2. Why is there no energy policy in the U.S. government?

3. What behavior in your lifestyle would you be unwilling to change to save energy?

4. Do the United States and other industrialized nations have a right to continue to use a disproportionate share of the world's energy? If not, what must be done?

5. What steps could be taken to get policymakers to use social science methods in energy savings?

6. Why is there no policy on nuclear waste?

7. What is the comparative success of antecedent and consequent strategies?

8. What is the comfort barrier?

9. Why has solar power not been used more?

10. What is the political opposition to better energy use?

13

Human Factors

Definition

At first blush, it would seem that *human factors* is a term synonymous with environment-behavior research. The problem is that human factors as a discipline began long before E&B research. Some claim it started with Quetelet's (1869, 1870) works while others see its beginnings around World War I. Whatever the origin, it was usually connected with engineering. Europeans refer to it as *ergonomics*. Some engineers call it *value engineering*; others call it *engineering psychology*. Much of it involves measurement of the physical attributes of the human body, called *anthropometry*. The way that human factors seems different from E&B was expressed by Henry M. Parsons (1972):

> Some of us in the human factors field who attend conferences and read the literature on environmental design discern such emphasis on subjective reactions that we are dismayed. We are not used to this. We are accustomed to in-put out-put models in which the important dependent behavior is what the individual does, not what he (she) feels. (pp. 370-371)

In other words, in the past, human factors used objective human behavior as its main independent variable and ignored any subjective aspects. After E&B and human factors researchers discovered one another, this changed and now both use subjective aspects of human behavior. But it must not be assumed that the fields have entirely merged. Although much overlap has occurred, there still remains an emphasis on the physical human measurements in human factors.

There is a Human Factors Society that organized in 1957 and publishes the journal *Human Factors*. Members are engineers, physiologists, psychologists, and "many other scientists who are concerned with the human element in operations, training and engineering" (quoted from the back cover of every issue of *Human Factors*).

Historical Perspective

Like many professionals in human factors, Adolphe Quetelet (1796-1874) was educated in one profession and wandered into another. He was a professional astronomer in Belgium and began studying anthropometrics (Quetelet, 1870), human abilities as they related to measurements of the body, and even such behaviors as propensity to commit crimes (see Quetelet, 1984).

Norman Triplett (1897) was another pioneer in human factors. He is best remembered for his work on bicycle races. The best strategy in any race is to wait until the last possible moment and then give forth the maximum effort. The psychology of being in front in the race created stress, which was the principle from which Triplett derived his strategy. He observed that racers were reluctant to take the lead for this reason. Hence the best strategy remains: Conserve that energy until the last moment.

Chapanis (1975) divided the history of human factors into four distinct periods: pre-World War I, the World War II and aerospace era, the era of sociotechnical systems, and the current or cosmopolitan era.

Actually, the pre-World War I era was fairly active in terms of human factors because it involved all the tools invented by humanity up to that time. Chapanis tends to slight this period because World War I gave impetus to the military aspects of human factors and began the work on the object that is probably the subject of more human factors research than any other: the airplane.

Airplanes were first used in World War I as substitutes for the slower observation balloons. As pilots flew over enemy territory, it became frustrating not to be able to shoot back at the troops who fired from below.

Gradually guns were introduced and then the arms race accelerated to machine guns. The problem was the machine gun was too efficient a hurler of bullets; the bullets found their way into the whirring propeller and the plane lost motive power and fell. With the intensity of battle, it was too much to expect the gunner to aim only to the side. There was a great need to fire forward. At first, metal "diverters" were fastened to the propeller so the bullets would be deflected. The trouble was they would be deflected to hit almost anywhere.

Anthony H. G. Fokker, a Dutch aircraft designer, noted the problem with machine guns and propellers and developed the "interrupter gear" so that the machine gun would only fire when the propeller was horizontal. This gave the Germans a tactical advantage and Fokker's 1915 monoplane became the terror of the skies. Only 400 were made before the allies learned to make their own interrupter gears by 1917.

The Sopwith Camel was a standard British fighter of this era. What is left out of popularization of the war is the fact that this airplane had a severe torque problem. *Torque* is the tendency of a spinning object to make the base to which it is attached spin in the opposite direction. The propeller on the airplane had a tendency to make the airplane spin the opposite way. This was countered by flying the plane as though it was always banking slightly. It was harrowing to have to remember not to fly exactly level.

It was not until the period between the first and second of Chapanis's eras that pilots learned how to get out of tailspins, which are now not the dreaded phenomenon they once were. A tailspin could just as well be called a nose spin from its appearance. The plane goes out of control and literally spins around its center of gravity, which is closer to the nose than the tail. It is not unlike a falling leaf. When a pilot stalled the plane or lost forward motion in a climb, a tailspin would often occur and the standard practice was to bail out. In the 1920s, General Billy Mitchell (1879-1936), famous for being the first to bomb battleships, learned that by gunning the engine the plane would stabilize and then the pilot could pull out of the dive and save both plane and pilot. Of course, problems have a way of returning, and the F-16 fighter plane of today has a nasty habit of going into a flat spin after a flameout, just to show how progress is not always in a straight line.

It was also the tendency in World War I to have pilots fly until they died. It was not until World War II that it was discovered motivation could be increased by limiting missions to a fixed number.

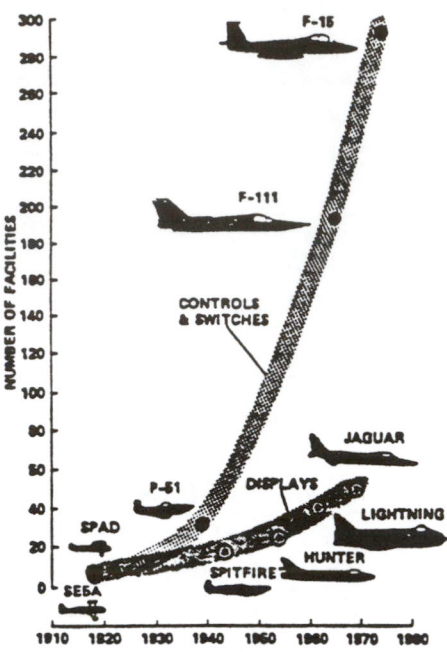

Figure 13.1. Cockpit Facilities Growth 1910-1980
SOURCE: Wickens and Rouse (1987).

The second era (World War II) ushered in a flood of human factors research connected with military weapons. The airplanes acquired metal skins, much more armament, and greater range and power. They also acquired greater complexity. Wickens and Rouse (1987) characterize military R&D as following a stereotyped pathway of invention and implementation before testing for human factors. In other words, weapons are created and manufactured before human limitations in operating these weapons are understood. Figure 13.1 shows the increase in complexity of the cockpit facilities of airplanes.

Figures 13.2 and 13.3 show this increase more concretely. Figure 13.2 is the cockpit of Lindbergh's plane, the Spirit of St. Louis, which flew the Atlantic in 1927. Figure 13.3 shows the training cockpit for the space shuttle at Johnson Space Center. Keep in mind that the photograph in Figure 13.3 does not show the entire cockpit.

So complex has the military airplane become that Wickens and Rouse (1987) point out the F-18 has 675 acronyms in three different display modes, 177 warning indicators, and six different auditory tones. There is simply

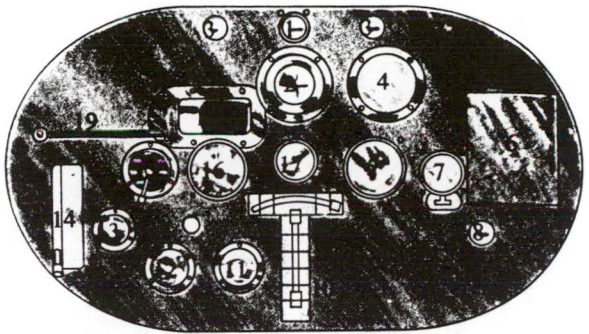

1 Mirror	10 Longitudinal level
2 Voltmeter indicator for Earth inductor compass	11 Oil-temperature gauge
	12 Fuel gauge
	13 Oil-pressure gauge
3 Instrument lights	14 Mixture control
4 Altimeter	15 Magneto switch
5 Airspeed indicator	16 Tachometer
6 Compass correction chart	17 Turn-and-bank indicator
7 Eight-day clock	18 Periscope
8 Primer operating knob	19 Periscope handle
9 Lateral level	

Figure 13.2. Cockpit Instrument Panel for the *Spirit of St. Louis*, 1927

not enough room for all the functions in the cockpit so each display and key must have several different functions. They report that one pilot felt he had accomplished something by learning only 3 of the 17 or 20 radar modes.

One of the complications of high-speed military aircraft is the phenomenon known as TLC. No, this does not mean tender loving care, it means *temporary loss of consciousness*. It was not discovered until pilots were filmed maneuvering aircraft. They were observed to lose consciousness without being aware of it. This happened during high-speed turns.

"Blacking out" was discovered early in the history of flight. It happened when a plane dived and then pulled out. The blood rushed from the pilot's head into the lower body and consciousness was lost. As the speed of aircraft increased, this began to happen even in turns. A pressure suit was invented to compress the lower body so that the blood would not have space to flee to. Yet, even with pressure suits, TLC (temporary loss of consciousness) occurred because of the high speed of jet aircraft.

Figure 13.3. Training Cockpit for the Space Shuttle

Modern military aircraft have developed to the point where they can operate by voice commands. A pilot can say "dive" and the plane will do so. A helmet is under development in which the pilot has only to look at a key or instrument to make it operate.

Chapanis's second era ended in 1969 when the focus changed from military and space to civilian needs. Although the work on military and space continued, human factors research expanded to consider populations it had not dealt with before such as the elderly and children and to problems dealing with urban design, airports, and office environments. And then, scarcely had this era started when the last era, the cosmopolitan one, began.

Essentially, the cosmopolitan era is the internationalization of human factors, when products must be produced for the world rather than any particular nation. This causes some interesting problems for human factors research.

Kennedy (1975) points out how the design of the airplane cockpit is affected by this new emphasis. Figure 13.4 shows the military standard

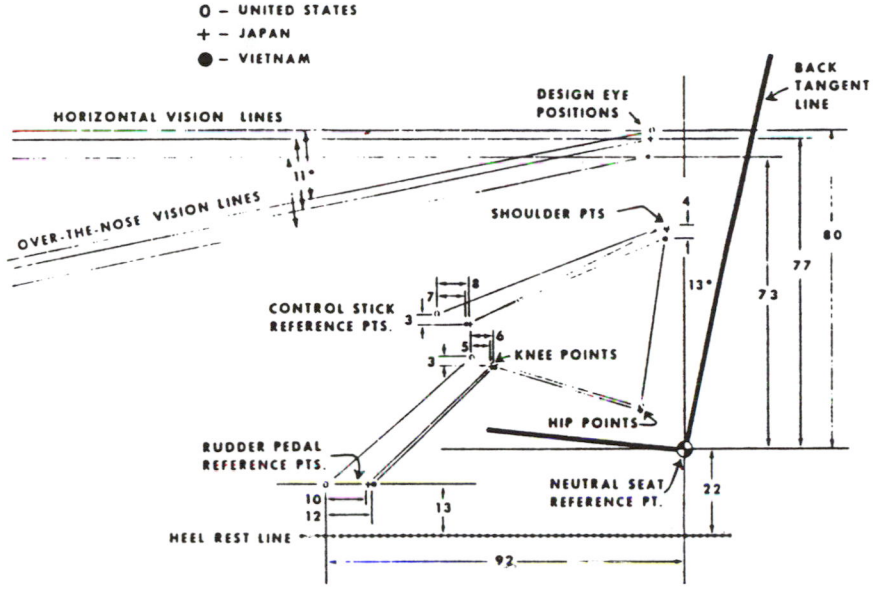

Figure 13.4. Military Standard Cockpit Configuration
SOURCE: K. Kennedy, "International Anthropometric Variability and Its Effects on Aircraft Cockpit Design," in A. Chapanis, editor, *Ethnic Variables in Human Factors Engineering* (1975), pages 47-66, figure 4. Reprinted by permission of the Johns Hopkins University Press.

for a cockpit. Note the *design eye position* (DEP) where the pilot must have his eyes to be able to see over the nose to the horizon. The *neutral seat reference point* (NSRP) is where the pilot must sit to be able to see and reach the stick, other hand controls, and foot pedals. The DEP and NSRP are exactly 80 centimeters apart. This is all very nice when such a stan- dard is made to fit U.S. males. But when pilots from Japan or Vietnam sit in this cockpit, they often can't see over the cowling. Raising the seat doesn't help because then they can't operate the foot pedals. In short, the cockpit must be reconfigured completely. Imagine how this applies to commercial and private aircraft as well.

Anthropometrics

Dreyfus Associates (Diffrient, Tilley, & Bardagjy, 1974) have developed charts (Figure 13.5) that show the measurements required for wheelchairs, car seats, cabinets, chairs, doors, and a host of other openings and furniture in the built environment. Although most of the illustrations on

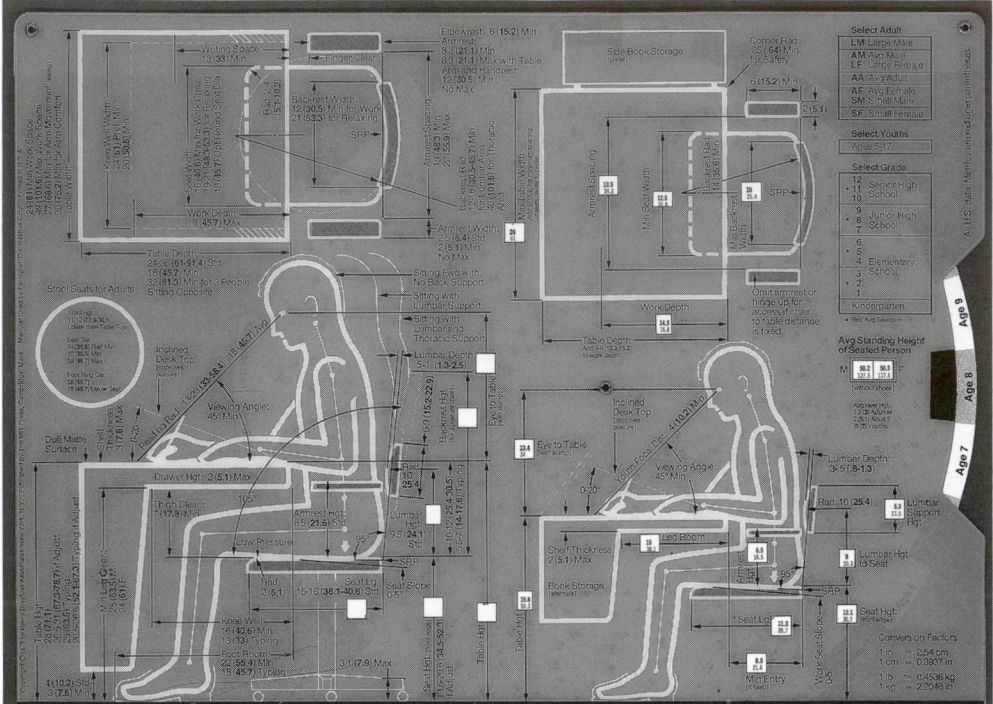

Figure 13.5. Anthropometry Chart From Dreyfuss Associates
SOURCE: Diffrient et al. (1974). © MIT Press. Used by permission.
NOTE: A good work chair permits many postures. Adjustable chair and table heights give maximum comfort for all users. Hip angles should be at least 90° for eating. Flat hard seats can be endured for 1 hr. Contoured seats with 1 (2.5) pad can be endured for 3 hrs. [avoid bucket seats]. To avoid "bottoming" install .5 (1.3) firm pad under the soft pad. Avoid the insecurity of flexing backrests. Armrests for relaxing chairs can be as long as the seat length; when used at tables 8.3 (21.1) is maximum. Upholstery should breathe and not be slippery or have an irritating texture. Chairs may require casters and swivels to move into other work positions.

airplane design have also considered anthropometry, the application to civilian enterprises is an example of Chapanis's last two eras of human factors. The use of anthropometrics has two inherent problems: the design measurement limits and the lack of data worldwide.

The first problem is essentially one of design limits. How can any design be made to fit 100% of the population? Should a doorway be high enough to admit a 7-foot basketball player without having to stoop? Most doorways are under 7 feet in height. What about cars, chairs, tables, and all the designed elements in civilization? The somewhat arbitrary decision has been to *design for the outer limits* and these were set at only 90% of the population measurements, which eliminates the upper and lower 5%. This is by no means a universally accepted standard.

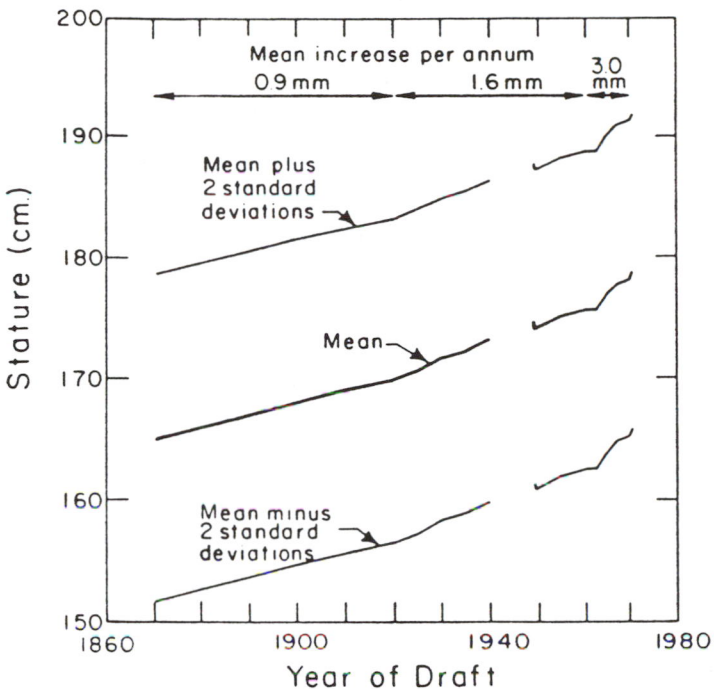

Figure 13.6. Growth of Dutch Conscripts
SOURCE: J. R. De Jong, "Introduction and Welcome," in A. Chapanis, editor, *Ethnic Variables in Human Factors Engineering* (1975), pages xv-xviii, figure 1. Reprinted by permission of the Johns Hopkins University Press.

The second problem of anthropometrics is the lack of data on various populations of the world. Most of the available data come from military measurements, even in the United States. White (1975) and Roberts (1975) cite these data and discuss the problems of dealing with them. The issue is further complicated by the fact that anthropometric measures of populations are changing.

De Jong (1975) described the increase in height of Dutch conscripts from 1860 through 1970 (Figure 13.6). They grew 3 mm. per annum in the last three decades! U.S. conscripts have grown an inch since World War I, and the Japanese are reputed to have grown a half inch since World War II.

The Bedroom

Parsons (1972) became the human factors poet laureate of the bedroom. He collected all work previously done on the bedroom and summarized it.

The main activities of the bedroom are (obviously) sleeping, sexual activity, sitting, housekeeping, and observing. Parsons also recognized several minor activities such as dressing, being sick, dying and giving birth, and occupational and recreational activities.

Lying behavior, according to Parsons, occupies 45% of the lives of every human. There are from 20 to 60 changes of position per night while lying in bed. Such movement is considered healthy, and rest is disturbed if a person is not free to move during sleep. Kleitman (1963) cites more than 300 U.S. patents granted for devices to prevent people from snoring.

Sexual behavior is associated with bed in our society. It was not always so. Mumford (1961) describes how sexual activity in medieval times was more often outside:

> In short, erotic passion was more attractive in the garden and the wood under a hedge, despite stubble or insects, than it was in the house, on a mattress whose stale straw or down was never quite free from musty dampness or fleas. (p. 286)

The bed was not considered such a private place then and the maid would often sleep at the foot of the bed to keep the feet of the master and mistress warm. Parsons found that most people were too inhibited to talk about sexual activity in the bedroom. A "surprising" number of married couples preferred twin beds.

The average housewife walks 4 miles and spends 25 hours each year making beds. Of the surveyed housewives, 84% indicated they make the bed each day and 15% cleaned or vacuumed the mattress after each sheet change.

Sitting is either sitting on the side of the bed or sitting up in bed, a custom practiced by ancient kings in state in which they would receive petitioners. The largest bed was the one used by Henry VIII, which accommodated 68 people. However, only 43% of the housewives surveyed would let anyone sit on the bed after it was made. And 4% admitted they had fallen out of bed recently.

By "observing," Parsons meant how the bedroom looked, and it seems the appearance of the bedroom is a big factor. Many recognized that the bedroom had a fundamentally feminine appearance. Of the housewives surveyed, 82% feel the bedroom has inadequate space for undressing and dressing; 25% said they dressed in the bathroom; 14% said they had their children come into the bed for one reason or another.

Parsons did not deal with bedrooms in prisons or other institutions. The main conclusion seems to be that the bedroom is mostly too small. Some researchers claim this is a class and status issue, with the size of the bedroom increasing with income. The presence of noise is questionable as an annoyance. Many claimed they went to sleep more quickly with noise such as traffic present. One of the reasons air-conditioning was liked was that it gave a reason to sleep under covers. The use of covers was mentioned frequently. Parsons speculated that the air-fluidized bed would replace the water bed. This device blows air against very tiny ceramic spheres to produce an air cushion. His prediction did not come true.

The Bathroom

In medieval times, there was no bathroom. One simply emptied the chamber pot into the street to add to the urban aroma of life. But this was too much atmosphere for Victorian England and an inventor who immortalized his device with his own name brought civilization a huge step forward: Thomas Crapper, the inventor of the flush toilet (see Figure 13.7). Crapper's invention has remained virtually the same up to the present time and it was not until quite recently that investigations were made into the adequacy of the bathroom itself. Kira (1966, 1976) looked into the commode, the bathtub, and the shower. He found that, in 1972, 275,000 people injured themselves in the bathtub. His remedy was to stop making bathtubs as shiny ceramic fixtures and instead make their surfaces nonslip with friction tape on the bottom of the tub. Most accidents were due to the slippery surface. He also proposed a seat and back rest in the tub and wanted to increase its depth by four inches.

For showers, there should be multiple heads and also an opportunity to sit down while showering.

It was the commode to which much of Kira's work was directed. He found that 96% of the women he surveyed claimed they did not sit down on public toilets because of fear of getting a venereal disease (trichomonas vaginalis). But it was to men that most of the findings were directed. Men stand up to urinate. This is a time-honored custom and seen to be a symbol of male virility. Hemingway waxes eloquent about the clear yellow stream springing forth into the air.

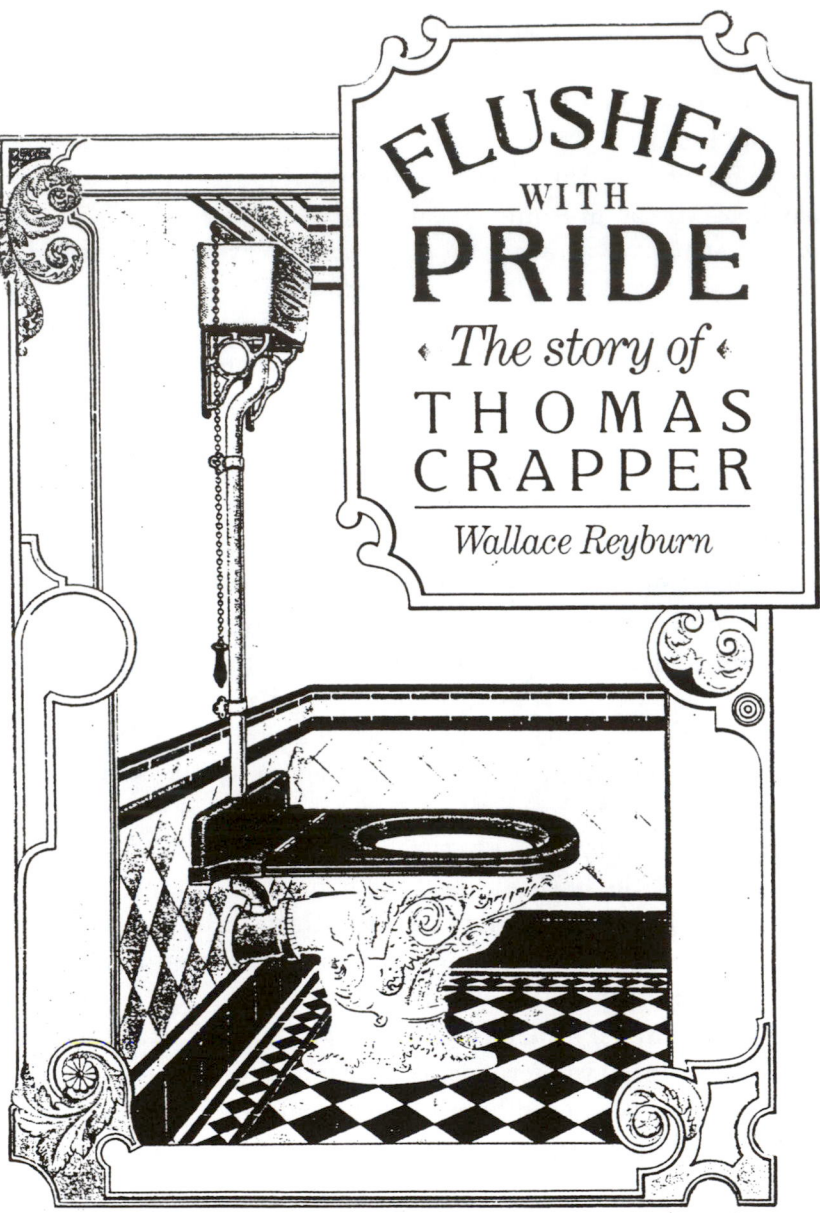

Figure 13.7. A Cult Book
SOURCE: Used by permission of Pavilion Books.

The trouble with this manly vision is that it is not very sanitary. The "clear yellow stream" is accompanied by a fine mist that coats the fixture that is designed to receive it. This is one reason women complain they can't keep bathrooms clean when men are around. If the seat is not raised for urination, then this fine spray will coat the seat. Women are not excused here, because if they do not sit down, they create more spray and thus coat the public toilets even more, the very thing they are so concerned about in trying to avoid trichomonas.

The solution is for men to sit down to urinate. It goes further than the private commode. Kira shows how urine in the public "stand-up" commodes splashes and coats the wall of the stall next to the commode. This means, in effect, there is a circle of spray that coats the trousers.

It is not customary in all societies for men to stand up to urinate. In Iran and other Middle Eastern countries, it is common to see men stoop down in public to urinate. It is not only more sanitary, it is also more modest. From this custom, it is easy to see why the Oriental toilet took the form it did (see Figure 13.8). Essentially, the toilet consists of a ceramic fixture in the floor. It is a much harder target to hit if one stands. But, alas, I cannot say from personal observation that it is more sanitary and this is because of the custom of using water to clean oneself rather than paper. Orientals consider the use of paper to be much less satisfactory than the use of water. The custom is to wash the anus after defecating and use paper only to blot dry. This sounds more sanitary except that I have seen mothers scoop the water right out of the fixture to wash their children.

A modern compromise in the Orient is the use of the Western commode with a tiny copper pipe that squirts water at the anus as the toilet is flushed. It is quite a shock to the uninitiated infidel.

What Kira did for urine in the bathroom, Gerba did for feces. Gerba, Wallis, and Melnick (1975) showed that bacteria and virus in the toilet bowl could not be eliminated by flushing no matter how many times the toilet was flushed. The bacteria remained in sufficient amounts to breed and multiply. Hence the only way to clean the toilet is with disinfectant.

In addition to this discovery is the fact that when the toilet is flushed after a bowel movement, it creates a fine aerosol spray that contains feces and the spray is inhaled by the person in the confined space of the stall or bathroom. Feces contain 20% live bacteria by weight (Rosebury, 1969). The same conditions found by Kira also apply to Gerba's findings. The wall behind the toilet is contaminated. Wooden toilet seats harbor bacteria. The principal viruses Gerba found were hepatitis A, which causes infectious hepatitis, and rotavirus, which causes diarrhea in children. Gerba's recommendation is to clean toilets and wipe down faucets and

Figure 13.8. The Oriental Toilet

door handles in public rest rooms once a day and, if someone is sick, once a day at home too. Once a week is sufficient if everyone is healthy at home.

Thus it would seem that the current object on which we sit so confidently does not do a good job of taking away that with which we no longer want to be associated.

Dieter Philippen of Germany and his Institute Technisch Lebensraumplanung für Behinderte und Alte Menschen have invented a new toilet seat whose main purpose is to bring together that which the common toilet seat wants to separate (Figure 13.9).

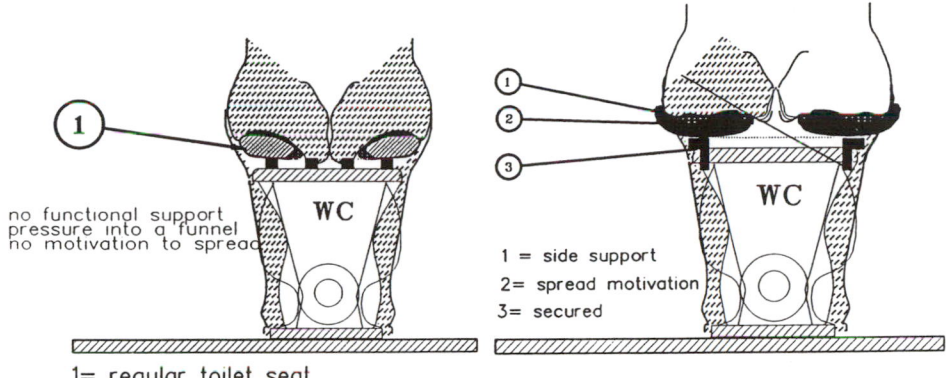

Figure 13.9. Seating With a Funnel Action or on a Presslit Ergosit
SOURCE: Reprinted by permission from Institut - T.L.P.e.V.

How Do You Do It Up There?

Pogue (1991), of *Skylab 4* fame, wrote a book titled *How Do You Go to the Bathroom in Space?* Pogue had spent more time in space than any U.S. citizen—84 days—until Thagard's excursion on *Mir* in 1995, which lasted over 90 days. But the Russians have a much greater record of over 439 days by Valery Polyakov. Nevertheless, the problems of both nations remain the same and the problem of elimination in space is a continuing one. Essentially, the elimination system is operated by vacuum (see the shuttle bathroom in Figure 13.10). Note the toilet seat is designed to eliminate any air space around the buttocks. Also, a fixture is attached for female urine (see Figure 13.11, which is a closeup of the space station toilet) and to pick up stray droplets that get out or don't make it into the vacuum.

The problem with going to the bathroom in space is that there is no gravity. What seems to fall to the ground naturally on Earth only eddies around the body in space and is inevitably sucked into the air circulation system unless otherwise dealt with.

The toilet is also equipped with straps, so that one is firmly held down on the seat, and with handles so that the least amount of space exists between cheeks and seat. As Pogue puts it: "Proper use of the toilet was essential if one wanted to avoid losing friends" (p. 52). The shuttle toilet shown in Figure 13.10 and the space station toilet in Figure 13.11 are unisex devices adapted for both sexes after careful research. If the sys-

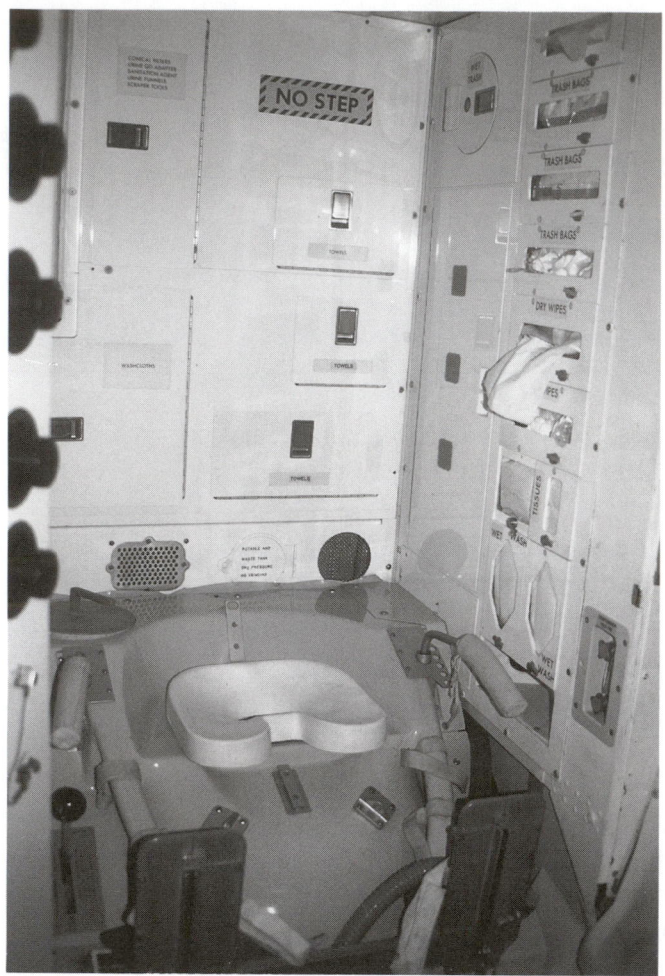

Figure 13.10. The Shuttle Bathroom

tem fails, NASA has available commercial adult diapers for each crew member.

Other Problems of Weightlessness

DeCampli (1986) raises the question of whether humans could actually survive a mission to Mars. After the 6-month stay aboard *Salyut 6*, the

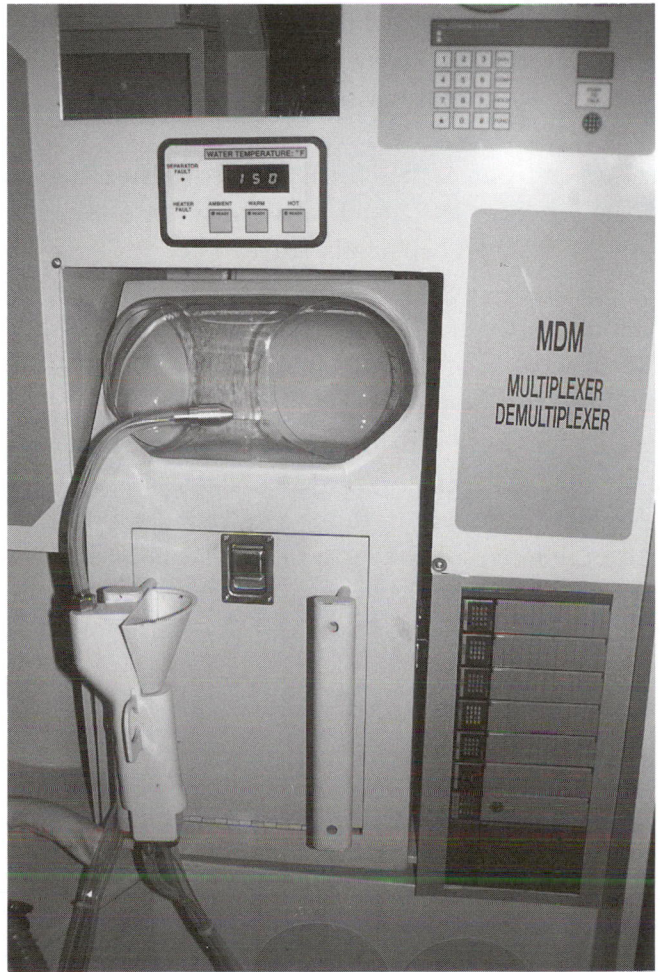

Figure 13.11. Closeup of Female Cup in Space Station Toilet

Russian crew *were physically unable to walk or care for themselves in Earth's gravity*. They were unable to stand up. Only after 5 days could they walk again. It was 6 weeks before they were declared fully recovered. Most serious was the loss of calcium from the bones. The issue of whether this could become permanent from long missions remains unsolved.

Pogue (1991) describes the physical sensations of weightlessness as a feeling of being flushed in the face, a throbbing in the neck, and a feeling of tumbling or spinning every time there is movement. There is a sensation of stuffiness in the head, which may become a bad headache. About 50% of the astronauts get space sickness and vomit. The same barf bags available to air travelers are used by astronauts on these occasions. Although most of the symptoms eventually abate, the head congestion may be permanent.

There is also the condition called "birdlegs," which comes about because the muscles of the leg force the blood into the softer tissues of the body and the legs become thinner, especially the calves.

DeCampli (1986) also stresses the radiation levels in space and calls attention to the fact that space missions so far have been able to escape radiation problems because of their short duration. He suggests a "storm" shelter with 10 times the shielding of the space shuttle.

Finally, there is the space station (Figure 13.12) and travel to Mars in the immediate future. Training for the space station is already taking place despite the many cuts in funds and resulting changes in its final form. These problems will have to be solved before space travel is practical.

Computers

Until computers came we did not know what computer anxiety was. Yes, there is computer anxiety and a scale to measure it (Chu, 1991). Anxiety about using computers is a very real factor in getting people to use them. Farina (1991) found that anxiety in general (trait anxiety) does predict whether a person will have computer anxiety. Swartz (1986) reports in the *APA Monitor* that executives profess admiration but don't use computers.

Yet there is more to computer use than anxiety. Until the widespread use of computers and typewriters, *carpal tunnel syndrome* was a painful condition suffered by butchers, meat packers, and an occasional carpenter. It was thought to be caused by use of the wrist under the considerable strain of hammering and pounding that took place in such professions. Then, with the longer use of computers, it was discovered that keyboard users were also prone to the syndrome. The syndrome is caused by the rubbing of tissue around the "tunnel" containing the median nerve that goes through the network of carpal bones, muscles, and tendons in the wrist (see Figure 13.13). This rubbing can produce irritation and swelling around the nerve, which causes a tingling sensation and numbness and,

Figure 13.12. Space Station Concept

if it continues, can result in such pain that it is difficult or too painful to use the hand. The remedy is an operation that cuts away tissue to free the tunnel.

Human factors analysis of carpal syndrome shows that it is repetitive kinds of motions that produce the swelling and pain. In most uses of the hand, the rubbing is not painful because the tissues have time to recover and rest. But when the same movement occurs over and over without recovery time, the irritation builds and the syndrome results.

The syndrome is complicated by several factors. There seems to be a genetic predisposition in that some people have less lubricating fluid in the wrist. Also, people with diabetes and gout seem to be more susceptible. Birth control pills also seem to increase the chances of the syndrome. And it is known that injury to the wrist can also bring on the syndrome.

How do we prevent this? Proper seating, keeping the hand level, and use of a wrist rest at the keyboard are some strategies. The elbow should form a 90-degree angle between upper and lower arm. Rests of about 10 minutes every hour are another strategy but so are exercises in which you make a tight fist, then stretch out the fingers and hold for 5 seconds, and then repeat. Most important is to keep from the constant repetition of the same movement. Variety of motion is the key.

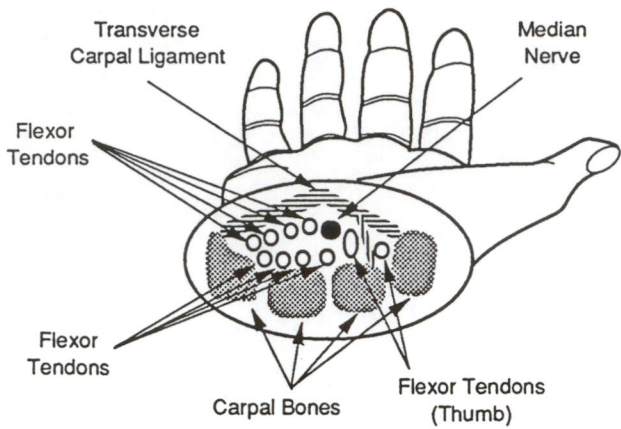

Figure 13.13. Anatomy of Carpal Tunnel Syndrome
SOURCE: Mark Sheehan, "Avoiding Carpal Tunnel Syndrome: A Guide for Computer Keyboard Users," *Computing & Communication News,* April-May 1991, University of Arizona; reprinted by permission.

Conclusions

Volkomir (1991), in a popular article in *Smithsonian*, describes how we are surrounded by a numberless variety of electronic gadgets including the computer, car radios, and the inscrutable VCR that are beyond the capacity of the average individual to operate, even with instructions. The reason for all this is that these devices, like the military hardware described above, were manufactured before the needs of humans to operate them were considered.

Most humans are like the astronauts of Tom Wolfe's *The Right Stuff* (1979); they tend to blame themselves when a mechanical device breaks down or can't be operated. In other words, if we had the right stuff, we could operate and fix these things. But with the bewildering array of gadgets and their increasing complexity, we are all being surrounded by complexity we cannot understand. An engineer cannot figure out how to warm coffee in a microwave, a parent is embarrassed to have to ask an offspring to program the VCR to record a future show, an airline traveler is confused by the flashing lights of the new public toilets in the Chicago airport, a driver can't figure out how to remove the key from the car he rented.

No wonder the complexity causes accidents like Three Mile Island or crashes in helicopters and commercial airlines. Human factors has simply not been considered enough in the design of an increasing number of things, or as Chapanis points out, cosmopolitanism has not yet reached every part of the world, and we are also experiencing the wrong anthropometry in foreign products. Clearly, there is a need to include human factors in the design of the everyday products that we use.

GOALS

Definitions and Concepts

- Ergonomics
- Human factors
- Cosmopolitanism
- DEP
- Anthropometry
- Tailspin
- Outside limits
- NSRP
- Carpal tunnel syndrome
- The right stuff
- Chapanis's four eras

Important Studies

- Wickens and Rouse (1987)
- Kennedy (1975)
- Diffrient et al. (1974)
- Parsons (1972)
- Kira (1966, 1976)
- Gerba et al. (1975)
- DeCampli (1986)
- Chu (1991)

QUESTIONS

1. Why has there not been more cooperation between human factors and environment behavior research?

2. What are the human factors complications of the cosmopolitan era?

3. What is the relationship between DEP and NSRP?

4. How does anthropometrics relate to human factors?

5. Why are populations not stable in height and weight?

6. Why should men sit down to urinate?

7. Why should disinfectant be used in toilets?

8. What is the greatest danger in space travel?

9. How can you avoid carpal tunnel syndrome?

10. Can you program a VCR?

14

POE-PDR

Definition

Just as in the previous chapter, where we saw that military hardware was often produced without considering human factors, so it is that buildings and most aspects of the built environment are constructed without sufficient reference to human needs. The assumption is that the designer knows enough about human needs based on personal experience. This assumption has been proven wrong too many times, hence the arrival of *postoccupancy evaluation* (POE).

It has been called by many different names. Some wanted to call it *postoccupancy assessment* so as to not frighten designers with the term *evaluation*. Others have suggested *sociophysical technology, user needs, design research*, and even *human factors*.

The British developed a *Housing Appraisal Kit* (Housing Development Directorate, 1978), a ready-made survey for doing POEs. But by the mid-1970s, the term *POE* had become universally accepted. The term comes from the occupancy permit issued by a building inspector to certify that a building can be occupied after construction is complete.

Although it is clear that a POE is an evaluation, there is still some debate as to what is evaluated. Some would hold that the design of a building is what is actually evaluated. The opposite position is that the design by itself is irrelevant, it is whether the building suits the users' needs. A middle position is that a POE evaluates both the design and the human needs in relation to each other. Whatever point of view is taken, the POE is very much an exercise in evaluation. It is not a method but uses several methods. It is not an experiment but it can take the form of one.

Many people who have heard of environmental psychology are unaware that POEs are a unique contribution of this discipline and that there are more POEs than any other kind of work done. Bechtel and Srivastava (1978) discovered more than 1,300 POEs done on housing alone by 1977 and many more have been done in all fields since.

Historical Perspective

It is easy to say that there has always been a need for POEs, given the evidence from so many being done. Cornell University Agricultural Experiment Station, for example, began a series of systematic studies of farmhouses by meticulously detailing all the activities that take place in the farmhouse and then designing for a fit with these activities. Figure 14.1 shows a housewife's arm extensions, very much like the anthropometric measures of the previous chapter. These recommendations were published in 1959 under the title *Farmhouse Planning Guides: Household Activity Data and Space Needs Related to Design*. This was an interesting example of a very thorough POE effort that got placed on the shelf and lost after local use.

The history of POEs is more convoluted and involves a slow evolution from class exercises and social science efforts to the final selling of POEs as a marketable product. It must be remembered from Chapter 3 that many of the early efforts of E&B research were directed at changing architecture through the use of POEs.

The Academic Type

The first type of POEs done are still the most numerous kind. These were done, usually informally, when an architecture professor asked students to go out of the classroom, find a building, and report back on what they thought of the design. Some of these were purely subjective, but a few involved some objective measures such as questionnaires or interviews. In any case, the academic POE gave birth to one of the most

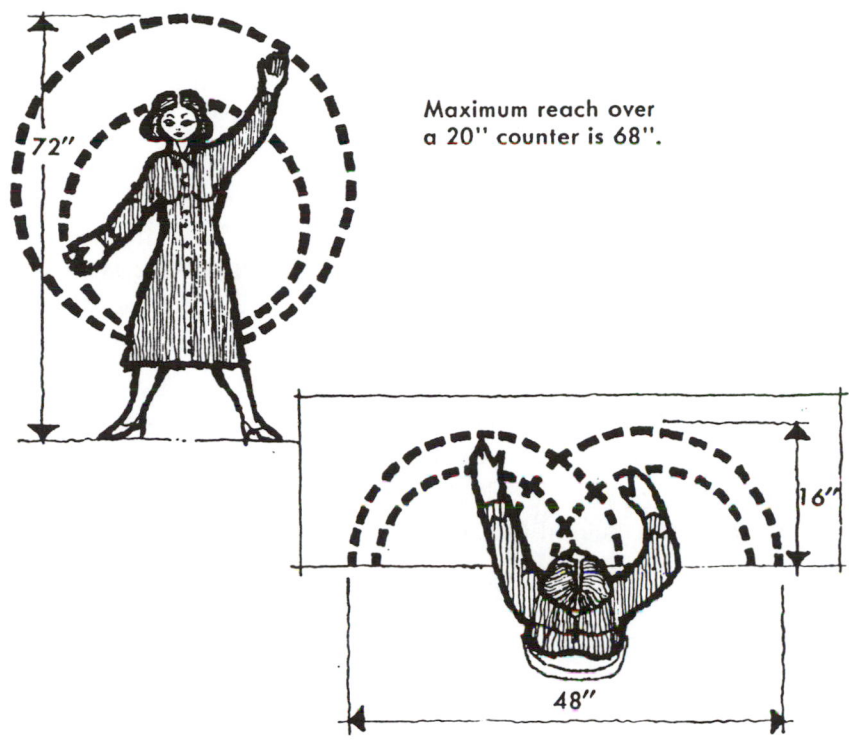

Figure 14.1. Standing and Sitting Reach Envelopes of the Housewife
SOURCE: Heiner and McCullough (1948); reprinted by permission.

ubiquitous methods used in POEs, the walkthrough. *Walkthroughs* are simply that, walking through the building, preferably with plans and/or the architect or occupants, asking questions, and getting familiar with all aspects of the building as it was constructed. Walkthroughs are a good method for discovering the differences between how the building was constructed and how it was designed.

Here it is necessary to become familiar with *change orders*. These are issued when the contractor wants to change some material or an aspect of the design; the orders must be signed by the architect to be legal. It is interesting to note that walkthroughs often uncover changes the architect never knew about. Some changes may be due to later modifications and additions.

Most academic POEs were not written for publication and were seen only as class assignments. Wolfgang Preiser, at my request, made a list of POEs he had done, and the list had over 150 entries. In my own office are more than 100 from my class in methods alone. This story could be repeated by professors all over the world. The number of POEs is truly impossible to count.

The Scientific POE

With the advent of environmental psychology and organizations such as EDRA, social science professors got into the POE business and began formulating social science methods for POEs. Statistical sampling of occupants of buildings with pretested interviews and questionnaires, use of control groups, or at least comparison groups (Carson, Carson, Margulis, & Wehrli, 1980) was the recommendation made to create scientifically respectable POEs. These began mostly in the 1960s and 1970s with a peak reached around 1973 (Bechtel & Srivastava, 1978). A social scientist or a team of social scientists would choose a building and evaluate it by identifying the users, sampling them, and then scientifically collecting and analyzing data with statistically supported conclusions.

The Collaborative Type

It was quickly discovered by social scientists that POEs done by social scientists alone did not get much use by designers. They were often seen as products of social science for social scientists. In some cases, the social scientists were seen as emphasizing problems and ignoring successes (AIA, 1977). For these reasons and because of a desire on the part of many designers to learn how to do POEs on their own, a number of collaborations developed between designers and social scientists. The earliest collaboration was between Ewing Miller, architect, and Lon Wheeler, psychologist (Wheeler, 1985). They collaborated on a truck dispatcher's station and later on dormitories for the University of Indiana. Other examples are Neal Deasy's works (e.g., Deasy, 1968) and Brolin and Zeisel (1968). Sometimes the collaborations were for just a single project; more often a relationship formed over several projects. Collaborations were never very numerous but they continue today to account for a small number of POEs.

The Institutional Type

Although most of the effort behind POEs was directed at the design practitioner, the clients of these practitioners, usually government agencies or large corporations, began to learn about the usefulness of POEs and to include them as part of the RFPs (requests for proposals). Often this was because someone inside the agency or corporation with knowledge of POEs managed to influence the agency in this direction. Chief among these were Andrew Euston at HUD (U.S. Department of Housing and Urban Design), Ron Reinsel (1985) at GSA (General Services Administration), and Karl Eichinger (1985) at the Veterans' Administration.

Andrew Euston, an architect, has a 30-year history at HUD. He is responsible for the phrase *sociophysical technology* (Euston, 1967), which did not catch on as the label for POEs but did become the title of several conferences sponsored by HUD. The first conference was held at the American Institute of Architects headquarters in Washington in 1967. Under Euston's guidance, HUD also instituted an annual housing design award based on users' needs.

Ron Reinsel at GSA reached the point where his agency was funding POEs of office buildings. GSA is the "builder" of the federal government. Any buildings for government agencies must go through this organization. Reinsel was the first to get a government agency to have an annual budget item for POEs.

Al Mioto and his colleague Karl Eichinger began doing POEs in the Veterans' Administration hospitals in the 1970s and developed an elaborate scheme for teams of doctors, health workers, and administrators to evaluate the success of hospital designs.

The common element of these types of POEs was that they became part of the institutional memory of each agency and influenced the way business was carried out.

The Entrepreneurial Type

The most recent evolution of the POE was the formation of organizations to do POEs either for profit or by contract with other agencies. The Buffalo Organization for Social and Technological Innovation (BOSTI) was the earliest, and although doing POEs was not their only reason for existence, the POE was part of their mainstay. Other organizations were Jay Farbstein and Associates, John Zeisel's Building Technology, Inc., and

Box 14.1

UC's "Building Pathologist"

Funny thing about the buildings we spend our public lives in. We almost never are asked, "Do they work."

I certainly have never been asked. But that's what Wolfgang Preiser does. He asks building users: "Does it work?"

And from that simple question, Preiser has built an international reputation. He keynoted a conference on building pathology a few weeks ago in England at Oxford and for want of a better term calls himself a "building pathologist."

His wife is a pathologist. He is a much-published architecture professor in the University of Cincinnati's College of Design, Architecture, Art and Planning, and certainly as a researcher and consultant, he does investigate building "diseases," including sick-building syndrome. But "building pathologist" doesn't encompass what he and others like him do. He could equally be called an "environmental psychologist" or a "building physiologist" because he studies how buildings perform and even the emotional effects buildings have on us.

Is the building safe? Do workers have to walk too far to do routine tasks? Are sinks the wrong height? Drawers the wrong size? Are elevators overloaded? Do tenants feel in control of public areas? Will the building accommodate technological advances? Does the space work for the purpose it was designed for? Will cheap materials cost more in maintenance over time?

Preiser found one vertical high-rise center in Kentucky isolated researchers on separate floors from each other. In Jerusalem at a blind handicapped children's home funded by Keren Or, Inc., he introduced double handrails equipped with Braille knobs which tell the kiddoes exactly where they are and on what floor. He had seen a similar system in Switzerland.

"The elevator at the home is the first Hebrew-speaking elevator in the world," he told me.

Min Kantrowitz Associates. Gerald Davis pioneered the POE enterprise in Canada with TEAG, the Environmental Analysis Group. See the box for a press report on Preiser's POEs.

These five types of POEs arose as the need for them changed over time. They began at different periods but continue on to the present day. One can see many academic types still originating from the classrooms of architectural schools. Some collaborations continue to be formed. The institutional types continue and change, and the entrepreneurial types also continue to grow. Although these types follow a rough chronological

---

Box 14.1 Continued

Preiser is best known for pioneering work with POEs (post-occupancy evaluations), but admits it is a misnomer since specialists like him are just as likely to be doing pre-occupancy evaluations. In fact, catching mistakes before they get built is the ideal. He is evaluating a 30,000-square-foot HMO prototype for Kaiser Permanente before they start building units all over the country.

Lawsuits against architects have doubled since the 1970s—mostly for building-performance problems. POEs not only identify mistakes that can be fixed in buildings already built, they also guide clients how to alter the next building cycle and set strategic building standards.

Preiser and research associate Ramaswarmy G. Krishman are attempting to build a computerized expert-system database that exists now only in architects' brains. It will be complete with video walk-through simulations and taped interviews to guide UC in designing or redesigning buildings to perform to the max. The database will be transferable later to other Ohio universities and beyond, and eventually will include a multitude of building functions. The database will be designed so small business people as well as big institutions can break out data-guides for their building projects.

Universities, UC included, and corporations are moving toward "asset management" whereby departments must pay for space. Unproductive departments lose space. Buildings often are designed by committee, and look and act like it. Departments fight over space. All the more reason for user evaluations and outsider analysis.

"Information transfer is what is at stake," Preiser says.

The toughest "transfer" of all may be to design buildings to anticipate both present and future users. At a recent "futures" meeting in Michigan, Preiser heard Disney is moving into the health-care industry. Instead of "How do you feel," discharged patients will be asked, "Did you have a good time?" Preiser speculates med centers someday may be attached to malls. Have a gall-stone removed, then shop at Sharper Image? But the key question about the building will still boil down to: "Does it work?"

SOURCE: *The Cincinnati Enquirer* (Oct. 29, 1991)/Tony Lang; reprinted by permission.

order, they differ mostly on the way they originate and what happens to them.

Controversies

Because so many people are involved (Bechtel & Srivastava listed over 1,000 worldwide participants in 1978) from so many different disciplines, controversies were bound to develop. These took several forms.

Designer Intentions

An early controversy arose over whether any building could be evaluated without knowledge of the designer's intentions. The argument went that it was not fair to evaluate a design without understanding what was intended. Despite what persons might say or do who live in the building, it may be that a particular section or the whole building was not designed for the way they are using it.

There are two problems with this argument. First is that most buildings are not designed by architects. Only 5% or less of all buildings are designed by an architect. Hence, if knowledge of the design intentions was required, 95% of all buildings would be eliminated. Second, there is so much slippage between the design and the building in terms of time, construction, and later changes that the original intentions may never have been incorporated in the final product.

One of the most common slippages occurs in university buildings where the time frame between original design and final occupancy is often so long that the design is no longer relevant. For example, a building may be originally intended for offices but by the time it is completed the need for classrooms is so great it gets converted to classroom space. The same thing often happens with industrial corporations, whose needs change rapidly.

The next most common slippage occurs when the contractor makes changes from the original design. This was mentioned previously in terms of change orders. Therefore, if the original designer is living and available, it is imperative to walk through the building to account for all the changes from the original design, some of which may be unknown or forgotten.

Ultimately, having the designer become part of the POE is a luxury but not a necessity for a POE to be done. Most buildings simply do not have original designers available.

The Time Controversy

When should a POE be done? Although the name comes from the permit of occupancy, it is obvious that people have to live or work in the building for some time before a POE can be done. Some say a whole "generation" should have passed, that is, all the original people who first moved into the building have been replaced. This gives time for the "newness" to wear off and for people to adjust. Another suggestion is to wait an arbitrary period of time such as 2 years so that the "newness" has had time to wear off. There is no definitive answer to this dilemma except to try to account for the fact that when people move into a building there is an effect of newness that may influence how people answer questions about the building's features.

The Political Dilemma

The POE is the most political of all social science evaluations. This has much more to do with the purpose of the POE than it does with the POE itself. Originally (as we can recall from above), the purpose of the POE was to influence the practice of architecture, that is, to evaluate designs so the architect would know what did and did not work and could benefit from both past mistakes and successes. This meant that the architect had to incorporate the POE into the daily way of doing business. Despite more than 30 years of POE work, it is safe to say that only a small fraction of the architectural profession use POEs. Why? Chiefly because POEs have been done from "outside" the agency or firm. The Canadian POE effort is a good example.

Jacqueline Vischer (1985) reports on the effort to incorporate POEs into the housing ministry of the Canadian government. This effort was one of the largest and most elaborate POE efforts ever made. It involved tens of millions of Canadian dollars and dozens of POEs done on Canadian government construction. In the end, it was to no avail and the government decided it did not "learn anything." The chief reason was that the top officials who could most benefit from the knowledge gained from POEs did not take part in the effort.

It became clear from this and from the many efforts to incorporate POEs in architectural practice that unless the chief decision makers were involved and committed to the POE process, it would be seen as either threatening or unnecessary. In other words, the chief decision makers had to "buy in" to the information and have an investment in the outcome.

Unfortunately, neglect becomes the fate of by far the majority of POEs for this reason. They were not part of the organizational will and so they were not incorporated into the way the organization operated.

Methods

It has become the common practice in doing POEs to use three or more methods (Bechtel & Srivastava, 1978). This is because the message of the social scientists had gotten through on the need for *convergence* of methods (Campbell & Fiske, 1959), that is, to have more than one method so that if the results are in agreement, one has more certainty of the validity of the results, and if they do not agree, one then suspects that something has gone wrong. The controversy is over whether to use control groups as in an experiment (Carson et al., 1980). Most POEs simply treat the population living in the building being evaluated as unique, with no comparisons with any other groups. Some, like Trites et al. (1970), used comparison groups. Although very few POEs use comparison groups of any kind, most use more than one method to attempt convergence.

Theory

A common criticism of POEs is that they contribute nothing to theory, either to social science theory or to architectural theory. Much of this evolves around Zimring and Reizenstein's (1980) concepts of *generality* and *focus*. They claim many POEs have too narrow a focus in terms of what physical parts of the building are evaluated and what range of behaviors are measured. Much of this criticism does not take into account the concept of *accretion* of knowledge. Even drugs, which are tested under strict experimental methods, depend on physicians' use for final acceptance. If any number of doctors find success with the drug, then it is accepted. Similarly, if many studies of offices, each done with differing methods and conditions, find the same results in human behavior, then it becomes accepted that this behavior is associated with offices. Such knowledge is collected by the process of accretion. It does not eliminate or substitute for experimental methods, it follows them as the final field trial of any product and is more the end point of a process than a process by itself. In this sense, POEs, even done sloppily, can contribute to knowledge by accumulating results.

Who Pays?

One of the most problematic issues is the one of who pays for the POE. Many architects have sought to do POEs on their buildings but can find no one willing to pay after a building is completed. Also, many architects, who already have many consultants to pay as part of the design process, are not willing to add another or pay out of their fee. Therefore, the problem of paying for POEs always remains a large one.

Who Does the POE?

This controversy is related to the political issue in that POEs should involve decision makers, but does this not raise the issue of who is qualified to do POEs? Social scientists, of course, insist that qualified persons trained in social science should be the only ones to do POEs. There was even an attempt to license POE workers at one time.

The problem is solved either by having social scientists do the POEs or by having a collaborative effort between designers and social scientists. And, of course, there are occasions when practitioners are trained as both designers and social scientists (Bechtel, 1983).

Financial Practices That Work Against POEs

The building industry can be characterized as a *walkaway system*. That is, the designer of the building "walks away" once the building is completed. Two societal forces operate to perpetuate this system: the contractual arrangements by which buildings get built and the reward system for architects.

An architect is legally bound by the final drawings of a building. Once the architect signs the drawings, she is legally liable for the building as specified in those drawings. Even if the building falls down and it is clearly the fault of the contractor, the architect must be sued, and then she can sue the builder. This means the architect's responsibility ends with the final drawing. Even though many architects today try to include a construction supervision clause in their contracts, the majority still walk away once the building is finished.

Drawings then become the basis of the chief reward system for architects. Architectural awards are given for the drawing, not the building. Judges don't visit the building to decide on an award, they look at a drawing. This follows from the concept that architecture is one of the fine arts like painting and sculpture and it further removes the architect from the building itself. Another way to look at it would be to say that architecture is more like painting than sculpture.

With these two forces operating on the architect, there is no incentive to become involved with the building itself, no way to learn about problems of living in or managing the building. Many architects express regret at this. When Bechtel and Srivastava (1978) surveyed architects, a majority expressed a desire to become more involved with buildings after they are built.

The way buildings are financed also contributes to separating the architect from the building. Most buildings are financed by a mortgage. Many commercial buildings have a 40-year mortgage. The owner of the building wants to have the lowest mortgage possible, obviously, so that the payments also will be low. This means the lowest possible cost of building. The emphasis becomes focused on keeping construction costs as low as possible because construction is seen as the chief item of cost. This creates two dilemmas for the use of POEs. First, cost cutting takes place as a part of the design process to keep money outlay within a given budget. Second, the construction cost is actually only a small fraction of the total cost over a building's 40-year life.

Cost cutting occurs after the architect presents the drawing to the client. The client is either happy or disappointed and then has the accountant go over the construction cost of the plans. Inevitably, the accountant says the plans will cost too much. Or, in another variation, the excavation or materials cost more than expected, so the construction cost must be lowered by *cutting something out of the design*.

Pruitt Igoe, a large public housing project in St. Louis, Missouri, was constructed in 1955-1956. It housed 12,000 people; most were on welfare. When the final plans were presented by the architect, the housing authority said it could not afford the building as shown in the plans. Something had to be cut. The decision was to cut the public toilets on the first floor, because everyone in the building had their own bathrooms. The elevators were scaled back to stop only on every other floor. Otherwise, the building was built as planned. The on-paper design won an award for multifamily housing. Twenty years later, the project was declared uninhabitable and blown up (Figure 14.2). Pruitt Igoe became the symbol of architectural arrogance and ignorance.

But it was not the architect's fault. Lee Rainwater (1966) studied the behavior at Pruitt Igoe before and during the many attempts to save it. By 1965, the project was already in trouble when Rainwater and his colleagues did a survey (Gouldner, Pittman, Rainwater, & Stroberg, 1966). Taking the first-floor toilets out meant that children who were playing outside and who had, as all humans do, to heed the call of nature, were not able to reach their apartments before nature overwhelmed them. They urinated and defecated in the elevators, in the elevator shafts, in the hallways, and anywhere that nature demanded they find a place.

Figure 14.2. Pruitt Igoe Being Blown Up

Having elevators stop on every other floor also caused undue exposure to women in the hallways. Instead of having just half a hallway to traverse to get to their apartments, about half of the women had to go up a stairway and down another hallway. There were predators waiting in the hallways and stairways.

Thus Pruitt Igoe became a symbol for inept design when it actually was a product of imprudent financing, a financial system that did not take into account human behavior of the simplest and most easily understood kind.

Brill studied the relative costs of three elements in putting up and maintaining a building: initial construction, furnishings and equipment, operations and maintenance, and salaries of the people who use the building (Villecco & Brill, 1981) (see Table 14.1).

In other words, when looking at the *true total cost* over the life of the building, even in the first year the personnel costs far exceed construction costs. Therefore, any mistake in design that does not address people costs could easily bankrupt (or, in the case of Pruitt Igoe, destroy) the building. The problem with the current system of finance is that it does not take into account the much higher personnel cost and instead bases all the

Table 14.1 True Costs of a Building: Percentages of Total Cost of Achieving the Mission of the Office (calculated in constant $)

Mission Cost Component	Time Frames for Costs in Years		
	1 year	10 years	25 years
1. Construction, furnishings & equipment	38.1%	5.8%	2.8%
2. Operations & maintenance	2.2%	3.4%	3.6%
3. Office workers' salaries	59.7%	90.8%	93.6%

SOURCE: Villecco and Brill (1981).

decisions on saving the construction cost, which is only 2.8% of the true cost over 25 years.

But what of the cost of doing a POE? Does it pay to do one in the terms Villecco and Brill describe? Trites et al. (1970) showed how a radially designed hospital can save thousands of dollars annually by eliminating the unnecessary travel of nurses. CERL, the Construction Engineering Research Laboratory, studied the cost of doing a POE on an office building and showed that the POE could save $77 dollars for every dollar spent (CERL, 1982).

Brill (1982) went on to show that design improvements can save money in productivity, lowering vandalism, improving management, and lowering accident rates.

POEs Over the World

John Daish (Daish & Kernohan, 1980; Daish, Kernohan, & Salmond, 1981) and Duncan Joiner undertook a project to incorporate POEs in the military housing of New Zealand. Ross Thorne (Szokolay, 1981; Thorne, 1982; Thorne & Arden, 1980) and his colleagues did POEs in Australia. A. Thorne (1980) sees the white man as a particularly recalcitrant intruder in the Australian ecology. Niit, Heidmets, and Kruusvall (1983, 1985) reported on a number of POEs of buildings in Estonia and the former Soviet Union. Euclides Sanchez and Esther Wiesenfeld are a collaborative team (Sanchez, Wiesenfeld, & Cronick, 1987) who have produced many POEs in Venezuela. Ornstein (1991) is at the center of the University of São Paulo efforts in POEs. Urbina-Soria, Mercado, and

Ortega head the environmental psychology program at the National University of Mexico (UNAM), where POEs are often the theses of students (Urbina-Soria, Ortega-Andeane, & Bechtel, 1991).

Europe has its own group of POE practitioners with Canter (Canter & Donald, 1987) leading the way in Britain; the Technological University of Delft led the way in the Netherlands; Gärling (1982) was a pioneer in Sweden; and the Swedish Building Institute (Dahlstrom, 1957) is an institutional example of POE use for the world. Kruse and Grauman (Kruse et al., 1990) have long been the chroniclers of environmental psychology in Germany. Levy-Leboyer (1980) pioneered in France.

Japan (Hagino & Ittelson, 1980; Ittelson, Asai, & Ker, 1986; Yoshitake, Takahashi, Bechtel, & Asai, 1990) has not emphasized POE work but concentrated more on problems related to traffic safety, community change, panic, and evacuation. This emphasis on disasters is an integral part of Japanese history (see Hagino, Mochizuki, & Yamamoto, 1987). There has not been the collaboration between architects and social scientists in Japan that has characterized much of the U.S. work, but architects such as Takahashi and Nishide (1990) emphasize behavioral factors in design.

Predesign Research

It only became apparent in the mid-1980s that much of the work already being done was not actually POEs as such but research *before* a building was designed. This has come to be more properly called *predesign research* (PDR). Some confusion arises because the first step in PDR is to collect POEs done on similar buildings. In other words, the first step in doing a PDR on a new office building is to collect all the POEs available on office buildings so as not to repeat work already done. Thus POEs are an integral part of PDR. PDR, of course, is more nearly like true research rather than the POE, which is an evaluation. PDR seeks to learn the profile of human needs so that the new building can be designed to take the findings into account.

Many of the same controversies that are part of POEs are also inherent in doing PDR. Who should do PDR? What methods should be used? What is the political nature of involving the decision makers? All these issues are part of PDR. However, funding is not usually the same kind of problem because PDR is often funded by the client who wants the building designed. In fact, there are many examples of a contract being awarded to an architect who did not know what PDR was and who then had to contract with a social scientist to do the work.

In light of the definition of PDR as research done *before* design, the farmhouse research cited earlier that was done by the Cornell University Agricultural Experiment Station (1959) might be seen as a PDR study. Housewives were carefully observed over time as they went about their work in farmhouses and then the data were accumulated for the future design of farmhouses. The title of the final report was *Farmhouse Planning Guides*. This was intended to be used by anyone planning to build a farmhouse. Nevertheless, it remains a true evaluation of past farmhouses, with no particular building in mind. In a similar vein, the famous Trites et al. (1970) study of three hospital designs was done to influence future design of hospitals. Trites et al. might seem a curious merging of POE and PDR because the evaluation of the hospital designs that were studied was immediately pertinent to any future design. However, because it was not done with any future building in mind, it stays in the POE category.

The CERL (1982) study cited earlier was a true PDR work. The FAA contracted with CERL, the Construction Engineering Research Laboratory, to study a proposed office complex in an old hangar. The contract cost a total of $28,000 but was able to save $2,160,000 by eliminating 21,600 square feet of unnecessary floor space and yet add 150 additional workers in the hangar space.

PDR research, like most POE work, remains mostly unpublished, but because of its nature, it gets used immediately on the project for which it was commissioned. For example, the research done by ERDF (Dumouchel, 1971) was used immediately by the Cuyahoga Housing Authority in Cleveland to remodel the Carver Park public housing project.

PDR and Programming

Programming (not the computer kind!) is the name given to collecting all the information necessary to design a building. Although programming is taught in most university departments of architecture, it remains true that most architects do not program today. Ideally, PDR should be an integral part of every program. Yet the way PDR is often contracted, it sometimes remains outside the programming operation and may be unused. The ideal of bringing PDR social science measures into programming remains pretty much of an ideal, much like the goal of incorporating POEs into architectural practice.

The New Nonsocial POE

Because of the new consciousness of the many chemicals that are present in modern buildings, and the airtight structures that are a product of modern construction, a new phrase has been coined to define the problem as the *sick building syndrome* (SBS).

Baird, Berglund, and Esfandabad (1994) provide an excellent example of this new type of nonsocial POE. To begin with, although SBS seems to refer to the building itself, it must be understood that only a portion of the people in a building are sensitive to whatever is in the air. Thus, although SBS refers to the building, it is measured through the people who are sensitive to it.

Baird et al. (1994) studied the staff at the University of Stockholm library. It was found that over half of the staff who reported symptoms (54.4%) described symptoms of both the eyes and upper air passages. Altogether, 91% of the 68 subjects reported some symptom of either the eyes, the upper air passages, or both. See Figure 14.3.

What is noteworthy, and typical, of these new nonsocial POEs is that they report nothing about how debilitating these symptoms are, how they interfere with work, or whether they are related to hours lost from work. Thus, although the SBS becomes a genre of evaluation all its own, it often does not relate to POE work previously done and does not become part of the larger picture of the indoor environment.

The Chinese Have a Different Word for It

Few Westerners encounter the ancient Chinese custom of *feng shui* (sometimes spelled *fung shui*). Boxer (1968) describes it as an ancient eclectic body of knowledge on how to deal with change, especially making physical changes such as moving into a building. In a more anecdotal fashion, Browning (1984) describes how Western occupants of a new building in Hong Kong improved their fate.

Under pressure from Chinese staff, the Westerner often employs a practitioner of the art of Feng Shui. After examining the office, the

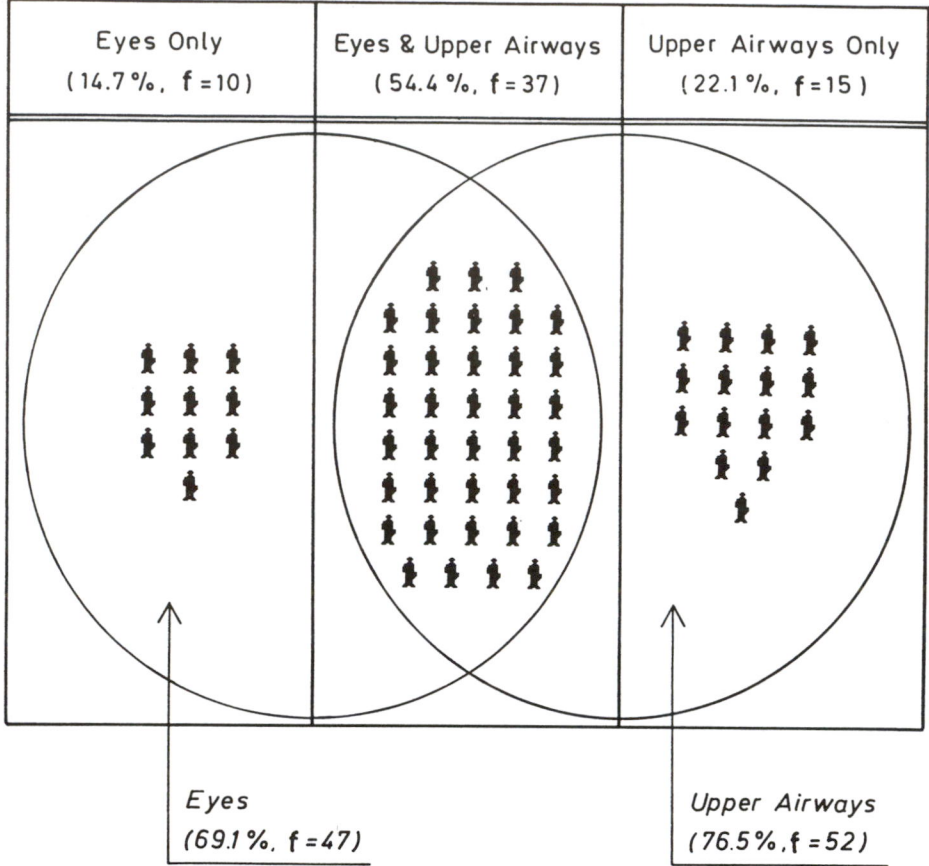

Figure 14.3. Staff Reporting Symptoms
SOURCE: Baird et al. (1994, p. 158); reprinted by permission.

practitioner will recommend such things as changing the way the desk faces or placing a fishbowl with six black fish on the desk to absorb the bad luck. Sometimes, the entire building must be vacated for a more favorable residence.

Boxer (1968) described how a village succeeded in getting the location of a reservoir changed because the suggested location would sever the veins of the invisible green dragon protecting the village. Financial compensation can also be paid to farmers who are harmed by new buildings interfering with their feng shui.

The only thing in common with the more Western POE is the walk-through taken by the feng shui practitioner. All data are collected in this single operation and the report of results is instantaneous. The consequences of a failure to heed these results according to the belief system can be serious illness and even death. The belief in this practice is much more widespread in China among the average citizen than is the POE among people of Western nations.

Conclusion: Quality Control

It was originally the purpose of POEs to become part of the design process of buildings. The proper place for a POE was in an archive of the designer that would be pulled out and used with each new design so that each new design could take advantage of the knowledge gained from previous designs. This use of POEs was intended to become cumulative and to result in *second and third generations* of POEs. After the first POE was done, a design would be derived from its knowledge and a second-generation POE done on that design, resulting in yet another design for which a third-generation POE would be done, and so on. There are some second-generation POEs but very few were ever done in the way originally intended. Part of this was due to the "walkaway" system described above and part due to the way design firms conduct business. Caudill, Rowlett & Scott claimed to use POEs this way.

This system, if it ever got into operation, would introduce quality control into the building system. *Quality control* is a familiar term in industry (see Chapter 17); it means constantly improving the manufactured product by a feedback process on its performance. In this way, defects are eliminated, the life of the product is extended indefinitely, and its function constantly improved. The feedback process in the building system is the POE. Each POE acts as a quality control mechanism to tell which elements of a building should be improved and which should be eliminated.

Currently, this goal remains more of an ideal than a reality, yet great numbers of POEs and an increasing number of PDRs continue to be performed.

GOALS

Definitions and Concepts

POE

PDR

SBS

Walkthrough

Collaborations

Change orders

The best time for a POE

Scientific POE

Walkaway system

Architecture as art

Convergence of methods

Cost cutting

Quality control

Nonsocial POE

Second-generation POE

Designer intentions controversy

Time controversy

Important Studies

Bechtel and Srivastava (1978)

CERL (1982)

Villecco and Brill (1981)

Wheeler (1985)

Gouldner et al. (1966)

Campbell and Fiske (1959)

QUESTIONS

1. Why has the POE not been adopted by many architects?

2. What is the best time to do a POE?

3. How does architecture as art interfere with POEs?

4. What is the walkaway system?

5. Who pays for POEs and PDR?

6. What does quality control have to do with POEs?

7. What is the evidence that POEs save money?

8. Explain the concept of the true cost of a building.

9. Why is the POE so political?

10. What became of the original idea to introduce POEs to architects?

Part III

The Study of Environments

15

The City

———— ⚬⚬ ————

Historical Perspective

How did cities begin in human history? Perhaps no other writer has given more thought to that question than Lewis Mumford (1961). Mumford sees the beginning evolving around the two poles of movement and settlement. At first, there was very little settlement. If we accept Leaky and Lewin's (1977) estimates, there were 23 million years of wandering before any settlement. In fact, until very recently, even in historic times, hunting-gathering bands spent most of their time moving in fairly regular patterns to gather food. The Inuit (the modern name for Eskimos) were only in recent times settled in villages (Condon, 1983) and Australian Aboriginals did not settle until the white man induced them (see Winterhalder & Smith, 1982, for Aboriginal foraging models). Even quite recently, there were efforts to settle wandering tribes such as the Qashqai in Iran (Bonine & Keddie, 1981).

The first settlement, Mumford claims, was the tomb. Once the custom of burying the dead arose, the burial place became the first permanent place that the wandering groups could return to. Mumford sees the tomb as the first break with what he calls the "animal counterparts." The territorial ranges of hunting-gathering tribes have their counterparts in territorial ranges of animals. Baboons have a highly social territorial

Figure 15.1. Temple I at Tikal: An Example of a Temple-Tomb

range, as do lions, hyenas, wildebeests, gorillas, pandas, and most other animals. These are similar to humans' ranges.

The significance of the tomb became further enhanced when it ultimately evolved into a temple where the dead were worshipped. Three parallel courses of city evolution can be seen in Mesopotamia, Egypt, and Yucatán. All three gave rise to pyramid-tombs, which then became the nucleus of ceremonial centers around which city development took place.

Figure 15.1 shows temple I of Tikal, the largest Mayan city, and Figure 15.2 shows the ceremonial courtyard and acropolis between the two main temples. At first, the Mayan temples were not thought to be tombs, but it was later discovered that under each pyramid were elaborate tombs for government officials or high priests. The acropolis in Figure 15.2 houses the tombs of such illustrious Mayan Kings as Curl Snout and Stormy Sky (see Schele & Freidel, 1990).

Egypt quickly developed the tomb complex as a ceremonial center. Figure 15.3 shows the first pyramid of Zoser (2780 B.C.) and Figure 15.4 shows the classical pyramids of Giza (2500-2200 B.C.). Egypt's pyramids did not become temples themselves, as did the Mayan, but had temples

Figure 15.2. Acropolis and Ceremonial Court, Tikal

connected to each; Figure 15.5 shows the temple at the corner of Cheops' pyramid. In addition, each pharaoh erected a major temple as he joined the Egyptian pantheon.

Figure 15.6 shows the temple of Queen Hatshepsut at Deir el-Bahri in Egypt (1520-1480 B.C.). Mumford points out that the temples and tombs acquired a monumental quality that would inspire awe. Figure 15.7 shows the hypostyle columns at Karnak, the most massive columns ever used in architecture in the history of the world. When a person entered these temples, the response was awe and a sense of being overwhelmed. Thus the temples aided in keeping the masses under control and satisfied that the gods were too powerful to resist.

But it must not be forgotten that the cave played a role in this sequence. Caves discovered at Altamira and Lascaux seem to have been ceremonial places. They are filled with elaborate paintings on the walls and were definitely not inhabited. Of course, there were other caves that were inhabited, but the main point is that temples and tombs were merging in history, and the cave became a part of this sequence in several areas.

Figure 15.3. First Pyramid of Egypt, Zoser's Step Pyramid

The first nucleus of the city was the ceremonial center, which was usually a collection of temple-tombs. But these were still only temporary meeting places. Mumford thought what was necessary to make a permanent settlement was the invention of agriculture. Only with permanent crops could the gathering cease and the settlements known as villages begin.

Mumford sees the Paleolithic period with its hunting as a more masculine culture; with the Neolithic period, the rise of the village brought about a mother culture. Mumford supports this thesis by pointing out that in Egyptian hieroglyphics, *house* or *town* can also stand for *mother*. Most languages that distinguish between masculine and feminine nouns designate *house* or *town* as feminine. The evolution from hunting-gathering to a village culture took place about 9000 B.C. to 4000 B.C.

More recent evidence (Lewin, 1988) shows that this sequence did *not* occur as Mumford imagined. It seems that the village appeared before agriculture and it was the village that spurred agriculture more than the other way around.

Figure 15.4. Classical Egyptian Pyramids at Giza

This merging of the hunting-gathering Paleolithic with the Neolithic created a new proto-urban milieu in which the more peaceful female influences with their female gods gave way to the harsher, more unforgiving masculine culture. Mumford (1961) put it more precisely:

> Woman's strength had lain in her special wiles and spells, in the mysteries of menstruation and copulation and child-birth, the arts and life. Man's strength now lay in feats of aggression and force, in showing his ability to kill and his contempt for death: in conquering obstacles and forcing his will on other men, destroying them if they resisted. (p. 27)

Please note the similarity to Taylorism in Chapter 17.

What Mumford is saying here is that the shift from the feminine ethos to the masculine caused the rise of cities, and the city is an instrument of power that made war possible (see Mumford, 1961, p. 43).

The next stage, after settlement of villages, was the collection of villages together as neighborhoods. An example of this is the ancient city

Figure 15.5. Temple at Corner of Cheops's Pyramid

of Chan Chan on the coast of Peru near Trujillo. Figure 15.8 shows the walls of these units that make up the city of Chan Chan. Chan Chan was more like a cluster of walled villages.

The next stage of development is the citadel, which is the military center, or fortress. The "last" of the Mayan cities, Mayapan, was a walled city for defense. Presumably, it developed as a response to pressure from invaders (Hardoy, 1968). Curiously, the Mayans never developed a citadel in the military sense Mumford described.

Figure 15.6. Temple of Queen Hatshepsut, Egypt

Another example of the rise of a city as a collection of villages comes from an architecture student's thesis at the University of Teheran describing Dezful, a city of Iran, which shows that human services such as bakeries, mosques, and groceries are duplicated for every 2,000 people (see Bechtel, 1975).

The hunters of the village became warriors and the domination of peasants became a part of the social structure. Weapons and armies were housed in the citadel. The male and male-dominant culture became preeminent. The citadel became the fortified house of the ruler.

A good example of the citadel is the fortress of Sacsahuaman in Cuzco, Peru (Figure 15.9). This massive fortress was the scene of a climactic battle between the conquistadors and the Incas. But Cuzco at that time was no city in the sense we understand it now. Cuzco was composed of six panacas. A *panaca* is a castle in which the mummy of the dead Inca sat on his throne attended by his court just as though he were alive. In other words, death was a fiction to the Inca. The mummy continued to rule from his throne.

Figure 15.7. Hypostyle Columns at Karnak, Egypt

But how did the other Incas get into the picture? The son of the Inca was heir to the throne but it was a new throne without lands to support it. It was up to the new Inca to go out and conquer new lands whose people would have to pay him royalties. Thus each Inca was responsible for supporting himself by new conquests. This accounts for the spread of the Inca empire. At the time of Pizarro's entrance into Inca history in 1532, Cuzco was an excellent example of the flowering of a true ceremonial center with a citadel.

Returning to the citadel as the home of brute force, because the ruler could not be constantly enforcing, he combined the citadel with the ceremonial center as a population placator to form the first ancient cities. This began about 3000 B.C.

Mumford differentiates the ancient city with its citadel and ceremonial center from the medieval city, which arose later. Hellenic and Roman cities had certain characteristics that were passed on to the medieval city.

Figure 15.8. Neighborhood Section Walls of the Ancient City of Chan Chan, Peru

Ancient classical cities such as Athens and Rome were not nice places to live. Mumford talks about the "barnyard" assortment in Athens and the pestilence of Rome. But the classical cities conveyed the ideal of the *citizen*, a person who was a member of the city and responsible for its welfare.

The disintegration of the classical cities after the fall of Rome led to the monastery as a kind of transition to the medieval. Monasteries were retreats from the chaos of the disintegration of the classical period and the medieval cities grew from a newer religious emphasis combined with the secular elements of commerce. Princes declared many of the medieval cities free of taxes, which permitted their growth and prosperity. Mumford favored the medieval city because of its balance between the religious and the secular and commercial elements. For a time stretching from about 1,000 A.D. to the 1500s, the medieval city flourished but within it began the process of its own demise, what Mumford calls "commercialism" (translation: capitalism).

Figure 15.9. The Fortress of Sacsahuaman, Cuzco, Peru

Figure 15.10 shows a view of Bruges, a well-reconstructed example of what a medieval city looked like. Actually it was Bruges that gave rise to the word *bourse* (or stock exchange) from the De Beurze banking house that was based there.

This commerce set up trade routes and a banking system superseding the cities and establishing an international commerce that made the industrial revolution possible. Mumford felt the medieval city was an ideal human environment because of its balance of political and social forces and its architectural and humanitarian qualities. In Bruges, one can see houses built for the poor. The hovels and mud huts of the classical cities were gone. The guilds, those organizations of tradesmen, made life for the common tradesman more bearable.

The modern city then became organized around industry. The social ecologists (Hawley, 1950) asserted that industrial cities followed natural sources of power, such as the fall lines along rivers. But, of course, these would only be the new cities such as Buffalo, New York, because older cities were already established. Mumford sees the industrial influence

Figure 15.10. Bruges, a Reconstructed Medieval City in Belgium

beginning about 1820. The industrial city was termed "coketown" by Mumford. Coketown was not a step upward. The working person lived in a crowded, dark house with scarcely enough room for children. The town was organized around the factory and access to it. Housing was minimal.

The most important aspect of the nineteenth-century industrial influence was the tremendous migration of population into the cities. Actually, this migration began earlier, about 1750. From 1750 until about 1945, the migration of the human population was from the countryside, where villages usually had populations of 250 or less, to what Vining (1982) calls the "core." The core is the primary industrial region of a country with the greatest density of population.

A striking feature of this migration, especially after World War II, has been the development of two urban patterns—the "hole" and the "doughnut." The "hole" cities are chiefly those in the United States where the center of the city decayed and became the recipient of the poorest migrants. The "doughnut" cities were those in the developing countries where the poorest migrants settled in a ring at the outer edges of the city.

Figure 15.11. Squatter Settlements Near Lima, Peru (Barriadas)

There is also a distinction in the kind of settlements that took place. In the more affluent United States, the migrants rented or sometimes bought the depreciated housing of the inner city, while in the poorer countries, the migrants are called squatters and took over either privately owned or government land and then erected their own makeshift housing. Dwyer (1975) calls these "spontaneous" settlements a major urban form, the largest urban form in developing countries. In fact, they are probably the largest urban form in existence today.

Both kinds of cities see the migrants as a major problem. They generally are too poor to pay for the services they need and their dwellings are considered a kind of urban blight by the more affluent. Figure 15.11 shows squatter settlements near Lima, Peru, and Figure 15.12 shows squatter settlements at Ankara, Turkey. Both countries show striking parallels in their squatter settlements. The squatters usually organize themselves into a sort of municipal council with a mayor, select their land, and put up dwellings in an organized fashion with a layout of streets. As time goes on, the dwellings get improvements such as sewers, electricity, better

Figure 15.12. Squatter Settlements at Ankara, Turkey (Gecekondu)

walls, and eventually such middle-class institutions as restaurants. See Weiker (1981) for a description of Turkish squatter settlements called *gecekondu*, and see Mangin (1967) for descriptions of Peruvian settlements called *barriadas*. Dwyer (1975) describes squatter settlements in several countries.

The "hole" cities have fared much better than the "doughnut" cities because of much greater resources. As an exception, Chicago never developed the blighted, inner-city look. At the extreme, New York, especially in the Bronx, developed square miles of burned-out blocks of housing. Urban renewal programs only partially remedied the inner-city problem by displacing the older housing with newer apartment buildings. Many cities have attempted downtown renewal projects, with mixed success.

Vining (1982) describes a new trend of migration away from the industrial core that began in the late 1940s but gained momentum in the 1970s. This pattern is seen chiefly in the United States but also occurs in Canada and northwestern Europe. The rest of the world continues to experience migration into the core, although this slowed toward the end of the 1980s, and in many core cities there is a loss of population, sometimes because of government policy.

This new trend was not foreseen by social scientists and may foretell an end to the most massive migration in human history. Indeed, the new trend is seen as a ray of hope in such countries as Mexico, where urban migration has become the most serious problem in the nation. But Vining feels this reversal cannot be expected in most countries because of the geographic and economic disadvantages that would need to be overcome. But Vining may be wrong. For example, the 1991 census of São Paulo shows only 9,480,427 people, not the more than 16 million often claimed (see Fox, 1984).

Finally, Mumford fears the coming of *megalopolis*, the expanding of the current cities until, for example, the East Coast of the United States is one continuous city from Boston to Miami.

In summary, Mumford's sequence of city development started with the tomb; went to the cave, which, with the tomb, became a temple; then came the village and a merging of Neolithic with Paleolithic culture; then the ceremonial center (which may have preceded the village); then the citadel, a merging of the temple and the citadel in the king's dwelling; the classical city; the medieval city; coketown; and, finally, the modern city, which may evolve into the megalopolis. What is important to understand in this evolution is the ideological growth that accompanied these changes. Most central was the evolution of the citadel from the village when an essentially female culture yielded to a harsh male culture and the city became the instrument of male expression: war.

Admittedly, this is a simplification of Mumford's revelation of a complex process. Each stage was a layering over of the previous stage. Mumford sees survivors of each stage in various aspects of human life. Hunting and fishing as sports are the survivors of hunting and gathering; gardening is the survivor of the agricultural period; neighboring is a survivor of the village life. Each stage added new dimensions but did not entirely eliminate the previous stage.

The Overload Hypothesis

With the publication of his article, "The Experience of Living in Cities," Stanley Milgram (1970) stimulated a series of studies that confirmed popularly held attitudes about cities and city life. The article contrasted behavior in cities with behavior in less urban areas.

A key aspect is the extreme density of an urban area. In suburbia, a 10-minute radius in all directions would encompass about 11,000 people. In Manhattan, it would take in 220,000. These numbers have consequences on behavior that are far reaching.

One of the most graphic illustrations of this effect was the car-stripping demonstration (done by Phil Zimbardo) in which one abandoned car was left in Manhattan and another in Palo Alto, California. Within 45 minutes, the car abandoned in Manhattan was stripped of removable parts, many taken by seemingly middle-class people. In Palo Alto, the hood was closed by a helpful passerby and the car had not been touched for 3 days when the demonstration ended.

Milgram felt that the stimuli were so intense and so varied in the city that residents suffered from an *information overload*. The only way to survive was to shut out stimuli and concentrate on only that information necessary for the immediate task.

There were six consequences of the overload: (a) Less time could be given to each interaction. (b) There was a disregard for lower power stimuli. (c) Boundaries were erected to keep out unwanted stimuli. (d) Access to self was cut. (e) The intensity of each input had to be increased. (f) Specialized institutions had to be created to handle human circumstances that were created by the extreme density (i.e., delinquency, poverty, issues of the elderly).

Cohen (1978) pointed out that it is easy to become overloaded just by trying to do two tasks at once. Most people will favor one at the expense of the other and usually will focus on central stimuli at the cost of peripheral. Cohen also speaks of the "capacity consuming nature" of irrelevant stimuli, which produces a cognitive fatigue effect. Fatigue is more likely to be experienced when the stimuli do not occur at a known time or at a pace set by the individual. Cohen's model of overload suggests that the capacity to process information is not fixed but shrinks when exposed to prolonged demands. Thus prolonged environmental stressors are likely to create overload resulting in ignoring of social cues, failing to provide help when it is needed, and an indifference to the welfare of others.

Milgram and Sabini (1978) did a study of subway travelers that seemed to contradict the lack of helpfulness hypothesis. An experimenter would enter a train, pick out a seated subject at random, and ask for the subject's seat. The results were that 68.3% yielded their seats. Upon reflection, however, it turned out the experimenters who asked for the seats felt so uncomfortable having to ask that the subjects may have responded to the distress of the experimenter. Another view is that the subway riders were intimidated because the experimenters wore leather jackets and might have been perceived as being from gangs.

Korte (1978) summarized much of the research relating to the findings that nonurban seemed to be more helpful than urban residents. Various methods have been used to demonstrate the lack of helpfulness of urban people. The "lost letter" technique consists of dropping addressed letters in public places to see whether they will be mailed back by passersby. According to Korte, these results are somewhat mixed because the differences are not always clear. For example, Hansson and Slade (1977) used lost letters addressed to the Communist Party and more of these were returned in urban rather than nonurban areas.

But when strangers asked to use the telephone, 72% in nonurban areas versus only 27% in urban areas offered to allow the use of their telephone, and when experimenters overpaid store clerks, 80% in nonurban versus only 55% in urban stores returned the change. And it was reported that urban people are less likely to report shoplifting (Korte, 1978).

Levine, Martinez, Brase, and Sorenson (1994) performed an experiment with six types of helping behavior across 36 U.S. cities. The best predictor of helping behavior was population density. However, Levine et al.'s study used cities of 300,000 and above, and this was not a test of urban versus nonurban helping. In an earlier study, Levine, Lynch, Miyake, and Lucia (1989) show that pace of life is generally related to the size of cities. The concept of an overload hypothesis is supported by these data.

The City as Pathogenitor

The city as an unhealthy place is a theme of research that has a substantial history. Much of this research follows Wirth's (1938) rather negative view of the effects of high densities. Faris and Dunham (1939) led the way with a study of Chicago that showed schizophrenia and some other forms of mental illness were associated with specific areas of the city. Faris and Dunham proposed isolation as the chief cause. Wilner et al. (1962) attempted to study the longitudinal effect of urban housing in

Baltimore on an experimental group of 400 families that moved to better housing as compared with a control group of 600 families that stayed in the slums. Wilner et al. did a review of 40 studies (24 U.S., 16 European) and found generally positive correlations between poor housing and poor health. In the Wilner et al. study, there were also correlations between general morbidity and poor housing. This was especially true for younger and older age groups. Considering episodes of illness for all kinds totaled, there were more episodes among the group that stayed in the slums.

The famous Midtown Manhattan study (Srole et al., 1975) found a difference in numbers of ambulant nonpsychotic mental patients at a ratio of 4 to 1 between Midtown Manhattan and New Haven, Connecticut. However, this difference was attributed to "intercommunity differences in outpatient treatment capacities." The overall impairment rate (of mental illness) was 23.4%, compared with a Baltimore, Maryland, study finding of 10.3%.

These studies were criticized from the point of view of the *ecological fallacy*, which states simply that merely because variables are associated geographically does not mean that they are causally related. For example, in public housing a large collection of single-parent, female-headed households is gathered because these are the people most qualified for government housing. It is also true that a great number of these households have children who are arrested or stopped by police on suspicion of criminal activity. Thus it would appear that juvenile arrests correlate with public housing, but no one is assuming it is the housing that caused the arrests. The more common assumption is that it is the lack of structure and parental guidance in the home.

Further, studies of rural morbidity and mental illness (Leighton, 1959) also show fairly high rates of mental impairment. Thus the case for the city as an unhealthy place has not been convincingly demonstrated by the studies cited, and is connected with the ecological fallacy.

City Size

Plato's ideal city size was 5,040 but this did not include the slaves, which would make the actual city size nearer 30,000. Estimates of ideal city size have been equally imprecise since Plato's time. Lamm (1973) compared the relative costs of various services. In towns of 10,000, for example, an average of only 8 square feet of road space is required per commuter. When a town reaches the size of 100,000, the number of square feet per commuter increases to 28, and when the city size is 1 million, the number of square feet is 97. In other words, an increase in population by a factor of 100 requires an increase in road space of 1,200!

These disproportionate increases seem to be typical as a function of city size although not usually as dramatic as the road space example. For example, a city of less than 50,000 will spend $12 per person on education while a city of 1,000,000 will spend $85. A city of less than 50,000 spends only $1 per welfare recipient while a city of 1,000,000 spends $88. Generally, across all services, a city of less than 50,000 spends $120 while a city of 1,000,000 spends $411 for the same services per person.

Lamm also speaks about the fact that mayors and city council members constantly preach the doctrine of obtaining new jobs and more industries for their cities. This is a self-defeating proposition because, although the tax base increases when people immigrate to the new jobs, the costs of services increase even more because the migration exceeds the number of jobs available. For example, it was found that when Albuquerque acquired new jobs, it got an increase in the unemployed and a decrease in population in the surrounding countryside. Similarly, when Detroit made a herculean effort to create 50,000 jobs for poor people, it found its unemployment rate had also increased. The lesson is obvious. More people looking for jobs move in than there are jobs available.

This same lesson was demonstrated, Mumford (1961) claims, when Rome exceeded its capacity in ancient times, but, lamentably, no one learned that lesson either.

Hoch (1976) examined the relationship of city size to wages and found that as city size increases, wages paid for the same jobs increase disproportionately. Richardson (1983), an economist, asserts that costs and benefits related to city size are the "products of imagination" reflecting value judgments rather than hard data. Further, he asserts that notions of a single optimal size do not take into account the hierarchical relationships of cities in a national system where imposing a single size on all cities would be inefficient.

Urban Villages

Herbert Gans's (1962) book *The Urban Villagers* made people aware that the so-called melting pot of the city was actually composed of ethnic enclaves in which the residents tried to preserve their own identity rather than merge with the majority culture. A number of studies have aimed at urban neighborhoods (Hannertz, 1969; Keller, 1968; Liebow, 1967; Suttles, 1968). Keller (1968) proposed that family relations and friends take precedence over neighborhoods and that neighborhoods that are distinctive are vanishing into the larger urban milieu.

It was also Gans (1967) who discovered suburbanites were relatively happier in their suburban homes than they were living in the city and that commuting was seen as a positive, not a negative, experience. This lesson was reinforced painfully during the energy crisis by the many failures in attempting to separate the driver from the automobile (Zerega, 1981). It turns out that the automobile is a place of maximum choice and control over one's environment.

Urban Activity Patterns

One of the problems of urban life has been the difficulty of studying urban behavior in its totality. Small samples of groups dealing with a specific problem such as commuter stress have been the norm. Chapin (1965, 1974) studied urban behavior to find out how urban residents spend their daily time because he felt this would be of use to planners. Chapin separates daily behavior into obligatory and discretionary activities. Obligatory are the activities devoted to the necessities of life such as work, education, transportation, medical care, and so on, and they form the most dominant part of time allocation. Discretionary time includes leisure activities and those things people don't "have" to do.

Curiously, the total amount of free time for adults showed little difference across Chapin's sample of urban blacks and whites of the Washington, D.C., area. Table 15.1 shows a breakdown of these discretionary activities. Some distinctive patterns emerge. Blacks spend more time on passive activities than nonblacks. The low-income status also emphasizes passive activities while the higher status emphasizes recreation diversions. In looking at stages in the life cycle, younger people favor recreation; senior citizens prefer passive forms of activity; the three middle stages are strongest on social interactions. Looking at days of the week, Sunday is the peak time for social interaction for everyone measured. The three middle life stages use Saturday for social interaction as well as Sunday. Recreation is highest for all except the elderly on Saturday. The elderly use Sunday as the primary recreation day.

Table 15.1 Urban Behavior Patterns

Activity Category	% Engaging in Activity		Mean Hrs. Devoted to Activity	
	Black (n = 358)	Nonblack (n = 1,309)	Black (n = 358)	Nonblack (n = 1,309)
Main Job	58.7	53.7	5.32	4.99
Eating	92.8	97.7	1.38 *	1.74
Shopping	19.3	40.3	.31 *	.63
Homemaking	70.9	77.9	2.63	2.76
Family Activities	12.9	35.3	.20 *	.60
Socializing	22.4	40.3	.48 *	.80
Participation (Ch. & Orgs.)	5.3	6.8	.11	.14
Recreation, Other Diversions	13.4	33.7	.36 *	.60
Watching TV	69.5	66.2	2.42 *	1.43
Rest & Relaxation	41.1	61.9	.98	.93
Miscellaneous	89.9	87.3	2.57	2.83
All Forms of Discretionary Activity	99.1	99.5	5.78	5.89

SOURCE: *Human activity patterns in the city: Things people do in time and in space,* F. Chapin, Copyright © 1974 John Wiley & Sons, Inc. Reprinted by permission of John Wiley & Sons, Inc.
*Differences in duration to left and right significant $p \leq .05$ in difference of means test.

The finding of a high degree of passive forms of recreation in urban life becomes an important policy issue. Are current policies forcing people into a more passive mode of recreation? Would the lower economic groups actually prefer more active modes? Because television is the largest of all forms of passive recreation, television becomes a major factor of influence across all groups. Next to TV watching and all forms of reading, more time is devoted to visiting than any other single activity. What are the implications of this for transportation planning? On Saturdays and Sundays, visiting takes the largest chunk of time spent for travel among all discretionary activities.

In partial answer to some of the above questions, Chapin analyzed some of his data to compare families who were "not making ends meet" with those who were considered to be "making it." The families who were not making ends meet showed considerably more passive activity in free time indicating it was economic circumstances that forced this pattern. Employment status and sex role were taken into account. This pattern was especially marked for poor blacks. By contrast, the families "making it" devoted more time to social communications and active diversions. Work status and sex were also controlled. Married women who worked had the least free time.

Lynch (1977) reports a cross-cultural study of adolescent behavior in Poland, Mexico, Argentina, and Australia. It is apparent that across all these cultures, the adolescents make use of the streets in a continual round of what appears to adults to be aimless behavior. But this only amounts to 5%-10% of their time during weekdays. The rest of their time is programmed by school, meals, and other activities. During weekends, unprogrammed time rises to 30%-35%. The Australians were the most mobile; the Poles the most restricted. All groups complained of boredom and little to do. A common experience is that there is no "place" for them. They have no place they own or place to gather except the streets or other public places. This finding is reinforced by Campbell, Smith, Steenberger, and Stucky's (1979) study of adolescent "hanging out."

Herbert Wright (1969) did a comparative study of children in large versus small towns, which helped to elucidate the differences between urban and small town experiences for children. Wright used two methods. One was to drive around with a child and ask questions about neighbors on either side of the child's house. The other was to ask the child to "build" the community using play blocks. The discovery was that children of small towns knew more details about neighbors than did children of large towns. Wright hypothesizes the reason for this difference is that the large town children are exposed to a great variety of people and places with little repetition. The small town children are exposed to much less variety but much more repetition. Thus the small town child learns more about a smaller environment because of repetitious exposure.

Karen Franck (1980) reports a study of newcomers to a town of 31,000 versus newcomers to New York City. Although initially there are large differences in friendship formation, favoring the smaller town, these differences disappear after 7 or 8 months. However, the urbanites report greater *difficulty* in forming friendships, so Franck hypothesizes the fear and distrust in a large city make friendship formation more difficult.

Classification of Cities

Up to this point, the term *city* has been used in a monolithic fashion. Already, from the data on size differences, it must be evident that size alone makes an important difference in the kind of city one lives in. But cities differ on many dimensions in addition to size. Some are smoggy; some have clear skies. Some are mountain cities; others are seaports. Is there any way to classify cities in some orderly fashion, or are they all unique? There have been more attempts at answering this question than might at first be thought. The classification of cities has been an ongoing interest of the International City Manager's Association. They have sponsored a series of American city classifications in their *Municipal Year Book* published since 1934. Ogburn (1937) pioneered an early classification. Chauncey Harris did an economic classification of cities in 1943. This interest in city classification is at once practical for the city managers and other policymakers as well as basic to E&B researchers who want to understand the forces that come to bear in city environments.

A tour de force in city classification began on June 24, 1965, when a conference was held on city classification to bring it up to date with the latest technology in analysis methods. A grant to do classification research was sponsored by the International City Manager's Association and the Resources for the Future organization. The results are reported in Berry (1972). It turns out that there are almost as many city typologies as there are questions that can be asked about cities. There are classifications by nonwhite population characteristics (Meyer, 1972), social and political dimensions of suburbs (Walter & Wirt, 1972), functional and social classes (Schnore & Winsborough, 1972), political outputs (Clark, 1972), Canada-U.S. comparisons (Ray & Murdie, 1972), time series (King & Jeffrey, 1972), land use (Sacks & Firestone, 1972), government images (Adrian, 1972), and social areas (Rees, 1972). It should be clear that there is no single classification for cities as a whole. The typologies are entirely dependent on the purposes for which they are made.

Berry earlier traced how cities are affected by environmental factors (Berry & Neils, 1969). There was a sequence of influences from the agricultural era when land, water, climate, and transportation dominated, to the industrial when mineral resources and hydropower were preeminent, to the service economy of post-World War II. In this economy, white-collar service skills are the chief influence combined with food service, recreation, and other service elements. The latter are far different in the way they interact with the environment than the agricultural or industrial eras. Berry (1972) posits a postindustrial city "in which industries, employees and their families are seeking out education, cultural attractions, open countryside, and other amenity resources" (p. 364). The example, created since Berry's book, is Silicon Valley.

Attempts to Create Models for the City

Three early theories attempted to explain the spatial organization of urban space. Harris and Ullmann (1945) describe a concentric zone theory, a sector theory, and a multiple nuclei theory (see Figure 5.13). Burgess (1925) used a concentric zone model to describe the growth of Chicago (Figure 15.15). This theory describes city development around a central business core that contains stores, banks, hotels, offices, and recreational centers (the Loop). Around the core is arranged the first zone of factories and the transition area (poor housing). There is a zone of blue-collar homes, followed by a residential zone and a commuter zone (today, this would be called the suburbs).

Hoyt (1939) examined rents in 142 cities and described a city of wedges rather than concentric circles. The sectors tend to follow transportation lines and natural features rather than concentric circles, hence their wedge shape.

The multiple nuclei theory does not follow either of the above but posits several nuclei around which housing and other features are grouped. This model would apply to many modern cities where the downtown is seen as only one center and other nuclei are created by shopping centers and suburban industries.

All three models have relevance to all cities. Chicago retains the downtown loop as a viable center because of its enormous building program. Other cities are variations of the sector and multiple nuclei concepts, some even within concentric zones. Superhighways, which came after these theories, cut many cities into wedges and multiple nuclei. The earlier concepts can be seen in the models described below.

The most frequently used economic model is described by Richardson (1983) as the *monocentric model*. Very simply, this is a "doughnut" model with work (or employment) in the hole and residents in the doughnut surrounding the hole. Richardson points out there are many variants of this model but basically it suffers from oversimplicity, and many attempts have been made to introduce a variety of elements into its equations. The main problem with the model, as Richardson points out, is that it cannot deal with the "polycentric" spatial structure characteristics of modern cities. Other problems with the monocentric model are that it does not deal with questions of urban planning and change, and it ignores the public sector. Richardson points out that the real usefulness of the

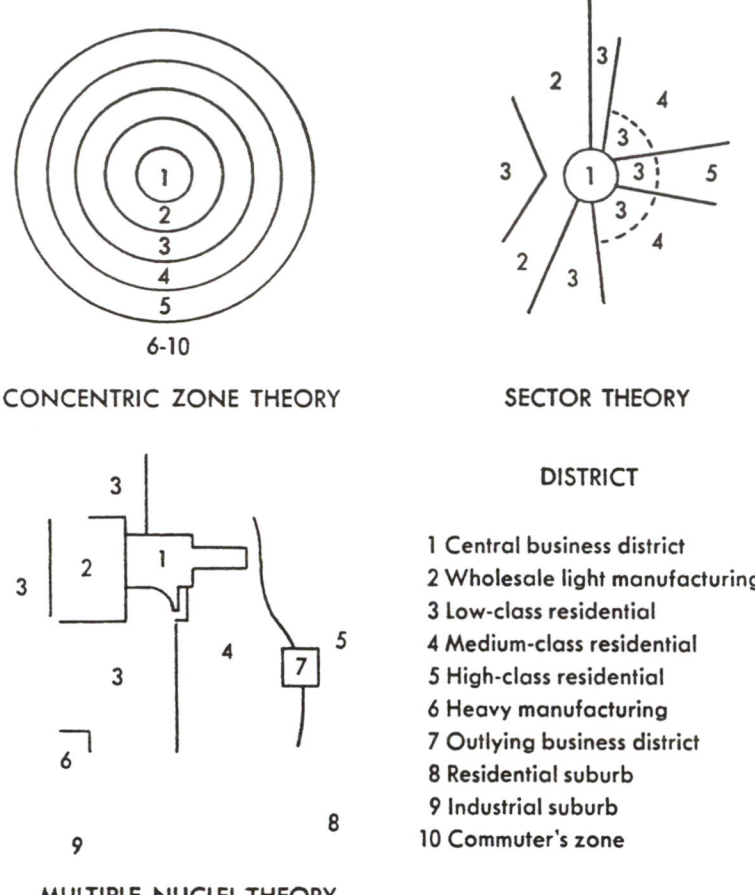

CONCENTRIC ZONE THEORY

SECTOR THEORY

DISTRICT

1 Central business district
2 Wholesale light manufacturing
3 Low-class residential
4 Medium-class residential
5 High-class residential
6 Heavy manufacturing
7 Outlying business district
8 Residential suburb
9 Industrial suburb
10 Commuter's zone

MULTIPLE NUCLEI THEORY

Figure 15.13. Internal Structure Models of Cities
SOURCE: From C. D. Harris and E. L. Ullman, "The Nature of Cities," *Annals of the American Academy of Political and Social Science,* November, 1945, p. 12.

monocentric model is to focus on a few key variables such as rent or housing rather than the total reality of a city. Computer simulations taking into account a greater complexity of variables would be more useful for a larger picture.

Wirth (1938) did not propose a complete model but did characterize urban living as a way of life. The features that made this way of life different than others are population size, density, and heterogeneity. The literature is mixed in supporting Wirth's notion of a way of life. Much of

Wirth's inference was that the interaction of three variables was negative in terms of quality of human life. Gans (1962) maintains that these three factors are negligible in considering effects on human life compared with social variables such as status and stage in the life cycle. Other researchers (Baldassare, 1983) also examine residential density and find that it is limited in its effects on social behavior. Others (Fischer, 1976; Freedman, 1975) describe positive benefits of dense urban settlement. Thus Wirth's somewhat negative view has not been upheld by modern research, but the more important issue of whether his original three elements produces a way of life has been taken up by the overload hypothesis.

Chapin (1974) proposes a general model for explaining activity patterns in the city (Figure 15.14). Chapin's model is based on his data from activity patterns of urban residents but one limitation is the lack of data on how opportunity would influence his model.

Note the feedback loops in Chapin's model that allow a change in activity based on one's experience with it as well as the influence of opportunities. Chapin's is the only truly behavioral model based on data. Unfortunately, it only has data from one city—Washington, D.C.

Models continue to influence many aspects of city planning. For example, a computer model is used to simulate traffic planning in urban areas (Cohn & McVoy, 1982). Origin and destination zones, where people begin and end buying trips, are considered a basis for economic planning. It is ironic that few of these models take into account what is known from empirical studies of human behavior.

The City as the Future

The views of the city as future are generally not optimistic. Mumford saw the citadel (read: Kremlin and Pentagon) as having taken over the city and moving all of civilization toward nuclear destruction. With the demise of the cold war, one hardly sees hope with the chaotic conditions in many smaller countries. The hope that Mumford sees lies in what is termed the *functional grid*. Unlike the old city where all power and wealth was collected in a central place like the citadel, modern electronics enables great dispersal and decentralization. Mumford's vision is not unlike a modern electrical power grid, where, if any part is damaged, other parts can take over. The network has a series of plants, some small, some larger, but no large central plant. The other analogy is the library

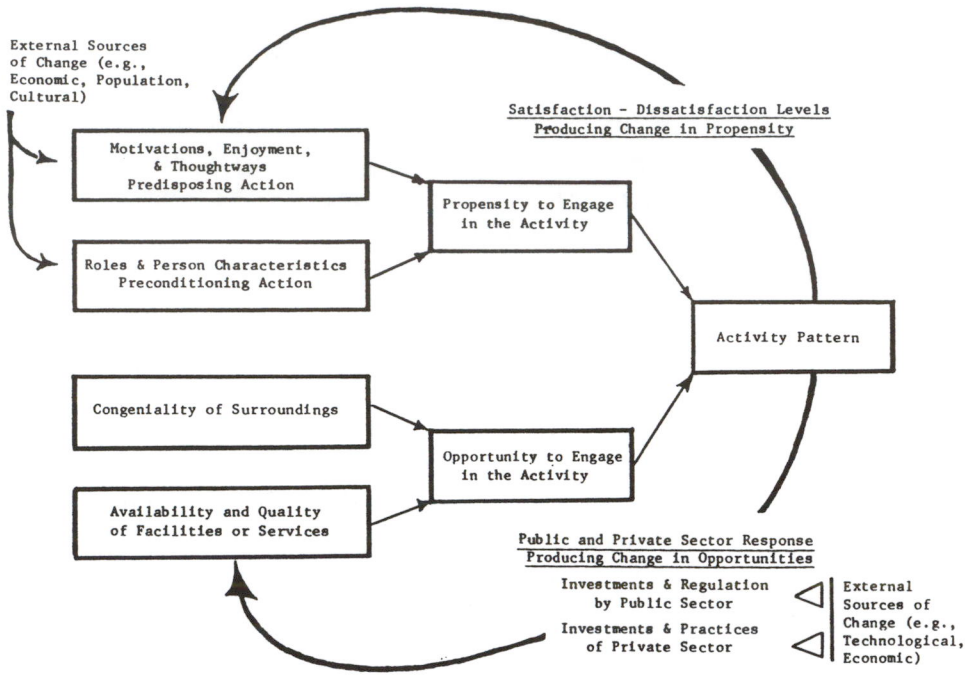

Figure 15.14. Chapin's Urban Activity Model
SOURCE: *Human activity patterns in the city: Things people do in time and in space,* F. Chapin, Copyright © 1974 John Wiley & Sons, Inc. Reprinted by permission of John Wiley & Sons, Inc.

loan system, whereby the smallest village has access to the huge information resources of the largest library.

Toffler (1980) agrees with Mumford's view in his own vision of the electronic cottage industry. Because of electronics, he sees a future where a significant number of white-collar workers do not have to leave home to do their work. Thus Mumford's electronic decentralization and Toffler's view coincide remarkably. Naisbitt's (1982) popularized predictions also agree with the electronic decentralization trend.

The most radical view of the city's future is provided by Paolo Soleri (1974), the Italian architect who wants to redesign the city to save the enormous land consumption that usually accompanies urban growth. Soleri's view is a single, megalithic structure that involves a high concentration of population with minimum land use, yet total self-sufficiency with food. Soleri has changed his ideal model somewhat, as Figures 15.15 and 15.16 indicate. Unlike the other visionaries of the city's future, Soleri

Figure 15.15. Soleri's Models for Future Cities (1)

is building his ideal community out of concrete and with human inhabitants at Cordes Junction, Arizona (Figure 15.17).

The population projections of the United Nations (Fox, 1984) paint a grim future for the cities of the world. In 1950, only 7 cities had more than 5 million people. In 1984, 34 cities have more than 5 million, and if current trends continue, by 2025, there will be 93, with 80% of these in emerging nations. The picture is not pretty.

> The upsurge in third world urban populations has overwhelmed resources. Sprawling slums, massive traffic jams, chronic unemployment, regular failure of electric and water services, strained educational and recreational facilities, and skyrocketing food and fuel costs are the stuff of daily existence. (Fox, 1984, p. 150)

But these abstract conditions are made real by Dwyer's description of Barrio 65 on the edge of Bogotá (Dwyer, 1975), typical of many of the spontaneous settlements of Third World cities. (The squatter settlement

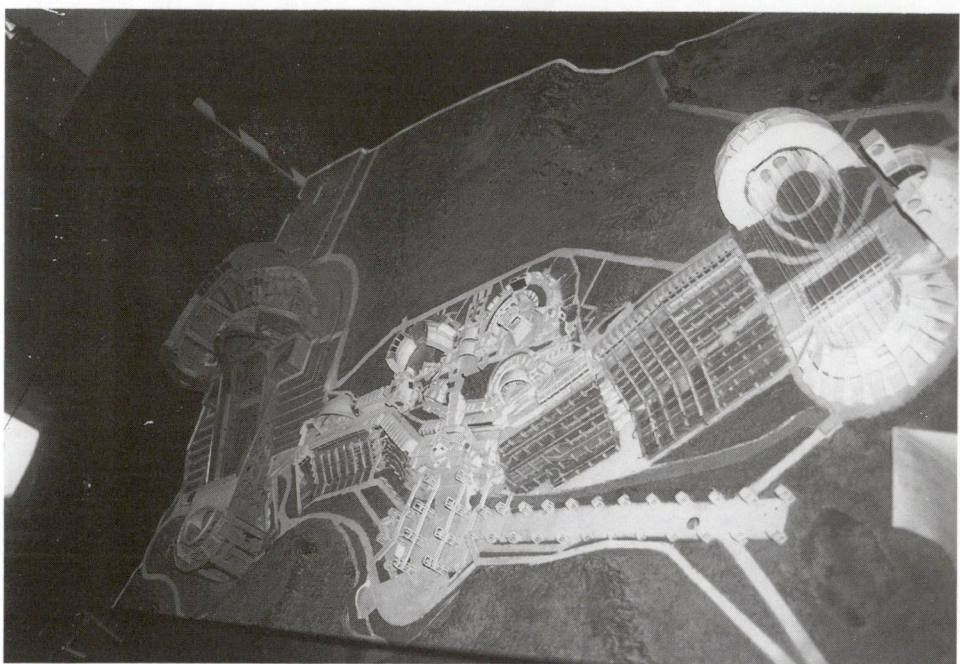

Figure 15.16. Soleri's Models for Future Cities (2)

is called a *barrio* in Colombia, a *barriada* in Peru, a *favela* in Brazil, and a *colonia* in Mexico.)

Urban services are practically non-existent in the Barrio of 65. Illness and mortality rates are exceptionally high. Water has to be fetched in old cans from a municipal hydrant at the base of the hill. There is no electricity, except for those few huts that illegally tap the electricity company's power line. For the most part, small wood fires have to suffice for cooking. A few privies belong to certain privileged families, their doors secured by padlocks. Fortunately, there are others that are not so exclusive. In either case, water carrying excrement from the privies runs almost continuously in black streams alongside the paths of the *barrio*. Children are playing everywhere so, not surprisingly, infant diarrhea and other intestinal complaints take a heavy toll. Measle outbreaks also kill large numbers; death from malnutrition is also known. Women here have many children—contraception even of the simplest kind is hardly understood—and it is a rare family in the *barrio* that does not speak of having one or more *angelitos* in heaven. (pp. 3-4)

Figure 15.17. Arcosanti at Cordes Junction, Arizona

This is more likely the vision of the future for most of the world's urban dwellers in the years to come.

Two views of future urban life emerge from environment and behavior studies. One is the depressing view of massive urban squatter settlements surrounding the developing cities of the world and overtaxing the potential resources of any country. The opposite view is the electronic cottage industry, separated from city density and offering a far greater choice of discretionary time and flexibility in labor. These two views are in sharp conflict. The major problem of the future is to determine how to deal with the swelling populations of the urban settlements without destroying the new vision of freedom and affluence that futurists espouse.

GOALS

Definitions and Concepts

Citadel

Tomb-temple

Coketown

Megalopolis

Core

Overload hypothesis

Arcosanti

Barriada

Ceremonial complex

Mother culture

Male-dominant culture

Hole and doughnut cities

Squatter settlements

New jobs fallacy

Ecological fallacy

City typology

Concentric circles (Burgess, 1925)

Wedges (Hoyt, 1939)

Multiple nuclei

Richardson's (1983) doughnut

Wirth's (1938) urban model

Free time

Important Studies

Mumford (1961)

Vining (1982)

Milgram (1970)

Cohen (1978)

Korte (1978)

Lamm (1973)

Gans (1962)

Berry (1972)

QUESTIONS

1. Has the male-dominant culture survived today?

2. How did the city make war possible?

3. Why didn't squatter settlements happen in North America?

4. What does Soleri hope to accomplish?

5. What is the possible influence of electronic media on the city?

6. What is the principal hope for squatter settlements?

7. What is the point of making a typology of cities?

8. What credence is there for the city as pathogenitor?

9. What is the principal difference between cities in North America and those in developing countries?

10. Who has the least free time of any population group?

16

Institutions That Shape Us

Definition

It might be said that environmental psychology had its beginnings with research in the mental hospital. All three of the earliest programs—Utah, CUNY, and ERF—were funded to do research in mental hospital environments. Thus these first efforts brought the inadequacies of the mental hospital to an early appraisal (Bechtel, 1977) and formed the basis for launching research into other institutions. It became obvious that the institutions provided environments that were different in many ways from the surrounding society.

Institutions have sometimes been defined as regularized ways of meeting human needs. Goffman (1961) defined a *Total Institution* "as a place of residence and work where a large number of like-situated individuals, cut off from the wider society for an appreciable period of time, together lead an enclosed, formally administered round of life" (p. xiii).

Although this definition may do for prisons and mental hospitals, it is too narrow for "less total" institutions such as medical hospitals, museums, zoos, and many others. Further, environment and behavior research at first emphasized the buildings and physical environments of these places rather than the rules and social aspects. Yet it is these rules of operation that defined the effects of the physical environments. Eventually, research accumulated to the point where the very necessity for many institutions that we take for granted came into question.

The Mental Hospital

We did not always lock up our mentally ill. Foucault (1973) argues that it was the Age of Reason in France that began the custom in our society. Prior to this, the mentally ill would wander the streets, but on one day, the "great confinement" of 1656, 1% of the population of Paris was locked up, many in chains. Confinement of the mentally ill is not peculiar to our society. The 12 tablets of Roman law prescribed what to do if a person was found "raving mad" in the streets. Baghdad had an asylum by the eighth century, and Damascus by the ninth.

Treatment of the mentally ill has had a history of wavering between humanitarian and punitive outlooks. Pinel, the French psychiatrist, freed those patients locked up in Paris, but Dr. Benjamin Rush at the Pennsylvania Hospital in Colonial America thought punishment an integral part of treatment: "Terror acts powerfully on the body through the medium of the mind and should be employed in the case of madness" (quoted in Deutsch, 1949, p. 80).

Yet in Belgium there existed a system of treatment of the mentally ill that is almost as old as any of these histories. At a place near the village of Geel in Belgium, a woman was pursued from Ireland by her mad father and beheaded in the year 600. The spot was revered when it was later discovered her remains were covered by white stones and she became the patron saint of mental illness, Saint Dimpna. Pilgrimages to the site of her grave led to the practice of housing the mentally ill there. It became a custom to board the mentally ill with families. The first hospital was built in 1286 and the annual pilgrimages in June continued until the demythologizing effort in the Catholic Church quite recently. Thus, for over 700 years, Geel has taken care of mental patients without hospitalization and been every bit as successful as modern methods (Roosens, 1979). The patients are called "boarders" and there are currently about 800 in the town, which has now grown to 30,000. Figure 16.1 shows the psychiatric center from which the patients are loosely monitored. The same system was adopted in the 1880s by another village in Belgium, Lierneaux, with much the same results. The existence of these places of enlightened treatment and their continued success with the most difficult

Figure 16.1. Psychiatric Monitoring Center at Geel

patients raises the question of whether mental hospitals in their current form are needed.

The history of mental treatment in the United States falls into three periods: moral treatment, custodial, and deinstitutionalization.

Moral Treatment

Moral treatment lasted from about 1840 to 1880. This was an enlightened period of treatment that taught that mental patients needed kindness. Dorothea Dix was a pioneer of this period and went about the country preaching for humane treatment. She is credited with establishing 30 state mental hospitals. During this period, the Association of Medical Superintendents of American Institutions for Insane (AMASAII) was established.

The physical form of most state hospitals was established by an architect named Thomas Kirkbride. He designed the first mental ward for the Philadelphia General Hospital in 1856, called the Kirkbride Day Hall. Figure 16.2 shows the design. Curiously enough, this design lasted well into the 1950s in general use and still can be seen in some state mental

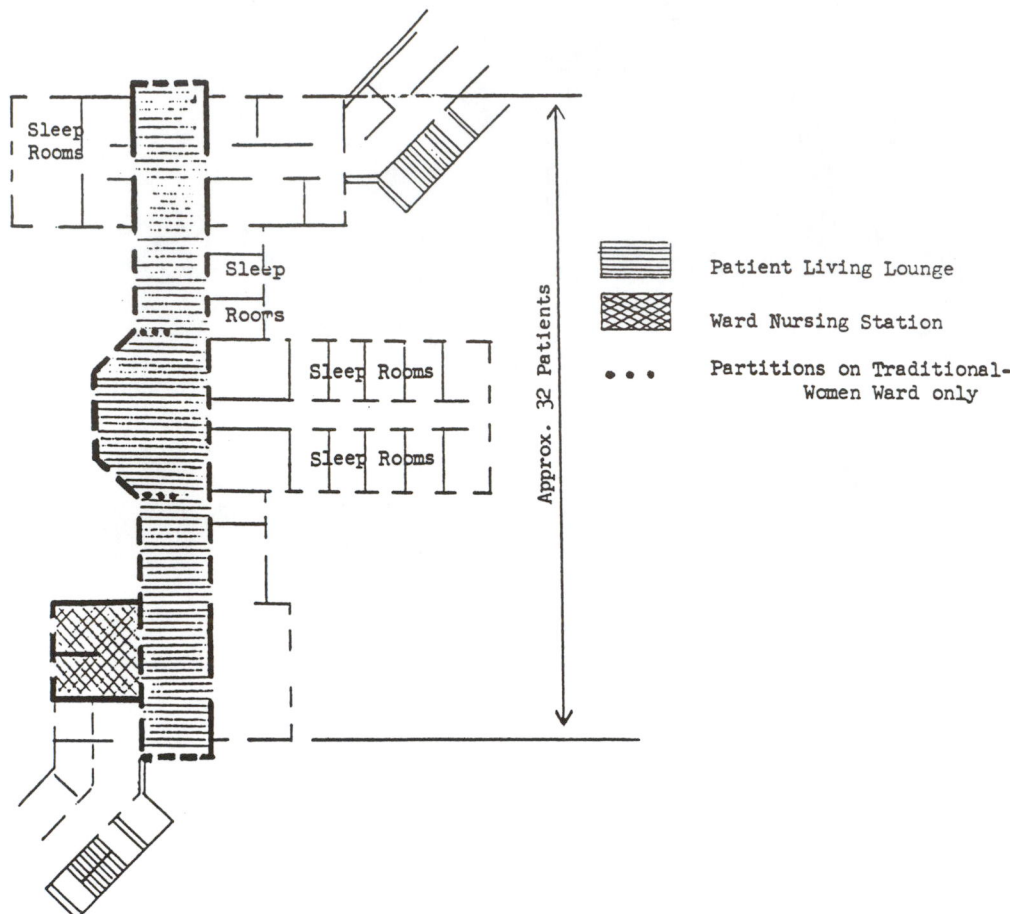

Figure 16.2. Kirkbride Day Hall for Mental Patients, 1856

hospitals today. Figure 16.3 shows a typical fortresslike exterior of a state mental hospital.

Custodial Period

This unfortunate period lasted from 1880 to the 1950s. Prior to 1845, the Pennsylvania Hospital had a discharge rate of 50%. By the period 1925 to 1934, this had fallen to 9% but in the 1940-1946 period rose to 22%. What happened was that the treatment of mental patients had lapsed into merely "warehousing" people.

Unfortunately, that is not the worst aspect of this period. Valenstein (1986) describes how the doctors Freeman and Watts perpetrated a fraud

Figure 16.3. Sample of Fortresslike Design of Mental Hospital

on the medical profession and mental patients by introducing lobotomy and lobectomy. Lobotomy was practiced both as prefrontal as well as postorbital, that is, going in behind the eye or cutting a hole in the temporal plate of the skull and inserting a skewer that was rotated to cut nerve connections in the brain. There was no credible evidence that this practice produced anything but vegetablelike humans. Nevertheless, the practice was widespread in mental hospitals up to the next period.

Deinstitutionalization

This began when pharmacists became aware that shamans in India were treating mental illness by having their patients chew the snakeroot plant, *rauwolfia serpentina*. This plant had long been used for treatment of snake bites, hence its popular name. But the particular plant in India seemed to have a calming and clarifying effect on schizophrenics. After a chemical analysis of the plant, two new drugs were derived, *reserpine* and

Box 16.1

The Plight of the "Deinstitutionalized" Mental Patient

Since 1955, when psychotropic drugs began to replace straitjackets and locked wards for psychiatric patients, an estimated 1.5 million long-term residents have been released from American mental hospitals. The exodus has swelled in recent years, now that "deinstitutionalization"—supplemented by community mental health centers—has become the dogma of the mental health extablishment.

Under the banner of "community-based care," perhaps 250,000 mentally and emotionally disabled persons are now in nursing homes, boarding houses, residential hotels, subsidized apartments, group homes, and halfway houses.

Sensible as that may sound, it hasn't been working out very well. For it seems no one gave very careful thought as to what would really happen to these mental patients once they were on their own. They all have a roof of some kind over their heads, and the means to acquire food and medical care if they are well-organized enough to do so. But for most the concept of "community care" is no more than a sad joke. Very few of these people are being systematically looked after by anyone; programs supplying vocational training, guidance in self-care, recreation, or simple opportunities for socialization are few. A large proportion of them (the figures are very blurry) have been placed in poor, crime-ridden areas that hardly qualify as "communities." And the real communities don't want former mental patients around.

The President's Commission on Mental Health, which issued its report in April, said that the "stigma" attached to the mentally ill was the largest single obstacle to rehabilitation of former mental patients.

The reason for this stigma, and what might be done about it, were the focus of a national conference held in May in Washington, D.C., sponsored by the Horizon House Institute of Philadelphia. Called "The Community Imperative," it drew some 450 people to figure out how to persuade communities to be more accepting of former mental patients. "The situation is getting out of hand in many cities," noted Tom Bryant, chairman of the presidential commission. "Retrenchment is being demanded in area after area." Because of community resistance, the number of halfway houses has remained almost static over the past decade. "It has been estimated," said another speaker, "that for every community program that is established and in operation, another has been prohibited or closed because of community opposition."

Perceived "dangerousness and unpredictability" of former patients are cited as the main reasons for public aversion. Television and the press took a drubbing at the conference for conveying the impression that to be mentally ill is to be a homicidal maniac, whereas such studies as there are indicate that former patients

Box 16.1 Continued

do not appreciably increase the crime rate—they are far more often withdrawn and fearful.

Aside from their misconceptions about mental patients, many people find it emotionally unsettling and aesthetically distasteful to be confronted with the sight of disheveled people engaged in bizarre if harmless behavior. This problem is aggravated by the fact that groups of patients are often clumped in one area resulting in what might be called oversaturation. A woman from the Dupont Circle Citizens Association in Washington complained, for example, that 1500 former patients from St. Elizabeth's Hospital had been relocated in her neighborhood. "We don't like it, and we are not going to have it," she proclaimed. People don't like having their parks taken over by patients who have nowhere else to go, or their local McDonald's "jammed with repulsive mental patients."

In happy contrast was a case history related by Geoffrey Greene of the West 87th Street block association in New York City. When 130 released patients were relocated in a hotel on the block, the association (representing an upper middle class neighborhood) set up a committee to help integrate the newcomers with the rest of the neighborhood. They obtained the services of several social workers to help the residents adjust, set up a lunch program for them, and persuaded the hotel to contribute recreation rooms; members of the community contributed furniture, clothes, books, and money. Now, says Greene, patients participate in social events and activities of the block association, and the whole community has found the exercise so therapeutic that "it has improved 200 percent."

Unfortunately, most communities with this sort of togetherness exercise it to exclude rather than integrate mental patients.

Many suggestions on how to improve community attitudes were bandied about at the conference. Much of it was PR: public education, programs to "sensitize the media," the introduction of new euphemisms (James Mancuso of the State University of New York at Albany proposed that former mental patients be thought of as "ceremony violators," so as to conceptually divorce their unorthodox behavior from its stigma-riddled cause.)

As for strategies for introducing patients into communities, the general feeling seemed to be that trying to sneak them in in "low-profile" fashion was likely to backfire, and the best course was to get community members actively engaged in decisions right from the beginning. Although improvements in servies and programs, better planning in site selection, and more training of community workers were seen as necessary, the concern always returned to public education. Until public attitudes are changed, said Bryant, "I suspect very little more will happen" in social integration of the mentally disabled.—C.H.

chlorpromazine, and the drug revolution in mental illness was on. For some patients, the drug's effect was immediate and dramatic. One day they would be hallucinating and unable to converse, the next they would wake up and say, "good morning," and appear as though they had never had an illness. For others, the change was less dramatic but nevertheless positive.

The net result was the great "emptying out" of the mental institutions in the 1953 to 1955 period. At about the same time, studies were being done to show that mental hospitals were *iatrogenic*, that is, creating the very illnesses they were supposed to solve.

The Joint Commission on Mental Illness and Health met during this period and recommended the abolishment of mental hospitals as they existed at that time and the establishment of treatment centers within the community. The result was the Community Mental Health Centers Act of 1963.

What has happened since the passage of this act? Kiesler and Sibulkin (1987) list five myths that have grown up in the period since deinstitutionalization.

Myth 1. The number of episodes of mental hospitalization has declined in recent years. *Fact:* There was a steady increase in the 15 years before 1987 but it was completely within general hospitals *without* psychiatric facilities. In total, there was a 57% increase in mental hospitalizations since 1965.

Myth 2. The length of stay in mental hospitals has declined. *Fact:* In most places, the length of stay has remained stable. The average stay in the 1980s was still 143 days but there is great variability with an 18 to 1 ratio across sites.

Myth 3. Only a small percentage of all hospital stays are for mental illness. *Fact:* One quarter (25%) of all days spent in hospitals are for mental illness.

Myth 4. For the small number of people with mental illness, they can best be treated in mental hospitals. *Fact:* The vast majority could be treated much more effectively outside mental hospitals. The mental hospital remains the place of last choice to send a person with mental illness.

Myth 5. More money is spent for psychotherapy than for mental hospitalization. *Fact:* Fully 70%-75% of expenditures for mental illness are for hospitalization, a prime reason insurance companies are so reluctant to cover mental illness.

Kiesler and Simpkins (1993) describe the recent trend of for-profit mental hospitals, increasing from 184 in 1980 to 314 in 1986. See also Culliton (1986) below on medical hospitals.

Kiesler and Simpkins (1993) pursued these trends with some difficulty from the establishment and found that by 1980 over 60% of all psychiatric inpatient episodes took place in general hospitals and of these over 60% in hospitals without psychiatric units. This population constitutes "the unnoticed majority" in inpatient psychiatric care and what Kiesler and Simpkins call the new *de facto system* of inpatient care. What is occurring is a merger of the former separation of medical and mental hospitals.

Although the "miracle" drugs were a prime force behind deinstitutionalization, they were found to have a surprisingly harmful effect on patients. After some time, patients who had taken chlorpromazine and reserpine began having tics and nervous twitches. These became more serious until the patient lost control of muscular activity. This condition is called *tardive dyskinesia*. Unfortunately, even modern drugs such as clozapine cause it (Kane, 1993).

It is also unfortunate that the newer drugs cause a new condition (Keck, 1991) called *neuroleptic malignant syndrome*. Initial signs are fever, severe muscular rigidity, and elevated heart rate and blood pressure. In some cases, there may be coma, kidney failure, brain damage, or death. These symptoms were found in 6 out of 679 patients followed who were taking antipsychotic drugs.

In the meantime, research was continuing within the mental hospitals that continued to survive the CMHC Act of 1963. At Topeka State Hospital in Kansas, Nick Colarelli and Saul Siegel (1966) began the *H WARD* project. They took 36 schizophrenics who had been abandoned by doctors as incurable and put them together on Ward H at Topeka State Hospital. Nine aides were assigned to care for these patients without the assistance of doctors or psychologists. When the aides asked what they should do, they were told to treat the patients just like they would anyone else.

For some time, there was a period of turmoil on the ward. The aides seemed to have no direction. A sociologist was called in to help. Contrary to what one might expect, the advice was to get the psychologists and doctors even *further* off the ward. They were still too accessible to the aides and this was the cause of the trouble—the aides were going to these experts for help.

In the period from 1960 to 1965, all but 5 of the 36 schizophrenics were discharged from the hospital and those remaining were in far better condition than they were in 1960. What happened? When asked how they did it, the aides would respond with statements like, "I just treated them like one of my kids." And they actually did. They took the patients home, brought them things, and even hit them if they got out of line. It was apparent that the patients got a lot of human care.

Perhaps as important as the change in patient behavior was the change in the behavior of the aides themselves. They began as somewhat passive individuals, lacking self-confidence. By 1965, they had become confident, independent in their thinking, and able to challenge authority.

George Fairweather (1969, 1974) went further by taking the patients entirely out of the mental hospital and placing them in a motel with the instructions to organize and earn their own living. He effectively reduced the recidivism rate (i.e., the percentage who return to the mental hospital) from 72% to 12%! The patients organize themselves into what Fairweather calls a "lodge" society and go about making a living. One of the most frequent methods is to organize a janitorial service. There are over 300 of these lodge societies operating today.

Thus it seems that the best way to deal with mental patients is to take them out of the physical environment of the mental hospital entirely and place them in a "normal" environment, exactly what the Belgian village of Geel has been doing for over 700 years.

But what is it about the mental hospital as an institution that makes it so harmful to the very patients who are supposed to be helped? Rosenhan (1973) provided one example. He had eight "pseudopatients" admitted to mental hospitals (Rosenhan was himself one of these pseudopatients). The pseudopatient presented a rehearsed set of symptoms to be admitted and, upon admission to the ward, immediately ceased having any symptoms. Most of these "patients" were surprised at how easily they were admitted. They had fully expected to be exposed as the frauds they were. Eventually, each patient was discharged with a diagnosis of "schizophrenia in remission," that is, not cured but not showing any symptoms.

Rosenhan claims that this exercise proves the professionals cannot recognize sanity. Once the pseudopatients were labeled schizophrenic, they remained schizophrenic for the rest of their lives. However, 35 of 118 of the *patients* recognized the pseudos. Some even said, "You're not crazy. You're a journalist."

A further experiment was performed at some of the hospitals to test these findings. The staff was told that during the next 3 months, one or more pseudopatients would try to be admitted to the hospital. Judgments were made on 193 patients and 41 were called pseudopatients. Actually, none was. This illustrated that when the rules were changed to *look* for pseudopatients, there was a willingness to find them. But it also showed the fallacy of judgments. Rosenhan (1973) concludes:

> It is clear we cannot distinguish the sane from the insane in psychiatric hospitals. The hospital itself imposes a special environment in which the meanings of behavior can easily be misunderstood. The consequences to patients hospitalized in such an environment—the powerlessness, depersonalization, segregation, mortification, and self-labeling—seem undoubtedly countertherapeutic. (p. 257)

Goffman labeled this process *mortification:* "In the accurate language of some of our oldest institutions, he (the patient) begins a series of abasements, degradations, humiliations, and profanations of self. His self is systematically, if often unintentionally, mortified" (p. 14).

Spivack (1984) describes this process as a stripping off of *behavior settings* so that the social support and places to do things in life are taken away. He calls the process a *setting deprivation.*

> Fear, isolation, and a sense of numbing helplessness characterize hospital experiences for the majority of patients. To enter a hospital, especially a mental hospital, either as a visitor or patient is to encounter an environment which has no equal in barrenness anywhere in our culture save for the prisoner's cell. (pp. 37-38)

Osmond (1957) described the Kirkbride Day Hall as a *sociofugal* space, which inhibits conversation, like a train terminal, essentially a place for waiting. He prescribed a more *sociopetal* space with a choice between the two for patients. Izumi (1957) designed the first remedial mental hospital based on these principles (see Figure 16.4).

More modern designs focus on community mental health centers or treatment in homes (Bechtel, 1979). Evidence from Geel, the H Ward study, and Fairweather's lodge societies indicate that the mental hospital is an outmoded institution but evidence from deinstitutionalization indicates the public is not ready to accept more communitylike solutions. Kiesler and Sibulkin (1987) claim the mental hospital survives because it was never questioned as a cure for mental illness.

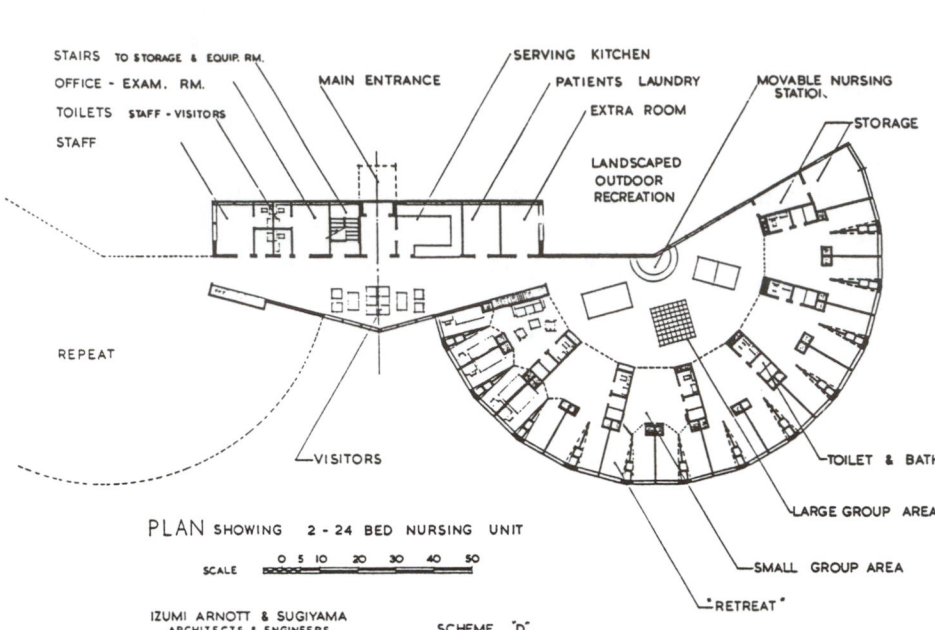

Figure 16.4. Mental Hospital Design
SOURCE: Izumi (1957).

Prisons

In her review of four books on prisons, Lennox (1990) repeated two quotations that summarize the state of prisons in three countries: the United States, Canada, and Great Britain. The first is a quote from di Gennaro and Lenci (1975): "Prisons are constructed in the interests of those who do not use them, thus there is no understanding of what makes them 'work' " (p. 275).

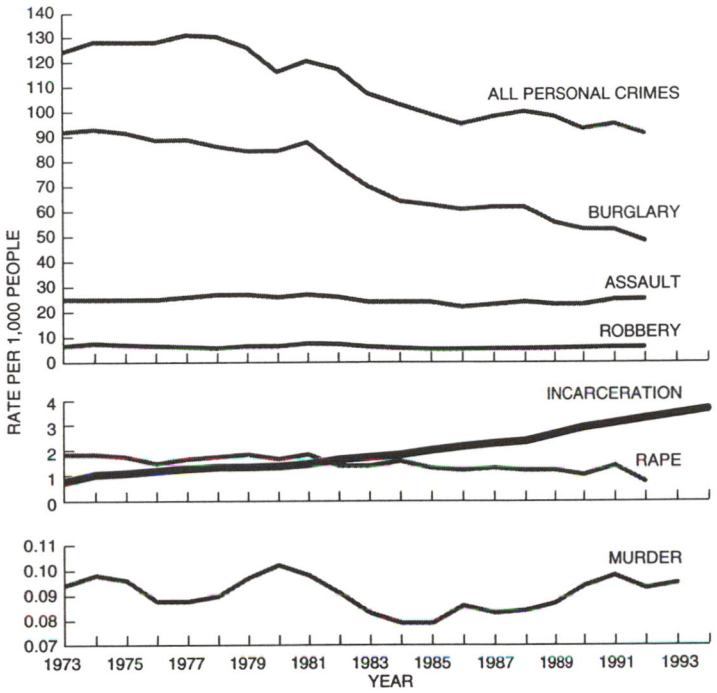

Figure 16.5. Population in Prison per 100,000 and the Result

SOURCE: FBI Bureau of Justice Statistics, the Sentencing Project.

NOTE: *Crime rates* have not responded consistently to "get tough" approaches to incarceration. Since the early 1970s the proportion of Americans behind bars has more than tripled. Property crime (including burglary, robbery and personal larceny) has dropped about 30 percent, but violent crime remains high.

The second is a quote from Rothman (1973, quoted in Yanich & Doig): "Each generation discovers anew the scandals of incarceration, each sets out to correct them, each passes on a legacy of failure—we inherit in essence a two hundred year history of reform without change" (p. 278).

The United States is perhaps the best example of these quotes. We are the most prison-minded nation in the world (Figure 16.4). We lock up more people per 100,000 population than any other country. Moyer (1975) points out that prisons have always been successful at retribution and punishment but remarkably unsuccessful at correction and rehabilitation.

Lennox (1990) sums up her review with five findings:

1. The prevalence of ill health is inevitably linked with imprisonment.
2. The incidence of problems is linked with the type of housing.
3. Prison crowding is more significant than social crowding.

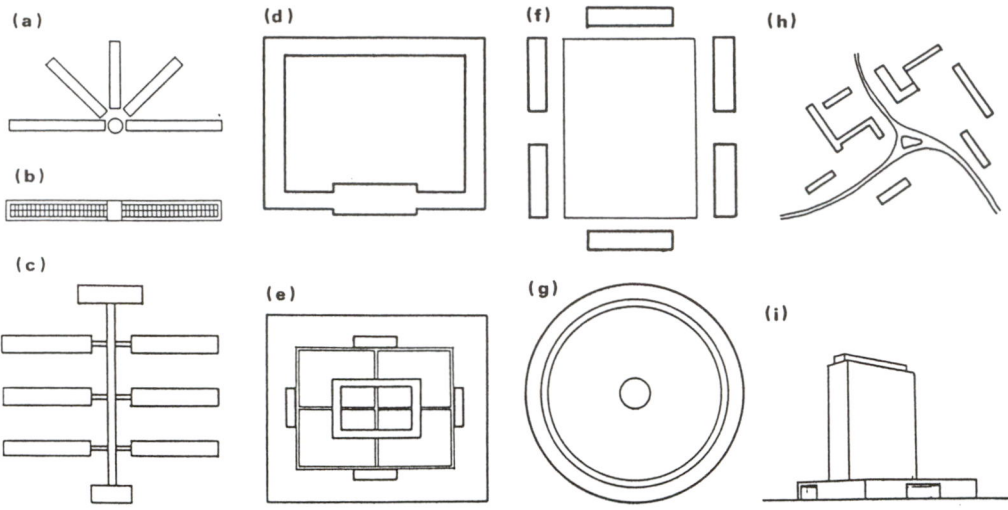

Figure 16.6. Prison Designs
SOURCE: Fairweather (1975). Used by permission.
NOTE: An architecture of association: (a) Radial plan, (b) Auburn/Sing plan, (c) Telephone pole plan, (d) Self-enclosing plan, (e) Courtyard plan, (f) Campus plan, (g) Free layout, (h) Panopticons, (i) Skyscrapers.

4. The variable effects on inmates are related to personal characteristics and backgrounds.

5. The reactions of inmates are related to their personal characteristics.

In short, some problems seem to be caused by the environment and others brought to the environment by the prisoners. Ill health and crowding are related to environment but many individual effects are more related to the qualities the inmates possess in their own characters.

Fairweather (1975) describes prison designs (Figure 16.6). We can see that a preponderance of these have been influenced by the radial design as was Izumi's design of mental hospitals. Indeed, the source of the radial concept was Jeremy Bentham's Panopticon.

But what about the effectiveness of prisons as opposed to alternatives such as probation or house arrest? Langan (1994), in one of the largest studies done of prison outcomes, compared prisoners who served time in prison sampled from 100 counties in 37 states in the United States versus probationers sampled from 32 counties in 17 states. The criterion was the number of rearrests between 1983, when the prisoners were released, and 1986, when the follow-up study was made. Of 109,000 released prisoners,

63% were rearrested within 3 years, while of 79,000 probationers, only 43% were rearrested. When these figures were corrected for number of prior arrests, however, the differences disappear. What this means is that the figures on probationers are inflated because they contain the best prospects for "going straight." Langan's conclusion is that neither prison nor probation is "clearly superior" to the other in deterring future crime. Then Langan goes further with an interesting analysis. Because probationers are free in the society at large, they can commit crimes, and some do. He calculates the number of crimes committed by probationers and concludes that putting the probationers in prison would decrease crime but by possibly unmeasurable amounts.

No account of prisons would be complete without a description of the aborted experiment by Zimbardo, Haney, Banks, and Jaffe (1968). The experiment was planned as a mock simulation of prison with college student volunteers as guards and prisoners. The prisoners were given mock arrests by the local police department and put into the basement of Stanford University's psychology building. They were read 16 rules of incarceration derived from studying real prisons, and housed in 6-foot-by-9-foot laboratory rooms for cells. There were volunteer guards, a warden, and toilet facilities without showers. The prisoners had uniforms and so did the guards. There were no clocks or windows.

Over time, the behavior of the guards became increasingly brutal. They increased the number of body counts after sleep. They began to work overtime. When they were bored, they began to taunt the prisoners. They made the prisoners clean toilets with their bare hands. The intrusions in the prisoners' lives increased until they were almost constant. The prisoners had to do push-ups, recite their numbers, and were encouraged to vilify and curse one another.

The prisoners became more and more passive, actually stimulating the guards to be more aggressive. The prisoners became isolated from each other as they followed the guards' suggestions.

As noted in Zimbardo et al. (1968): "It was remarkable how readily we all slipped into our roles, temporarily gave up our identities, and allowed these assigned roles and the social forces of the situation to guide, shape and eventually to control our freedom of thought and action" (p. 12).

The experiment ended because the participants had gone too far. The experiment only lasted 6 days of the planned 2 weeks. Zimbardo was astounded that things had gotten out of hand so quickly. Four prisoners had to be released because of extreme emotional depression or anxiety attacks and, in one other instance, a psychosomatic rash.

Of the five prisoners who remained, it was clear they were more authoritarian in their belief system as measured by the F Scale. It must be remembered that the participants in this experiment were ordinary college students screened to be emotionally stable, physically healthy, mature, and law-abiding. There was no measurable difference between those who were assigned to be guards and those assigned to be prisoners. Assignments were random. Zimbardo concludes that it was the *situational* forces that elicited this behavior in what would ordinarily be "nice" people. No one has done an experiment like this since. In fact, given the current requirements for assurances against potential harm, it is unlikely such an experiment could be performed today.

Given our society's punitive attitude, it is unlikely prisons will do anything but increase in number. A recent trend is to privatize prisons by contracting them out to a for-profit organization (Logan, 1990). This trend parallels the private for-profit hospital (see below).

Medical Hospitals

The most famous study on medical hospital design was the Trites et al. (1970) comparison of radial, single corridor, and double corridor designed hospitals at Rochester, Minnesota (Table 16.1). After collecting these data and replicating it for two other shifts, Trites et al. concluded that the radial design was superior in every way.

The radial design had fewer absences and accidents; it was much preferred by the nurses, but even more important, it saved time in nurses' trips from nursing station to patient. This was the most critical element of all. It meant that each nurse in the radial unit spent 97 hours more per year with the patients as opposed to traveling the halls.

The Trites et al. study is one of the most successful environmental design studies ever done. It has influenced hospital design, especially for intensive care units, all over the world.

A second classic experiment with hospital design was performed by Roger Ulrich in 1984. He was able to locate a hospital where a certain number of patients had a window looking at a brick wall while another room looked out on trees and landscaping. Fortunately, he was able to match patients with the same operation, gall bladder surgery, across both

Table 16.1 Selected Data From Hospital Design Study

		Radial	Single	Double
169 RNs	Absences	135	206	211
43 PNs	Accidents	4	13	6
	Preferences			
	RN	86.5%	6.2%	7.3%
	PN	81.4%	11.6%	7.0%

SOURCE: Trites et al. (1970).

Table 16.2 Comparison of Patients Seeing Trees Versus Bricks Out the Window

	Seeing Trees	Seeing Bricks
Number of days in recovery	7.96	8.70
Number and strength of analgesics	.96	2.48
Nurses' notes	1.13	3.96

SOURCE: Data compiled from Ulrich (1984).

rooms with the same nurses, and able to match for sex, age, smoking, weight, and previous hospitalization. There were 46 patients in 23 matched pairs. Data are shown in Table 16.2.

In all cases, the patients seeing only bricks out the window took longer to recover in the hospital, required more and stronger doses of analgesics, and had more nurses' notes on problems. Thus the importance of viewing greenery for recovery was established. Yet, ironically, landscaping is typically viewed as the first item to cut in building projects such as hospitals because it is seen as the least necessary element in the building.

The number of days in recovery is especially important because hospitals are reimbursed by government programs such as Medicare on a DRG basis. *DRG* stands for diagnostic related groups, a method of reimbursement based on the diagnosis. For example, a gall bladder operation will be given a fixed amount regardless of the number of days the person spends in the hospital. Therefore, to make a profit on the hospital stay, it would be most important to find a general method whereby hospital stays could be shortened. Under pressure from the DRG system, hospitals are indeed sending patients home early, and this has given rise to a whole new set of programs called Home Health Care Agencies.

Many hospitals today will have Home Health Care Agencies as an adjunct care operation that will set up and manage care in the home after the patient is discharged. Comparable costs of home care compared with hospital care are often of the magnitude of $35 versus $600, so it can be well understood why home health care agencies are proliferating. Thus the real importance of Ulrich's study in terms of hospital design is to show the financial significance of a design element hitherto considered superfluous in regard to health care.

Stevens (1989) documents why medical hospitals in the United States have turned from the charitable, nonprofit orientation of former years and become since the 1960s more "capitalistic," which is seen as the principal cause of the trouble with health care today. The emphasis now is to show a profit rather than to provide a service.

Culliton (1986) describes how this profit motive has influenced hospitals by the rise of for-profit hospitals that siphon off the high-paying patients and leave the charity hospitals bankrupt. In 1975, only 375 hospitals, or 6% of the total, were for-profit institutions. By 1986, this figure had more than doubled to 878, or 13%.

Cousins (1979) describes how hospitals have become so technologically oriented and directed toward the convenience of the doctors that "a hospital is no place for a person who is seriously ill" (p. 29). And although Trites et al. (1970) may have outlined the design for intensive care units, these have become stressful in their own right. The *American Journal of Nursing* describes how sound levels are enough to interrupt sleep at 80 decibels 125 times per night. Further, patients are interrupted at least once an hour night and day by caregivers or visitors ("Din of Alarms," 1994, p. 9).

The noise is mainly from the more than 33 alarm systems that surround the patient. These signal at a rate of 50 times per hour. When doctors and nurses were asked to identify the source of these sounds, they answered only 43% correct on the total alarms and 50% on the most critical ones. The conclusion is that there simply are too many alarms.

To counter these kinds of problems, the Plane Tree Model Hospital Project at the Pacific Presbyterian Medical Center in San Francisco (see Malkin, 1992, for a description and photographs) has created an environment that is truly patient centered. The philosophy of Plane Tree is to put the responsibility for care more squarely in the patient's hands. The patient has a choice of whether he or she wants nurturing care, active involvement, family support, and privacy. There is direct access to medical charts. The patient can go directly to the nursing station and inquire.

There is a medical library made more user-friendly than most medical libraries with tapes on various illnesses, operations, and drugs. There is a kitchen where patients can prepare their own food. There are reading rooms and places for family and friends to stay overnight.

Plane Tree clearly runs counter to the way most hospitals operate today. The emphasis on patient responsibility interferes with the customary procedures most hospitals feel it is necessary to use to provide the best care. Documentation on Plane Tree is not yet available, but anecdotal evidence indicates it is the kind of environment patients prefer.

As the result of an extensive research program, Carpman and Grant (1993) present exterior and interior wayfinding schemas for modern hospital complexes. Their research shows that most hospitals today have systems of signage that are far too complex.

Museums and Art Galleries

Bitgood and Loomis (1993) divide the history of museum research into three periods: the 1920s and 1930s, the 1960s and 1970s, and the more modern period, which includes the present time. Up until the 1970s, most research was done by researchers outside the museum such as Robinson et al. (1928) and Melton (1935), the early pioneers. But after the 1970s, museum professionals made the research a more "internal" process. Wolf (1980) introduced a more holistic approach to museum research while Diamond (1982), Rosenfeld (1979), and others used ethological methods.

Arthur W. Melton (1935) conducted the classic study of museum and art gallery visitors during the Depression. This study was reprinted (Parsons, 1972) and it should be read by every museum official today. Melton discovered some basic behavioral facts that are relevant to any institution that wants visitors to see displays.

(1) Intrinsic value. The basic assumption of most professionals is that any artwork has an intrinsic value that will manifest itself no matter where or how the work is displayed. Melton showed how this was almost never true but that where and how the object is displayed overwhelm whatever intrinsic value the object may have. The object may be ignored by more than half of the visitors if it happens to be on the left side of a room where there is a doorway dividing the room in half. Visitors will enter by one door and leave by another opposite door.

Further, it turns out that there are intrinsic *classes* of art objects. For example, paintings are always preferred over furniture. In fact, pictures placed in a furniture exhibit to fill the empty spaces will be more attended to than the furniture on display.

(2) Crowding and isolation. Most exhibitors feel that crowding distracts and that more attention will be paid to an isolated object. This turns out to be true but there are limits. Once there are 12 objects in a room, the effect is much less when more are added than when there are only 6 objects in the room. In other words, crowding has a fairly quick *saturation* effect.

(3) Period exhibits. Many museums have period or style rooms where objects of a certain period or style are exhibited with the idea that this will increase visitor interest. These exhibits have been consistently unsuccessful by themselves. They do, however, serve as a kind of "oasis" in terms of the other exhibits and have a relief effect on the museum visitor; that is, here is something I don't have to pay so much attention to.

(4) Museum fatigue. It was Gilman (1916) who first used the term *museum fatigue*. Melton found that museum fatigue is not a uniform phenomenon. The time visitors spend on each object does not decrease appreciably over time, but the *number of stops* does. By the end of the visit, the visitor will be making two thirds fewer stops than at the beginning. Furthermore, this can be observed even when the entire time in the museum is as little as *four minutes*.

(5) Position in the gallery. Three quarters of the people who enter a room turn right. Therefore, exhibits should be arranged in a right-to-left sequence rather than left to right. More than half of the people entering a room will only look at exhibits on the wall to which they turn, ignoring the opposite wall. Which brings up the importance of exits. Any exit to a room will successfully compete with exhibits. Thus, if a person enters a museum room by one door and sees another door immediately across the room, he or she will tend to enter, turn right, go along the wall, and exit by the second door, missing half of the room. When Melton experimented with a room by adding a second door, he cut down the visitor time in that room from 73 seconds to 23!

One of the most important aspects of Melton's work is that it makes clear the best internal museum design is the *cul de sac*, that is, a room with only one entrance. This is the best physical design to guarantee maximum exposure to what is in the room.

Screven (1969, 1974) did a series of experiments in which he tried to test the learning that took place within a museum. He had subjects attempt to memorize the names of three fossil human skulls and found that he could not succeed in getting what were known to be normal learning results. There seemed to be something about the environment of the museum that pulled people away from the task at hand. Finally, he put the exhibit in a room away from the flow of traffic and got the results he at first expected. This is also instructive of the nature of museum environments. They are not primarily a place where one focuses exclusively on exhibits, but because of the need to traverse the floor plan and get through a strange place, a certain amount of energy is devoted to *exploratory behavior* (Bechtel, 1967). In an exploratory mode, the animal is concerned with finding environmental cues as to how to proceed, and this interferes to some extent with learning about the objects on display. Screven (1990) went on to develop a model for evaluation of exhibits (see Bitgood & Loomis, 1993).

Much has been learned about museums and human behavior in them. Hood (1993), for example, has learned that people respond more readily to museums that show some concern for the visitor by providing comfort. Hard benches without backs are an example of lack of caring in a museum. This is somewhat similar to Sommer's (1974) *hard architecture* concept in which the environment is hardened to prevent damage but also communicates an uncaring message. Kaplan, Bardwell, and Slakter (1993) also explore the museum as a restorative environment but find something less than the ideal. Many find museums tedious and tiring. Those who feel comfortable in museum settings because of previous experience are more likely to receive the restorative benefits.

Zoos

In her doctoral dissertation, Joyce Shettle-Neuber (1986) investigated what she called "second" and "third" generations of exhibits in zoos. This reflects the evolution of zoo exhibits first described by Campbell (1984) as the simple cages or deep pits in the nineteenth century and well into the twentieth (first generation) to those most prevalent today, the cement enclosures surrounded by dry or water-filled moats (second generation), to the third generation exhibits, which are an attempt to display the animal in its natural habitat with as much space and native vegetation as is possible. Controlling for animals by keeping the same species across second- and third-generation exhibits, she interviewed visitors and staff, did behavioral mapping, and timed visitors at each exhibit. Generally, visitors stayed longer at the new exhibits but there were some exceptions and these were due to the fact that animals were sometimes more visible at the older exhibits.

This illustrates, of course, the basic conflict between visitors' and animals' needs at the zoo. What is good for the animal in terms of providing a less stressful environment does not always coincide with the motive of the visitor in coming to the zoo. In fact, research on zoos can be characterized as forming largely around this dilemma, trying to accommodate both the animals' and the visitors' needs. The staff is also involved by presenting a third level of needs, in terms of having access to the animals for service.

Martin and O'Reilly (1988) describe the various kinds of research projects that have centered on zoos, and there are certain similarities to the museum research of Bitgood and Loomis's (1993) compendium. There are the academic researchers and the "inside" researchers. Terry Maple (1983) is an example of an outside researcher who became an insider as director of Atlanta's zoo.

Conclusions

Institutions, according to Milgram (1970; see Chapter 15), are a result of overcrowded circumstances, such as cities, and are developed to deal with the problems that arise from too many people and too many demands. Although some institutions clearly serve a good purpose and enhance the lives of many, some of our institutions such as prisons and mental hospitals have become dysfunctional and seem to cause as many or more problems than they solve. What is interesting is that, despite the mounting evidence of their iatrogenic nature, they continue to be supported as cornerstones of our own social ideology of how to deal with deviants. The evidence remains, but in a nonscientific society changes come from sources other than scientific evidence.

Nevertheless, E&B research has compiled an impressive record of testing improved designs for medical and mental hospitals, zoos, museums, prisons, and other institutional environments.

GOALS

Definitions and Concepts

Institution

Kirkbride Day Hall

Iatrogenic

Tardive dyskinesia

Neuroleptic drugs

Museum fatigue

Generational zoo exhibits

Hard architecture

Cul de sac design

Plane Tree model

Mortification

Sociopetal-sociofugal

De facto inpatient system

Plane Tree model

Important Studies

Roosens (1979)

Kiesler and Sibulkin (1987)

Kiesler and Simpkins (1993)

Colarelli and Siegel (1966)

Fairweather (1969, 1974)

Rosenhan (1973)

Zimbardo et al. (1968)

Lennox (1990)

Trites et al. (1970)

Ulrich (1984)

Melton (1935)

Langan (1994)

QUESTIONS

1. Why do we continue to have mental hospitals?

2. Why are the number of prisons increasing?

3. Should we consider alternatives to prison?

4. How can the people of Geel tolerate crazy people in their homes?

5. Why are people with mental problems going to general hospitals?

6. What is the effect of private, for-profit hospitals?

7. Should anyone take neuroleptic drugs for a long period of time?

8. How can the untrained people in Ward H cure schizophrenics?

9. What is the best museum design and why?

10. Why do museums sometimes have trouble with education?

17

The Changing Work Environment

ॐ

Definition

It is difficult to define *work*, let alone the *work environment*. The standard definition is "paid employment," but that hardly does justice to volunteers or housewives. The more general definition is "an activity that creates something of value to others." Yet this "activity" often cannot be separated from other activities because work is usually embedded in a social and cultural context. Do football players work when they play? Is playing football only work when the players get paid?

Work becomes difficult to define in more complicated ways when one wants to define what work *means*. For work to be "meaningful," the worker requires that it should contribute to a sense of identity. No one wants to do work that is degrading. Yet societies often define low-status jobs as those particularly close to the physical environment such as farming or tanning hides (see Chapter 2). Work often serves to define a person's importance. Each society tends to identify a person's status by the work he or she does. Thus work tends to stratify a society and organize it into levels of functioning.

The average person will spend 40 to 45 years at work. Each year, about 2,000 hours will be spent in a full-time job. Work occupies half or more of our waking hours.

Historical Perspective

Clark Clifford, former adviser to several presidents, divides the history of labor in the United States into five periods:

(1) The wave of immigrants and the rise of heavy industry from the 1880s on. This period was characterized by a shortage of labor and a welcoming of immigrants to work in the new industries being established. Actually, immigration increased markedly following the Civil War and has continued to be a significant part of the labor picture, turning from the welcoming of immigrants to the fear of them in more recent times.

(2) The internal migration from the farms and villages to the cities during and following World War I. This migration was covered in detail in Chapter 15.

(3) The period of social controls from the 1930s through the 1960s. This period marks the end of child labor, the beginning of women's entry into the workforce, the consolidation of labor union gains, and the battles for racial equality.

(4) A cultural evolution during the 1970s, which brought even more social issues into the workplace. This period continues into the present with such issues as sexual harassment.

(5) Automation from the 1980s onward. The technology of automation dominates much of management thinking but the social and cultural struggles continue in importance.

These periods are similar to Muchinsky's (1993) history of Industrial/Organizational Psychology with the exception that the period after World War II was called the era of "specialization," and the period from 1964 onward called the era of "government intervention."

Like many of the historical perspectives presented so far in this book (for human factors, for cities, for POEs), each period does not end at a specific time but continues on into the next several periods. The problems of automation are covered over with the social struggles of sex and race and interwoven with the diminishing numbers of nuclear families and changing values.

Drucker (1993) would add a sixth period, the *postcapitalist* or (called by some) the *information age*. This means that the basis of the economy and the value of labor has shifted from production of goods to organizing all economic activity around the production of information.

The Great and Fallen Hawthorne Study

Books on environmental psychology (Canter, 1972) and industrial psychology often begin with the famous studies done by Elton Mayo and his colleagues (Roethlisberger & Dickson, 1939), and cite them as the beginning of the scientific study of work. As much as anything in psychology can be called a tradition, the Hawthorne studies took their place as a landmark and have been cited everywhere as the prime example of how making a group special, simply by studying it, will make them perform better. Thus was born the prime excuse for deception in psychology: If the people being studied *know* they are being studied, it will ruin the results.

Although anyone who reads the original study can see problems with the above reasoning (Gillespie, 1991), it is interesting to note that few have troubled to do so. For example, the main study concentrated on a group of workers who were wiring an electrical assembly. A group of six young women were used as a *control* group in the study. The experimental group received an increase in lighting level to try to demonstrate that lighting level would cause an increase in productivity. And so it did. The trouble was that the six young women *also* increased their productivity level. In fact, they were able to sustain an increase in productivity at a lighting level that approximated moonlight! The conclusion of Mayo was that the mere knowledge that they were being studied caused the women to work harder. When the same study (Roethlisberger & Dickson, 1939) was done on men, the results were not equal. Apparently, either the men already felt special enough or were embedded in a social system the women did not share.

Gillespie (1991, p. 56) points out, however, that "the change in pay may be the most significant variable" in explaining why the six women did better than they should have as a control group. Mayo neglected to take into account that the control group received an increase in pay during the experiment.

The ladies themselves had their own explanations as to why their group had an increase in productivity. They had rest periods during which they had refreshments and this made them less tired. And they also claimed they received less variety in the relays they wired so it took less time than learning new ones. Mayo failed to mention any of these factors.

Thus one of the icons of scientific studies of the workplace falls from grace. Gillespie (1991) claims this is because "meaning is not discovered, it is imposed" (p. 4). Another view might be Barker's (see Chapter 10) that psychologists should be *transducers* rather than *operators*, allowing the data to convey their meaning rather than imposing a theory too early.

The Environment-Work Interface

Another aspect that has become clear over time about work environment studies is that cultural values and management styles are so intertwined with the physical form of the work environment that they cannot be seen as separate. In other words, a particular work environment may look and be shaped the way it is because it was determined by a particular management set of beliefs. Or the converse may be true. A particular physical aspect of an environment may be obstructive or not facilitative because it does not suit a particular management style.

For example, when some early studies were being done on mental hospital design (Bechtel, 1977), the management styles of several mental hospitals were undergoing radical change. The old style of having psychiatrists in one set of offices, psychologists in another, and nurses in their own enclave was giving way to the *treatment team* concept in which a team consisting of a psychiatrist, psychologists, nurses, social workers, and aides worked together as a unit. Consequently, it was decided the team should have offices next to each other so it would be easier to communicate. This caused a radical change in design from the previous arrangements of collegial offices.

Similarly, some managers feel they have to be able to watch employees as they work or employees will not work at the level they should. This belief dictates a design of visual access from the manager's office. Some managers believe in lunchrooms where workers can socialize; others feel such places are an invitation to socialize at the expense of work.

Thus the management styles and the design of the workplace are so intertwined that both must be understood as part of the environment. One cannot just talk about the physical environment in a workplace. It must always be placed in the management context to understand the effect of the environment on the workers. Barker (1968) refers to this link between behavior and physical environment as *synomorphy*. It means simply that environment and behavior cannot be separated. A good example is a chair. Even though no one may be sitting in the chair, it is obvious that the chair is for sitting, and even though people can sit in many places, they most often take the form of sitting that fits into a chair.

It must also be understood that any normal physical aspect of the workplace is of "marginal utility" (Brill, Margulis, & Konar, 1984) in enhancing worker perceptions of jobs. It is most important to keep in mind the larger issues of pay, status, responsibility, and management variables to keep the physical environment in proper perspective. Of course, extremes of noise and lack of lighting and ventilation will have an influence. The following are some physical aspects of the work environment that have been studied by environmental psychologists.

Windows in the Workplace

There seems to be a widespread desire for windows in the place of work. Wotten, Blackwell, Wallis, and Barkow (1982) found three out of four employees wanted a window near their workstation. Butler and Biner (1989) found all of the college students they surveyed felt windows were preferred in an office setting. But, unfortunately, most workers do not have access to windows. Edwards (1978) found that most of the 1,200 workers he surveyed worked in the "windowless core" of buildings.

Heerwagen and Orians (1986) formulated the *compensation hypothesis*, meaning that employees without access to windows would compensate by hanging pictures, putting up plants, and so on. To test this hypothesis, Biner, Butler, Lovegrove, and Burns (1993) conducted a series of studies to determine how and why workers would compensate. They found that workers do indeed hang pictures and plants but that this is done regardless of whether they have access to windows or not. In fact, these studies are a confirmation of *personalization* because this was one of the most important reasons given for hanging pictures and displaying plants and other objects.

Wells (1965) claims windows are connected to status, such that those nearest to or with a window have higher status than those without one.

Lighting

About 100 foot-candles are required to read. Some work tasks require more. The fabled Hawthorne studies (Roethlisberger & Dickson, 1939) were supposed to measure the critical difference that increased lighting would make in productivity. Instead, they showed that other factors could easily overcome lighting effects. Nevertheless, lighting is still a critical issue in the workplace. Marans and Yan (1989) found that lighting was the second factor related to satisfaction with the environment in offices. (Size of work surfaces was first.)

Noise

The Occupational Safety and Health Administration (OSHA) (1974) has worked out a complex procedure for measuring exposure to noise. Although some want to define noise as unwanted sound, Burrows (1960) treats it as surplus information in regard to the task. Sound frequencies are measured by a unit called Hertz (Hz). Most frequencies audible to humans are below 1,000 Hz but we are more sensitive to high frequencies than lower ones so that a high frequency tone will sound subjectively louder than a lower frequency. Therefore, sound measurements are weighted by frequency to take into account this difference, and the EPA (1974) has adopted a standard to approximate the sensitivity of the human ear. Decibels (dB) are a measure of loudness. This can get quite complex in that a measure of 1,000 Hz of 40 dB (decibels) is equal to a 50 Hz tone at 40 Db, illustrating that the high frequency is equal to the lower in subjective loudness.

Not only intensity but also the length of exposure must be measured, so the EPA (1974) arrived at an equivalent sound level (Leq), which is dBs of a constant noise over time. To get some idea of sound levels (see Table 1.3 in Chapter 1), a conversation should be around 30 dB while any sound interfering with conversation is considered disruptive. Most hearing loss occurs with exposure over time and starts with the upper ranges (4,000 Hz). Sound levels around 90 to 100 dB are considered harmful even if not prolonged. Many industrial workers are continuously exposed to such levels during their 8-hour shift. But most noise is not at this level.

Sundstrom, Bell, Busby, and Asmus (1994) found that 54% of the 2,391 workers they asked at 58 sites were bothered *often* by noise. Most of this was the human voice, talking on telephones. Satisfaction on the job was negatively related to increasing noise. The Research Lab (1992) found 50% of their workers rated noise as between extremely annoying and unbearable. To mask the conversational noise that is actually the most troublesome, many organizations introduce *white noise* (Beattie, 1982).

The general conclusion is that the effect of noise on task performance is minimal except at extremes (Sanders & McCormick, 1993). Gawron (1982) reviewed 58 noise experiments and found 29 showed hindrance and 22 had no effect. Seven studies actually facilitated performance under noise. Broadbent (1976) had tried to explain such differences earlier by his "funneling of attention" hypothesis. At high levels of noise, the worker focuses only on the most important aspects of a task. If relevant information is missed by this narrowing of focus, performance suffers. But for simple tasks, the narrowing of focus may actually improve performance.

One aspect does seem to be impaired by noise and that is the semantic comprehension of written material. Smith (1989) found that understanding of verbal materials was compromised by noise. Weinstein (1974, 1977) used a proofreading task to measure noise effects and found it affected location of grammatical errors but did not affect the ability to detect spelling errors. Smith and Stansfield (1986) discovered that people in high aircraft noise zones failed to retain the meaning of read material.

The Open Office

In the late 1950s and early 1960s, a West German furniture manufacturer, Eberhard and Wolfgang Schnelle, introduced a new design for offices called the *landscaped office* (Bürolandschaft). Later it was called the *open office*. The concept was to eliminate all the individual cubicles that formerly housed individual office spaces and mass them together in one space. Partitions, lighting, heating, and cooling were eliminated from interior spaces and the construction cost savings were considerable. Further, it was also easier to have visual access to all the workers in this huge space, so this was very appealing to the direct supervision style of management.

The greatest promise was the potential for being able to organize a company around its own self-styled management system and to change and even experiment to arrive at the best network possible. Promoters of the scheme claimed that a new, more coherent social cohesion would form. It was called a "sociologist's dream." Figure 17.1 shows a typical open office plan. Note the clusters of desks and communication spaces in between. The open office also promised ease of reorganization. New groupings of desks could be easily accomplished without having to move walls. This plan found acceptance worldwide.

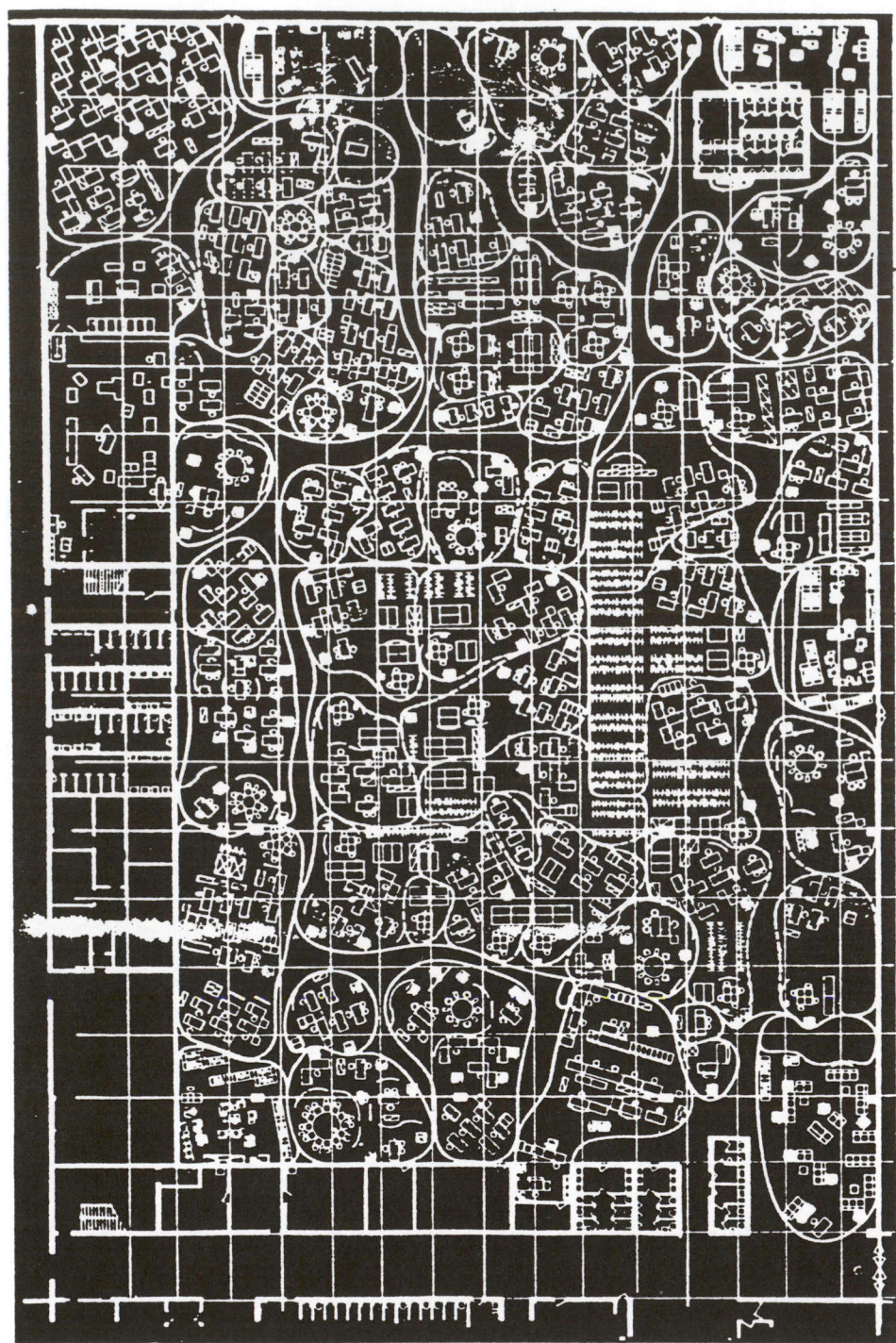

Figure 17.1. Landscaped Office

SOURCE: Brookes and Kaplan (1972). Reprinted with permission from Malcolm Brooks and from *Human Factors,* Vol. 14, No. 5, 1972. Copyright 1972 by the Human Factors and Ergonomics Society. All rights reserved.

NOTE: Plan view of a typical office which has been laid out according to a landscape plan. The conventional rectilinear geometry of small offices, partitions, corridors, and rows of desks in a bullpen is replaced by a casual geometry purported to reflect work groupings.

Brookes and Kaplan (1972) did one of the first social science tests of this concept. As they pointed out, the open office concept was introduced and accepted without any data to support its efficacy. It was sold purely on the unstated claims of its proponents. Zeitlin (1969) had reported rumored 40%-50% reductions in space requirements, a 20% decrease in maintenance costs, a 95% reduction in setup costs, and 10%-20% increases in productivity but was unable to support any of these claims from his own study of the New York Port Authority. Zeitlin (1969) concludes that it is not possible for the design of the office, whether landscaped or conventional, to instill motivation in the workforce.

Bates (1971) reported a "loss of identity" on the part of workers on moving to a landscaped office. Hundert and Greenfield (1969) found little difference on comparing a conventional with a landscaped office. Brookes and Kaplan (1972) supported the findings of Zeitlin and Hundert and Greenfield by showing their 100 subjects experienced increased noise, visual bustle, lack of privacy, loss of personal space control. There may be increased social cohesiveness but Brookes and Kaplan felt their data did not conclusively support this. The conclusion was the open office plan was not actually distinguishable from conventional offices in terms of function.

These data were later confirmed by other studies (Marans & Spreckelmeyer, 1982). Thus one of the most extensive changes in office environments in this century was shown not to be an improvement over the old design *except in initial construction costs.*

Taylorism

The fact that management style interacts inseparably with the physical design of the workplace is nowhere illustrated better than in the influence of Frederick Winslow Taylor on U.S. management philosophy.

Taylor (1856-1915) is popularly called "the Father of Scientific Management" but this is misleading because he was not *scientific* in the accepted definition of the term. Copley (1923) wrote the first biography of Taylor but subsequent biographies (Kakar, 1970; Nelson, 1980; Zalesnik, 1966) have been more critical of Taylor's philosophy and methods. What is important is the influence Taylor had on management in the United States and how this influenced the impersonalization of work and the work area.

He began as a mechanical engineer, getting his degree in June 1883 from the Stevens Institute of Technology, and then was an apprentice machinist and pattern maker. At the Midvale Steel Company in Philadelphia, he spent 3 years trying to bend workers to his will. Taylor's aim was to take control of the workplace from the worker and place it entirely in the hands of the manager. For 15 years, he worked during various periods to determine how many foot-pounds of work a man could do in a day. Taylor's view was of the worker as a machine. Yet, it is ironic that the most central discovery of his 15-year work was that every task has a natural pace that requires periods of rest. Unfortunately, this central fact was forgotten and the "legacy" of his work was to try to force as much work as possible into the work period without regard to the rest periods that are so essential to maximum performance.

One of his favorite speeches would begin, "What is the name of the man you are working for? What does he want you to do *now?*" Taylor considered the working man was "stupid and phlegmatic, a man like an ox" (Nelson, 1980, p. 172).

Although Taylor's influence was great, his own professional society, the American Society of Mechanical Engineers, refused to publish his chief work, *Principles of Scientific Management*, and it was not published until after his death. His followers banded together to form the Taylor Society.

In addition to the control-over-work philosophy, the most visible legacy of Taylor was the time-motion study. Although others had done it before him and most of the credit should go to Gilbreth and Thompson, his followers, the time-motion study was accepted by unions in the 1920s. Time-motion studies are done by watching a worker perform a given task, noting the time and placing a monetary value on the task by which the worker would be paid according to the time it took to perform it. To make more money, the worker would have to decrease the time it took him to perform the task.

Zalesnik (1970) claims that "no single figure in the history of industrialization did more to affect the role of manager than Taylor and, in fact, those who came after him had to take Taylor's work into account" (p. ix). Even today, managers are routinely taught in management schools how to impose their will on workers. Although Taylor died in 1915, the view of worker as machine lives on and with it such views as the necessity for visual oversight of the workers and all the other physical requirements of absolute control.

Job Enrichment

Frederick Herzberg (1968) introduced the term *job enrichment*, which redefined work as a group task. Taylor's view was of work as an individual enterprise, the single worker at a station. Job enrichment redefined work as a group undertaking with individual tasks able to be changed at the will of the worker. The group decided which person would do which task and would allow variation within tasks as well as persons switching roles.

Drucker claims "job enrichment has been around for 60 years. It's been successful every time it has been tried, but industry is not interested" (quoted in Tarrant, 1976, p. 257). Why should this be the case? Part of the reason is Taylorism, the view that the workplace should be entirely in the control of management. But job enrichment places a major portion of control back in the hands of the workers. This goes contrary to current beliefs and traditional practice in U.S. industry.

What is interesting about job enrichment is this fact, that although it has been successful, it has not been accepted by industry. In other words, it is another example of scientific evidence that goes contrary to current belief systems and is ignored.

Walton (1977) showed how the Pet Food plant in Topeka, Kansas, adopted job enrichment and increased profits the first year. Davis and Cherns (1975) summarize many studies and show that in most cases job enrichment has succeeded. The cases where it has not worked reveal managers unwilling to share profits and power with the workers. This brings up a distinction between *job enlargement* and *job enrichment* (Herzberg, 1968). What many of the industries that failed at job enrichment have tried is merely enlarging the jobs rather than truly enriching the work experience. The workers were quick to perceive that they were merely having to do more work for the same amount of pay.

What then actually distinguishes job enrichment from merely doing more work? The example of the Volvo plant in Sweden is a good illustration (Gyllenhammer, 1977). The plant managers had become painfully aware that the quality of their automobile had deteriorated sadly. The plant had increased absenteeism, lots of job-hopping, and even malicious vandalism. Something needed to be done. A new plant at Kalmar, Sweden, became the place to try new innovations in the working force. First, the physical surroundings were changed and made more pleasant. The dullest jobs were mechanized. Workers were divided into groups, each responsible for a clearly defined part of the car. One group had the electrical system, another had charge of doors, another the interior. Each group does its own inspections, works at its own pace.

Later, each worker learned all of the operations in the plants, even the Torslanda plant with 8,000 workers. Sweden actually has a law that mandates that workers must take part in all decisions from the shop floor to the corporate boardroom. Thus the workers took responsibility for deciding on every aspect of how they should do their work.

When U.S. unions visited Sweden, they declared it could never work in the United States. But, of course, it has worked in the United States and in the rest of the world (Davis & Cherns, 1975).

Control of the Workplace

The conflict between the Taylor style of management and the more democratic job enrichment movement raises the question of how important it is for workers to control the workplace. Symme (1986) sees this as a broader issue of democracy related to the political system in a country. *Industrial democracy* is a movement that has taken hold in Europe and mandates worker participation in industrial decisions similar to the situation described above in Sweden.

As previously mentioned (in Chapter 11 on stress), Karasek and Theorell (1990) studied work from the point of view of control and found that workers who had least control (decision making) and most pressure to perform had the highest likelihood of heart disease. See Figure 17.2.

They conclude, however, that

in spite of the entirely different and glitteringly successful examples of alternative work design in Western Europe, Japan and the United States, Taylor's principles are still at the core of Industrial Engineering curricula when it comes to the design of the worker's task. (Karasek & Theorell, 1990, p. 24)

Further, "low levels of decision latitude carry the double penalty of high stress and loss of innovative potential" (p. 199).

Thus the work environment today is not only undergoing a great amount of change but is also remaining in a state of conflict in the United States between the Tayloristic education of most managers and the engineers who design workstations, and the participatory movement of job

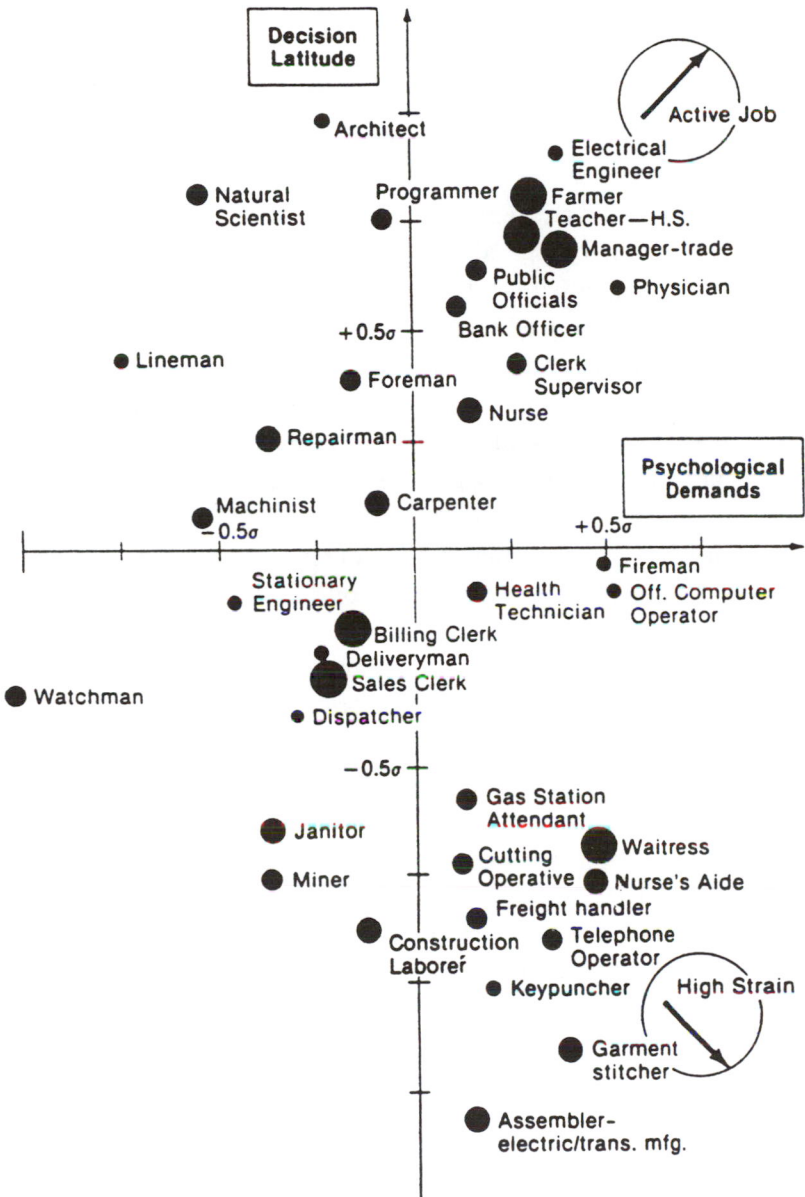

Figure 17.2. Demands and Decision Latitude in Jobs

SOURCE: Data from Quality of Employment Surveys 1969, 1972, 1977 (Karasek & Theorell, 1990, p. 67). Copyright © 1990 by Robert Karasek. Reprinted by permission of BasicBooks, a division of HarperCollins Publishers, Inc.
NOTE: The occupational distribution of psychological demands and decision latitude (U.S. males and females, N = 4,495).

enrichment and industrial democracy. In European industry, the industrial democracy movement is becoming standard.

Deming

Unknown in the United States until 1980, W. Edwards Deming wore a modest pin in his lapel. It was about the size of a dime. On very close scrutiny and after intense translation, the information on this pin reads roughly as follows: "The Second Order of Treasure. The Japanese People attribute the rebirth of Japanese industry and its worldwide success to W. Edwards Deming." In other words, when Emperor Hirohito presented this award, it was to make Deming a national treasure because he was the person responsible for the Japanese economic success after World War II.

No discussion of the management influence on the working environment would be complete without recognition of his revolutionary influence, still being resisted in much of U.S. management circles. Deming (1986) proposed 14 radical measures to transform Japanese industry. It is often claimed these are "hard to understand" because they fly so blatantly in the face of what is being taught in management schools today.

Deming says, for example, that all merit pay, inspectors, annual evaluations, competitive bidding, and bonuses must be eliminated. No order (request) should be made without a reason. What must be managed is the *system*, not people. Once these changes are in place, the system must be constantly improved so that there is practically *no* rejection rate.

As an example of the exactness that can be achieved, Deming had parts manufactured in the United States compared with those in Japan. The parts in the United States had been failing at an unacceptable rate. By the measurements made by inspectors, all the parts passed with flying colors. When the Japanese parts were measured, it was thought the calipers had broken because all parts were essentially identical. In other words, by the standards used in the United States, there were *no* tolerances.

The essence of Deming's message is that everyone in the organization must work for the same goal: the nearest to perfection possible. This is not accomplished by any one method but by a great number of small changes and adaptations (see Chapter 2 on evolution) that are continually refined. The process never ends.

One of Deming's most important points is that work should be a joy! A more complete story of the Japanese success is contained in Halberstam (1986). Despite the undeniable success of the Japanese, much of U.S. industry still resists the insights Deming offered. Taylorism is still very much alive.

The Social Climate Scales

The *Social Climate Scales* developed by Rudolph Moos and his associates at Stanford Medical School attempt to combine the social and environmental elements in work settings (Moos, 1986). The *Work Environment Scale* (WES) contains 10 subscales: Involvement, Peer Cohesion, Supervisor Support, Autonomy, Task Orientation, Work Pressure, Clarity, Control, Innovation, and Physical Comfort. The latter scale measures to what extent the physical surroundings contribute to a work experience. Other subscales are obviously related to such issues as Taylorism and industrial democracy. Work settings that are high on Taylorism will have high scores on task orientation, work pressure, and control and low scores on involvement, peer cohesion, supervisor support, and autonomy. Settings with industrial democracy or job enrichment will have high scores on involvement, peer cohesion, supervisor support, autonomy, and clarity and low scores on control.

Brady, Kinnaird, and Friedrich (1980) found that employees who scored higher on involvement, cohesion, support, autonomy, and innovation had higher job satisfaction. Morale seems to be lower among employees where peer relationships are strained or distant, the job is chaotic or poorly planned, and supervisors are highly controlling (Berkeley Planning Associates, 1977).

The WES has been used in a variety of work settings as well as internationally (see Moos, 1986, the *Work Environment Scale Manual*, second edition).

The Future Work Environment

Most authorities agree (Howell, 1993) that the most important aspect of the future work environment is change. Spreckelmeyer (1993) claims: "There is considerable evidence to suggest that environmental change has caused—or at least exacerbated—conditions that cause increased levels of dissatisfaction, displacement and inefficiency among office workers" (p. 182). Fraser (1989) goes farther: "Despite the amelioration of physical conditions achieved over the last half century and more, the ambience of work is becoming increasingly less tolerable in most levels of working society" (p. 118).

In other words, the future work environment is already here and its chief characteristic is constant change. How does one deal with this new environmental element? Few environmental studies deal with change as an environmental factor (Wapner, 1992). Hakken (1993) stresses that work has not changed so much, and especially discounts the influence of computers in bringing about change. Howell (1993) claims that the changes require a new focus on two areas: understanding and coping with complex task demands and accommodating and exploiting individual differences.

There is no doubt that technology is demanding increasingly complex tasks from workers. Computer software and hardware are a good example; both can become obsolete faster than their operations can be learned. Are "pull-down" menus more quickly learned than the old keyboard commands? The investigation of such questions can be quite circular and elusive (Cooke, 1992; Howell, 1993).

One of the concepts that emerges from investigation of how people approach complex problems is *situation awareness* (SA). As contrasted to the more general *savoir faire*, which is a personality trait of being able to deal appropriately with *every* situation, situation awareness is more of a learned capacity to deal with certain specific situations. Howell (1993) complains that SA is not consistently defined across studies even though each researcher seems confident of its usage.

One insight that seems to have been gained under this concept is to train for specific aspects of a situation rather than under the complexity of "real-life" circumstances. For example, Kass, Herschler, and Companion (1991) trained subjects to recognize muzzle flashes in a simpler situation and found this helped more than trying to train under more complex battlefield simulations.

Human factors, engineering psychology, and industrial/organizational psychology have all emphasized the normal or statistically average person in the design of the workplace. What has happened is that this concept has been made invalid by the introduction of so many new variables such as sex, race, ethnicity, and age. This has meant the more complex task of

designing for these many differences. Thus the new task is to accommodate and even exploit these individual differences to advantage. *Hardiness* (remember Kobasa?) has become a subject of individual differences
(Westman, 1990).

Aging has become a hot topic in measures of individual differences
because the workforce is aging rapidly. It is becoming clear that chronological age itself is not a good predictor of risk. Aging people find a variety
of ways to compensate for diminishing abilities.

The result of this new emphasis on change is to design and train for an
increasingly more specific set of tasks and to customize design and
training to more selected workers. In short, the designing and training
for work is acquiring a new situational awareness of its own.

Conclusions

Almost all authorities agree that the most common element in the
workplace today is change. In the United States, there still exists the
conflict between the Victorian ideology of Taylorism and the more democratic methods of Deming. What is amazing to behold is the resistance to
such programs as job enrichment despite their proven success. The future
seems to demand more generalists than specialists, with people trained
to constantly adapt to change.

GOALS

Definitions and Concepts

Compensation hypothesis

Funneling of attention

Open office

Job enrichment

Job enlargement

WES

Situation awareness

Social Climate Scales

Postcapitalist age

Synomorphy

Taylorism

Industrial democracy

Deming's method

Important Studies

Roethlisberger and Dickson (1939)

Gillespie (1991)

Biner et al. (1993)

Sundstrom et al. (1994)

Broadbent (1976)

Brookes and Kaplan (1972)

Walton (1977)

Karasek and Theorell (1990)

Questions

1. Why does noise sometimes improve performance?

2. Do people make up for a lack of windows by using pictures?

3. Is the open office a success or failure?

4. What is the critical difference between job enlargement and job enrichment?

5. Why does the name of the Social Climate Scales use the word *social* instead of *environmental?*

6. What is the age of information?

7. What is the real secret behind Deming's methods?

8. Why is Taylorism so popular?

9. What is the main difference between U.S. and foreign workers?

10. What is the chief environmental element in the future workplace?

18

Recreational Environments

Definition

Barker (1968) defines *recreational behavior* as "behavior that gives immediate gratification; consummatory behavior" (p. 64). In other words, this is behavior engaged in for its own sake, not like work, which is, presumably, done for money. Cheek (1971) simply calls all leisure and recreation *not work*. There are overlaps because many volunteers work without pay and, presumably, do this for its own sake or for "higher" motives such as altruism. Similarly, many players who are paid enjoy their work so much they could not do otherwise. A good example is the hockey player in Studs Terkel's (1974) volume on work, who could not resist a frozen puddle on the street, who put on his skates and went "flying."

Some attention must also be given to the concept of *leisure*. Many authorities (Haywood, Kew, & Bramham, 1989; Kraus, 1994) prefer this term but use it almost synonymously with *recreation*. Leisure seems to connote more than recreation in that it encompasses contemplative free time that does not necessarily involve any activity. Thus Kraus (1994) speaks of leisure *and* recreation. For heuristic purposes, however, let us consider the two terms to be synonymous.

Historical Perspective

Most texts on recreation (Chubb & Chubb, 1981; Haywood et al., 1989; Kraus, 1994) provide detailed historical backgrounds for recreation that go back to Neolithic times. What seems to emerge from these historical ramblings is the fact that the industrial revolution had a profound effect on recreation by sequestering work in time and place. The industrial revolution had the effect of taking work out of the home into the factory or office and segregating time for work so that recreation and work became largely separated. Thus a major effect of the industrial revolution was to contrast work with recreation. There was a time for work and a time for play.

A second effect was to change the character of recreation from its largely homespun, spontaneous nature to a more commercial product. One did not pay for recreation in preindustrial days. It was spontaneous and did not involve purchased items. But with the concentration of populations, commercial recreation became possible and, with it, the rise of recreation as an industry in its own right. Today it is common to speak of the recreational industry comprising everything from the tourist and travel industry to commercial sports, hotels, amusement parks, movies, and even paid television.

A third effect was to increase the kind of recreation from individual and more active behavior to more passive, sitting-and-watching types of behavior. Television viewing is the most obvious example. Nevertheless, the variety of recreational pursuits is such that recreation is never thought of in a narrowly defined sense. It is always seen to encompass the full range from active to passive pursuits.

Although "not work" may seem clearly separated from work in our own society, historical precedents exist where games, for example, were actually more than recreation as it is understood today. An example is the famous "ball game" of the Mayan Indians (Schele & Friedel, 1990). This game was played with a basketball-sized solid latex rubber object that was batted through a stone ring. The losers lost their heads! Figure 18.1 shows a bas relief mural at the ball court in Chichén Itzá on the Yucatán Peninsula of Mexico. The "winner" on the left keeps his head while the loser on the right loses his. Stylized streams of blood flow from the loser's neck and the winner holds the head of the loser. Streams of blood from the neck of the loser become snakes heads. A death's-head is at the bottom

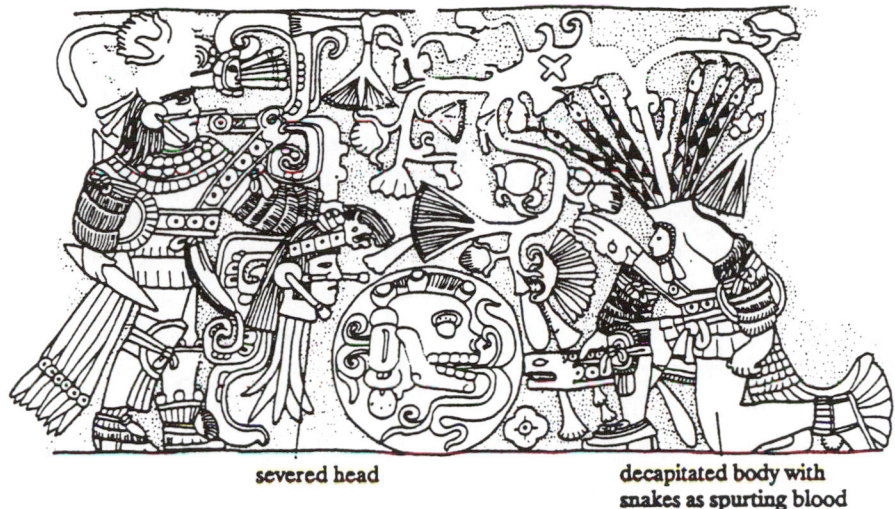

severed head   decapitated body with
                                snakes as spurting blood

Figure 18.1. Ball Game Panel at Chichén Itzá

center of the panel, and this symbolism leads archaeologists to see the ball game as a reenactment of Mayan mythology whereby Hero Twins tricked the Lords of Death into sacrifice. The Mayans believed rebirth could come about through decapitation. It was often the custom to have captured rulers play this game to the death. Therefore, the game served many functions in religion and government, not the least of which was unifying the social order.

Mumford (1961) also saw the unifying element of games in his description of Rome. In fact, the emperors of Rome became so dependent on the games as a sop to the public that by A.D. 354, there were 175 days a year devoted to games and the total number of holidays was 200! As Mumford puts it (1961), "No body of citizens, not even the Athenians at the height of their empire, ever had such an abundance of idle time to fill with idiotic occupations" (p. 231).

In earlier times, games were often a direct product of the state with a view to pacifying and unifying the population. Games may serve these same functions today without being direct products of government and religion. To paraphrase and somewhat stretch another theoretician, games were clearly the opiate of the people in historic times.

Social Focus of Recreation

Cheek, Field, and Burdge (1976) proposed the thesis that recreation is essentially a *group* behavioral phenomenon. This means that all forms of recreation are primarily attended by people in groups, and the most frequent group found is the family. Next most frequent are groups of friends and families with friends. The point of making this distinction is that it shows how recreation sites should be organized to accommodate this family orientation rather than the activities per se.

Cheek et al. distinguish recreation from work by showing that work participation is largely *individual* in nature. A person goes to work alone and, even though working in groups, does not go to work as part of a group. This view has certain advantages for the design and management of recreational places. If it is assumed that the units coming to the site are families, then the design of all physical accommodations must take this into account from reception, through participation, and to the last exit.

But there is a more profound meaning intended by Cheek et al., which is that people don't go to a place to take part in an activity, they go there to be together. The family doesn't just go boating or picnicking or visiting the zoo, they want to do something *together*. The conclusion, say Cheek et al., is to design recreation for this sense of gathering, not just in terms of the activity itself.

Looking at the broad spectrum of recreational activities, they found that 96% were engaged in them with a group at parks and beaches; 91% at playgrounds, schools, tracks, stadiums, and ballparks; and even 69% engaged with groups at their own homes or the home of a relative or friend. Table 18.1 shows the breakdown of kinds of groups by place. The home is the place where most people recreate alone. All other places are largely for group events.

In another study based on a national sample, subjects were asked to indicate where they spent their leisure time with friends, and the home was clearly the place where most leisure time was spent alone or with friends (see Table 18.2).

What is interesting about these findings is that most recreation is thought of as outdoors and not much thought is given to the home as a site for recreation. Bechtel (1989) found that homes in Alaska, Iran, and Saudi Arabia also had recreation as the most frequent use of time in the home, yet the home is the least designed for recreation of all environments!

Table 18.1 Proportion of Individuals Who Participated With Someone Else in a Recreation Place

Place	Percentage	N
Neighborhood; at home or the house of a friend or relative	69	340
Parks	96	268
Playgrounds, schools, tracks, stadiums and ballparks	91	347
Beaches, lakes, rivers	97	525

SOURCE: Cheek et al. (1976).

Table 18.2 Group Composition by Recreation Place

	Percentage					
Place	Alone	With Friends	Family	Family & Friends	Other	N
Neighborhoods, at home or the house of a friend or relative	31	11	43	14	1	340
Parks	4	22	51	22	1	268
Playgrounds, schools, tracks, stadiums, and ballparks	9	28	44	16	3	347
Beaches, lakes and rivers	3	20	50	26	1	529

SOURCE: Cheek et al. (1976).

Theories of Recreation

As early as the psychologist McDougall (1918), theoreticians were claiming recreation, or play, was a socializing force in development. Play either practiced instincts, rehearsed social norms, got rid of surplus energy, acted as a catharsis, or exercised growing abilities. Veblen (1899), contrary to most theorists, saw leisure as a sign of decadence and an example of economic exploitation.

Csikszentmihalyi (1976, 1990) developed the *flow model* of recreation, which he later extended to other areas of life such as work. From his earlier model of voluntary involvement, free time, enjoyable experience, and structured activity (1976), he enlarged to an eight-part model that contained (a) an appropriate skill, (b) focused attention, (c) clear goals, (d) immediate feedback, (e) deep involvement, (f) sense of control, (g) the dissipation of self-absorption, and (h) the sense of time being altered.

Csikszentmihalyi's book (1990) is titled *Flow: The Psychology of Optimal Experience*. The central point seems to be a near-transcendental experience where the person is taken out of the self by the experience but has the sense of self increased at the same time. This theory came from many observations of people enjoying themselves in recreational pursuits but it was later observed to be present in almost any activity. Hence the free time aspect was dropped in the later model. One can experience the same sense of flow in an enjoyable work experience. As such, Csikszentmihalyi's model is no longer just a recreational theory but one that applies to many aspects of human life.

The aspect of control is a central part of Ajzen and Driver's (1992) *planned behavior* model. Readers will remember the Fishbein and Ajzen model of attitudes from Chapter 4. This is an updated version of that model. Three components make up the model: attitude toward the behavior, subjective norms, and degree of perceived behavioral control. Often control is seen as the person's sense of how easy it is to perform the behavior (play tennis, dance, and so on). The basic idea is that people decide to engage in these behaviors (recreation) when these three factors operate favorably. Their data show that when the perceived behavioral control is measured, it considerably improves the predictability that a recreational behavior will be engaged in.

Haggard and Williams (1992) assert that we select leisure activities on the basis of our ability to affirm valued aspects of our identities. McIntyre (1992) developed an *adventure model* of recreation and sees risk-taking kinds of recreation as an arena for adventure.

Much has been written about the international aspects of recreation. Scitiovsky (1992) uses a stimulus-seeking model similar to Berlyne's and notes that Europeans are educated for enjoyment of the "finer things" while the United States educates people for jobs, which results in more pedestrian pursuits that are more an escape from work than a pursuit of finer things.

Jackson (1991) sees most leisure research divided into how people use their time versus the experience and meaning of leisure and recreation. Thus the time studies seldom relate what the behavior means to the person and simply list hours spent per week, month, or year, assuming this is important in itself. The "meaning" studies attempt to interpret the nature of the experience and place a value on it. Shaw (1992), for example, looks at the experiences of men versus women in the so-called family recreational pursuits and find the meaning for men and women quite different because the work to be done in preparation and execution of family outings is unequally divided, with women doing most of the work. Consequently, even though the events may be valued by both men and women, the meaning is most often different, with women seeing it as far less leisurely than the men. Henderson (1992) pursues the meaning-for-women issues and finds that the "ethic of caring" most typifies the kinds of activities women most often volunteer for.

And What Is Fun?

Poldichak (1991) attempts to define the undefinable, the word *fun*. He argues that *fun* and *leisure* are not actually synonymous: "You cannot have fun by yourself." His definition: "Fun is a socio-emotional, international process wherein persons deconstruct social biographical inequalities to create a with-equal-other, social human bond" (p. 124).

The Modern Trend

In an exhaustive analysis of recreation expenditure records, Blaine and Golam (1991) looked at recreational expenditures from 1946 to 1988 and found that, directly as a result of women entering the labor force, the amount of leisure time available to families decreased. As a further result, consumers increased the buying of "market-purchased goods." They conclude:

> Extrapolating this to the future conjures up disturbing images of a society virtually devoid of leisure but loaded with gadgets in attempts to make up for the loss of time, where books are replaced by TV, quiet walks by high speed vehicles, chess by high tech video games, and so forth. (p. 121)

Social Worlds of Recreation

Hobbies create social worlds of their own. There are bridge players, stamp collectors, coin collectors, members of tennis clubs, and so on. Each of these can gather a nationwide or even worldwide following that is held together by newsletters, conventions, commercial publications, awards, and local clubs. Stamp collectors, for example, have a hierarchy of worldwide, national, and local stamp shows attended by various levels of devotees from the very wealthy to the relatively poor. There are stamp magazines and newspapers, and worldwide, national, and local clubs. The hobby is said to number into the millions. Much the same is also true of coin collectors.

Marks (1991) details the social world of hunting in the southern United States. Hunting is seen as an exclusive male activity that has survived and flourished throughout our 200-year history. Hunting asserts the superior position of the male in society and becomes increasingly important in a world where the lines between masculine and feminine activity are becoming blurred. In many ways, hunting is a refuge for males, a place to escape from female influence into a completely male-dominated world. Trophy heads are seen as symbols of the masculine mystique.

Yet environmental degradation of the landscape is a serious problem for the hunters. They see the loss of habitat as threatening their very existence as game, especially small game, gets scarcer. At the same time, the hunters are the bulwark of the National Rifle Association and strongly defend the right to bear any arms. Yet they feel they must support conservation avidly.

Hunting also serves as the school for young men into the masculine world. The father-son aspect of hunting serves to perpetuate the hunting myth from generation to generation and becomes the vehicle for the relationship to the father. One must wonder whether similar behavior is associated with fishing, golf, and other recreational pursuits.

The Biophilia Hypothesis

Wilson (1984) proposed the biophilia hypothesis, which is an evolutionary concept that ties humans to the terrestrial landscape. In other words, humans are attached genetically to the landscape by the process of evolution and it is now coded in the genes to prefer natural environments. Some of this concept was encountered in Chapter 2 in Appleton's (1975) prospect and refuge theory and Balling and Falk's (1982) preference for savannas. The biophilia hypothesis is much broader, however, and does not limit itself to specific kinds of environments such as savannas.

Ulrich (1993) focuses on the *restorative* aspect of natural settings. His research and that of several others shows that exposure to natural environments reduces stress and therefore restores the person to a more healthful state. For example, Ulrich, Dimberg, and Driver (1991) showed 120 subjects a stressful movie and then split the group into two, showing half urban settings and the other half natural settings. Those who saw the natural settings recuperated much faster and more thoroughly than those exposed to the urban settings by four physiological measures such as heart rate, skin conductance, muscle tension, and pulse transit time and also self-reports on such things as positive feelings and feelings of anger and fear. Thus the people seeing a natural environment recovered faster, in four to six minutes, but also in more lasting and beneficial ways.

These findings can be extended to practical aspects of the environment. Judy Heerwagen (1990) reduced the amount of stress in a dental office by hanging a mural of a landscape on the wall.

It would seem that the biophilia hypothesis is still in need of a great deal of research before the genetic aspect is demonstrated but the preference for natural environments is well on its way to acceptance. Ulrich (1993) has extended the hypothesis from merely a preference for natural environments to a *restorative* response.

Conclusions

In historical times, recreation was used by the state to unify people. Since the industrial revolution, recreation has become more of a foil to work—free time contrasted to bought time. With women entering the workforce and work time increasing, recreation has become more commercialized and technology oriented. Although some theories such as flow theory see recreation as self-actualizing, other theories such as the biophilia hypothesis see it as acting out genetic imperatives. Problems of definition remain. Some characterize recreation as "not work" while others see it as a by-product of groups meeting. In any case, it is increasing and changing with our society, becoming more commercial and passive.

GOALS

Definitions and Concepts

Recreation

Leisure

Commercial recreation

Group behavioral aspect

Social worlds of recreation

Restorative aspects

Flow model

Planned behavior model

Adventure model

Fun

Biophilia hypothesis

Important Studies

Cheek et al. (1976)

Csikszentmihalyi (1976)

Ajzen and Driver (1992)

Blaine and Golam (1991)

Marks (1991)

Appleton (1975)

Ulrich et al. (1991)

QUESTIONS

1. Why is recreation seen as an interest of governments?

2. What role does recreation have in modern life?

3. What is the significance of the restoration hypothesis?

4. What is the evidence for biophilia?

5. Of what importance is the flow model?

6. What role does recreation play in your own identity?

7. How much time do you spend in recreational pursuits?

8. What is the cost per week of recreation in your life?

9. Did recreation play a role in the downfall of the Roman Empire?

10. Does recreation play a role in national identity?

19

Extreme Environments

Definition

In many places on our globe, we encounter environments that are considered extreme relative to the temperate climate of North America. What is considered extreme, however, can often be a matter of ethnocentric viewpoint. I can remember well the look of disdain from ARAMCO (Arabian American Oil Co.) officials when a colleague of mine referred to the local climate of eastern Saudi Arabia as extreme. To them it was natural. It is a good thing to recognize that the classification of any extreme environment is purely a relative matter. To a resident of any climate, what is extreme is something not experienced.

Nevertheless, with our rapidly expanding population, we are creating living environments in places where people would ordinarily not choose to live. This is especially true in new technological areas such as space travel. We are literally creating new environments where humans could not exist without a complete life support system. These environments are currently tailor-made to the astronauts. Futuristic environments are being hypothesized by scientists (Johnson & Holbrow, 1977) who plan space colonies (see Figure 19.1).

On Earth, new environments are being created in previously uninhabited areas to make mining communities, weather and radar stations, military outposts, and experimental communities tied to space exploration.

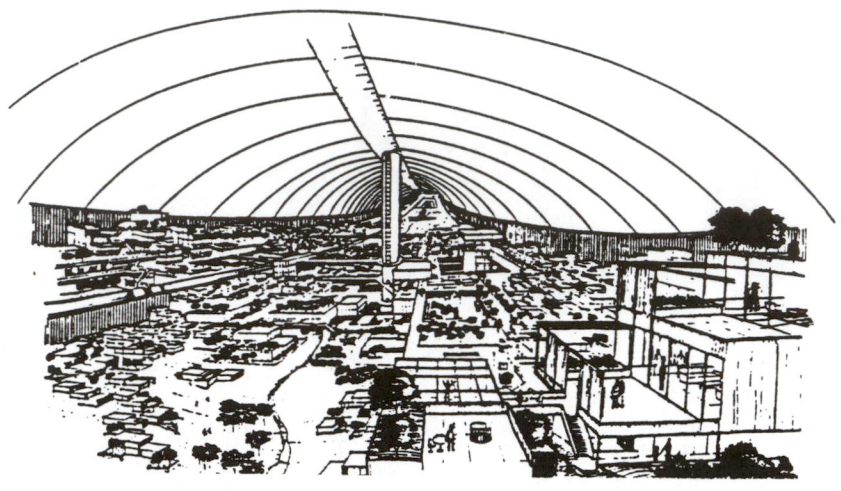

Figure 19.1. NASA Concept of Space Colony

At first it might seem as though they are living laboratories for testing all the design principles that can be used for the entire human race, but it is now known that the people who go to these communities have a special quality and that the challenge of the community itself attracts professional people who are highly motivated to endure extremes.

Therefore, although extreme environments are still places where it is most critical to understand human behavior, it must be recognized that the findings do not always generalize to the world at large or even necessarily to other extreme environments.

As was discovered in the Tektite and the MacDonald and Oden studies (see Chapter 9), the "selection factor" operates to draw highly motivated people to places where there are professional challenges. These kinds of people can be seen as the "hardy" types (see Chapter 11) who respond to a challenge that most people would prefer not to endure.

Deserts

Definition

It seems that there is no agreement as to what constitutes a desert (Landsberg, 1978; McGinnies, Goldman, & Paylore, 1965). Some restrict the definition to areas where there are 2 inches of rainfall per annum while others would include up to 15 inches of rainfall per year. And, although it is recognized that variables other than rainfall must be included in the definition, there is no common agreement as to what these variables might be.

Golany (1978) points out that the climates of desert areas are determined by four variables: latitude, which determines amount of solar radiation; distance from the sea; elevation; and topography. There exists a literature on studies of deserts or arid lands (Givoni, 1969; Golany, 1978) and the subject area exists as a discipline despite the lack of a universally agreed upon definition.

One common problem worldwide is the tendency toward *desertification*, that is, the tendency of many formerly productive lands to turn into deserts (Spooner & Mann, 1982). The general conclusion is that desertification is caused by political and social problems at the local and regional levels.

A second problem derives from irrigation of desert areas in an attempt to make them productive. Although this seems a wise thing to do at first, the eventual result could be that the very land to be saved will be destroyed by *salinization*, which is the result of salt deposits left on the land surface after water has evaporated (Solomon, 1985). Large areas of California have been abandoned because of selenium salts. When I was in the Turkmenistan Republic, I saw the Kara Kum Canal, which carried water from the Caspian Sea to Ashkhabad, the capital. Land on both sides of the canal was white with salt encrustation because the canal was not lined and water seeped into the soil and evaporated, leaving the salts behind. Salinization is a worldwide problem.

Quality of the Environment

Arid lands problems can be juxtaposed against those of cold regions with surprising results: They are not as different as one might first imagine. In fact, the problems are so similar that Australian arid lands specialists invited Canadian specialists to their UNESCO conference in 1973 (Australian National Commission for UNESCO, 1976).

As further evidence for the perceived similarity, Bechtel administered a list of adjectives to U.S. residents of Saudi Arabia and found the ranking of adjectives correlated to the rankings from the study of a Canadian community by a rho of +.825 (Bechtel, Ittelson, & Wheeler, 1978).

Several anecdotes will suffice to convey the flavor of desert life. The most common experiences have to do with attempting to transfer Western temperate-climate architecture and building techniques to the desert area. A common example is Venetian blinds. These metal objects, which were invented to keep out sun, serve to collect heat from the sun and act as radiators, making the air conditioner work harder.

Few designs take into consideration how the air blast of the air conditioner will have an impact in relation to the furniture arrangements. One third of the subjects questioned in one study (Bechtel, 1975) complained of sinus headaches due to the impact of air-conditioning drafts. In one case, the bedrooms of a series of residences were so small that the sleeper could not escape the full blast of the air conditioner. The only choice was to have a supercooled head or to turn the bed around and have supercooled feet.

Rugs undergo unusual wear because of the abrasive character of the truly ever-present dust and sand. I remember being amused at how outside light globes would fill up with sand. The sand is so abrasive that paint finishes on houses and automobiles will show wear spots within a 3-year period, depending on one's location.

Pouring concrete can be a futile exercise in the hot desert sun but it is possible if one has a large supply of ice chips to mix in with the concrete. Caulking that is perfectly satisfactory in the U.S. Midwest cracks and crumbles in the desert air. Asphalt shingles melt, tar paper cracks, and ordinary paints, drapes, and carpets fade quickly if exposed to the desert sun.

Yet not all of the problems are from dryness. On the coasts of many deserts (remember, closeness to the sea is a critical variable, according to Golany), one can get the extremes of dryness and humidity only days apart. I remember sitting in the air-conditioned dining room of the Al Gosaibi Hotel in Al Khobar, Saudi Arabia, and watching the moisture from outside air collect in streams of water and run down the panes almost as if it were raining.

The traditional garb Arabs developed helps them deal with the intense sun of their desert. The whole body is covered with a white, loose-fitting garment called a *thobe*. The advantage of this garment is that it protects from the rays of the sun and allows proper cooling from perspiration because of its looseness. The head is protected by a *gutra*, which is held in place by a doubled band called an *agaal*. Western Arabs have a white gutra while eastern Arabs have a checked pattern. I was disappointed to see that the gutra I bought was made in Japan.

Older Arab houses, before air-conditioning, had an underground room where the residents would go in late morning and remain until sunset. With the advent of central air, this custom has been quickly vanishing.

Desert areas, then, present many challenges to the design and construction professionals as well as the environmental psychologists who try to work there. Not the least of these problems is a desire on the part of government officials in many Middle Eastern, African, and South American arid lands to adopt U.S. and western European methods and styles to their own countries without first considering whether these elements are suitable, or even harmful, to their own residents. For example, the "latest" in hospital design was demanded for a large medical hospital in Saudi Arabia without consideration of the need for separate male and female entrances and waiting rooms, which their culture dictates. There are many horror stories of attempts to bring Western capital-intensive building technology to Third World countries.

Shay Gap: A Planned Desert Community

In an unpublished survey of arid lands studies done in 1976, 379 studies were surveyed of which only 76 were concerned with some physical aspect of the geography such as erosion or the water table. This shows a dearth of material when compared with the studies done on cold regions.

Shay Gap, Western Australia,[1] is a prime example of a community designed specifically for one of the hottest deserts in the world. In many ways, it exemplifies an attempt to provide the best that is known in design and technology to suit the demands of a harsh environment and provide a comfortable human existence.

Lawrence Howroyd, the architect, studied Middle Eastern desert communities for clues about how towns could be designed to adapt to the heat and wind extremes of the desert. He found that the concept of the medieval wall was both a physical and a psychological barrier, keeping the desert outside the community. For these reasons, Shay Gap was placed in a location sheltered by hills on three sides.

Houses placed close to each other multiply the shade available. Streets between these houses also become more tolerable for walking when shaded. The conclusion was to place houses close enough together to

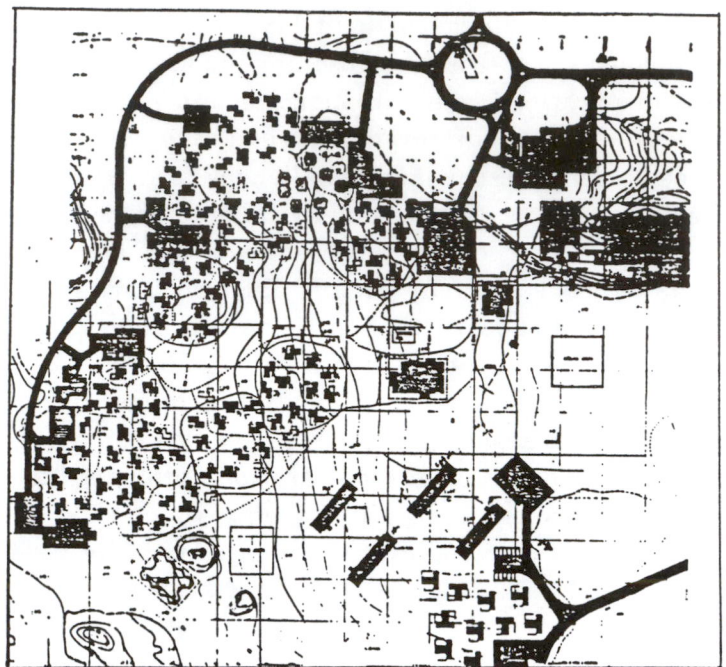

Figure 19.2. Plan of Shay Gap
SOURCE: Bechtel, Ledbetter, and Cummings (1980).

provide some overlapping shade. Further, Howroyd was impressed by the fostering of social contacts that the Middle Eastern communities provided so he banned automobiles from the living areas and made all amenities within walking distance. Figure 19.2 shows the site plan for Shay Gap. Note the clustering of homes and the closeness of facilities to housing.

(1) Methods. The study of Shay Gap is an example of postoccupancy evaluation (POE) done by directly testing the design hypotheses of the architect. After talking with the architect Lawrence Howroyd, in his office in Perth, Western Australia, the researchers were able to discern 55 distinct hypotheses. These were then tested by use of the behavior setting survey and by a questionnaire (see Bechtel, Ledbetter, & Cummings, 1980, App. B).

From the 173 families and 357 single people living in Shay Gap at the time of the study, 73 subjects were selected at random. These people were administered the questionnaire, which combined design questions and the behavior setting survey.

(2) Results. The main innovations of Shay Gap proved to be successful. The prohibition of cars resulted in a consensus that it was a safe environment for children; 42% felt it was the safest of any place they had lived in recently. Asked to rate the surrounding hills, residents reacted favorably. Out of ratings 1 through 5, with 5 most favorable, the mean was 4.15; that is, 63% favored the hills (combining ratings of 4 and 5).

The closeness of houses (average 12 feet) was not seen as a problem (Figure 19.2). Part of this may be due to the fact that windows could not be opened because of the central air-conditioning.

The shopping center was a success as the behavioral focal point of the community and the social club was the place for most recreation.

The deliberately bland off-white interiors were designed by Howroyd to provide for the maximum individual expression of residents. He realized the mining families accumulated possessions that they would bring with them and would need an interior environment that would not clash with a wide range of colors and objects. The success of the off-white interior was confirmed in other studies in Iran, Israel, the United States, and Saudi Arabia (Bechtel, 1975, 1976).

In general, then, Shay Gap seems to be a place successfully designed to meet the needs of a remote desert mining community. It stands as an example of planning and design for this extreme environment.

Cold Regions

Definition

What are cold regions? In terms of the globe, the Arctic is defined as all areas lying above the Arctic Circle (lat. 66°33′ N). Most of this is actually the permanently frozen Arctic Ocean. The significance of the Arctic Circle is that above it the sun does not appear over the horizon in midwinter. There are very few communities above the Arctic Circle; Tromso and Hammerfest in Norway, Kiruna in Sweden, Nanisivik and Fort McPherson in Canada, and some places in Siberia such as Ust-Chann, Ambarchik, Srednekolymsk, Chokurdakh, and Verkhoyansk. Alaska's few communities include Point Barrow; the oil communities of Prudhoe Bay; and Wainwright, Point Hope, and Kotzebue, the latter three being Inuit communities. (See Figure 19.3, left side.)

Climatologically, an arbitrary temperature is used to define *polar climate* as one where the mean temperature of the warmest month does

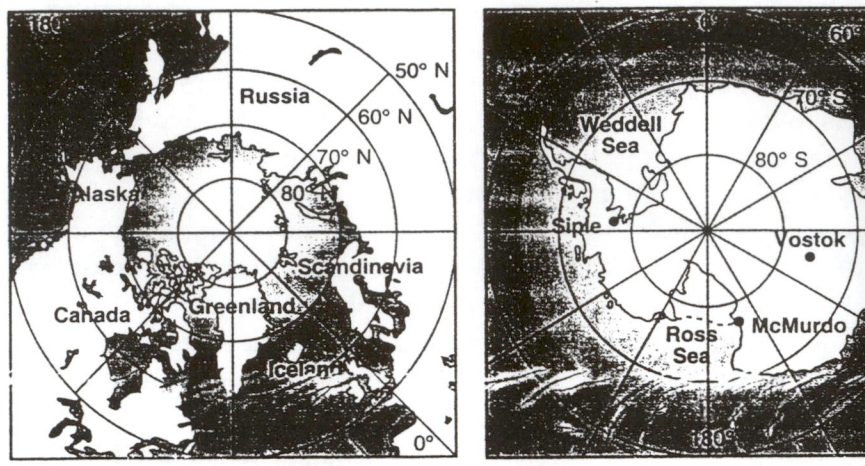

Figure 19.3. The Arctic and Antarctic
SOURCE: Reprinted with permission. Copyright by the American Association for the Advancement of Science.
NOTE: A different world: For polar researchers, this is how to look at the earth.

not exceed 50°F (10°C). This more or less follows the northern limit of trees.[2] But for our purposes, we go much further south and include areas of northern Montana, North Dakota, Minnesota, Wisconsin, northern New England, and all of Canada.

These are places where most of the anecdotal experiences noted below are known, and they constitute an area where cold regions design is a significant element. Correspondingly, this takes in large parts of Norway, Sweden, and Finland, most of Russia, and, of course, all of Greenland and Alaska.

Quality of the Environment

The Cold Regions Habitability Project, begun by Burgess Ledbetter for the Cold Regions Research and Engineering Laboratory in 1972, and lasting through 1978, provided opportunities to study humans living in the extreme climate of Alaska. Other projects such as the Canadian Polar Psychology Project (Suedfeld, Bernaldez, & Stossel, 1989) improved and internationalized polar studies.

Much has been written about the legendary cold of Alaska but until one has experienced the wind and dryness of the cold, there is little appreciation of what a truly severe climate it is. A few descriptive anecdotes will suffice.

On one of our trips to Murphy Dome, a study site near Fairbanks, we started out in an army vehicle that simply refused to operate in the −60° weather. We were forced to walk back to our starting point, which was only three blocks. I can remember feeling my nostril hairs freeze to needles as I inhaled.

I wish I had remembered to spit at that time because native Alaskans told me that one of the ways to tell if it is 50° below is to open the door and spit out. If the spit freezes before it hits the ground, it is at least 50 below.

Hoods are required with parkas and are lined with wolf hide (as are army parkas) because wolf hair is the only substance that will not frost up from breathing. Most of us were wearing "bunny" boots issued by the army. These are specially made boots filled with air as insulation and they must be deflated for air travel. Those without this protection complained of pain in their feet from the cold.

Houses suffer greatly in the north. During winter, the extreme dryness of the out-of-doors creates a hydrostatic pressure that will peel paint off logs just from the force of moisture passing through. A pin hole in the vapor barrier of the insulation (9 inches thick recommended) will cause a grapefruit-sized peeled area in outside paint in just one winter. This is true of any porous material such as wood, cement block, or brick.

Frost boils and condensed icicles can build up to such an extent that when spring comes, there will literally be a flood that stains and weakens walls, carpets, and any fixtures on the walls.

The water pump (or the steam pump) in the heating system is a critical element and, if it goes out, plumbers estimate about 45 minutes before the house or apartment freezes up, pipes burst, and the place becomes uninhabitable.

Automobiles must be winterized to survive in the north. Extra thin motor oil is used as well as special hydraulic fluids for the transmission and brake systems. The car must be fitted with an electric blanket around the battery and an electric dip stick in the motor. Unless the car is plugged in or the motor is running, it will freeze and have to be left for spring. Finding a vacant head bolt to plug into is more vital than finding a place to park.

Frostbite is an ever-present danger. The military coined a phrase for troops to memorize: 30-30-30. It stands for the fact that human flesh freezes in 30 seconds in a 30-mile-an-hour wind at 30° below zero. But wind chill factors of −100 occur. Any movement increases the risk. A forgetful person will run across a street in shirt sleeves and freeze his earlobes. A pilot opens up the window of the helicopter and looks out at the rotor blade and freezes his cheeks. The heater on the truck fails and the driver freezes the skin on his thighs under his clothes because that is where the draft was.

Ice fog is condensed human (and animal) breath. In some places, it is called habitation fog. It becomes so dense that reflectors must be placed at regular intervals along every road so that a person does not lose the road in the fog.

It has only recently been recognized that the lack of sunlight produces a particular kind of depression known as seasonal affective disorder, or SAD, which is alleviated by exposure to intense light (Bower, 1989, 1990). It has been known for some time that light acts as a "clock-setting" stimulus to human circadian rhythms. Czeisler et al. (1986) show how a woman's 24-hour rhythm was shifted by 6 hours after exposure to 4 hours of bright light for seven evenings. But an estimated 4% of the people in *middle* latitudes also suffer from SAD (Rosenthal & Wehr, 1987). Symptoms are a drop in mood, lack of energy, oversleeping, overeating, and carbohydrate craving. There is also a summer SAD, which peaks in July and August. Both are treated with exposure to bright lights in the evenings between 8 to 11 p.m. Estimates are that one in twenty Alaskans suffer some form of this malady.

These anecdotes serve to alert one to the fact that an Alaskan winter is, indeed, an extreme environment. What is not so obvious is that the summer is considered by many to be extreme also. Many have difficulty with the long hours of daylight. Blackout shades are considered a standard method for trying to maintain standard sleeping hours. Most people admit to sleeping less in summer and more in winter. In my research in Alaska, I encountered a person who hadn't slept in 10 days one summer.

(1) Methods. The method used for the cold regions project was the behavior setting survey developed by Roger Barker (1968) (see Chapter 10). This technique was adapted and validated for use in evaluating the behavior needs of cold regions residents. The data were then used to develop better criteria for designing cold regions building and communities (Ledbetter, 1978).

Before deciding which communities to study, it was felt necessary to classify the government communities of Alaska to determine whether they were all of one stripe or of many different kinds. Because these designs were for the government, civilian communities were not included. Had they been, the results would have been very different.

(2) First phase. Few environmental studies had been done on a region the size of Alaska. Therefore, it is worth considering the steps and methods in some detail. First, how does one go about studying such a large area? The purpose of the study is contained in the questions that needed answering from the point of view of the Cold Regions Habitability Project. The central aim was to arrive at knowledge that would enable architects and engineers to build better environments. The most central question to ask in attacking such a problem is whether Alaska is one single monolithic environment or a series of smaller environments. We know intuitively that it cannot be monolithic. Conditions vary so greatly in different parts that the next question becomes the focus of inquiry: What variables define the environments that make up Alaska?

There are two choices to make at this point. One can search for all the variables anyone has ever used to classify environments and come up with an exhaustive list. One can also be realistic and search for the data that are already available on Alaska and thus save the prohibitively costly venture of going there and collecting the information on-site. We did a little of both. Literature on Alaska emphasized variables of climate, geography, physical plant, and sociopsychological aspects. Climate was obvious and measures of temperature, wind velocity, amount of snow, and days of overcast were available from the federal government on a daily basis.

Geography includes climate, of course, but it was also used to include latitude and longitude, probability of earthquake based on past data, presence or absence of trees, and age of underlying rocks.

Physical plant refers to the age of buildings, type and number of buildings, cost per square foot to maintain, square feet of work space available (per person), square feet of housing available, and square feet of recreational space available.

Sociopsychological variables were the largest group of variables including the population of workers, presence or absence of wives and/or children, distance to nearest large town, rank of service, and percentage of housing units occupied. In all, 41 variables were used (see Bechtel, 1973, table 1).

Because this was a study of government installations, no civilian communities were included. This meant that Alaska's two largest cities,

Anchorage and Fairbanks, would only be represented by respective military installations near them. More important, the government installations were populated by a temporary population, that is, professionals sent for a specific tour of duty and not native Alaskans. This had a defining influence on the results (remember the "selection" effect).

We selected 61 sites for study. These included three army bases, 17 air force sites, and 40 independent Federal Aviation Administration (FAA) sites with 6 FAA sites overlapping air force sites.

These data produce a 41 × 61 matrix. How can one possibly analyze such an unwieldy amount of information? Fortunately, computers allow the handling of such data with ease. The BCTRY system (Tryon & Bailey, 1970) allowed us to find out (a) what variables are important in defining the environments we have chosen and (b) how the environments can be classified by these variables.

(3) Results. The analysis of variables showed latitude as the primary determiner of environments in Alaska. Mean annual temperature, daylight hours on shortest day, permafrost,[3] moisture, probability of earthquake, age of underlying rocks, amount of overcast, and altitude were all highly related to latitude. Correlations range from −.836 to −.920 for most, only .765 for permafrost.

Other important definers, in decreasing order of importance, were number of recreation buildings, dependents living on base, cost of housing construction, wind, and distance to Anchorage. These variables became the points of measures that were used to classify the environments themselves.

The computer threw out annual snowfall, age of buildings, and distance to nearest town. Snowfall? Irrelevant in Alaska? Yes! Because snowfall varies so greatly that it relates to no other variable. Extremes are 317 inches at Yakutat to only 20 inches at Barrow with many variations in between. Thus amount of snowfall, an extremely important variable in construction of roofs and general quality of the environment, cannot be used in defining the environments of a large region because it varies too much locally. This is an important concept to understand in trying to study any large unit. It is much like saying we cannot deal with differences among individuals when we study groups. Yet, these differences may be important (see Bechtel, 1989).

By contrast, age of buildings also could not be used because it varied very little. A majority of the buildings were built in the 1950s. This is like saying we can't use a variable because it does not vary enough. Thus only descriptors that vary (but not too much) get used.

The 61 environments were rescored by the computer on the six clusters of variables mentioned above (latitude, number of recreational buildings, and so on) and classified according to how well their score profiles on those six areas matched. Eleven types of environments resulted (see Table 19.1).

First, an important fact was observed in the classification. The large bases grouped together in their own type (Fort Richardson, army; Fort Wainwright, army; and Elmendorf, air force), and the next-to-large grouped into their type (Fort Greely, army; Eilson, air force). *But all other types did not mix the kind of service.* Thus we have six FFA types and six AF types. In other words, once the larger bases are selected out, the main classifications are by type of service. Within each type of service, the external variables of geography then determine most of the classifications. These are central FAA, Middle FFA I & II, low latitude FAA, South Coast FFA, and one type low on dependents. Air force bases are Western Southwest and those low on dependents. Low on dependents was a tertiary variable for classification.

What have we learned from this classification? It told us that of the 41 variables we used, latitude was the most powerful in determining major aspects of the environment. A surprise, even earthquakes were related to latitude. However, when it came down to classifying each environment, size of the population of the site, type of administration, and absence of dependents were the important descriptors. These are also the main variables determining quality of life at the sites.

The classification also helped to determine a lower number of sites to study because we can now randomly sample within each type to test a representative sample. Unfortunately, only seven sites were finally studied because of the convenience of overlapping of air force and FAA sites. For example, Murphy Dome is a site that has an FAA and an Air Force Station together. It was cheaper to study these than to select a remote site in the Aleutians. Weather also made a study in the Aleutians problematic.

(4) Second phase. Data from seven sites were collected using a questionnaire to perform an abbreviated behavior setting survey (Bechtel & Ledbetter, 1976). The data show that several issues need to be considered in design for cold regions.

Table 19.1 Eleven Types of Environments in Alaska

Type 1	Western AC&W Sites		Type 6	Middle FAA (Type II)
7	Cape Lisburne (AF)		22	Aniak (FAA)
9	Cape Romanzof (AF)		31	Cold Bay (FAA)
14	Kotzebue (AF)		33	Dillingham (FAA)
18	Tin City (AF)		41	Homer (FAA)
			42	Iliamna (FAA)
			44	King Salmon (FAA)
Type 2	Central FAA		49	Middleton Island (FAA)
21	Anchorage (FAA)			
47	Lake Hood Seaplane Towers (FAA)			
50	Murphy Dome (FAA)		Type 7	Large Bases
51	Nenana (FAA)		1	Fort Richardson (Army)
			2	Fort Wainwright (Army)
			3	Elmendorf AFB (AF)
Type 3	AC&W Low on Dependents on Base			
6	Campion (AF)			
11	Fort Yukon (AF)		Type 8	Next-to-Large Bases
12	Indian Mountain (AF)		3	Fort Greely (Army)
15	Murphy Dome (AF)		5	Eielson AFB (AF)
16	Sparrevohn (AF)			
17	Tatalina (AF)			
19	Galena (AF)		Type 9	Low Latitude FAA
			23	Annette (FAA)
			34	Duncan Canal (FAA)
Type 4	Middle FAA With Dependents		40	Gustavus (FAA)
27	Big Delta (FAA)		46	Level Island (FAA)
28	Big Lake (FAA)		54	Sisters Island (FAA)
35	Farewell (FAA)			
36	Fire Island (FAA)			
39	Gulkana (FAA)		Type 10	South Coast FAA
48	McGrath (FAA)		29	Biorka Island (FAA)
56	Skwentna (FAA)		30	Yakataga (FAA)
57	Summit (FAA)		32	Cordova (FAA)
58	Talkeetna (FAA)		43	Johnston Point (FAA)
			55	Sitka (FAA)
			61	Yakutat (FAA)
Type 5	Middle FAA (Type I)			
25	Bethel (FAA)			
26	Bettles (FAA)		Type 11	AC&W Southwest
37	Fort Yukon (FAA)		8	Cape Newenham (AF)
38	Galena (FAA)		10	Cold Bay (AF)
45	Kotzebue (FAA)		13	King Salmon (AF)
52	Nome (FAA)		20	Shemya (AF)
53	Northway (FAA)			
60	Unalakleet (FAA)			

SOURCE: Bechtel (1973).
NOTE: Site left out of classification: Barrow.

Site selection and design. One of the critical variables of site design is the separation (or mixing) of single men with families. Inevitably, the married men become suspicious of the single men, and the slightest provocation, such as a single man walking through the family area, can start rumors flowing. This conflict between marrieds and singles is further complicated by the fact that single quarters are universally disproportionately smaller than married quarters. Single workers feel they have no room to entertain and, consequently, feel dependent on invitations from families.

This single versus married conflict is a universal phenomenon found not only in military sites but also in mining, construction, oil, and research communities throughout the world (Goering & Bechtel, 1979). One way to deal with it is to design a site so that the families and singles do not have to go through each other's territories to get to the amenities such as shopping centers, churches, work, and school. Figure 19.4 shows an ideal site scheme for such a plan.

Another and preferable way to deal with it is to completely integrate the singles within the community. Nanisivik (Bechtel & Ledbetter, 1980) is an example of successful integration even though not all singles are integrated. Single apartments with two to four men are side by side with married couples and families. One of the variables that helps make this mixture successful is small size. Nanisivik had less than 300 workers. Another variable is work. All women had jobs at Nanisivik as well as working 9 or more hours a day for 6 days. Thus there were fewer opportunities for singles and marrieds to come in contact outside the work situation.

Site design is heavily influenced by whether the policy is to separate or mix the singles with the rest of the community. The larger the site and the more leisure time available, the more difficult it is to bring about a successful mix.

Howroyd (Bechtel et al., 1980) raised the issue of whether desert sites should be protected from the elements. Zrudlo (1972) points out this is especially necessary for Arctic and Antarctic sites because of the severe wind chill factor and drifting snow. Further, one should plan to take maximum advantage of what little sun is available. Knowles (1977) has worked out the most advantageous site plan to take advantage of sunlight for a location near Anchorage. Knowles's techniques can be applied to any location (Knowles, 1974).

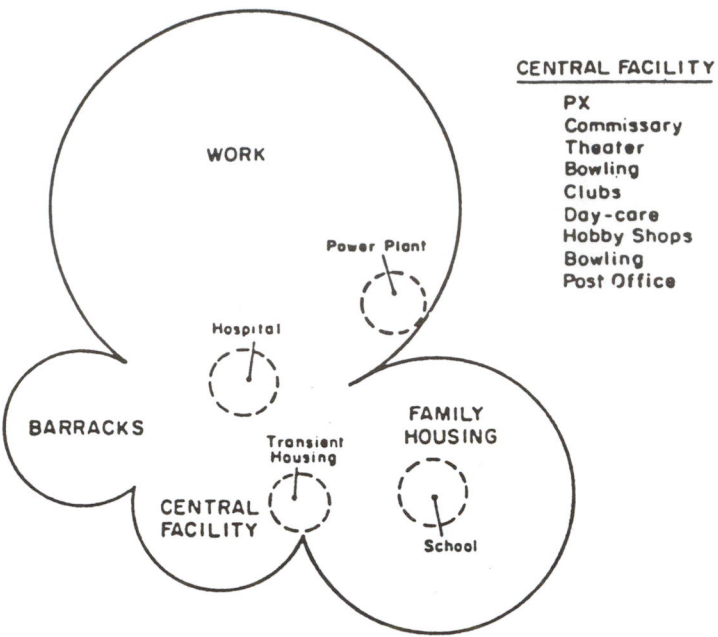

Figure 19.4. Ideal Site Plan for Separation of Singles and Marrieds

Housing Design

The military as well as many governmental agencies and even international developers still tend to assume that the same basic house style can be built with minimum modification in any climate. This assumption is a major source of difficulty in the north. Windows at all sites studied were failing. They would develop a "leak" that allowed cold air to come in and moisture to condense until the sill and pane were frozen over. By no means do all windows fail in this way, but enough do to be troublesome.

Many residents simply cover the windows with Reynolds wrap or some other material during the entire winter. Triple-paned windows have been developed and have since become the norm for new construction.

Other problems are encountered in back doors that freeze open because of condensation when they are opened frequently. This problem is dealt with by building an Arctic entrance for both back and front doors. Bathroom fans can actually bring the house down to freezing temperatures if left on for long and used at the speeds customary in more temperate climates.

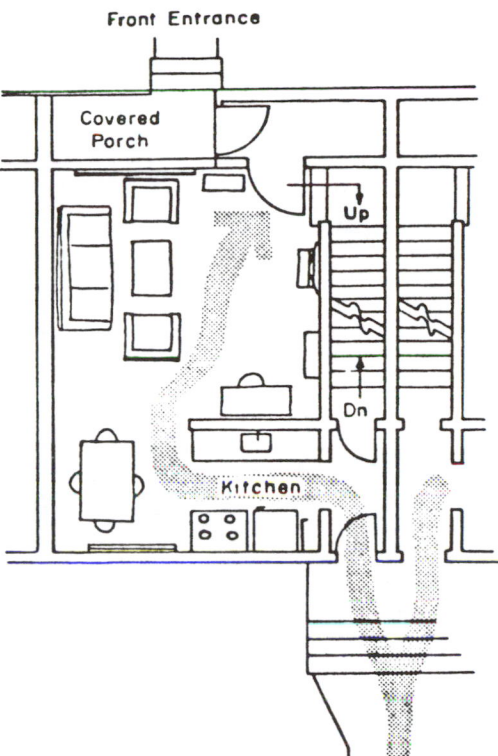

Figure 19.5. Typical Military House Plan
NOTE: Fort Wainwright family housing traffic pattern through living room.

The most central issue of house design, however, is not the technical issues of windows, doors, fans, and other details, troublesome though these are. The most important factor is a design that allows the adults and children to live in the house without constant interference. Figure 19.5 shows a typical house plan at Fort Wainwright near Fairbanks (it is also typical of many military houses in Georgia, Texas, and California).

This particular style creates problems because the children must interrupt adults every time they go to the bathroom. The only bathroom is upstairs. If someone is in the kitchen or watching TV in the living room, the children must pass either in front of them or very close to them. And those who have children know that it is almost never a mere passing by.

These contacts are not necessarily the cause of the much touted "cabin fever" of the housewife but they add to and exacerbate the feeling of never

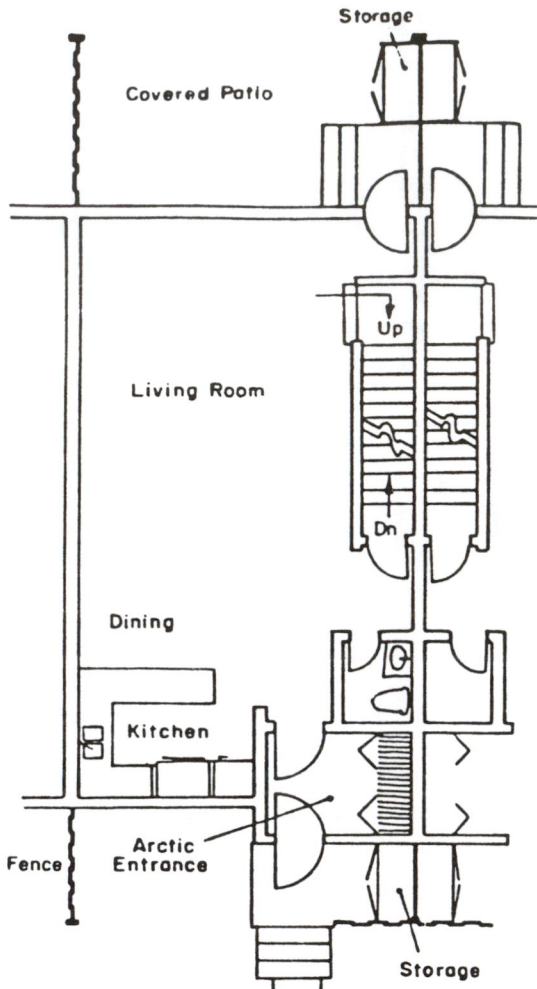

Figure 19.6. House Plan Solving the Children Traffic Pattern

having time to oneself and never being alone. A solution to this problem is a second bathroom on the first floor as in Figure 19.6.

The "housewife" syndrome is the bane of the north. Psychiatrists and ministers are constantly sought out by housewives who seemingly spend the entire winter indoors. One can easily understand why there are so many pressures to do so. Getting children and oneself dressed for the cold can take up to 45 minutes (as timed by observers). By the time the housewife goes through this ordeal, she becomes convinced it is not worth the effort. Our data (Bechtel & Ledbetter, 1976) indicate that women without jobs spend on an average 20 hours and 30 minutes out of 24 hours a day in the house compared with their husbands, who spend only 14 hours and 45 minutes in the house. In fact, most of the time out of the house occurs in summer. Some housewives claim they never leave the house from October until May.

Cabin fever can take a severe form. One example was a man who shot his wife during our stay. Such behavior is not limited to the government stations. Foulks (1972) describes the Arctic hysterias that occur among the native populations.

This intense exposure to the indoors produces a heightened sensitivity to noise and other interference with tasks. The best solution is a room where one can go (or send the children) to be alone. Refinishing cellars into recreation rooms is one solution. Using daybeds in the bedrooms facilitates their use by children during the day.

Nature of the Population

One aspect of the Cold Regions Habitability Project that differs from the Tektite studies was that residents were not all highly motivated volunteers. Although some military and nearly all FAA personnel sought out Alaska, most of the military simply drew it as one of their assignments.

Furthermore, even if the males were enthusiastic, their wives more often were not. Therefore, the cold regions study approached the test of how a "normal" population would react to design more than the Tektite studies did. Nevertheless, another element crept in to mar the generalizations. This was the temporary nature of the time spent in Alaska. Few people retire in Alaska. In 1990, Alaska had the lowest percentage of elderly (4%) of any state in the union. Most, even in civilian settlements, see it as a place to visit, and make a living for a time, but not to stay permanently. Of course, this makes the native Alaskans irate and they resent the carpetbag nature of so many inhabitants they call *chacheekos*.

That many people living in the environments we studied did not take the environment seriously was a complicating factor. Despite Arctic training, frostbite occurrences were high. Many did not try to integrate with the surrounding communities, which meant more time was on their hands with little to do. The FFA communities, where terms in Alaska averaged 8 years, were a contrast, and some residents would even run for political office in the surrounding communities.

The chief result of this temporary nature of the involvement was that 78% of the available time in homes was spent in recreational activities in, for example, the Fort Wainwright housing. This contrasted to only 24% in FAA homes, a difference of more than three times! The result is pressure on the house to perform as a recreational vehicle, for which it was not designed. Residents complained they did not have room for their activities or space to store the equipment they brought with them or purchased.

The pressure to make the house more recreational seemed to foreshadow new housing designed for the rich (Demarest, 1981) and may indicate a major trend in housing design, provided the financing for amenable housing becomes available again.

Juxtaposition of Desert and Cold Regions Findings

Comparisons between cold and hot regions design requirements are as follows.

1. Both require the equivalent of an Arctic entrance, a vestibule with a second door so that temperature and condensation problems are lessened by closing the outer door before the inside one is opened. In hot regions, a grid or sand trap should be provided while in cold regions the grid is for stamping off the snow. Cold regions require a mud scraper.

2. Both require heavy insulation. Nine inches of batting with a vapor barrier *inside* is becoming a standard for both kinds of environments. The insulation and vapor barrier combination provides help in keeping moisture inside the house. Actually, dryness is more of a problem in cold regions and humidifiers are more frequently seen there.

3. Both require thermal pane windows. Double panes are a minimum and triple panes are now being used. Materials are important. Wood cracks in both places but aluminum conducts heat and cold. A partial solution is to have windows that cannot be opened. This was successful at Shay Gap and at Cape Lisburne in Alaska.

Figure 19.7. Partially Earth-Sheltered House Saving on Energy Costs and Ideal for Cold Regions

4. Both climates tend to keep people indoors in severe weather. This makes interior design more critical, and the houses have to serve as primary recreational enclosures in addition to the minimal functions for which they are usually designed. The more remote the community, the more this requirement gains in priority.

5. Future solutions to both kinds of severe climates are partially sought in underground housing. Actually, this is actually part underground housing arranged so windows on one side get maximum sun penetration (University of Minnesota, 1979; see also the issues of *Underground Space*, a journal published by Pergamon Press). The advantage of earth-sheltered housing is that it provides a tremendous energy savings (up to 60%) and is less subject to wear from the elements. Figure 19.7 illustrates an earth-sheltered house seen as acceptable to respondents given a questionnaire (Bechtel, 1978b).

6. Both types of environments prohibit leaving children unattended in cars for obvious reasons. Military police in cold regions check cars in supermarket parking lots for children left alone. In deserts, the temperature of parked cars can reach over 160°F.

This also applies to leaving pets in cars. Hot regions are probably worse in this regard because of rapid dehydration.

7. Both deserts and cold regions need to conserve water. Many areas in the north that are snow covered are actually deserts. This is especially true of Antarctica (see below). The following expression is one used in remote regions to conserve water by minimizing the number of times the toilet is flushed: "If it's brown, wash it down; if it's yellow, let it mellow." It applies equally to hot and cold regions.

Antarctica

Environment and behavior research in Antarctica only has a very recent history. Antarctica represents 10% of the Earth's land mass (see Figure 19.3, right side) but holds 70% of its fresh water in the form of ice. No one lives in Antarctica except as part of some governmental research operation. Despite all of this ice, the interior of Antarctica is actually a desert. A feature that makes Antarctica so different than the Arctic is its high altitude. The nations who use Antarctica have signed a treaty to use it for scientific purposes only. The International Geophysical Year in 1957 marked the beginning of permanent habitation in Antarctica and since that time several countries have kept stations occupied the year round.

Research in Antarctica has taken on a new character as a "surrogate" for space communities (Harrison, Clearwater, & McKay, 1991). Unfortunately, little E&B work went into the designing of most of the present structures (see the box), but the Australian bases at Mawson, Davis, and Casey (Incoll, 1990) were designed according to E&B research and theory and seem to have been successful (Nelson, 1992).

High Altitudes

World War II aircraft required oxygen use at 10,000 feet. Some peoples of the world live at this altitude or higher. Figure 19.8 shows a man carrying kindling on his back at high altitudes in the Andes of Peru. The burden weighs over 100 pounds and the man will run for 20 miles (yes, I said *run*). Native peoples at this altitude adapt over many generations and have smaller stature and more red blood cells as well as a higher concentration of hemoglobin, a condition known as *polycythemia.*

Box 19.1

A Design for Life in the Freezer

For an architect, drawing up a blueprint for a new station at the South Pole is about as tough a challenge as terrestrial design gets. Eight inches of snow accumulate every year and never melts. A steady wind creates drifts that can bury low-lying buildings in months. Temperatures routinely hit minus 100 degrees Fahrenheit. The "ground" itself—really a glacier almost 2 miles deep—slides an average of 33 feet toward the sea each year, and adjacent spots can move at different speeds, ripping apart structures. And then there's the task of designing facilities that will help the station's two dozen or so winter inhabitants endure near-total isolation from the outside world during 6 sunless months.

Given these challenges, it's no wonder the National Science Foundation (NSF) has spent 4 years chewing over more than a dozen different configurations to replace the current station, built in 1975. Proposals, fluctuating between the aesthetic and the practical, have ranged from half-buried mounds to a globe on stilts. But the first solid design is finally emerging from the cloud of half-formed ideas.

This week, NSF is expected to propose a structure consisting of three horizontal U-shaped modules on stilts, connected by flexible enclosed walkways. Each of the elevated modules will have two floors; some will contain sleeping and personal space, others will have lab areas, recreational rooms, a cafeteria, and conference rooms. At 120,000 square feet, the new station will be some 33,000 square feet larger than the existing dome and underground arches that comprise the current station. It will be able to house 150 people in summer—25 more than the current overcrowded accommodations—and 50 in winter, compared with the current overcapacity of 29. But the biggest difference is in the way each person will be housed: Individual rooms and workspaces, windows, and a mix of common and team space will allow for efficient working conditions even during the depths of winter.

The design is dominated by the need to prevent the relentless drifts from burying the station. Today, bulldozer crews spend nearly the entire summer digging the current dome out from its winter accumulation; to avoid a "bowl" effect, they now have to push the snow nearly a mile away. The new station will be almost maintenance free, with each module perched on legs above the ice. The raised modules will have their leading edges sloped to deflect a nearly constant 10- to 15-mph wind and accelerate it underneath the structure, thereby reducing the accumulation of snow. Because some drifting is inevitable, the modules are designed to be raised when the "ground" gets too close. Likewise, because the ice sheet on which the new station will be built is moving, the walkways that connect the modules are flexible.

(continued)

Box 19.1 Continued

Inside the station, quarters will seem luxurious compared to the existing berths, whose welders' curtains often provide the only privacy and metal lockers the only personal storage. The station will also have a gym, a room with a ceiling high enough for volleyball (a game played with a beanbag instead of a ball), and a sound-proofed practice room for the pick-up rock bands that have become a South Pole tradition. NSF's polar operations manager, Erick Chiang, hopes the new station will feel "like a reasonably good motel," with at least one special feature: a 3000-square-foot area in which treated sewage fertilizes vegetables and perhaps some fruit.

As for working conditions, laboratory space will consist mostly of flexible work stations, open areas, and a machine shop. Power will be provided initially by the same sort of diesel-electric power plants that provide heat and electricity for the current station. But NSF is also planning on some passive solar heating—during the summer months, the pole is the sunniest spot on Earth—as well as exploring photovoltaics and wind turbines for supplemental power. To ease fuel consumption, the new station will be insulated to a value nearly five times that of the average U.S. residence.

Outside, the surrounding ice will be divided into science sectors: "Dark" for astrophysics; "Quiet" for seismology; "Clean air" for atmospheric sampling; and perhaps a balloon launch sector as well. A fifth sector is the actual pole, a significant geopolitical feature as well as a tourist attraction.

Symbolism is important when redesigning South Pole station, says Joseph Ferraro, with the Honolulu firm of Ferraro, Choi & Associates, Ltd., the proposed new station's chief architect. "NSF wants a really impressive shape," he says, as well as a way to clean up the surrounding area, now littered with crates and temporary scientific structures. One option would give the station the look of a wing by connecting the modules with a flexible mesh.

One symbol that is not expected to survive the redesign is the familiar dome. Although the dome will be used to house the estimated 80 workers and their equipment during the 8 years of construction, it will be taken down when the new station is finished. Not only would the dome continue to present a drifting problem, says Chiang, but "we just didn't feel it would be right to turn the symbol into a shed."

—Christopher Anderson

SOURCE: *Science,* Vol. 264, June 24, 1994. Reprinted with permission. Copyright by the American Association for the Advancement of Science.

A disadvantage of this condition is that if one wants to come to lower altitudes, corpuscles may clump together and form clots that can be life threatening if the clots block the blood supply to lungs or the brain. The only visible aspect of polycythemia is the red cheeks of the children.

Figure 19.8. Fuel Gatherer in the Peruvian Altiplano

West (1984) describes the more temporary adjustments that interlopers to high altitudes, such as mountain climbers, must make to endure climbing such extremes as Mt. Everest. Figure 19.9 shows the stages at which measurements were taken up to 29,028 feet, the summit.

Climbers have no time to grow significantly more blood cells but must simply learn to breathe harder by "an enormous increase in ventilation." Actually, they are helped by the fact that the atmosphere above Mt. Everest, because it is near the equator, is significantly more dense.

Hypoxia, or lack of oxygen, can be a life-threatening circumstance and can lead to life-threatening behavior in less severe forms. For example, one traveler in the Andes was nearly killed when her companion began hallucinating due to lack of oxygen and tried to switch off the headlights

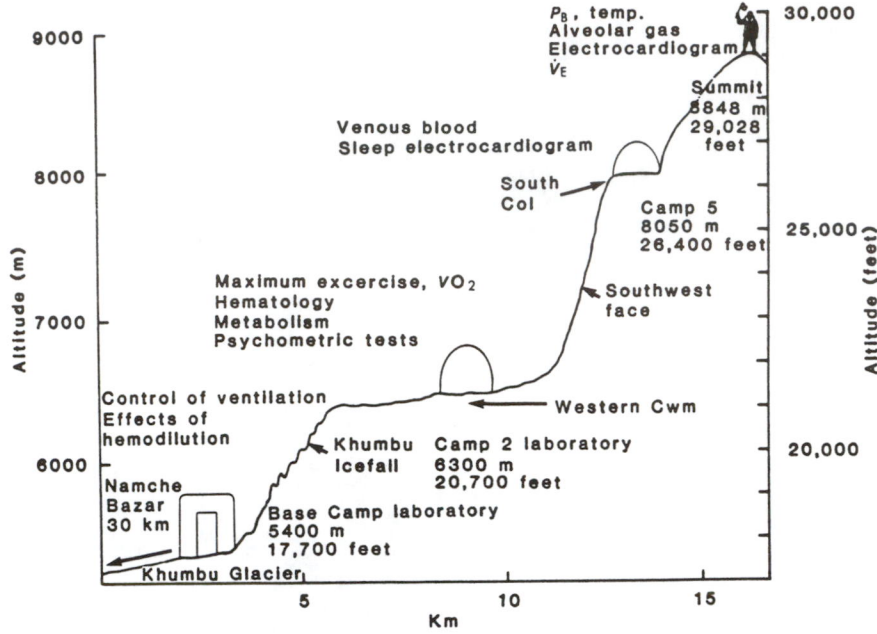

Figure 19.9. Altitudes Where Hypoxia Was Measured on Everest Expedition
SOURCE: West (1984). Reprinted with permission. Copyright by the American Association for the Advancement of Science.

of the car while they were driving down a narrow mountain road. I can remember when one of my companions essentially went blind and walked into a wall; fortunately, there were no injuries. The condition of hypoxia in the Andes is called *soroche* by the natives and they are quite used to the strange behavior of the tourists who succumb to it. A temporary antidote is to have lots of caffeine, but *not* alcoholic beverages, which will make it worse. Some persons may react by swelling of the lung tissues and accumulation of fluid, and this may cause death by suffocation. On the other hand, because mountains also have more positive ions in the air, they almost always cause a feeling of elation, and one must think carefully about whether the feeling is due to hypoxia or the more benign ions.

Life in the Altiplano of Peru is harsh and unforgiving. The average life span is still in the forties.

Adaptation to high altitudes is made through an organ located at the place where the carotid arteries divide called the *carotid body*. This is a very small organ weighing only about 20 mg. in persons living at sea level but enlarged to 60 mg. in persons living at high altitude (Ward, Milledge, & West, 1989). Most people only experience the "normal" effects of altitude but others may suffer from the "malignant" swelling of the lungs (pulmonary edema) and the brain (cerebral edema). Both of the latter are life threatening.

Conclusions

It was once thought that extreme environments would be an ideal testing ground for E&B studies because the extreme outside conditions would force people to remain indoors more than in temperate climates and this would provide a more severe test of design. As these places were studied, however, it became clear that there were two factors affecting results, the selection factor and adaptation.

As was apparent in the crowding and cold regions studies, the kind of person sent to such places was highly motivated and therefore likely to endure extreme conditions to advance on the career ladder. As was also evident, any accompanying wives and children were not equally motivated.

In high altitudes and in the native communities of cold regions, adaptation was the second factor that qualified any data collected. Native people had centuries to adapt to the local conditions and had physiological changes and cultural practices that were not shared by visitors. Thus, although the extreme places are interesting, the findings don't generalize without caution.

Notes

1. Work performed on the study of Shay Gap was under contract No. DACA 89-78-M-2086 with the Cold Regions Research and Engineering Laboratory, Hanover, New Hampshire.

2. Antarctica is a special case because it was uninhabited until 1956 and to this day houses only a handful of scientists. Studies are reported in the more than 20 volumes of the American Geophysical Union (see Gunderson, 1974).

3. *Permafrost* is ground that is permanently frozen the year round. It never thaws in summer. It is hard to predict just where permafrost will be in the marginal areas below the Arctic Circle. It creates problems of construction. In some cases, the foundation of a building must be refrigerated so that its weight does not melt the permafrost and cause the building to sink.

GOALS

Definitions and Concepts

Deserts

Hydrostatic pressure

Cold regions

Permafrost

Vapor barrier

Arctic entrance

Carotid body

Cabin fever

30-30-30

Single versus married conflict

Housewife syndrome

Selection factor

Condensation problems

SAD

Arctic summer

Salinization

Important Studies

Bechtel and Ledbetter (1976)

Bechtel and Ledbetter (1980)

Golany (1978)

Australian National Commission
for UNESCO (1976)

QUESTIONS

1. What are the chief ways in which extreme environments differ from those less extreme?

2. How do desert and tundra dwellings differ? How are they similar?

3. What cautions must be used in drawing conclusions from studies done in extreme environments?

4. What are the hazards of irrigation?

5. What are the differences between an Arctic and a tropical entrance?

6. What are the chief lessons to be learned in designing environments for extreme climates?

7. What community principles have been learned about extreme climates?

8. Why are government employees of extreme climate locations different than the average person?

9. What are the periods of most stress in extreme climates?

10. How does Antarctica differ from the Arctic?

20

Children's Environments

Historical Perspective

Although most cultures profess to love and cherish children, the facts of some historical times and some cultures tell a less positive story. The Chinese, up to recent times, bound the feet of girls in a most cruel fashion. Sometime between the ages of 5 and 7, the girl's feet were bound by cloths that were gradually tightened until the instep broke and the foot doubled up on itself. The ideal was to reach a length that did not exceed *3 inches*. Lindquist (1975) quotes a Chinese woman who described her experience: "The lot of a natural footed woman and mine is like that of heaven and hell" (p. 4).

An ancient Egyptian papyrus says, "The ear of a boy is in his back: He listens when he is beaten." In ancient Greece, if the father thought a child was sickly or he was unable to support it, he was sanctioned by custom to abandon it on a remote hillside to die. More girl babies met this fate than boys. Roman children were thrashed with a cane or leather strap and it was thought that the endurance of pain was a good discipline to learn.

The Ottoman Empire recruited children of Christians (Janissaries) to become the bureaucratic slaves of the government. These children were taken from their families and told to think of their parents as dead. They were disciplined by eunuchs and were not allowed to talk without permission.

At this point, the reader may feel that the view of children's lot presented here is somewhat biased and misleading. Surely, the fate of children in general is not so dismal. Yet, this is the view considered by Alice Miller (1981) in learning about her own childhood. Trained as a psychoanalyst, it was only after throwing over the doctrine of psychoanalysis that she was able to encounter and deal with the painful realities in her childhood. In other words, there is a tendency in all societies to paint a rosy picture of childhood not unlike the "undoing" of negative events from Taylor's (1991) minimization hypothesis. Thus, if there were negative aspects, they tend to be covered over and forgotten. Although this may have some survival value, it also often prevents a realistic look at what children actually encounter.

Not all cultures had such harsh views of raising children and disposing of them. The Shawnees, for example, had a very enlightened view of how to raise children. Eckert (1992) describes the Shawnee methods of child rearing:

> As for the Shawnee punishment of children, such a thing was virtually unknown. Punishments and threats were never used to make them obey. Instead, it was the child's pride that was appealed to in order to have him or her carry out the parents' wishes and it was a method that worked inordinately well. A parent who wanted to have an errand run or a chore taken care of only needed to say, in the presence of his children, what it was he wished and often with the comment added, "I wonder if there is any good child anywhere around who would do this." Normally there would be a scramble among the children as they vied to fulfill the wish of mother or father. Praise from a parent or neighbor was a cherished reward. And there was always community support in supplying such praise. It was not uncommon for anyone witnessing a child performing a task to wonder aloud, "Whose good child is this who does such a thing so nicely?" and, if told who the parent was, to exclaim, "My! Has so-and-so got such a good child as that?" In cases where a child did something bad, it was probably never done again, simply by the parent saying something like, "Oh, how sad I am that my child has done this bad thing. I truly hope he will never do it again." (p. 53)

Is this the memory you have of your childhood? More than likely you were punished and grew up with an orientation to avoid punishment as Piaget (1932) says is typical of our society. But the Shawnee view of child rearing is similar to that of Maria Montessori (1964), who emphasizes that mistakes not be noticed, let alone punished.

Aries (1962) traces the evolution of childhood as it has come to be known in our current time. He feels that past times have featured "privileged" ages. Youth, or young adulthood in our terms, was featured in the seventeenth century while childhood was featured in the nineteenth and adolescence in the twentieth centuries. Before the seventeenth century, childhood was a brief transition period passed through quickly. In medieval society, the idea of childhood as we know it did not exist. As soon as the child was independent of mother or nanny, it was considered part of adult society.

Hernandez (1993) cites eight "revolutions" in the lives of children in the United States in the twentieth century: (a) disappearance of the two-parent farm family, (b) decrease in number of siblings, (c) increase in level of parent's education, (d) increase in number of mothers in the workforce, (e) decrease in father's full-time employment, (f) rise of the single-parent, female head-of-household family, (g) disappearance of the intact, never-divorced, two-parent, two-child family, and (h) the reappearance of widespread poverty. Hernandez is critical of typical developmental psychology, which he sees as reductionistic and "obsessed" with the individual.

Definition

Children's environments are usually defined by adults in terms of what they feel is proper for children. Burnett (1974) was the first to describe a constructed environment that was physically compatible with the psychological development of children. The Durham learning environment was designed to correspond to the learning stages in development as described by Piaget (1954) and Bruner (1966). The environment considered two stages: In the first, the infant learns to distinguish him- or herself as an object (Figure 20.1); in a later stage, the infant expands attention and begins to engage in "purposeful movement" (Figure 20.2).

Strictly speaking, Skinner (Gewirtz, 1992; Hawkins, 1990) was earlier in attempting an environment dictated by developmental needs with his invention of the "aircrib," a simple rectangle in which he placed his infant daughter.

The front of the box was glass so the infant could look out. The temperature was controlled so that it was never necessary to wear more than

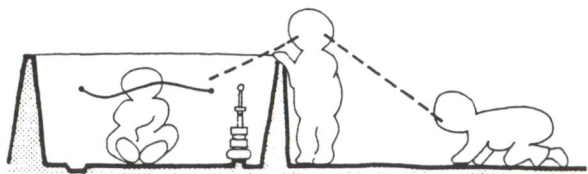

Figure 20.1. Self-Defining
SOURCE: Burnett (1974); reprinted by permission.

Figure 20.2. Purposeful Movement
SOURCE: Burnett (1974); reprinted by permission.

a diaper. This prevented rashes and did not require the constant dressing that takes place with most infants. The floor was a plastic sheet the texture of linen and it was on a roller so it could be rolled out from under the baby as soon as it became soiled. Then it was washed, dried, and returned in a continuous loop. Because this seemed inhumane to many people, the aircrib was never adopted by the public.

Barbey (1974) asked children to draw their "ideal home" (Figure 20.3) and he observed that their drawings did not reflect the adult view of privacy. Children tended to be more open in their ideal homes. He also observed a pervasive theme of grottolike spaces that seemed to symbolize both dependence and independence, noting that the grotto is more symbolic than the house. It is both open and closed in nature, with no break between ground, walls, and ceiling, which form a softly linked, continuous surface. The children ignored all of the more ostentatious aspects of design and showed a world much different than that of adults.

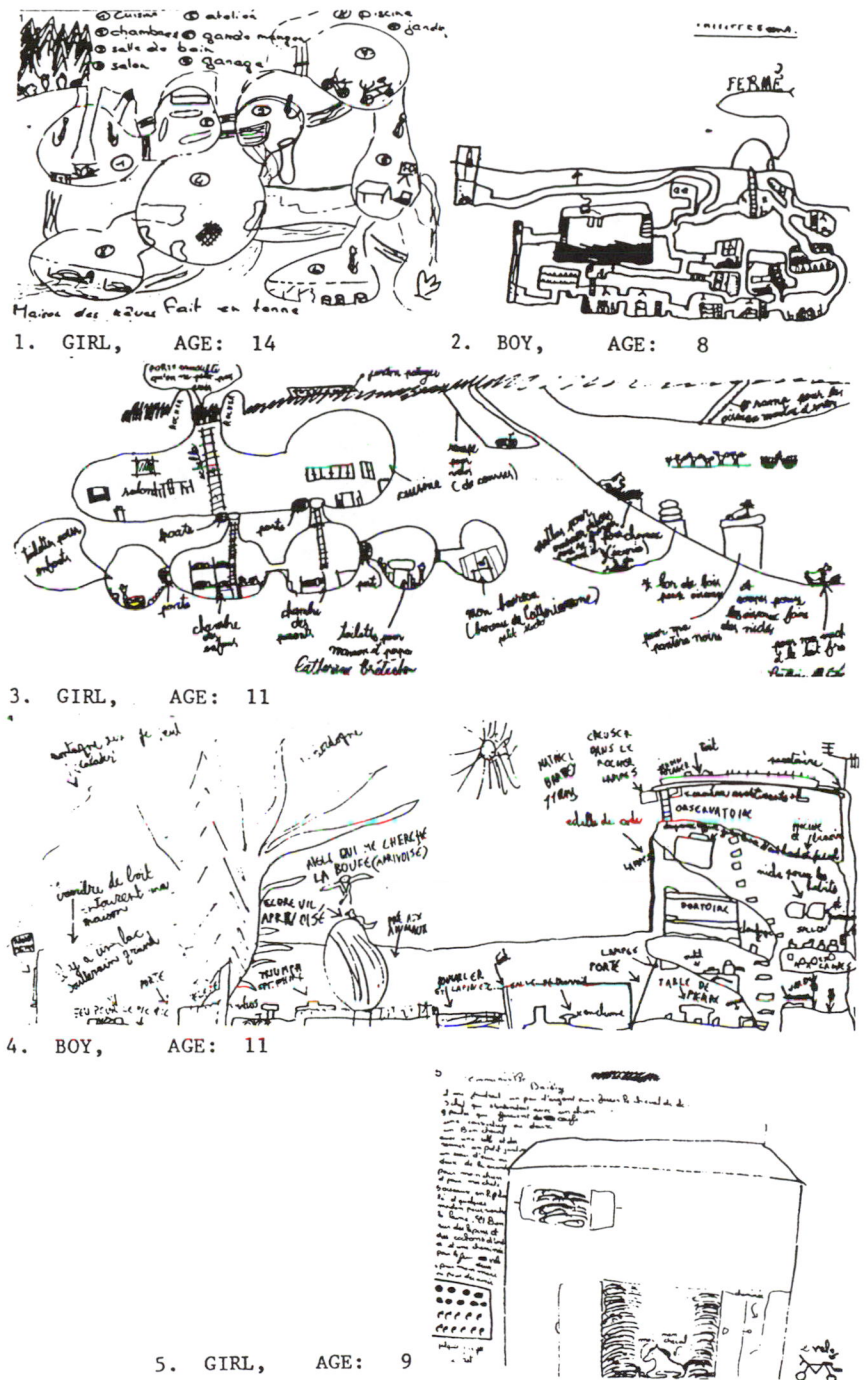

1. GIRL, AGE: 14 2. BOY, AGE: 8

3. GIRL, AGE: 11

4. BOY, AGE: 11

5. GIRL, AGE: 9

Figure 20.3. Barbey's Children's Drawings
SOURCE: Barbey (1974, p. 145); reprinted by permission.

Thus attempts to construct an environment just for children have been few and the definition of children's environments remains that part of the adult environment largely made by adults for children. Chief of these are the home, the neighborhood, schools, and the larger world.

The Home Environment

The home environment is not as safe as some adults assume it to be. Kaminer and Sandler (1994) point out that 100 children a day die in their homes in the United States. The chief villain is the stairway and its banisters, between which a child can wedge its head and strangle. Poisons, vitamins, and other medicines are a second hazard and must be kept in cabinets that are locked and out of reach. Hot stoves, houseplants (of the poisonous variety), glass-top tables, and electrical outlets are other hazards from which curious children can be protected.

Prescott (1973) showed that children who lived in high-rise apartments would show interiors while children who lived in single-family houses would show exteriors when asked to draw their homes. The implication is that the physical environment influences what the child thinks of as "home."

Children tend to get spaces in the house that are left over after adults claim the places they want (Zimring, Reizenstein Carpman, & Michelson, 1985). White et al. (1979) claim that children from 1 to 3 spend 80%-90% of their waking hours interacting with the physical environment directly. As Michelson (1985) points out, however, whether this is the physical environment at home or in a day care center depends on whether the mother works. In 1990, 54% of mothers in the United States with children under 6 were in the workforce (Hofferth & Phillips, 1991), and this was predicted to reach 66% by 1995. This considerably decreases the amount of time spent in the home environment.

Sebba and Churchman (1983) asked 185 family members, "To whom does each place in the apartment belong?" Of the children, 98% had their own place at the table but only 38% had a place in the living room. The only place in the apartment where the child could exhibit any ownership was the bedroom.

Rochberg-Halton (1984) asked members of 82 three-generation families (N = 315) about the objects that surrounded them in their homes. The purpose was to search out the environmental landscape of the house. It was discovered that different family members often inhabit different symbolic environments even though living in the same house. The main discovery was that "special" objects differed by generations considerably (see Chapter 8, Table 8.1, for a list of objects chosen). Children tended to choose more action-oriented objects such as stereos while adults and the elderly chose more objects of contemplation such as photographs. More important, however, from the point of view of home environments, was that almost half of the children's objects (ages 8 to 14) were in their bedrooms. The importance of the bedroom declines with age until in adulthood only 11% of the objects were in the bedroom, but then the bedroom increases until at age 70, 24% of the objects are located in the bedroom. Thus it would seem that the bedroom is a special arena for childhood.

When Rochberg-Halton asked, "Where in your home do you feel most at home?" over half of all children felt most at home in their bedrooms. Autonomy and privacy were the reasons most given for selecting the bedroom.

Neighborhood

Wright (1969) demonstrated that children of small towns knew more about their immediate neighborhoods than did children of larger towns and cities. Wright accompanied children on walks around their towns and asked them questions about who lived in the houses and what they did. He also asked them to play a block game by constructing the town from wooden blocks. In both cases, children in small towns knew more about their environments than did children in larger communities. Wright feels that the main reason for the familiarity of children with small towns is that they have more frequent daily contacts than do children of the larger communities. The children in small towns see the same faces more, have less distance to travel, and hence see the same places more. More recently (Gaster, 1991), fear of crime has entered the picture, which tends to prevent children from going outdoors as much.

Gaster (1991) investigated the access children had to their neighborhood in a specific section of New York City from 1915 to 1976 and found that access had been reduced in this time period. The age at which children were allowed free access increased from an average of 5.5 to 7.55. The number of sites visited decreased while obstacles and barriers increased. It seemed as though parent-imposed restrictions decreased but

Figure 20.4. The Traditional Playground
SOURCE: *Childhood City* (1974); reprinted by permission from the Environmental Design Research Association.

the number of professionally supervised activities increased. In some ways, this parallels the findings of Blaine and Golam (1991) that recreation is moving toward paid activity.

Aiello, Gordon, and Farrell (1974) and Clare Cooper Marcus (1974) both found that children seem to prefer the paved areas of the environment more than the natural areas. This would seem to contradict the biophilia hypothesis, but the reasons are complex. Part of the choice is because of the heavy use of bicycles, tricycles, wagons, and so on; part is because some parents are afraid of the natural areas.

Playgrounds

Rothenberg, Hayward, and Beasley (1974) described three types of playgrounds (Figures 20.4, 20.5, 20.6). A traditional playground has the most commonly recognized equipment of slides, swings, teeter-totters and is usually part of a school, housing project, or park.

The contemporary playground emphasizes novel forms and different textures and is more design conscious. This type may also contain traditional equipment but have other attractions such as tunnels, statuary, and tree houses. Adventure or "junk" playgrounds let the children design and build their own play area with materials supplied such as old tires, large blocks of wood, gardening tools, and scrap materials.

Figure 20.5. The Contemporary Playground
SOURCE: *Childhood City* (1974); reprinted by permission from the Environmental Design Research Association.

Figure 20.6. The Adventure Playground
SOURCE: *Childhood City* (1974); reprinted by permission from the Environmental Design Research Association.

The authors' observations showed that younger children with their caretakers generally concentrated at the traditional playgrounds while older, unaccompanied (by caretakers) children used the contemporary along with teenagers and some adults. Of the children Rothenberg et al. observed at adventure playgrounds, 96.7% arrived by themselves or with a peer, thus reinforcing the child-user image of the adventure playground.

Coates and Bussard (1974) observed 35 children at natural play in the environment of a housing development in a small city. They looked at three aspects of the children's play: the home base, territorial range, and chaperoned travel. As children aged, they made more use of and enlarged the territorial range. Chaperoned travel increased for girls but decreased for boys. An interesting finding is that children were kept away from grass, similar to the cautionary behavior of parents in regard to the natural areas. Urban playgrounds are vacant during 88% of the peak time for playing (Dee & Liebman, 1970; Wade, 1968). I observed in foreign countries such as Iran that most of the time children were not using playgrounds because there was no adult supervision. The use of these playgrounds depended upon having adults there to watch.

Schools

Aries (1962) points out that what we see as our current school system is a direct descendent of the cathedral school of medieval times. There was a radical break between the ancient schools of Greece and Rome and the medieval concept of education, which was solely for recruiting monks. By medieval times, it is often said that one in ten persons was either in or attached to a monastery.

We also tend to feel that our times of violence are something new. In 1680, the College de Bourgogne had a rule: "Neither firearms nor swords are to be retained in pupils' rooms and those who possess such weapons must hand them over to the principal who will keep them in a place chosen for that purpose" (Aries, 1962, p. 315). In France, there were armed school mutinies that tended to decline by the twelfth century, but in England they got worse. Children were given swords at the age of 5.

Sommer (1967; Sommer & Olsen, 1980) investigated the effects of "soft" classroom design versus the usual "hard" design (see Figures 20.7 and 20.8). The soft classroom is not without its problems; that is, it is harder to maintain because even though it is cheaper to clean rugs than to keep tile clean, there usually are no rug cleaners kept as part of routine maintenance equipment. Nevertheless, participation rates for students in the soft classroom were two to three times higher than in conventional seminar classrooms, and voluntary participation was 79% versus 51%.

Glass, Cohen, Smith, and Filby (1982) did a meta-analysis of 725 studies done on class size. Their conclusion was that very small classes

Figure 20.7. Hard Classroom (before)
SOURCE: Sommer (1967); reprinted by permission.

are much better than even relatively small classes. Performance decreases until, when large class sizes are reached, the addition of even many more students makes no difference. They also found that class size has more influence on teacher attitudes than on pupils. Teachers' attitudes tend to get more negative as class size increases.

Where one sits in class has long been a subject of inquiry. As early as 1921, Griffith claimed there was a peak in grades in the fourth row. He formulated the *eye contact hypothesis* to account for why pupils in the front did better. Even as late as 1984, Moore and Glynn claimed that students' physical location in the classroom can significantly affect both their behavior and their academic achievement levels.

But, like so many cherished beliefs, this one did not stand the scrutiny of science. Montello (1988) did a meta-analysis of seven independent classroom seating studies representing thousands of students and came

Figure 20.8. Soft Classroom (after)
SOURCE: Sommer (1967); reprinted by permission.

to the conclusion that if there is an effect of seating location on academic grades, it is so small as to be insignificant. Montello cautions, however, that his study holds only for seating *without choice*. If students get to choose their own seats, then a selection factor may account for differences, and this is when most studies find a correlation with grades. There is, however, an influence on participation and attitudes toward the teacher, those in the front being more likely to participate more and have a better attitude than those in the rear.

Sommer's (1967) classic study on classroom ecology demonstrated that pupils will respond favorably and with better grades to an environment that is more humanely designed with rugs on the floor and pictures on the wall. Unfortunately, the vast majority of classrooms remain the "hard architecture" type that Sommer describes as typical of schools and prisons because the priority is expense of maintenance. It might be said that the design of classroom interiors is for the convenience of janitors more than pupils.

School Size

School size is a topic studied thoroughly by Barker (1968) and his colleagues (Barker & Gump, 1964; also see Chapter 10). Barker (1965) summarized the advantages of small schools over large ones. Generally, students in smaller schools have greater satisfaction related to the development of competence, being challenged, taking part in more important actions, being involved in group activities, being valued more, and gaining more cultural and moral values.

By contrast, pupils in larger schools report having fewer satisfactions in vicarious enjoyment, being affiliated with larger entities, learning about other persons and activities, and gaining "points" with participation. Wicker (1969) supported these findings and Baird (1969) confirmed them with a national sample of 21,000 students.

Perhaps school size has something to do with Skinner's (1984) denunciation of our current school system. He points out that with existing technology, pupils could learn twice the amount in the time given compared with what they now accomplish in a standard school.

Teacher Expectations

Rosenthal conducted classic research referred to as *the pygmalion studies* (Rosenthal & Jacobsen, 1968). Two groups of children were matched for abilities. The teacher of the first group was told to expect about an average performance from these students. The teacher of the second group was told to expect an outstanding performance. At the end of the grading period, the students "performed" according to the expectations of the teachers. Thus it was demonstrated that the expectations the teachers had was a powerful influence on how students performed and were graded.

Schools and Delinquency

Lee Robins (1966) compared 524 students who were referred to a clinic to 100 controls who represented the student population at large. The main characteristic that seemed to separate the study group was its antisocial behavior, which was characterized as psychopathic. Usually this meant theft but also running away, truancy, bad company, sexual activities, and staying out late. The girls were characterized mainly by sexual activity. The antisocial behavior was measured by its variety, the number of episodes, and the seriousness of the offenses. It seemed that the behavior pattern was clear by the age of 7. Aggressiveness was an especially stable trait in the boys. Robins (1966) questions many commonly held beliefs, based on her results. Among these is the assumption "that behavior defined as legally antisocial is 'normal' in lower class men" (p. v). The schools accept such behavior and generally do not deal with it.

Olweus (1978) found that 10% of the boys in grammar and secondary schools engage in bullying behavior on the school grounds. The bully picks out a whipping boy and torments him in public on a fairly continuous basis. But the most harmful aspect is the "mobbing" behavior that occurs when a number of passive individuals watch the bullying and do not interfere with the bully because of fear. This creates the illusion of support for the bully and the image that the peer world (and even the school itself, by default) is against the whipping boy. Olweus became interested in this behavior when he heard about boys committing murder and suicide as a result of such mobbing.

His advice is for the school to directly interfere and prevent bullying rather than accepting it because "boys will be boys." Apparently, there is a common belief that such behavior builds character and strength in men and that they must learn "to fight their own battles." The problem with such logic is that the bully picks a whipping boy who has little chance of fighting back. Olweus advises boys to fight back no matter what, however, because bullies want only passive whipping boys.

Since 1983, there has been a nationwide program in Norway to educate teachers and parents about bullies and their victims. There are many misconceptions about bullies. They are not failures in school who pick on others to compensate for their own insecurity. Bullies are usually self-confident and are popular with their fellow students up through the sixth grade. They are good at talking their way out of situations and are effective at using others for their own ends. Even though bullies break the rules at home as well as school, parents are often unaware that their sons are bullies. Bullies are universal; they operate in rural as well as urban schools, large as well as small schools.

In another longitudinal study, Ahlstrom and Havighurst (1971) followed 400 "losers" through their school careers. At first, their project was an attempt to intervene in delinquent behavior at the eighth grade but they quickly discovered it was too late. By the third grade, the pattern is already set. The careers of their study group were fraught with violence: 10 were killed by violence or accidents, 30 were knifed or shot, 55% showed serious maladjustment, 65% were arrested for other than traffic offenses.

What contributes to such an end? Many factors operate in the environment. These include lack of an opportunity to be a man, lack of family support, having a neighborhood that exposes them to trouble, a lack of a sense of control over the environment and therefore limited attempts to do anything to adapt. Critical in their list of things to do to correct these situations is the choice of the right kinds of persons to teach in inner-city schools. Patient but determined teachers who can be flexible are important, but *male* teachers are very important because they can provide a relationship with boys that is lacking to those most in need.

These studies point out that schools are a most important factor in delinquency because they do not directly deal with the character-building aspects so important in the lives of young men and boys. More attention must be paid to the male-modeling aspects of education and the fact that interference in antisocial behavior must take place before the third grade.

Widom (1989) makes a very important point in regard to the effects of violence and abuse on later development. Although there is strong support for the *cycle of violence hypothesis*, as well as neglect and other forms of abuse leading to violent and criminal behavior in later life, the facts show that, although 26% of child abuse and neglect victims had later juvenile offenses, *74% did not*. Although 11% did have an arrest for a violent criminal act, *89% did not*.

Although this means there is great potential for prevention programs narrowing these figures even more, the overwhelming fact remains that most victims of neglect, violence, and abuse do not turn out to be criminals! Granted, some of this may be because other, unrecorded behaviors may occur such as suicide and depression, but the fact remains there is little understanding of the main effect, which is that most people survive. Widom calls for a greater understanding and study of the processes involved in how people survive and protect themselves against the negative effects. The problem is that our research is directed toward negative effects.

But what does work with delinquency? Wolf described a successful effort to reform delinquents by use of a token system that rewarded the

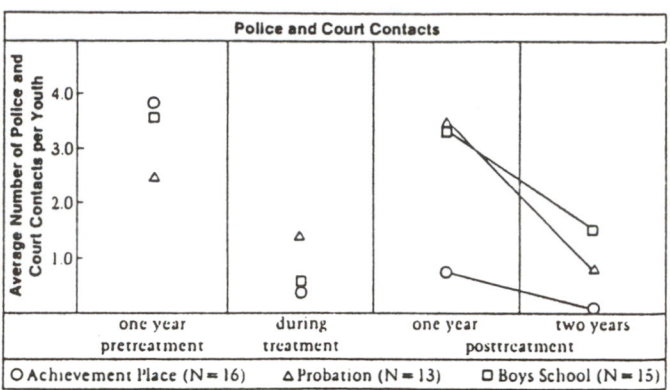

Figure 20.9. Comparison of Police and Court Contacts
SOURCE: Used by permission from *Psychology Today*.

learning of social behaviors. Wolf was convinced that many delinquents simply never learned the social skills necessary to get along. He set up a system of basic learning of social, academic, and self-help skills. It was a success. He demonstrated that he had effectively turned potential criminals into potentially productive citizens (see Phillips et al., 1973, and Figure 20.9.)

According to Figure 20.9, the Achievement Place Youth began with the highest average number of police and court contacts prior to treatment and in comparison with a sample of 13 boys on probation and 15 in a boys' school. During treatment, they moved to the lowest number in comparison with these two other groups, and 1 year and 2 years later were still far lower in these contacts than the other two groups who seemed to stay at the pretreatment level.

But when Wolf tried to replicate the system a second time, it failed. What happened? Fortunately, the two efforts had been heavily recorded with videotape so it was possible to compare the process in both attempts. It soon became clear that although both sets of surrogate parents had administered the scripts of the program similarly, those in the successful first attempt had gone beyond the script to express feelings of concern, explain more carefully the taking away of credits, and in general be more caring and warm toward the boys. It was an important lesson.

In a later study, Wolf (1987) suggested that "the realistic goal for some persons with serious delinquent behavior may be extended supportive and socializing treatment" (p. 347). He found that serious delinquency "robustly eludes" short-term treatment and may be an interaction of environmental and constitutional variables.

Oriental Schools Versus U.S. Schools

Stevenson (1992) reports on five collaborative studies done across schools in the United States, China, Taiwan, and Japan. Much has been written about the inadequacy of U.S. schools but Stevenson blames it on the fact that U.S. schools "strayed from the effective application of well-known teaching methods" (p. 70), a criticism echoed by Skinner (1984).

U.S. and Asian students do not start out with a wide disparity in ability but by the fifth grade, for example, the average score of one Chicago school was only as high as the worst of all the Asian schools tested. Clearly, this is a problem of school instruction and not native ability. Americans perform better than Asian students in reading in the first grade but are even by the sixth grade. Despite this, U.S. mothers in Minneapolis were three times more satisfied with their children's performance in school than their Asian counterparts. The U.S. students were also positive about their progress. U.S. students also tended to wish more for money and objects while Asian students wished more for educational goals such as completing college.

Examples of how the Asian schools are more effective are as follows: Study is dispersed among frequent periods of activities that are more "fun" to students. Longer and more frequent recesses also characterize the Asian schools. Thus Asian students see school as more enjoyable. Asian students may spend as much as four times more hours in homework than the U.S. students and do a lot more reading for pleasure. Consequently, much less time is spent watching TV. Contrary to the U.S. stereotype, Asian students do not experience more stress.

Teachers in Asian schools have more time for students because they actually spend less time in class and more time with individual students who need help. Beijing teachers are in class only 3 hours a day compared with U.S. teachers, who spend most of their school day in the classroom. Also, Asian teachers see themselves more as guides rather than as dispensers of information. Students are regarded as active *participants* in the process. Asian students were observed attending to the teacher 80%

of the time as opposed to only 60% in the United States. Stevenson attributes this as much to the spacing of lessons with breaks as to the effectiveness of the teachers.

Wiatrowski, Gottfredson, and Roberts (1983) found two environmental factors influenced disruptive behavior in schools. These were called "urban social disorganization" and "academic suburbanism." In other words, the inner-city schools tend to experience more disruptive behavior while at the same time occupying buildings that have fewer facilities. These are compared with the newer suburbs, where parents have higher educations and incomes and the buildings have many more facilities for the activities.

The Open School Plan

The *open school plan* refers to a design for schools without interior walls. Ordinary schools typically have classrooms opening off of each side of a corridor, called a double loaded corridor. The open school, like the open office (see Chapter 17), has a large open interior. The savings on initial construction are considerable. There are no interior walls, heating ducts, or electrical outlets within walls. On the other hand, sound travels across the open space, and people are visible no matter where they are in the open plan.

Gump (1987) summarizes research on the open plan and shows that there are several responses: (a) reduction of the space by use of barriers, (b) introduction of "quiet" spaces, and (c) reduction of activities that interfere across the space.

When Gump measured the erection of barriers across the open spaces in 21 schools (Gump & Ross, 1979), it was discovered that 38% of the openness had been reduced by erection of barriers such as bookcases, cabinets, coatracks, and other devices to shield students and teachers from each other.

Quiet rooms are physical spaces entirely enclosed and buffered from sounds from the rest of the school by insulation. It is like a room within a barn. This is done to enclose such noisy activities as band practice. In a way, this is a more extreme example of the first response, erection of barriers.

The third response is what Gump characterizes as a "rigidity" of programs. This means that teachers stopped noisy activities and planned movements about the open space more carefully. There is some suggestion that this results in a regimentation more severe than would occur in a conventional classroom.

The construction of open classrooms has declined, and new schools have returned to the more classical double loaded corridors. Yet many of the open schools will remain for quite some time and students will continue to be educated in their somewhat more restrained environment. It was an experiment that did not work.

More important, just as the open office was an attempt to save on construction cost, so the open school was a promise to provide savings *without investigation of the behavioral response beforehand*. Society has had to spend untold amounts in these experiments, all of which could have been saved by doing proper research to determine whether they worked before they were built. Now generations of students and workers will have to live with the less than satisfactory open plans until they are eventually replaced.

Vandalism

In a classic paper, Zeisel (1974) described how about half of the vandalism that occurs in schools is not actually intentional but the result of poor design or, simply, accidents. By focusing on these kinds of damage, Zeisel (1976) was able to write a handbook on how to prevent such damage. An example of his checklist for formal school play areas is shown in Figure 20.10. Zeisel went on to teach students and teachers how to recognize the environmental sources in many facilities that caused them to deteriorate, which could be changed to prevent further physical problems formerly classed as vandalism.

The Hooper Avenue School

Neal Deasy was one of the first architects to promote collaboration between architects and social scientists (Deasy, 1970). He established a long-term relationship with Thomas Lasswell, a social psychologist. When asked to improve the Hooper Avenue School in Los Angeles, Deasy and Lasswell investigated the needs of the surrounding community and did the necessary social psychological research to give them information on how the school could be improved. What is especially interesting about the project was that the data they collected provided "an accurate measure of the real concerns of the neighborhood, concerns which proved to be

PLAY: Formal Play Areas

What have you done to minimize breakage of objects around playgrounds and basketball courts?

	YES	NO
There is sufficient space around formal play areas for normal play	[ ]	[ ]
Ground surfaces in and around formal play areas have no major irregularities or hindrances to play.	[ ]	[ ]
Wall surfaces around formal play areas can be used to bounce balls back to players.	[ ]	[ ]
Low lighting fixtures and other hardware are out of the way of ball playing.	[ ]	[ ]
Lines on walls and on ground accommodate local street games.	[ ]	[ ]
There is a buffer between formal play areas and the school building.	[ ]	[ ]
There are no windows or glass doors around formal play areas.	[ ]	[ ]
Glass around formal play areas is specially protected.	[ ]	[ ]
There is no damageable planting immediately adjacent to formal play areas.	[ ]	[ ]

PLAY: Pick-up Play Areas

What have you done to be sure that objects will not be broken around pick-up play areas — areas near buildings like entry ways and pathways with hard ground surfaces, a wall, and enough room to throw or hit a ball?

	YES	NO
There are consciously designed areas for pick-up play.	[ ]	[ ]
There is no low lighting or other fixtures which can be hit by balls in pick-up play areas.	[ ]	[ ]
Walls and ground surfaces in pick-up play areas are the same as in formal play areas.	[ ]	[ ]
There are no windows in pick-up play areas.	[ ]	[ ]
Any windows near pick-up play areas are protected from balls and sticks.	[ ]	[ ]

Figure 20.10. Checklist for Play Area Vandalism
SOURCE: John Zeisel (1976). Used by permission.

quite different from the highly publicized demands that have been made upon the board of education" (Deasy, 1970, p. 1).

In other words, the social research provided data for a much different environment, one that was more suited to the students and the neighborhood. It was the forerunner for many studies to come.

In conclusion, it would seem that there are many significant influences of the school environment. Among these are size of the school, size of the classroom, physical appearance of the classroom, teacher expectations, bullying, and mobbing. Delinquency seems to be encouraged more by a lack of opposition to it than any purposive behavior, but it can be remedied by token economies and a caring environment. Schools are far behind what Skinner (1984) has demonstrated they are capable of, and it seems most U.S. schools simply fail to use educational techniques already shown to be successful.

The Environment of Divorce

I did not think of divorce as an environmental concept until my youngest daughter, then in grade school, came to me one day and asked when I was going to get an apartment. So many of her friends had parents who were divorced that it seemed natural for fathers to have their own apartments. Later, one of my graduate students did an unpublished study of how much time it took to arrange the logistics of reconstituted families. I was impressed with how the situation of divorce forces people, especially children, into certain modes of behavior. I feel it would be remiss to conclude a chapter on children's environments without reviewing the environmental constraints that divorce imposes.

By 1993, half of all marriages contained at least one partner who had been previously married. Often this would mean that a child or children would be brought from the previous marriage to be joined by children of the current marriage. Divorce directly affects more than 1 million children a year in the United States.

Hetherington has studied the circumstances of divorce for long periods (Hetherington, Cox, & Cox, 1976, 1978, 1979). She found that the circumstances produced a situation where the mothers felt trapped and the fathers felt as though they were shut out. As a result, the mothers would become overly strict toward the children while the fathers tended to become much more permissive. Both parents felt incompetent, lonely, alienated, and depressed the first year.

Part of the reason mothers feel so trapped is that their incomes are sharply reduced so they are forced to work and care for the children at the same time. Weitzman (1985) showed that the average divorced mother's income is reduced by 73% while the divorced father's income *increases* by 42%.

In a meta-analysis of 72 studies on the effects of divorce on children, Amato and Keith (1991) showed that children of divorce score lower than those in nondivorced families by an average of .14 standard deviations on many standard tests. They stress, however, a family conflict model rather than just a divorce effect per se.

The children of divorced parents, according to the Hetherington studies, showed much less affection and less social compliance than children of nondivorced parents. The relations between mothers and sons become particularly strained. As the mother becomes more strict, the son tends to rebel.

At the end of 2 years, most of the debilitating effects seem to abate but Hetherington stresses that there is no such thing as a "victimless" divorce.

Wallerstein and Kelly (1974, 1975) and Kelly and Wallerstein (1975, 1976, 1977) did similar studies of divorced children in Marin County, California, and essentially replicated Hetherington's findings. However, they investigated the age relationship to divorce and added some dimensions. Ages 7-8 were less able to deny the divorce circumstances and were usually more sad in appearance than younger children. Those 9-10 were better able to manage but showed more shame and anger. These behaviors continued for some after a 1-year follow-up.

Kulka and Weingarten (1979) attempted to study the long-term effects on adults who had been children of divorce. They reassessed in 1976 individuals who were measured in 1957. The results were somewhat questionable because of the difficulty in isolating one event as the cause. In general, they did not find as many differences as they expected from those of nondivorced families.

Cherlin et al. (1991) did a longitudinal study in England similar to the Hetherington et al. and Wallerstein and Kelly studies with the same kinds of results but they factored out behavioral problems present *before* the parents divorced. Their conclusion is that "much of the effect of divorce on children can be predicted by conditions that existed well before the divorce occurred" (p. 1386).

This leaves several questions unanswered such as when children begin to experience the process that precedes a divorce, and whether dysfunctional families can be distinguished from functional families that get a divorce. Nevertheless, these results from both the U.S. and the British studies indicate that more attention should be paid to the processes that occur in troubled families, not just the effect of parents' separation.

Franklin, Janoff-Bulman, and Roberts (1990) echoed these findings when they asked college students of divorced versus nondivorced parents about their chances of future marriage prospects. Children of divorced parents were less optimistic and had less trust in future spouses than those from nondivorced families but this was affected by whether there was continuous conflict in the family.

Child Care Environments

Scarr, Lande, and McKartney (1989) point out that in the nineteenth century, child care was seen as a way to keep deprived children off the streets even though well-to-do families had child care in the form of hired help in the home. It was only in the 1980s that child care gained public acceptance because so many middle-class mothers stayed in the workforce after giving birth. By 1990, about half of all preschoolers in the United States with employed mothers were in some form of care that did not involve relatives. Over a quarter were in center-based care environments. These child care centers are licensed enterprises that are either specially built or remodeled specifically for that purpose and may house up to 175 children of different age groups. The other 51% of working mothers place their children with grandparents or with other relatives.

When evaluating these environments, health and safety have been the main emphasis. Booth (1992) points out that there actually is no consensus on what child care is or should be. Because the United States has lagged behind so many other countries in supporting child care (see Kamerman, 1991), the Family and Medical Leave Act of 1993 was passed to provide some financial support for working families. Lowry (1993) demonstrates that children prefer private places to play and these are often in short supply in child care centers. To avoid a sense of being crowded in day care centers, Lowry suggests small 30" × 30" enclosed structures that children can crawl into.

When outcome measures were compared between children exposed to centers versus homes, Scarr and Eisenberg (1993) found few differences. This is because employed parents actually spend as much time with their children as parents who are not employed. Employed parents spend time with children by letting the housework go, giving up time for personal leisure, and even sleeping less so as to be with their children. This accounts for the few differences between children in child care centers and those who are cared for at home. Although this is generally true across a broad cross section of children, it should be pointed out that child care for children at risk from dysfunctional homes and deprived backgrounds is of proven benefit.

The Environment of Poverty

Between 1960 and 1990, there were 64 million children in the United States, and this figure remained constant throughout the 30-year period (Fuchs & Reklis, 1992). Because the number of adults increased in proportion to the children (ages 18-64 from 100 to 152 million), it would be fair to assume this would increase the welfare of children. Just the opposite occurred. In 1988, 20% of children of aged 3-17 had one or more developmental, learning, or behavioral disorders. By the time these children reached 12-17, the rate was one in four, or 25%. Children in poverty increased even though adult poverty levels remained the same.

Why has children's well-being suffered this setback? Huston (1991) points out that minority groups are disproportionately involved because they have more children. The work of the parents is often on the lower scale and insufficient for their needs. Benefits are decreasing, both welfare and medical, and poor children are not receiving a sufficient education to participate in the economy. The conclusion is very clear that children born in poverty have little chance of escaping it, especially if they are minority children. The environment of poverty is very confining.

This vision is multiplied once one moves outside the United States: One hundred million people worldwide are homeless, living on sidewalks, in garbage dumps, and under bridges (Durning, 1989). Four hundred million are so undernourished they are likely to suffer stunted growth, mental retardation, or death before they mature. In 1988, 14 million children died of simple diseases that it would have cost only $5 to cure.

Robert McNamara (1981), when head of the World Bank in 1978, defined poverty as "a condition of life so limited by malnutrition, illiteracy, disease, squalid surroundings, high infant mortality and low life expectancy as to be beneath any reasonable definition of human decency" (pp. 238-239).

Rigoberta Menchú (1983), a spokeswoman for the poor and refugees of Guatemala, who won the Nobel peace prize in 1992, described how her little brother died of the effects of a pesticide being used in the fields where the family was working:

> The little boy died early in the morning. We didn't know what to do. Our neighbors were anxious to help my mother but they didn't know what to do either—not how to bury him or anything. Then the overseer told my mother she could bury my brother in the plantation but she had to pay a tax to keep him buried there. My mother said, "I have no money at all." He told her: "Yes, and you already owe a lot of money for medicine and for other things, so take his body and leave." . . . It was impossible to take his body back to the highlands . . . so my mother decided that, even if she had to work for a month without earning, she would pay the tax to the landowner, or the overseer, to bury my brother in the plantation. . . . One of the men brought a little box, a bit like a suitcase. We put my brother in it and took him to be buried. . . . That night the overseer told us: "Leave here tomorrow." (p. 88)

Poverty as an environmental variable has only been studied by anthropologists and sociologists, seldom by psychologists (see Harrington, 1962; J. Lewis, 1988; O. Lewis, 1961). Kotlowitz (1991) documents the plight of black children in public housing in Chicago. Lapierre (1985) describes the lives of Calcutta's poor, and Lobo (1982) describes life in Peru's barriadas. Poverty remains the most pervasive of all environmental influences on the lives of children worldwide.

Adolescent Environments

The period in life known as adolescence is very much a creation of industrial society. As Aries points out, preindustrial children went right from childhood to adulthood. Only when the child labor laws of the early twentieth century took effect was there time for adolescence.

Lynch (1977) did a study of adolescents in four countries: Australia, Argentina, Mexico, and Poland. Just as in children's environments, it seems adolescent environments are those that are left over after adults have taken theirs. Lynch calls these spaces "unprogrammed," which means, largely, of no use to adults. These spaces are usually outdoors, on the streets, in parks, or in "wasteland" areas not used by adults. The behavior in these areas is described by the adolescents as "messing around" or "hanging out." This is seen by adults as useless and unproductive but to the adolescents it is a necessary period of socialization. The adolescents can be observed as constantly talking with one another. Pennartz and Elsinga (1990) confirm this socialization by results from their own group of adolescents in Arnhem, the Netherlands. They chose communication/contact with people as the most important aspect of the adolescents' behavior that they looked at compared with the behaviors of adults and architects.

What becomes apparent from observing adolescents is that they have difficulty finding places to hang out. Anthony (1985) describes the mall as a "teenage hangout" and finds teenagers spend 1 to 5 hours at a time, most traveling in groups of two or three.

Perusse (1978) studied four middle-class communities in the suburbs in the Kansas City area and found the major problem was finding a place to "hang out." The teenagers would constantly discuss what to do and often get in trouble by "raiding" record stores or creating nuisances in public places.

Bronfenbrenner's Ecology of Human Development

Urie Bronfenbrenner (1979) proposed an ecological schema for human development that is more detailed in terms of personal contacts than the ecological psychology of Barker (see Chapter 10). Bronfenbrenner emphasizes such smaller units as *dyads, tetrads*, and *ecological transitions*. As the child develops in the dyad with the mother or other caregivers, developmental changes take place in both the infant and the caregiver. Bronfenbrenner sees the ecological environment as a series of nested shells like Russian dolls, with the smallest at the dyad level and the largest at the cultural or *macrosystem* level.

He (1979) takes a dim view of schools in the United States as "one of the most potent breeding grounds of Alienation in American society" (p. 53). The main cause of this alienation is the lack of any contact with *caring* environments. U.S. children grow up in the educational system without having to *care* for anyone such as a sick person, an elderly person, or a handicapped person. The physical isolation of the school as it moves further from the home and becomes larger in size (see Barker & Gump, 1964) results in peer group influences on the average student that are contrary to parental influence. Peer groups tend to encourage egocentrism, aggression, and antisocial behavior.

A solution suggested by Bronfenbrenner is to develop a *Curriculum for Caring* so that students would learn about and become concerned with the needs of others. Bronfenbrenner cites research that reinforces the findings already discussed for divorce. He also sees divorce as an environmental circumstance that generates special kinds of behavior.

Conclusions

What can be said about children's environments? Despite the knowledge gained in many research projects (e.g., Barker & Gump, 1964; Glass et al., 1982; Olweus, 1978; Rosenthal & Jacobsen, 1968; Skinner, 1984), there is a surprising lack of application of what is known. As Stevenson (1992) pointed out, U.S. schools don't apply the standard educational tools already well established in other schools of the world, let alone the research results referred to above.

Schools remain larger despite the evidence that small schools are so much better. The belief in economy of scale is best exemplified by my own experience with the Kansas City School District in the early 1970s. The district had some 70 schools at the end of the 1960s and was contemplating closing the smaller schools as an efficiency measure. The district hired a research team to study the problem, and, of course, the study found the small schools should be closed. Taking the same data from the hired study, I reanalyzed it by dividing the schools into those above 300 pupils and those below. On the Iowa basic skills test, the pupils in the schools with fewer than 300 pupils scored 12 points better than the average pupil in schools with more than 300 students. Further, using the data on heating and cooling, it was cheaper to heat and cool the small schools than it was to maintain the larger one. Despite knowledge of these data, the smaller schools were closed. Once again, our belief systems rule our behavior rather than data derived from scientific evidence.

GOALS

Concepts and Definitions

Medieval childhood

Eye contact hypothesis

Seating position in class

School size

Violence hypothesis

Participation in learning

Divorce effects

Hanging out

Poverty environments

Adolescent

Children's environments

Traditional playground

Contemporary playground

Adventure playground

Open school plan

Vandalism

Pygmalion studies

Child care environments

Important Studies

Montessori (1964)

Piaget (1932)

Sebba and Churchman (1983)

Wright (1969)

Gaster (1991)

Rothenberg et al. (1974)

Glass et al. (1982)

Sommer (1967)

Olweus (1978)

Widom (1989)

Bronfenbrenner (1979)

QUESTIONS

1. Why are parents unconcerned over bullying behavior?

2. Why have U.S. schools failed to incorporate educational practices known to be effective?

3. How do untested concepts such as the open school become so popular?

4. Why is the United States so far behind other countries in child care?

5. Why don't we study the fact that most children *don't* become delinquent, even when exposed to violence and abuse?

6. If we know small schools and small classrooms are so much more effective, why do schools and classrooms keep getting larger?

7. If Wolf's methods were so effective, why weren't they adopted?

8. What is the most important lesson to be learned from vandalism?

9. What can be done to counter the pygmalion effect?

10. Why do we profess such love for children yet neglect them?

21

Environments for the Elderly

The Problem of Aging

Why do we grow old? Is there a genetic code that could be fixed to eliminate aging? Or do we just "wear out" like a machine? Rose (1991) offers some hope that successive generations could be bred to live longer. He has done this with fruit flies. Not only do the fruit flies live longer, they are also hardier and healthier.

Then there is the *disposable soma* hypothesis. This view sees the body as a vehicle to bring about reproduction by preserving the body until reproduction is over, about age 40, and then just living off the reserves until death. This is somewhat like the sociobiology of Wilson (1975) but hypothesizes less directiveness on the part of the genes. Rusting (1992) reviews much of the research related to the disposable soma hypothesis and concludes there are newly discovered factors such as the effects of free radicals in the body that may be more significant.

All of us breathe oxygen but it has only recently been discovered that oxidized lipids accumulate in aging cells. Furthermore, there is some evidence that DNA itself is influenced by oxidation, which causes loss of effectiveness in mitotic replication. Another effect is to harm the mitochondria in cells, which are the energy supply, and thus, as the body ages, cells become deprived of energy. These new results are tantalizingly close

---

Box 21.1

How to Live to Be 120

To grasp what it means to be 120 years old, consider this: a woman in the U.S. now has a life expectancy of 79 years. Jeanne Calment of Arles, France, reached that advanced age back in 1954, when Eisenhower was in the White House and Stalin had just passed from the scene. Twenty-two years later, at age 100, Calment was still riding her bicycle around town, having outlived both her only child and grandchild. And 20 years after that, she was charming the photographers and reporters who arrived in droves last week, along with the French Minister of Health, to mark her 120th birthday.

The woman certified by the *Guinness Book of World Records* as the oldest living human allowed that she was "very moved" by the celebration. How does she feel? Like half the people over 85, she no longer hears very well. A broken hip five years ago left her unable to walk, and cataracts have robbed her of vision. (She has refused surgery, says her physician, Victor Lèbre, because "she thinks it's normal at 120 not to see.") But there is no question that her wit is intact. Asked what kind of future she expects, Calment didn't miss a beat: "A very short one." As for her Methuselan achievement, "It's not impressive at all," she insisted. "It's natural to grow old."

True, of course, but 120 borders on the unnatural. It is at the uppermost limit of what biologists believe is the maximum human life-span. Calment, says Harvard geriatrician Dr. Thomas Perls, "is the Michael Jordan of aging," genetically blessed with extraordinary physical gifts that favor survival. "The chances of you or me getting to be her age are similar to our chances of playing basketball like Jordan." Only one other person is known to have lived as long: Shigechiyo Izumi of Japan, who died in 1956 at 120 years.

Whereas few of us can expect to be longevity superstars, demographic trends show that more and more of us will at least make it into the big league. The "oldest old"—those 85 and older—make up the fastest-growing segment of the population in the U.S. and other prosperous nations. Between 1960 and 1990, while the overall U.S. population grew 39%, the ranks of those 85 and older jumped 232%. The U.S. Census Bureau projects that by the year 2040, there will be 1.3 million Americans 100 years or older; some demographers put the figure at 4 million.

The picture of 4 million doddering, medically needy centenarians is not pretty, but the prospect may not be so grim. People who make it past 85 are a hardy group, says Richard Suzman of the National Institute on Aging. About 30% still live in

---

but not yet at the conclusive stage. They suggest that all kinds of "aging" diseases such as diabetes, Alzheimer's, and Parkinson's may be related to the oxidation process in cells. Hayflick (1994) discovered what is now called "Hayflick's Limit." When he grew human cells in vitro, he found

Box 21.1 Continued

the community and "are robust in the sense that they are able to lift shopping bags, walk half a mile and climb stairs."

The oldest old are healthier than the merely old in several respects. Heart disease and stroke, for instance, have their greatest impact in the 50s through 80s for men and about 10 years later for women. Those who make it past the danger zones are less apt to be stricken at all. Similarly, Alzheimer's disease usually picks off its victims by the mid-80s. Perls found that men in their 90s outperformed octogenarians in tests of mental function.

The Grim Reaper himself may slow his pace for the oldest old. While the chance of dying increases exponentially with each year from 50 to 90, the odds rise less steeply after 90.

The vigor of the very old has a simple explanation, says Perls: "The genetically weak die off, and what is left is an enriched group of healthy, strong individuals." This weeding-out process is most evident among those for whom the selection pressures are greatest. For instance, while death rates are higher for African Americans than for whites up to age 75, blacks who make it to 75 have superior health and longevity. Similarly, although men have a shorter average life-span than women, males who do survive into extreme old age tend to be in better shape than women. Men make up 20% of 100-year-olds and 40% of 105-year-olds.

If there's a secret to long life, it is surely in the genes. Calment's mother lived to 86, her father to 93. Scientists speculate that long-lived people may carry genes that confer special resistance to the assault of free radicals, chemical residues of metabolism that do increasing damage to DNA as the years roll by. Researchers are also looking at apolipoprotein E, a substance that ferries cholesterol to and from cells. People vulnerable to Alzheimer's and heart disease tend to have a certain type of gene for this protein, while those who live longest tend to have another type.

Temperament, also genetically mediated, may play a role in longevity too. Perls, who is studying 100 Boston-area centenarians, notes that whereas they all have seen their children, siblings and friends die, they "handle stress incredibly well." A life-style of moderation and exercise also helps, as does education. Studies suggest that, on average, better-educated people suffer less mental deterioration in old age.

As for Jeanne Calment, she seems to embody the calm resilience associated with long life. "I took pleasure when I could," she said last week. "I acted clearly and morally and without regret. I'm very lucky."

SOURCE: *Time* (March 6, 1995, p. 85). © 1995 Time Inc. Reprinted by permission.

that they stopped reproducing after 50 generations. Other researchers do not necessarily accept this limit as the program of death because it may be due to the oxidation effects described above.

As yet there is no unified theory of aging but many advise the use of antioxidants to counter the oxidizing effect. Olshansky, Carnes, and Cassel (1990) examine data that seem to show the upper limits of the human life span have just about been reached given current technology. The age of 80 is about the most that can be expected given the limits of today's medicine. Of course, much of the world has yet to reach that limit but the United States is nearly there with a life expectancy of about 75 in 1988. The difficulty in reaching a higher limit is shown by the fact it would take a 12% reduction in overall mortality for females in the United States and a 48% reduction in mortality for males just to reach a life expectancy of 80 years for both males and females. This is not likely in the near future. "It is our opinion that with existing medical technology, declines in mortality comparable to the total elimination of all circulatory diseases, diabetes, and cancer combined is highly improbable" (Olshansky et al., 1990, p. 638).

More important to Olshansky et al. are the *number* of elderly who survive because of their impact on social security and health care. Because these numbers have been so severely underestimated in the past, the lack of planning has placed a strain on governmental and private resources that is unprecedented in our history. The question remains: Have we gained longer life at the cost of longer frailty?

Rowe and Kahn (1987) point out that nearly all research on the elderly has lumped together all people at a certain age without regard to how large the differences are in health among all the members of age groups after 65. They attack the current concepts of normality and suggest that age cohorts be separated by *usual* versus *successful* aging. Usual aging is what we consider "normal" today, but, in fact, the many ailments we see as "normal," such as diabetes, osteoporosis, and loss of cognitive function, are actually the results of improper diet, lack of exercise, smoking, and other habits that cause the apparent losses so much accepted as common to aging.

Another cause of debilitation in aging is loss of autonomy and control over one's life. Studies on aging populations, such as those of Shupe (1985), Krantz and Shulz (1980), Langer and Rodin (1976), and Mercer and Kane (1979), show that loss of control is associated with a deteriorating condition and even death while gaining control brings improved health and outlook. In fact, doing things to help the elderly often results in "infantilization." Successful aging results from good habits practiced over a lifetime with continuous control while usual aging is the result of harmful practices that are the result of poor habits in earlier life.

The famous "Termite" studies were not about insects but about the most famous cohort in the history of psychological studies (Friedman et al., 1995). Lewis Terman selected 1,528 very bright California schoolchildren in 1921 to study them through school into their adult lives. This cohort became known as the "Termites" because of their association with Terman. By the last decade of the twentieth century, about half the cohort had died so it was possible to correlate their life habits with death versus those who survived. The results confirm Rowe and Kahn's (1987) assertions. Smoking and drinking predicted premature mortality. Obesity was not a factor because not enough of the cohort were overweight. More interesting were the psychological factors of dependability, trust, and lack of impulsiveness (sometimes called ego strength) were related to good health. Echoing the previous chapter, divorce "clearly predicted premature mortality."

Finally, an important perspective to keep in mind concerning all research on the elderly is the tendency to attribute behaviors to the state of being elderly rather than the environment in which the elderly person or group is found. Rodin and Langer (1980) illustrate how easily this happens with an experiment showing that loss of memory—which in a popular misconception about the aging process is assumed to happen "naturally" with the elderly—is easily improved by making the environment more conducive and more demanding of thought and memory.

Historical Perspective

Hareven (1994) provides an illuminating historical perspective on the changes in generational relations in U.S. society. There is the common myth that the United States once had a majority of extended families living under one roof. In fact, such families rarely existed. North American households from colonial times have had a nuclear composition. One reason is that fewer people lived to old age in earlier times, but the more prevalent reason is that when the older people did survive, they lived in separate houses near their children in what is a "modified extended family system" (Greven, 1970). This was different than the extended family system in Europe. In addition, Hareven points out, there was never a "golden age" in family relations with older people. The elderly were always insecure even though they were regarded more highly in the past. This system is characterized by Hareven (1994) as "intimacy from a distance." Although the generations did not necessarily live under the same roof, they were in constant contact. This pattern has existed in the United States since the earliest settlements.

What has happened is that family support for the elderly has eroded even as the numbers of elderly and their survival to older ages has increased. It used to be that one of the children would move in with the elderly to take care of them. That is increasingly rare today. Offering boarders lodging was a frequent strategy for the elderly to keep the home intact. About one third of young men and women in their twenties and thirties lived with families other than their own in the late nineteenth century United States. These periods served as a transition to establishing their own families.

Hareven claims that the most profound change since World War II has been the *empty nest* stage. Several factors have produced this. Among them are people living longer, having fewer children, spacing the children closer together, and the children leaving home earlier. The net result is a couple left alone in their home at a relatively early stage, even in their forties and fifties. In older times, the nest was almost never empty because the births of children were much more spaced out over the childbearing period and children tended to stay longer before leaving.

Of interest, divorce may now be stepping in to fill the nest again. Data show that reconstituted families are once again blurring the generational differences. Since the 1980s, more erratic and flexible family patterns have been emerging.

Definition

Neugarten (1975) divided the elderly into two groups: the young-old (55-75) and the old-old (75+). Carp (1987) and others tend to repeat this distinction. Those 85+ are the largest growing segment of this population (according to the 1990 U.S. Census). Those 65 and older constituted 12.6% of the population in 1990. The American Association for Retired Persons (AARP, 1990) predicts there will be 66 million persons over 65 by the year 2030.

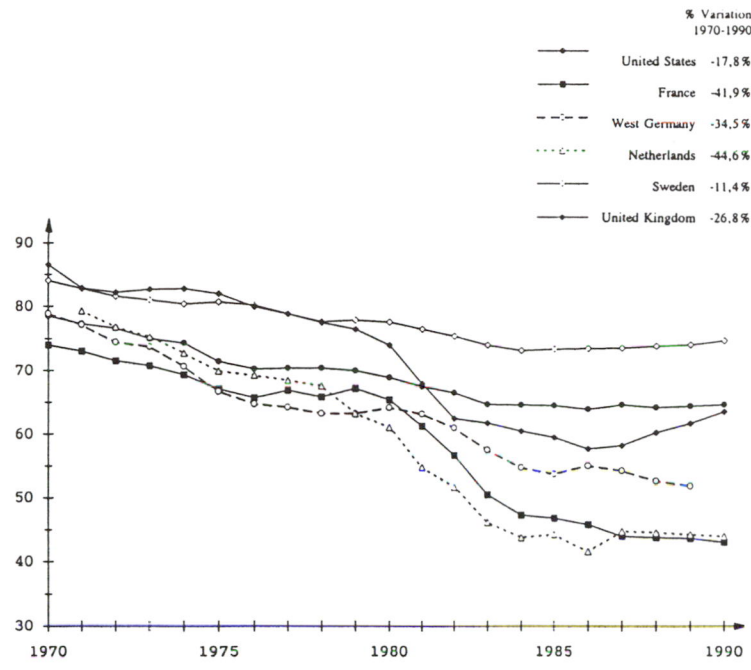

Figure 21.1. Employment Rates for Men 55-64 Years Old
SOURCE: OED Labor Force Statistics from Guillemard and Rein (1993). Reproduced, with permission, from the *Annual Review of Sociology* Volume 19, \cpr 1993, by Annual Reviews Inc.
NOTE: International time series of employment activity rates of men from 55 to 64 years old.

There was once a consensus that being elderly started at age 65. The U.S. census still uses that definition. But fundamental changes are occurring in the age of retirement (Guillemard & Rein, 1993) such that increasing numbers are retiring before the age of 65 (Figure 21.1).

Thus old age is now a *postretirement* stage characterized by the quick slide into death. By 1983, the amendments to the Social Security Act were nudging the retirement age to 67 by 2027. Current proposals in Congress would bring it up to 70 well before that date. Other countries such as Sweden and Japan are also trying to raise the retirement date. These efforts may eventually turn the tide of early retirement, but, for now, the trend has serious budget consequences for all Western nations. The most severe strain comes from the demands for medical care. General Motors, for example, spends more on medical care for its employees than it does on steel. Older persons typically require more medical care and so the cost of retirement brings an increasing medical care cost.

Figure 21.1 shows the dropping age levels for retirement since 1970. Guillemard and Rein call this phenomenon a new "third stage" in the life course. According to them, the pension system has created a new stage between adulthood and advanced old age. Two distinctions must be made about this new stage. One is that leaving the work market after 60 is not necessarily retirement. For example, 70% of the workers who stop working before 65 in Germany, France, and the Netherlands do so well before receiving a pension. This phenomenon is called "early exit" by Guillemard and Rein to distinguish it from leaving the labor market and having a pension.

Early exit is a growing phenomenon that is causing concern in governments throughout the world. Although private pension systems seem to be encouraging early exit because it is cheaper for them, government pension systems find early exit burdensome because of the increasing numbers. In 1962, the U.S. government lowered the retirement age of men to 62. Immediately, more than half of those eligible exercised the option and the number has been increasing. Consequently, in 1983, amendments to the Social Security Act began raising the age of benefits to 66 in 2009 and 67 in 2027. Similar measures have taken place in Germany and Sweden but failed in Japan.

Private corporations find themselves saddled with pension and medical benefit expenses so these are being cut with increasing frequency. One response to these opposing forces is for retirement to become a part-time work situation where the employee negotiates an early retirement with lowered job responsibilities (Conrad, 1991).

Theoretical Perspectives

The above discussion on definition has consequences for the theoretical perspective on aging. Most aging theories do not take into account environmental influences (Carp, 1987). Yet, it is clear from the social cushion changes cited above that the character of aging is changing because of private and government pension policies. In fact, if Guillemard and Rein (1993) are correct, another stage in the life cycle has been added, inserted between adulthood (working) and old age. This retirement-early exit stage is the direct product of industrial society just as adolescence was carved out of late childhood and early adulthood.

Typical of the theories that do not take into account environmental influences is the staged theory of Erikson (1959), who sees the main problem of life as establishing basic trust with other humans. Once this is established, the other stages can proceed, but without basic trust, mental illness such as schizophrenia develops. Erikson sees adulthood (ages 20-40) as a period of generativity, if successful, or stagnation, if not. Maturity (ages 40-60) results in integrity, if successful, or despair on the negative side. Erikson was the first theoretician to extend developmental theory into older ages. Previous theories such as those of Freud, Jung, and Adler thought development ended by late childhood or adolescence at best.

It is in the last stage, 60+, that Erikson runs afoul of the more modern evidence. Erikson sees this period of 60+ as being preoccupied with death. The newer evidence would suggest that retirement becomes a bigger question than death and that preoccupation with death, if it ever occurs, is put off until a later period.

A more ecological theory is that proposed by Lawton and Nahemow (1973). This is called the *environmental docility* hypothesis because get-ting older is seen to be increasing dependence on the environment as ability to fend for oneself decreases. Ideally, a person's abilities would match the environmental demands but eventually the demands exceed the ability to respond successfully and the environment must become more prosthetic.

Lawton (1990) expresses the counterpart of docility as the *environmental proactivity* hypothesis. This is the opposite because, "as personal competence increases, the variety of environmental resources that can be used in satisfaction to the person increases" (p. 639). Proactivity operates also as an explanation of growth in childhood and adulthood. But it can be applied to the elderly because if the environment is made proactive, the elderly will respond.

Perhaps the most prominent theory on the elderly in their environments is that of *psychological control*. Langer (1983, 1989) is the chief proponent of this theory, beginning with her work with Rodin (Langer & Rodin, 1976; Rodin & Langer, 1977). The original experiments involved two floors of a nursing home with matched subjects and two different messages delivered by management about the care the subjects were to receive. One message assured the subjects they would be taken care of and made comfortable. The other message said they would have to make their own decisions and be responsible for many aspects of their own care. Later evidence at 18 months showed that the persons given the responsibility message were much more active, healthier, and in better spirits than those given the "care" message. In fact, 7 out of 47 died in the "responsible" group while 13 out of 44 died in the "care" group, a death rate of about half. This strongly suggests that control is directly related to longevity.

Rodin (1986) expanded this concept to epidemiology and was able to show that the elderly who had more control over their lives had less disease and lived longer. But the concept of control is not without its problems. Langer (1983) discusses these by contrasting Averill's (1973) distinction of three kinds of control: (a) the behavioral, which is a direct action to influence some threatening event; (b) cognitive, which interprets the threat; and (c) decisional, which is the ability to choose among possible actions. Langer adds her own dimension, which is the *awareness* of alternatives that must hold for each of Averill's types of control. In other words, unless the person is aware of the consequences of the threat and decisions to influence the outcome, there can be no sense of control. This is particularly important in the laboratory, where the experimenter most often defines the consequences for the subject rather than letting the subject define them. Langer (1983) concludes: "People experience control as they master their own internal (mental) or external environments—as they make the unfamiliar familiar" (p. 19). She later renames this awareness *mindfulness* (Langer, 1989).

Fry (1989) expanded the notion further and showed the negative potential for carrying the control theory too far. The losses that occur with age tend to undermine the older person's confidence and self-esteem. Medical people tend to reward dependent rather than independent behavior. And, when circumstances are such that the environment is more than the person can respond to, the inability to take control can have devastating effects. Failure to achieve control can result in depression, self-blame, and corresponding deterioration. Nevertheless, having the elderly accept as much control as possible remains a goal for most environments for the elderly (Altholz, 1988; Barker, 1988; Feingold, 1990).

Housing for the Elderly

Housing for the elderly is divided into several large categories. First, most elderly continue to live in their own homes. This is sometimes called "in place" housing. Of the total number of households in the United States in 1990 (91,947,410), 8,824,845, or 9.59%, are householders 65 years old or older. This is by far the largest elderly housing group.

Group quarters constitutes the next largest group but these account for only 1,730,982 of the elderly. Group quarters can be *congregate housing*. This is housing where meals are served in a common dining room, and housekeeping and nursing services are provided, even though individuals live in their own quarters. Some congregate housing can be of the *continuing care* type, which is a more intensive community geared to providing health care and maintenance services until death. *Shared* housing describes the type in which at least two unrelated persons live together in a dwelling unit, each one having one's own private space and sharing other common areas such as a kitchen, dining room, and/or living room.

Of those 60-64 years of age, only ½ of 1% are in *nursing homes;* 1.3% of those 65-74 are in nursing homes, but 10.06% of those 75+ are in nursing homes. Clearly, very few elderly are in nursing homes, and residence in nursing homes is a function of increasing age.

Moos and Lempke (1994) report on research evaluating 300 elder care facilities in the United States. Moos and his associates have pioneered the development of the Multiphasic Environmental Assessment Procedures (MEAP). These are questionnaires administered to staff and residents to evaluate five features of a facility: (a) residents and staff, (b) physical and architectural features, (c) policies and programs, (d) social climate, and (e) outside observer ratings. The places rated fall under three broad categories: nursing homes, residential care, and congregate apartments. Nursing homes tended to make the bottom of the list, especially in regard to the autonomy of the residents. But also, in comparing the kinds of ownership and management, the nonprofit facilities clearly came out best. "In general these findings confirm the advantages of non profit facilities, particularly in areas more difficult to regulate, such as the comfort of the physical environment, policies that enhance residential self direction and the quality of the social environment" (Moos & Lempke, 1994, p. 237).

The most significant change in housing for the elderly in the United States in recent years has been the rise of the *segregated elderly* community. The first of these was Youngtown, Arizona, in 1957, and it was quickly followed by Sun City (phases 1, 2 and 3, and Sun City West), all at the same location northwest of Phoenix, Arizona. Many similar communities were developed throughout the United States. The reason for such communities was the rapid rise in income of the elderly (Hurd, 1989) more than other groups. Thus, for the first time, the elderly can afford to move into communities built just for their needs. Nevertheless, these are still a small minority and are included partly under the "in place" category because the elderly are still living in their own homes.

Hunt and Hunt (1985) describe *naturally occurring retirement communities* that can be as small as one building or constitute a whole neighborhood. These are places that attract the elderly because of the companionship of other persons their own age but that also have handy amenities like grocery stores. These places are usually older housing that has not been built specifically for the elderly as in the Sun City model. The advantage of the naturally occurring retirement community is its connectedness to an existing community with intergenerational ties.

It is very clear that most elderly wish to remain in their own homes (Filion, 1992; Groves, 1992; Saup, 1986; Struyk, 1987; Tinker, 1987). This is largely because they feel most control there but also because they have a network of support. There are some differences in the research about whether the neighborhood or the physical features of the structure are the more important aspects of this "in place" dwelling. Jirovec (1985) finds it is the quality of the surrounding neighborhood. This echoes an earlier finding by Havighurst (1969). But Windley (1983) found it was the specific housing features. Christensen, Carp, and Cranz (1992) found structural adequacy the most important factor in housing satisfaction. Some of the reasons for these differences may be the character of the neighborhood itself. The elderly are much more affected by crime than people of other ages (Fashimpar, 1984; Normoyle, 1987, 1988), and it may be that in neighborhoods where crime exists, they rely less on neighborhood support.

Living alone, regardless of housing type, seems to be less of a problem for the elderly than might be imagined. Hiner (1987) finds there is not a loss of quality of life or a health risk in living alone for the elderly. Hartwigsen (1986) agrees and shows that her widows living alone have better functional status than comparable married women. Wister (1985) finds that elderly persons living alone give up some advantages in social exchanges but gain in privacy.

Independence and control seem to be the most important aspects of elder housing in whatever housing type. Berkowitz (1988) interviewed residents of self-help housing for the elderly and reported that the self-help aspect enhances control and self-esteem. Altholz (1988) claims fostering autonomy has many positive benefits across housing types. When Barker (1988) looked at how landlords evaluated elderly applicants for private housing, independence was the main criteria for approval. Residents who were evicted were expelled for outlandish behavior, not for physical impairment. Vallerand and O'Connor (1989) claim that nursing homes by themselves do not have detrimental effects, it is actually the link between self-determination and life satisfaction. Hinrichsen (1985) found high-density senior housing to have positive benefits. De Grace (1987) did not find loneliness connected to any housing type.

Certain types of buildings do seem to have an effect, however. Ekblad (1990) found the high rises in Beijing were not beneficial to either the elderly or children. Imamoglu (1992) had similar conclusions about Turkish elderly. Heller (1984) found a low negative correlation between building height and sociability. Husaini (1991) found black elderly were worse off in high-rise buildings. Normoyle (1988) asserts that building height has a significant effect on reactions to crime but the actual fear of crime seems to be less among high-rise dwellers. Duffy (1984) concludes that elderly people in high-rise buildings are higher in morale but not in physical or mental health.

Despite these few negative experiences among high-rise residents who are elderly, the overall experience in the urban United States is that elderly prefer and feel safer in high-rise buildings.

Several efforts are being made to improve the lot of the elderly in various forms of housing. Thompson (1985) reports on Victoria Plaza in San Antonio as being the first public housing for the elderly to include the "introduction of beauty." Czaja (1988) describes the new "smart houses" for the elderly that have electric outlets and appliances designed to reduce chances of electric shock, that provide hot water heaters that won't send out water that is too hot, and have increased security, entertainment, and communication services.

Delaski-Smith (1984) reports that the elderly in intergenerational housing have greater self-esteem and satisfaction but at the expense of privacy, yet Weinstein (1988) shows that elderly in age segregated communities are more sexually active.

Finally, Walker (1991) finds that 53% of her elderly subjects reported having fallen in recent years and that fear of falling ranked first among common fears.

The conclusions from the housing studies seem to support a proactive-docility hypothesis. Being proactive is very similar to taking control. Independence and self-help correlate with satisfaction across housing types but many factors can enter the equation. There are many examples of housing built specifically for the elderly and these range from the smart-built individual homes to the Sun City communities of the world. As the elderly population continues to grow, more accommodations will be made and the variety of choices can only increase.

Nofim

Nofim is the Hebrew word for "beautiful view." Starting in 1977 (Bechtel, 1991), an association of retired schoolteachers and other professionals in Jerusalem decided to build a retirement community of their own. As far as I can determine from an informal survey of active researchers, this is the only example of an elderly group building their own quarters. They hired an engineering firm and ERDF (see Chapter 3) to help them design this environment.

As an environmental psychologist, I directed these clients to address four main issues of design: (a) admittance and discharge from the facility, (b) the cost and size of the apartments, (c) the range of services that the facility can provide, and (d) whether residents could work on the staff of the facility. A committee was formed to address each issue and later committees were formed to deal with essential issues of Jewish life such as food. The first question was the hardest because all of them wanted a place they couldn't be thrown out of no matter how ill they became. But this was not possible because it would make the cost of each unit prohibitive. They had to work out a compromise among themselves based on the money available.

As a social scientist, this was my first opportunity to present data to a client group and let them draw their own conclusions and derive their own design principles. Thus the future residents of Nofim were empowered to take control of the process of design.

Groundbreaking was on November 15, 1978, and the building was completed in 1984. Once more, it must be emphasized that Nofim was the first building for the elderly in which the residents themselves designed, built, and managed the property. Although the building is not remarkably different than those designed by developers (Figure 21.2), it is the process itself that empowered the residents to take control of their own environment.

Figure 21.2a. External View From Nofim

Figure 21.2b. Internal Views From Nofim

Adriana Plotkin (1990), an architecture student from the Technion in Israel, did a POE (Chapter 14) of Nofim and found that

> Nofim is a good example of successful sheltered housing for the elderly, in which we find the declining capabilities of the elderly were taken into consideration. This is a supportive and helpful environment especially regarding the elderly's need for independence, freedom of choice and independent action. Nofim is a building which includes all of the characteristics of a regular building in addition to several services that are highly valued by the residents, and that include support and help in time of need and the achievement of social contacts through activities which encourage contact among residents. (p. 24)

Nofim is far from perfect. It turned out that the site was not an especially good one. Despite the "beautiful view" of its name, it was too far from a shopping center and too close to a noisy street. Also, the compromise in design to preserve the view meant construction delays that discouraged some original subscribers.

In the passage of time, Nofim has become an example of housing for the elderly in Israel. It is very much an international community of elderly retired who have migrated to Israel for ideological or religious reasons.

Conclusions

The accumulated support for the docility-proactivity hypothesis and the evidence for the efficacy of control in environments of the elderly make it very clear that these environments should be shaped to encourage maximum control. But the counterdanger of sudden loss of faculties, mental and physical, makes it a requirement just as important that the prosthetic aspects of the environment be immediately available.

Koncelik (1976) and others outline what kinds of amenities are needed for frail elderly in nursing homes. Yet even independent housing must have wheelchair accessibility if residents are to remain in their dwellings after incapacity. The issues of environments for the elderly remain under continuous research, but it also seems clear that, for the elderly, remaining in their own homes is the preferred and best choice.

The docility hypothesis, along with its proactive counterpart, has been used by several researchers and found to have currency in evaluating and designing environments for the elderly.

GOALS

Definitions and Concepts

Disposable soma hypothesis

Hayflick's Limit

Empty nest

In place housing

Congregate housing

Adulthood (Erikson)

Maturity (Erikson)

Environmental docility
hypothesis

Environmental proactivity
hypothesis

Shared housing

Congregate housing

Young-old

Old-old

Psychological control

Mindfulness

Usual aging

Successful aging

The "third stage"

Continuing care communities

Age segregated communities

Naturally occurring retirement
communities

Important Studies

Hayflick (1994)

Langer and Rodin (1976)

Rodin and Langer (1977)

Rowe and Kahn (1987)

Hareven (1994)

Friedman et al. (1995)

Olshansky et al. (1990)

Lawton and Nahemow (1973)

Lawton (1990)

QUESTIONS

1. Why do the elderly prefer their own homes?

2. Why are age segregated retirement communities successful?

3. What are the limits on empowering elderly to take control of their environment?

4. What is the difference between what we think of as usual aging and what aging can be?

5. Is the environmental docility hypothesis actually dependency?

6. Why should the elderly in intergenerational housing have better self-esteem?

7. How does gaining control lead to longer life?

8. What is the significance of mindfulness versus taking control?

9. How does a continuing care community differ from congregate housing?

10. What do the elderly fear more than death?

22

The House and Housing

Historical Perspective

Why do we live in houses? Where did the idea of a house come from? Watkins (1990) describes the earliest archeological evidence of a house from excavations at Quermez Dere in northern Iraq. These ruins date from circa 8,000 B.C.E., and the evidence pushes back the beginning of the Neolithic period to that date. Actually, there were three houses excavated but they were all built on top of each other (Figure 22.1). Essentially the houses were subterranean in character, and each older house was filled in before the pit of the the new one was dug. In the center of each house was a "scorched" area with a few stones set in plaster around it, and each house had a strange pillar-type object that did not hold up the roof but may have been an altar.

Watkins sees these three objects as evidence of a change of definition of the house from being just a temporary shelter to the house as a "home," the center of the family with symbolic representation (the pillar-altar) of values. For a thorough discussion of the concept of home, see Benjamin et al. (1995).

Other aspects of the house show it was kept clean because careful excavation failed to reveal any floor debris, and it was constantly repaired so there was a concern with keeping up its appearance. Watkins (1990) sees the(se) house(s) as "the private and concrete expression of a particu-

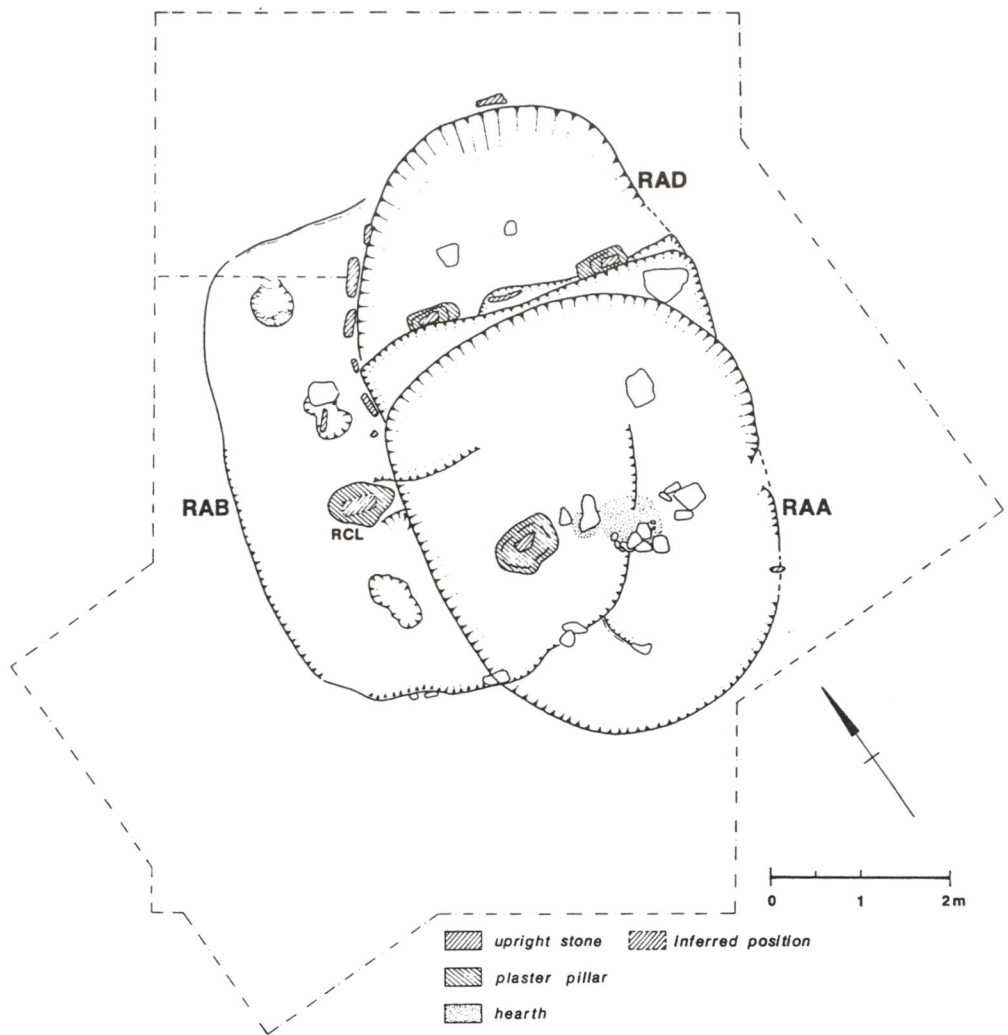

Figure 22.1. House Excavations in Northern Iraq
SOURCE: Watkins (1990).

lar family group" (p. 344). Previous to this period, there were many
temporary shelters in evidence but none with these permanent qualities.

Coulanges (1864/1955) claims that the origin of the house in Western
society was the field. At first the field was surrounded by a wall for
protection, but in the center was an altar for the sacred fire, the primitive
religion that preceded organized religion in the Greco-Roman tradition.
Then, as time passed, the altar was enclosed to protect it from the

elements and this became the house. This is not too different than Raglan's (1964) claim that the house originated as a temple. In a very real sense, the primitive house of Greco-Roman origin *was* a temple because it housed the sacred fire.

The sacred fire was the religion of the family. The father was the high priest and each family had its own ceremonies and traditions related to the fire. The fire was never to be extinguished. The first son became the inheritor of the priestly office. This tradition later was codified as *primogeniture*, the law of inheritance passing from father to first son.

The consequences of this law were far reaching because it settled the problem of inheritance of the primary means of subsistence by ruling out all the subsequent sons and all women as well. Women had the lowest status because they would leave the family religion and worship at another house when they married. They fared no better at the husband's house because they came to worship a strange god. Here is a significant place to note the denigration of women that is a continuing force in our society.

There is at least some evidence for the house-temple concept (or origin) in Mayan civilization. Figure 22.2 shows a typical house in the Yucatán in the present day. Figure 22.3 shows the Temple of the Magician at Uxmal, an ancient Mayan City. Note that in the center of the temple building at the top of the circular pyramid is a representation of a house very much like the one in Figure 22.2. Gallenkamp (1976) describes how the first Mayan houses were built on slightly raised earth platforms to help with drainage. At first, the temple, or house of God, was hardly different than the other houses but gradually the "house" of God was raised until it became a pyramid.

Coulanges quotes ancient Greek documents that state how the sacred fire taught men to build houses. It is thought that the hearth, with its mantle, is the remnant of this ancient tradition. In any case, the form the house took was that of a courtyard. Courtyard houses are everywhere throughout Europe, Asia, and Africa. They did not exist in North or South America until the Spaniards arrived. The Spanish house is essentially an Arab house. This came about when Spain was conquered by the Moors, who were Arabs. Many famous Arab buildings, such as the Alhambra Palace, are tourist attractions in Spain. Figure 22.4 shows a typical Arab house with its courtyard arrangement. This is the model for Spanish houses today. Following the ancient tradition, the wall is built first. Most Arab houses cannot afford the two-courtyard system for separation of males and females, so a compromise left only one courtyard.

Figure 22.2. Native House In Yucatán

Part of the tradition that developed in the Arab world was to have the entrance provide some sense of entering a temple so the house was made holy by the presence of a quotation from the Koran over the doorway. This tradition is followed via other historical pathways in Jewish houses, where scriptures are enclosed in a small tube or case called the *mezuzah* attached to the doorpost. They are found even on hotel doorposts in Israel.

In Roman times, the sacred entrance was a bit more literal. In richer homes, the visitor would pass by a miniature version of a Roman temple such as that pictured in the entrance to a house in Pompeii. Figure 22.5 shows the courtyard of the Domus Vettiorum, a wealthy house in Pompeii. Figure 22.6 shows a miniature temple in the entrance of another Pompeii house. These entrance temples vary in size and detail but the idea of the holy entrance is clear.

It is often not realized how literal was the transfer of Arab architecture to the New World via Spain. Figure 22.7 shows a house in Lima, Peru, dating from early settlement times. Note the intricate wooden coverings on the windows. These are exact copies of wooden coverings existing in

Figure 22.3. House of the Magician Temple at Uxmal

Arabia today (Fadan, 1983) called *raushan*. These coverings had a practical value because they allowed free circulation of air while at the same time providing privacy. In time, the coverings gave way to the simple wooden shutters seen on most Spanish houses today.

In medieval times, the courtyard house was elaborated on to contain quarters for apprentices, sheds for cattle and livestock, and spaces for looms (Mumford, 1961). The medieval house was a self-sustaining industrial site where the inhabitants made their own clothes, grew their own food, and manufactured a product.

It was the industrial age that gave us the form of the house most frequently seen in cities in North America and Europe. Many of these workers' houses can be seen in older industrial cities such as Manchester, England. Mumford (1961) calls the first industrial cities "coketowns."

As this transition unfolded, the original courtyard house that was "inward looking" gave way to the industrial workers' house, which became "outward looking." There were no windows in the outside walls of the courtyard house. In many Spanish and Arab cities, one can walk down

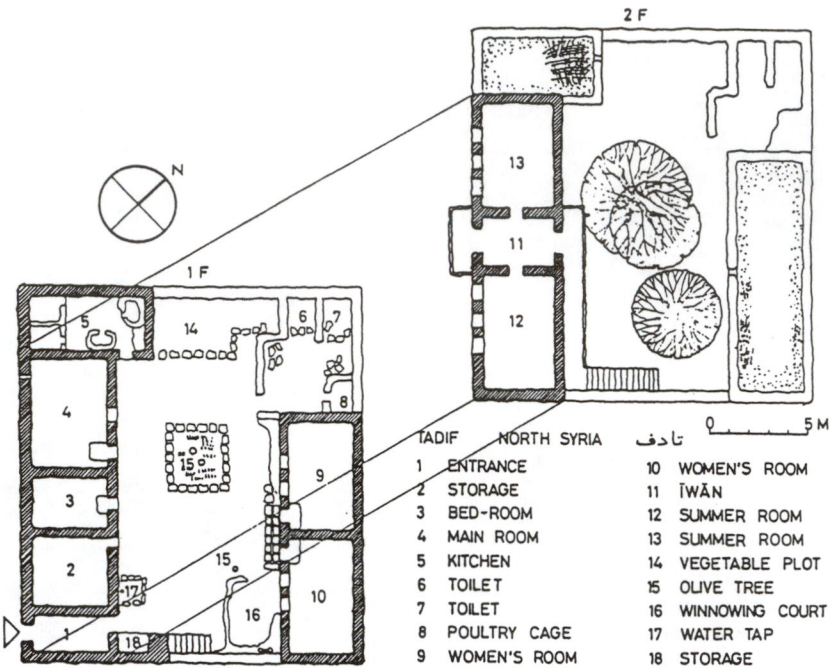

Figure 22.4. Arab Courtyard House Plan

streets for blocks without seeing a window. The industrial house acquired windows to the outside. The front yard became a semipublic space. The parlor was where visitors were received. English parlors of Victorian times were only opened to receive visitors on Sunday afternoon. The rest of the week, the parlor furniture was covered with cloths to keep it from getting dusty.

Mumford (1961) decries this turn of events: "Today, the degradation of the inner life is symbolized by the fact that the only place sacred from intrusion is the private toilet" (p. 269). Compare this with the last refuge of male territory in the house in Chapter 8.

Definitions

When is a house a home? Hayward (1975) reviewed research on this topic and showed that the concept overlaps between the physical dwelling

Figure 22.5. Roman Courtyard House at Pompeii

and the neighborhood. In fact, it was only after the seventeenth century that the concept of home focused on the house. Prior to that the "home" was the village of origin.

Other cultures have different ideas of home. When I was investigating Shay Gap, Australia, an Aboriginal answered the question about where he was from by saying, "Me b'long Nimingarra." Nimingarra was an uninhabited place near Shay Gap where he could not have lived unless he camped there. Further conversation revealed that this was his *spiritual* home, his place of spiritual origin where his clan group had emerged.

A similar but more literal belief exists among the Hopi. The place of origin for all Hopi is the *Sipapu*, the place where they came out of the ground into this world. Supposedly, this is a spring in the Grand Canyon.

Thus the meaning of home varies with time and culture. Other meanings explored are those such as *refuge*, the place where a person can go to find solace and restoration. Despite what Mumford says, most people look at their home as a place of privacy (Fried, 1963; Hayward, 1975; Seeley, Sim, & Loosely, 1956).

Figure 22.6. Miniature Temple at Entrance to House, Pompeii

Many people also express the concept of a "childhood home." This may refer to a specific house, a neighborhood, or a town. Fried (1963) described how people mourn the loss of a home, particularly when this is a home where one grew up.

House and Identity

The home is also seen as a personalized place (see the discussion of territoriality in Chapter 8). Clare Cooper Marcus (1974) detailed how people pick out a house that expresses their identity and then personalize it to complete the process. By contrast, when they cannot choose a house that expresses identity, they tend to feel the house may threaten their identity, especially if it is an anonymous high rise. The identity expressed by the house is the one people want others to see. Kron (1983) develops this concept as display. People surround themselves with objects that display the identity they want to project.

Figure 22.7. House in Lima, Peru With Arab Window Coverings

Jung (Jaffe, 1979) is often described as having coined the idea that the house can be an expression of the entire psyche. His famous dream (see the box) portrays a house that is symbolic of his innermost thought processes. In fact, this dream was a turning point in his life. It marked his break with Freud and his discovery of the collective unconscious. His dream was evidence that he was tapping into the collective unconscious of all humanity. The lower portions of the house represented ancient civilizations that were not just part of his own experience but went beyond

Box 22.1

Jung's Dream

This was the dream. I was in a house I did not know, which had two stories. It was "my house." I found myself in the upper story, where there was a kind of salon furnished with fine old pieces in rococo style. On the walls hung a number of precious old paintings. I wondered that this should be my house, and thought, "Not bad." But then it occurred to me that I did not know what the lower floor looked like. Descending the stairs, I reached the ground floor. There everything was much older, and I realized that this part of the house must date from about the fifteenth or sixteenth century. The furnishings were medieval; the floors were of red brick. Everywhere it was rather dark. I went from one room to another, thinking, "Now I must really explore the whole house." I came upon a heavy door, and opened it. Beyond it, I discovered a stone stairway that led down into the cellar. Descending again, I found myself in a beautifully vaulted room which looked exceedingly ancient. Examining the walls, I discovered layers of brick among the ordinary stone blocks, and chips of brick in the mortar. As soon as I saw this I knew that the walls dated from Roman times. My interest by now was intense. I looked more closely at the floor. It was of stone slabs, and in one of these I discovered a ring. When I pulled it, the stone slab lifted, and again I saw a stairway of narrow stone steps leading down into the depths. These, too, I descended, and entered a low cave cut into the rock. Thick dust lay on the floor, and in the dust were scattered bones and broken pottery, like remains of a primitive culture. I discovered two human skulls, obviously very old and half disintegrated. Then I awoke.

* * *

It was plain to me that the house represented a kind of image of the psyche —that is to say, of my then state of consciousness, with hitherto unconscious additions. Consciousness was represented by the salon. It had an uninhabited atmosphere, in spite of its antiquated style.

The ground floor stood for the first level of the unconscious. The deeper I went, the more alien and the darker the scene became. In the cave I discovered remains of a primitive culture, that is, the world of the primitive man within myself—a world which can scarcely be reached or illuminated by consciousness. The primitive psyche of man borders on the life of the animal soul, just as the caves of prehistoric times were usually inhabited by animals before man laid claim to them. . . .

. . . My dream thus constituted a kind of structural diagram of the human psyche; it postulated something of an altogether *impersonal* nature underlying the psyche. . . .

SOURCE: Jung (1963, pp. 158-159).

to a common experience shared by all humanity. Jung would go on to have other dreams about houses that would also add to his inner knowledge.

Roberta Feldman (1990) discovered that people also have what she calls *settlement identity*. Of her 1,648 subjects in Denver, 84.3% identified some settlement identity. Most common was "city person," or a suburbanite. Others identified themselves as "small town" persons, "country/ mountain persons," and about 15% did not identify with any settlement type. Feldman claims the settlement identity is important in a culture such as that in the United States, where there is a lot of movement from house to house within the settlement type. Thus people move from one city location to another or from one suburban location to another but seldom switch settlement types.

Theoretical Perspectives

Werner, Altman, and Oxley (1985) detail the *transactional theory* of house occupancy (see Figure 22.8). Although it is true that Barker (1968) uses a transactional view, the transactional view that Werner et al. (1985) expound includes an internal sense of meaning. In fact, they say, "Transactional processes in homes occur at the level of action and at the level of meaning; they can be events, activities, meanings, evaluations or any other psychological process" (p. 2). Another difference from the ecological psychology perspective is that, while Barker emphasized the stability of behavior settings, the transactional view emphasizes the changing nature of the house and its environment.

Others (Cohn, 1979; Egenter, 1992; Rapoport, 1969) emphasize the cultural and ethnic character of house design and describe how houses take their form from cultural expression. Colloredo-Mansfeld (1994) describes how architecture of houses can be an expression of conspicuous consumption à la Veblen (1899). There is no question that culture plays a significant role in the way a house looks. But, as Werner et al. (1985) point out, this form changes with time in a dynamic process involving culture, behavior, and economics.

Many researchers have asked the question about what aspects of a house create *satisfaction* (Christensen et al., 1992; Francescato, Weidemann, Anderson, & Chenoweth, 1979; Weidemann, Anderson, Butterfield, & Odonnell, 1981). The answer seems to be that satisfaction is determined by a mix of factors that include not only the house and its physical

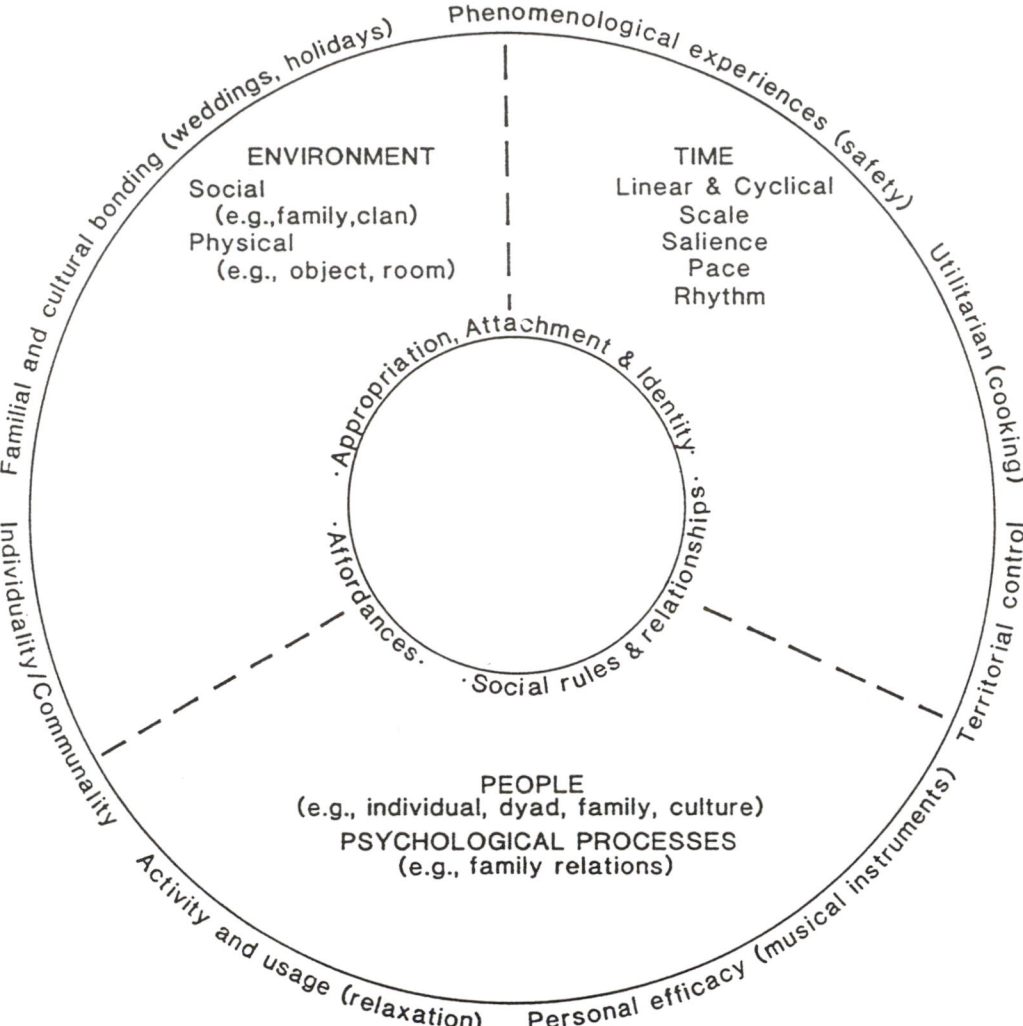

Figure 22.8. The Home as a Transactional Unity
SOURCE: Werner et al. (1985, p. 2). Used with permission.

qualities but also the surrounding neighborhood and the social quality of
the surround. For example, Francescato et al. (1979) found that satisfaction depended on three elements: the design, the management practices
(in public housing), and the surrounding social aspects. Weidemann et al.
(1982) distributed a massive questionnaire of 236 questions and derived
several factors. The most important was a general factor that contained

the attractiveness of the home, the suitability of recreational facilities, and police response (also in public housing).

Safety plays a major role when homes are in large cities. Williamson (1981) found that satisfaction was conditioned by physical aspects but also by the ability to form social networks.

Housing satisfaction clearly has both design (physical) and social components. Whether the social component contains safety concerns depends on the location. As a further illustration of this, Churchman and Ginsberg (1984) found Israelis did not have negative images of high-rise housing as seen in most of the other studies done because Israelis live in a relatively safe environment and do not fear crime.[1]

Inside the House

Weisner and Weibel (1981) studied 200 California families using 38 variables. They found four factors to describe the inner appearance of the houses: (a) disorder/functional complexity (the funky factor), (b) decorative complexity (how filled the place looked), (c) warm/children oriented, and (d) books. Much of what they found was woven into the lifestyles of the families but it was clear that the "lived in" look and the funky factor made a better environment for children.

Pennartz (1986) tried a more phenomenological approach. It must be remembered that phenomenology regards each person's experience as unique and not replicable. Pennartz asked: Where in the house is it most pleasant? And when is it most pleasant? The answers seemed to be centered on five themes. The first was a children-come-home-from-school sort of theme where everybody collects to greet and exchange the news of the day. The second theme was also of togetherness but more when everyone is at home but doing separate things. The third theme was doing things alone when no one else was home, and the fourth theme was Sunday, which had its own list of activities. The final theme is the only negative one and it occurs when a person is alone with nothing to do. Pennartz finds a relationship between the physical arrangements because they will either facilitate or hamper the people in the house being together. Size and number of rooms and the relationship among rooms are critical aspects.

Sandy Smith (1994) analyzed the home episodes of her 21 subjects and found four clusters (see Table 22.1). These were recreation, chores, social interaction, and housework.

Table 22.1 Clusters of Home Episodes

Recreation
R1	Reading or writing for pleasure
R2	Thinking, relaxing, [meditating], praying, etc.
R3	Listening to radio or music
R4	Watching television
R5	Speaking on the telephone
R6	Drinking tea/coffee/juice/beer/wine
R7	Studying or working at home
R8	Sleeping or resting

Social Interaction
S1	Being intimate with partner
S2	Talking with partner
S3	Spending time with children, e.g., helping with homework
S4	Eating a meal with partner
S5	Entertaining or being with friends
S6	Caring for child(ren); washing, bathing, dressing, feeding, putting to bed

Chores
C1	Eating a meal alone
C2	Spending time with pets, e.g., feeding, grooming, playing with them
C3	General personal hygiene, e.g., showering, bathing, cleaning teeth, using toilet, etc.
C4	Dressing, undressing, applying make-up
C5	Gardening, watering, mowing lawn

Housework
H1	Ironing, folding clothes
H2	Laundry: washing, hanging out clothes
H3	Tidying house, e.g., making bed, putting things away
H4	Cleaning house; dusting, polishing, vacuuming, taking out garbage
H4	Clearing, washing or drying dishes
H5	Preparing food, cooking meals

SOURCE: Smith (1994). Used by permission from Academic Press.

Bechtel (1989) reported behavior in a house selected from each of three countries—the United States (Alaska), Iran, and Saudi Arabia—and concluded that the most dominant behavior was recreation (see Table 22.2). The conclusion from these studies, however, is not easy to implement. Recreation is the activity the house is least designed to accommodate.

Housing in most cultures has been so *shelter* oriented that little consideration is given to providing space for recreation. A modest concession is the recent addition of the den. In U.S. homes, the practical solution to this problem is for the TV set to take over the living room with furniture rearranged to accommodate TV viewing.

Table 22.2 Comparison of Recreation in Homes of Three Countries

Sites	Dominant Recreational Pattern	Design Consequences
Alaska		
Fort Wainwright	TV, children's play	increase play space
FAA sites	TV, children's play	increase play space
Iran	TV, visiting	expand kitchen
Saudi Arabia	cooking, entertaining, reading	expand kitchen and dining room, provide quiet space

SOURCE: Bechtel (1989).
NOTE: Major conclusion: increase recreational space across all sites

International Perspective

The United States and most industrialized countries of Europe and Asia take for granted the presence of single-family dwellings as the ideal for families. This remains so for the United States even though the intact family with mother and father living at home and mother *not* working is now the minority.

The rest of the world has to be satisfied with self-built houses (Dwyer, 1975; United Nations, 1992). These range from the cane mat houses in the barriadas of Peru to the brick gecekondu of Turkey (see Chapter 15, "The City"). It must be recognized that these self-help housing examples are *not* a solution to the worldwide housing problem.

It is now commonly accepted that most government housing programs worldwide have been failures. None is more graphic than the Peruvian government's effort to supply housing to people living in its barriadas. The reasons for the failures are as many as the countries involved. In Peru (see Figure 22.9), it was because the people were so poor they could not afford the electricity and water provided for each of the housing lots. In Iran, it was because the housing was located too far from the city where the occupants worked. In India, it was largely because the population was simply too great for the problems. This is often a common denominator. In many cases where housing is provided for one family by a government, other families move in to help pay the rent, and thus the crowding is perpetuated. Lang (1989) also points out that much of the housing provided ignores the basic principles of urban design and does not provide an urban infrastructure of parks and other public places.

Figure 22.9.   Empty Developed Land Intended for Housing in Peru

The unfortunate result is that in so many of the large cities of the world such as Mexico City, São Paulo, Calcutta, Hong Kong, Cairo, and many others, the self-built house of squatter settlements will remain the chief form of housing for some time to come. Yet, despite van Vliet's (1987) admonition against sweeping generalizations about world housing, it seems clear that the poor people of the world have taken the housing problem into their own hands because the governments do not have the resources. Further, Mangin's (1973) generalization more than 20 years ago—that the squatter settlements are continuously improved by their owners until, after 15 or more years, they cannot be distinguished from middle-class housing—is also true. An outstanding example is Nezahual-coyotl in Mexico City, the largest squatter settlement on Earth, which is now almost indistinguishable from nonsquatter parts of the city.

Technological Perspective

It was the architect Le Corbusier who said the house is a "machine for the living." No one has carried that principle to the extreme that R. Buckminster Fuller did with his *dymaxion house*. The original patent for the dymaxion house was taken out in 1927. It was literally a machine for living. The concept appeared to be something like a tree house because it was supported by a central mast that contained the heating, lighting, and plumbing (Marks & Fuller, 1973). Most of the dymaxion house is manufactured elsewhere and simply connected on site. Cars are parked under the house. Obviously, it did not catch on.

Czaja's (1988) *smart house* looks very much like any ordinary house except it has more sophisticated appliances that are programmed for greater safety and convenience.

Toffler's (1980) *electronic cottage* has already been realized in many locations. Ahrentzen (1990) describes the boundary problems entailed in working at home: A truly modern complication of technology occurs when children at home want to use the computer for their games. Also, a result of working at home not yet being an accepted part of daily life is that others often do not take seriously the work done at home. As a whole, Ahrentzen found there were not as many conflicts over work at home as might be expected but this may have been because her average subject had already been working at home about 4 years and may have long ago worked out these conflicts.

Underground Housing

One of the most efficient ways to save energy is to place the house underground. Most of the research on underground housing took place in the 1970s under the Carter administration when it was investigated as an energy-saving solution (Moreland, 1981). The Earth serves as an insulator from temperature extremes and can act to modify both hot and cold climates. Some countries, such as China, Tunisia, and Turkey (Kostof, 1972), have areas where numbers of people have been living in underground housing for centuries. According to Wells (1977), the main psychological problem with adjusting to underground living is the unusually quiet background. On a more physical basis, the placement of the auto-

Box 22.2

Dymaxion House

PLAN - ISOMETRIC - AND - ELEVATION OF A MINIMUM DYMAXION HOME

SOURCE: Marks and Fuller (1973, p. 88); courtesy Buckminster Fuller Institute, Santa Barbara.

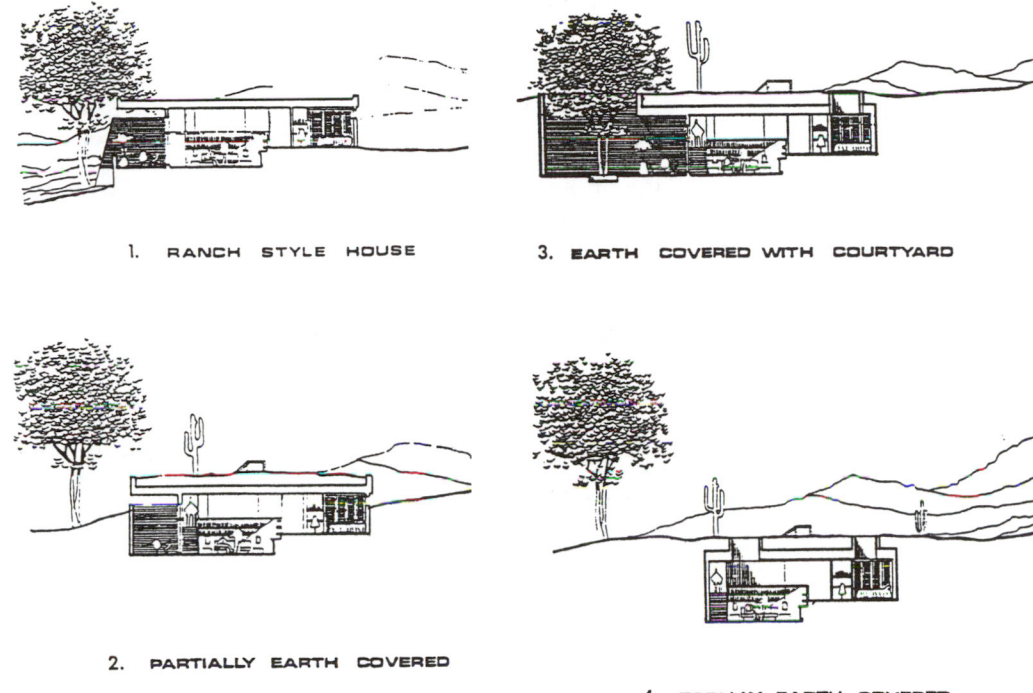

Figure 22.10. Earth-Sheltered Housing Types

mobile is a more serious problem because of the tendency of heavier gases such as carbon dioxide to stay in underground places.

Baggs (1977) describes Coober Pedy, an Australian opal mining town that has had underground housing since the 1930s. The complete community is underground, including offices, swimming pools, and houses. An interesting feature of living underground described by Baggs is that, because the air is generally cooler, dust is blown *away* from the dwelling, resulting in a more dust-free environment than might be expected.

Bechtel (1981; see Figure 22.10) shows several kinds of underground dwellings contrasted to a ranch house: partially earth covered, earth covered with courtyard, and totally earth covered. Although most people in the Yuma sample preferred the ranch house to the other types, a significant minority picked the partially earth covered. The completely underground model, however, is most efficient.

It was interesting to note that when Baggs asked residents of Coober Pedy to choose from the same types of houses, the residents rejected the ranch house as being "too hot" because it would need too much air-conditioning. The differing results can be seen from the point of view of what kind of house the residents are most used to living in.

There exists a negative image of underground housing explored by Bligh (in Gorman, 1976), who questioned 80 persons working in a Sears store. The respondents overwhelmingly rejected the idea of working underground. When it was pointed out to 30 of these workers that they *already were* working underground, they promptly changed their minds. Sommer (1974) also reported that people who work underground reported feeling like "moles."

By the 1980s, there were about 600 to 800 underground buildings of all types in the United States but these were mostly *not* houses.

Mobile Homes

According to the U.S. census of 1990, there were 7,399,837 mobile home dwelling units in the United States. South Carolina had the largest percentage of mobile homes (16.9%) while Hawaii had the smallest (.1%). Similar to underground housing, the use of mobile homes was promoted by research and building programs in the 1970s. In 1969, George Romney, secretary of the Department of Housing and Urban Development (HUD), began Operation Breakthrough to produce industrialized housing. The unfortunate outcome of this program was that the local laws and ordinances in the counties, states, and cities were so tangled and entrenched that it was impossible to get through them to produce affordable housing. To make housing units that were cheap enough, they had to be uniform for all locations.

Wallis (1991) describes the history of mobile homes in stages beginning with the Depression, where they served as shelter for itinerant workers, as temporary housing during World War II, then as mobile housing, and finally as affordable detached housing. He sees the use of mobile homes declining but still the only significant alternative to the "stick-built" house.

Of course, there has always been a question of whether a mobile home is truly a "home," and many laws and ordinances have been passed to restrict its use. It is the accumulation of these laws that defeated the

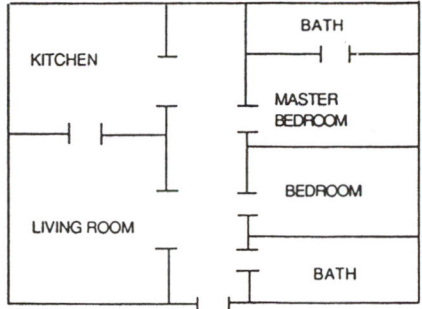

Figure 22.11. Architectural Depth Schema
SOURCE: Evans et al. (1996). Copyright © 1996 by the American Psychological Association. Reprinted with permission.

attempt to make mass-produced mobile homes in Operation Breakthrough. Thus the ideology of a "proper home" has held sway against this type of technological solution to the housing problem.

House Design and Crowding

Evans, Lepore, and Schroder (1996) compared residents of houses that have architectural "depth" with those living in houses that have less depth. They found that the deeper houses provided environments that had somehow fostered less psychological distress and less social withdrawal. Figure 22.11 shows the schema for depth calculation. The master bedroom has a depth of two because one has to go through two spaces to reach it, the doorway and the hallway. The bath of the master bedroom would have a depth of three because there is the additional space of the master bedroom to go through. Evans et al. feel it is the social withdrawal that this depth permits that accounts for the relief from crowding. In other words, the architectural depth of a house can act as a mediator to crowding.

The Future

Franck and Ahrentzen (1989) describe households of the future. These include collective housing, communal housing, single-parent households,

single-room hotels, and other forms of experimental and successful housing innovations throughout the world. The main thesis is that, with the changing structure of the family, the design of housing must be changed to suit the current needs. Housing design in the past has relied on the assumption that the world was made up of intact, nuclear families while the increasing numbers of single-parent families and single individuals have not been accommodated. The future of housing seems to evolve around these new demands.

Conclusions

Primogeniture was a solution to an environmental problem: how to keep the land intact from generation to generation. The result was the superior status that men have claimed over women throughout all cultures. This ideology was implanted in religion, law, and custom and remains pretty much in force throughout the world today. The house remains as the physical remnant and, ironically, in Western civilization, the house is seen as the place where women are most dominant.

Housing, like work, children's environments, and environments for the elderly is evolving to meet changing population needs. Traditional ideologies are closely tied to what constitutes a proper place for a family home, and these ideologies are being tested by social developments. New forms are being experimented with and technology is helping to change the interior arrangements of housing design. Nevertheless, most of the world struggles with housing for the poor and governments have been unable to meet the demand. In the face of this, the poor of the world have taken matters into their own hands and are building houses on their own. The contrast between housing for the rich and the makeshift housing for the poor is increasing.

Note

1. I remembered this statement when Arza Churchman was telling me about the scud missiles landing near her neighborhood during the Persian Gulf War. Her granddaughter slept through the episode wearing a gas mask.

GOALS

Definitions and Concepts

House versus home

Origin of the Western house

House as temple

Courtyard house

Medieval house

Inward- versus outward-looking
    houses

Home as refuge

Shelter orientation

House as expression of self

Electronic cottage

Self-built house

Primogeniture

Settlement identity

Transactional theory

Housing satisfaction

Architectural depth

Important Studies

Watkins (1990)

Coulanges (1864/1955)

Francescato et al. (1979)

Hayward (1975)

Mumford (1961)

Fried (1963)

Mangin (1973)

Marks and Fuller (1973)

Marcus (1974)

Wallis (1991)

Franck and Ahrentzen (1989)

QUESTIONS

1. How is ideology tied in with the origin of the house?

2. What problem was primogeniture designed to solve?

3. What was the religious reason for the low status of women?

4. What basic change occurred in the transition from medieval to industrial housing?

5. What basic theoretical problem does transactional theory solve?

6. What is the evolution of squatter settlements?

7. What are the elements of housing satisfaction?

8. What basic needs are not met by housing design, and why?

9. How would the electronic cottage help environmental problems?

10. What forms is housing of the future likely to take?

23

Disasters

Historical Perspective

By any definition, the greatest disaster in human history was the Black Death caused by the plague in the fourteenth and fifteenth centuries. It cost upward of 25 million lives, which was about one quarter of the entire population of Europe at that time.

Although the first worldwide disaster relief effort was begun in October 1914,[1] Sutlive (1986) claims that the first modern study of disasters was not until Prince (1920). Looking at where disasters have taken place recently (Sutlive, 1986), the largest toll from 1970 to 1980 seems to have been in Central America and the Caribbean from hurricanes (Table 23.1).

Definition

Defining a disaster is not as easy as it may at first seem. A hurricane at sea is not a disaster until it comes in contact with humans and causes damage. A disaster requires some natural or human agent affecting a human population and/or property. Fritz (1961) gives a more formal definition:

Table 23.1 Deaths From Disasters 1970-1980

	Deaths per Million
North America	31.5
Europe	38.57
Central America/Caribbean	918.16
South America	341.33
Asia	376.28
Africa (excluding drought)	117.05
Australia/Oceania	323.5

SOURCE: Sutlive (1986). Reprinted by permission.

Disasters are: Events observable in time and space, in which societies or their larger subunits (e.g., communities, regions) incur physical damages and losses and/or disruption of their routine functioning. Both the causes and consequences of these events are related to the social structures and processes of societies and their subunits. (p. 655)

Note that the social elements of society are emphasized as being inextricably bound to the event. Both Fritz (1961) and Kreps (1984) stress that disasters are events that have impacts on social units that respond to the impacts; each of these can be studied.

Schlager (1994) and others make the distinction between *natural* disasters and human-made or *technological* disasters. So far, natural disasters outrank technological ones in terms of damage and loss of human life, but as Baum (1993) points out, the technological disasters are increasing in scope.

Theoretical Perspective

Disasters have been measured in many ways: property damage, loss of life, and, more recently, psychiatric impairment. White and Haas (1975) did a review of disaster research in 1975 and concluded that up to that point, the research had been concentrated on technological solutions instead of focusing on the social, economic, and political factors that would also yield useful findings. They also pointed out that the United States was increasingly vulnerable to natural disasters because of increasing urbanization in locations where natural disasters occur such as floods, hurricanes, and earthquakes. They noted the lack of any theoretical perspective in the research.

Subsequent reviews have not indicated a great deal of improvement in theoretical points of view (Kreps, 1984; Quarantelli & Dynes, 1977). The sociologists still tended to use disasters as a kind of test of the existing social structure and felt they could learn from the way how the social structure responded.

In 1983, Drabek and Key applied the *therapeutic community* concept, proposed by Fritz (1961) and Barton (1970), in their study of the Topeka tornado in 1966. The therapeutic community is brought into being by the disaster itself. It did not exist prior to the event. After the disaster, people are brought together in response to the event who would have had no reason for contacting one another before. Social bonds are created through these contacts and some relationships enhanced that were already in existence. The establishment of these social bonds is not random but a direct response to the disaster. These bonds of friendship can be found with persons who come to the disaster site as part of a formal organization such as the Red Cross or some local rescue unit, or they can be informal through actions of neighbors or persons who volunteer locally. Many of these bonds will continue after the event.

Other researchers such as Fairchild and White (1981) and Tierney and Baisden (1979) have also used the therapeutic community concept. But a problem with the concept became evident when it was used with disasters of severe magnitude such as the Buffalo Creek dam break (Erikson, 1976), where virtually every family had injury or death. In these cases, the social fabric is destroyed and the community is incapable of any response. In other words, there have to be enough people left alive and uninjured to be able to respond for the therapeutic community to operate. The Buffalo Creek dam flood was unusual, however, and the concept of a therapeutic community still holds for most locations where disasters occur.

Kreps (1984) follows Fritz (1961) in suggesting four core elements of disasters: (a) They are *events* that can be studied in themselves. (b) They have *impacts* in various ways. (c) There are *social units* involved. (d) There are *responses* of various kinds and at various levels. Kreps goes on to classify 24 types of disasters with more than 40 forms of association. All of these can be linked with human ecology, complex organizations, collective behavior, environmental sociology, and environmental psychology.

Table 23.2 First Actions Taken in a Fire

Behavior category	Percentage of participants undertaking this as their first action
1. Take some firefighting action	15
2. Contact fire brigade	13
3. Investigate fire	12
4. Warn others	11
5. Do something to minimize danger	10
6. Evacuate oneself from building	9.5
7. Evacuate others from building	7

SOURCE: Cantor (1980, table 6.1).
NOTE: These seven classes of action describe almost 80 per cent of the first actions taken.

Disaster Prevention

Much of the reason for studying disasters is to learn how better to prepare for them so as to minimize losses in life and property damage. One axiom, introduced by Quarantelli (1954), seems to hold for *immediate* danger: When people are confronted by imminent danger, they react rationally and in an adaptive fashion. Studies by Perry, Lindell, and Green (1981) and Leik, Leik, Ekker, and Gifford (1982) seem to confirm this proposition that most people do the right thing when threatened with immediate disaster.

But is this always true? Canter (1980) and his colleagues find that there is often panic and irrational behavior during fires. Wood (1980) summarizes behavior from 952 fires. He found that 95% of the people behave in what can be considered an appropriate fashion and only 5% did something that could "increase the risk." Table 23.2 summarizes 80% of the behavior.

Sime (1980) examines the concept of panic in fires and concludes that it is overemphasized and often confused with flight behavior, which is not panic at all. Panic has very limited usefulness in designing or planning for fires. In a later test of a panic model, Simes (1983) found people choose a more affiliative model in escape behavior. In short, they try to be with family or friends when getting out in a hurry.

So it seems, in most disaster situations, people do behave in the appropriate manner. When it comes to long-term preparation, however, another kind of psychology takes over. Most people *don't* do the right thing.

Studies by Kunreuther, Ginsberg, Miller, Sagi, and Slovic (1978), Burby and French (1980), Mader, Spangle, and Blair (1980), Turner et al. (1980), and Rossi, Wright, and Weber-Burdin (1982) show that preparation is low on the priority list of politicians or anyone else not directly connected with disaster prevention. Universally, disaster managers' recommendations are met with inaction or even outright opposition from local politicians when they suggest spending money for disaster preparation or prevention. Kreps (1984) concludes that this is not because people deny or do not fear disasters, but "they are necessarily preoccupied with the immediate problems and concerns of daily living" (p. 321). This is an excellent example of being unable to plan to prevent future disaster because of preoccupation with current concerns (see Chapter 2).

A classic study of disaster prevention was the work of Sims and Bauman (1972). They studied the prevention behavior of samples from the northern and southern regions of the United States. The finding was that more people were killed by tornadoes in the South because of their fatalistic attitude. Why run into a shelter if your end is already predestined? People of the North were more practical minded and took precautions.

Psychological Impairment

Until recently (Kreps, 1984), it was commonly accepted that disasters produce, at best, only temporary psychological impairment. That picture has changed with the study by Rubonis and Bickman (1991) that used a meta-analysis of 52 disaster studies in which psychological impairment was quantitatively measured. The results show an overall increase of 17% compared with surrounding populations. But the effects are not uniform. Women are more likely to be victims than men and they tend to suffer from depression and anxiety. There is further confirmation that the true impact of a disaster should be measured in terms of human lives rather than any other measure. The effect of psychological impairment was directly related to the magnitude of loss of life. Obviously, this is influenced by grieving.

Also important is the fact that the way the psychological impairment is measured can influence the severity. Retrospective measures show higher disaster-psychopathology relationships than standardized measures. This is an important finding because it supports the use of standardized measures of psychological impairment (Dohrenwend, 1975). Questionnaires also seemed to result in higher effects than interviews. As in all disaster studies, the longer the time after the event, the less was the effect of psychological impairment.

Finally, natural disasters were more harmful than technological ones. This may only be because of magnitude but it is also easier to *blame* someone for technological disasters.

Rubonis and Bickman suggest that psychological counseling be provided for future disasters (see Addison, 1992) with special concern for grieving.

Chernobyl

The world's worst nuclear disaster occurred on April 26, 1986, when two explosions blew out unit four of the Chernobyl nuclear plant located 70 miles north of Kiev, the capital of the Ukraine. Only two people were killed immediately, but within 2 weeks, 31 workers exposed to radiation also died, and radioactive fallout equal to 10 times that of the Hiroshima bomb was released over Europe.

The reactor was an RBMK type, which was not used in any other country. It was deliberately chosen by the former Soviet Union because it produced nuclear power at the same time that it produced plutonium for nuclear weapons (Schlager, 1994). At first, Soviet officials tended to blame the operators but later they conceded some design changes were needed. Unfortunately, these were design changes already incorporated in the rest of the world so nothing new was learned.

At first about 135,000, and later another 2,000,000, local people were evacuated from the surrounding area near Chernobyl, but some were taken to places more contaminated than the places they fled and had to be moved again.

Fallout was so extensive that Lapland reindeer herders in Norway were told they could not eat their reindeer. A Canadian customs official refused vegetables from Italy contaminated by iodine 31.

But perhaps most significant was Chernobyl's disastrous effects on attitudes toward nuclear power in the world. Renn (1990) summarized the studies done on the Chernobyl disaster and noted that it was a watershed in attitude change (Figure 23.1).

Increase of opponents in %

The changes of public opinion before, directly after, and one year after the Chernobyl accident in selected countries. ▨ = 1987; ■ = after; □ = before.

Figure 23.1. Public Opinion After Chernobyl
SOURCE: Original data from various authors; used by permission from Academic Press.

In their review of Chernobyl studies, Earle and Cvetkovich (1990) raise the issue of *defensive avoidance*. They maintain that too many researchers accept this mode of denial without considering that there might be subjective reasons for people "just not being interested" in matters like Chernobyl. Readers of this volume may notice a similarity between defensive avoidance and Kreps's (1984) finding with respect to people being too interested in daily affairs to take a long-term view.

Conclusion

Disaster studies are a classic example of the mobilization-minimization hypothesis of Taylor (1991). People confronted with a negative event manage to mobilize and behave reasonably well. But in terms of preparation to prevent future disasters or to minimize their effects, most people are either defensively avoiding or preoccupied with current events. This is, of course, typical of the larger picture of behavior toward all environmental disasters.

Note

1. It was called the Commission for Relief in Belgium and was headed by Herbert Hoover. In over 5 years of existence, it moved 28 million tons of supplies to war-torn Europe at the then current cost of $3.9 million, with the incredibly low overhead rate of .43%. Needless to say, the fame from this effort propelled Hoover into the presidency of the United States.

GOALS

Definitions and Concepts

Disasters

Natural disasters

Technological disasters

Mobilization-minimization
   hypothesis

Blame factor

Panic

Defensive avoidance

Therapeutic community

Core elements of disasters

Immediate versus long-term
   threat

Use of standardized measures of
   psychological impairment

Important Studies

Prince (1920)

Fritz (1961)

Wood (1980)

Kreps (1984)

Rubonis and Bickman (1991)

Renn (1990)

Taylor (1991)

Sims and Bauman (1972)

QUESTIONS

1. Why were there more deaths in the Central American/Caribbean area than any other place in the world due to disasters?

2. What do sociologists study in disaster research?

3. What is the most significant way to measure disaster impact?

4. What is the rate of psychological impairment in disasters?

5. What limits the therapeutic community concept?

6. Did this concept operate in the Oklahoma City bombing?

7. Do most people react well in disasters?

8. Why is panic a limited concept?

9. What is the essential difference in response to immediate disasters versus long-term preparation and prevention?

10. What is the concept of defensive avoidance?

Part IV

Conclusions

24

Theories in
Environment and Behavior

Definition

What is a theory? A good definition might be that a theory is an *understanding* of some phenomenon: why it happens, what causes it, and what limits it. But for a long time, scientific theories were thought to be *mathematical predictions*, that is, an ability to predict when a phenomenon will occur. The preciseness of the prediction was a measure of the "goodness" of the theory.

Modern consensus, however, demands a little more. A good theory should be one that (a) predicts, (b) summarizes, (c) provides understanding, and (d) is heuristic. The last word demands some understanding itself. *Heuristic* means "tending to provoke discovery." E&B theories presented in this book are listed in Table 24.1.

One of the earliest theories proposed in E&B was a concept that fits under the label *environmental determinism*. This concept holds that all human behavior is caused by the environment. B. F. Skinner, with his version of *behaviorism* (Chapter 2), stands out as one proponent of this concept, asserting that all human behavior is "shaped" by the environment. Lacey (1979) asserts that "Skinner does not deny that there are

Table 24.1 Theories by Chapter

Chapter	Theories
2	sociobiology, RRR, evolutionary psychology, ethnocentrism, mobilization-minization, control, transactional view, harm avoidance, refuge
3	ecological psychology, proxemics, personal space
4	belief systems, sociopetal-sociofugal, HEP-NEP, Gray's model, Fishbein-Ajzen model, GAIA, tragedy of the commons, social traps
5	ecological perception, adaptation level, attribution
6	cognitive maps, wayfinding
7	personal space, expectancy theory, reciprocity
8	defensible space, personalization, object identity
9	crowding
10	ecological psychology
11	stress, GAS, life events, ambient stressors, type A, hardiness
12	behaviorism
13	human factors
14	POE, PDR
15	overload hypothesis, male-dominant culture
16	cul de sac design, hard architecture, Geel model
17	compensation, funneling, situation awareness, Taylorism, Deming's method
18	biophilia hypothesis, flow model
19	selection factor
20	participation in learning, divorce
21	Hayflick's limit, disposable soma, mindfulness, successful aging, proactivity
22	primogeniture, architectural depth, inward versus outward
23	therapeutic community, defensive avoidance, blame factor

inner events. Rather he maintains they are fully functions of external forces" (p. 6).

But Skinner was not the only proponent of environmental determinism. Richard Neutra, a "world-class" architect, gave an address at the University of Kansas in 1965 in which he said with confidence that he could build a house in such a way that he could guarantee that any couple who lived in the house would divorce within a month. Perhaps this is more *architectural determinism* than just environmental, but it expressed the belief of some architects that their designs control human behavior. This is one of the sources of resistance to the use of social science in architectural design (see Chapter 3).

Another, what might at first seem an obvious, candidate under this concept is ecological psychology. Barker (1968) sees behavior and environment so closely linked that his work is often labeled deterministic. However, his work is more accurately classified in terms of a *transactional view* because behavior and environment are seen as interacting. The environment often is as much changed by the behavior as is the behavior by the environment.

An area that might seem outside the theoretical realm is that of POE and PDR. These, after all, are just evaluations of environments and are essentially atheoretical. The problem with that view is that the purpose of the use of both POEs and PDR is to introduce a system of quality control not unlike that envisioned by W. Edwards Deming. Thus POE and PDR are actually part of a systematic approach that includes not only work and architectural environments but also schools, hospitals, and other institutions. In fact, this is also essentially a transactional viewpoint because the chief goal is to make the institution or organization truly responsive to the environment.

And this leads to the theories about beliefs, attitudes, and values regarding the environment. What has been found is that belief systems are largely inadequate for dealing with the environment or even most human situations. The goal here as well is to open the system up to more environmental inputs.

So now we arrive at the point where *all* environmental theories are involved in creating greater and more adequate responses to environmental stimuli. Much of what has been talked about in this book is opening up the social cushion with its full-blown complexity of beliefs and sociocultural groups to more adequate environmental message receipt.

The theories listed in Table 24.1 can be classified into four fundamental points of view: (a) the "true" E&B theories, which emphasize the environment-behavior connection as inseparable; (b) the person-in-the-environment theories, which emphasize the individual organism's responses as essentially continuing across any environmental context; (c) the social psychological theories, which concentrate on the social context of the organism; and (d) the environment-on-the-person theories, which emphasize what the environment does to any person. See Table 24.2.

Some of these theories that are outside the usual domain of E&B research and others that are more familiar bear closer examination to see how they relate.

Table 24.2 Four Groups of Theories

E&B	Person-in-Environment	Social-Psychological	Environment-on-Person
ecological	personal space	crowding	evolution
transactional	proxemics	beliefs	GAIA
sociofugal	control	attribution	sociobiology
stress	privacy	mobilization-minimization	biophilia
Deming	personalization	HEP-NEP	overload
POE-PDR	flow	commons	defensible space
Gibson	adaptation level	social traps	behaviorism
proactivity	wayfinding	expectancy	harm avoidance
	object identity	reciprocity	successful aging
	Taylorism	compensation	cul-de-sac
	situation awareness	divorce	hard architecture
	human factors	social cushion	Hayflick
	mindfulness	ethnocentrism	disposable soma
	selection	attitudes	
	hardiness	culture	
		therapeutic community	
		primogenture	
		defensive avoidance	
		blame	

GAIA

First proposed by James E. Lovelock in his 1979 book, *GAIA: A New Look at Life on Earth*, the central proposition in this theory is that the atmosphere is maintained at a remarkably constant level by a combination of bacteria, plants, and animals that act together like a living organism (GAIA) to keep the gas levels stable. This process began in Precambrian times when aerobic and anaerobic bacteria had a struggle for dominance and the aerobic bacteria won. Since that time, the atmosphere has been maintained at pretty close to the same level of approximately 20% oxygen and 80% nitrogen. Even slight variations would be disastrous to various forms of life. And, of course, there were such fluctuations, but the system was always able to correct itself and restore the balance even though species may have been wiped out.

A serious problem with this theory is that it was interpreted as though the Earth were actually a purposeful organism, GAIA, and many religious people deluged Lovelock with letters, testimonials, and admonitions, treating him as a priest of a new religion. Lovelock acknowledges his own responsibility for this by admitting that his earlier writing tended to be more "poetic than scientific." Lovelock's position, however, is "that the nonliving and living represent a self-regulating system that keeps itself in a constant state" (Kerr, 1988a, p. 393). This tamer version is not without its supporters (Schneider & Boston, 1991).

The GAIA hypothesis is most related to concerns about preserving the ozone layer, climatological warming, and atmospheric pollution because it tries to show the natural limits of preserving the balance and how our interference interrupts that process (see Chapter 1).

Sociobiology

E. O. Wilson's *Sociobiology* (Wilson, 1975) sets forth one of the most radical propositions about human behavior in the twentieth century. Briefly, the central concept is that it is the *genes* that determine behavior. The brain and body are simply envelopes to hold the genes for propagation. Human motivation is directed entirely at propagating genes. Each person tries to maximize propagation of the genes in his or her body and will eliminate others' genes or prevent them from reproducing. This leads to a capsulizing of the idea as the "selfish gene" (Dawkins, 1976).

The sociobiologists have some clever evidence to support their central hypothesis. A study of family killings in Canada, for example, shows that stepchildren are much more likely to be killed than genetic children, by 60-70 times. In England and Wales, it is only 15-20 times as great, but still highly significant. Wilson concludes, "Living with a stepparent is the single most powerful risk factor for child abuse that has yet been identified" (Gibbons, 1993, p. 987). Thus the main cause of child abuse is having the wrong genes.

And why do we go to war? One reason, according to sociobiologists, is for men to acquire women with whom they can propagate their genes (Gibbons, 1993)!

One serious problem the sociobiologists have is to explain altruism. If the genes are truly selfish, how do we explain the soldier who throws himself on a hand grenade to save the lives of his buddies, who carry foreign genes? Or, put another way, the sociobiologists cannot explain Mother Teresa. Even Darwin described altruistic behavior in animals.

The compromise most often used is to see closely related groups as "saving" the genes in a more complex way. Thus saving two siblings is equal to saving one offspring (or four cousins, aunts, or uncles). But this still doesn't translate into altruism for complete strangers.

Biophilia

It is seldom realized that Wilson (1984) proposed the *biophilia hypothesis* on an equal plane with selfish genes. This hypothesis was described as "the innate tendency to focus on life and lifelike processes" (p. 1). Thus we feel a kinship to animals and trees and it is in our selfish interest to preserve them. This innate tendency is what enables us to heal more quickly by looking at trees as opposed to brick walls (Ulrich, 1993), and can form the basis for all kinds of behavior that may or may not be seen as altruistic. Thus we have two innate tendencies, to propagate our genes but also to preserve the habitat in which they can grow.

Biophilia, of course, goes beyond just preserving habitat to preferences for the out-of-doors, or, according to Appleton (1975), savannahs. Wilson pleads that any ethics to preserve the environment, however, must be expressed in *selfish* terms to take advantage of these innate propensities.

Overload

Milgram's (1970) simple hypothesis describing urban life (Chapter 15) explained a number of behaviors as being due to an overload of the perceptual processing system. There are so many stimuli in the urban environment that every person there must adjust by reducing the stimulus load. This is done by eliminating contacts below a certain threshold, shortening but intensifying those remaining, and creating access barriers to oneself up to a total of six consequences, including the creation of certain institutions. The idea is a very simple one. We have only a limited capacity to process information, so when we are overloaded there are only so many strategies we can use to decrease the load to a manageable level.

Understimulation

A slightly more complex theory evolved from understimulation, or not having enough stimuli to function properly. This theory tries to explain things such as cabin fever in extreme climates (Chapter 19) or possible psychological problems from extended space travel.

As Zubeck (1969) described 15 years of *sensory deprivation* research, which is another name for understimulation, it was first thought that putting people in a sensorially deprived environment would make them mentally ill. It was not recognized until later (Suedfeld, Ballard, & Murphy, 1983) that the *under*-stimulation presented was actually *monotonous* in nature.

In the first experiments begun at McGill University in the early 1950s, the established procedure was to place the experimental subjects in a large white dome so as to reduce visual background, introduce white noise to mask as much of the immediate ambient noise, and place their hands in cotton batting. About the only stimuli allowed were eating, sleeping, and going to the bathroom. These are the conditions that only later seemed to be monotonous in character. The common response to these conditions was to report hallucinations, which are manifest symptoms of mental illness. This began to be a regular finding of these studies (Zubeck, 1969).

As Suedfeld et al. (1983) point out, there were positive aspects of the original sensory deprivation experiments, but these were lost in the more sensational reports of hallucinations. Much if not all of the hallucinatory response is now thought to be due to suggestion. Orne (1982) reports how he planted a microphone under the desk of the secretary recruiting subjects for the experiments. Even though the subjects were not supposed to know how long the experiment would last, the recording of the conversations with the secretary and the subjects left no doubt that the subjects had a good idea of how long the experiment would last. A subject would make comments like, "I have an exam next Thursday." The secretary would then remark something like, "That should be no problem." The result was that subjects knew the length of time and would begin hallucinating about halfway through the experiment.

Suedfeld reported that when a flotation tank method was used and total darkness and silence became the standard environment, subjects in the *reduced environmental stimulation therapy* (REST) reported no hallucinations, a pleasant experience, and, in fact, by later experiments, a positively therapeutic benefit.

The conclusion of this was that sensory deprivation began as a method for bringing about mental illness symptoms and ended up at the opposite pole, removing symptoms. This was achieved by separating the effects of suggestion and monotonous stimulation from a true reduced environmental stimulation circumstance.

Organismic-Holistic

It is obvious that deprivation and overload are at the opposite ends of the stimulus continuum. Organismic theory is in between. The basic premise of organismic theory is the philosophy of holism, expressed by Smuts (1973): "The cells don't make the plant, the plant makes the cells." This means the organism must be seen as a holistic entity, not just the sum of any of its parts. Overload and sensory deprivation then are minitheories dealing only with extreme ranges of the organism's behavior while organismic theory sees the organism as trying to maintain a path between overload and deprivation. The organism seeks an *optimal* level of stimulation. Thus, in organismic theory, the organism would avoid sensory deprivation or overload and seek out environments that were in a more comfortable middle. But here there is a veering from the environmentally caused to the self-directed.

Sociopetal and Sociofugal

We will recall (from Chapter 3) that Humphrey Osmond (1957) first coined the terms *sociofugal* and *sociopetal* to describe two kinds of space that inhibit and encourage conversation. This was E&B's first minitheory, which is definitely related to an environmental cause of behavior. Sociofugal space, because of its large volume, high ceilings, and high lighting, tends to discourage conversation, while sociopetal space, because of its more intimate dimensions with low ceilings, close lighting, and smaller volume, encouraged conversation. Sociofugal space is typical of train, airport, and bus terminals while sociopetal space is found in homes, restaurants, and private offices. This theory served as a guide for many architects but it was Sommer (1972) who pointed out that places like airports needed both kinds of spaces because some people wanted to have intimate departure conversations while others wanted the anonymity of sociofugal space.

Theories Originating Within the Person

It was an unfortunate circumstance of history that our civilization followed the Platonic separation of mind from body. This has created a spate of theories conceived as originating from within the self, mind, soul, or whatever internal existence that is seen as relatively independent from the body and the environment (Altman & Rogoff, 1987). The astute reader will also notice that some of the theories already mentioned can also be seen as having originated from within the self. Type A and hardiness can also be viewed as *traits* of personality.

The essence of trait theory is that it is seen as a characteristic of the personality that is relatively independent of the social surroundings and/or the physical environment. An important distinction must be made here. Trait theories operate independently of situations. People are seen as essentially consistent across all situations. This opposes *situational determinism*, which sees behavior as determined by the situation and all traits as irrelevant. Trait theory sees human behavior as a result of what is brought to each situation. Situational determinism sees behavior within any situation as universal and regardless of individual differences.

Stress

Selye's (1956) discovery of what is now called stress is very much like an E&B theory. Difficulties of defining stressful events have already been discussed (see Chapter 11). Nevertheless, the fact that environments can be stressful, and thus debilitating, is accepted within these limitations, and many practical ways have been prescribed to make many environments less stressful. Having control is an important way to reduce stress

(Langer, 1983). And, as Antonovsky (1979) has pointed out, one of the ways people exercise control over their lives is by having a "coherent view" of the universe. Belief systems, with their attendant clusters of attitudes, are a central aspect of how people deal with their world.

Belief Systems

Spicer (1971) described what he called *identity systems*. These are belief systems by which a group of individuals affiliate with certain symbols and what they stand for, and achieve a high degree of internal social solidarity that may have more consistency and longer life than larger social entities such as cultures or corporations. Although Spicer discussed this more than 25 years ago, the 1990s have produced more than their share of these identity systems in the forms of Jonestown, the Branch Davidians, state militias, and neo-Nazi groups in many countries. But these are the figures that stand out from a background. All of us operate within belief systems. They are socially reinforced and, more often than not, independent of environmental influence.

Nothing brings out belief systems more than trying to convince people to conserve environmental assets. Chief of these is the HEP (Human Exceptionist Paradigm) formulated by Dunlap and Van Liere (1978b) (Chapter 4). Any person adhering to this belief system is relatively immune to entreaties to conserve because the environment exists to be used by humans. Anyone who wants to "save" it is immediately suspect. Save it for whom? Because it is to be used, and you don't want *me* to use it, then *you* must have motives to use it yourself. This and many other arguments arise spontaneously from those who hold the HEP because it is not conceivable that someone would not want to exploit the environment.

Belief systems are particularly difficult to penetrate. They are internally consistent and capable of instant explanations for any event that might disturb that belief. For example, when a Texas group was dedicating a memorial to the Branch Davidians in Waco on April 19, 1995, and they heard of the destruction of the federal building in Oklahoma City, the immediate response was that it was probably done by the federal government itself to take publicity away from their dedication of the memorial.

It is too easy to label such thinking "sick" and dismiss it as of no importance. Unfortunately, too many people in the world hold to such belief systems and too many people are being killed for the reason that they don't think in a similar vein. Such ideological thinking is everywhere. If you think you are immune, ask yourself if you believe in economic growth, paying only what it costs to extract oil and minerals, putting people in prison for crimes, or in mental hospitals for mental illness. All of these beliefs are irrational and without scientific foundation. They are part of our own cherished belief system.

The most important problem of our time is not whether we will destroy our planet but whether we can deal with people who do not believe as we do. This is the central issue of our time because if we cannot learn to deal with people of different beliefs without imposing our will by force, then the issue of the environment will not even be addressed. We will continue to be preoccupied with fighting each other, and, of course, the environment will continue to be eroded by these very struggles.

The enemy is not "us" but the belief systems within each of us. The belief system each person holds is the most important tool in keeping control of the world. Each person sees his or her belief system as the "right way" to deal with life and the environment (as if they were different). In short, the belief system gives one at least the illusion of control, and to give this up is to invite chaos. As is all too evident, too many people are willing to kill (but not necessarily die) for their beliefs. Mumford (1961) traces such thinking back to the postagricultural revolution (see Chapter 15).

Control

And this brings us to the theories of control. Langer (1983) performed her classic experiment with the elderly in a nursing home (see Chapter 21). The experimental group was given control over their environment. The control group was simply taken care of and made comfortable by staff. Those who had control lived longer and were healthier, and, by some measure, were even happier. Karasek and Theorell (1990) (see Chapter 17) found that the workers who had the least control over their environments were the least healthy.

But Rodin (1986) and Evans, Shapiro, and Lewis (1993) point out that taking control is not always efficacious. In fact, Evans et al. describe 12 conditions of control, half of which are negative in outcome. Why? Because the ability to take control (behavioral competence), the belief in ability to control (control cognition), and control motivation operate in situations such that being placed in circumstances where ability, beliefs, or motivation are exceeded produces negative results. In short, control is only beneficial when the person is capable, believes he or she is capable, and wants to take control.

None of the research known to me actually deals with those who simply don't want to take control. Some work (Chesney et al., 1981) comes close when Type B managers are placed in situations with low control and like it. But Fromm (1969) deals with the issue of Germans wanting to give up control. His book is titled *Escape From Freedom*. A question remains in many of the identity groups that exist today: How much of the motivation of followers is to relinquish control to a leader? As Fromm cautions, it can happen anywhere.

Ecological Psychology

The ecological psychology of Roger Barker (1968), like the transactional viewpoint of Altman and his colleagues (Altman & Rogoff (1987), shares a place in theories that blend or mix the environment with the organism. Humans and behavior settings are inseparable. The transactional view (see Chapter 22) goes further than the ecological in that it allows personality and other variables. Although ecological psychology does not disallow personality, most of the studies simply ignore it as a variable (see Chapter 10).

Ecological psychology is the most like an E&B model of any of the theories in E&B. The behavior setting is seen as a context from which any individual's behavior can be predicted with high accuracy despite any personality traits. The transactional view also tries to take time more into account while ecological psychology emphasizes the permanence of behavior settings, even though Allan Wicker (1979) discusses the birth and death of behavior settings.

The transactional view emphasizes meaning and understanding more than the ecological but the ecological has, at least so far, higher predictability. Ecological psychology emphasizes that a simple manipulation of the variable of size can have profound consequences on human behavior, and there is a fair listing of reasons this happens. So far, the transactional view has not had time to produce a similar magnitude in findings.

Conclusions

Good theories should have predictive value, provide understanding, summarize data well, and be heuristic. In at least some measure, all of the theories described above have fulfilled these requirements. The social psychology theories are no doubt the most heuristic by producing the most research. Ecological psychology is the least heuristic, producing the least number of research findings; yet, it has the largest number of citations (see Chapter 3). Not all E&B researchers would agree with Holahan (1982) that Barker was the first environmental psychologist. The E&B field has probably been the most interdisciplinary of all the social sciences. But the consequence of that has been to bring in so many diverse theories. Most of these, such as expectancy, attribution, reciprocity, overload, and control, are actually theories of social psychology. It is as though many of the theories of the disciplines have converged on E&B, not adapted to it or helped synthesize it. Each has brought important insights, valuable to whatever side of the person/environment equation they were on. But in the end, we must be dissatisfied because there is no coherent view, no unified field theory. Attempts have been made through the transactional view to synthesize as many of the theories as was possible. But perhaps the subject (or subjects) is actually too diverse to be easily encompassed by any theory at this time. In addition, the way the social sciences are institutionalized in universities does not actually permit the formation of new departments and more interdisciplinary programs. The retrenchment goes on and may grow worse (see Chapter 3). This means that research will be more a captive of the disciplines than ever before and faculty members who want tenure had better keep within the fold.

But the problems of the environment continue unabated. No matter how the social cushion may try to protect us from reality, it has a way of intruding. The question is this: At what point will that intrusion become so insistent that even the true believers cannot ignore it. Will it be too late? This is not a question that will be settled by theory.

GOALS

Definitions and Concepts

Theory

Overload

Architectural determinism

Heuristic

Biophilia hypothesis

Trait theory

Belief systems

HEP

GAIA hypothesis

Environmental determinism

Sociobiology

Situational determinism

Pleasure dimension

Identity systems

Understimulation

REST

Important Studies

Milgram (1970)

Lovelock (1979)

E. O. Wilson (1975)

Suedfeld et al. (1983)

Dawkins (1976)

QUESTIONS

1. What theories show the most promise in explaining why it is so difficult to conserve our resources?

2. What theory comes entirely from the physical environment?

3. What social science has given rise to most of the theories?

4. What three theories seem to combine naturally?

5. Why are belief systems so difficult to penetrate?

6. What forces exist to operate against uniting the academic disciplines?

7. Which theory attempts to unify concepts the most?

8. What do you think of the evidence for sociobiology?

9. What were the mistakes made in sensory deprivation research?

10. Which theory has amassed the most evidence?

25

The Third Revolution in Thinking

The will to believe is perhaps the most powerful, but certainly the most dangerous human attribute.

—John P. Grier

Historical Perspective

Two major revolutions in thinking have forced humans to radically alter their view of themselves and the universe. The first was the Copernican revolution. Nicolaus Copernicus had his major work, *On the Revolutions of Heavenly Bodies*, published in 1543 as he lay dying. It is hard for us to imagine today the upheaval caused by overthrowing the Ptolemaic view of the universe with Earth as the center. But it was not just the position of celestial bodies being argued. It was the symbol of *man* at the center of the universe that was being overthrown. This was unthinkable.

Galileo published his own work supporting the Copernican view in 1632 *(Dialogue on the Great World Systems)*. He was tried by the Inquisition as defending a heretical system of thought. Rather than risk being burned at the stake, he recanted but was under house arrest for the remainder of his life. It took hundreds of years for acceptance of the Copernican view.

The second revolution of thought was the Darwinian. Charles Darwin's publication of *Origin of Species* in 1859 marked the beginning of this second revolution. As the Copernican revolution was repulsive in its humiliating message, so the Darwinian was unbearably degrading in its message that *man* was a lowly animal. Darwin was accused of demoralizing humanity. It is very evident that many people today are unable to accept the basic message of Darwin, less than 200 years afterward.

So, with the second revolution of thought still unacceptable to a segment of our population, we are already thrust into the third revolution, which, for lack of a better term, is Dunlap and Van Liere's *New Environmental Paradigm*, or NEP. This is an equally humiliating and degrading message for it makes *man* a part of nature and subject to nature's laws rather than above them. Needless to say, many are unable to follow the implications of this message, let alone accept its central premise.

Notice that all three of these revolutions have one thing in common: They displace human beings as the center of the universe. The effect is to deprive human beings of a cherished view of themselves as the center of all things. This is also similar to other social revolutions such as civil rights, women's rights, gay rights. Each of these also dethrones dominant groups from their positions of power. But we miss the main point when we see these simply as power contests. It is important to realize that it is a *worldview* that is being overthrown, a view of how one relates to the rest of the universe and how one's identity is formed. The white male is overthrown from his view of himself as the head of a pyramid of social order.

As Ronnie Janoff-Bulman (1992) proposes in her new theory of post-traumatic stress disorder, the real trauma of life comes not from physical injury or psychological abuse but from the destruction of basic assumptions about one's position in the universe and identity. She specifically aims at the belief that the world is benevolent and meaningful and that the individual person is worthy. When these assumptions are violated, trauma occurs. Thus it is not easy to have one's assumptive worldview violated and remain intact.

Present Perspective

Perhaps now we can better understand the difficulty people have in accepting a less than dominant position in relation to the world. Let us take, for example, a hypothetical rancher in Montana (I could have said practically any other state as well). He has lived on his land all his life. He is part of the third generation to do so. The more than 100 years of living on the land has built a tradition in his family. He has raised cows for more than 40 years. He learned from his father, who learned from his father. He is master of his domain. When he gets up in the morning and walks outside, he can look to the far ranges of the mountains and feel that this land is his and that he belongs to it.

Yet everywhere he turns, there are messages to undermine this comforting view. A government agent tells him to reduce his herd because he is overgrazing the land—the *nerve* of this agent who just came from some eastern city to tell him what to do on his own land. What does this guy know about raising cattle? He got his learning from some eastern *college*.

And he has had to reduce his herd anyway. People aren't buying good beef anymore. They want the stringy, lean kind that comes from Brahmas, those damned cows from India. Some professor told people they were eating too much fat. He always ate steak with lots of fat on it. Everyone knows that's what makes meat taste good.

His daughter comes home from college and calls him a chauvinist. His wife seems to agree. Damn these women! What's happening to them? A man can't get any respect these days. Even his son shows no interest in running the ranch. He wants to live in the city!

And, worst of all, the price of land has risen so much *that he can't even afford to leave his land to his children!* The city people are moving in everywhere and driving the value of his land up. He reads in the local paper that the days of raising cattle are numbered. The world can no longer afford to cycle its food through a cow but must take the food directly to people.

Wherever he looks, he is beleaguered by change he doesn't understand or, worse, thinks he understands as a deliberate attempt to take his land. There is no area that is safe, no place to go. The only solution is to fight these incursions just as his ancestors fought the Indians and squatters and sheep men. He is angry, frustrated, and confused.

This diversion may seem too fanciful to some, but this same story with variations is the story of every human being on this planet. All of us are being threatened by the third revolution in thought. Toffler (1980) calls it *the Third Wave*. Drucker (1993) calls it *postcapitalist society*. Whatever term it may be given, it is easily recognized as a change that seems forced upon everyone by governments, movements, unrecognizable sources, or some scapegoated group such as liberals or conservatives. The fact is, it is all of these and more. As many groups react to the changes, they form countermovements to prevent change, which provoke further countermovements.

We feel much like the people of the Copernican and Darwinian revolutions. Things are falling apart. We reach out for some security, some sense of safety and order. But the pressure is unrelenting. Each day, we read of some new discovery or event that threatens to overturn some cherished belief.

But no one looks to his or her own belief system as the villain in this universal dilemma. The people of the Copernican revolution did not fault their beliefs about the place of the Earth in the heavens. They wanted to shut up Galileo. The natural reaction is to rail against the message and the messenger, to attack the source as untrustworthy, to attribute to it motives that are unacceptable. The government wants to destroy us, say the militiamen. What do you say?

The only path left is to question beliefs themselves. No one will accept the concept that all belief systems are incomplete and dated, no matter what the evidence. We, of course, have no trouble accepting the falsity of some belief other than our own, but ours seems like the true belief.

Better, then, to preach moderation in belief. After all, we accept that eating too much and drinking too much are not good practices. For the sake of those around us, we must come to accept that believing too much is perhaps an even greater problem, especially for those outside our group of believers. Let *moderation* in all beliefs be the watchword of our survival! We must learn to recognize a person drunk with belief, someone who has overindulged and lost judgment. We must publicize belief binges and orgies as they appear on television and in public places and recognize them for the excess that they are. We must come to accept that beliefs are dangerous substances and must be regulated by at least the same amount of common sense we say we try to use for other dangerous potions.

In short, the third revolution says there is nothing sacred about beliefs. They are all incomplete views of the universe. They all fall short of their own stated purposes, and they have an uncanny way of getting everybody into trouble. We can no longer afford to overindulge in this druglike luxury.

It is fortunate that science has no problem with this view because science is ever ready to overturn any theory or any hypothesis with new evidence. Science is the only contingency belief system. This can only remain true if scientists hold all propositions tentatively. And so it must be with everyone: Hold all views in moderation, tentatively, and with some suspicion that they may not be the final answer.

A Final Perspective

The facts of our environment must be the basis for whatever belief system we ascribe to. If any belief system is contrary to a test of these facts, it will be in continual conflict with what we call nature. In effect, this is how we have lived our entire history. *All* belief systems (or, at least, as we practice them) have been at least in some part in conflict with nature. This is simply because our understanding of nature keeps changing. The Ptolemaic view once was valid.

We have been able to survive because, prior to this time, there weren't enough human beings to deplete the resources of our planet. Now we are beginning to make such inroads and at such an accelerated pace that specific end points can now be calculated. The first predictions of the Club of Rome (Meadows et al., 1972) were exceeded in many areas by the time the second set of predictions was modeled (Meadows et al., 1992).

The facts are that the current population of the world cannot find sufficient resources to live at the level of the United States at this moment. This is not a future calamity. It is simply not possible for the rest of the world to live at the level of the United States *now*!

The only way an increase in population can be accommodated is to keep them in abject poverty and/or reduce the standard of living for those already here. And, because this increase is already happening, standards of living are already being reduced. It is noticed most in the United States but is happening everywhere (Durning, 1989).

Therefore, not to deal with the population issue is to begin a slow but accelerating lowering of the world's standard of living. But to deal with the population issue is to lock horns with many militant groups that are opposed to any attempt to control births. And one doesn't have to point at specific churches or movements, much more widespread are cultural imperatives throughout the world.

What Can You Do?

(1) Start with yourself. Have you stopped smoking? Have you encouraged your friends to stop as well. Do you protest others smoking in your presence?

Consider your diet. Ornish (1990) provides recipes for a low-fat diet that can reverse heart disease.

Learn to work differently. Being in a job with low decision power is a stressful situation (Karasek & Theorell, 1990) that can have life-threatening consequences. Follow Deming's (1986) concepts (Chapter 17) about participant decision making on the job.

Learn to think differently. Remember that this is not a scientific thinking society. Question the sources and facts behind everything you hear on TV or from your friends. Insist on getting further evidence. Libraries with electronic access make it easier today than ever before to get useful information.

Learn to learn differently. Follow Skinner's proven path to make learning a self-rewarding part of your life (Chapter 20). In addition, only an informed electorate can elect informed candidates.

(2) Deal with the difficult issues. We have arrived at the custom of avoiding difficult issues. But abortion, birth control, women's rights, poverty, and the environment are all so closely tied together that one cannot deal with one without coming upon the others. Remember the first ethical law of the environment (Chapter 4)? You can't do just one thing. Everything is related.

Nowhere is this more true than for the population question. People in the industrial world are so removed from the environment and protected by the social cushion that they are blind to the everyday realities of most of the people of the world, especially those in Asia, Africa, and South America.

How are these elements so closely linked together? Consider a poor family in India. The women do most of the gathering of water and wood (Chapter 11) and feed the children. But the environment must provide the water and wood, so it becomes stripped of vegetation and the watering places dry up. Consequently, the journey to water gets longer and the time it takes to gather wood gets longer also. Hence more children are needed to help in the chores. Further, they are the only insurance against starving in old age. The spiral begins and widens. As there are more children, more wood and water are needed, the journeys get longer, and so even more children are needed. The trap is fatal; millions can no longer survive and flee to the cities.

Women's position in this cycle is critical. They get less pay than a man for the same job. They literally have to spend half of their lives either being pregnant and carrying or lactating and feeding babies. At the same time, they must continue to provide wood, water, and food. Even in modern industrial societies, married women with children are the most stressed segment of our society (Chapter 11).

Basic statistics show that as employment of women for cash increases, the number of children goes down (Dasgupta, 1995). Women who have 0-5 children are 30.5% employed while women who have 7 or more are only 10.6% employed across 79 Third World countries. Thus increasing the status of women reduces the number of children.

But this does not necessarily translate into a blanket concept that increasing economic prosperity will decrease population, and therefore, this should be the best way to decrease population. Robey, Rutstein, and Morris (1993) show that the birthrates of some 30 developing countries have declined due to the use of family planning methods. With the exception of China, 38% of married women in childbearing years in developing countries now use some form of birth control. This accounts for 90% of the decrease in birthrates. Thus, even when there is no increase in economic gains for women, birth control methods can and do make a difference even in the poorest of countries.

And, yes, even abortion is part of this picture. And it is closely linked with contraception. For example, seven out of ten women who use a 95% effective contraception method would still need at least one abortion to maintain a two-child family (Jacobson, 1992). This means that introducing birth control methods can actually increase abortions because no birth control method is 100% effective. Nevertheless, generally speaking, over the population as a whole, abortions tend to decrease when birth control is introduced. Abortion still remains the most frequently used birth control method in the world (Jacobson, 1992).

Thus poverty, women's rights, abortion, population control, and the environment are inextricably bound together, and one cannot deal with environmental problems without dealing with these difficult issues.

(3) Don't look to institutions. From the evidence presented (see Chapter 16), it should be evident that our usual way of dealing with problems by creating institutions often has a way of increasing the problem. Institutionalizing the mentally ill has actually increased the problem. Putting people in jail makes them worse criminals. Not all institutions are necessarily this way, but one should be suspicious because institutions have a way of taking off with a life of their own that may have nothing to do with the reason they were created. Examine carefully the way any institution operates with "underpersoning theory" in mind (see Chapter 10). Almost all corporations,

SOURCE: David Fitzsimmons (Sept. 7, 1995), © The Arizona Star; reprinted by permission.

institutions, or organizations operate at an overstaffed level. The recent "downsizing" of most U.S. industry is a painful case in point.

A very strong part of this problem is the almost intractable belief in growth as a necessity for the health of any organization. We seem to find it inconceivable that we would belong to any organization that is not growing. Our schools must be growing. Our cities and towns must be growing. Our churches must be growing. Not to grow is to decline.

Perhaps nothing needs more of a change in our thinking than this pernicious belief. And don't be fooled by phrases like *sustainable growth*. We can have sustainable agriculture. It is easy to do with a renewable natural resource. But we cannot have sustainable growth in anything. It is a basic contradiction in terms; in fact, the phrase is an oxymoron. The question to ask is, At what point does whatever is sustainable stop growing? Never? Well, how can anything exist that will grow forever? If your state or city grows forever, at what point will it reach the boundaries of another? Does this not mean ultimate conflict? Once again, we have the shortsighted thinking of the commons, the inability to think into the future. Growth, all growth, has to end somewhere. When will we come to grips with this simple fact?

(4) Learn to get along with everyone. Don't accept negative comments, thoughts, or feelings about any ethnic or minority groups no matter how bad they may look. We cannot survive if we are consumed by strife, especially the kind of strife that sanctions ethnic cleansing, bombing public buildings, or even excluding ethnic minorities. Beware of the constant need of political leaders to join in scapegoating minorities. Remember how easily Hitler won over a whole nation by uniting them behind hatred of the Jews (Shirer, 1960).

And do not think that such blaming to gain power is a thing of the past. Consider how Jews, refugees, immigrants, welfare mothers, and hosts of other groups including environmentalists are blamed today by numerous groups and politicians in a deliberate attempt to gain power. This demon may be with us forever; we must never relax in vigilance. Whenever anybody begins blaming some group for the troubles of the world, be automatically suspicious.

(5) Fight myths and deliberate misinformation. As part of the response to the third revolution, myths and misinformation are generated. Some of these are more easily dealt with than others. An example is the myth of lost jobs (see the first box).

Another myth that is similar is that environmental regulations threaten economic health (see the second box).

Don't ever listen to anyone who says it can't be done. The example of Curitiba shows that it can (Moore, 1994). Curitiba is a city of 1.6 million people about 260 miles south of São Paulo in Brazil. The average family earns about $100 per week. It has its *favelas* just like São Paulo and Rio de Janeiro, but there is a striking difference.

1. Curitiba probably has the best bus system in the world. The cost of a ride is about 5 cents. The average wait for a bus is 5 minutes. The buses hold 270 passengers. It is one of the few public transit systems that pays

Box 25.1

Employment Blues:
Nothing to Do With Being Green

As the battle between jobs and the environment rages, at least one economist says he has reason to call a truce. Eban S. Goodstein of Skidmore College and the Economic Policy Institute in Washington, D.C., recently published his study tracking the number of jobs lost because of environmental legislation. Using U.S. Department of Labor statistics from 1987 through 1990, Goodstein found that for that period an average of only 0.1 percent of all larger-scale layoffs nationwide were the result of environmental regulations, such as the Clean Air Act—according to employees' own estimates. Changes in a company's ownership, in contrast, accounted for almost 35 times the number of jobs being terminated.

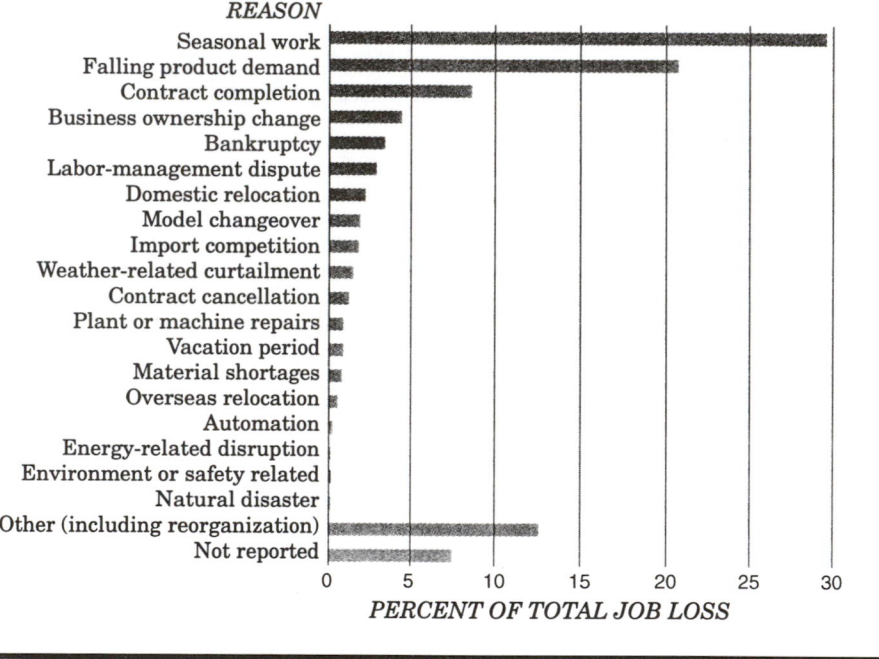

REASON

Seasonal work
Falling product demand
Contract completion
Business ownership change
Bankruptcy
Labor-management dispute
Domestic relocation
Model changeover
Import competition
Weather-related curtailment
Contract cancellation
Plant or machine repairs
Vacation period
Material shortages
Overseas relocation
Automation
Energy-related disruption
Environment or safety related
Natural disaster
Other (including reorganization)
Not reported

0   5   10   15   20   25   30

PERCENT OF TOTAL JOB LOSS

for itself. Even though Curitiba has a higher car ownership than all but three of Brazil's other cities, the equivalent of two thirds of the city's residents ride the buses because they are faster, cheaper, and more comfortable than cars. The air of Curitiba is smog-free because of the transportation system.

Box 25.2

Clean Environment
and Strong Economy Mix Well

The argument that strong environmental standards threaten economic development is a popular theme these days. But a state-by-state study completed late last year by the Institute for Southern Studies shows the argument holds little merit. The institute, a social-policy research group, found that states with the best environmental records also offer the best job opportunities and climate for long-term economic development.

"The choice is not jobs versus the environment," says Bob Hall, the institute's research director. "The states that do most to protect natural resources wind up with the strongest economies." Nine of the top 12 states in the environment category ranked in the top 12 on the strong-economy list, while nine of the 12 bottom-Nmost states in the environmental list ranked in the dozen lowest in the economic list.

The study corroborates work by other researchers. Stephen Meyer, of the Massachusetts Institute of Technology, recently analyzed 20 years of economic performance and concluded, "States with stronger environmental standards tended to have the higher growth in their gross state products, total employment, construction employment and labor productivity than states that ranked lower environmentally."

Environmental regulations may prove too costly for some companies, but only if other factors already have undermined a firm's financial stability, says Hall. "In other words," he explains, "a particular factory may be so marginal that the cost of environmental controls pushes it over the competitive edge, but the demand for safeguarding public health is not to blame. A facility this fragile is operating on borrowed time, forcing someone else, such as taxpayers, to subsidize its true costs to the environment and the public."

In conferring rank among the states, the institute used 20 economic and 20 environmental indicators, including worker health, accident statistics, health-insurance coverage, toxic-chemical discharges, fertilizer use and state spending on the environment. Copies of the report are available from the institute at P.O. Box 531, Durham, North Carolina 27702.

The nine states that ranked among the top 12 in both the environmental and economic categories:	*The nine states that ranked among the bottom 12 in both the environmental and economic categories:*
Colorado	Alabama
Hawaii	Kentucky
Maryland	Louisiana
Massachusetts	Mississippi
Minnesota	Oklahoma
New Hampshire	South Carolina
Oregon	Tennessee
Vermont	Texas
Wisconsin	West Virginia

SOURCE: The National Wildlife Federation, *National Wildlife Magazine* (June-July 1995, p. 5); reprinted by permission.

2. Trees and green space are increasing because the government made it a crime to cut down a tree. When any tree is removed, two trees must be planted. In 1965, there were 5 square feet of green space per person. Today there are 540 square feet of green space per person.

3. Garbage is traded for food. Using funds that ordinarily would be used for garbage collection, a system of local neighborhood centers was established where poor people can trade six bags of garbage for one bag of food: 102,000 people are fed and 400 tons of garbage are collected each month.

4. Almost three quarters of the paper and over half of the metal, glass, and plastic are recycled in Curitiba. This is accomplished by recruiting children in the schools to instruct their parents on how to recycle; cart people, recruited from the favelas, wheel carts to pick up recycled goods that can be sold, and regular street sweepers are employed by the city. The recycling has decreased the amount of waste going to landfills by 50% in volume.

5. Free health care is given to poor people. This is coupled with free child care centers.

All this was accomplished by Jaime Lerner, former mayor, architect, and city planner. In a slow and difficult process, he has brought about these changes by appealing to diverse groups of people to become involved in solutions to several problems at once. The buses, for example, solved the problems of air pollution *and* cheap transportation for the poor.

* * *

Finally, perhaps the most pernicious deliberate misinformation is that environmental "extremists" are more concerned about owls and wolves than they are about people. This lie does not require any data, it needs only a slight bit of thought to understand that the goal of all environmentalists, whether extreme or not, is to save human lives. The whole point is to make the Earth habitable again for human beings. How extreme is it to want to save human lives? Should we become less extreme by not saving as many lives? It is not that we are saving the Earth for the owls and wolves and the future even though that needs to be done too; the point is to save the people who are dying now; to save the people who are needlessly dying of cancer because of contaminants such as asbestos, dioxins, CFCs, and other carcinogens.

What is at stake is nothing less than life on this planet.

> You must be the change you wish to see in the world.
>
> —Gandhi

GOALS

Definitions and Concepts

Sustainable growth

Underpersoning theory

Institutions

Environmental extremists

The third revolution in thinking

PTSD

Curitiba

New Environmental Paradigm

Declining birthrates in developing countries

The poverty-women's rights-environment cycle

Important Studies

Copernicus (1543)

Darwin (1859)

Meadows et al. (1972)

Meadows et al. (1992)

Janoff-Bulman (1992)

Dasgupta (1995)

Jacobson (1992)

1. What personal things can you do to help alleviate environmental stress?

2. What concept is at the heart of previous views on the place human beings have in the universe?

3. Does this concept still operate?

4. How are group conflicts related to environmental loss?

5. What is the relationship among women, poverty, and the environment?

6. What is the relationship between environmental regulation and the economy?

7. What is the relationship between environmental regulation and jobs?

8. Why do environmentalists emphasize saving animals?

9. Why do most of us have to eat differently?

10. What needs the most change in your own thinking?

References

AARP (American Association of Retired Persons). (1990). *A profile of older Americans: 1990*. Washington, DC: Author.

Abbott, B., & Badia, P. (1986). Predictable versus unpredictable shock conditions and physiological measures of stress: A reply to Arthur. *Psychological Bulletin, 100*, 384-387.

Abbott, B., Schoen, L., & Badia, P. (1984). Predictable and unpredictable shock: Behavioral measures of aversion and physiological measures of stress. *Psychological Bulletin, 96*, 45-71.

Abelson, P. (1987). World food. *Science, 236*, 9.

Addison, D. (1992). Psychologists help alleviate hurricane Andrew's havoc. *Psychological Monitor, 23*, 22.

Adler, L., & Granbert, J. (1976). Projected social distances from mental patient-related stimuli in cross national perspective: Four English speaking countries. *International Journal of Group Tensions, 6*, 15-25.

Adrian, C. (1972). A comparative typology of urban government images. In B. Berry (Ed.), *City classification handbook: Methods and applications* (pp. 247-262). New York: John Wiley.

Agarwal, A. (1988). Beyond pretty trees and tigers in India. In D. Pitt (Ed.), *The future of the environment* (pp. 93-125). Boston: Routledge.

Ahlstrom, W., & Havighurst, R. (1971). *400 losers*. San Francisco: Jossey-Bass.

Ahmed, S. (1979). Invasion of personal space: A study of departure time as affected by sex of the intruder, sex of the subject and saliency condition. *Perceptual & Motor Skills, 49*, 85-86.

Ahrentzen, S. (1990). Managing conflict by managing boundaries: How professional homeworkers cope with multiple roles at home. *Environment and Behavior, 22*, 723-752.

AIA Research Corporation. (1977). *Post occupancy evaluation*. Washington, DC: American Institute of Architects.

Aiello, J. (1987). Human spatial behavior. In D. Stokols & I. Altman (Eds.), *Handbook of environmental psychology* (pp. 389-504). New York: John Wiley.

Aiello, J., Baum, A., & Gormley, F. (1981). Social determinants of residential crowding stress. *Personality & Social Psychology Bulletin, 7*, 643-649.

Aiello, J., Epstein, Y., & Karlin, R. (1975). Effects of crowding on electrodermal activity. *Sociological Symposium, 14*, 42-57.

Aiello, J., Gordon, B., & Farrell, T. (1974). Description of children's outdoor activities in a suburban residential area: Some preliminary findings. In *Childhood city* (Man-Environment Interactions: Evaluations and Applications: The State of the Art in Environmental Design Research, Vol. 12, D. Carson, General Ed., pp. 187-196). Washington, DC: Environmental Design Research Association.

Ajdukovic, D. (1988). A contribution of the methodology of personal space research. *Psychologische Beitrage, 30*, 198-208.

Ajzen, I., & Driver, B. (1992). Application of the theory of planned behavior to leisure choice. *Journal of Leisure Research, 24*, 207-224.

Akhtar, S. (1990). Concept of interpersonal distance in borderline personality disorder. *American Journal of Psychiatry, 147*, 260-261.

Albrecht, G., Walker, V., & Levy, J. (1982). Social distance from the stigmatized: A test of two theories. *Social Science & Medicine, 16*, 1319-1327.

Aldwin, C., & Stokols, D. (1988). The effects of environmental change on individuals and groups: Some neglected issues in stress research. *Journal of Environmental Psychology, 8*, 57-75.

Alexander, C. (1964). *Notes on the synthesis of form*. Cambridge, MA: Harvard University Press.

Alexander, C., Silverstein, M., Angel, S., Ishikawa, S., & Abrams, D. (1977). *A pattern language*. Oxford: Oxford University Press.

Allen, G. (1981). A developmental perspective on the effects of subdividing macrospatial experience. *Journal of Experimental Psychology: Human Learning and Memory, 7*, 120-132.

Altholz, J. (1988). Fostering autonomy in living environments: A psychosocial perspective. *Journal of Housing for the Elderly, 5*, 67-81.

Altman, I. (1975). *The environment and social behavior*. Pacific Grove, CA: Brooks/Cole.

Altman, I. (1982). Some observations on the institutional status of environmental psychology. *Division 34 Newsletter, 9*, 3-4.

Altman, I. (1992). A transactional perspective on transitions to new environments. [S. Wapner (Ed.), Special issue: Transitions] *Environment and Behavior, 24*, 268-280.

Altman, I., & Rogoff, B. (1987). World views in psychology: Trait, interactional, organismic and transactional perspectives. In D. Stokols & I. Altman (Eds.), *Handbook of environmental psychology* (Vol. 1, pp. 1-40). New York: John Wiley.

Altman, I., & Wohlwill, J. (1976a). *Human behavior and environment: Advances in theory and research* (Vol. 1). New York: Plenum.

Altman, I., & Wohlwill, J. (1976b). *Children and the environment* (Vol. 3). New York: Plenum.

Altman, I., & Wohlwill, J. (1976c). *Environment and culture* (Vol. 4). New York: Plenum.

Amato, P., & Keith, B. (1991). Parental divorce and the well being of children: A meta analysis. *Psychological Bulletin, 110*, 26-46.

Amdur, M. (1976, March 3-5). Toxicological guidelines for research of sulfur oxides and particulates. In American Statistical Association, *Statistics and the environment* (Proceedings of the fourth symposium), Washington, DC.

American Psychiatric Association. (1994). *Diagnostic and statistical manual* (4th, rev. ed.). Washington, DC: American Psychiatric Press.

Ames, A. (1951). Visual perception and the rotating trapezoidal window. *Psychological Monographs, 65*(Whole no. 324).

Anderson, J., Tooney, D., & Brune, W. (1991). Free radicals within the Antarctic vortex: The role of CFCs in the Antarctic ozone loss. *Science, 251*, 39-46.

Anderson, L. (1981). Land use designations affect perception of scenic beauty in forest landscapes. *Forest Science, 27*, 392-400.

Anderson, N. (1965). Averaging versus adding as a stimulus-combination rule in impression formation. *Journal of Personality and Social Psychology, 2*, 1-2.

Anderson, P., & Sull, K. (1985). Out of touch, out of reach: Tactile predispositions as predictors of interpersonal distance. *Western Journal of Speech Communication, 49*, 57-72.

Anooshian, L., & Siegel, A. (1985). From cognitive to procedural mapping. In C. Brainerd & M. Pressley (Eds.), *Basic processes in memory development: Progress in cognitive development research* (pp. 47-101). New York: Springer-Verlag.

Anthony, K. (1985). The shopping mall: A teenage hangout. *Adolescence, 20*, 307-312.

Antonovsky, A. (1979). *Health, stress and coping*. San Francisco: Jossey-Bass.

Appleton, J. (1975). *The experience of landscape*. New York: John Wiley.

Appleyard, D. (1981). *Liveable streets*. Berkeley: University of California Press.

Appleyard, D., & Craik, K. (1978). The Berkeley Environmental Simulation Laboratory and its research programme. *International Review of Applied Psychology, 27*, 53-55.

Aragones, J., & Arredondo, J. (1985). Structure of urban cognitive maps. *Journal of Environmental Psychology, 5,* 197-212.

Ardrey, R. (1966). *The territorial imperative.* New York: Atheneum.

Argyle, M., & Dean, J. (1965). Eye-contact, distance and affiliation. *Sociometry, 28,* 289-304.

Aries, P. (1962). *Centuries of childhood.* New York: Knopf.

Arthur, A. (1986). The stress of predictable and unpredictable shock. *Psychological Bulletin, 100,* 379-383.

Askins, R. (1995). Hostile landscapes and the decline of migratory songbirds. *Science, 267,* 1956-1957.

Australian National Commission for UNESCO. (1976). *Man and the environment: New towns in isolated settings.* Canberra: Author.

Averill, J. (1973). Personal control over aversive stimuli and its relationship to stress. *Psychological Bulletin, 80,* 286-303.

Baggs, S. (1977). *The dugout dwellings of an outback opal mining town in Australia* [Mimeo]. Kensington, NSW, Australia: University of South Wales, Department of Landscape Architecture.

Bailey, R., Branch, H., & Taylor, C. (1961). *Architectural psychology and psychiatry: An exploratory national research conference.* Salt Lake City: University of Utah Press.

Baird, J., Berglund, B., & Esfandabad, H. (1994). Longitudinal assessment of sensory reactions in eyes and upper airways of staff in a sick building. *Environment International, 20,* 141-160.

Baird, L. (1969). Big school, small school: A critical examination of the hypothesis. *Journal of Educational Psychology, 60,* 253-260.

Baldassare, M. (1983). Residential crowding and social behavior. In J. Pipkin, M. LaGory, & J. Blan (Eds.), *Remaking the city* (pp. 148-161). Albany: SUNY Press.

Balling, J., & Falk, J. (1982). Development of visual preference for natural events. *Environment and Behavior, 14,* 5-28.

Balogun, S. (1991). Personal space as affected by religions of the approaching and approached people. *Indian Journal of Behavior, 15,* 45-50.

Balsam, P., & Tomie, A. (Eds.). (1985). *Context and learning.* Hillsdale, NJ: Lawrence Erlbaum.

Bandura, A. (1979). *Social learning theory.* Englewood Cliffs, NJ: Prentice Hall.

Banks, W., & Krajicek, D. (1991). Perception. In M. Rosenzweig & L. Porter (Eds.), *Annual review of psychology* (Vol. 42, pp. 305-331). Palo Alto, CA: Annual Reviews.

Barbey, G. (1974). Anthropological analysis of the home concept: Some considerations based on children's drawings. In *Childhood city* (Man-Environment Interactions: Evaluations and Applications: The State of the Art in Environmental Design Research, Vol. 12, D. Carson, General Ed., pp. 143-149). Washington, DC: Environmental Design Research Association.

Barker, J. (1988). Gate-keeping: Residential managers and elderly tenants. *Gerontologist, 28*, 610-619.

Barker, R. (1965). Explorations in ecological psychology. *American Psychologist, 20*, 1-14.

Barker, R. (1968). *Ecological psychology*. Stanford, CA: Stanford University Press.

Barker, R., Dembo, T., & Lewin, K. (1941). *Frustration and regression: A study of young children* (University of Iowa Studies in Child Welfare, No. 18). Ames: University of Iowa.

Barker, R., & Gump, P. (1964). *Big school, small school*. Stanford, CA: Stanford University Press.

Barker, R., & Schoggen, P. (1973). *Qualities of community life*. San Francisco: Jossey-Bass.

Barker, R., & Wright, H. (1951). *One boy's day*. New York: Row Peterson.

Barker, R., & Wright, H. (1955). *Midwest and its children*. Evanston, IL: Row Peterson.

Barker, R., & Associates. (1978). *Habitats, environments and human behavior*. San Francisco: Jossey-Bass.

Barkow, J., Cosmides, L., & Tooby, J. (1992). *The adapted mind: Evolutionary psychology and the generation of culture*. New York: Oxford University Press.

Barnard, W., & Bell, P. (1982). An unobtrusive apparatus for measuring interpersonal distances. *Journal of General Psychology, 107*, 85-90.

Baron, R., Mandel, D., Adams, C., & Griffen, L. (1976). Effects of social density in university residential environments. *Journal of Personality and Social Psychology, 34*, 434-446.

Bartecchi, C. E., MacKenzie, T. D., & Schrier, R. W. (1995, May). The global tobacco epidemic. *Scientific American*, p. 49.

Barton, A. (1970). *Communities in disaster*. Garden City, NY: Anchor Doubleday.

Bates, A. (1971). *Office planning for business information systems*. Paper presented at the Symposium of Human Factors in Business Systems, Human Factors Society meeting, New York.

Baum, A. (1993). Implications of psychological research on stress and technical accidents. *American Psychologist, 48*, 665-672.

Baum, A., & Koman, S. (1976). Differential response to anticipated crowding: Psychological effects of social and spatial density. *Journal of Personality and Social Psychology, 34*, 526-536.

Baum, A., & Paulus, P. (1987). Crowding. In D. Stokols & Altman (Eds.), *Handbook of environmental psychology* (Vol. 1, pp. 533-570). New York: John Wiley.

Baum, A., & Singer, J. (1981). *Advances in environmental psychology: Vol. 3. Energy: Psychological perspectives*. Hillsdale, NJ: Lawrence Erlbaum.

Beattie, R. (1982). Effects of white noise on the most comfortable level for speech. *Journal of Auditory Research, 22*, 71-76.

Bechtel, R. (1967). Hodometer research in museums. *Museum News, 45*, 23-26.

Bechtel, R. (1973). *Classification of selected federal operations sites in Alaska*. Hanover: Cold Regions Research & Engineering Laboratory.

Bechtel, R. (1975). User data. Chap. 3 in *Studies and planning services to develop and apply performance specifications in procurement and evaluation of housing* (Data analysis report, pp. 18-87). Silver Spring, MD: Tadger, Cohen, Shifferman & Bigelson.

Bechtel, R. (1976). *Profile of housing needs of ARAMCO employees*. Washington, DC: Real Estate Research Corporation.

Bechtel, R. (1977). *Enclosing behavior*. Stroudsberg, PA: Dowden, Hutchinson & Ross.

Bechtel, R. (1978a). *What are post occupancy evaluations? A laymen's guide to the POE*. Washington, DC: U.S. Department of Housing and Urban Development.

Bechtel, R. (1978b). Human factors preliminary report. In E. K. Chann (Ed.), *Engineering feasibility study interim report: Meso environmental quadraplex housing units* (pp. 101-118). Tucson: Earl Kai Chann, Architecture & Planning.

Bechtel, R. (1979, May). *The institutional use of the house*. In the Symposium on Residential Treatment Homes for Correctional Youths, R. Srivastava (Chair), EDRA 10, Buffalo, NY.

Bechtel, R. (1981). Psychological response to earth covered housing. In F. Moreland (Ed.), *Earth covered buildings: An exploratory analysis for hazard and energy performance* (Report prepared for the Federal Emergency Management Agency, Washington, DC).

Bechtel, R. (1983). We've looked at both sides now: A work shop of the dual educated. In D. Amedeo, J. Griffin, & J. Potter (Eds.), *EDRA* 23. Washington, DC: Environmental Design Research Association.

Bechtel, R. (1989). Behavior in the house: A cross cultural comparison using behavior setting methodology. In S. Low & E. Chambers (Eds.), *Housing, culture and design*. Philadelphia: University of Pennsylvania Press.

Bechtel, R. (1991). Nofim: The beautiful vision of a retirement community in Israel. In W. Preiser, J. Vischer, & E. White (Eds.), *Design intervention toward a more humane architecture*. New York: Van Nostrand Reinhold.

Bechtel, R. (in press). The paradigm of environmental psychology: A reply to Stokol's paradox. *American Psychologist*.

Bechtel, R., Ittelson, W., & Wheeler, L. (1978). Environmental psychology and housing design in arid urban areas. In G. Golany (Ed.), *Urban planning for arid zones* (pp. 75-86). New York: John Wiley.

Bechtel, R., & Ledbetter, C. E. (1976). *The temporary environment*. Hanover: Cold Regions Research & Engineering Laboratory.

Bechtel, R., & Ledbetter, C. E. (1980). *Post occupancy evaluation of a planned Arctic community*. Hanover: Cold Regions Research & Engineering Laboratory.

Bechtel, R., Ledbetter, C. E., & Cummings, N. (1980). *Post occupancy evaluation of a remote Australian community: Shay Gap, Australia*. Hanover: Cold Regions Research & Engineering Laboratory.

Bechtel, R., & Srivastava, R. (1978). *Post occupancy evaluations in housing*. Washington, DC: Department of Housing and Urban Development.

Becker, F. (1982). *Workspace: Creating environments in organizations*. New York: Praeger.

Becker, L., Seligman, C., Fazio, R., & Darley, J. (1981). Relating attitudes to residential energy use. *Environment and Behavior, 13*, 590-609.

Bell, P., Fisher, V., Baum, A., & Greene, T. (1990). *Environmental psychology* (3rd ed.). New York: Holt, Rinehart & Winston.

Bell, P., Fisher, J., Baum, A., & Greene, T. (1996). *Environmental psychology* (4th ed.). New York: Harcourt Brace.

Bell, P., Fisher, V., & Loomis, R. (1978). *Environmental psychology*. Philadelphia: W. B. Saunders.

Bell, P., Kline, L., & Barnard, W. (1988). Friendship and freedom of movement as moderators of sex differences in interpersonal distancing. *Journal of Social Psychology, 128*, 305-310.

Bem, D. (1972). Self perception theory. In L. Berkowitz (Ed.), *Advances in experimental social psychology* (Vol. 6). San Diego, CA: Academic Press.

Benedick, R. (1991). *Ozone diplomacy*. Cambridge, MA: Harvard University Press.

Benedict, R. (1959). *Patterns of culture*. Boston: Houghton Mifflin.

Benjamin, D., et al. (1995). *The home: Words, interpretations, meanings and environments*. Brookfield: Avebury.

Berkeley Planning Associates. (1977). *Evaluation of child abuse and neglect demonstration projects: Project management and worker burnout* (Vol. 9, NTIS No. PB 278 446). Berkeley, CA: Author.

Berkow, R., et al. (Ed.). (1977). *The Merck manual of diagnosis and therapy*. New York: Merck, Sharp and Dome Laboratories.

Berkowitz, M. (1988). The effects of a resident self-help model on control, social involvement and self-esteem among the elderly. *Gerontologist, 28*, 620-624.

Berlyne, D. (1963). Complexity and incongruity variables as determinants of exploratory choice and evaluative ratings. *Canadian Journal of Psychology, 17*, 274-290.

Berry, B. (Ed.). (1972). *City classification handbook: Methods and applications*. New York: John Wiley.

Berry, B., & Neils, E. (1969). Location, size and shape of cities as influenced by environmental factors. In H. S. Perloff (Ed.), *The quality of the urban environment*. Baltimore, MD: Johns Hopkins University Press.

Bharucha-Reid, R., & Kiyak, A. (1979). The concept of dissonance and too much personal space. *Journal of Nonverbal Behavior, 4*, 123-125.

Bharucha-Reid, R., & Kiyak, A. (1981, April). Personality and environmental determinants of seating choice. In *EDRA 12* (pp. 265-271). Washington, DC: Environmental Design Research Association.

Biner, P., Butler, D., Lovegrove, T., & Burns, R. (1993). Windowlessness and the workplace: A reexamination of the compensation hypothesis. *Environment and Behavior, 25*, 205-227.

Birdsell, J. (1953). Some environmental and cultural factors influencing the structuring of Australian Aboriginal populations. *American Naturalist, 87*, 171-207.

Birdwhistell, R. (1970). *Kinesics and context: Essays on body motion communication.* Philadelphia: University of Pennsylvania Press.

Bitgood, S., & Loomis, R. (1993). Introduction: Environmental design and evaluation in museums. [S. Bitgood & R. Loomis (Eds.), Environmental Design & Evaluation in Museums]. *Environment and Behavior, 25*, 683-697.

Blaine, T., & Golam, M. (1991). An empirical assessment of US consumer expenditures for recreational goods and services 1946-1988. *Leisure Sciences, 13*, 111-122.

Blaustein, A., & Wake, D. (1995). The puzzle of declining amphibian populations. *Scientific American, 272*, 52-57.

Bonine, M., & Keddie, N. (1981). *Continuity and change in modern Iran.* Albany: SUNY Press.

Booth, A. (1976). *Urban crowding and its consequences.* New York: Praeger.

Booth, A. (Ed.). (1992). *Child care in the 1990s: Trends and consequences.* Hillsdale, NJ: Lawrence Erlbaum.

Bouchard, T. (1994). Genes, environment and personality. *Science, 264*, 1700-1701.

Boucher, J., & Osgood, C. (1969). The pollyanna hypothesis. *Journal of Verbal Learning and Verbal Behavior, 8*, 1-8.

Bower, B. (1989). Sizing up SADness according to latitude. *Science, 136*, 198.

Bower, B. (1990). Bright light therapy expands its horizons. *Science, 137*, 325.

Bowman, C., & Fishbein, M. (1978). Understanding public reaction to energy proposals: An application of the Fishbein model. *Journal of Applied Social Psychology, 8*, 319-340.

Boxer, B. (1968). Space, change and feng-shui in Tseun Wan's urbanization. *Journal of Asian & African Studies, 3*, 226-240.

Bradburn, N. (1969). *The structure of psychological well-being.* Chicago: Aldine.

Brady, C., Kinnaird, K., & Friedrich, W. (1980). Job satisfaction and perception of social climate in a mental health facility. *Perceptual & Motor Skills, 51*, 559-564.

Brechner, K. (1977). An experimental analysis of social traps. *Journal of Experimental Social Psychology, 13*, 552-564.

Brechner, K., & Linder, D. (1981). Social trap analysis of energy distribution system. In A. Baum & J. Singer (Eds.), *Advances in environmental psychology* (Vol. 3, pp. 27-52). Hillsdale, NJ: Lawrence Erlbaum.

Brehm, S., & Brehm, J. (1981). *Psychological reactance: A theory of freedom and control.* New York: Academic Press.

Brill, M. (1982). *Do buildings really matter?* Academy for Educational Development, Educational Facilities Laboratory [no listed location].

Brill, M., Margulis, S., & Konar, E. (1984). *Using office design to increase productivity: Vol. 1. Workplace design and creativity.* Washington, DC: National Science Foundation.

Broad, W. (1979). High anxiety over flights through ozone. *Science, 205,* 767-769.

Broadbent, D. (1971). *Decision and stress.* San Diego, CA: Academic Press.

Broadbent, D. (1976). "Funneling of attention" hypothesis: Noise and the details of experiments. A reply to Poulton. *Applied Ergonomics, 7,* 231-235.

Brody, A. (1990). Chrysotile, tremolite and mesothelioma [Letters to the editor]. *Science, 248,* 794-795.

Brolin, B., & Zeisel, J. (1968, July-August). Mass housing: Social research and design. *Architectural Forum,* pp. 66-71.

Bronfenbrenner, U. (1979). *The ecology of human development.* Cambridge, MA: Harvard University Press.

Brookes, M., & Kaplan, A. (1972). The office environment: Space planning and affective behavior. *Human Factors, 14,* 373-392.

Brown, B. (1987). Territoriality. In D. Stokols & I. Altman (Eds.), *The handbook of environmental psychology* (pp. 505-531). New York: John Wiley.

Brown, B. (1992). The ecology of privacy and mood in a shared living group. *Journal of Environmental Psychology, 12,* 5-20.

Brown, B., & Altman, I. (1983). Territoriality, defensible space and residential burglary: An environmental analysis. *Journal of Environmental Psychology, 3,* 203-220.

Brown, D. (1991). *Human universals.* Philadelphia: Temple University Press.

Brown, G., & Harris, T. (Eds.). (1989). *Life events and illness.* New York: Guilford.

Brown, R. (1967). *Social psychology.* Glencoe, IL: Free Press.

Brown, T., & Daniel, T. (1984). *Modeling forest scenic beauty: Concepts and applications to Ponderosa Pine* (USDA Forest Service Research Paper RM-256). Fort Collins, CO: Rocky Mountain Forest and Range Experiment Station.

Browning, E. (1984). When fung shui speaks, business listens. *International Wildlife, 14,* 36-37 (originally from the *Wall Street Journal*).

Brune, W., Anderson, J., Toohey, D., Fahey, D., Kawa, S., Jones, R., Mckenna, D., & Poole, L. (1991). The potential for ozone depletion in the Arctic polar stratosphere. *Science, 252,* 1260-1266.

Bruner, J. (1966). *Toward a theory of instruction.* Cambridge, MA: Harvard University Press.

Brunswik, E. (1956). *Perception and the representative design of psychological experiments.* Berkeley: University of California Press.

Brush, R., & Palmer, J. (1979). Measuring the impact of urbanization on scenic quality: Land use change in the Northeast. In *Proceedings of Our National Landscape: A conference on applied techniques for an analysis and management of the visual resource.* Berkeley, CA: USDA Forest Service.

Burby, R., & French, S. (1980). The U.S. experience in managing flood plain use. *Disasters, 4,* 451-457.

Burch, M., et al. (1978). Effects of population density and information overload on state anxiety and crowding perception. *Psychological Record, 28,* 207-214.

Burgess, E. (1925). The growth of the city: An introduction to a research project. In R. Park & E. Burgess (Eds.), *The city* (pp. 47-62). Chicago: University of Chicago.

Burgess, J. (1981). Development of social spacing in normal and mentally retarded children. *Journal of Nonverbal Behavior, 6,* 89-95.

Burgess, J. (1983a). Interpersonal spacing behavior between surrounding nearest neighbors reflects both familiarity and environmental density. *Ethology & Sociobiology, 4,* 11-17.

Burgess, J. (1983b). Developmental trends in proxemic spacing behavior between surrounding companions and strangers in causal groups. *Journal of Nonverbal Behavior, 7,* 158-169.

Burgoon, J., & Jones, S. (1976). Toward a theory of personal space expectations and their violation. *Human Communication Research, 2,* 1131-1146.

Burnett, C. (1974). Mental image and design. In J. Lang, C. Burnette, W. Moleski, & D. Vachon (Eds.), *Designing for human behavior* (pp. 169-182). Stroudsberg, PA: Dowden, Hutchinson & Ross.

Burnham, J. (1987). *How superstition won and science lost.* Rutgers, NJ: Rutgers University Press.

Burrows, A. (1960). Acoustic noise, an informational definition. *Human Factors, 2,* 163-168.

Burton, I. (1962). *Types of agricultural occupance of floodplains in the United States* (Paper No. 75). Chicago: University of Chicago, Department of Geography Research.

Burton, I., Kates, R., & White, G. (1978). *The environment as hazard.* Oxford: Oxford University Press.

Butler, D., & Biner, P. (1989). Effects of setting on window preferences and factors associated with those preferences. *Environment and Behavior, 21,* 17-32.

Byrd, G., & Guyot, G. (1979). Altering classroom seating and serial order. *Perceptual & Motor Skills, 49,* 658.

Cadwallader, M. (1979). Problems in cognitive distance: Implications for cognitive mapping. *Environment and Behavior, 11,* 559-576.

Calhoun, J. (1962). Population density and social pathology. *Scientific American, 206,* 139-148.

Calhoun, J. (1973). Death squared: The explosive growth and demise of a mouse population. *Proceedings of the Royal Society of Medicine, 66,* 80-88.

Calhoun, J. (1976). Scientific quest for a path to the future. *Populi, 3* [Special, unnumbered sec.].

Campbell, D. (1965). Ethnocentric and other altruistic motives. In D. LeVine (Ed.), *The Nebraska Symposium on Motivation*. Lincoln: University of Nebraska Press.

Campbell, D., & Fiske, D. (1959). Convergent and discriminant validation by the multitrait multimethod matrix. *Psychological Bulletin, 56*, 81-105.

Campbell, D., & Lancioni, G. (1979). The effects of staring and pew invasion in church settings. *Journal of Social Psychology, 108*, 19-24.

Campbell, E., Smith, T., Steenberger, B., & Stucky, R. (1979). *Evaluation of the Carriage House Mobile Counseling Project* [Mimeo]. Lawrence: University of Kansas.

Campbell, J. (1983). Ambient stressors. *Environment and Behavior, 15*, 355-380.

Campbell, S. (1984). A new zoo? *Zoonooz, 55*, 4-7.

Can buildings make you sick? (1996). [Video]. Boston: WGBH.

Cannon, W. (1932). *The wisdom of the body*. New York: Norton.

Canter, D. (1972). *Psychology for architects*. New York: Applied Science Publishers.

Canter, D. (Ed.). (1980). *Fires and human behavior*. New York: John Wiley.

Canter, D., & Donald, I. (1987). Environmental psychology in the United Kingdom. In D. Stokols & I. Altman (Eds.), *Handbook of environmental psychology* (Vol. 2, pp. 1281-1310). New York: John Wiley.

Canter, D., & Tagg, S. (1980). The empirical classification of building aspects and their attributes. In G. Broadbent, R. Bunt, & T. Llorens (Eds.), *Meaning and behaviour in the built environment* (pp. 1-19). New York: John Wiley.

Cantril, H., & Ittelson, W. (1954). *Perception: A transactional approach*. Garden City, NY: Doubleday.

Caplan, M., & Goldman, M. (1981). Personal space violations as a function of height. *Journal of Social Psychology, 114*, 167-177.

Caporeal, L., & Brewer, M. (1991). Issues in evolutionary psychology. *Journal of Social Issues, 47*(3), special issue.

Carducci, B., & Webber, A. (1979). Shyness as a determinant of interpersonal distance. *Psychological Reports, 44*, 1075-1078.

Carp, F. (1987). Environment and aging. In D. Stokols & I. Altman (Eds.), *Handbook of environmental psychology* (Vol. 1). New York: John Wiley.

Carpenter, C. (1934, May). Behavior and social relations of the howling monkey. *Comparative Psychology Monographs* (entire issue).

Carpman, J., & Grant, M. (1993). *Design that cares* (2nd ed.). Chicago: American Hospital Publishing.

Carpman, J., Grant, M., & Simmons, D. (1984). *No more mazes: Research about wayfinding in hospitals*. Ann Arbor: University of Michigan, Hospitals Patient and Visitor Participation Project.

Carrick, R. (1963). Ecological significance of territory in the Australian magpie (Gymnorhina tibicen). *Procedures of the XIII International Ornithological Congress*, pp. 740-753.

Carroll, J. (1956). *Language, thought and reality: Selected writings of Benjamin Lee Whorf*. New York: John Wiley.

Carson, D., Carson, F., Margulis, S., & Wehrli, R. (1980). Post occupancy housing evaluations: A practical strategy for obtaining control groups. *Environment and Behavior, 12*, 541-550.

Carson, R. (1962). *Silent spring*. Boston: Houghton Mifflin.

Cavallin, B., & Houston, B. (1980). Aggressiveness, maladjustment, body experience and the protective function of personal space. *Journal of Clinical Psychology, 36*, 170-176.

CERL (Construction Engineering Research Laboratory). (1982). *Return on investment case study* (Vol. R5). Champaign, IL: Author.

Cha, J., & Nam, K. (1985). A test of Kelley's cube theory of attribution: A cross-cultural replication of McArthur's study. *Korean Social Science Journal, 12*, 158-180.

Chapanis, A. (1975). Cosmopolitanism: A new era in the evolution of human factors engineering. In A. Chapanis (Ed.), *Ethnic variables in human factors engineering* (pp. 1-10). Baltimore, MD: Johns Hopkins University Press.

Chapin, F. (1965). *Urban land use planning*. Urbana: University of Illinois Press.

Chapin, F. (1974). *Human activity patterns in the city: Things people do in time and in space*. New York: John Wiley.

Cheek, N. (1971). Toward a sociology of non-work. *Pacific Sociological Review, 14*, 245.

Cheek, N., Field, D., & Burdge, R. (1976). *Leisure and recreation places*. Ann Arbor, MI: Ann Arbor Sciences Publishers.

Cherlin, A., Furstenberg, F., Chase-Lansdale, P., Kiernan, K., Robins, P., Morrison, D., & Teitler, J. (1991). Longitudinal studies of effects of divorce on children in Great Britain and the United States. *Science, 252*, 1386-1389.

Cherulnik, P. (1993). Promoting energy conservation. In P. Cherulnik, *Applications of environment-behavior research* (pp. 241-263). Cambridge: Cambridge University Press.

Chesney, M., Sevelius, G., Black, G., Ward, M., Swan, G., & Rosenman, R. (1981). Work environment, type A behavior and coronary heart risk disease factors. *Journal of Occupational Medicine, 23*, 551-555.

Choldin, H. (1978). Urban density and pathology. *Annual Review of Sociology, 4*, 91-113.

Christensen, D., Carp, F., & Cranz, G. (1992). Objective housing indicators as predictors of the subjective evaluations of elderly residents. *Journal of Environmental Psychology, 12*, 225-236.

Christian, J., Flyger, V., & Davis, D. (1960). Factors in mass mortality in a herd of sika deer. *Chesapeake Science, 1*, 79-95.

Chu, P. (1991). Validating the computer anxiety rating scale: Effects of cognitive style and computer courses on computer anxiety, MBA vs. college students. *Computers in Human Behavior, 7*, 7-21.

Chubb, M., & Chubb, H. (1981). *One third of our time: An introduction to recreation behavior and resources*. New York: John Wiley.

Churchman, A., & Ginsberg, Y. (1984). The image and experience of high rise housing in Israel. *Journal of Environmental Psychology, 4*, 27-42.

Ciolek, T. (1980). Spatial extent and structure of the field of co-presence: Summary of findings. *Man Environment Systems, 10*, 57-62.

Ciolek, T. (1983). The proxemic lexicon: A first approximation. *Journal of Nonverbal Behavior, 8*, 55-79.

Ciolek, T., & Furnham, A. (1980). Subjective interpersonal distance in a public setting: Effect of situation and ecology. *Man Environment Systems, 10*, 107-116.

Cisneros, H. (1995). *Defensible space: Deterring crime and building community*. Washington, DC: Department of Housing and Urban Development.

Clamp, P. (1976). Evaluating English landscapes: Some recent developments. *Environment and Planning, 8*, 79-82.

Clark, T. (1972). Urban typologies and political outputs. In B. Berry (Ed.), *City classification handbook* (pp. 152-178). New York: Wiley.

Clarke, P. (1986). Theoretical and measurement issues in the study of field phenomena. *Advances in Nursing Science, 9*, 29-39.

Cline, R., & Puhl, C. (1984). Gender, culture and geography: A comparison of seating arrangements in the US and Taiwan. *International Journal of Intercultural Relations, 8*, 199-219.

Cloninger, C., Svaric, D., & Prysbeck, T. (1993). A psychobiological model of temperament and character. *Archives of General Psychiatry, 50*, 975-990.

Coates, G., & Bussard, E. (1974). Patterns of children's spatial behavior in a moderate density housing development. In *Childhood city* (Man-Environment Interactions: Evaluations and Applications: The State of the Art in Environmental Design Research, Vol. 12, D. Carson, General Ed., pp. 131-142). Washington, DC: Environmental Design Research Association.

Cochran, C., & Hale, W. (1984). Personal space requirements in indoor versus outdoor locations. *Journal of Psychology, 117*, 121-123.

Codol, J. (1985). The estimation of physical distance between people: Am I as far from you as you are from me? *Année Psychologique, 85*, 517-534.

Codol, J., Jarymowicz, M., Kaminska-Feldman, M., & Szuster-Zbrojewicz, A. (1989). Asymmetry in the estimation of interpersonal distance and identity affirmation. *European Journal of Social Psychology, 19*, 11-22.

Cohen, S. (1978). Environmental load and the allocation of attention. In A. Baum, J. Singer, & S. Valins (Eds.), *Advances in environmental psychology: Vol. 1. The urban environment* (pp. 1-29). Hillsdale, NJ: Lawrence Erlbaum.

Cohen, S., Krantz, D., Evans, G., Stokols, D., & Kelly, S. (1981). Aircraft noise and children: Longitudinal and cross-section evidence on adaptation to noise and the effectiveness of noise abatement. *Journal of Personality & Social Psychology, 40*, 331-345.

Cohn, J. (1979). *The palace or the poorhouse: The American house as a cultural symbol*. Lansing: Michigan State University Press.

Cohn, L., & McVoy, G. (1982). *Environmental analysis of transportation systems*. New York: John Wiley.

Colarelli, N., & Siegel, S. (1966). *Ward H: An adventure in innovation*. New York: Van Nostrand.

Cole, R. E. (1971). *Japanese blue collar: The changing tradition*. Berkeley: University of California Press.

Cole, R. E. (1980). *Science, 209*, 476-477.

Collet, P., & Marsh, P. (1980). Seat choice in an airport lounge. *Man Environment Systems, 10*, 83-106.

Colloredo-Mansfeld, R. (1994). Architectural conspicuous consumption and economic change in the Andes. *American Anthropologist, 96*, 845-865.

Condon, R. G. (1983). *Inuit behavior and seasonal change in the Canadian Arctic*. Ann Arbor: UMI Research Press.

Conniff, R. (1990). You never know what the fire ant is going to do next. *Smithsonian, 21*, 48-59.

Conigliaro, L., Cullerton, S., Flynn, K., & Roeder, S. (1989). Stigmatizing artifacts and their effect on personal space. *Psychological Reports, 65*, 897-898.

Conrad, C. (1991). The emergence of modern retirement: Germany in an international comparison (1850-1960). *Population, 3*, 171-200.

Conservation Foundation. (1982). *State of the environment, 1982*. Washington, DC: Author.

Conway, D. (Ed.). (1977). *Human response to tall buildings*. Stroudsberg, PA: Dowden, Hutchinson & Ross.

Cooke, N. (1992). Eliciting semantic relations for empirically derived networks. *International Journal of Man-Machine Studies, 37*, 721-750.

Cooper, K. (1984). Territorial behavior among the institutionalized: A nursing perspective. *Journal of Psychosocial Nursing and Mental Health Services, 22*, 6-11.

Cooper Marcus, C. (1974). Children's play behavior in a low rise, inner city housing development. In *Childhood city* (Man-Environment Interactions: Evaluations and Applications: The State of the Art in Environmental Design Research, Vol. 12, D. Carson, General Ed., pp. 197-211). Washington, DC: Environmental Design Research Association.

Copley, F. (1923). *Frederick W. Taylor, father of scientific management*. New York: Harper.

Cornell University Agricultural Experiment Station (with the New York State College of Home Economics). (1959). *Farmhouse planning guides*. Ithaca, NY: Author.

Cothern, C., & Ohanian, E. (1987). Paper delivered at Health Physics Society annual meeting, Salt Lake City.

Cothern, C., & Smith, J. (1987). *Environmental radon*. New York: Plenum.

Coucelis, H., Golledge, R., Gale, N., & Tobler, W. (1987). Exploring the anchor point hypothesis of spatial cognition. *Journal of Environmental Psychology, 7*, 99-122.

Coulanges, F. (1955). *The ancient city*. Garden City, NY: Doubleday Anchor. (Original work published 1864).

Council on Environmental Quality. (1980). *Environmental quality: 1980*. Washington, DC: Government Printing Office.

Council on Environmental Quality and U.S. Department of State. (1980). *The global 2000 report to the president: Entering the twenty first century: Vol. 1. Summary report*. Washington, DC: Government Printing Office.

Cousins, N. (1979). *Anatomy of an illness*. New York: Norton.

Coward, H. (1995). *Population, consumption, and the environment*. Albany: SUNY Press.

Cox, V., Paulus, P., & McCain, G. (1984). Prison crowding research: The relevance for prison housing standards and a general approach to the crowding phenomena. *American Psychologist, 39*, 1148-1160.

Cox, V., Paulus, P., & McCain, G. (1986). Not for attribution: Reply to Bonta. *American Psychologist, 41*, 101-103.

Cox, V., Paulus, P., McCain, G., & Karlovac, M. (1982). The relationship between crowding and health. In A. Baum & J. Singer (Eds.), *Advances in environmental psychology* (Vol. 4, pp. 271-294). Hillsdale, NJ: Lawrence Erlbaum.

Craik, K., & Zube, I. (1976). *Perceiving environmental quality*. New York: Plenum.

Crane, D., Russell, J., & Griffin, W. (1983). Personal space: An objective measure of marital quality. *Journal of Marital & Family Therapy, 9*, 325-327.

Crump, K. (1990). [Letter to the editors]. *Science, 247*, 799.

Csikszentmihalyi, M. (1976). *Beyond boredom and anxiety*. San Francisco: Jossey-Bass.

Csikszentmihalyi, M. (1990). *Flow: The psychology of optimal experience*. New York: Harper & Row.

Csikszentmihalyi, M., & Rochberg-Halton, E. (1981). *The meaning of things: Domestic symbols and the self*. Cambridge: Cambridge University Press.

Culliton, B. (1986). For-profit hospitals loom large on health care scene. *Science, 233*, 928-930.

Curran, J., & Stanworth, J. (1978, December). Some reasons why small is not always beautiful. *New Society*, pp. 627-629.

Czaja, S. (1988). Safety and security of the elderly: Implications for smart house design. *International Journal of Technology & Aging, 1*, 49-66.

Czeisler, C., Allan, J., Strogatz, J., Ronda, J., Sanchez, R., Rios, D., Freitag, W., Richardson, G., & Kronauer, R. (1986). Bright light resets the human circadian pacemaker independent of the timing of the sleep-wake cycle. *Science, 233*, 667-671.

Daish, J., & Kernohan, D. (1980). *Annotated bibliography on post occupancy evaluation of government buildings*. Wellington, New Zealand: University of Wellington, School of Architecture.

Daish, J., Kernohan, D., & Salmond, A. (1981). *Post occupancy evaluation trial studies*. Wellington, New Zealand: University of Wellington, School of Architecture.

Daly, H. (1991). *Steady state economics*. Washington, DC: Island.

Danford, S., & Willems, E. (1975). Subjective responses to architectural displays: A question of validity. *Environment and Behavior, 7*, 486-516.

Daniel, T. (1976). *Prediction of scenic quality from manageable forest landscape features* (Final report). Tucson: University of Arizona.

Daniel, T., & Boster, R. (1976). *Measuring landscape esthetics: The scenic beauty estimation method* (Research paper RM-167). Fort Collins: Rocky Mountain Forest and Range Experiment Station, USDA Forest Service.

Daniel, T., & Ittelson, W. (1981). Conditions for environmental research: Reactions to Ward and Russell. *Journal of Experimental Psychology: General, 110*, 153-157.

Darwin, C. (1859). *On the origin of species*. London: Murray.

Dasgupta, P. (1995). Population, poverty and the local environment. *Scientific American, 272*, 40-45.

D'Atri, D. (1981). Crowding in prison: The relationship between changes in housing mode and blood pressure. *Psychosomatic Medicine, 43*, 95-105.

Davis, L., & Cherns, A. (Eds.). (1975). *The quality of working life* (Vols. 1-2). New York: Free Press.

Davis, L., & Lennon, S. (1983). Social stigma of pregnancy: Further evidence. *Psychological Reports, 53*, 997-988.

Dawes, R., Faust, D., & Meehl, P. (1989). Clinical versus actuarial judgment. *Science, 234*, 1668-1674.

Dawkins, R. (1976). *The selfish gene*. Oxford: Oxford University Press.

Dean, L., Pugh, W., & Gunderson, E. (1975). Spatial and perceptual components of crowding: Effects on health and satisfaction. *Environment and Behavior, 7*, 225-236.

Dean, L., Pugh, W., & Gunderson, E. (1978). The behavioral effects of crowding: Definitions and methods. *Environment and Behavior, 10*, 419-431.

Deasy, C. (1968, January). When a sociologist gets into the act. *American Institute of Architects' Journal*, pp. 72-76.

Deasy, C. (1970). When architects consult people. *Psychology Today, 3*, 54-57, 78-79.

DeBeer-Kelston, K., Mellon, L., & Solomon, L. (1986). Helping behavior as a function of personal space invasion. *Journal of Social Psychology, 126*, 407-409.

DeCampli, W. (1986, September-October). The limits of manned space flight. *The Sciences*, pp. 47-52.

DeCarlo, T., Sandler, H., & Tittler, B. (1981). The role of personal space in family therapy. *Family Therapy, 8*, 255-266.

de Charms, R. (1968). *Personal causation*. San Diego, CA: Academic Press.

Dee, N., & Liebman, J. (1970). A statistical study of attendance in urban playgrounds. *Journal of Leisure Research, 2*, 145-159.

De Grace, G. (1987). The psychosocial characteristics associated with loneliness in the elderly and their homes, according to the type of housing. *Canadian Journal of Behavioural Science, 3*, 298-313.

De Jong, J. (1975). Introduction and welcome. In A. Chapanis (Ed.), *Ethnic variables in human factors engineering* (pp. xv-xvii). Baltimore, MD: Johns Hopkins University Press.

Delaski-Smith, D. (1984). Housing the elderly: Intergenerational family settings. *Journal of Housing for the Elderly, 2*, 61-70.

De Long, A. (1981). Phenomenological space-time: Toward and experiential relativity. *Science, 213*, 681-683.

Demarest, M. (1981). Entertainment on the house. *Time, 118*, 76-77.

Deming, W. (1986). *Out of the crisis*. Cambridge: MIT Center for Advanced Engineering Study.

Department of Energy. (1989). *Applied research, development, demonstration, testing and evaluation plan for environmental restoration and waste management*. Washington, DC: Government Printing Office.

Deutsch, A. (1949). *The mentally ill in America: A history of care and treatment from colonial times*. New York: Columbia University Press.

DeWailly, E., Nantel, A., Weber, J., & Meyer, F. (1989). High levels of PCBs in breast milk of Inuit women from Arctic Quebec. *Bulletin of Environmental Contamination and Toxicology, 43*, 641-646.

Dewar, R. (1984). Environmental productivity, population regulation and carrying capacity. *American Anthropologist, 86*, 601-614.

Diamond, J. (1982). *The gloom of the museum*. Woodstock, VT: Elm Tree Press.

Diffrient, N., Tilley, A., & Bardagjy, J. (1974). *Humanscale 1/2/3*. Cambridge: MIT Press.

di Gennaro, G., & Lenci, S. (1975). Architecture and prisons. In *Prison architecture*. London: Architectural Press.

Din of alarms hurts patients, caregivers. (1994). *American Journal of Nursing, 94*, 9.

Dobzhansky, T. (1964). *Heredity and the nature of man*. New York: Harcourt, Brace & World.

Dodge, M. (1972). *Modification of littering behavior: An exploratory study*. Unpublished master's thesis, Utah State University.

Dogan, M., & Rokkan, S. (Eds.). (1969). *Quantitative ecological analysis in the social sciences*. Cambridge: MIT Press.

Dohrenwend, B. (1975). Sociocultural and socio-psychological factors in the genesis of mental disorders. *Journal of Health and Social Behavior, 16*, 365-392.

Dohrenwend, B., & Dohrenwend, B. (1974). *Stressful life events: Their nature and effects*. New York: John Wiley.

Dohrenwend, B., Dohrenwend, B., Dodson, B., & Shrout, P. (1984). Symptoms, hassles, social supports and life events: Problem of confounded measures. *Journal of Abnormal Psychology, 93*, 222-230.

Downey, R. (1978). Differences between entering freshmen from different high schools. *Journal of College Student Personnel, 19*, 353-359.

Downs, R., & Stea, D. (1973). *Image and environment: Cognitive mapping and spatial behavior*. Chicago: Aldine.

Downs, R., & Stea, D. (1977). *Maps in minds*. New York: Harper & Row.

Drabek, T., & Key, W. (1983). *Conquering disaster: Family recovery and long-term consequences*. Irvington.

Dreyfus, H. (1972). *Symbol sourcebook*. New York: McGraw-Hill.

Drucker, P. (1993). *Post capitalist society*. New York: Harper Business.

Duffy, M. (1984). The role of design factors of the residential environment in the physical and mental health of the elderly. *Journal of Housing for the Elderly, 2*, 37-45.

Dumouchel, J. (1971). *Arrowhead final report*. Kansas City, MO: Environmental Research and Development Foundation.

Dunlap, R., & Catton, W. (1994). Struggling with human exceptionalism: The rise, decline and revitalization of environmental sociology. *American Sociologist, 25*, 5-30.

Dunlap, R., & Van Liere, K. (1978a). *Environmental concern: A bibliography of empirical studies and brief appraisal of the literature*. Monticello, IL: Vance Bibliographies.

Dunlap, R., & Van Liere, K. (1978b). The "new environmental paradigm." *Journal of Environmental Education, 9*, 10-19.

Durning, A. (1989). *Poverty and the environment: Reversing the downward spiral* (Worldwatch Paper 92). Washington, DC: Worldwatch Institute.

Dwyer, D. (1975). *People and housing in Third World cities*. White Plains, NY: Longman.

Dyson, F. (1984). *Weapons and hope*. New York: Harper & Row.

Eaker, E., & Castelli, W. (1988). Type A behavior and mortality from coronary disease in the Framingham study. *New England Journal of Medicine, 319*, 1480-1481.

Earle, T., & Cvetkovich, G. (1990). What was the meaning of Chernobyl? *Journal of Environmental Psychology, 10*, 169-176.

Earthworks Group. (1989). *50 simple things you can do to save the Earth*. Berkeley: Earth Works Press.

Eastwood, L. (1985). Personality, intelligence and personal space among violent and nonviolent delinquents. *Personality and Individual Differences, 6*, 717-723.

Ebstein, R., Novick, O., Umansky, R., Priel, B., Bennett, E., Nemanov, L., Katz, M., & Belmaker, R. (1996). Dopamine D4 receptor exon III polymorphism associated with the human personality trait of novelty seeking. *Nature Genetics, 12*, 78-80.

Eckert, A. (1992). *A sorrow in our heart: The life of Tecumseh*. New York: Bantam.

Edelstein, M. (1988). *Contaminated communities*. Boulder, CO: Westview.

Edmonson, B., & Han, S. (1983). Effects of socialization games on proximity and prosocial behavior of aggressively mentally retarded institutionalized women. *American Journal of Mental Deficiency, 87*, 435-440.

Edwards, D. (1980). Perception of crowding and tolerance for interpersonal proximity and separation in South Africa. *Journal of Social Psychology, 110*, 19-28.

Edwards, J. (1978). *Daylighting as supplement to electric illumination*. B.T. architectural dissertation, Ryerson Polytechnical Institute, Toronto.

Egenter, N. (1992). *Architectural anthropology*. Lausanne: Structura Mundi.

Eggington, J. (1982). *The poisoning of Michigan*. New York: Norton.

Ehrlich, P., & Ehrlich, A. (1970). *Population, resources, environment: Issues in human ecology*. New York: Freeman.

Eichinger, C. (1985). In search of innovation: Examining the POE process in the VA. In S. Klein, R. Wener, & S. Lehman (Eds.), *Environmental change / social change* (EDRA Vol. 16). Edmond, OK: Environmental Design Research Association.

Eisenberg-Berg, N., Hand, M., & Haake, R. (1981). The relationship of preschool children's habitual use of space to prosocial, antisocial and social behaviors. *Journal of General Psychology, 138*, 11-121.

Eiser, J. R. (1990). Nuclear attitudes after Chernobyl: A cross national study. *Journal of Environmental Psychology, 10*, 101-110.

Ekblad, S. (1990). Housing and health in Beijing: Implications of high-rise housing on children and the aged. *Journal of Sociology and Social Welfare, 17*, 51-77.

Ekland-Olson, S. (1986). Crowding, social control and prison violence: Evidence from the post-Ruiz years in Texas. *Law & Society Review, 20*, 389-421.

Eldridge, R. (1978). 1977 update for land disposal practices survey. *Waste Age*, 35.

Elgin, D. (1981). *Voluntary simplicity: An ecological lifestyle that promotes personal and social renewal*. New York: Bantam.

Eliot, E., & Cohen, J. (1981). Social facilitation effects via interpersonal distance. *Journal of Social Psychology, 114*, 237-249.

Enstrom, J. (1979). Rising lung cancer mortality among non-smokers. *Journal of the National Cancer Institute, 62*, 755.

EPA (Environmental Protection Agency). (1974). *Information on levels of environmental noise requisite to protect public health and welfare with an adequate margin of safety* (EPA 550/9-74-004). Washington, DC: Author.

Epstein, Y. (1981). Crowding stress and human behavior. *Journal of Social Issues, 37*, 126-144.

Erikson, E. (1959). The problem of ego identity. *Psychological Issues, 1*, 101-164.

Erikson, E. (1963). *Childhood and society*. New York: Norton.

Erikson, K. (1976). *Everything in its path*. New York: Simon & Schuster.

Esser, A. (Ed.). (1971). *Behavior and environment: Use of space by animals and men*. New York: Plenum.

Euston, A. (1967, April 19). *Socio-physical design policy*. Paper prepared for presentation to the Senate Subcommittee on Executive Reorganization of the Government.

Evans, G. (1979a). Behavioral and physiological consequences of crowding in humans. *Journal of Applied Social Psychology, 9*, 27-46.

Evans, G. (1979b). Graduate programs. In W. White (Ed.), *Resource in environment and behavior* (pp. 37-94). Washington, DC: American Psychological Association.

Evans, G., & Carrere, S. (1991). Traffic congestion, perceived control and physiological stress among urban bus drivers. *Journal of Applied Psychology, 76*, 658-653.

Evans, G., & Cohen, S. (1987). Environmental stress. In D. Stokols & I. Altman (Eds.), *Handbook of environmental psychology*. New York: John Wiley.

Evans, G., & Lepore, S. (1992). Conceptual and analytical issues in crowding research. *Journal of Environmental Psychology, 12*, 163-173.

Evans, G., Lepore, S., & Schroeder, A. (1996). The role of interior design elements in human responses to crowding. *Journal of Personality and Social Psychology, 70*, 41-46.

Evans, G., Palsane, M., Lepore, S., & Martin, J. (1989). Residential density and psychological health: The mediating effects of social support. *Journal of Personality & Social Psychology, 57*, 994-999.

Evans, G., Shapiro, D., & Lewis, M. (1993). Specifying dysfunctional mismatches between different control dimensions. *British Journal of Psychology, 84*, 255-273.

Fadan, Y. (1983). Traditional houses of Makka: The influence of socio-cultural themes upon Arab-Muslim dwellings. In A. Germen (Ed.), *Islamic architecture and urbanism* (pp. 295-326). Dammam, KSI: King Faisal University.

Fairchild, T., & White, D. (1981). *Organizational response to mental health needs of elderly disaster victims*. North Texas State University, Center for the Study of Aging.

Fairweather, G. (1969). *Community life for the mentally ill*. Hawthorne, NY: Aldine.

Fairweather, G. (1974). *Creating change in mental health organizations*. Elmsford, NY: Pergamon.

Fairweather, L. (1975). The evolution of the prison. In *Prison architecture*. London: Architectural Press.

Farbstein, J. (1983). Comments on his dual education. In D. Amedo, J. Griffin, & J. Porter (Eds.), *EDRA 14* (p. 276). Washington, DC: Environmental Design Research Association.

Farina, F. (1991). Predictors of anxiety towards computers. *Computers in Human Behavior, 7*, 263-267.

Faris, R., & Dunham, H. (1939). *Mental disorders in urban areas*. Chicago: University of Chicago Press.

Farley, F. (1990, May). The Type T personality, with some implications for practice. *California Psychologist*, p. 29.

Fashimpar, G. (1984). Criminal victimization and its effects upon elderly residents of public housing. *Journal of Housing for the Elderly, 2*, 3-15.

Faust, D., & Ziskin, J. (1988). The expert witness in psychology and psychiatry. *Science, 241*, 31-35.

Fawl, C. (1978). Disturbances children experience in their natural habitat. In R. Barker & Associates, *Habitats, environments and human behavior*. San Francisco: Jossey-Bass.

Feingold, E. (1990). Supporting the independence of elderly residents through control over their environment. *Journal of Housing for the Elderly, 6*, 25-32.

Feldman, R. (1990). Settlement-identity: Psychological bonds with home places in a mobile society. *Environment and Behavior, 22*, 183-229.

Feldman, S. (1966). Motivational aspects of attitudinal elements and their place in cognitive interaction. In S. Feldman (Ed.), *Cognitive consistency*. San Diego, CA: Academic Press.

Filion, P. (1992). Subjective dimensions of environmental adaptation among the elderly: A challenge to models of housing policy. *Journal of Housing for the Elderly, 10*, 3-32.

Finighan, W. (1980). Some empirical observations on the role of privacy in the residential environment. *Man Environment Systems, 10*, 153-159.

Finnie, W. (1973). Field experiments in litter control. *Environment and Behavior, 5*, 123-144.

Fischer, C. (1976). *The urban experience*. Orlando, FL: Harcourt Brace Jovanovich.

Fishbein, M., & Ajzen, I. (1975). *Belief, attitude, intention and behavior: An introduction to theory and research*. Reading, MA: Addison-Wesley.

Fisk, E. (1983). *The peacocks of Baboquivari*. New York: Norton.

Fiske, S., & Taylor, S. (1991). *Social cognition* (2nd ed.). New York: McGraw-Hill.

Flavin, C., & Lenssen, N. (1994). Reshaping the power industry. In *State of the World, 1994* (pp. 61-80). Washington, DC: Worldwatch Institute.

Fleming, I., Baum, A., & Weiss, L. (1987). Social density and perceived control as mediators of crowding stress in high-density residential neighborhoods. *Journal of Personality & Social Psychology, 52*, 899-906.

Folarin, B. (1983). The influence of sex of the approached child on the personal space of the approaching child. *Journal of Environmental Psychology, 3*, 157-160.

Folarin, B. (1989). Comparison of personal space as a function of grade and sex of interacting pairs of children. *Perceptual and Motor Skills, 68*, 873-874.

Ford, J., & Hoebeke, S. (1980). Distant personal spacing and psychological distance. *Psychological Reports, 46*, 1299-1303.

Foucault, M. (1973). *Madness and civilization: A history of insanity in the age of reason.* New York: Random House.

Foulks, E. (1972). *The Arctic hysterias of the north Alaskan Eskimo.* Washington, DC: American Anthropological Association.

Fox, K. (1984). Behavior settings and eco-behavioral science: A new arena for mathematical social science permitting a richer and more coherent view of human activities in social systems, Part I. *Mathematical Social Sciences, 7*, 117-135.

Fox, R. (1984). The world's urban explosion. *National Geographic, 166*, 179-185.

Francescato, G., Weidemann, S., Anderson, J., & Chenoweth, R. (1979). *Residents' satisfaction in HUD assisted housing: Design & management factors.* Washington, DC: U.S. Department of Housing and Urban Development.

Franck, K. (1980). Friends and strangers: The social experience of living in urban and non-urban settings. *Journal of Social Issues, 36*, 52-71.

Franck, K., & Ahrentzen, S. (1989). *New households, new housing.* New York: Van Nostrand Reinhold.

Frankenhaeuser, M., Lundberg, U., & Mardberg, B. (1990). *The total workload of men and women as related to occupational level and number and age of children* (Reports from the Department of Psychology, No. 726). Stockholm: Stockholm University.

Franklin, K., Janoff-Bulman, R., & Roberts, J. (1990). Long-term impact of parental divorce on optimism and trust: Changes in general assumptions or narrow beliefs. *Journal of Personality & Social Psychology, 59*, 743-755.

Fraser, T. (1989). *The worker at work.* London: Taylor & Francis.

Freedman, J. (1975). *Crowding and behavior.* New York: Viking.

Freedman, J., & Perlick, D. (1979). Crowding, contagion, & laughter. *Journal of Experimental Social Psychology, 15*, 295-303.

Frew, J. (1983). Clarity of boundary conditions in interpersonal contact. *Gestalt Journal, 6*, 117-123.

Fried, J. (1963). Grieving for a lost home. In L. Duhl (Ed.), *The urban condition* (pp. 151-171). New York: Basic Books.

Friedman, M., & Rosenman, R. (1959). Association of specific overt behavior patterns with blood and cardiovascular findings, blood cholesterol level, blood clotting time, incidence of arcus senilis, and clinical artery disease. *Journal of the American Medical Association, 169*, 1286-1296.

Friedman, M., Thoresen, C., Gill, J., Ulmer, D., Powell, L., Price, V., Brown, B., Thompson, L., Rabin, D., Breall, W., Bourg, E., Levy, R., & Dixon, T. (1986). Alteration of Type A behavior and its effect on cardiac recurrences in post myocardial infarction patients: Summary results of the recurrent coronary prevention project. *American Heart Journal, 112*, 653-655.

Friedman, H., Tucker, J., Schwartz, J., Tomlinson-Keasey, C., Martin, L., Wingard, D., & Criqui, M. (1995). Psychosocial and behavioral predictors of longevity: The aging and death of the "Termites." *American Psychologist, 50*, 69-78.

Fritsch, A., & Castleman, B. (1974). *Lifestyle index*. Washington, DC: Center for Science in the Public Interest.

Fritz, C. (1961). Disasters. In R. Merton & R. Nisbett (Eds.), *Social problems*. New York: Harcourt, Brace & World.

Fromm, E. (1969). *Escape from freedom*. New York: Avon.

Fromme, D., Jaynes, W., Taylor, D., & Hanold, E. (1989). Nonverbal behavior and attitudes toward touch. *Journal of Nonverbal Behavior, 13*, 3-14.

Fry, P. (1989). *Psychological perspectives of helplessness and control in the elderly*. Amsterdam: North Holland.

Fuchs, V., & Reklis, D. (1992). America's children: Economic perspectives and policy options. *Science, 255*, 41-46.

Fukuhara, S. (1977). An experimental study of visual behavior in social interaction: Eye contact in a dyad as affected by interaction distance and affiliation need. *Japanese Journal of Experimental Social Psychology, 17*, 30-38.

Fukui, S. (1983). Psychopathology of psychiatric patients in terms of personal space: A comparative study of schizophrenic, depressive and neurotic patients. *Kyushu Neuropsychiatry, 29*, 181-204.

Funk, S., & Houston, B. (1987). A critical analysis of the hardiness scale's validity and utility. *Journal of Personality and Social Psychology, 53*, 572-578.

Gallenkamp, C. (1976). *Maya: The riddle and rediscovery of a lost civilization*. New York: David McKay.

Ganjavi, O., Schell, B., Cachon, J., & Poporino, F. (1985). Geophysical variables and behavior: XXIX. Impact of atmospheric conditions on occurrences of individual violence among Canadian penitentiary populations. *Perceptual & Motor Skills, 61*, 259-275.

Gans, H. (1962). *The urban villagers*. New York: Free Press.

Gans, H. (1967). *The Levittowners: Way of life and politics in a new suburban community*. New York: Vintage.

Gärling, T. (1982). Swedish environmental psychology. *Journal of Environmental Psychology, 2*, 233-251.

Gärling, T. (1989). The role of cognitive maps in spatial decisions. *Journal of Environmental Psychology, 9*, 269-278.

Gaster, S. (1991). Urban children's access to their neighborhood: Changes over three generations. *Environment and Behavior, 23*, 70-85.

Gawron, V. (1982). Performance effects and noise intensity, psychological set and task type & complexity. *Human Factors, 24*, 225-243.

Geller, B., Winett, R., & Everett, P. (1982). *Preserving the environment*. Elmsford, NY: Pergamon.

Geller, E. S., Witmer, J. F., & Orebaugh, A. L. (1976). Instructions as a determinant of paper-disposal behaviors. *Environment and Behavior, 8*, 417-439.

Geller, E. S., Witmer, J., & Tuso, M. (1977). Environmental interventions for litter control. *Journal of Applied Psychology, 63*, 344-351.

Gerba, C., Wallis, C., & Melnick, J. (1975). Microbiological hazards of household toilets: Droplet production and the fate of residual organisms. *Applied Microbiology, 30*, 229-237.

Gewirtz, J. (1992). B. F. Skinner's legacy to human behavior and development. [K. Lattal (Ed.), Special issue: Reflections on B. F. Skinner and Psychology] *American Psychologist, 47*, 1411-1422.

Gibbons, A. (1993). Evolutionists take the long view on sex and violence. *Science, 261*, 987-988.

Gibbs, J. (1983). Problems and priorities: Perceptions of jail custodians and social service providers. *Journal of Criminal Justice, 11*, 327-338.

Gibson, J. (1979). *The ecological approach to visual perception*. Boston: Houghton-Mifflin.

Giel, R., & Ormel, J. (1977). Crowding and subjective health in the Netherlands. *Social Psychiatry, 12*, 37-42.

Gifford, R. (1983). The experience of personal space: Perception of interpersonal distance. *Journal of Nonverbal Behavior, 7*, 170-178.

Gifford, R., & O'Connor, B. (1986). Nonverbal intimacy: Clarifying the role of seating distance and orientation. *Journal of Nonverbal Behavior, 10*, 207-214.

Gillespie, R. (1991). *Manufacturing knowledge*. Cambridge: Cambridge University Press.

Gilman, B. (1916). Museum fatigue. *Scientific Monthly, 12*, 62-64.

Gilmour, D., & Walkey, F. (1981). Identifying violent offenders using a video measure of interpersonal distance. *Journal of Consulting & Clinical Psychology, 49*, 287-291.

Givoni, B. (1969). *Man, climate and architecture*. Amsterdam: Elsevier.

Gladhart, P., Zuiches, S., & Morrison, B. (1978). Impacts of rising prices upon residential energy consumption, attitudes and conservation policy acceptance. In S. Warkov (Ed.), *Energy policy in the United States: Social and behavioral dimensions*. New York: Praeger.

Glaser, U. (1985). The tavern as psychosocial encounter setting: Approaches and results of an empirical study. *Gruppen Dynamic, 16*, 351-359.

Glass, D., & Singer, J. (1972). *Urban stress: Experiments on noise and social stressors*. San Diego, CA: Academic Press.

Glass, G., Cohen, L., Smith, M., & Filby, N. (1982). *School class size: Research and policy*. Beverly Hills, CA: Sage.

Goering, P., & Bechtel, R. (1979). *Recommendations for single worker accommodation, Town of Pine Point, N.W.T.* Report to Cominco, Ltd., Canada.

Goetzberger, A. (1993). Solar energy contributions for sustainable development. In M. Prince (Ed.), *Advances in solar energy* (Vol. 8, pp. 14-22). New York: American Solar Energy Society.

Goffman, I. (1961). *Asylums: Essays on the social situation of mental patients and other inmates*. Garden City, NY: Doubleday.

Golany, G. (1978). *Urban planning for arid zones*. New York: John Wiley.

Gold, R. (1985). *Ranching, mining and the human impact of natural resource development*. New Brunswick, NJ: Transaction.

Goldhaber, M., Houts, R., & Disabella, R. (1982). Moving after the crisis: A prospective study of Three Mile Island area population mobility. *Environment and Behavior, 15*, 93-120.

Goldsmith, E., & Hill, R. (1986). Family development theory and space utilization: A review and synthesis. *Journal of Social Behavior and Personality, 1*, 223-232.

Golledge, R. (1978). Learning about urban environments. In T. Carlstein, D. Parkes, & N. Thrift (Eds.), *Timing space and spacing time*. London: Edward Arnold.

Good, L., Seigel, S., & Bay, R. (1965). *Therapy by design: Implications of architecture for human behavior*. Springfield, IL: Charles C Thomas.

Gorman, J. (1976). The Earth's the ceiling. *The Sciences, 16*, 16-20.

Gough, H. (1962). Clinical versus statistical prediction in psychology. In L. Postman (Ed.), *Psychology in the making* (pp. 526-584). New York: Knopf.

Gould, S. (1989). *Wonderful life: The Burgess shale and the nature of history*. New York: Norton.

Gouldner, A. (1960). The norm of reciprocity. *American Sociological Review, 25*, 161-178.

Gouldner, A., Pittman, D., Rainwater, L., & Stroberg, J. (1966). *A preliminary report on housing and community experiences of Pruitt-Igoe residents*. St. Louis, MO: Washington University.

Gove, W., Hughes, M., & Galle, O. (1979). Overcrowding in the home: An empirical investigation of its possible pathological consequences. *American Sociological Review, 44*, 59-80.

Grad, F., Rosenthal, A., Rockett, L., Fay, S., Heywood, J., Kain, J., Ingram, G., Harrison, D., & Tietemberg, T. (1975). *The automobile and the regulation of its impact on the environment*. Norman: University of Oklahoma Press.

Grant, E. (1965). An ethological description of some ecological patterns of schizophrenic behavior. *Proceedings of the Leeds Symposium on Behavioural Disorders* (pp. 3-14).

Gray, D. (1985). *Ecological beliefs and behaviors*. Westport, CT: Greenwood.

Gray, D., Eckles, C., & Fuehrer, R. (1982). *The relative predictive power of primary and derived ecological beliefs*. Paper presented at the meeting of the Eastern Psychological Association, Baltimore.

Grden, J. (1974). Anxiety or caffeinism: A diagnostic dilemma. *American Journal of Psychiatrists, 131*, 1089-1902.

Greenbaum, P., & Rosenfeld, H. (1980). Varieties of touching in greetings: Sequential structure and sex-related differences. *Journal of Nonverbal Behavior, 5*, 13-25.

Greven, P. (1970). *Four generations: Population, land and family in colonial Andover, Massachusetts*. Ithaca, NY: Cornell University Press.

Griffith, C. (1921). A comment upon the psychology of the audience. *Psychological Monographs, 30*, 36-47.

Groves, M. (1992). To move or not to move? Factors influencing the housing choice of elderly persons. *Journal of Housing for the Elderly, 10*, 33-47.

Guillemard, A., & Rein, M. (1993). Comparative patterns of retirement: Recent trends in developed societies. *Annual Review of Sociology, 19*, 469-503.

Gump, P. (1974). Operating environments in open and traditional schools. *School Review, 84*, 575-593.

Gump, P. (1987). School and classroom environments. In D. Stokols & I. Altman (Eds.), *Handbook of environmental psychology* (Vol. 1, pp. 691-732). New York: John Wiley.

Gump, P., & Ross, R. (1979). What's happening in schools of open design? *JSAS Catalogue Selected Documents in Psychology, 9*, 1816.

Gunderson, E. (1974). *Human adaptability to Antarctic conditions* (Antarctic Research Series, Vol. 22). Washington, DC: American Geophysical Union.

Gyllenhammer, P. (1977). *People at work*. Reading, MA: Addison-Wesley.

Haber, G. (1980). Territorial invasion in the classroom: Invadee response. *Environment and Behavior, 12*, 17-31.

Haddon, A. (Ed.). (1901). *Reports of the Cambridge anthropological expedition to the Torres Straits* (Vols. 1-2). Cambridge: Cambridge University Press.

Haggard, L., & Williams, D. (1992). Identity affirmation through leisure activities: Leisure symbols of the self. *Journal of Leisure Research, 24*, 1-18.

Hagino, G., & Ittelson, W. (Eds.). (1980). *Interaction process between human behavior and the environment*. Tokyo: University of Tokyo Press.

Hagino, G., Mochizuki, M., & Yamamoto, T. (1987). Environmental psychology in Japan. In D. Stokols & I. Altman (Eds.), *Handbook of environmental psychology* (Vol. 2, pp. 1155-1170). New York: John Wiley.

Hakken, D. (1993). Computing and social change: New technology and workplace transformation. *Annual Review of Anthropology, 22*, 107-132.

Halberstam, D. (1986). *The reckoning*. New York: William Morrow.

Hall, E. (1959). *The silent language*. Garden City, NY: Doubleday.

Hall, E. (1966). *The hidden dimension*. Garden City, NY: Doubleday.

Hall, E. (1974). *Handbook for proxemic research*. Washington, DC: Society for the Anthropology of Visual Communication.

Hamilton, V., & Sanders, J. (with Y. Hosoi, Z. Ishimura, N. Matsubara, H. Nishimura, N. Tomita, & K. Tokoro). (1983). Universals in judging wrongdoing: Japanese and Americans compared. *American Sociological Review, 48*, 199-211.

Handwerker, W. (1986). Modern demographic transition: An analysis of subsistence choices and reproductive consequences. *American Anthropologist, 88*, 400-417.

Hannertz, U. (1969). *Soulside: Inquiries into ghetto culture and community*. New York: Columbia University Press.

Hansell, S. (1991). The meaning of stress. *Contemporary Psychology, 36*, 112-114.

Hansen, J. (1988, June 23). *The greenhouse effect: Impacts of current global temperature and regional heat waves*. Testimony before the Committee on Energy and Natural Resources, U.S. Senate.

Hansen, J., Johnson, D., Lacis, A., Lebedeff, S., Lee, R., Rind, D., & Russell, G. (1981). Climate impact of increasing atmospheric carbon dioxide. *Science, 213*, 957-966.

Hansson, R., II, & Slade, K. (1977). Altruism toward a deviant in city and small town. *Journal of Applied Social Psychology, 7*, 272-279.

Harada, J., & Araragi, C. (1981). The effects of interpersonal distance and number of potential helpers on helping behavior. *Japanese Journal of Experimental Social Psychology, 21*, 35-39.

Hardin, G. (1968). The tragedy of the commons. *Science, 162*, 1243-1248.

Hardoy, J. (1968). *Urban planning in pre-Columbian America*. New York: Braziller.

Hareven, T. (1994). Aging and generational relations: A historical and life course perspective. *Annual Review of Sociology, 20*, 437-461.

Harrington, M. (1962). *The other America: Poverty in the United States*. New York: Macmillan.

Harris, C. (1943). A functional classification of cities in the United States. *Geographical Review, 33*, 86-99.

Harris, R., Hohenemser, C., & Kates, R. (1978). Our hazardous environment. *Environment, 20*, 6-15, 38-41.

Harris, C., & Ullman, E. (1945). The nature of cities. *Annals of the American Academy of Political and Social Science, 242*, 7-17.

Harrison, A., Clearwater, Y., & McKay, C. (1991). *From Antarctica to outer space: Life in isolation and confinement*. New York: Springer.

Hart, F., & Associates. (1979). *Preliminary assessment of cleanup costs for national hazardous waste problems*. Prepared for the Environmental Protection Agency, Washington, DC.

Hart, R., & Moore, G. (1973). The development of spatial cognition: A review. In R. Downs & D. Stea (Eds.), *Image and environment* (pp. 246-288). New York: Aldine.

Harter, S. (1978). Effectance motivation reconsidered: Toward a developmental model. *Human Development, 21*, 34-64.

Hartwigsen, G. (1986). Older widows in a retirement community: The case of Sun City area in Arizona. *Journal of Housing for the Elderly, 4*, 37-51.

Havighurst, J. (1969). A report to a special committee of the Gerontological Society. *The Gerontologist, 9*, 4, Pt. 2.

Hawkins, R. (1990). The life and contributions of Burrhus Frederick Skinner. *Education & Treatment of Children, 13*, 258-263.

Hawley, A. (1950). *Human ecology*. New York: Ronald.

Hayduk, L. (1983). Personal space: Where we now stand. *Psychological Bulletin, 94*, 293-335.

Hayduk, L. (1985). Personal space: The conceptual and measurement implications of structural equation models. *Canadian Journal of Behavioural Science, 17*, 140-149.

Hayduk, L., & Mainprize, S. (1980). Personal space of the blind. *Social Psychology Quarterly, 43*, 216-223.

Hayes-Roth, B., & Hayes-Roth, F. (1979). A cognitive model of planning. *Cognitive Science, 3*, 275-310.

Hayflick, L. (1994). *How and why we age*. New York: Ballantine.

Hayward, J. (1975). Home as an environment and psychological concept. *Landscape, 20*, 2-9.

Hayward, J. (1983). Comments on his dual education. In D. Amedo, J. Griffin, & J. Potter (Eds.), *EDRA 14* (p. 276). Washington, DC: Environmental Design Research Association.

Haywood, L., Kew, F., & Bramham, P. (1989). *Understanding leisure*. Orleans, MA: Hutchinson Education.

Heberlein, T. (1974). *Beliefs about sanctions, norm activation and violation of the anti-littering norm*. Paper presented to the Rural Sociological Meeting, Montreal.

Hediger, H. (1950). *Wild animals in captivity*. Newton, MA: Butterworth's Scientific.

Hediger, H. (1955). *Studies of the psychology and behavior of captive animals in zoos and circuses*. Newton, MA: Butterworth's Scientific.

Heerwagen, J. (1990, April). The psychological aspects of windows and window design. In K. Anthony, J. Choi, & B. Orland (Eds.), *Proceedings of the 21st Annual Conference of the Environmental Design Research Association*, Champaign, IL.

Heerwagen, J., & Orians, G. (1986). Adaptations to windowlessness: A study of the use of visual decor in windowed and windowless offices. *Environment and Behavior, 18*, 623-639.

Heft, H. (1988). The vicissitudes of ecological phenomena in environment-behavior research: On the failure to replicate the "angularity effect." *Environment and Behavior, 20*, 92-99.

Heider, F. (1944). Social perception and phenomenal causality. *Psychology Review, 51*, 358-374.

Heider, F. (1958). *The psychology of interpersonal relations*. New York: John Wiley.

Heiner, M., & McCullough, H. (1948). *Functional kitchen storage* (Cornell University Agricultural Experiment Station, Bulletin 846). Ithaca, NY: Cornell University.

Heise, D. (1969). Some methodological issues in semantic differential research. *Psychological Bulletin, 72*, 406-422.

Heller, T. (1984). Impact of environment on social and activity behavior in public housing for the elderly. *Journal of Housing for the Elderly, 2*, 17-25.

Helmreich, R. (1974). Evaluation of environments: Behavioral observations in an undersea habitat. In J. Lang, C. Burnette, W. Moleski, & D. Vachon (Eds.), *Designing for human behavior*. Stroudsberg, PA: Dowden, Hutchinson & Ross.

Helmreich, W. (1992). *Against all odds: Holocaust survivors and the successful lives they made in America*. New York: Simon & Schuster.

Helson, H. (1964). *Adaptation level theory*. New York: Harper & Row.

Henderson, K. (1992). Invisible pioneers? The impact of women on the recreation movement. *Leisure Sciences, 14*, 139-153.

Herman, J. (1988). On the failure to replicate the "angularity effect": Reply to Heft. *Environment and Behavior, 20*, 100-102.

Herman, J., Miller, B., & Shiraki, J. (1987). The influence of affective associations on the development of cognitive maps of large environments. *Journal of Environmental Psychology, 7*, 89-98.

Herman, J., Norton, L., & Klein, C. (1986). Children's distance estimates in a large scale environment: A search for the route angularity effect. *Environment and Behavior, 18*, 533-558.

Herman, J., Norton, L., & Roth, S. (1983). Children and adults' distance estimations in a large-scale environment: Effects of time and clutter. *Journal of Experimental Child Psychology, 36*, 453-470.

Hern, W. (1991). Proxemics: The application of theory to conflict arising from antiabortion demonstrators. *Population and Environment: A Journal of Interdisciplinary Studies, 12*, 379-388.

Hernandez, D. (1993). *America's children: Resources from family, government and the economy*. New York: Russell Sage.

Herzberg, F. (1968). One more time: How do you motivate employees? *Harvard Business Review, 46*, 1.

Herzog, T. (1989). A cognitive analysis of preference for urban nature. *Journal of Environmental Psychology, 9*, 27-43.

Hetherington, M., Cox, M., & Cox, R. (1976). Divorced fathers. *Family Coordinator, 25*, 417-428.

Hetherington, M., Cox, M., & Cox, R. (1978). The aftermath of divorce. In J. Stevens & M. Matthews (Eds.), *Mother-child, father-child relations*. Washington, DC: NAEYC.

Hetherington, M., Cox, M., & Cox, R. (1979). Stress and coping in divorce: A focus on women. In J. Gullahorn (Ed.), *Psychology and women in transition*. Washington, DC: B. H. Winston.

Hieb, L. (1977). *Space, time, world view and architecture form* [Mimeo]. Pullman: Washington State University.

Higashiyama, A., & Ono, H. (1988). "Koko," "soko," and "asoko," (here and there) as verbal dividers of space. *Japanese Psychological Research, 30*, 18-24.

Hill, R., Blackman, R., & Crane, D. (1982). The effect of the marital relationship on personal space orientation in married couples. *Journal of Social Psychology, 118*, 23-28.

Hiner, S. (1987). Health status and quality of life among elderly public housing residents. *Journal of Applied Gerontology, 6*, 405-414.

Hinrichsen, G. (1985). The impact of age concentrated, publicly assisted housing on older people's social and emotional well-being. *Journal of Gerontology, 40*, 758-760.

Hirst, E., & Hannon, B. (1979). Effects of energy conservation in residential and commercial buildings. *Science, 205*, 656-661.

Hirtle, S., & Jonides, J. (1985). Evidence of hierarchies in cognitive maps. *Memory and Cognition, 13*, 208-217.

Hoagland, W. (1995). Solar energy. *Scientific American, 273*, 170-173.

Hoch, I. (1976). City size effects, trends and policies. *Science, 193*, 856-863.

Hodges, B. (1974). Effect of valence on relative weighting in impression formation. *Journal of Personality and Social Psychology, 30*, 378-381.

Hodgson, R., & Thayer, R. (1980). Implied human influence reduces landscape beauty. *Landscape Planning, 7*, 171-179.

Hofferth, S., & Phillips, D. (1991). Child care policy research [S. Hofferth & D. Phillips (Eds.), Special issue: Child Care Policy Research]. *Journal of Social Issues, 47*, 1-14.

Holahan, C. (1982). *Environmental psychology*. New York: Random House.

Holmes, G., Karst, R., & Erhart, S. (1990). Proxemics and physical disability: Etiology and interactional barriers. *Journal of Applied Rehabilitation Counseling, 21*, 25-31.

Holmes, T., & Rahe, R. (1967). The social readjustment scale. *Journal of Psychosomatic Research, 4*, 189-194.

Holz, R., Brannigan, G., & Schofield, J. (1980). The kinetic family drawing as a measure of interpersonal distance. *Journal of Genetic Psychology, 137*, 307-308.

Homma, M. (1990). A Japanese perspective on crowding: How well have the Japanese adjusted to high density? *Psychologia: An International Journal of Psychology in the Orient, 33*, 128-137.

Hood, M. (1993). Comfort and caring: Two essential environmental factors. *Environment and Behavior, 25*, 710-724.

Housing Development Directorate. (1978). *Housing appraisal kit* (Vols. 1 & 2). London: Greater London Council, Department of Environment.

Howell, W. (1993). Engineering psychology in a changing world. In *Annual review of psychology* (Vol. 44, pp. 231-263). Palo Alto, CA: Annual Reviews.

Hoyt, H. (1939). *Structure and growth of residential neighborhoods in American cities*. Washington, DC: Federal Housing Administration.

Hundert, A., & Greenfield, N. (1969). Physical space and organizational behavior: A study of an office landscape. *Proceedings of the 77th Annual American Psychological Association, 4*, 601-602.

Hunt, J. M. (1944). *Personality and behavior disorders*. New York: John Wiley.

Hunt, M., & Hunt, G. (1985). Naturally occurring retirement communities. *Journal of Housing for the Elderly, 3*, 3-32.

Hurd, M. (1989). The economic status of the elderly. *Science, 244*, 659-664.

Husaini, B. (1991). Social and psychological well being of black elderly living in high rises for the elderly. *Journal of Gerontological Social Work, 16*, 57-78.

Huston, A. (1991). *Children in poverty: Child development and public policy*. Cambridge: Cambridge University Press.

Hutchison, S. (1990). How to protect yourself from your environment. *National Wildlife, 28*, 30-42.

Huxley, J. (1974). *Evolution: The modern synthesis* (3rd ed.). Sydney, Australia: Allen & Unwin.

Imamoglu, E. (1992). Housing and living environments of the Turkish elderly. *Journal of Environmental Psychology, 12*, 35-43.

Incoll, P. (1990). The influences of architectural theory on the design of Australian Antarctic stations. *Proceedings of the Fourth Symposium on Antarctic Logistics and Operations*, São Paulo.

Insel, P., & Lindgren, H. (1978). *Too close for comfort: The psychology of crowding*. Englewood Cliffs, NJ: Prentice Hall.

Ittelson, W. (1961). *Some factors influencing the design and function of psychiatric facilities* (Progress report). Brooklyn, NY: Brooklyn College.

Ittelson, W., Asai, M., & Ker, M. (Eds.). (1986). *Cross cultural research in environment and behavior*. Tucson: University of Arizona.

Ittelson, W., Proshansky, H., Rivlin, L., & Winkel, G. (1974). *An introduction to environmental psychology*. New York: Holt, Rinehart & Winston.

Iverson, R., et al. (1981). Physical effects of vehicular disturbances in arid lands. *Science, 212*, 915-916.

Iwai, K. (1986). The most appropriate space in special education—the most appropriate space between mentally retarded children and teacher. *Japanese Journal of Special Education, 24*, 35-42.

Iwata, O. (1978). Human spatial behavior. *Annual Review of Sociology, 4*, 29-56.

Iwata, O. (1980). Territoriality orientation, privacy orientation and locus of control as determinants of the perception of crowding. *Japanese Psychological Research, 22*, 13-21.

Izumi, K. (1957). An analysis for the design of hospital quarters for the neuropsychiatric patient. *Mental Hospitals, 8*, 31-32.

Jackson, E. (1991). Introduction. [Special issue: Leisure constraints/constrained leisure] *Leisure Sciences, 13*, 273-278.

Jackson, J., & Latane, B. (1981). Strength and number of solicitors and the urge toward altruism. *Personality and Social Psychology Bulletin, 7*, 415-422.

Jacobson, J. (1992). *Gender bias: Roadblock to sustainable development* (Worldwatch Paper 110). Washington, DC: Worldwatch Institute.

Jaffe, A. (1979). *Apparitions: An archetypal approach to deaths, dreams and ghosts.* Irving, TX: Spring.

Jain, U. (1987). Effects of short term density on personal space. *Indian Journal of Current Psychological Research, 2,* 25-31.

Janoff-Bulman, R. (1992). *Violated assumptions.* New York: Free Press.

Jewell, P. (1966). The concept of home range in mammals. In P. Jewell & C. Loizos (Eds.), *Play, exploration and territory in mammals* (pp. 85-109). New York: Academic Press.

Jirovec, R. (1985). Residential satisfaction as a function of micro and macro environmental conditions among urban elderly men. *Research on Aging, 7,* 601-616.

Johanson, D., & Shreeve, J. (1989). *Lucy's child.* New York: William Morrow.

Johnson, R. D., & Holbrow, C. H. (1977). *Space settlements: A design study.* Washington, DC: National Aeronautics and Space Administration.

Johnson, W., Stolzfus, V., & Craumer, P. (1977). Energy conservation in Amish agriculture. *Science, 198,* 373-378.

Jones, E. (1985). Interpersonal distancing behavior of hearing impaired versus normal hearing children. *Volta Review, 87,* 223-230.

Jones, P., & Wigley, N. (1990). Global warming trends. *Scientific American, 263,* 84-91.

Jouriles, E., Bourg, W., & Farris, A. (1991). Marital adjustment and child conduct problems: A comparison of the correlation across subsamples. *Journal of Consulting & Clinical Psychology, 59,* 354-357.

Jung, C. (1963). *Memories, dreams, reflections.* London: Collins & Routledge & Kegan Paul.

Kakar, S. (1970). *Frederick Taylor: A study in personality and motivation.* Cambridge: MIT Press.

Kamerman, S. (1991). Child care policies and programs: An international overview [S. Hofferth & D. Phillips (Eds.), Special issue: Child Care Policy Research]. *Journal of Social Issues, 47,* 179-196.

Kaminska-Feldman, M. (1988). Conditions of social deindividuation and asymmetry in rating self-others distance. *Polish Psychology Bulletin, 19,* 241-248.

Kaminski, G. (1983). The enigma of ecological psychology. *Journal of Environmental Psychology, 3,* 85-94.

Kanaga, K., & Flynn, M. (1981). The relationship between invasion of personal space and stress. *Human Relations, 34,* 239-248.

Kane, J. (1993). Does clozapine cause tardive dyskinesia? *Journal of Clinical Psychiatry, 54,* 327-330.

Kannel, W., & Thomas, H. (1982). Sudden coronary death: The Framingham study [H. Greenberg & E. Dwyer (Eds.), Special issue: Sudden Coronary Death]. *Annals of the New York Academy of Sciences, 382,* 3-21.

Kanouse, D., & Hanson, L. (1971). Negativity in evaluations. In E. Jones et al. (Eds.), *Attribution: Perceiving the causes of behavior*. Morristown, NJ: General Learning Press.

Kaplan, K., Firestone, I., Klein, K., & Sodikoff, C. (1983). Distancing in dyads: A comparison of four models. *Social Psychology Quarterly, 46*, 108-115.

Kaplan, R. (1994, February). The coming anarchy. *Atlantic Monthly*, pp. 44-76.

Kaplan, S. (1972). The challenge of environmental psychology: A proposal for new functionalism. *American Psychologist, 27*, 140-143.

Kaplan, S. (1987). Aesthetics, affect and cognition: Environmental preferences from an evolutionary perspective. *Environment and Behavior, 19*, 3-32.

Kaplan, S., Bardwell, L., & Slakter, D. (1993). The museum as a restorative environment. *Environment and Behavior, 25*, 725-742.

Kaplan, K., Firestone, I., Klein, K., & Sodikoff, C. (1983). Distancing in dyads: A comparison of four models. *Social Psychology Quarterly, 46*, 108-115.

Kaplan, S., & Kaplan, R. (1982). *Cognition and environment: Functioning in an uncertain environment*. New York: Praeger.

Karasek, R., & Theorell, T. (1990). *Healthy work: Stress, productivity and reconstruction of working life*. New York: Basic Books.

Kass, S., Herschler, D., & Companion, M. (1991). Training situational awareness through pattern recognition in a battlefield environment. *Military Psychology, 3*, 105-112.

Kates, R., & Wohlwill, J. (1966, October). Man's response to the physical environment [Special issue]. *Journal of Social Issues, 22*.

Katz, L. (1964). Effects of different monetary gain and loss on sequential two-choice behavior. *Journal of Experimental Psychology, 68*, 245-249.

Keating, C., & Keating, E. (1980). Distance between pairs and acquaintances and strangers on public benches in Nairobi, Kenya. *Journal of Social Psychology, 110*, 285-286.

Keck, P. (1991). Epidemiology of neuroleptic malignant syndrome. *Psychiatric Annals, 21*, 148-151.

Keller, S. (1968). *The urban neighborhood: A sociological perspective*. New York: Random House.

Kelley, H. (1967). Attribution theory in social psychology. In D. Levine (Ed.), *Nebraska Symposium on Motivation, 15*. Lincoln: University of Nebraska Press.

Kelly, G. A. (1955). *The psychology of personal constructs*. New York: Norton.

Kelly, J., & Wallerstein, J. (1975). The effects of parental divorce: I. The experience of the child in early latency: II. The experience of the child in late latency. *American Journal of Orthopsychiatry, 45*, 253-254.

Kelly, J., & Wallerstein, J. (1976). The effects of parental divorce: Experiences of the child in early latency. *American Journal of Orthopsychiatry, 46*, 20-32.

Kelly, J., & Wallerstein, J. (1977). Brief interventions with children in divorcing families. *American Journal of Orthopsychiatry, 47*, 23-39.

Kempton, W., Darley, J., & Stern, P. (1992). Psychological research for the new energy problems. *American Psychologist, 47*, 1213-1223.

Kennedy, K. (1975). International anthropometric variability and its effects on aircraft cockpit design. In A. Chapanis (Ed.), *Ethnic variables in human factors engineering* (pp. 47-66). Baltimore, MD: Johns Hopkins University Press.

Kerr, R. (1988a). No longer willful, Gaia becomes respectable. *Science, 240*, 393-395.

Kerr, R. (1988b). Indoor radon: The deadliest pollutant. *Science, 240*, 606-608.

Kerr, R. (1991). Global temperature hits record again. *Science, 251*, 274.

Kerr, R. (1994). Antarctic ozone hole fails to recover. *Science, 266*, 217.

Kerr, R. (1995). It's official: First glimmer of greenhouse warming seen. *Science, 270*, 1565-1567.

Kerr, R. (1996). Ozone destroying chlorine tops out. *Science, 271*, 32.

Kiesler, C., & Sibulkin, A. (1987). *Mental hospitalization*. Newbury Park, CA: Sage.

Kiesler, C., & Simpkins, C. (1993). *The unnoticed majority in psychiatric inpatient care*. New York: Plenum.

King, L., & Jeffrey, D. (1972). City classification by oblique factor analysis of time series data. In B. Berry (Ed.), *City classification handbook: Methods and applications* (pp. 211-224). New York: John Wiley.

King, J., Marans, R., & Solomon, L. (1982). *Preconstruction evaluation: A report on the Full Scale Mock-Up and Evaluation of Hospital Rooms*. Ann Arbor: University of Michigan, Architectural Research Laboratory.

Kinloch, G. (1986). A multivariate analysis of social distance in Hawaii. *Journal of Social Psychology, 126*, 137-139.

Kira, A. (1966). *The bathroom*. New York: Viking.

Kira, A. (1976). *The bathroom: Criteria for design* (2nd ed.). New York: Viking.

Kirmeyer, S. (1978). Urban density and pathology: A review of research. *Environment and Behavior, 10*, 247-269.

Kleeman, W. (1981). *The challenge of interior design*. Boston: CBI.

Kleeman, W. (1983, April). Paper presented at the Information Technology and Office Design workshop, *EDRA 13*, Lincoln, NE.

Kleeman, W. (1991). *Interior design of the electronic office*. New York: Van Nostrand Reinhold.

Klein, G. S., & Holt, R. P. (1960). Problems and issues in current studies of subliminal activation. In J. Pretman & E. Hartley (Eds.), *Festschrift for Gardner Murphy*. New York: Harper.

Klein, J. (1991). Negativity effects in impression formation: A test in the political arena. *Personality and Social Psychology Bulletin, 17*, 412-418.

Kleinke, C. (1980). Interaction between gaze and legitimacy of request on compliance in a field setting. *Journal of Nonverbal Behavior, 5*, 3-12.

Kleitman, N. (1963). *Sleep and wakefulness*. Chicago: University of Chicago Press.

Kline, L., & Bell, P. (1983). Privacy preference and interpersonal distancing. *Psychological Reports, 53*, 1214.

Kline, L., Bell, P., & Babcock, A. (1984). Field dependence and interpersonal distance. *Bulletin of the Psychonomic Society, 22*, 421-422.

Kluckhohn, F., & Strodtbeck, F. (1961). *Variations in value orientations*. Evanston, IL: Row, Peterson.

Knowles, R. (1977). *Energy and form*. Talk given at the Alaskan Urban Design Forum, Alaska State Council on the Arts, Anchorage.

Knowles, R. (1981). *Sun rhythm form*. Cambridge: MIT Press.

Kobasa, S. (1979). Stressful life events, personality and health: An inquiry into hardiness. *Journal of Personality and Social Psychology, 37*, 1-11.

Kolata, F. (1982). Value of low-sodium diets questioned. *Science, 216*, 31-39.

Koncelik, J. (1976). *Designing the open nursing home*. Stroudsberg, PA: Dowden, Hutchinson & Ross.

Koncelik, J. (1982). *Aging and the product environment*. Stroudsberg, PA: Dowden, Hutchinson & Ross.

Kornhauser, A. (1965). *Mental health of the industrial worker*. New York: John Wiley.

Korte, C. (1978). Helpfulness in the urban environment. In A. Baum, J. Singer, & S. Valins (Eds.), *Advances in environmental psychology: Vol. 1. The urban environment*. Hillsdale, NJ: Lawrence Erlbaum.

Korte, C. (1980). *Urban-nonurban differences in social behavior and social psychological models of urban impact*. New York: Lawrence Erlbaum.

Korzybski, A. (1958). *Science and sanity: An introduction to non-Aristotelian systems and general semantics*. Lakerville, CT: Institute of General Semantics.

Kostof, S. (1972). *Caves of god*. Cambridge: MIT Press.

Kotlowitz, A. (1991). *There are no children here*. New York: Anchor.

Krantz, D., & Schulz, R. (1980). Personal control and health: Some applications to crisis of middle and old age. In A. Baum & J. Singer (Eds.), *Advances in environmental psychology* (Vol. 2). Hillsdale, NJ: Lawrence Erlbaum.

Kraus, R. (1994). *Leisure in a changing America: Multicultural perspectives*. New York: Macmillan.

Kreps, G. (1984). Sociological inquiry and disaster research. *Annual Review of Sociology, 10*, 309-330.

Kron, J. (1983). *Home-psych: The social psychology of home and decoration*. New York: Potter.

Kruse, L., & Arlt, R. (1984). *Environment and behavior: An interdisciplinary and multi-disciplinary bibliography, 1970-1981* (Vols. 1 & 2). Munich: Sauer.

Kruse, L., Grauman, K., & Lantermann, E. (1990). *Ökologische Psychologie*. München: Psychologie Verlags Union.

Kruskal, W. (1975). Statistics, energy and lifestyle [Letter to the editor]. *Science, 187*, 10.

Kuethe, J. (1962). Social schemas. *Journal of Abnormal and Social Psychology, 64*, 31-38.

Kuhn, T. (1970). *The structure of scientific revolutions* (2nd ed.). Chicago: University of Chicago Press.

Kulka, R., & Weingarten, H. (1979). The long-term effects of parental divorce in childhood on adult adjustment [T. Levitin (Ed.), Special issue: Children of Divorce]. *Journal of Social Issues, 35*, 50-78.

Kunreuther, J., Ginsberg, R., Miller, L., Sagi, P., & Slovic, P. (1978). *Disaster insurance protection: Public policy lessons*. New York: John Wiley.

Kunzendorff, R., & Denney, J. (1982). Definitions of personal space: Smokers versus nonsmokers. *Psychological Reports, 50*, 818.

Lacey, H. (1979). Control, perceived control and the methodological role of cognitive constructs. In L. Perlmuter & R. Monty (Eds.), *Choice and perceived control* (pp. 5-16). Hillsdale, NJ: Lawrence Erlbaum.

Lacey, J. (1967). Somatic response patterning and stress: Some revisions of activation theory. In M. Appley & R. Trumbull (Eds.), *Psychological stress* (pp. 14-37). Norwalk, CT: Appleton-Century-Crofts.

Lamm, R. (1973). Local growth: Focus of a changing American value. *Equilibrium, 1*, 4-8.

Landsberg, H. (1978). Planning for the climatic realities of arid regions. In G. Golany (Ed.), *Urban planning for arid zones* (pp. 23-37). New York: John Wiley.

Lang, J. (1989). Cultural implications of housing policy design. In S. Low & E. Chambers (Eds.), *Housing, culture and design* (pp. 375-392). Philadelphia: University of Pennsylvania Press.

Langan, P. (1994). Between prison and probation: Intermediate sanctions. *Science, 264*, 791-793.

Lange, H., Mueller, C., & Donnerstein, E. (1979). The effects of social, spatial and interference density on performance and mood. *Journal of Social Psychology, 109*, 283-287.

Langer, E. (1983). *The psychology of control*. Beverly Hills, CA: Sage.

Langer, E. (1989). *Mindfulness*. Reading, MA: Addison-Wesley.

Langer, E., & Rodin, J. (1976). The effects of choice and enhanced personal responsibility for the aged: A field experiment in an institution. *Journal of Personality & Social Psychology, 34*, 191-198.

Lapierre, D. (1985). *City of joy*. New York: Warner.

Larson, J., & Lowe, W. (1990). Family cohesion and personal space in families with adolescents. *Journal of Family Issues, 11*, 101-108.

Latane, B., & Nida, S. (1981). Ten years of research on group size and helping behavior. *Psychological Bulletin, 89*, 308-334.

Lave, L., Hendrickson, C., & McMichael, F. (1995). Environmental implications of electric cars. *Science, 268*, 995.

Lawton, M. P. (1990). Residential environment and self-directedness among older people. *American Psychologist, 45*, 638-640.

Lawton, M. P., & Nahemow, L. (1973). Ecology and the aging process. In C. Eisdorfer & P. Lawton (Eds.), *The psychology of adult development and aging*. Washington, DC: American Psychological Association.

Lazarus, R. S., & McCleary, R. (1951). Autonomic discrimination without awareness: A study of subception. *Psychological Review, 58*, 113-122.

Leaderer, B. (1982). Air pollutant emissions from kerosene space heaters. *Science, 218*, 1113-1115.

Leakey, R., & Lewin, R. (1977). *Origins*. New York: E. P. Dutton.

Lecompte, W., & Willems, E. (1970). Ecological analysis of a hospital. In J. Archea & C. Eastman (Eds.), *EDRA 2* (Proceedings of the Second Annual Conference, pp. 421-425). Washington, DC: Environmental Design Research Association.

Ledbetter, C. B. (1978). *Developing functional requirements for facilities in cold regions: Social aspects*. Hanover: Cold Regions Research & Engineering Laboratory.

Lee, T. (1968). Urban neighborhood as a socio-spatial schema. *Human Relations, 21*, 241-267.

Lee, T. (1978). A theory of socio-spatial schemata. In S. Kaplan & R. Kaplan (Eds.), *Humanscape: Environments for people*. North Scituate, MA: Duxbury.

Leighton, A. (1959). *My name is legion*. New York: Basic Books.

Leik, R., Leik, S., Ekker, K., & Gifford, G. (1982). *Under the threat of Mount Saint Helens*. Washington, DC: National Science Foundation.

Lennox, A. (1990). Decoding the imagery of prisons: What role for environmental psychology? *Journal of Environmental Psychology, 10*, 273-284.

Leonard, J., & Newman, R. (1970). Three types of maps for blind travel. *Ergonomics, 13*, 165-179.

Lerner, D. (1958). *The passing of traditional society: Modernizing the Mideast*. New York: Free Press.

Lerner, M. (1980). *The belief in a just world*. New York: Plenum.

Levine, A. (1982). *Love Canal: Science, politics & people*. Lexington, MA: D. C. Heath.

Levine, M. (1982). You-are-here maps: Psychological considerations. *Environment and Behavior, 14*, 221-237.

Levine, M., Marchon, I., & Hanley, G. (1984). The placement and misplacement of you-are-here maps. *Environment and Behavior, 16*, 139-157.

Levine, R., Lynch, K., Miyake, K., & Lucia, M. (1989). The Type A city: Coronary heart disease and the pace of life. *Journal of Behavioral Medicine, 12,* 509-524.

Levine, R., Martinez, T., Brase, G., & Sorenson, K. (1994). Helping in 36 U.S. cities. *Journal of Personality & Social Psychology, 67,* 69-82.

Levitt, L., & Leventhal, G. (1978). Effect of density and environmental noise on perception of time, the situation, oneself and others. *Perceptual & Motor Skills, 47,* 999-1009.

Levy-Leboyer, C. (1980). *Psychologie et environnement.* Paris: Presses Universitaires de France.

Lewin, K. (1951). *Field theory in social science.* New York: Harper.

Lewin, R. (1988). A revolution of ideas in agricultural origins. *Science, 240,* 984-986.

Lewin, R. (1989). *Human evolution: An illustrated introduction* (2nd ed.). Boston: Blackwell.

Lewis, J. (1988). *Strengthening the poor: What we have learned.* New Brunswick, NJ: Transaction.

Lewis, O. (1961). *The children of Sanchez.* New York: Random House.

Lewis, T. (1995). The difficult quest of Herbert Needleman. *National Wildlife, 33,* 20-25.

Liddell, C., & Kruger, P. (1989). Activity and social behavior in a crowded South African township nursery: A follow-up study on the effects of crowding at home. *Merrill-Palmer Quarterly, 35,* 209-226.

Liebow, E. (1967). *Tally's corner.* Boston: Little, Brown.

Liimets, H., Niit, T., & Heidmets, M. (Eds.). (1983). *Man in the psychophysical environment.* Tallinn: Estonian Branch of the Soviet Psychological Society and Tallinn Pedagogical Institute.

Likens, G., Driscoll, C., & Buso, D. (1996). Long term effects of acid rain: Response and recovery of a forest ecosystem. *Science, 272,* 244-246.

Lindquist, H. (1975). *China: Focus on revolution.* Englewood Cliffs, NJ: Prentice Hall.

Little, B. (1972). Psychological man as scientist, humanist and specialist. *Journal of Experimental Research in Personality, 6,* 95-118.

Lobo, S. (1982). *A house of my own.* Tucson: University of Arizona Press.

Logan, C. (1990). *Private prisons: Pros and cons.* Oxford: Oxford University Press.

Lombardo, J. (1986). Interaction of sex and sex role in response to violations of preferred seating arrangements. *Sex Roles, 15,* 173-183.

Lombardo, T. (1987). *The reciprocity of perceiver and environment: The evolution of James J. Gibson's ecological psychology.* Hillsdale, NJ: Lawrence Erlbaum.

Long, G. (1984). Psychological tension and closeness to others: Stress and interpersonal distance preference. *Journal of Psychology, 117,* 143-146.

Loo, C. (1992). *Chinatown.* New York: Praeger.

Louw, G. N. (1971). Water economy of certain Namib desert animals. *South African Journal of Science, 67*(3), 119-123.

Louw, G., & Seely, M. (1982). *Ecology of desert organisms*. White Plains, NY: Longman.

Love, K., & Aiello, J. (1980). Using projective techniques to measure interaction distance: A methodological note. *Personality & Social Psychology Bulletin, 6*, 102-104.

Lovejoy, C. O. (1981). The origin of man. *Science, 211*(4480), 341-350.

Lovelock, J. (1978). *The ages of GAIA*. New York: Norton.

Lovelock, J. (1979). *Gaia: A new look at life on Earth*. Oxford: Oxford University Press.

Lowrey, P. (1993). Designing for the child's privacy in the preschool environment. In R. Feldman, G. Hardie, & D. Saile (Eds.), *Power by design: EDRA 24* (pp. 180-188). Edmond, OK: Environmental Design Research Association.

Ludlow, L., & Levy, S. (1984). Personal space as a function of infant illness: An application of multidimensional scaling. *Journal of Pediatric Psychology, 9*, 331-347.

Lumsden, C., & Wilson, E. O. (1981). *Genes, mind and culture*. Cambridge, MA: Harvard University Press.

Lynch, K. (1960). *Image of the city*. Cambridge: MIT Press.

Lynch, K. (1977). *Growing up in cities: Studies of the spatial environment of adolescence in Cracow, Melbourne, Mexico City, Salta, Toluca and Warszawa*. Cambridge: MIT Press.

Lynch, K. (1981). *A theory of good city form*. Cambridge: MIT Press.

MacDonald, J., & Gifford, R. (1989). Territorial cues and defensible space theory: The burglar's point of view. *Journal of Environmental Psychology, 9*, 13-21.

MacDonald, W., & Oden, C. (1973). Effects of extreme crowding on the performance of five married couples during 12 weeks of intensive training. *Proceedings of the 81st Annual Convention of the APA* (Vol. 8, 209-210). Washington, DC: American Psychological Association.

Madden, T., Ellen, P., & Ajzen, I. (1992). A comparison of the theory of planned behavior and the theory of reasoned action. *Personality and Social Psychology Bulletin, 18*, 3-9.

Mader, G., Spangle, W., & Blair, M. (1980). *Land use planning after earthquakes: Final report*. Spangler.

Magenau, E. (Ed.). (1959, March 10-12). *Research for architecture: Proceedings of the AEA-NSF Conference* (Ann Arbor, MI). Washington, DC: NSF.

Maki, R. (1981). Categorization and distance effects with spatial linear orders. *Journal of Experimental Psychology: Human Learning and Memory, 7*, 15-32.

Malkin, J. (1992). *Hospital interior architecture*. New York: Van Nostrand Reinhold.

Malt, H. (1972). *An analysis of public safety as related to the incidence of crime in parks and recreational areas in central cities*. Washington, DC: Department of Housing and Urban Development.

Manaster, G., Cleland, C., & Brooks, J. (1978). Emotions as movements in relation to others. *Journal of Indian Psychology, 34,* 244-253.

Mandal, M., & Maitra, S. (1985). Perception of facial affect and physical proximity. *Perceptual & Motor Skills, 60,* 782.

Mangelsdorf, A. (1985). Lessons learned and forgotten: The need for prevention and mental health intervention in disaster preparedness. *Journal of Community Psychology, 13,* 239-257.

Mangin, W. (1967). Squatter settlements. *Scientific American, 217,* 21-29.

Mangin, W. (1973). Squatter settlements. In K. Davis (Ed.), *Cities, their origin, growth and human impact.* New York: Freeman.

Mann, C. (1991). Lynn Margulis: Science's unruly earth mother. *Science, 252,* 378-381.

Mannheim, K. (1956). *Essays on the sociology of culture.* London: Routledge & Kegan Paul.

Maple, T. (1983). Environmental psychology and great ape reproduction. *International Journal for the Study of Animal Problems, 4,* 295-299.

Marans, R., & Spreckelmeyer, K. (1982). Measuring overall architectural quality: A component of the building environment. *Environment and Behavior, 14,* 652-670.

Marans, R., & Yan, X. (1989). Lighting quality and environmental satisfaction in open and enclosed offices. *Journal of Architecture and Planning Research, 6,* 118-131.

Marcus, C. (1974). The house as symbol of the self. In J. Lang, C. Burnette, W. Moleski, & D. Vachon (Eds.), *Designing for human behavior* (pp. 130-146). Stroudsberg, PA: Dowden, Hutchinson & Ross.

Mardberg, B., Lundberg, U., & Frankenhaeuser, M. (1990). *The total workload of male and female white collar workers: Construction of a questionnaire and a scoring system* (Reports from the Department of Psychology, No. 714). Stockholm: Stockholm University.

Marks, R., & Fuller, R. (1973). *The dymaxion world of Buckminster Fuller.* New York: Anchor.

Marks, S. (1991). *Southern hunting in black and white.* Princeton, NJ: Princeton University Press.

Markus-Kaplan, M., & Kaplan, K. (1979). The typology, diagnosis, pathologies and treatment of Hellenic versus Hebraic personality styles: A proposal on the psychology of interpersonal distancing. *Journal of Psychology & Judaism, 3,* 153-167.

Marshall, E. (1982). EPA may allow more lead in gasoline. *Science, 215,* 1375-1378.

Marshall, E. (1985). The rise and decline of Temik. *Science News, 229,* 1369-1371.

Martin, J., & O'Reilly, J. (1988). Contemporary environment-behavior research in zoological parks: Editors' introduction. *Environment and Behavior, 20,* 387-395.

Martin, P., & Klein, R. (Eds.). (1989). *Quarternary extinctions: A prehistoric revolution.* Tucson: University of Arizona Press.

Mason, J., Maher, J., Hartley, L., Moughey, E., Perlow, M., & Jones, L. (1976). Selectivity of corticosteroid and catecholamine responses to various natural stimuli. In G. Serban (Ed.), *Psychopathology of human adaptation* (pp. 147-171). New York: Plenum.

Matlin, M., & Strang, D. (1978). *The Pollyanna principle: Selectivity in language, memory and thought*. Cambridge, MA: Schenkman.

Matthews, K. (1988). Coronary heart disease and Type A behaviors: Update on an alternative to the Booth-Kewle and Friedman (1987) quantitative review. *Psychological Bulletin, 104*, 373-380.

Maykovich, M. (1980). Social distance between Chinese and Americans. *Acta Psychologica Taiwanica, 22*, 1-12.

Mazur, A., & Rosa, E. (1974). Energy and lifestyle. *Science, 186*, 607-610.

McCarthy, D., & Saegert, S. (1978). Residential density, social overload and social withdrawal. *Human Ecology, 6*, 253-272.

McClelland, L., & Belsten, L. (1979). Prompting energy conservation in university dormitories by physical, policy and resident behavior changes. *Journal of Environmental Systems, 9*, 29-38.

McDougall, W. (1918). *Social psychology*. Boston: John W. Luce.

McGinnies, E. (1949). Emotionality and perceptual defense. *Psychological Review, 56*, 244-251.

McGinnies, W. J., Goldman, B. J., & Paylore, P. (Eds.). (1965). *Deserts of the world*. Tucson: University of Arizona Press.

McGurk, B., Davis, J., & Grehan, J. (1981). Assaultive behavior personality and personal space. *Aggressive Behavior, 7*, 317-324.

McIntyre, N. (1992). Involvement in risk recreation: A comparison of objective and subjective measures of involvement. *Journal of Leisure Research, 24*, 64-71.

McKechnie, G. (1974). *Manual for the Environmental Response Inventory*. Palo Alto, CA: Consulting Psychologists Press.

McKechnie, G. (1978). The Environmental Response Inventory in application. In K. Craik & G. McKechnie (Eds.), *Personality and the environment*. Beverly Hills, CA: Sage.

McNamara, R. (1981). *The McNamara years at the World Bank: Major policy addresses of Robert S. McNamara 1968-81*. Baltimore, MD: Johns Hopkins University Press.

Meadows, D., Meadows, D., & Randers, J. (1992). *Beyond the limits*. Mills, VT: Chelsea Green.

Meadows, D., Meadows, D., Randers, J., & Behrens, W. (1972). *The limits to growth*. New York: New American Library.

Megargee, E. (1977). The association of population density, reduced space and uncomfortable temperatures with misconduct in a prison community. *American Journal of Community Psychology, 5*, 289-298.

Melges, F., & Swartz, M. (1989). Oscillations of attachment in borderline personality disorder. *American Journal of Psychiatry, 146,* 1115-1120.

Melton, A. (1935). *Problems of installation in museums of art* (New Series No. 14). Washington, DC: American Association of Museums.

Meltzer, D. (1983). Temperature and distance as technical dimensions of interpretation. *Revista Uruguaya de Psicoanalysis, 62,* 15-24.

Menchú, R. (1983). *I, Rigoberta Menchu: An Indian woman in Guatemala.* London: Verso.

Mendel, G. (1865). *Verhandlungen des Naturforschenden Vereines in Brunn* (bd. iv.). Anderson, CT.

Mercer, S., & Kane, R. (1979). *Health social work.*

Merzbach, R. (1975). *Dodge Daily Journal,* p. 1.

Metzger, W. (1966). Figural-Wahrnehmung. In W. Metzger (Ed.), *Handbuch der Psychologie* (pp. 693-744). Bern: Hogrefe.

Meyer, D. (1972). Classification of U.S. metropolitan areas by the characteristics of their nonwhite populations. In B. Berry (Ed.), *City classification handbook* (pp. 61-94). New York: John Wiley.

Michelson, W. (1968). Most people don't want what architects want. *Trans-Action, 5,* 37-43.

Michelson, W. (1985). Basic dimensions for the analysis of behavioral potential in the urban environment II: An update on methodological and substantive results. In W. Ittelson, M. Asai, & M. Ker (Eds.), *Cross cultural research in environment and behavior: Proceedings of the Second Japan-US Conference on Environment and Behavior* (pp. 195-208). Tucson: University of Arizona.

Mikkin, H. (1988). *Environmental conditions for group activities.* Tallinn, Estonia: Tallinn Pedagogical Institute.

Milgram, S. (1970). The experience of living in cities. *Science, 167,* 1461-1468.

Milgram, S. (1973). [Chapter 2 introduction]. In W. Ittelson (Ed.), *Environment and cognition.* New York: Seminar.

Milgram, S., & Sabini, J. (1978). On maintaining urban norms: A field experiment in the subway. In A. Baum, J. S. Singer, & S. Valins (Eds.), *Advances in environmental psychology: Vol. 1. The urban environment* (pp. 31-56). Hillsdale, NJ: Lawrence Erlbaum.

Miller, A. (1981). *The drama of the gifted child.* New York: Basic Books.

Miller, N. E. (1944). Experimental studies of conflict. In J. M. Hunt (Ed.), *Personality and the behavior disorders* (pp. 431-465). New York: Ronald.

Miller, O. (1984). Culture and development of everyday social explanation. *Journal of Personality and Social Psychology, 46,* 961-978.

Miller, T., Turner, C., Tindale, S., Posavac, E., & Dugoni, B. (1991). Reasons for the trend toward null findings in research on Type A behavior. *Psychological Bulletin, 110,* 469-485.

Mitchell, R. (1971). Some social implications of high density housing. *American Socio-logical Review, 36,* 18-29.

Mitchell, R. (1980). Public opinion and nuclear power before and after Three Mile Island. *Resources, 64,* 5-9.

Monbiot, G. (1994). The tragedy of the enclosure. *Scientific American, 270,* 159.

Monk, T. (1987). Coping with the stress of jet lag. *Work and Stress, 1,* 163-166.

Montello, D. (1988). Classroom seating location and its effects on course achievement. *Journal of Environmental Psychology, 8,* 149-157.

Montello, D. (1991). Spatial orientation and the angularity of urban routes: A field study. *Environment and Behavior, 23,* 47-69.

Montessori, M. (1964). *The Montessori method.* Cambridge, MA: Schocken.

Moore, C. (1994). Greenest city in the world! *International Wildlife, 24,* 38-43.

Moore, D., & Glynn, T. (1984). Variation in question rate as a function of position in the classroom. *Educational Psychiatry, 4,* 232-248.

Moore, E. (1982). A prison environment's effect on health care service demands. *Journal of Environmental Systems, 11,* 17-34.

Moore, G. (1968). *Emerging methods in environmental design & planning* (Proceedings of the first Design Methods Group conference). Boston: DMG.

Moore, G., & Howell, S. (1982). *A research agenda for the eighties.* Washington, DC: Environmental Design Research Association.

Moos, R. (1986). *Work Environment Scale Manual* (2nd ed.). Palo Alto, CA: Consulting Psychologists Press.

Moos, R., & Lempke, S. (1994). *Group residences for older adults.* Oxford: Oxford University Press.

Moran, R., & Dolphin, C. (1986). The defensible space concept: Theoretical and opera-tional explication. *Environment and Behavior, 18,* 396-416.

Moreland, F. (1981). *Earth covered buildings: An exploratory analysis for hazard and energy performance.* Report prepared for the Federal Emergency Management Agency, Washington, DC.

Morell, D. (1981). Energy conservation and public policy: If it's such a good idea, why don't we do more of it? [C. Seligman & L. Becker (Eds.), Special issue] *Journal of Social Issues, 37,* 8-30.

Morris, E., & Smith, G. (1980). A functional analysis of adult affection and children's interpersonal distance. *Psychological Record, 30,* 155-163.

Moses, S. (1989, October). Food coloring may alter kid's behavior. *Monitor,* p. 9.

Moss, F. (1924). Study of animal drives. *Journal of Experimental Psychology, 8,* 165-185.

Mossman, B., Bignon, J., Corn, M., Seaton, A., & Gee, J. (1990). Asbestos: Scientific developments and implications for public policy. *Science, 247,* 294-301.

Mowat, F. (1963). *Never cry wolf.* Boston: Little, Brown.

Moyer, F. (1975). The architecture of closed institutions. In *Prison architecture*. London: Architectural Press.

Muchinsky, P. (1993). *Psychology applied to work* (4th ed.). Belmont, CA: Brooks/Cole.

Mumford, L. (1961). *The city in history*. New York: Harcourt, Brace.

Murdock, G. P. (1931). Ethnocentrism. [E. R. A. Seligman (Ed.)] *Encyclopedia of the Social Sciences, 5*, 613-614.

Murphy-Berman, V., & Berman, J. (1978). The importance of choice and sex in invasions of interpersonal space. *Personality & Social Psychology Bulletin, 4*, 424-428.

Murtha, M. (1988). Information resource for post occupancy evaluation. *Journal of Architectural and Planning Research, 5*, 321-338.

Nagar, D., Pandey, J., & Paulus, P. (1988). The effects of residential crowding experience on reactivity to laboratory crowding and noise. *Journal of Applied Social Psychology, 18*, 1423-1442.

Naisbett, J. (1982). *Megatrends*. New York: Warner.

NASA (National Aeronautics and Space Administration). (1988). *Executive summary of the Ozone Trends Panel*. Washington, DC: Author.

National Academy of Sciences (NAS). (1979). *Stratospheric ozone depletion by halocarbons: Chemistry and transport*. Washington, DC: National Academy Press.

National Academy of Sciences (NAS). (1983a). *Acid deposition: Atmospheric processes in eastern North America*. Washington, DC: National Academy Press.

National Academy of Sciences (NAS). (1983b). *Changing climate*. Washington, DC: National Academy Press.

National Academy of Sciences (NAS). (1984). *Toxicity testing: Strategies to determine needs and priorities*. Washington, DC: National Academy Press.

National Bureau of Standards. (1973). *Technical options for energy conservation in buildings* (Technical Note 784). Gaithersburg, MD: Author.

National Institute for Occupational Safety & Health (NIOSH). (1975). *The Federal Coal Mine Health Program in 1973*. Washington, DC: U.S. Department of Health, Education and Welfare.

National Research Council. (1982). *Diet, nutrition and cancer*. Washington, DC: National Academy Press.

National Research Council. (1986). *Environmental tobacco smoke: Measuring exposures and assessing health effects*. Washington, DC: National Academy Press.

Needleman, H., Bellinger, D., Schnell, A., Leviton, A., & Allred, E. (1990). The long term effects of exposure to low doses of lead in childhood. *New England Journal of Medicine, 322*, 83-88.

Needleman, H., et al. (1979). Deficits in psychologic and classroom performance of children with elevated dentine lead levels. *New England Journal of Medicine, 300*, 689-695.

Neisser, U. (1967). *Cognitive psychology*. Norwalk, CT: Appleton-Century-Crofts.

Neisser, U. (1990). Gibson's revolution. *Contemporary Psychology, 35*, 749-750.

Nelson, D. (1980). *Frederick W. Taylor and the rise of scientific management*. Milwaukee: University of Wisconsin Press.

Nelson, L. (1992). *To thrive—not just survive: A study of the habitability of Australian Antarctic buildings* (ASAC Project No. 505). Melbourne, Australia: ASAC.

Nero, A. (1988). Controlling indoor pollution. *Scientific American, 258*, 42-48.

Nesnow, S., & Huisingh, S. (1974, December 3). *Mutagenic and carcinogenic potency of extracts of diesel and related environmental emissions: Summary and discussion of results*. Paper presented at the International Symposium on Health Effects, Cincinnati.

Neugarten, B. (1975). The future and the young-old. *Gerontologist, 15*, 4-9.

Newell, R., Reichle, H., & Seiler, W. (1989). Carbon monoxide and the burning Earth. *Scientific American, 261*, 82-89.

Newman, O. (1972). *Defensible space*. New York: Macmillan.

Newman, O. (1980). *Community of interest*. Garden City, NY: Anchor Press/Doubleday.

Nice, M. (1941). The role of territory in bird life. *American Midlands Naturalist, 26*, 44-487.

Nicholson, W., Johnson, E., Harington, J., Melius, J., & Landrigan, P. (1990). Reply to Mossman, et al. *Science, 248*, 796-799.

Niemi, T. (1975). The time-space distances of suicides committed in the lock-up in Finland 1963-1967. *Psychiatrica Fennica*, pp. 267-270.

Niit, T., Heidmets, M., & Kruusvall, J. (1983). *Psychology and architecture* (Vols. 1, 2). Tallinn, Estonia: Estonian Branch of the Soviet Psychological Society and the Tallinn Pedagogic Institute.

Niit, T., Heidmets, M., & Kruusvall, J. (1985). *The sociopsychological basis of environmental design*. Tallinn, Estonia: Estonian Branch of the Soviet Psychological Society and the Tallinn Pedagogic Institute.

Noejirwan, J. (1978). A laboratory study of proxemic patterns of Indonesians and Australians. *British Journal of Social & Clinical Psychology, 17*, 333-334.

Norberg-Schulz, C. (1971). *Existence, space and architecture*. London: Studio Vista.

Nordhoff, C. (1960). *The communistic societies of the United States*. New York: Hillary House.

Normoyle, J. (1987). Fear of crime and satisfaction among elderly public housing residents: The impact of residential segregation. *Basic and Applied Social Psychology, 8*, 193-207.

Normoyle, J. (1988). The defensible space model of fear and elderly public housing residents. *Environment and Behavior, 20*, 50-74.

Noshpitz, J. (1984). Narcissism and aggression. *American Journal of Psychotherapy, 38*, 17-34.

Nriagu, J., & Pacyna, J. (1988). Quantitative assessment of world wide contamination of air, water and soil by trace metals. *Nature, 333*, 134-139.

Occupational Safety and Health Administration (OSHA). (1974). Occupational noise exposure: Proposed requirements and procedures. *Federal Register, 39*, 37773-37777.

Odum, E. (1971). *Fundamentals of ecology* (3rd ed.). Philadelphia: W. B. Saunders.

Ogburn, W. (1937). *Social characteristics of cities*. Chicago: International City Manager's Association.

Ogunlade, J. (1980). Social distance among the Yoruba of Nigeria. *Social Behavior & Personality, 8*, 121-123.

Okabe, A., Aoki, K., & Hamamoto, W. (1986). Distance and direction judgment in a large scale urban environment: Effects of a slope and a winding trail. *Environment and Behavior, 18*, 755-763.

O'Keefe, J., & Nadel, L. (1978). *The hippocampus as a cognitive map*. New York: Oxford University Press.

Olshansky, S., Carnes, B., & Cassel, C. (1990). In search of Methuselah: Estimating the upper limits to human longevity. *Science, 250*, 634-640.

Olweus, D. (1978). *Aggression in the schools: Bullies and whipping boys*. New York: Halstead.

O'Neal, E., Brunault, M., Marquis, J., & Carifio, M. (1979). Anger and the body buffer zone. *Journal of Social Psychology, 108*, 135-136.

O'Neal, E., Schultz, J., & Christenson, T. (1987). The menstrual cycle and personal space. *Journal of Nonverbal Behavior, 11*, 26-32.

O'Neill, M. (1991). Evaluation of a conceptual model of architectural legibility. *Environment and Behavior, 23*, 259-284.

Orians, G. (1980). Habitat selection: General theory and applications to human behavior. In J. Lockard (Ed.), *The evolution of human social behavior*. New York: Elsevier.

Orians, G. (1986). An ecological and evolutionary approach to landscape aesthetics. In E. Penning-Roswell & D. Lowenthal (Eds.), *Meanings and values in landscape*. Sydney, Australia: Allen and Unwin.

Orne, M. (1982, March). [Remarks delivered at the meeting of the Society for Behavioral Medicine, Chicago].

Ornish, D. (1990). *Dr. Dean Ornish's program for reversing heart disease*. New York: Ballantine.

Ornstein, S. (1991). Large scale POE on university campus, São Paulo, Brazil. *Design Research News, 22*, 7, 26.

Orr, D. (1979). Catastrophe and social order. *Human Ecology, 7*, 41-52.

Osmond, H. (1957). Function as the basis of psychiatric ward design. *Mental Hospital, 8*, 23-30.

Oxley, D., & Barrera, M. (1984). Undermanning theory and the workplace: Implications of setting size for job satisfaction and social support. *Environment and Behavior, 16*, 211-234.

Page, J. (1990). Pushy and brassy, the starling was an ill-advised import. *Smithsonian, 21*, 76-85.

Park, R., & Burgess, E. (1925). *The city*. Chicago: University of Chicago Press.

Parsons, H. M. (1972). The bedroom. [H. Parsons (Ed.), Special issue: Environmental design] *Human Factors, 14*, 421-449.

Parsons, R. (1991). The potential influences of environmental perception on human health. *Journal of Environmental Psychology, 11*, 1-24.

Paslawskyj, L., & Ivinskis, A. (1980). Dominance, agonistic and territorial behavior in institutional mentally retarded patients. *Australian Journal of Developmental Disabilities, 6*, 17-24.

Passini, R. (1984). *Wayfinding in architecture*. New York: Van Nostrand Reinhold.

Passini, R., & Proulx, G. (1988). Wayfinding without vision: An experiment with congenitally totally blind people. *Environment and Behavior, 20*, 227-252.

Patterson, M. (1975). Personal space: Time to burst the bubble? *Man Environment Systems, 5*, 67.

Patterson, M. (1979). Seating arrangement, activity and sex differences in small group crowding. *Personality & Social Psychology Bulletin, 5*, 100-103.

Patterson, M., Roth, C., & Schenk, C. (1979). Seating arrangement, activity and sex differences in small group crowding. *Personality and Social Psychology Bulletin, 5*, 100-103.

Paulus, P. (1991). Perspectives on research classics: I've done my time. *Contemporary Social Psychology, 15*, 9-11.

Paulus, P., & McCain, G. (1983). Crowding in jails. *Basic & Applied Social Psychology, 4*, 89-107.

Paulus, P., McCain, G., & Cox, V. (1978). Death rates, psychiatric commitments, blood pressure and perceived crowding as a function of institutional crowding. *Environmental Psychology & Nonverbal Behavior, 3*, 107-116.

Pederson, D. (1978). Effects of group characteristics on social space. *Perceptual & Motor Skills, 47*, 1307-1321.

Pegan, G., & Aiello, J. (1982). Development of personal space among Puerto Ricans. *Journal of Nonverbal Behavior, 7*, 59-68.

Pennartz, P. (1986). Atmosphere at home: A qualitative approach. *Journal of Environmental Psychology, 6*, 135-154.

Pennartz, P., & Elsinga, M. (1990). Adults, adolescents and architects: Differences in perception of the urban environment. *Environment and Behavior, 22*, 675-714.

Perkins, D., Meeks, J., & Taylor, R. (1992). The physical environment of street blocks and resident perceptions of crime and disorder: Implications for theory and mea-sure-ment. *Journal of Environmental Psychology, 12*, 21-34.

Perkins, K., & Marsha, A. (1978). The effect of increased knowledge of body systems and functions of attitudes toward the disabled. *Rehabilitation Counseling Bulletin, 22*, 16-20.

Perlmuter, L., & Monty, R. (1979). *Choice and perceived control*. Hillsdale, NJ: Lawrence Erlbaum.

Perry, R., Lindell, M., & Green, M. (1981). *Evacuation planning and emergency management*. Lexington, MA: D. C. Heath.

Perusse, L. (1978). *Attitudes and self-reported behaviors of teenage boys in four middle-status communities toward physical and social environments of their neighborhoods*. Unpublished doctoral dissertation, University of Missouri.

Peters, H. (1990). Chernobyl and the nuclear power issue in West German public opinion. *Journal of Environmental Psychology, 10*, 121-134.

Peterson, K., Roscoe, B., & Draper, D. (1982). Utilization of appropriate projective techniques in assessing preschool children's personal space and bodily orientation. *Perceptual and Motor Skills, 54*, 67-70.

Phillips, J. (1979). An exploration of perception of body boundary, personal space and body size in elderly persons. *Perceptual & Motor Skills, 48*, 299-308.

Phillips, E., Phillips, E., Fixsen, D., &Wolf, M. (1973). Behavior shaping works for delinquents. *Psychology Today, 7*, 74-79.

Piaget, J. (1932). *The moral judgment of the child*. London: Kegan Paul, Trench & Trubner.

Piaget, J. (1954). *The child's construction of reality*. New York: Basic Books.

Picasso, G. (1985). Corporate assessment of real estate: An exploratory study. In a symposium on the successful use of POEs in Building Delivery Systems, *EDRA 16*. Edmond, OK: Environmental Design Research Association.

Platt, J. (1973). Social traps. *American Psychologist, 28*, 641-651.

Plotkin, A. (1990). *Post occupancy evaluation of Nofim: An Israeli experiment in housing for the elderly*. Master's thesis, Israel Institute of Technology.

Pogue, W. (1991). *How do you go to the bathroom in space?* New York: Tom Doherty Associates.

Poldichak, W. (1991). Establishing the fun in leisure. *Leisure Sciences, 13*, 123-136.

Poporino, F. (1986). Managing violent individuals in correctional settings. *Journal of Interpersonal Violence, 1*, 213-237.

Preiser, W. (1985). A combined tactile-electronic guidance system for visually impaired person in indoor and outdoor spaces. In *International Conference on Building Use and Safety Technology* (pp. 54-59). Washington, DC: National Institute of Building Sciences.

Preiser, W., Rabinowitz, H., & White, E. (Eds.). (1988). *Post occupancy evaluation*. New York: Van Nostrand.

Prescott, A. (1973). *The exterior individualization of the living unit: Its significance as expressed by children's drawings*. Unpublished master's thesis, Rensselaer Polytechnic Institute.

Prince, M. (Ed.). (1993). *Advances in solar energy* (Vol. 8). New York: American Solar Energy Society.

Prince, S. (1920). *Catastrophe and social change*. Halifax: Kind.

Proshansky, H. (1973). Theoretical issues in environmental psychology. *Representative Research in Social Psychology, 4*, 93-107.

Proshansky, H. (1987). The field of environmental psychology: Securing its future. In D. Stokols & I. Altman (Eds.), *Handbook of environmental psychology* (pp. 1467-1488). New York: John Wiley.

Proshanky, H., Ittelson, W., & Rivlin, L. (1970). *Environmental psychology: Man in his physical setting*. New York: Holt, Rinehart & Winston.

Proshanky, H., Ittelson, W., & Rivlin, L. (1976). *Environmental psychology* (2nd ed.). New York: Holt, Rinehart & Winston.

Quarantelli, E. (1954). The nature and conditions of panic. *American Journal of Sociology, 60*, 267-275.

Quarantelli, E., & Dynes, R. (1977). Response to social crisis and disaster. *Annual Review of Sociology, 3*, 23-49.

Quetelet, A. (1869). *Soziale Physik*. Brussels: C. Muquardt.

Quetelet, A. (1870). *Anthropometrie*. Brussels: C. Muquardt.

Quetelet, A. (1984). *Research on the propensity for crime at different ages*. Cincinnati: Anderson.

Rabkin, J., & Streuning, E. (1976). Life events, stress and illness. *Science, 194*, 1013-1020.

Rachlinski, J., Foltin, R., & Fischman, M. (1989). The effects of smoked marijuana on interpersonal distances in small groups. *Drug and Alcohol Dependence, 24*, 183-186.

Raglan, L. (1964). *The temple and the house*. New York: Norton.

Ragland, D., & Brand, R. (1988). Coronary heart disease mortality in the Western Collaborative Groups Study: Follow up experience of 22 years. *American Journal of Epidemiology, 127*, 462-475.

Rainwater, L. (1966). Fear and house as haven in the lower class. *Journal of the American Institute of Planners, 32*, 23-31.

Raloff, J. (1982). Noise can be hazardous to our health. *Science News, 12*, 377-381.

Raloff, J. (1984). Surviving salt. *Science News, 126*, 314-317.

Raloff, J. (1989). Dioxin: Paper's trace. *Science News, 135*, 104-106.

Ramanathan, V. (1988). The greenhouse theory of climate change: A test by inadvertent global experiment. *Science, 240*, 293-299.

Rapoport, A. (1969). *House form and culture*. Englewood Cliffs, NJ: Prentice Hall.

Rapoport, A. (1974). Aging-environment theory: A summary. In P. Windley, T. Byerts, & F. Ernst (Eds.), *Theory development in environment and aging* (pp. 263-282). Washington, DC: Gerontological Society.

Rathje, W., & Murphy, C. (1992). *Rubbish! The archaeology of garbage: What our garbage tells us about ourselves*. New York: HarperCollins.

Rathje, W., & Ritenbaugh, C. (Eds.). (1984). Household refuse analysis [Special issue]. *American Behavioral Scientist, 28*(1).

Ray, D., & Murdie, R. (1972). Canadian and American urban dimensions. In B. Berry (Ed.), *City classification handbook: Methods and applications* (pp. 181-210). New York: John Wiley.

Ray, J. (1984). Authoritarianism and interpersonal spacing behavior. *Personality & Individual Differences, 5*, 601-602.

Redding, B., Mefford, R., & Wieland, B. (1967). Effect of observer movement on monocular depth perception. *Perceptual and Motor Skills, 24*, 725-726.

Reed, E. (1988). *James J. Gibson and the psychology of perception*. New Haven, CT: Yale University Press.

Reed, E., & Jones, R. (Eds.). (1982). *Reasons for realism: Selected essays of James J. Gibson*. Hillsdale, NJ: Lawrence Erlbaum.

Rees, P. (1972). Problems of classifying subareas within cities. In B. Berry (Ed.), *City classification handbook: Methods and applications* (pp. 265-330). New York: John Wiley.

Reid, D. (1980). Spatial involvement and teacher-pupil interaction patterns in school biology laboratories. *Educational Studies, 6*, 31-41.

Reinsel, R. (1985). Symposium: Successful uses of POEs in building delivery systems. In S. Klein, R. Wener, & S. Lehman (Eds.), *Environmental Change/Social Change: EDRA 16* (pp. 340-341). Edmond, OK: Environmental Design Research Association.

Reiss, A. J. (1961). *Occupations and social status*. New York: Free Press.

Renn, O. (1990). Public responses to the Chernobyl accident. *Journal of Environmental Psychology, 10*, 151-168.

Repace, J., & Lowrey, A. (1980). Indoor air pollution, tobacco smoke and public health. *Science, 208*, 464-472.

Research Lab. (1992). Noise in multiple-workstation open-plan computer rooms: Measurements and annoyance. *Journal of Human Ergology, 21*, 69-82.

Rettig, S., & Pasamanick, B. (1964). Differential judgment of ethical risk by cheaters and non-cheaters. *Journal of Abnormal and Social Psychology, 69*, 109-113.

Revelle, R. (1976). Energy use in rural India. *Science, 192*, 969-974.

Revelle, R. (1982). Carbon dioxide and world climate. *Scientific American, 247*, 35-43.

Richardson, H. (1983). The contribution of ban economics to city planning and spatial structure. In J. Pipkin, M. LaGory, & J. Blau (Eds.), *Remaking the city* (pp. 203-228). Albany: SUNY Press.

Richey, M., McClelland, L., & Shimkanas, A. (1967). Relative influence of positive and negative information in impression formation and persistence. *Journal of Personality and Social Psychology, 6*, 322-327.

Rivano-Fischer, M. (1984). Interactional space: Invasions as a function of the type of social interaction. *Psychological Research Bulletin, 24* (Lund University, 15 pp.).

Rivano-Fischer, M. (1988). Micro-territorial behavior in public transport vehicles: A field study on a bus route. *Psychological Research Bulletin, 28* (Lund University, 18 pp.).

Roberts, D. (1975). Population differences in dimensions, their genetic basis and their relevance to practical problems of design. In A. Chapanis (Ed.), *Ethnic variables in human factors engineering* (pp. 11-30). Baltimore, MD: Johns Hopkins University Press.

Roberts, L. (1991). High dioxin dose linked to cancer. *Science, 251*, 625.

Robey, B., Rutstein, S., & Morris, L. (1993). The fertility decline in developing countries. *Scientific American, 269*, 60-67.

Robins, L. (1966). *Deviant children grown up*. Baltimore, MD: Williams & Wilkins.

Robinson, E., et al. (1928). *The behavior of the museum visitor* (New Series No. 5). Washington, DC: American Association of Museums.

Rochberg-Halton, E. (1984). Object relations, role models and cultivation of the self. *Environment and Behavior, 16*, 335-368.

Rodin, J. (1976). Crowding, perceived choice and response to controllable and uncontrollable outcomes. *Journal of Experimental Social Psychology, 12*, 564-578.

Rodin, J. (1986). Aging and health: Effects of the sense of control. *Science, 233*, 1271-1276.

Rodin, J., & Langer, E. (1977). Long-term effects of a control-relevant intervention with institutionalized aged. *Journal of Personality & Social Psychology, 35*, 12-29.

Rodin, J., & Langer, E. (1980). Aging labels: The decline of control and the fall of self-esteem. *Journal of Social Issues, 36*, 12-29.

Roethlisberger, F., & Dickson, W. (1939). *Management and the worker*. Cambridge, MA: Harvard University Press.

Roger, D. (1982). Body image, personal space and self esteem: Preliminary evidence for "focusing" effects. *Journal of Personality Assessment, 46*, 468-476.

Rokeach, M. (1968). *Beliefs, attitudes, and values*. San Francisco: Jossey-Bass.

Rokeach, M. (1973). *The nature of human values*. New York: Free Press.

Roodman, D., & Lenssen, N. (1995). *A building revolution: How ecology and health concerns are transforming construction* (Worldwatch Paper 124). Washington, DC: Worldwatch Institute.

Roosens, E. (1979). *Mental patients in town life: Geel—Europe's first therapeutic community*. Beverly Hills, CA: Sage.

Rose, M. (1991). *Evolutionary biology of aging*. Oxford: Oxford University Press.

Rosebury, T. (1969). *Life on man*. New York: Viking.

Rosenfeld, A., & Hafemeister, D. (1988). Energy efficient buildings. *Scientific American, 258*, 78-85.

Rosenfeld, H., Breck, B., & Smith, S. (1984). Intimacy mediators of the proximity-gaze compensation effect: Movement, conversational role, acquaintance and gender. [Special issue: Nonverbal Intimacy and Exchange] *Journal of Nonverbal Behavior, 8*, 235-249.

Rosenfeld, S. (1979). The context of informal learning in zoos. *Journal of Museum Education, 4*, 1-3, 15-16.

Rosenhan, D. (1973). On being sane in insane places. *Science, 179*, 250-258.

Rosenman, R., Brand, R., Jenkins, C., Friedman, M., Straus, R., & Wurm, M. (1975). Coronary heart disease in the western collaborative group study: Final follow up of 8½ years. *Journal of the American Medical Association, 233*, 872-877.

Rosenthal, N., & Wehr, T. (1987). Seasonal affective disorder with summer depression and winter hypomania. *American Journal of Psychiatry, 144*, 1602-1603.

Rosenthal, R., & Jacobsen, L. (1968). *Pygmalion in the classroom: Teacher expectation and pupil's intellectual development*. New York: Holt Rinehart.

Ross, L. (1977). The intuitive psychologist and his shortcomings: Distortions in the attribution process. In L. Berkowitz (Ed.), *Advances in experimental social psychology* (Vol. 13). San Diego, CA: Academic Press.

Ross, R., & Campbell, D. (1978). A review of EDRA proceedings: Where have we been? Where are we going? W. Rogers & W. Ittelson (Eds.), *New directions in environmental design* (EDRA 9; pp. 43-59). Tucson: University of Arizona.

Rossi, P., Wright, J., & Weber-Burdin, E. (1982). *Natural hazards, and public choice: The state of local politics of hazards mitigation*. San Diego, CA: Academic Press.

Roth, A., & Bechtel, R. (1972, June 30). *Measuring the impact of vertical policing upon residents: An evaluative approach*. Kansas City, MO: Greater Kansas City Mental Health Foundation.

Roth, D., Wiebe, D., Fillingim, R., & Shay, K. (1989). Life events, fitness, hardiness and health: A simultaneous analysis of proposed stress-resistant effects. *Journal of Personality and Social Psychology, 57*, 136-142.

Rothenberg, M., Hayward, D., & Beasley, R. (1974). Playgrounds for whom? In *Childhood city* (Man-Environment Interactions: Evaluations and Applications: The State of the Art in Environmental Design Research, Vol. 12, D. Carson, General Ed., pp. 121-130). Washington, DC: Environmental Design Research Association.

Rotter, J. (1966). Generalized expectancies for internal vs. external control of reinforcement. *Psychological Monographs, 80*(Whole No. 609).

Rovine, M., & Weisman, G. (1989). Sketch-map variables as predictors of way-finding performance. *Journal of Environmental Psychology, 9*, 217-232.

Rowe, J., & Kahn, R. (1987). Human aging: Usual and successful. *Science, 237*, 143-149.

Ruback, R. (1987). Deserted (and non-deserted) aisles: Territorial intrusion can produce persistence, not flight. *Social Psychology Quarterly, 50*, 270-276.

Ruback, R., & Carr, T. (1984). Crowding in a women's prison: Attitudinal and behavioral effects. *Journal of Applied Social Psychology, 14*, 57-68.

Ruback, R., Carr, T., & Hopper, C. (1986). Perceived control in prison: Its relation to reported crowding, stress and symptoms. *Journal of Applied Social Psychology, 16*, 375-386.

Ruback, R., & Pandey, J. (1991). Crowding, perceived control and relative power: An analysis of households in India. *Journal of Applied Social Psychology, 21*, 315-344.

Ruback, R., Pape, K., & Doriot, P. (1989). Waiting for a phone: Intrusion on callers leads to territorial defense. *Social Psychology Quarterly, 52*, 232-241.

Rubonis, A., & Bickman, L. (1991). Psychological impairment in the wake of disaster: The disaster-psychopathology relationship. *Psychological Bulletin, 109*, 384-399.

Rushton, J. (1991). Mongoloid-caucasoid differences in brain size from military samples. *Intelligence, 15*, 351-359.

Russell, A., Milford, J., Bergin, M., McBride, S., McNair, L., Yang, Y., Stockwell, W., & Croes, B. (1995). Urban ozone control and atmospheric reactivity of organic gases. *Science, 269*, 491-495.

Russell, J., & Lanius, U. (1984). Adaptation level and the affective appraisal of environments. *Journal of Environmental Psychology, 4*, 119-135.

Russell, J., & Pratt, G. (1980). A description of the affective quality attributed to environments. *Journal of Personality and Social Psychology, 38*, 311-322.

Russell, J., & Ward, L. (1982). Environmental psychology. In *Annual review of psychology* (Vol. 33, pp. 651-688). Palo Alto, CA: Annual Reviews.

Russell, J., Ward, L., & Pratt, G. (1981). Affective quality attributed to environments: A factor analytic study. *Environment and Behavior, 13*, 259-288.

Rust, D. (1982). Solar flares, proton showers and the space shuttle. *Science, 216*, 939-945.

Rustemli, A. (1986). Male and female personal space needs and escape reactions under intrusion: A Turkish sample. *International Journal of Psychology, 21*, 503-511.

Rustemli, A. (1988). The effects of personal space invasion on impressions and decisions. *Journal of Psychology, 122*, 113-118.

Rusting, R. (1992). Why do we age? *Scientific American, 267*, 131-141.

Ruttan, V. (Ed.). (1992). *Sustainable agriculture and the environment*. Boulder, CO: Westview.

Saarinen, T., & Sell, J. (1981). Environmental perception. *Progress in Human Geography, 5*, 525-547.

Saarinen, T., & Sell, J. (1987). *International directory of environment-behavior-design*. Tucson: University of Arizona Press.

Sacks, S., & Firestone, R. (1972). Dimensions and classifications of British towns on the basis of new data. In B. Berry (Ed.), *City classification handbook: Methods and applications* (pp. 211-224). New York: John Wiley.

Sadalla, E., & Magel, S. (1980). The perception of traversed distance. *Environment and Behavior, 12*, 65-80.

Sadalla, E., & Staplin, L. (1980). The perception of traversed distance: Intersections. *Environment and Behavior, 12*, 167-182.

Sanchez, E., Wiesenfeld, E., & Cronick, K. (1987). Environmental psychology from a Latin American perspective. In D. Stokols & I. Altman (Eds.), *Handbook of environmental psychology* (Vol. 2, pp. 1337-1358). New York: John Wiley.

Sanchez-Bedolla, M. (1981). Effects of space resources and affective relationships on social interaction behavior. *Revista de la Associacion Latinoamericana de Psicologia Social, 1*, 241-272.

Sanders, J. (1978). Relation of personal space to the human menstrual cycle. *Journal of Psychology, 100*, 275-278.

Sanders, J., Hakky, U., & Brizzolara, M. (1985). Personal space among Arabs and Americans. *International Journal of Psychology, 20*, 13-17.

Sanders, J., Thomas, M., Suydam, M., & Petri, H. (1980). Use of an auditory technique in personal space measurement. *Journal of Social Psychology, 112*, 99-102.

Sanders, M., & McCormick, E. (1993). *Human factors in engineering and design* (7th ed.). New York: McGraw-Hill.

Sanoff, H., & Cohen, S. (1969). *EDRA 1: Proceedings of the First Environmental Design Research Association Conference*. Washington, DC: Environmental Design Research Association.

Saup, W. (1986). Housing in old age: Psychological aspects. *Zeitschrift für Gerontologie, 5*, 342-347.

Scarr, S., & Eisenberg, M. (1993). Child care research: Issues, perspectives and results. In L. Porter & M. Rosenzweig (Eds.), *Annual review of psychology* (Vol. 44, pp. 613-644). Palo Alto, CA: Annual Reviews.

Scarr, S., Lande, J., & McKartney, K. (1989). Child care and the family: Cooperation and interaction. In J. Lande, S. Scarr, & N. Guzenhauser (Eds.), *Caring for children: Challenge to America* (pp. 1-20). Hillsdale, NJ: Lawrence Erlbaum.

Schaeffer, M., Baum, A., Paulus, P., & Gaes, G. (1988). Architecturally mediated effects of social density in prison. *Environment and Behavior, 20*, 3-19.

Schele, L., & Friedel, D. (1990). *A forest of kings: The untold story of the ancient Maya*. New York: William Morrow.

Schelling, T. (1971). The ecology of micromotives. *Public Interest, 25*, 61-98.

Schindler, D. (1988). Effects of acid rain on freshwater ecosystems. *Science, 130*, 215.

Schlager, N. (1994). *When technology fails*. Detroit: Gale.

Schneider, S., & Boston, P. (1991). *Scientists on Gaia*. Cambridge: MIT Press.

Schnore, L., & Winsborough, H. (1972). Functional classification and the residential location of social classes. In B. Berry (Ed.), *City classification handbook: Methods and applications* (pp. 124-151). New York: John Wiley.

Schnorr, J., & Levi, D. (1984). Diffusion of solar technology: Alternative perspectives. *Environment and Behavior, 16.*

Schoggen, P. (1989). *Behavior settings*. Stanford, CA: Stanford University Press.

Schwartz, S. (1994). Are there universal aspects in the structure and content of human values? *Journal of Social Issues, 50,* 19-45.

Schwartz, S., & Bilsky, W. (1990). Toward a theory of the universal content and structure of values: Extensions and cross-cultural replications. *Journal of Personality and Social Psychology, 58,* 878-891.

Schwartz, S., & Sagiv, L. (1995). Identifying culture specifics in the content and structure of values. *Journal of Cross-Cultural Psychology, 26,* 92-116.

Scitiovsky, T. (1992). *The joyless economy: The psychology of human satisfaction* (rev. ed.). Oxford: Oxford University Press.

Scott, J. (1984). Comfort and seating distance in living rooms: The relationship of interactants and the topic of conversation. *Environment and Behavior, 16,* 35-54.

Screven, C. (1969). The museum as a responsive learning environment. *Museum News, 47,* 7-10.

Screven, C. (1974). *The measurement and facilitation of learning in the museum environment: An experimental analysis*. Washington, DC: Smithsonian Press.

Screven, C. (1990). The uses of evaluation before, after and during exhibit design. *ILVS Review: A Journal of Visitor Behavior, 2,* 36-67.

Sears, D. (1983). The person-positivity bias. *Journal of Personality and Social Psychology, 44,* 233-250.

Sebastian, R., Bignon, J., & Martin, M. (1982). Indoor airborne asbestos pollution: From ceiling to floor. *Science, 216,* 1410-1412.

Sebba, R., & Churchman, A. (1983). Territories and territoriality in the home. *Environment and Behavior, 15,* 191-210.

Seeley, J., Sim, R., & Loosely, E. (1956). *Crestwood Heights*. Toronto: University of Toronto Press.

Seligman, M., & Miller, S. (1979). The psychology of power: Concluding comments. In L. Perlmuter & R. Monty (Eds.), *Choice and perceived control*. Hillsdale, NJ: Lawrence Erlbaum.

Selye, H. (1956). *The stress of life*. New York: McGraw-Hill.

Selye, H. (1976). *The stress of life* (rev. ed.). New York: McGraw-Hill.

Severy, L., Forsyth, D., & Wagner, P. (1979). A multimethod assessment of personal space deviations in female and male, black and white children. *Journal of Nonverbal Behavior, 4,* 68-86.

Shadish, W. (1984). Policy research: Lessons from the implementation of deinstitution-alization. *American Psychologist, 39*, 725-738.

Sharp, E., & Hall, D. (1979, December 12). Haulers fouling state with deadly chemicals. *Detroit Free Press*, p. 19A.

Shaw, S. (1992). Dereifying family leisure: An examination of women's and men's everyday experiences and perceptions of family time. *Leisure Sciences, 14*, 271-286.

Shettle-Neuber, J. (1986). *Zoo exhibit design: Post occupancy evaluation and comparison of animal enclosures*. Unpublished doctoral dissertation, University of Arizona, Tucson.

Shirer, W. (1960). *The rise and fall of the Third Reich: A history of Nazi Germany*. New York: Simon & Schuster.

Shupe, D. (1985). Perceived control, helplessness, and choice. In J. Birren & J. Livingston (Eds.), *Cognition, stress and aging*. Englewood Cliffs, NJ: Prentice Hall.

Siegel, A., & White, S. (1975). The development of spatial representations of large scale environments. In H. Reese (Ed.), *Advances in child development and behavior* (pp. 9-55). San Diego, CA: Academic Press.

Sigelman, C., & Adams, R. (1990). Family interactions in public: Parent-child distance and touching. *Journal of Nonverbal Behavior, 14*, 63-75.

Silka, L., & Brasier, F. (1980). *The national assessment of the ground water contamination potential of waste impoundments*. Washington, DC: Environmental Protection Agency.

Sime, J. (1980). The concept of panic. In D. Canter (Ed.), *Fires and human behavior*. New York: John Wiley.

Sims, J., & Baumann, D. (1972). The tornado threat: Coping styles of the North and South. *Science, 176*, 1386-1391.

Sinha, S., & Mukerjee, N. (1990). Marital adjustment and personal space orientation. *Journal of Social Psychology, 130*, 633-639.

Skinner, B. (1984). The shame of American education. *American Psychologist, 39*, 947-954.

Skogan, W. (1990). *Disorder and decline*. New York: Free Press.

Slane, S., Dragen, W., Crandall, C., & Payne, P. (1980). Stress effects on the nonverbal behavior of repressors and sensitizers. *Journal of Psychology, 106*, 101-109.

Slane, S., Petruska, R., & Cheyfitz, S. (1981). Personal space measurement: A validational comparison. *Psychological Record, 31*, 145-151.

Slovic, R., Fischoff, B., & Lichtenstein, S. (1981). Perception and acceptability of risk from energy systems. In A. Baum & J. Singer (Eds.), *Advances in environmental psychology* (Vol. 3, pp. 155-169). Hillsdale, NJ: Lawrence Erlbaum.

Slovic, R., & Lichtenstein, S. (1968). Relative importance of probabilities and payoffs in risk taking. *Journal of Experimental Psychology, 78*, Pt. 2, pp. 1-18.

Smetena, J., Bridgeman, D., & Bridgeman, B. (1978). A field study of interpersonal distance in early childhood. *Personality & Social Psychology Bulletin, 4*, 309-313.

Smith, A. (1989). A review of the effects of noise on human performance. *Scandinavian Journal of Psychology, 30*, 185-206.

Smith, A., & Stansfield, S. (1986). Aircraft noise exposure, noise sensitivity and everyday errors. *Environment and Behavior, 18*, 214-216.

Smith, B., & Cantrell, P. (1988). Distance in nurse-patient encounters. *Journal of Psychosocial Nursing and Mental Health Services, 26*, 22-26.

Smith, H. (1981). Territorial spacing on a beach revisited: A cross-national exploration. *Social Psychology Quarterly, 44*, 132-137.

Smith, R. (1982). Hawaiian milk contamination creates alarm. *Science, 217*, 137-140.

Smith, R., Alexander, R., & Wolman, G. (1987). Water quality trends in the nation's rivers. *Science, 235*, 1607-1615.

Smith, R., & Knowles, E. (1978). Attributional consequences of personal space invasions. *Personality & Social Psychology Bulletin, 4*, 429-433.

Smith, S. (1994). The psychological construction of home life. *Journal of Environmental Psychology, 14*, 125-136.

Smuts, J. (1973). *Holism and evolution*. Westport, CT: Greenwood.

Snell, J., Achenbach, S., & Peterson, S. (1976). Energy conservation in new housing design. *Science, 192*, 1305-1311.

Snyder, C., & Endelman, J. (1979). Effects of degree of interpersonal similarity on physical distance and self-reported attraction: A comparison of uniqueness and reinforcement theory predictions. *Journal of Personality, 47*, 492-505.

Socolow, R. (1978). *Saving energy in the home*. Cambridge, MA: Ballinger.

Soleri, P. (1974). *Arcology: The city in the image of man*. Cambridge: MIT Press.

Solomon, K. (1985). Adjusting water production functions to account for salinity. In E. Whitehead, C. Hutchinson, B. Timmerman, & R. Varady (Eds.), *Arid lands, today and tomorrow* (pp. 195-203). Boulder, CO: Westview.

Solomon, R., & Wynne, L. (1953). Traumatic avoidance learning: Acquisition in normal dogs. *Psychological Monographs, 67*(354, 19 pp.).

Sommer, R. (1967). Classroom ecology. *Journal of Applied Behavioral Sciences, 3*, 489-503.

Sommer, R. (1969a). *Personal space: The behavioral basis of design*. Englewood Cliffs, NJ: Prentice Hall.

Sommer, R. (1969b, April). The lonely airport crowd. *Air Travel*, pp. 16-18.

Sommer, R. (1972). *Design awareness*. New York: Holt, Rinehart & Winston.

Sommer, R. (1974). *Tight spaces*. Englewood Cliffs, NJ: Prentice Hall.

Sommer, R., & Olsen, H. (1980). The soft classroom. *Environment and Behavior, 12*, 3-16.

Spector, A. (1978). *An analysis of urban spatial imagery*. Unpublished doctoral dissertation, Ohio State University, Department of Geography.

Speelman, D., & Hoffman, C. (1980). Personal space assessment of the development of racial attitudes in integrated and segregated schools. *Journal of Genetic Psychology, 136*, 307-308.

Speth, G., Yarn, J., & Harris, R. (1980). *Environmental quality: The Eleventh Annual Report of the Council for Environmental Quality*. Washington, DC: Government Printing Office.

Spicer, E. (1971). Persistent cultural systems. *Science, 174*, 795-800.

Spigelman, A., & Spigelman, G. (1991). The relationship between parental divorce and the child's body boundary definiteness. *Journal of Personal Assessment, 56*, 96-105.

Spivack, M. (1984). *Institutional settings*. New York: Human Sciences Press.

Spooner, B., & Mann, H. (1982). *Desertification and development: Dryland ecology in social perspective*. San Diego, CA: Academic Press.

Spreckelmeyer, K. (1993). Office relocation and environmental change: A case study. *Environment and Behavior, 25*, 181-204.

Srivastava, P., & Mandal, M. (1990). Proximal spacing to facial affect expressions in schizophrenics. *Comprehensive Psychiatry, 31*, 119-124.

Srole, L., Langer, T., Kirkpatrick, P., Michael, S., Opler, M., & Rennie, T. (1975). *Mental health in the metropolis: The Midtown Manhattan Study*. New York: Harper.

Starr, N. (1979). The invalidity of subjective ratings of the physical environment. In W. Rogers & W. Ittelson (Eds.), *New directions in environmental design research (EDRA 9)*, 428-443.

Starr, N., & Danford, S. (1979). The invalidity of subjective ratings of the physical environment. In W. Rogers & W. Ittelson (Eds.), *New directions in environmental design (EDRA 9)*, 428-443. Tucson: University of Arizona.

Stephens, K., & Clark, D. (1987). A pilot study on the effect of visible physical stigma on personal space. *Journal of Applied Rehabilitation Counseling, 18*, 52-54.

Stern, P. (1992). What psychology knows about energy conservation. *American Psychologist, 47*, 1224-1232.

Stern, P., Dietz, T., & Guagnano, G. (1995). The new ecological paradigm in social-psychological context. *Environment and Behavior, 27*, 723-743.

Stern, P., & Gardner, G. (1981). Psychological research and energy policy. *American Psychologist, 36*, 329-342.

Stern, P., & Kirkpatrick, E. (1977). Energy behavior. *Environment, 19*, 10-15.

Stern, P., & Oskamp, S. (1987). Managing scarce environmental resources. In D. Stokols & I. Altman (Eds.), *Handbook of environmental psychology* (Vol. 2, pp. 1043-1088). New York: John Wiley.

Stevens, R. (1989). *American hospitals in the twentieth century*. New York: Basic Books.

Stevenson, H. (1992). Learning from Asian schools. *Scientific American, 267*, 70-77.

Stokols, D. (1976). The experience of crowding in primary and secondary environments. *Environment and Behavior, 8*, 49-86.

Stokols, D. (1977a). Origins and directions of environment behavior research. In D. Stokols (Ed.), *Perspectives on environment and behavior theory, research, and applications* (pp. 5-36). New York: Plenum.

Stokols, D. (1977b). *Perspectives on environment and behavior.* New York: Plenum.

Stokols, D. (1978a). Environmental psychology. *Annual Review of Psychology, 29,* 253-295.

Stokols, D. (1978b). A typology of crowding experiences. In A. Baum & Y. Epstein (Eds.), *Human response to crowding.* Hillsdale, NJ: Lawrence Erlbaum.

Stokols, D. (Ed.). (1983). [Special issue: Theory] *Environment and Behavior, 15.*

Stokols, D., & Altman, I. (Eds.). (1987). *Handbook of environmental psychology* (Vols. 1-2). New York: John Wiley.

Stokols, D., Ohlig, W., & Resnick, S. (1975). Perception of residential crowding, classroom experiences and student health. *Human Ecology, 6,* 233-252.

Stone, D., Fitzgerald, M., & Kinsella, T. (1990). A study of behavioral deviance and social difficulties in 11 and 12 year old Dublin school children. *Irish Journal of Psychiatry, 11,* 12-14.

Strodtbeck, F., & Hook, L. (1961). The social dimensions of a twelve man jury table. *Sociometry, 24,* 397-415.

Strube, M., & Werner, C. (1983). Interpersonal distance and personal space: A conceptual methodological note. *Journal of Nonverbal Behavior, 6,* 163-170.

Strube, M., & Werner, C. (1984). Personal space claims a function of interpersonal threat: The mediating role of need for control. *Journal of Nonverbal Behavior, 8,* 195-209.

Struever, S., & Holton, F. (1979). *Koster.* New York: Anchor/Doubleday.

Struyk, R. (1987). Aging at home: How the elderly adjust their housing without moving. *Journal of Housing for the Elderly, 4,* 192.

Subcommittee on Oversights and Investigations of the House Committee on Interstate and Foreign Commerce. (1979). *Hazardous waste disposal report.* Washington, DC: Government Printing Office.

Suedfeld, P., Ballard, E., & Murphy, M. (1983). Water immersion flotation: From stress to experiment to stress treatment. *Journal of Environmental Psychology, 3,* 147-156.

Suedfeld, P., Bernaldez, J., & Stossel, D. (1989). The polar psychology project (PPP): A cross national investigation of polar adaptation. *Arctic Medical Research, 48,* 91-94.

Sullivan, H. (1945). *The interpersonal theory of psychiatry.* New York: Norton.

Sun, M. (1982). Use of super-plus tampons discouraged. *Science, 216,* 1300.

Sun, M. (1987). In search of Salmonella's smoking gun. *Science, 226,* 30-32.

Sundstrom, E. (1978). Crowding as a sequential process: Review of research on the effects of population density on humans. In A. Baum & Y. Epstein (Eds.), *Human response to crowding.* Hillsdale, NJ: Lawrence Erlbaum.

Sundstrom, E., Bell, P., Busby, P., & Asmus, C. (1994). Environmental psychology 1989-1994. *Annual Review of Psychology, 47,* 485-512.

Supancic, P. (1988). *Suicide and attempted suicide in prisons: Links with stress in an adaptation to prison*. Unpublished doctoral dissertation, University of Texas, Austin.

Sussman, N., & Rosenfeld, H. (1978). Touch, justification and sex: Influences on the aversiveness of spatial violations. *Journal of Social Psychology, 106*, 215-225.

Sussman, N., & Rosenfeld, H. (1982). Influence of culture, language and sex on conversational distance. *Journal of Personality & Social Psychology, 42*, 66-74.

Sutlive, V. (1986). *Natural disasters and cultural responses* (Publication No. 36). Williamsburg, VA: College of William and Mary, Department of Anthropology.

Suttles, R. (1968). *The social order of the slum*. Chicago: University of Chicago Press.

Symme, B. (1986). Industrial democracy and the worker. *International Review of Applied Psychology, 35*, 101-120.

Szokolay, C. (Ed.). (1981). *Understanding the built environment: Proceedings of the Australian and New Zealand Architectural Science Association 1981 Canberra Conference*, Brisbane: University of Queensland.

Takahashi, T., & Nishide, K. (1990). Behind a mask: Personal territory and spatial articulation. In Y. Yoshitake, R. Bechtel, T. Takahashi, & M. Asai (Eds.), *Current issues in environment-behavior research* (pp. 199-210). Tokyo: University of Tokyo.

Tarrant, J. (1976). *Quotations from Drucker: The man who invented corporate society*. Boston: Cahner.

Taylor, C., Bailey, R., & Branch, H. (1967). *The Second National Conference on Architectural Psychology*. Salt Lake City: University of Utah.

Taylor, R. (1988). *Human territorial functioning: An empirical, evolutionary perspective on individual and small group territorial cognitions, behaviors and consequences*. Cambridge: Cambridge University Press.

Taylor, S. (1991). Asymmetrical effects of positive and negative events: The mobilization-minimization hypothesis. *Psychological Bulletin, 110*, 67-85.

Terkel, S. (1974). *Working*. New York: Pantheon.

Thalhoffer, N. (1980). Violation of a spacing norm in high social density. *Journal of Applied Social Psychology, 10*, 175-183.

Thompson, D., Aiello, J., & Epstein, Y. (1979). Interpersonal distance preferences. *Journal of Nonverbal Behavior, 4*, 113-118.

Thompson, M. (1985). The first public housing for the elderly. *Generations, 9*, 11-15.

Thorne, A. (1980). The arrival of man in Australia. In A. Sheratt (Ed.), *The Cambridge encyclopedia of archeology*. Cambridge: Cambridge University Press.

Thorne, A. (1982). *Housing evaluation in Australia* (Occasional paper, Ian Buchan Fell Research Project). Sydney: University of Sydney.

Thorne, R., & Arden, S. (Eds.). (1980). *People and the man-made environment*. Sydney: University of Sydney.

Tierney, K., & Blaisden, B. (1979). *Crisis intervention programs for disaster victims: A sourcebook and manual of mental health.* Bethesda, MD: National Institute for Mental Health.

Tinker, A. (1987). A review of the contribution of housing to policies for the frail elderly. *International Journal of Geriatric Psychiatry, 2,* 3-17.

Tobiasen, J., & Allen, A. (1983). Influence of gaze and physical closeness: A delayed effect. *Perceptual & Motor Skills, 57,* 491-495.

Toffler, A. (1980). *The third wave.* New York: William Morrow.

Tolman, E. (1938). The determiners of behavior at a choice point. *Psychological Review, 45,* 1-41.

Tolman, E. (1948). Cognitive maps in rats and men. *Psychological Review, 55,* 189-208.

Train, R. (1978). The environment today. *Science, 201,* 320-324.

Trefil, R. (1990). Modeling Earth's climate requires both science and guesswork. *Smithsonian, 21,* 29-37.

Triplett, N. (1897). The dynamogenic factors in pacemaking and competition. *American Journal of Psychology, 9,* 507-533.

Trites, D., Galbraith, F., Sturdavant, M., & Leckwert, J. (1970). Influence of nursing unit design on the activities and subjective feelings of nursing personnel. *Environment and Behavior, 3,* 303-334.

Tryon, R., & Bailey, D. (1970). *Cluster analysis.* New York: McGraw-Hill.

Turner, R., Nigg, J., Paz, D., & Young, B. (1980). *Community response to earthquake threat in Southern California: Final report* (10 vols.). Los Angeles: UCLA, Institute for Social Science Research.

Ugwuegbu, D., & Anusiem, A. (1982). Effects of stress on interpersonal distance in a simulated interview situation. *Journal of Social Psychology, 116,* 3-7.

Ulrich, R. (1979). Visual landscapes and psychological well-being. *Landscape Research, 4,* 17-23.

Ulrich, R. (1983). Aesthetic and affective response to natural environment. In I. Altman & J. Wohlwill (Eds.), *Behavior and the natural environment.* New York: Plenum.

Ulrich, R. (1984). View through a window may influence recovery from surgery. *Science, 224,* 420-421.

Ulrich, R. (1993). Biophilia, biophobia and natural landscapes. In S. Kellert & E. Wilson (Eds.), *The biophilia hypothesis.* Washington, DC: Island.

Ulrich, R., Dimberg, U., & Driver, B. (1991). Psychophysiological indicators of leisure benefits. In B. Driver, P. Brown, & G. Peterson (Eds.), *Benefits of leisure.* Washington: Venture.

Ulrich, R., & Simons, R. (1986). Recovery from stress during exposure to everyday outdoor environments. In *Proceedings of the 17th Environmental Design Research Association Conference,* Atlanta.

Umpleby, S. (1987). World population: Still ahead of schedule. *Science, 237,* 1555-1556.

United Nations. (1992). *Housing in the world: Graphical presentation of statistical data.* New York: U.N. Publications.

University of Minnesota. (1979). *Earth sheltered housing design* (The Underground Space Center). New York: Van Nostrand.

Urbina-Soria, J., Ortega-Andeane, P., & Bechtel, R. (1991). *Healthy environments (EDRA 22).* Mexico City: National Autonomous University of Mexico (UNAM).

U.S. Department of Health, Education & Welfare. (1979). *Smoking and health: A report of the surgeon general* (Publication 79-50066). Washington, DC: Government Printing Office.

U.S. Environmental Protection Agency. (1976). *Guideline for public reporting of daily air quality: Pollutant standards index.* Washington, DC: Government Printing Office.

U.S. Environmental Protection Agency, Office of Water and Waste Management. (1980). *Everybody's problem: Hazardous waste.* Washington, DC: Government Printing Office.

Valenstein, E. (1986). *Great and desperate cures: The rise and decline of psychosurgery and other radical treatments for mental illness.* New York: Basic Books.

Valins, S., & Baum, A. (1973). Residential group size, social interaction and crowding. *Environment and Behavior, 5,* 421-440.

Vallerand, R., & O'Connor, B. (1989). Life satisfaction of elderly individuals in regular community housing, in low-cost community housing and high and low self esteem determination nursing homes. *International Journal of Aging & Human Development, 28,* 277-283.

Valway, S., Martyny, J., & Miller, J. (1989). Lead absorption in indoor firing range users. *American Journal of Public Health, 79,* 1029-1032.

van Vliet, W. (1987). Housing in the Third World. [W. van Vliet & S. Fava (Eds.), Special issue: Housing in the Third World.] *Environment and Behavior, 19,* 267-285.

Vargas, F. (1984). Intimate space and psychoneurendocrinology of chronic stress. *Revista Chilena de Neuro-Psiquiatria, 22,* 259-264.

Veblen, T. (1899). *Theory of the leisure class.* New York: Macmillan.

Verplanken, B. (1989). Beliefs, attitudes and intentions toward nuclear energy before and after Chernobyl in a longitudinal within-subjects design. *Environment and Behavior, 21,* 371-392.

Villecco, M., & Brill, M. (1981). *Environmental design research: Concepts, methods and values.* Washington, DC: National Endowment of the Arts.

Vining, D. (1982). Migration between the core and the periphery. *Scientific American, 247,* 45-53.

Vischer, J. (1985). Post occupancy evaluation in public works, Canada (Symposium: Successful Uses of POEs in Building Delivery Systems). In S. Klein, R. Wener, & S. Lehman (Eds.), *Environmental change / social change* (pp. 340-341). Edmond, OK: Environmental Design Research Association.

Vogt, W. (1948). *Road to survival*. New York: W. Sloane Associates.

Volkomir, R. (1991). Falling into the gadget gap—and it's not our fault. *Smithsonian, 22,* 65-75.

von Foerster, H., Mora, P., & Amiot, L. (1960). Doomsday: Friday 13, 2026. *Science, 132,* 1291.

Vonnegut, K. (1981, August). A truly modern hero. *Psychology Today,* pp. 9-10.

Wachs, T. (1979). Proximal experience and early cognitive-intellectual development: The physical environment. *Merrill-Palmer Quarterly, 25,* 3-41.

Wade, G. (1968). *A study of free play patterns of elementary school-aged children in playground equipment areas*. Unpublished master's thesis, Pennsylvania State University.

Wald, N., Boreham, J., Bailey, A., Ritchie, C., Haddow, J., & Knight, G. (1984, January 28). Urinary cotinine as marker of breathing other people's tobacco smoke. *Lancet,* pp. 23-231.

Walker, J. (1991). Falls and fear of falling among elderly persons living in the community: Occupational therapy interventions. *American Journal of Occupational Therapy, 45,* 119-122.

Waller, G. (1986). The development of route knowledge: Multiple dimensions? *Journal of Environmental Psychology, 6,* 109-120.

Waller, M. (1984). The development of children's judgment of the distance-signalizing content of ordinary question as dependent on their syntactical form and the speech level of the question object. *Sprache und Kognition, 3,* 185-196.

Wallerstein, J., & Kelly, J. (1974). The effects of parental divorce: The adolescent experience. In J. Anthony & C. Koupernik (Eds.), *The child and his family: Children at psychiatric risk*. New York: John Wiley.

Wallerstein, J., & Kelly, J. (1975). The effects of parental divorce: The experiences of the preschool child. *Journal of the American Academy of Child Psychiatry, 14,* 600-616.

Wallis, A. (1991). *Wheel estate*. Oxford: Oxford University Press.

Walter, B., & Wirt, F. (1972). Uses of city classification in social and political research. In B. Berry (Ed.), *City classification handbook* (pp. 97-123). New York: John Wiley.

Walton, N. (1977). Work innovations at Topeka: After six years. *Journal of Applied Behavioral Science, 13,* 422-433.

Wapner, S. (1992). [Special issue] Transitions. *Environment and Behavior, 24.*

Wapner, S., Cohen, S., & Kaplan, B. (1976). *Experiencing the environment*. New York: Plenum.

Ward, M., Milledge, J., & West, J. (1989). *High altitude medicine and physiology*. Philadelphia: University of Pennsylvania Press.

Warden, C. (1931). *Animal motivation studies: The albino rat*. New York: Columbia University Press.

Washburn, S., & Devore, I. (1961). Social life of baboons. *Scientific American, 204,* 62-71.

Watkins, T. (1990). The origins of house and home? *World Archaeology, 21*, 336-347.

Webb, W., Worchel, S., & Brown, E. (1986). The influence of control on self-attributions. *Social Psychology Quarterly, 49*, 260-267.

Webber, D. (1982). Is nuclear power just another environmental issue? An analysis of California voters. *Environment and Behavior, 14*, 72-83.

Weber, P. (1993). *Abandoned seas: Reversing the decline of the oceans* (Worldwatch Paper 116). Washington, DC: Worldwatch Institute.

Weber, P. (1994). *Net loss: Fish, jobs and the marine environment* (Worldwatch Paper 120). Washington, DC: Worldwatch Institute.

Weidemann, S., Anderson, J., Butterfield, D., & Odonnell, P. (1981). Residents' perception of satisfaction and safety: A basis for change in multifamily housing. *Environment and Behavior, 14*, 695-724.

Weigel, R., & Newman, L. (1976). Increasing attitude-behavior correspondence by broadening the scope of the behavioral measure. *Journal of Personality and Social Psychology, 33*, 793-802.

Weiker, W. (1981). *The modernization of Turkey*. New York: Holmes and Meier.

Weinberg, A. (1976). The maturity and future of nuclear energy. *American Scientist, 64*, 16-21.

Weiner, J. (1994). *The beak of the finch*. New York: Knopf.

Weinstein, N. (1974). Effects of noise on intellectual performance. *Journal of Applied Psychology, 59*, 548-554.

Weinstein, N. (1977). Noise and intellectual performance: A confirmation and extension. *Journal of Applied Psychology, 62*, 104-107.

Weinstein, S. (1988). Senior adult sexuality in age segregated and age integrated communities. *International Journal of Aging and Human Development, 27*, 261-270.

Weintraub, B. (1991). Mystery of the shrinking red deer. *National Geographic, 180*, p. xv.

Weisburd, S. (1986). One ozone hole returns, another is found. *Science News, 130*, 215.

Weisman, J. (1981). Evaluating architectural legibility. *Environment and Behavior, 13*, 189-204.

Weisner, T., & Weibel, J. (1981). Home environmental and family life styles in California. *Environment and Behavior, 13*, 417-460.

Weiss, J. (1970). Somatic effects of predictable and unpredictable shock. *Psychosomatic Medicine, 32*, 399-408.

Weitzman, L. (1985). *The divorce revolution: The unexpected social and economic consequences for women and children in America*. New York: Free Press.

Wellens, A. (1979). Quantitative balance theory and the interpersonal liking-proximity relationship: A replication and extension of previous findings. *Journal of Psychology, 10*, 237-239.

Wells, B. (1965). The psycho-social influence of building environments: Sociometric findings in large and small office spaces. *Building Science, 1*, 153-165.

Wells, M. (1977). *Underground designs.* (Published by the author, Brewster, PA).

Wener, R., & Kaminoff, R. (1983). Improving environmental information: Effects of signs on perceived crowding behavior. *Environment and Behavior, 15*, 3-20.

Wener, R., & Keys, C. (1988). The effects of changes in jail population densities on crowding, sick call and spatial behavior. *Journal of Applied Social Psychology, 18*, 852-866.

Werner, C., Altman, I., & Oxley, D. (1985). Temporal aspects of homes: A transactional perspective. In I. Altman & C. Werner (Eds.), *Home environments* (pp. 1-32). New York: Plenum.

West, J. (1984). Human physiology at extreme altitudes on Mount Everest. *Science, 223*, 784-788.

Westman, M. (1990). The relationship between stress and performance: The moderating effect of hardiness. *Human Performance, 3*, 141-155.

Wheatstone, C. (1828). Contributions to the physiology of vision: Part I. *Philosophical Transactions of the Royal Society of London*, pp. 371-394.

Wheatstone, C. (1852). Contributions to the physiology of vision: Part 2. *Philosophy Magazine, 35*, 504-523.

Wheeler, L. (1985). Behavior and design: A memoir. *Environment and Behavior, 17*, 133-144.

White, B., Kaban, B., & Attanucci, J. (1979). *The origins of human competence.* Lexington, MA: D. C. Heath.

White, G. (1988). Challenges for the future. In C. Whitehead, C. Hutchinson, B. Timmerman, & R. Vavrady (Eds.), *Arid lands, today and tomorrow* (pp. 1423-1426). Boulder, CO: Westview.

White, G., & Haas, J. (1975). *Assessment of research on natural hazards.* Cambridge: MIT Press.

White, L. (1967). The historical roots of our ecological crisis. *Science, 155*, 1203-1207.

White, R. (1959). Motivation reconsidered: The concept of competence. *Psychological Review, 66*, 297-323.

White, R. (1975). Anthropometric measurements on selected populations of the world. In A. Chapanis (Ed.), *Ethnic variables in human factors engineering* (pp. 31-46). Baltimore, MD: Johns Hopkins University Press.

White, R. (1991). *It's your misfortune and none of my own: A new history of the American West.* Norman: University of Oklahoma Press.

White, W. (1979). *Resources in environment and behavior.* Washington, DC: American Psychological Association.

White, W. (Ed.). (1984). *EDRA membership handbook, 1983-1984.* Edmond, OK: Environmental Design Research Associates.

Whitehead, A. (1961). *The interpretation of science: Selected essays*. Indianapolis, IN: Bobbs-Merrill.

Wiatrowski, M., Gottfredson, G., & Roberts, M. (1983). Understanding school behavior disruption: Classifying school environments. *Environment and Behavior, 15*, 53-76.

Wickens, C., & Rouse, W. (1987). The role of human factors in Military R&D. In F. Farley & C. Null (Eds.), *Using psychological science: Making the public case* (pp. 167-178). Washington, DC: Federation of Behavioral, Psychological & Cognitive Sciences.

Wicker, A. (1969). Attitudes vs. actions: The relationship of verbal and overt behavioral responses to attitude objects. *Journal of Social Issues, 25*, 41-78.

Wicker, A. (1974). *Yosemite Valley employee survey*. Claremont, CA: Claremont College Print Shop.

Wicker, A. (1979). *Introduction to ecological psychology*. Pacific Grove, CA: Brooks/Cole.

Widom, C. (1989). The cycle of violence. *Science, 244*, 160-166.

Wiebe, D. (1991). Hardiness and stress moderation: A test of proposed mechanisms. *Journal of Personality and Social Psychology, 60*, 89-99.

Willems, E., & Raush, H. (1969). *Naturalistic viewpoints in psychological research*. New York: Holt, Rinehart & Winston.

Williamson, R. (1981). Adjustment to the highrise: Variables in a German sample. *Environment and Behavior 13*, 289-310.

Willis, F., Carlson, R., & Reeves, D. (1979). The development of personal space in primary school children. *Environmental Psychology and Nonverbal Behavior, 3*, 195-204.

Willis, F., & Hamm, H. (1980). The use of interpersonal touch on securing compliance. *Journal of Nonverbal Behavior, 5*, 49-55.

Wilner, D., Walkley, R., Pinkerton, T., & Tayback, M. (1962). *The housing environment and family life: A longitudinal study of the effects of housing on morbidity and mental health*. Baltimore, MD: Johns Hopkins Press.

Wilson, E. (1975). *Sociobiology*. Cambridge, MA: Belknap.

Wilson, E. (1984). *Biophilia*. Cambridge, MA: Harvard University Press.

Wilson, J. (1977). A test of the tragedy of the commons. In G. Hardin & J. Baden (Eds.), *Managing the commons*. New York: Freeman.

Wilton, R. (1979). Knowledge of spatial relations: A specification from the information used in making inferences. *Quarterly Journal of Experimental Psychology, 31*, 133-146.

Windley, P. (1983). Housing satisfaction among rural small-town elderly: A predictive model. *Journal of Housing for the Elderly, 1*, 57-68.

Wineman, J. (1982). Office design and evaluation, Parts I, II [Special issue]. *Environment and Behavior, 14*.

Winett, R. (1978). Prompting turning out lights in unoccupied rooms. *Journal of Environmental Systems, 6*, 237-241.

Winett, R., Hatcher, J., Leckliter, I., Ford, T., Fishback, J., Riley, A., & Lowe, S. (1981). *The effects of videotape modeling and feedback on residential comfort, the thermal environment and electricity consumption: Winter and summer studies*. Unpublished manuscript, Virginia Polytechnic Institute and State University, Department of Psychology.

Winett, R., Neale, M., & Grier, H. (1979). The effects of self-monitoring and feedback on residential electricity consumption. *Journal of Applied Analysis, 12*, 173-184.

Winette, R., Neale, M., Williams, K., Yokley, J., & Kauder, H. (1979). The effects of individual group feedback on residential electricity consumption: Three replications. *Journal of Environmental Systems, 8*, 217-233.

Winkel, F., Koppelaar, L., & Vrij, A. (1988). Creating suspects in police-citizen encounters: Two studies on personal space and being suspect. *Social Behavior, 3*, 307-318.

Winnicott, D. (1958). *Transitional objects and transitional phenomena*. New York: Basic Books.

Winterhalder, B., & Smith, E. (Eds.). (1982). *Hunter-gatherer foraging strategies*. Chicago: University of Chicago Press.

Wirth, L. (1938). Urbanism as a way of life. *American Journal of Sociology, 4*, 1-24.

Wister, A. (1985). Living arrangements and choices among the elderly. *Canadian Journal on Aging, 4*, 127-144.

Wittig, M., & Solnick, P. (1978). Status versus warmth as determinants of sex differences in personal space. *Sex Roles, 4*, 493-503.

Wohlwill, J. (1974). Human adaptation levels of environmental stimulation. *Human Ecology, 2*, 127-147.

Wohlwill, J. (1979). What belongs where: Research on fittingness of man-made structures in natural settings. In T. Daniel, E. Zube, & B. Driver (Eds.), *Assessing amenity resource values* (General Technical Report RM-68). Ft. Collins: USDA, Rocky Mountain Forest and Range Experimental Station.

Wohlwill, J., & Harris, G. (1980). Response to congruity or contrast for man-made features in natural recreation settings. *Leisure Sciences, 3*, 349-365.

Wolf, M. (1987). Serious delinquent behavior as part of a significantly handicapping condition: Cures and supportive environments. *Journal of Applied Behavior Analysis, 20*, 347-359.

Wolf, R. (1980). A naturalistic view of evaluation. *Museum News, 58*, 39-45.

Wolfe, T. (1979). *The right stuff*. New York: Farrar, Straus & Giroux.

Wood, B., & Talmon, M. (1983). Family boundaries in transition: A search for alternatives. *Family Process, 22*, 347-357.

Wood, P. (1980). Survey of behaviour in fires. In D. Canter (Ed.), *Fires and human behavior* (pp. 83-96). New York: John Wiley.

Wormith, J. (1984). Personal space of incarcerated offenders. *Journal of Clinical Psychology, 40*, 815-827.

Wotten, E., Blackwell, H., Wallis, D., & Barkow, B. (1982). *An investigation of the effects of windows and lighting in offices*. Ottawa: Department of National Health and Welfare, Canada.

Wright, H. (1969). *Children's behavior in communities differing in size, Parts I, II, III* [Mimeo]. Lawrence: University of Kansas, Department of Psychology.

Wright, H. (1971). Urban space as seen by the child. *Courier, 21*, 1-24.

Yaezawa, T., & Yoshida, F. (1981). The changes of physiological and cognitive responses caused by approaching of other person. *Japanese Journal of Psychology, 52*, 166-172.

Yanich, B., & Doig, J. (1973). *Criminal corrections, ideals, and realities*. Lexington, MA: Lexington.

Yeung, Y. (1977). High rise, high density housing: Myths and reality. *Habitat, 2*, 587-594.

Yoshitake, Y. (1990). *Current issues in environment-behavior research*. Tokyo: University of Tokyo.

Yoshitake, Y., Takahashi, T., Bechtel, R., & Asai, M. (Eds.). (1990). *Current issues in environment-behavior research*. University of Tokyo.

Young, A., & Guile, M. (1987). Departure latency to invasion of personal space: Effects of status and sex. *Perceptual and Motor Skills, 64*, 700-702.

Zalesnik, A. (1966). *Human dilemmas of leadership*. New York: Harper.

Zalesnik, A. (1970). Foreword. In S. Kakar, *Frederick Taylor: A study in personality and motivation*. Cambridge: MIT Press.

Zeisel, J. (1974). Designing out intentional school property damage: A checklist. In *Childhood city* (Man-Environment Interactions: Evaluations and Applications: The State of the Art in Environmental Design Research, Vol. 12, D. Carson, General Ed., pp. 173-186). Washington, DC: Environmental Design Research Association.

Zeisel, J. (1976). *Stopping school property damage*. New York: American Association of School Administrators.

Zeitlin, L. (1969). *A comparison of employee attitudes toward the conventional office and the landscaped office*. New York: Port Authority.

Zerega, A. (1981). Transportation energy conservation policy: Implications for social science research. *Journal of Social Issues, 37*, 31-550.

Zimbardo, P., Haney, C., Banks, W., & Jaffe, D. (1968). *The psychology of imprisonment: Privation, power and pathology* [Mimeo]. Stanford, CA: Stanford University, Department of Psychology.

Zimring, C. (1981). Stress and the designed environment. *Journal of Social Issues, 37*, 145-171.

Zimring, C., & Reizenstein, J. (1980). Post occupancy evaluation: An overview. *Environment and Behavior, 12*, 429-450.

Zimring, C., & Reizenstein, J. (1981). A primer on post occupancy evaluation. *AIA Journal, 70*, 52-54.

Zimring, C., Reizenstein Carpman, J., & Michelson, W. (1987). Design for special populations: Mentally retarded persons, children, hospital visitors. In D. Stokols & I. Altman (Eds.), *Handbook of environmental psychology* (Vol. 2, pp. 919-950). New York: John Wiley.

Zrudlo, L. (1972). *Psychological problems and environmental design in the north*. Quebec: Université Laval.

Zube, E. (1980). *Environmental evaluation: Perception and public policy*. Pacific Grove, CA: Brooks/Cole.

Zube, E., & Moore, G. (Eds.). (1989). *Advances in environment, behavior, and design* (Vol. 1). New York: Plenum.

Zube, E., Pitt, D., & Anderson, T. (1974). Perception and prediction of scenic resource values of the northeast. In E. Zube, R. Brush, & J. Fabos (Eds.), *Landscape assessment: Values, perceptions and resources* (pp. 151-167). Stroudsberg, PA: Dowden, Hutchinson & Ross.

Zubeck, J. (1969). *Sensory deprivation: Fifteen years of research*. Norwalk, CT: Appleton-Century-Crofts.

Zuravin, S. (1986). Residential density and urban child maltreatment: An aggregate analysis. *Journal of Family Violence, 1*, 307-322.

Author Index

Abbott, B., 260
Abelson, P., 34
Achenback, S., 279
Adams, C., 217
Adams, R., 172
Addison, D., 534
Adler, L., 169
Adrian, C., 356
Agarwal, A., 259-260
Ahlstrom, W., 466-467
Ahmed, S., 175
Ahrentzen, S., 519, 523
AIA Research Corporation, 314
Aiello, J., 166-167, 168-169, 178, 181, 216, 217, 460
Ajdukovic, D., 179
Ajzen, I., 112-113, 121, 416
Akhtar, S., 169
Albrecht, G., 170
Aldwin, C., 252
Alexander, C., 76, 77, 81
Alexander, R., 27
Allen, A., 175
Allen, G., 153
Allred, E., 9
Altholz, J., 492, 494
Altman, I., 62, 87-88, 89, 90-91, 96, 185, 189, 190, 198, 513, 549, 552
Amato, P., 474

American Association for Retired Persons (AARP), 488
American Psychiatric Association, 33
Ames, A., 132-135
Amiot, L., 37
Anderson, J., 6, 513
Anderson, L., 140
Anderson, N., 67
Anderson, P., 177
Anderson, T., 140
Anooshian, L., 153
Antonovsky, A., 260-261, 550
Anusiem, A., 179
Aoki, K., 155
Appleton, J., 45, 140, 145, 418, 546
Appleyard, D., 96, 135
Aragones, J., 151
Araragi, C., 177
Archea, J., 84
Arden, S., 324
Ardrey, R., 186, 187, 193
Argyle, M., 180
Aries, P., 455, 462
Arlt, R., 93
Arredondo, J., 151
Arthur, A., 260
Asai, M., 325
Asmus, C., 396

Subject Index

About the Author

Robert B. Bechtel is a graduate of Susquehanna University and received his M.A. and Ph.D. from the University of Kansas with his dissertation under Roger Barker. Previous books are *Enclosing Behavior* and *Methods in Environmental and Behavioral Research* (edited with Robert Marans and William Michelson). He was president of the Environmental Research and Development Foundation (1974-1984) and is currently Professor at the University of Arizona and editor of *Environment and Behavior*. His main interest continues to be ecological psychology, and he has worked on housing projects in Alaska, Australia, Canada, Iran, Israel, Saudi Arabia, and the United States. His community service includes many committees in the Presbyterian Church, as well as serving refugees from Central America and working with the Habitat for Humanity. He is also chairman of the Postal History Foundation. The latter stimulated a third volume: *The Arizona Statehood Postmark Catalogue*.

DATE

MA